BLOOD
MONEY

BLOOD MONEY

How Criminals, Militias, Rebels, and Warlords Finance Violence

MARGARET D. SANKEY

Naval Institute Press
Annapolis, Maryland

Naval Institute Press
291 Wood Road
Annapolis, MD 21402

ISBN 978-1-68247-437-2 (hardcover)
ISBN 978-1-68247-751-9 (eBook)

Library of Congress Cataloging-in-Publication Data is available.

♾ Print editions meet the requirements of ANSI/NISO z39.48-1992 (Permanence of Paper).
Printed in the United States of America.

30 29 28 27 26 25 24 23 22   9 8 7 6 5 4 3 2 1
First printing

The appearance of U.S. Department of Defense (DoD) visual information does not imply or
constitute DoD endorsement.

CONTENTS

PREFACE

When the U.S. Air Force Air War College hired me in 2015, it was not because of my historical expertise in eighteenth-century Scotland but because I could wrangle their computer systems and coax good research out of O-5 and O-6 students as their director of research and electives. Quickly, however, Uncle Sam and my dean, Dr. Chris Hemmer, offered generous support and opportunities for transforming what I knew about determined Jacobite efforts to hide money, lie to the courts, fund their exiles, and generate subsequent waves of insurgency in the British Isles into something of more twenty-first-century interest. Thanks to a Minerva grant (and prodding from my colleague Dr. Paul Springer), I began work on a new elective course, Dirty Money, and on the research that has turned into this book, starting with visits to the Interdisciplinary Art Crimes Conference and the Carabinieri of Italy's Il Comando Carabinieri Tutela Patrimonio Culturale.

Along the way, I discovered that not much had changed since the eighteenth century. Illicit actors were not plying their trades in dark corners but out in the open, entwined with everyday activities and tolerated to various degrees by the local authorities (it just takes a lot less time these days to hide money in the Cayman Islands). Violent nonstate actors reach into every sector of the mainstream financial system, from charities to car lots to real estate, not to mention innovative spaces like internet commerce and synthetic drug manufacturing.

Another substantial chunk of money and leave from my new boss, Dr. Mehmed Ali, at Air University's Academic Services allowed me to attend a Marshall Center seminar on Countering Trans-National Crime, an opportunity that put me in rooms with Ukrainian anticorruption auditors, Seychelles tax fraud prosecutors, and Senegalese customs inspectors. Their experiences and insights, as well as those of the four years of Air Command and Staff College students in Dirty Money, have added immeasurably to this project.

Most of my research before this book has involved sitting quietly in temperature- and humidity-controlled archives, puzzling out eighteenth-century handwriting, so it has been a professional upheaval to be out talking to Border Patrol agents in Arizona and seeing a demonstration of a confiscated marijuana-bale canon, sitting in on online art auctions, and getting a crash course in Bitcoin. Much of the scholarship on twenty-first-century illicit finance sits not in manuscript archives but online, in the form of blogs, caches of documents like the Panama Papers and Wikileaks, and the brave and relentless work of reporters who, in the absence of local print journalism, go to meetings, blow whistles, and cover things that sometimes risk their lives. Many thanks to the people who shared their expertise and continue to do the hard work.

The "buckle down and write it" portion of this project took place in the very strange year 2020, necessitating the extremely efficient and inventive efforts of the Air University Library, director Alisha Miles, and her outstanding staff to get me an eccentric roster of interlibrary loans and collection requests under challenging circumstances. That this was completed without throwing my laptop into the yard is due to my amazing in-house computer wizard, steady household manager, and human/genius, Ian.

The conclusions and opinions expressed in this research are those of the author and do not necessarily reflect the official policy or positions of the U.S. government, Department of Defense, or the Air University.

1
SHOW ME
THE MONEY

In his latest incarnation on premium cable, Tom Clancy's intrepid CIA analyst Jack Ryan pleads with his new boss to flag a newly identified threat: "9/11 cost half a million dollars! If he is real, what do you think he can do with twenty times that amount of money?" Dr. Ryan is half right—according to estimates made by the FBI, the 2001 attack on the World Trade Center and Pentagon cost between $300,000 and $500,000, which, with nineteen participants requiring expensive flight training and time, sits at the high end of operations budgets for terrorist attacks.[1] Even some of the most devastating attacks cost very little, including the 2002 bombings in Bali ($20,000), the 1993 World Trade Center Bombing ($19,000), the 7/7 London bombings in 2005 (€15,000), and the 2004 Madrid train bombs (€10,000–40,000).[2]

For operations that do not require training, long stays in a foreign country, or elaborate planning, the costs plummet drastically. The Pentagon's Joint IED Defeat Organization published a kind of 2012 "price list," estimating that a car bomb runs about $13,000–20,000 to produce, depending on the cost of the vehicle, suicide vests run about $1,200, and reliable remote-controlled

bombs cost about as much as an iPhone 5, $400.[3] The two men who con-
ducted the 2007 attack on the Glasgow airport used a Jeep Cherokee they
already owned and employed petrol bombs and easily obtained propane
canisters, while another pair of would-be bombers caught on their way to
the 2006 World Cup soccer matches in Cologne had suitcase devices made
of "a propane tank, alarm clock, batteries and a plastic bottle filled with gas,"
assembled for less than $500.[4] Internet-available handbooks make it easy
to put together nail bombs from the contents of a local hardware store,
like those used in right-wing extremist David Copeland's 1999 three-week
violent spree against Bangladeshis in Brick Lane, LGBTQ people in SoHo,
and multicultural Brixton.[5] In a conflict zone like Iraq or Syria, freelance IED
cells can assemble a team of team of six to eight people, including a money
man, explosives expert, placer, and triggerman, on short notice for as little
as $50, and they can be contacted on the internet for convenience.[6]

That so little can wreak such disproportionate carnage and mayhem is
one of the most insidious features of asymmetric warfare. Aside from the
tragic loss of lives, bombings and other methods of terrorist attacks can
devastate an area's livelihood derived from tourism for years after the event;
disable the physical infrastructure a population depends on for energy,
communications, and transport in ways that take a long time to repair; and
commit state security forces to huge budgets and cadres of personnel in an
attempt to be informed and on guard all the time, versus attackers needing
to be lucky just once in order to do massive damage.[7] Extensive records
from the British government's engagement with terrorism in Northern
Ireland allow for a startling extrapolation of long-term financial effects: For
every £1 the Irish Republican Army (IRA) and its splinter groups raised, they
could force the government into spending £130 on various attempts to stop
them and repair the damage done.[8] Al-Qaeda was extremely efficient in
producing a "violence product" for about $2,700 (40 percent of an average
Iraqi household income), with similar results against the North Atlantic
Treaty Organization (NATO) and the United States.[9]

Where Dr. Ryan's analysis is wrong is that any organization capable of
pulling off an attack like 9/11 has probably *already* spent many times more
than half a million dollars. A group that wants to capitalize on its bombing,

kidnapping, bank robbery, or seizure of a diamond field must have a supporting organization to carry forward its goals beyond the death or capture of the people who carried out the operation. Lone wolves may have no further goals than to live on as martyrs and to collect admirers, but groups "have to cross a divide that separates those who live a hand-to-mouth existence from those who can actually plan ahead" in order to have any chance of making their long-term plans a reality, whether that is to establish a separatist state, overthrow a government, or impose their religious views on another group.[10] A cut-price attack has behind it the entirety of the day-to-day business of the planners and agents who carry it out.[11] Just as with conventional military forces, illicit, violent nonstate actors (VNSA) require organizations to provide the mechanism that transforms resources into effective combat power and apply that generated power against an enemy.[12]

As a result, a group must consistently generate far larger amounts of money. In the 1990s the yearly IRA operating budget was usually a relatively modest £15 million, while the Kurdish Workers Party (PKK) needed $86 million every year, and Hezbollah, with extensive expenses because of its state-building and charity activities, had to acquire a conservative estimate of $100–200 million.[13] Even much less significant concerns, like a regional drug cartel or a small-time warlord, have bills to pay in order to continue existing, which requires structures and planning that, to add to the complexity and challenge, almost always encounter the additional friction of coming from the illicit economy, with all kinds of topped-up expense for secrecy, delivery to remote regions, surcharges by money launderers, and losses converting a commodity like diamonds or coltan into cash. If there's a truism about counterterror financing, it is that car bombs are cheap, and sustainment is where the money goes.

▪ Necessary Outflows

When I teach my Dirty Money course as an elective at Air University's Air Command and Staff College, it makes for an excellent first-day activity to ask students where all the money is hemorrhaging. Once they get warmed up, Air Command and Staff College students are remarkably good at this. As majors

(O-4), they—like their middle-management counterparts in illicit organizations—have the vantage point of being indispensable to making the system work but not yet enjoying the senior perks of their superiors, and they see it all. A limited survey of the expenses necessary for a VNSA to function involves, depending on the purpose and structure of the group, most of the following.

VNSAs need to recruit people, and if their plans involve more than expending cannon fodder, they need high-quality human capital. This means being visible within some tolerable degree to the wider world and presenting advantages (however they are defined, martyrdom included) to potential joiners. This may mean committing acts purely to demonstrate resolve and effectiveness to an audience of recruits, having a vivid and alluring presence in internet chat rooms to lure foreign-fighter volunteers, running youth clubs and soccer teams to inculcate the group's values at an early age, or—as the Japanese terror group Aum Shinrikyo did—paying fees to access databases of recent graduates of the hard sciences in order to target their marketing more precisely.[14] The consequences for relying on incompetent or untrainable recruits are substantial and embarrassing and can damage a VNSA significantly should, for example, one of the people chosen for a task prove completely unable to grasp the concepts at flight school.[15]

Compared to adversaries with the status of Westphalian states, VNSAs almost always start off with a big disadvantage in terms of acquiring hardware and weapons since they lack the ability to direct the tax and industrial base to support them or the diplomatic status to request restricted materials like currency-capable printing presses and biological weapons or to make large purchases like aircraft and maritime vessels.[16] State sponsorship, like Hezbollah's relationship with Iran, can open the door to receiving missiles, rockets, and other expensive equipment, which then requires storage, spare parts, and upkeep.[17] Through state sponsorship, wealth, and longevity, the Liberation Tigers of Tamil Eelam (LTTE) in Sri Lanka eventually fielded an air force and a navy to support their ground troops, but this added substantial complexity to their training programs and committed them to the care of a whole inventory of valuable assets.[18]

For those less well connected, getting weapons and military-grade equipment like night vision goggles, encrypted satellite phones, and chemicals will involve reaching into the black market or scrounging them off the battlefield. Since the end of the Cold War, the availability of mass-produced weapons has driven down the price, but a VNSA still needs to have the cash to be attractive to brokers and will pay for the friction of needing to avoid licensing or end-use certificates, to get discreet delivery, and to set up secure storage. VNSAs also need to factor in the possibility that they will have to abandon or destroy stockpiles of material and replace them somewhere else if forced to relocate.[19]

Few recruits come to a VNSA with the skills required to advance the group's agenda or to understand it. Major investment must be made in indoctrination, whether it is learning the history and pan-African orientation of the Black Kings gang in Chicago or the interpretation of Islamic law peculiar to the Taliban.[20] For groups with their own territory or a safe haven, it makes sense to set up a permanent training camp with a full curriculum and experienced instructors, perhaps even mock-ups of the different environments in which the group expects them to operate.[21] For operatives meant to go to the Global North, there's a "charm school" for wearing upper-middle-class clothing, sitting comfortably next to women, and practicing grooming expected of white-collar professionals.[22] There may be different courses for specialized skills like explosives, kidnapping, surveillance, or driving, beyond what is necessary to turn out disciplined foot soldiers.[23] Few groups have the resources or want to go as far as Revolutionary Armed Forces of Colombia (FARC), which began sending selected members to universities to major in subjects they found valuable (chemistry, accounting, law, engineering), eventually creating their own staff college, the Hernando Gonzales Military School in Llanos del Yarí, to teach their doctrine, but receipts from al-Qaeda in the Islamic Maghreb (AQIM) show regular payments for "workshops" on desirable skills like computer basics and weapons training.[24]

Knowing tradecraft in theory is a long way from being able to execute it reliably or skillfully, so the penalty for not investing in practice and dry runs is substantial. Defendants at their 2004 trial for conspiracy to plan a bombing campaign in the United Kingdom complained that their training camp in Pakistan had been so reluctant to allow noise from their firing range, which would alert neighbors, that "everyone waited until the last day to fire their weapons," which is hardly a recipe for competent marksmen.[25] Other plans

Hamas training camp. Maintaining training camps like this Hamas property in Gaza is a significant expense for a VNSA but allows the group to hone tradecraft and ensure standardized education in doctrine. *Courtesy Israeli Defense Forces Spokespersons Unit*

failed or left distinctive clues for investigators because various participants blew themselves up accidentally, got speeding tickets and were aggressive with the traffic cops, became nervous about how cars were to be parked on a ferry, were too insecure to travel separately as instructed, or got lost and called in repeatedly for directions to their target, most of which could have been avoided with practice and mastery of basic skills.[26]

In a closely related cluster of expenses, a VNSA needs to put money into maintaining covers for their operatives in hostile territory or conducting operations. They must have carefully forged identification that stands up to scans at airports and train stations, travel visas, and memberships in the professional organizations that match their personas. To avoid police sweeps, they may need to live in "nice" neighborhoods or in proximity to their targets, requiring pricey, long-term apartment rentals and maintenance, with instructions to keep up lawn care and participate in neighborhood social activities. Dedicated fundraisers in the Global North need to keep up appearances and represent themselves as respectable, prosperous, and nonthreatening, a level of comfort that requires eight times as much as the support given to families of martyrs.[27] The covers likely encompass disguises and costuming to fit in, which, in the case of al-Qaeda's instructions to the 9/11 hijackers, incorporated jewelry brought in from Bangkok to accessorize the first-class cabin and an alcohol and strip club allowance to create an image of a "bro" lifestyle that obscured their real orientation as religious ascetics.[28] Shoe-bomber Richard Reid violated nearly every one of these rules, including paying for a ticket in cash, turning up at De Gaulle Airport disheveled and without luggage, and looking so utterly unlike a first-class passenger en route to a Caribbean holiday that a fellow passenger told authorities, "I was immediately struck by how bizarre he looked."[29]

Keeping a standing force is a massive commitment of resources for a VNSA, especially one with pretensions of functioning like a licit army, where salaries and benefits are expected. Being able to pay, particularly at above-market rates, makes membership attractive in comparison to underemployment, unavailable civil service careers, and corrupt competition for educational opportunities. Boko Haram members cited the $42 they received for blowing up a church in Borno State as the most significant reason they had acted.[30] Public sector wages in Syria, especially after the nosedive of the Syrian pound in 2013, could not compete with ISIS's relatively generous package of salary and family subsidy ($400–600 per month, with extra for each wife and child); al-Nusrah Front fighters were peevish that their cousins had joined the Islamic State of Iraq and Syria because "the pay was better."[31] For recruits with special skills and education, the expectation can be even higher, leading Jordan's King Abdullah to complain that "as we try to create jobs [for the youth] . . . ISIS today is providing $1,000 a month in Saudi, which to people in Jordan is a middle class to higher middle class income."[32] Even a group that doesn't fancy itself an establishment probably needs to keep a portion of its membership entirely devoted to training, fundraising, and operations rather than to compete with regular employers for their time and energy, so they'll have to pay wages to keep them on a kind of illicit retainer.[33]

Once established, failing to deliver these salaries is a dangerous cause of division, resentment, and cleavage in the organization. ISIS put considerable effort into making sure that it issued and honored IOUs when revenues were low in Mosul and paid up when their treasury was once again flush, but this level of trust was not available to individual al-Shabaab commanders, whose credibility was damaged when they had empty coffers.[34] A dip in wages or members' loss of confidence that they'll be paid opens a door for an enemy to outbid the VNSA for the loyalty of its members in key jobs, which works in favor of counterterrorism agents investigating AQIM's border sector personnel in North Africa.[35]

Frequently an operation requires expertise that a VNSA may not have the capacity to field, or that requires an expert to detach from them for strategic purposes. Contracting with a "fixer" or money launderer with ties to the broader illicit world is easier than cultivating a whole network sui generis and provides more opportunities as well as the shielding offered by the fixer's value to other dangerous groups. Assassins possess expertise that gets the desired job done without being a direct link to the hiring VNSA. El Loco, for instance, worked indiscriminately for Mexico's cartels and made it possible for them to pick off rivals without incriminating themselves.[36] More mundane talents, like accounting, computer engineering, and logistics, are a matter of wealthy VNSAs affording better-than-licit fees, especially in any environment where privatization has cut loose a large number of former state employees, as in the post-Soviet 1990s.[37] Hiring experts always costs less overall than making expensive mistakes, as the IRA did in 1982, sending an inexperienced team into Western Europe to buy illicit weaponry and promptly getting scammed.[38]

Creating a media narrative is essential to wringing the most out of a VNSA's operations. Handheld camcorders and cell phones make it simple to record, edit, and promulgate a version of events that enhances the prowess and reputation of the group. Al-Qaeda learned that passing videotapes on to Al-Jazeera only led to the news network editing them for journalistic purposes, and that uploading curated versions via the internet was a far more effective means of distributing propaganda.[39] ISIS has taken this a step further by acquiring extensive equipment to produce professional-quality film and audio products; as a potential studio employee marveled, "They offered me $1,500 a month, plus a car, a house and all the cameras I needed. . . . I remembered looking around the office. It was amazing the equipment they had in there."[40] With these assets, ISIS cranks out hundreds of films, including *Clanging of the Swords, Part IV*, which competes for the attention of viewers with access to Hollywood blockbusters, using accomplished editing techniques and extensive drone footage soaring over Fallujah.[41] Once polished, these can be distributed online, copied as DVDs, and screened for more or less captive audiences in occupied towns where the internet is inaccessible or too slow.

It is in aid of these media portrayals and identity that a VNSA might spend money on things that do not add to their tactical capabilities or long-term strategy but are just *cool*. Cartels and gangs have trademark leather jackets and alligator boots, *narcocorridos*, and feral hippos, while militias and paramilitary groups raise morale with parades, sexy uniforms, and nicknames. Flashy but unnecessary weapons demonstrations, promoting catchy *nasheeds* (a cappella hymns), showcasing foreign fighters swigging Red Bull and driving around in sports cars is all part of ISIS building a brand, one that boosts recruiting and public popular support, and taps into much older characteristics of social banditry as resistance fighter and avenger.[42]

Even better than creating a media narrative is controlling it. ISIS branched out into traditional media in 2014, publishing a glossy, high-quality, English-language magazine, *Islamic State News*, and a radio station, Al-Bayan, in Mosul, which can broadcast battlefield updates, sermons, and Quran recitations to anyone with a receiver.[43] VNSAs with deeper pockets and experience have established and run TV stations, like Hezbollah's Al-Manar (The Lighthouse), complete with children's programming featuring a knock-off Mickey Mouse; the PKK's TV and satellite network MED TV; the LTTE National Television of Tamileelam, which can reach central Asia; and Paris-based Tamil Television Network for Europe and the Middle East.[44] VNSAs can own and operate publishing houses to print textbooks, distribute newspapers, and coordinate propaganda messaging across platforms.[45] In some cases a VNSA has purchased a media outlet to stifle investigations and criticism of its activities.[46]

VNSA real estate needs are more complex than those of a licit business too. Safe houses need to be acquired and maintained over the course of years and provide features like multiple entrances, ground floor access points, garages, and viewpoints to spot approaching law enforcement, and the safe houses need to be away from local businesses with cameras (increasingly difficult in places like the United Kingdom, which has extensive closed-circuit television coverage). Bomb building needs to take place away from prying eyes or in a basement with excellent noise insulation, while storage for other illicit materials should allow trucks to deliver discreetly and not trigger suspicions from multiple visitors at all hours. In many locations property owners run the real risk of being prosecuted or having the building destroyed or confiscated by the government, so inflated rent and hush money is expected. Sympathetic or collaborationist landlords still need to be paid off, with protection, gifts, or bribes, like the series of Provisional Irish Republican Army "rest house" hosts, who the organization compensated for their loyalty with alcohol and Christmas bonus baskets.[47]

For those participants in operations who die or are captured, the behavior of the VNSA toward them and their surviving family members has huge repercussions for the group's recruiting, effectiveness, and security. Suicide bombers expect ritualistic preparation, videotaping of their manifestos, and protection and pensions for their families after the act, with the whole community watching to see if the VNSA leadership pays a visit to console the extended clan and deliver succor in the form of food or cash. Gangs and cartels are expected to organize and deliver lavish, elaborate funerals, which may involve large donations to a church in order to get permission for interment but which can serve as a massive display of public support and a propaganda coup. Keeping the memory of the dead alive is good messaging and is expected from the survivors, so a VNSA may pay to have memorials erected, community murals painted and posters unfurled, ballads composed, or graves meticulously tended like those of the Black Tiger LTTE martyrs in Sri Lanka.[48]

Imprisoned members expect protection from guards and rival groups to be purchased for them, pensions paid to their wives and children, and legal representation to be set in motion to free them and air the group's grievances in court. Those who can be ransomed or bailed out must be retrieved before they can be interrogated or turned against the organization. Failing to uphold the VNSA's end of the illicit bargain can deter new recruits, lead angry and disappointed hangers-on to become informers, or advertise weakness to rivals and law enforcement.

Wounded comrades must be looked after and patched up, which can take the form of training street medics, having a Rolodex of ethically shady surgeons (or ketamine-adjacent vet students), and providing field hospitals all the way up to fully staffed medical centers, which may also form part of the group's outreach to the wider community. Should survivors need prosthetics, physical therapy, or continued treatment for chronic problems, the group is on the hook for a lifetime supply of glass eyes, canes, and oxygen tanks, lest they show themselves to be callous toward their heroes. If these treatments exceed what is available to most of the population, it can be a significant perk to recruitment and retention and an implied criticism of a state enemy.

Depending on the local tolerances for the VNSA, they may have a political wing that can compete in the open electoral marketplace. Waging a political campaign is expensive, from advertising, speaking tours, buttons, and local offices to employing consultants and speechwriters. This is usually the purview of a deeply rooted and mature VNSA, like the IRA, but can pay off spectacularly with public opinion gains and a seat at the negotiating table. Sinn Féin sucked up huge sums of money to maintain a headquarters in Parnell Square, Dublin, and thirty-two regional offices, with the U.K. government estimating that Gerry Adams spent £1.30 per vote (total: £137,000, far over licit U.K. campaign finance regulations) in the 1980s–1990s.[49] For those needing a softer touch, expensive K Street lobbyists and their colleagues in the Global North can be hired, like the D.C. firm Black, Manafort, Stone and Kelly, to put a shine on VNSAs like Angola's UNITA (the National Union for the Total Independence of Angola) and its leader, Jonas Savimbi, and make a strong case for state sponsorship and indulgence.[50] Even the most violent and incorrigible groups can find well-connected and eloquent defenders for the right price.

If they are not allowed to act openly in civil affairs, a VNSA probably pays gargantuan sums in bribes. Greasing palms gets a beat cop to turn a blind eye to corner drug deals or a customs agent to wave through a truck, keeps landlords from looking in suspicious crates in the basement, incentivizes an airline baggage handler to put smuggled cash and night vision goggles in the hold of an international flight, or affects the decision of a local politician about giving contracts to a VNSA business. On a bigger scale, Chechen militias paid Russian military commanders a $100,000 bribe for allowing them to retreat safely from Grozny during Operation Wolf Hunt and later paid airport workers to board terrorists wearing suicide bombs, despite intelligence services flagging them for screening.[51] A regional law enforcement structure riddled with paid informers will keep a VNSA safe from unannounced raids, undermine investigations, and—if the payment is big enough—function as a literal "get out of jail free" card. It is safe to assume that the amount of a bribe will never go down, forcing a group to evaluate the risk-return on meeting escalating demands versus killing the bribe recipient and starting over with someone else.

Getting safe haven and keeping good relationships with the local population, especially if the VNSA claims legitimacy on the basis of their relationship to them, requires putting in a lot of money. When they first arrived around Timbuktu, the Groupe salafiste pour la prédication et le combat was fastidious about overpaying their local hosts for food and lodging in order to buy themselves goodwill; they also offered medical treatment and shared their cellphone network.[52] Many conflict areas suffer from being underserviced by their governments, whether because of underlying prejudice against the population or social services cuts driven by economic austerity, leaving a gap into which VNSAs can pour resources and win friends. Gangs can sponsor youth basketball tournaments, insurgents can fund schools and soup kitchens, and terrorists can try to win Robin Hood reputations for swooping in to pay for weddings or clear a debt. Where a VNSA has taken on the mantle of a fully fledged government, like the LTTE, FARC, Moro National Liberation Front, Naxalites, or ISIS, those expenses rise precipitously as people expect everything from trash services to pothole repair.[53]

To plan operations, a VNSA should have established sources of intelligence, from corner lookouts to highly placed informants, so they can have situational awareness of their opponents' resources, plans, and weak points. Some of this can be achieved with the world's oldest human intelligence strategies, observation, and cash. A recent ethnographic study of sex workers in Nairobi found that al-Shabaab, which deplores prostitution among its own women, paid retainers to Tanzanians and Kenyans to pass along pillow talk.[54] The

IRA moved away from entirely self-contained teams into tasking specialized intelligence and surveillance personnel to provide background on a continual basis, generating a pool of blackmail possibilities and extortion calculations beyond the information needed for one operation.[55] With time and effort, a VNSA can acquire and build databases of car registrations, bank accounts, and personnel records as well as monitor cell phone transmissions and track the movement of law enforcement and military assets, sometimes better than their own commanders.

Even after spending all of this to make operations possible, a VNSA needs to keep an open hand with their budget. Attacks cost comparatively little, so it is best to avoid being too frugal and committing errors like those of the first World Trade Center bombers, who drew unnecessary attention to themselves by purchasing a child's (and thus discounted) airline ticket as part of their escape plan and insisting on getting a $400 deposit back from the truck rental company in order to upgrade the ticket; then some of the group engaged in petty theft and credit card fraud in Canada to support themselves in hiding. This cascading series of errors might have been avoided if the operations plan had included more padding and contingency.[56]

■ Even VNSAs Have Red Tape

No matter how determined a group is to be lean, stay agile, bend like the willow, achieve continual process improvement, or eat soup with a knife, the group will inevitably spawn a bureaucracy to manage things—a point that always elicits a chuckle from my Dirty Money students, thinking about their own experience in a licit military. Mob accountants are a feature of criminal life known from Scorsese movies, but behind almost every VNSA is a clerk with a spreadsheet: the Chicago Black Kings' treasurer, the IRA's finance department, Hezbollah's Jihadic Committee for the Support of the Islamic Resistance, Mau Mau receipt collectors, and some anonymous poor soul in the Warsaw Ghetto Uprising's audit department keeping track of rounds of ammunition on scraps of paper.[57] When this works well, the group has a basis for making advantageous decisions about how much to budget, how much wastage to tolerate, and how much friction they are willing to pay for in the process of planning and executing their activities. A group choosing not to develop this capability, like the Ulster loyalist militias, can find themselves at a disadvantage vis-à-vis their more capable rivals.[58]

Bureaucracies, though, can take on a life of their own, sometimes adopting the worst forms of their licit counterparts—lumbering, bound by hierarchy, persnickety, and focused on the forest instead of the trees. ISIS required receipts for even the smallest purchases, consuming bureaucratic time logging $1.80 bars of soap and a $3 broom.[59] Captured al-Qaeda documents show an accounting department as relentless as the Department of Defense's Defense Travel System in pursuing minutely itemized vouchers, with Mohammed Atef dispatching a disciplinary memo to a spendthrift agricultural engineer: "I was very upset by what you did. I obtained 75,000 rupees for you and your family's trip to Egypt. I learned that you did not submit the voucher to the accountant and that you made reservations for 40,000 rupees and kept the remainder, claiming you have the right to do so." Atef also chastised the engineer for a conflict over possession of an air conditioner shared with other al-Qaeda members.[60] Pushed too far, members frustrated by bureaucratic nickel-and-diming can also drop a dime, taking their embezzled funds and running to defect, like Jamal Ahmed al-Fadl, who testified in the African Embassy bombing cases after getting fed up with tight discipline and decamping with his loot.[61]

Financial Frameworks

Because of this whole raft of expenses, any VNSA must develop sources of income since there is no free lunch, even for the most austere, ideologically sustained believers. Surviving to fight another day means supporting yourself and accepting the pros and cons of whatever method brings in the resources. There's no one-size-fits-all method for illicit financing, only a group's skill in understanding their own goals, context, and resources, which can change dramatically over time and circumstances. One of the frustrating challenges of doing counterterrorism or counter-criminal finance is the depth of knowledge needed about the social, political, and economic factors unique to the operational environment and the ability to confront ambiguity and gray areas of policy—why, for example, the United States was alarmed by the collection of donations for Hezbollah in Detroit but allowed "Derry cans" on the bar of every faux-Irish pub on the East Coast, or that figuring out how the Boston bombers planned and financed their attack offers no insight into the machinations of a Shining Path raid on a police station.[62] In general, this is a constantly evolving quadrangulation among four factors: what sort of VNSA is it, where are they in terms of their longevity and maturity, what sort of resources do they have in terms of location and personnel, and what risk factors are present in their area of operation?[63]

What a VNSA is and what it wants are the basic factors in exploring what revenue streams will be available to it. If a VNSA's primary purpose is to make money, like a drug cartel, and to get away with making money as long as possible, its financing decisions are pretty flexible and opportunistic. After that things get complicated. Movements that are proxies for a state sponsor will have constraints on their fundraising to the taste of their patron, along with the advantage of a steady stream of money. Insurgents pursuing a war of national liberation or secession have to answer to diaspora expectations and calculate despoliation of the very land they hope someday to rule. Claiming to carry out the will of the people in demanding redress via terrorist acts means that those "people" will have a say in how much extraction of money or application of violence is too much, making a group like the PKK or Quebec Liberation Front much like a "publicly traded company," with shareholders who vote with their cooperation and support.[64]

Where the VNSA is in a life cycle of development also affects where the money comes from. Early in its existence, a group's needs are likely small and sustainable on robberies or minor handouts that R. T. Naylor characterizes as "blue collar" crime, but these needs will escalate as the organization gains in membership, popularity, and notoriety.[65] National or international reach opens new opportunities, including the credibility to claim "revolutionary taxes" and more predictable exploitation of a local asset like a diamond mine or a trafficking network's control of a key route. A fully matured VNSA has territory under its control and may act more like a sovereign state or multinational corporation, operating its own army and navy, diversifying revenue streams, and moving what were illicit transactions into the mainstream of the formal economy in a process that transforms a parasitical attachment to the state into the state.[66]

Where the VNSA operates and the personnel available to it will also be determining factors in what fundraising is possible. On the human capital side,

Mosul car bomb, 2004. Very inexpensive to produce, car bombs like this one at the main gate of Mosul Airfield are capable of killing large numbers of bystanders and inflicting widespread property damage, all for the cost of explosives and a used Chevy Caprice. *139th Mobile Public Affairs Detachment, Illinois National Guard, Defense Visual Information Distribution Service*

sociology offers a menu of resources: moral (legitimacy, solidarity, sympathy); cultural (collective identities, media); socio-organizational (social networks, formal organizations); human (labor, skills, experience, expertise); and material (money, property, equipment). What this means for a VNSA is that a rural peasant insurgency lacking literate personnel probably won't be running sophisticated bank scams, but a right-wing militia drawn from men employed in trades can likely extort construction sites profitably. The physical location of the group's primary area of operation matters too. An urban VNSA has higher chances of finding wealthy kidnap targets, banks to rob, and buyers for untaxed cigarettes but will encounter greater contact with law enforcement and surveillance. A rural sphere of action may contain space to cultivate the drugs, hiding places for smuggling, antiquities to dig up, or desperate people to traffic.

Dr. Michael Freeman, of the Naval Postgraduate School, has concise and practical criteria for what a VNSA wants out of any funding source. Of course, any group will prioritize getting money in as large a quantity as possible, as "more money allows terrorist groups to be stronger and more effective," and avoid fundraising again in favor of conducting their agenda.[67] Depending on their purpose, groups may want to tailor fundraising to sources that do not too badly damage their legitimacy in the eyes of their constituents, diaspora, state sponsors, or the general public, with drugs and kidnapping being particularly radioactive to the heroic reputations of the VNSA. It is helpful if the extraction of a funding source is secure and does not pose additional risks of detection or infiltration to the group or distract too significantly from the core mission, so petty crimes that up the odds of arrest or provoke rivals are a bad gamble. The money should flow reliably so that the group doesn't have to continually find new sources, scale up operations to acquire it, or hinder long-term planning. Once acquired, a smart VNSA wants access to and control of the money and its source, so having it pulled on the whim of a state sponsor or offended diaspora leader, or buried in an offshore account (or, literally, underground in a bag), is less desirable than being unbeholden and unfettered.[68] Finally, in a kind of Occam's razor of illicit violence, simple methods are best and are preferable to those necessitating overhead, special skills, extensive efforts, and expenditure of personnel.

Within these generalities, there are endless permutations of what VNSAs have done, are doing, and will do as future threats. While this work cannot catalog every form or offer encyclopedic coverage of the world's VNSAs, it can establish categories and popular sources and demonstrate patterns that constitute a useful background for understanding both what a group might do in the future and why that will be just as hard to intercept and prevent as the extraction that has come before. Let's get into the dirty money.

2
CROSSING
THE STREAMS

Café Milano in Georgetown is a nice place that bills itself as the "ultimate place to see and be seen" in Washington, D.C., as lawmakers, diplomats, and neighborhood residents sip wine, nibble carpaccio, and enjoy the sunny patio. The Saudi ambassador to the United States, Adel al-Jubeir, particularly enjoyed having dinner there, making reservations several times a week, which is why the Islamic Revolutionary Guards Corps of Iran decided it would be the ideal place to assassinate him. The overall plan allegedly came down from Maj. Gen. Qasem Soleimani, commander of the elite Quds Force and coordinator of covert global operations. He delegated the assassination to Abdul Reza Shahlai, whose greatest success had been in 2007, organizing a strike team, disguised in U.S. and Iraqi uniforms, to attack a provincial administration building in Karbala, Iraq. The raid killed five Americans and wounded three, and the sheer audacity of the attempt was meant to unsettle the Iraqi government. Shahlai took on the new assignment, assuring his superiors that, well, he knew a guy.[1]

That guy was Shahlai's cousin Mansour Arbabsiar, with whom he grew up in Bakhtaran, Iran. Arbabsiar emigrated to Texas before the Iranian Revolution but failed to prosper in Texas as a car salesman. With a track record of failed jobs and separated from his wife, he returned to Iran in 2011 and visited family. Whether it was an attempt to impress or a chance at an alternate career, Arbabsiar assured Shahlai that, indeed, he could line up expertise from a Mexican cartel to carry out a bombing at the restaurant. Briefed that the plan might kill 100–150 customers during a dinner service, he was nonchalant. "No big deal."[2]

Returning from Iran in the summer of 2011 with contact information for Shahlai's deputy, Gholam Shakuri, Arbabsiar started looking for a hitman, approaching a female friend whose nephew was rumored to be a member of Los Zetas, the Mexican drug cartel. At their meetings he quizzed the nephew on his knowledge of explosives and floated plans for an extended campaign of not just assassination but bombings of the Saudi and Israeli embassies. To underscore the high level of Iranian interest, he described Shahlai as someone wanted by the law in America and who had "been on CNN." Satisfied with the interviews, Arbabsiar arranged the transfer of $100,000 from accounts associated with Iran into those held by the nephew as a down payment on an eventual $1.5 million operations budget.[3] There was just one problem: the nephew wasn't a member of Los Zetas; he was a Drug Enforcement Administration informant, and he answered not to a kingpin but to a handler in Houston.[4]

When the informant notified his superiors of the plot, U.S. officials thought it was . . . bonkers. Who cold-calls cartel hitmen? Engages in a clumsy wire transfer of money? Talks on the phone about a mass casualty assassination event with no better code than "buying a Chevy"?[5] Two things made this more credible. Hezbollah has, and continues to organize, a dangerous presence in Latin America, with recent efforts to expand into Mexico using the Lebanese diaspora. In 2006 a Mexican newspaper reported that members of the Sinaloa cartel were receiving training from the Iranian Revolutionary Guard Corps (IRGC) in explosives and firearms, traveling to Tehran via Venezuela.[6] Additionally, analysts suspected that the Iranian Guards just might not be as good as they used to be. At the same time this plot was in motion, they partnered with criminal gangs in Baku, Azerbaijan, to assassinate the Israeli ambassador to Azerbaijan in a similar way, and Shahlai may have overestimated his cousin's actual acumen and knowledge of America. "What we're seeing would be inconsistent with the high standards we've seen in the past," one U.S. official said, but others thought that the brazen and aggressive nature of the plan reflected hardened religious leadership with no experience of tradecraft. They want what they want and tell the Quds group to make it happen, with people like Arbabsiar as "a throwaway."[7]

Federal agents picked him up in New York on September 29, 2011, where he was waiting for a connecting flight back to Texas from Mexico, and he confessed to organizing the plan, eventually pleading guilty in federal court. In asking for leniency, his lawyers citied Arbabsiar's manic depression and disorganization, promising that he developed "sincere remorse." Wanting to issue a deterrent, the judge sentenced him to twenty-five years, and the prosecutor cautioned that "the dangerous connection between drug trafficking and terrorism cannot be over-stated."[8] A former business partner with whom he co-owned a car lot offered a different assessment: "If they wanted 007, they got Mr. Bean."[9]

■ ■ ■

Outside of the intelligence community, we'll probably never know how serious this plot really was. The Iranian government promptly disavowed it, leading to suspicions of a rogue faction within the IRGC. Certainly, a couple of bumblers with a bomb *can* kill one hundred people in a restaurant, just as a domestic terrorist with an RV can level a city block. The contours of this incident, the emergence of an unholy alliance between two known genres of threats—terrorists and criminals—with appealing shades of conspiracy and skulduggery, play right into a popular vision of security threats, that a mass, monolithic convergence of all the bad guys is coming for your freedoms. At its most cartoonish, it looks like the ridiculous scene in *The Naked Gun*, with Leslie Nielson's Frank Drebin busting into a conference room where a whole cast of nefarious leaders (Arafat, Qadhafi, the Ayatollah, Gorbachev) are plotting the end of Western civilization.[10] It's not so cartoonish to hear it from a security studies professional who, with a straight face, informs me that thousands of MS-13 members are massing on the southern border of the United States to march on Austin, Texas, and install Venezuelan Chavismo.[11] Certainly, MS-13 does violent and terrifying things, but their ultimate goal is not the destruction of the Westphalian state but instead carving out a lawless space within it to make money and exercise power without the responsibilities of governance.

It is important to note that this is also not a new pattern. VNSAs whose priority is ideologically driven intersect with VNSAs who exist to make money because they share many of the same spaces and frequently find one another convenient, even if those goals eventually drive the groups apart. Historically, this exists as far back as you can find terrorists and criminals, although post–Cold War politics and media increased both the reasons and the opportunities for it to happen as well as the means by which mainstream citizens found out that it was happening. On a psychological level, the public and the security apparatuses that they produce feel most comfortable ranged against a solid enemy, even if the one they find is a huge, scary one. Lacking the Soviet Union as a focus, experts in the 1990s turned to "pax Mafiosi" and "global conglomerates of crime" or the insistence that Narco-terrorism was "a communist plot to undermine Western society."[12]

This simplistic understanding, which is still a popular shibboleth, does real damage to efforts in understanding, curtailing, and preventing the ways in which VNSAs finance themselves. It is much harder work to see VNSAs as independent actors, driven by their own grievances, profit motivations, ideological priorities, and available resources, even if it offers means to pick apart their alliances with each other and possibly nip some of their options in the bud. In some cases, lumping them together actually fuels the sense that their demands won't be addressed, whether it is rights for a minority group, mitigation of climate disruption, equitable resource sharing, or anticorruption campaigns. There are VNSA demands that a liberal international order cannot abide, but a South African gang that smuggles abalone because of fishing restrictions is more available for negotiation than the secessionist national group on whose ships the contraband travels, and the smugglers can be peeled off.[13]

Mara Salvatrucha (MS-13) originated in Southern California among the Salvadoran diaspora in the 1970s but doubled back to Central America with early 1990s deportations of its members into post–civil war El Salvador. It is currently designated by Executive Order 13581 as a Transnational Criminal Organization. *Photograph by Michael Johnson, U.S. Immigration and Customs Enforcement, Defense Visual Information Distribution Service*

It's especially crucial to understand for the purpose of VNSA finance that the forces allegedly most threatened by these groups—globalization and sovereignty—are also the props that make it possible for them to generate revenue, even if the stated goal of the group is to stop the forces of globalization and change or tear down existing borders.

■ A Hamburger Story

Because they're so often taught in undergraduate international relations and political science classes, Thomas Friedman's "Golden Arches" theory of conflict and his expanded meditation on globalization in *The Lexus and the Olive Tree* offer a good framework for examining the balance between globalism and sovereignty (of borders as well as cultural traditions).[14] The theory goes that countries that have McDonald's franchises won't go to war with one another because, having reached a point in which bourgeoisie, globalized culture, foreign investment, and supply chains make an American fast food chain viable, the residents share enough common values and access to resources that conflict is less productive than peaceful engagement.[15] We know now that this is not strictly true: Israel and Saudi Arabia both have branches, as do other iconic enemies, but the metaphor serves to highlight positives of globalization. The other side of the bun is that, within the standards of the franchise, each is allowed to customize depending on the desires of local customers, so Israel's are kosher, India's have a meatless burger, and Canadians can poutine-ize theirs.[16] If this balance worked consistently, giving the world a Coke (not coke) would be easy.

The problem is that every feature of globalization that makes international communications, commerce, interconnection, and spread of ideas faster and smoother also enables illicit actors. Global reach isn't new, it just works with jet engines and electronic bank transfers instead of mule trains and bullion ship convoys, and this speed exacerbates processes that a slower evolution might have mitigated with controls and other support structures. McDonald's and the prosperity it represents didn't land evenly in new locations, so while there might be "a new urban-oriented consumer culture; and new farmer entrepreneurs," those excluded have no reason to love Big Macs and lots of animosity for new types of "economic, cultural and social capital" that arrived in its wake.[17]

For a group antagonized enough to turn to violence, globalization offers a whole package of tools. The information revolution that puts the movie inspiration for the Happy Meal toy on every billboard also enables a group operating from a frontier town to propagandize online, use Google street views to scope out an ambush point, and summon a weapons dealer using a satellite phone. The fast-tracked customs agreement that gets lettuce and tomato onto the burger year-round facilitates illicit materials hitching a ride, sometimes in the same efficiently containerized shipping and produced by the same labor pool. The capital to buy a franchise, made more easily available through global banking and crowdfunding, is the same system entwined with laundering, shell companies, and tax evasion. Even the carefully chosen locations for franchises, with freeway access, easy left turns from drive-throughs, and big parking lots, mirror the reduction of friction in crossing borders, acting beyond the reach of the state, and steamrolling existing inconveniences out of the way to build free ports, distribution hubs, and enterprise zones. One of the most pressing security tensions in the post-9/11 environment has been attempting to balance the open access and efficiency demanded by commerce against the traditional tools of control like border crossings, inspections, restrictions on capital flight, and emigration.[18]

What makes illicit trade profitable, though, is the second part of the equation: sovereignty, in which Westphalian nations set their own legal boundaries for what is allowed and taxed, and in what availability. To extend our hamburger story, consider an extreme example: the Spam and Oreo burger. McDonald's China branches, as a promotional act, offered a limited-time menu item, crafted with a Hormel patty covered in cookie crumbs and special sauce. Someone of sufficient connection and means in San Francisco can't get it at the local drive-through, but with a couple of phone calls and enough financial incentive, can have one in the lunch bag of an air crew member leaving Shanghai and passed through borders into his hands at the speed of commercial air travel.[19] Aside from crimes against good taste and the minor risk to agricultural production via the introduction of nonnative food products, no real harm done except flouting the rules imposed by customs inspections. But imagine if it were drugs, or guns, or underage sex workers, or a looted antiquity. What drove the activity was arbitrage—skillfully manipulating what is legal (or tolerated) and available in one place into another where it is in demand, taxed, or forbidden. In business school, this is "buy low, sell high." In VNSA hands, it is the lifeblood of financing.[20]

What economists term "deviant globalization" has tracked closely against developments in the transnational licit organization of multinational corporations and global markets. Household names like Nestlé sought out areas that would cooperate with their purchase of water supplies in ways that Global North democracies would not countenance, production shifted to areas with less labor regulation and minimum wage expectations, and raw materials are sought where they can be extracted with the fewest obstacles in the form of environmental controls.[21] This is so deeply entrenched as practice that security language targeted at VNSA defaults to MBA PowerPoint jargon— "stop payment," or "new economy of terror"—but acknowledges that without any checks at all (like customers demanding fair trade, or the image of the organization), illicit versions can move faster, respond more with more agility, and find partners without consulting shareholders.[22]

Untangling "good" and "bad" money for the purposes of counterterror or counter–transnational criminal financing is extremely difficult since the arbitrage extends to how participants see the illegality of the actions. Deviant globalization offers opportunities for people shut out of the legitimate economy, is rarely "the worst choice available, or irrational," and injects cash into the economy of developing countries in ways that employ people (doctors, lawyers, bankers, chemists) who continue to participate in the licit economy.[23] Attempts by receiving countries to prohibit, prosecute, and intervene can be met with offense and incomprehension—the practice being complained about isn't a priority in the country of origin, the demand is coming from elsewhere, and the money it brings in is a useful form of development, even if it isn't the kind donors favor. Most countries demanding compliance with international prohibitions also want sovereignty for themselves, setting up an additional conflict: How can a state like the United States "respond effectively and not lose legitimacy—the perception and acceptance that power is used legitimately and justly—when violating the sovereignty of other states becomes necessary?"[24] If your island nation's economy is grounded in generating shell companies, who is to say you're wrong?

■ The Nexus

Back to the potential amalgamation of bad actors, Voltron-like, into a super-VNSA powered by the illicit economy. It seems that they have enough in common to stick together or at least coexist easily. They are premised on a contempt for the rule of law (at least where it prevents them from doing what they want), have personnel who have a strong esprit de corps and few options to leave, exploit violence and the threat of violence, and often operate in the same spaces where they can access vendors and resources covertly.[25] Is this enough to identify a convergence?

Dr. Tamara Makarenko set out a useful framework for exploring the intersections of crime and terror. Her 2004 article, based on a decade of security work and observation of the post–Cold War landscape, positions the platonic ideals of each category at opposite ends of a spectrum.[26] On the terror end, VNSAs are defined by prioritizing ideology, outcome over profits (a showy attack versus steady access to money), long horizons for achieving goals, discrimination in targeting who can be exploited, wanting to have their deeds publicized and gain a following, little to no interest in the state continuing in its present form, and conviction that they represent a righteous cause. At the other end, criminal organizations are motivated by profits, the secure continuation of those profits, immediate needs for those profits to materialize, far more inclusive views of who can be victimized, no real desire for wider publicity and recruitment, and, although often at odds, a need for states to provide arbitrage structures and maintain enough law and order for there to be a host for parasitical exploitation.

Things get really interesting when the groups take steps toward one another, although outside observers rarely get a full account of how the decisions are made to do so. A rebel group needs money; a criminal group needs expertise in building car bombs to eliminate a new reformist leader who threatens them. The rebels get hold of some gold or diamonds and need a buyer. The criminals want links in a country where the terrorists have compatriots. Since crime and terrorism usually end up in siloed law enforcement channels, it may be unnoticed by the authorities until long past the point at which "one person's terrorist is another person's gangster."[27] In extreme cases, they meet in the middle, forming what Makarenko terms "a black hole"—a fully criminalized political entity like North Korea or those on the slippery slope to it like Afghanistan, Angola, Myanmar, or Tajikistan. Black holes still need the rest of the world to function as a market for their enterprises, but they form dangerous safe havens and sources of illicit materials.[28]

VNSAs emerge and operate effectively in areas where something has badly broken down or didn't exist in the first place. High poverty, low educational levels, alienation from authority because of lack of access, or corruption-sustaining inequity and dysfunction create spaces where opportunistic illicit acts are a social safety net and widely tolerated. VNSAs have a ready pool of recruits: young people (usually men, but young women are increasingly involved) who see no future for themselves in the current system if they behave in licit ways. This doesn't exclude the scions of middle-class and wealthy people, either, as being shut out of political power is as motivating as financial mobility in many cases. This makes countries with recently demobilized soldiers or refugees from a nearby conflict especially fertile ground. Criminals and terrorists fish from the same pond of potential members, looking especially for those with lowered thresholds for violence and useful experience, putting people in each group who have known each other since childhood. Either way, a state that loses its motivated, capable, and ambitious young people to crime or ideologically motivated VNSAs is sabotaging its own future.

In general, career criminals aren't particularly impressed with ideology. Taking risks "without any prospect of getting rich" seems "downright weird." Old-school motorcycle gangs making money on drugs and guns don't want a politically motivated one like the Aryan Brotherhood drawing attention to motorcycle clubs unnecessarily and ruining business for everyone.[29] Although organized criminal groups can miscalculate and use more force than the public will accept, they aren't okay with the level of mayhem a terrorist attack entails, and they want corrupt and inept public officials to remain in office, not be replaced by a new regime.[30] In fact, most mafiosos understand that, at the core of a terrorist group, there are true believers who will turn on them as soon as they gain power, as Chinese and Russian gangsters learned as Mao Zedong and Joseph Stalin went from learning to rob banks and trains to putting their erstwhile partners in camps. Tribal smugglers in league with al-Qaeda in Iraq lost patience with having terms dictated to them and seeing a future where hard-nosed and austere theocrats were in charge.[31]

When criminal VNSAs get involved in politics, it is usually to bend them for their own purposes. In the early 1990s, organized crime in Italy generated around 7 percent of the gross domestic product, so when prosecutors mounted an aggressive campaign to curtail their activities, the Mafia struck back with a series of violent car bombings in Rome and Florence to send a message to the Christian Democrats in parliament. Drug lord Pablo Escobar and the Medellín cartel began attacking Colombia's political establishment when it adopted a policy of extraditing to the United States.[32] In April 2002 a new Brazilian administration cracked down on drug trafficking, including isolating kingpins in the prison system. Members of the affected criminal organizations launched attacks on government buildings and police officers and firebombed buses until the prosecutors folded and offered immunity to some of the leaders and a free pass for operations.[33] VNSAs usually don't win such an overwhelming victory with these tactics, but they can disrupt investigations, deter informers, derail passage of anticrime legislation, coerce judges, and pick off high-profile officers of the court.

Criminal VNSAs, however, can have surprisingly sentimental and nationalist attachment to their ethnic affinity, religion, or homeland. The Chechen Mafia, with its business centered in Moscow, saw both opportunity in keeping strict Russian control out of Chechnya and an obligation to uphold honor and donate funds and resources to enable Shamil Basayev's militias. Chinese triads in Latin America have no compunction working with Hezbollah since the effects are targeted far away from their interests and base of operations but will have nothing to do with Islamist Uyghur separatists in Xinjiang who threaten the Chinese state.[34]

States, especially their intelligence and clandestine services, frequently leverage this VNSA tendency, involving Mafias, gangs, and drug rings in political causes. U.S. military doctrine cites the importance of special operations forces using connections within available criminal networks, using World War II as an example.[35] Mafia in Sicily *really* hated Benito Mussolini and fascist attempts to crack down on their control of the island, while American commanders wanted information in advance of landings in Italy and mob cooperation in handling dockworkers and draft boards in New York and Boston. Vito Genovese and Lucky Luciano saw opportunity when it knocked and validated Office of Naval Intelligence officer Lt. Cdr. Charles Radcliffe Haffenden's willingness to "talk to anybody: a priest, a bank manager, a gangster, the devil himself." As their reward, the clearly antifascist godfathers were left in charge as the Allies moved north, entrenching a generation of criminal power.[36] The CIA partnered with gangsters, gun runners, and cartels throughout the Cold War, with 1962's Operation Mongoose signaling to a whole "generation of entrepreneurs" that playing ball with Uncle Sam yielded outstanding rewards in the name of national security.[37]

Similarly, the Japanese Yakuza operated as right-wing enforcers in the 1920s, both in the home islands against communist students as well as in colonial areas as goons. In the late 1940s Yoshio Kodama, who made his fortune in the

Chinese Civil War, parlayed cash into founding what became the Democratic Party (in the majority in Japan's Diet most of the time) and overtly used the Yakuza, with U.S. Occupation approval, to tamp down disruption and challenges to conservative capitalist revival of business.[38] As the Soviet Union tottered, KGB officers were busy stashing state funds in foreign bank accounts, shell companies, and assets like gold and diamonds, maybe as much as $600 billion. To do it, they needed to enlist the aid of Russian *vory* to manage the sheer scale of chicanery and necessary international connections, a devil's bargain the Mafia has flipped around on the surviving state apparatus.[39] A regime under sanction like Saddam's Iraq or apartheid South Africa may turn to criminals to provide goods expected of the state, from hard currency to powdered milk, but saddle itself with powerful, entitled VNSAs.[40]

If the group finds it necessary to undertake criminal activity, it has to establish the moral event horizon beyond which it and the people it claims to fight for can't accept. In Northern Ireland, the IRA—and its offshoots—justified crime as a way to undermine the political regime, codifying this in its *Green Book* of doctrine, and its supporters expected resistance as a symbol that "not everyone has to be oppressed."[41] It can maintain this balance by disciplining criminal connections who go too far, as with the execution of Martin Cahill in 1994, but it is also useful to point to their rivals as being much worse. One PIRA spokesman insisted, "You're better off looking at the Loyalists. Drugs, extortion . . . from criminal psychology and so forth, it's easy to see how this kind of activity has developed" among the Ulster Defence Association Protestants.[42] Hezbollah successfully uses a similar justification and has convinced a sizable portion of the Lebanese diaspora into legitimizing their actions.[43]

In 1996 the PIRA rushed to distance themselves from the murder of Irish Garda officer Jerry McCabe, phoning in an announcement that "there was absolutely no IRA involvement" as a "damage-limitation exercise." Gerry Adams pushed hard for the IRA to behave within bounds and not tarnish the prospects of Sinn Féin by losing the perceived moral high ground, threatening to resign in 1993 if members were indicted for extortion.[44] Eamon Collins regretted the loss of the romantic image of the IRA to the greed of a colleague who, after a bombing in County Down, "robbed the tills . . . took the shine off the operation and made the IRA look like common criminals."[45] The Zapatista

Army of National Liberation in Chiapas, Mexico, publicly debated getting involved with drug trafficking to raise money but thought it would damage their legitimacy as a political force in Mexico, shying away from the Tijuana and Juarez cartels. VNSAs that maintain a reputation as freedom fighters, whether true or not, have a re-entry path to society that criminals do not and are very conscious of the need to retain it.[46]

If the ideological VNSA does dabble with criminals, the dangers besides loss of reputation are acute. The organization may lose control over the members tasked with conducting joint operations with criminals, whether through greed or the attraction of being independent and having a freer hand with assets to carry out attacks their own way. Being in bed with criminals leaves the group open to infiltration by law enforcement, who may pick up on activities through peripheral contact, especially if the crimes involved are of special interest to prosecutors and law enforcement with focused resources, like drugs, human trafficking, or guns, or if they catch a whiff that an ideological VNSA is also involved.

Some ideological VNSAs make a point of being performatively frugal and austere to demonstrate that their funds go entirely to the cause. Al-Qaeda demanded receipts for a sixty-cent piece of cake, choosing to commit their accountants to managing the wave of paper. In the PIRA, one senior figure famously eschewed fancy meals and literally passed the hat for gas money at meetings, "and when he does come, he'll eat sandwiches and that's that . . . I don't think it rubs off on anyone to that degree, but you have to admire his attitude to money."[47]

It is far more common for leadership in an ideological VNSA to start sliding toward lifestyles more common among their criminal counterparts, with the expectation that great sacrifice for the cause entitles a certain comfort in lifestyle. Loyalist chiefs in Northern Ireland had a regular skim from the £5–6 million they raised every year, making it possible to build vacation houses in Tenerife, take holidays in Florida, and adopt a gold chain, spray-tan "player" flavor that was extremely conspicuous and angered a core of true believers who "did not become paramilitaries to threaten building contractors and sell pornography."[48] The IRA had a similar problem, although maybe a less glitzy one, with "Green Godfathers" like Thomas Murphy using part of his EU tax fraud for "a very nice lifestyle" and refusing to stop.[49] Hezbollah, whose fundraisers in Europe and the United States already expect to get eight times the pay of an operative in Lebanon, fell victim to lifestyle inflation in 2008, when their financier, Salah Ezzedine, involved the organization's leadership in the Middle Eastern version of Bernie Madoff's pyramid scheme.[50] Their high living—$300 headscarves, fancy dining, and SUVs—raised eyebrows, and the ensuing crash and loss of the money forced Iran to step in and prop up basic operations.[51]

This disparity can undermine the group's ideology and give low-level members implicit permission to lean criminal themselves. Life dedicated to conflict tends to skew profitable at the top but not trickle down. One former jihadi, in the process of deradicalization, said, "Initially, I was of the view that the leaders were doing jihad, but now I believe that it is a business and people were earning wealth. . . . First I was there for jihad; now I am there for my financial reasons."[52] Former al-Qaeda member L'Houssaine Kherchtou turned informant after being disgusted with "un-Islamic" embezzlement while being denied a $500 C-section for his wife. Junior loyalists in the Ulster Defense Association turned their attention to building their own "feather bed" following the example of their leadership.[53]

Some junior people join an ideological VNSA explicitly in search of financial gain, which can be a smart and pragmatic move. Speaking of a captured jihadi in India's borderlands, one official said, "He looks like a part-time jihadi, part-time criminal; if his criminal connections are backed by jihadi connections, it all becomes easier for him. As a jihadi, he gets access to certain people and places; as an ordinary criminal, he wouldn't find his way."[54] Detainee programs in Afghanistan and Nigeria report that many of their prisoners joined "inspired by money" and for tacit permission to do what they wanted under the banner of ideology.[55] Yugoslav gangsters returning home to join militias in the 1990s thought of it explicitly in these terms of "patriotic costume," as did some of the key Chechen guerrillas. A journalist ruefully admitted that after interviewing Bislan Gantemirov of the "Islamic Renaissance Party" in 1992, "so help me, I took this title seriously . . . when what his presence really demonstrated was an expansion of the used car market."[56] These participants tend to make finding end states to conflicts much more difficult because they benefit from continued instability and predation, as "one avoids battle but picks on unarmed civilians and perhaps eventually acquires a Mercedes . . . makes more sense than risking death . . . with little or no prospect of significant financial gain."[57]

Countries that incarcerate political and criminal offenders in the same institutions facilitate meetings between the two ends of the spectrum. Prisons, like military service, offer a mechanism in which people can size one another up for loyalty, skills, and trustworthiness as well as serve as a fermentation site for grievances. An International Centre for the Study of Radicalisation report laid out that jails are "places of vulnerability in which extremists can find plenty of 'angry young men' with criminal pasts who may experience cognitive openings and are ripe for extremist radicalisation and recruitment . . . and therefore create opportunities for collaboration and skills transfers."[58] A criminal with the ability to clone debit cards plays chess or lifts weights every day with a radicalized white supremacist or religious extremist, to the utility of both parties. Ideological VNSAs find that criminal prisoners, often realizing that their pasts make them unlikely to rejoin society on mainstream terms, can find redemption and new purpose. "Big A," a Danish-born career criminal, was in prison when he learned that his brother had cancer and turned to jihadi cellmates to prepare as a convert and foreign fighter bound for Syria on release. "Some people have died of my hands. . . . This is a big problem when I meet Allah. . . . It's just not good enough to be praying with all the shit I've done."[59]

When ideological VNSAs slide further into crime, it is usually for one of three reasons: funding changes, leadership transition, or a morphing of the conflict itself. The end of the Cold War meant the closing of U.S. and Soviet credit lines for long-standing actors, who had to choose between empty pockets and picking pockets, with all of the calculations about reputation, legitimacy, and distraction that went with it.[60] Deaths among the group's leadership, from targeted assassination or old age, can also signal a change in priority. Without Abdurajak Abubakar Janjalani, dead in a 1998 shootout with police in the Philippines, at its center, Abu Sayyaf kept its orientation to extremist Islam but embraced far more lawless means of support, including kidnapping and extortion.[61] The nature of the conflict itself may change as the group achieves some of its goals like power sharing or resource allocation or realizes that their push was hopeless. The IRA, surrounded by a far more prosperous economy with social mobility and outlets for Catholics, found support for its ideology (and the corresponding donations) waning.[62] Conversely, some gangs, founded with a strong "brotherhood" or ethnic identification, have foundered on continued exclusion and, like the Black Kings in Chicago, abandoned their ideology in the 1980s for what their leadership decried as the ghetto version of yuppie materialism.[63] Some scholars of VNSAs see this evolution from ideology to crime as the norm since, as the group expands, new followers equate achieving the goals of the group with financial benefit for themselves, eventually orienting themselves and the actions they take to reach those ends.

When groups do reach across the crime/terror divide, the results can be alarming and spectacular. In 1976 the Palestine Liberation Organization and the Christian Phalange—bitter enemies—teamed up with professional safe crackers affiliated with the Corsican Mafia to carry out a heist at the British Bank of the Middle East in Beirut, hauling off £25 million after blasting a hole through the wall of the Catholic church next door.[64] In the 1980s the Italian Red Brigades opened a deal with the Camorra for gangster hitmen to carry out paid assassinations for them in a temporary contract arrangement whose target list pleased both. After Manuel Noriega shut down First InterAmericans bank at the behest of the United States, angry cartel leaders asked the Basque nationalist and separatist group ETA to kill him in Europe.[65]

On a more casual basis, a VNSA may subcontract with another to acquire one-time use of a needed skill, perhaps relying on middlemen to broker relationships among a "Kevin Baconing" of known talents.[66] Pablo Escobar hired bomb makers from the National Liberation Army (ELN) in Colombia to plant car bombs in 1993, as grassroots jihadi networks hire youth street gangs to "smurf" their stolen credit cards, move guns, and sell drugs.[67] Recently a former police chief in Parwan Province, near Bagram Airfield, suggested that the Taliban was hiring freelancers from among local criminals to kidnap American personnel to collect Russian-paid bounties.[68] These alliances are mutually beneficial, but almost all are temporary and will shatter once the money runs out, priorities conflict, or it becomes useful to turn on one another, a feature that presents opportunities for law enforcement and counterterrorism to exploit.

■ Why Does the Nexus Matter?

Complicating efforts to investigate, interrupt, and deter ongoing VNSA financing is the tracked nature of law enforcement and military responses. At the international level, UN resolutions separate terrorist financing from transnational crime, each triggering different agreements about how to proceed. Individual nations, including the United States, have profoundly separate rules of engagement and legal options, depending on whether an organization is a foreign terror organization (FTO) or domestic terror organization (DTO).[69] Additionally, where a group traffics in narcotics, U.S. law allows designation as a "kingpin," causing overlap where a group is a DTO *or* FTO and kingpin, but none has so far been both. Late in the Trump administration, officials raised the possibility of labeling Mexican DTOs as FTOs, which would immediately have ramifications for companies doing business in Mexico, insurance companies, banks, and any commercial activity that could conceivably be seen as providing material support to terrorism.[70]

By the time a conflict grinds down, the society left to rebuild has been hugely altered. Sanctions have bonded smugglers and criminals to crucial sectors of the legitimate government and elevated dangerous bandits and guerrillas to positions in which they expect a say in subsequent policy and administration. Counterinsurgency creates a "dirty war forever," with lingering grudges, easily available weapons, and frayed social relationships and with a police force attuned to using kidnappings, torture, and their own criminal connections.[71] As mentioned earlier, there may be a faction of VNSA members whose horizons are short-term profits and who think they do far better continuing the conflict than making peace, or whose demands make them spoilers in any negotiation where they cannot be accommodated.

Peter Andreas' work on Sarajevo tracks the postwar ascension of a rogue's gallery of profiteers, militia chiefs, and goons-turned-guerrillas that really stands in for most fractious asymmetrical conflicts, including the American Revolution. R. T. Naylor's observation that the "steel of capitalism [is] often forged in the heat of war" is an apt description for people like Hasib Salkic who, in retrospect, saw his time during the siege of Sarajevo as "the best course in market economy one can get. I learnt it and use it today."[72] The transition of known crooks into founding fathers can be embraced by the public or deeply resented if the money being kept came from the population and not foreigners or a collective enemy. The day before a plebiscite to approve peace in Colombia, FARC's disclosure of their vast wealth antagonized voters who saw themselves as victims of the long-running violence.[73]

Rank-and-file members, especially if their financial prospects after demobilization are poor, are at high risk for using their skills in criminal enterprise. Well-planned and resourced demobilization, disarming, and deradicalization (DDR) programs can succeed if they contain "quick-impact" projects and are pragmatic about meeting the expectations of unsympathetic figures to divert them from predation.[74] This worked in Uganda, sending young men with few marketable skills into farming communities with incentives for locals to reintegrate them, lowering crime in the region by 7 percent because "the boys on the technicals (pickups with machine guns) are themselves tired. They see no benefit, only death. . . . Some of them in secure jobs now include some who were the worst gangsters. They prefer the $200 that comes with a settled job."[75] In some cases the winning government can channel former VNSA members into official units, balancing the risk of an insider threat against the very real skills they bring to the table; for example, the Philippine army absorbed members of the Moro Liberation Front in the 1990s, and the Russians turned Chechen guerrillas into brutal counterinsurgency specialists.[76]

Much more likely, though, the de-mobbed will form a reservoir for potential challengers to the government or will strike out on their own as criminal entrepreneurs. After the suppression of the Huk Rebellion in the Philippines, disgruntled former guerrillas headed off into the hills to be bandits or positioned themselves around the burgeoning U.S. military bases to run gambling rackets or prostitution rings and to extort other businesses, finding "that the fundraising skills they had developed during the insurgency could be put to good use for personal enrichment."[77] Hutu rebels from the National Forces of Liberation in Rwanda and Burundi, many of them former child soldiers, have lost their roots in the community with the deaths of their families in the conflict, and they feel that the new regime targeted them as enemies. Twenty-one-year-old Claude can only see his days in the bush as preferable to now "because [then] you could make an ambush for cars and steal things. Now I have to struggle so that my small brothers live . . . there is no hope."[78]

The immense commitment needed by all participants in a conflict, as well as peacekeepers and neighbors, to a legal and economic "reset" may be aided by inclusion of specialized expeditionary police, especially those experienced in anti–organized crime investigations like those offered by

Canada's International Peace Operations Branch of the Royal Canadian Mounted Police. With careful DDR programs and acknowledgment of the entwined forces of ideological and criminal VNSAs, there's a chance to pry them apart.

■ Or Can You Pry Them Apart?

Plots like the Iranian-cartel team-up are deeply unsettling. The expanded reach of VNSAs to places previously shielded from their activities magnifies the fear that people have little control over their environment and can't avoid being entangled with threats in some way by just transacting normal commerce in the mainstream economy. Are your avocados funding a gang? Is your bank laundering money for drug lords? Do you carry insurance run by a shell company? Is your great-uncle's internet girlfriend a Boko Haram catfisher? The sheer powerlessness of trying to be good while in a system oriented to cooperation with bad makes it easy to conceptualize conspiracies and amalgamation of threats into one giant convergence.

Experts who study transnational crime think of VNSAs like MS-13 as "third-generation" gangs, criminally oriented groups with the reach to operate across borders and the political aims to get rid of interference in their activities, a goal that can align them with political VNSAs under the conditions discussed above.[79] Unlike the traditional conception of the Mafia, they don't have a hierarchy with a decision-making godfather at the top to apply conservative brakes on plans that literally explode their presence on normies and bystanders who expect to be shielded from them. The 'Ndrangheta and the Russian *vory* are examples of criminal networks with aggressively creative tactics for making money and a tolerance for risk, prison terms, and death that are deeply shocking to outsiders. It works for those who survive and claim the profits at the top, producing an economy worth $2.5 trillion a year in the illicit economy, at least some of it coming from working in concert with insurgents, terrorists, and warlords.[80]

The new generation of politically minded VNSAs seems far less shy about including overtly criminal organizations in their "network of networks," providing resilience and agility. "Flattened" structures, rather than hierarchical command chains, allow junior members to collaborate with their counterparts in loose, decentralized ways, and they are more willing to act independently, especially if they're expected to take a do-it-yourself approach to financing. Some of them may even consider themselves as participating members in both VNSAs and juggle the priorities of profit and ideological motive as long as they can, making it hard for law enforcement to identify them, "as if such operatives carry membership cards in their wallets."[81]

Familiar with the language and tactics of an ideological group, anyone can use it as cover for their moneymaking and can claim sympathy and excuses, as well as co-opt scary reputations. It's facetious, but bizarrely, as Hans Gruber's schtick in *Die Hard* wasn't untethered from what actual VNSAs do: "The following people are to be released from their captors: In Northern Ireland, the seven members of the New Provo Front. In Canada, the five imprisoned leaders of Liberte de Quebec. In Sri Lanka, the nine members of the Asian Dawn Movement . . . (aside to the goons) I read about them in *Time* magazine."[82] Spy novelist Ian Fleming had figured out the appealing potential of this threat nearly thirty years before: a crime management organization that used the various flavors of political extremism to create circumstances in which criminal activity could flourish unimpeded.[83]

It may be especially cold comfort that even if such supervillains existed, they don't want to break down the system to the extent that they have to take on responsibilities for running a whole state effectively before their final victory (if that is what they're trying to do), and they need the globalization and arbitrage created by Westphalian boundaries, as much as they might rail against them for corrupting people, exploiting their constituents, or adding friction to their schemes. Thinking about the IRA's Marxist aims in the 1980s, James Adams made an observation that applies just as well to twenty-first-century VNSAs who "set out to overthrow the society in which they are operating. However, the more they succeed, the richer they become and the more dependent they are on the survival of that society for a regular source of income to fund the revolution."[84] The gamble is that the real-life organizations revel in the black holes and can judge when to stop for their own benefit.

3
CRIME

Bob Fromme, an Iredell County sheriff's deputy, was moonlighting as a security guard at the JR Tobacco Outlet in Statesville, North Carolina, when he noticed that the same group of buyers came in regularly, purchased 299 cartons at a time, and paid in cash, often a wad of $20,000 from a plastic bag. At first, he thought they were Mexicans laundering drug money, but from listening, "knew soon enough [their language] was Arabic." He took down the license plate of their minivan but found that the manager of the outlet and, indeed, local law enforcement were uninterested. After all, the outlet was located right off the interstate to encourage people to stock up on cigarettes, and in the tobacco heartland of the United States, it was insane to discourage the sale.[1]

What Fromme was trying in vain to report was a genuine plot to raise money for Hezbollah. Mohammed Hammoud, recruited as a teenager in Beirut, came to the United States in the late 1980s via the Tri-Border Area (TBA) of South America and established a group of foreign students and additional diaspora emigrants from among his relatives and neighbors.[2] Hammoud had noticed that in smoke-happy North Carolina, cigarette taxes were extremely low, while in Michigan, which contained a critical mass of Shi'ite diaspora business owners, the state had recently raised taxes to pay for a school levy. Quickly, he had regular routes with drivers ferrying 1,500 cartons cross-country, yielding $1–2 each, disguising the loads by using minivans driven by American women the group recruited (and, in some cases, married bigamously). Since this was a tax violation rather than a violent crime, the risk was low, the convenience store owners were eager distributers, and the venture eventually made $7,457,239 while cheating Michigan of nearly $4 million in revenue.[3]

With almost two dozen confederates, Hammoud's cigarette smuggling branched out into a whole cluster of shady businesses, including faking green-card marriages, using the IDs of foreign students who had returned home to get duplicate drivers' licenses and credit cards that would then be maxed out, and running an online porn business. Hammoud and his American wife, Angie Tsioumas, diversified the scheme into legitimate paths convenient for laundering the proceeds, including getting a small business loan to run a Middle Eastern restaurant, buy a BP gas station, and rent warehouses, while holding Hezbollah video viewing parties at their suburban home. The money generated was going back to Lebanon via "tourist" couriers and more than eight hundred bank accounts linked to the stolen IDs or was being used to purchase dual-use equipment like stun guns, night vision goggles, GPS systems, and laser range finders and having them delivered to Lebanon.[4]

The Bureau of Alcohol, Tobacco, Firearms, and Explosives got interested in 1996, followed by the FBI in 1999, once it became clear that this was a national security issue and not just one state undermining another's tax regime, leading to the 2001 grand jury indictment of twenty-five people for money laundering, cigarette trafficking, conspiracy, and immigration violations, one of the first applications of the material support statute.[5] Said Harb, who ran the porn business, turned informer for a lesser sentence of 3.5 years, while Hammoud, as the leader, received 150 years, although this was adjusted to 30 after appeal in 2011.[6] When asked about the role of their product in this case, the response of tobacco company representatives was to point to the high level of taxes on cigarettes and suggest that states should reduce them and cut the arbitrage available to organized crime.[7]

▪ ▪ ▪

Like Hammoud and his network, VNSAs just getting started in a new place, or without the deep pockets of a state sponsor or monopoly of a resource they can extract, can turn to a whole menu of crime, some of which may evolve (for money laundering or because of its success) into legitimate contributors to the local economy.[8] A smart and careful group will not rush into smash-and-grab robberies but will study the available opportunities for things that fit in Freeman's criteria—quantity, legitimacy, security, control, and simplicity. During the second week of my Dirty Money course, once students are warmed up to putting on the role of bad guys, I send them the link to ESRI's online Tapestry Segmentation lookup and ask them to plug in zip codes from places they have lived and worked.[9] The arbitrages appear quickly, with would-be kingpins noticing that an area with a large population of middle-income retired people might be ripe for a phone scam requesting bail for grandchildren jailed in Mexico, a low-income community next to a shipping hub is convenient for setting up a recycling center to buy stolen scrap metal and things that "fell off the truck," an underpopulated rural area with access to cheap water and electricity is a good location for a marijuana growing operation, and a wealthy community with seasonal vacation homes is the place to burgle. It is a convenient exercise relevant (and fascinating) to consider for a domestic community as well as for any area of operations to which military or law enforcement personnel deploy.

▪ Fraud

VNSAs may not agree on *why* they flout laws and regulations—for an ideological movement, their defiance is propaganda by deed in undermining the illegitimate authority of a government and legal or financial structure they wish to replace, and their frauds deny funds to that establishment as part of a process to make the state ungovernable. A gang or a criminal organization doesn't want to give up profit, or sees those who have it as undeserving or suckers. Whatever their motivations, they engage in a dazzling array of schemes to pull money from tax fraud, credit abuse, insurance policies, social welfare payments, and con games.

A steady stream of trucks crosses the Afghanistan-Pakistan border, following long-established trade (and smuggling) routes, taking advantage of the 1965 Asia Pacific Trade Agreement (updated in 2010). *Photograph by Staff Sgt. Ryan Matson (2011), 2nd Brigade Combat Team, 34th Infantry Division, Defense Visual Information Distribution Service*

High-tax regimes, like those in Western Europe, are prime candidates for VNSA members finding loopholes to avoid paying surcharges and pocketing the money for their own purposes. In Sweden, the son of the ISIS chief in Mosul set up a company to import iPhones from Lithuania, which he then sold at bargain prices made possible by not paying the hefty VAT (7.1 million in kroner). Abu Hamza, part of a Scandinavian-based al-Qaeda affiliate, imported German chickens and cheese into Denmark, hiding his evasion of VAT in a series of shell companies until the loss to the Danish government topped three million krone ($460,000). Another scheme involved selling fraudulent carbon-tax credits from the Italian SF Energy company to companies in Western Europe, building a war chest of €1.15 billion sent to the Taliban in 2014 via banks in Cyprus.[10]

One of the most pressing issues of the Brexit settlement is the possibility of rehardening the border between the Republic of Ireland and Northern Ireland, which has been open since about 2005. The old border, with checkpoints and drastically different tax incentives, was an IRA arbitrage scam for decades. Thomas "Slab" Murphy, who got his nickname by dropping cement blocks to break legs, mastered European Union export subsidy programs and purchased a barn straddling the border. His Irish pigs and cattle crossed the border into Ulster, earning a subsidy per head, then he smuggled them back south, repeating the game so often that people joked that the animals had been trained to walk in a circle. After being investigated in 1985, he switched to a similar grain subsidy dodge, sending trucks loaded with sand (and a top layer of wheat) to collect over and over.[11] At its most efficient, Murphy's routine, U.K. tax inspectors guessed, earned the PIRA £20 million a year.[12]

Businesses run to finance VNSAs, with the expectation that they will come to the attention of authorities and can be abandoned, can forgo paying taxes entirely. In 2004, a French security firm run by Algerians with links to al-Qaeda used the firm to train foreign fighters sent to Afghanistan, in the process managing to get payment from the French government as a contractor but then failing to pay taxes on any of their profits, costing the state $500,000.[13] At least four Finnish citizens lied on their personal taxes to accumulate refunds used to finance extremists in Syria, while Jonathan Paul Jimenez in the United States claimed three fraudulent dependents on his 2010 income taxes, netting a large refund he planned to use to become a foreign fighter. In the United States, the complexity of the tax code and numerous state and federal loopholes and exemptions as well as cutbacks in auditing and IRS enforcement make this a useful source of funding, especially if the plotter expects a one-way trip.[14]

When members of a VNSA plan to be martyrs or to flee the country, it is no big deal to rack up high-interest consumer debt. Using their own or a stolen ID, someone wanting to raise cash can, as advised in Bali bomber Imam Samudra's prison-written primer on terror financing, apply for multiple credit cards and then max them out with daily ATM withdrawals or the purchase of easily fenced items like jewelry.[15] The cell that carried out the 2004 Madrid attacks lived on unpaid credit card balances, while Norwegian lone wolf terrorist Anders Behring Breivik took out twelve credit cards and ran up 30,000 kroner in cash advances and purchases of uniforms, weapons, and ammunition in preparation for his plans.[16] Multiple cards and high levels of debt don't trip the algorithms because they are a common status for consumers, one that generates large revenue in the form of interest, so there is little reason for banks to discourage the behavior.

Borrowers unable to get the freedom offered by credit cards turn to applying for loans, sometimes with forged pay slips, to buy large items like expensive cars, which banks assume they will be able to repossess. Instead, like Amedy Coulibaly, the gunman in the 2015 Paris Hypercacher Kosher Supermarket siege, a scammer can trade the newly acquired car to a chop shop for weapons and cash, or even take the car to Syria, where it is a valuable commodity donated by foreign fighters to be retrofitted with weapons and used in combat.[17] At that point the possibility of a bank repossessing the vehicle or recovering the money is zero. Collaborations with mortgage brokers open bigger horizons for bank fraud based on very large purchases. In a complicated Illinois case, a Saudi financier donated money to the Qur'anic Literacy Institute, itself connected to the Holy Land Foundation and Hamas. That money went to purchase land in DuPage County that was set up as Woodbridge Fountain, a housing development. Subsequent real estate deals involving the property generated money that went back to Hamas and allegedly purchased arms used in 1996 attacks in Jerusalem, including one that killed a nineteen-year-old U.S. citizen.[18]

Another permutation of VNSA fraud generating funds is lying to insurance companies. Gangs have long been party to arson for hire, asking for a cut of the payout in exchange for providing the fire, but Northern Irish loyalist militias made it part of their financial portfolio, tailoring their actions—whether the full destruction of the building, vandalism and broken windows, or the spoilage of specific unsellable merchandise that could then be claimed as an insured loss—to the needs of the business owner.[19]

Because most Global North states require substantial auto insurance, defrauding the companies through staged car accidents is another lucrative avenue. Fender benders with extensive whiplash injuries were a specialty of one of the wealthiest Russian mob factions in Brighton Beach, New York, until investigated by the police as Operation Boris (for "big organized Russian insurance scam"). Movement for Unity and Jihad in West Africa volunteers in Spain drew attention to themselves in 2012 with too many traffic accidents, prompting an investigation that exposed the whole cell.[20] In 2006 Karim Koubriti, insured by the American company Titan, avoided being in a car accident at all, filing an entirely made-up claim for his injuries, medical bills, and lost wages as part of an "economic jihad." It was too big a reach when two jihadists in Germany planned to fund their travel to Iraq after claiming that one of them died in a faked traffic accident. The insurance company refused to entertain the $1 million claim without a body.[21]

A VNSA with a well-educated diaspora may tap into insurance fraud from another side, co-opting medical providers or having members with the professional credentials inflate the billing and share the proceeds (coerced or voluntarily). An Armenian American *vor* coordinated a network of 118 clinics in twenty-five states, generating $100 million in sketchy claims before being caught in 2010, with U.S. Attorney Preet Bharara marveling at the "profitability, geographic scope, and sheer ambition" of the scheme, for which Armen Kazarian received only thirty-seven months in a low-security prison.[22] In 2013 a naturalized Iranian American urologist was indicted for extensive medical fraud billing, with the proceeds sent to Iran via *hawala* transfer. Auditors caught him by noticing that he was not just generating claims during times he was out of the country but was charging them to multiple health care entitlement programs.[23]

The grisliest version of this is using insurance as a kind of bounty on the lives of VNSA members. From tapped communications, the United States knew that a Hezbollah cell in Canada seriously discussed, but then decided against, taking out policies on their foreign fighters bound for Lebanon in order to collect the payout after they died as suicide bombers. Chechen guerrilla chief Shamil Basayev, in a gesture of both bravado and financial planning, tried to insure his men with a Moscow life insurance company, although there is no account of whether he was successful. The technocratic death cult Aum Shinrikyo, though, made $5 million this way, requiring inpatients of their "Astral Hospital" to buy policies and name the cult as the beneficiary, and then murdering them.[24]

Participants in VNSAs, by being students, unemployed, refugees, or other status, may be entitled to social welfare benefits from the state where they live. Some fundraisers have abused these programs in creative ways to underwrite support. Taimour Abdulwahab, who detonated a suicide bomb in Stockholm in 2010, forged university records to receive a 450,000 kroner bursary to study medical science through the Centrala student loan program, although he did not attend any program. Administrative cracks in the Danish, British, French, Dutch, and Belgian benefit systems allowed young men and women who ventured to Syria as foreign fighters to continue receiving support payments and regularly withdraw cash from ATMs in Turkey for as long as two years before being found out and removed from welfare rolls for not residing at their registered addresses.[25]

The IRA had a well-deserved reputation for mastery of the United Kingdom's benefits system in England and Northern Ireland, with West Belfast regularly referred to as a "social welfare black hole." Any members working under the table, perhaps in construction, were also expected to claim unemployment payments, lessening the organization's obligation to support them with a living wage. Those with time on their hands manufactured multiple identities, with the most skillful juggling up to forty, each claiming housing, pension, unemployment, and dependent support.[26] VNSAs with connections to authorized retail outlets can convert some welfare benefits, like electronic benefits cards or food benefits through the Women, Infants, and Children nutritional program, into cash with the connivance of store managers who take a cut.[27]

What makes this form of financing insidious is that the practice, or even the appearance, of welfare fraud does irreparable harm to vulnerable communities in the eyes of voters and the governments supplying the benefits. At the height of Somali American youth disappearing from Minneapolis to become foreign fighters, accusations surfaced that Somali-run childcare centers in the Twin Cities were bilking the state's Child Care Assistance program, with fraudulent counts of families served and kickbacks paid to parents to sign in to plus-up the reimbursements. Coupled with anecdotal stories about "suitcases full of cash" headed out at the Minneapolis–St. Paul airport, rumors spiked that millions of dollars were going to al-Shabaab.[28] Eventually investigators proved that there *was* systemic fraud, to the personal profit of several daycare operators, but no link was ever established that money was going to a VNSA (suitcases full of money *were* going as *hawala* exchanges to legitimate recipients among the senders' families). The hostility generated made it significantly harder to manage the crisis of disappearing teenage boys, which alienated both the Somali refugees and the host community.[29] Demands that groups be excluded from benefits based on their religious or ethnic identification can exacerbate isolation and poverty and make it even more likely that radicalization can occur.

VNSAs profile the populations they plan to exploit, looking for a scheme that pairs their resources with the vulnerabilities of the people around them. In 2015 a cell of ISIS supporters in England looked for small towns where the population consisted of pensioners, who they assumed (correctly, as it turned out) would not be tech-savvy and would respond best to telephone contact. With phone books in hand, they systematically dialed and pretended to be police officers investigating compromised bank information. They then advised the panicked recipients of this news that they could transfer money to a "safe" account to protect it, and the callers would be delighted to help set that up. The victims of the scam weren't users of their banks' online features; they trusted authority and were too embarrassed to alert others, making this a lucrative investment in fraud.[30]

A target population with just enough computer savvy to log on but not to exercise critical thinking makes for a rich environment for a VNSA employing familiar con games. Nigerian 419 online schemes are already widespread and put money into the hands of criminal gangs, but beginning in 2014, reports surfaced that Boko Haram recruiters were engaged in "romance fraud and sextortion."[31] Come-on emails have been sent to thousands of targets, promising financial returns and ongoing connection and attention if the recipient of the message would only lend their bank accounts to help transfer huge riches out of a vulnerable situation.[32] The framing of the scam, complete with lavish salutations, misspellings, and melodramatic plot twists (deaths in assassinations, car accidents, orphans, hidden gold stashes) play into Global North expectations of developing country stereotypes, allowing a middle-aged woman in Ohio to "rescue" a high ranking and good looking, sweet-talking government official in exotic Lagos.[33] The framing stories change quickly with international news, tracking new crises to make the target feel involved with global affairs and in a position to do something, most recently tapping into fears about the COVID-19 pandemic.[34]

A VNSA operating in a low-income area can target deeper pockets, aiming for local big-box stores or companies. In the 1980s Richard Lee Guthrie of the Aryan Republican Army supplemented his income between armed robberies by executing an elaborate buy-and-return scam at Kmarts in Maryland, with most of the money going to Richard Butler at the Aryan Nation's headquarters in Idaho.[35] A Hezbollah cell in Texas skulked around Walmarts, changing barcodes so that Enfamil baby formula, which retailed at ten dollars a can, rang up as fifty-seven cents, allowing the group to resell it at a huge profit. In a related grocery store plan, another Hezbollah cell with friendly links in store management trawled through thousands of trashed Sunday newspapers for coupons, which the stores redeemed for them and handed back the resulting checks from Kraft, Johnson & Johnson, and other large food companies. Since stores get a handling fee for each coupon, the managers still made money; the plan only imploded when spreadsheets implied that the stores must have been selling a ridiculously disproportionate amount of certain items.[36]

The deepest pockets of all may seem to be a casino, which, since the advent of electronic gaming machines, can set the payout rates, thereby guaranteeing (within the parameters of state gaming regulations) that the house has a fixed mathematical edge. A Russian gang affiliated with *vor* Razhden Shulaya was willing to take the risk of running a con on a casino, acquiring a computer program purported to analyze the patterns of video slot machines using a cellphone app and signal the player when to press the spin button.[37] Casinos, with their own surveillance regimes and predictive algorithms, spotted the men wandering around filming with cell phones the slot machines at the Lumiere Place in St. Louis and immediately tagged in the FBI to share the footage.[38]

■ Fakers

Gray market goods permeate everyday life. Globalization creates international brands but also creates demand that far exceeds supply or the ability of consumers to purchase products. VNSAs find it lucrative to fill that gap, often tagging on to tolerated practices and established routes already being used by more powerful entities. Some fakes are made in the same factories as their luxury twins, lacking only registration with Prada or Fendi, while others are shoddy within the tolerance of the person who bought them. With the rare exceptions of machine parts, medicines, and food, a pair of knockoff Nikes or a bootleg copy of *Avengers: Endgame* is unlikely to harm an individual consumer, leading to the public perception that this is a victimless crime, but a bad actor can, with little risk, bring in huge sums of money to fund itself on high-margin, easily smuggled items.

Counterfeiting national currency is a time-honored tactic to fund operations while undercutting an enemy's economy and their public's trust. Nazi Germany coerced the labor of skilled forgers and printed £630 million in U.K. notes during World War II's Operation Bernhard, channeling the money into intelligence networks and international purchases. During the Cold War, East Germany pirated West German currency for the same dual reasons—ideological opposition to capitalist systems and purchasing power abroad.[39] Using the resources of the U.S. Treasury, the CIA counterfeited enemy money repeatedly, attaching propaganda to forged North Vietnamese dong and paying the mujahideen with $20 million in Afghan notes, with the expectation that when the deception became apparent, it would undermine the Kabul government.[40]

When counterfeiting, state sponsorship offers significant advantages, including access to printing presses and special paper sold only to sovereign nations. North Korea exploited this from the outset, acquiring a restricted Swiss-made Giori press and plates via fraudulent loans, then immediately putting them to use in the work of Bureau 39, producing as much as $100 million in $100 U.S. "supernotes," laundered through North Korean accounts in Macau and Hong Kong banks and sold to VNSAs around the world.[41] Iran offers similar services to Hezbollah, with its counterfeiting affiliates occasionally partnering with al-Qaeda in Egypt and Chechens when profitable or useful. Israeli counterterrorism officials made official complaint to the U.S. Treasury about notes they recovered in Lebanon and in circulation in Israel, only to be asked their estimate of the total value: $50 million. "That's all?" was the dismissive answer, along with an explanation that the United States prefers to redesign its notes frequently rather than deal with individual cases in such small quantity.[42]

Without state sponsorship, counterfeiting currency is a much more difficult task and is only really worthwhile if the notes are simple, like post-Saddam dinars, or if multiple banks issue notes, like in Northern Ireland, making it hard to spot fakes.[43] The PKK and LTTE have attempted to forge U.S. dollars and Sri Lankan currency, with the PKK employing high-quality color copy machines, but authorities detected the fakes and arrested the counterfeiting rings.[44] Because of the ideological attraction of refusing the legitimacy of U.S. currency, white power and sovereign citizen movements have repeatedly attempted to use counterfeiting money to fund themselves. Two Aryan Nation members with a church printing press made $50 bills that, despite being aged with coffee grounds, were immediately suspect to local merchants. Gale Nettles, planning to bomb the Dirksen Federal Building in Chicago in 2005, tried to finance his operation by making $20 bills (all with the same serial number) sold at a discount to an undercover FBI informant.[45]

VNSAs need visas, passports, drivers' licenses, and other crucial documents in order to operate in countries with robust bureaucracies. In many cases, forgeries are no longer enough, as the documents tie to an online database maintained by law enforcement and government agencies. A friendly or coercible diaspora population is a ready pool of available passports, drivers' licenses, and student documents, which the LTTE exploited extensively in Canada and Australia, reusing photo IDs and trusting that immigration officers would think most Tamils look alike.[46] An organization that has an inside track, perhaps a friendly connection at the Department of Motor Vehicles or someone in a university's ID office, can sell that expertise to others.

Areas with poor access to health care and haphazard regulatory structures are easy targets for drug counterfeiting, which has small startup costs and carries far lower penalties than narcotics trafficking. Dealing in "medicines," whether formulary knockoffs or completely worthless adulterations, can be more palatable in terms of reputation than being labeled as "drug dealers" if this is important to a VNSA.[47] Hezbollah uses a regional network to distribute a wide variety of counterfeit pharmaceuticals, from antimalarial treatment to the HIV/AIDS drug AZT, tapping into an illicit sector estimated at $75 billion annually and comprising as much as 10 percent of the world's prescription drug market.[48] The consequences of this are obvious and extremely dangerous: drugs with inconsistent dosages, deaths from useless knockoff insulin, public health crises as people with untreated HIV go about their lives, and declining quality of life because of ineffective deworming and malaria prevention, which also undermines trust in the medical and governmental systems responsible for a population's health and safety. One of the most popular counterfeits, available online with no questions asked, is Viagra and its knockoffs, which yield a far higher profit margin than cocaine and have almost no disgruntled customers willing to complain.[49]

Other bogus products are dangerous because they evade inspection and regulation meant to protect consumers from adulteration and shoddy production. Italian organized crime is a longtime player in the "Agromafia," which dilutes olive oil and engages in other lucrative food fraud that undermines *appellation d'origine contrôlée*, or AOC, designations and passes off cheap imitations and fillers for premium wines, cheeses, and aged vinegars.[50] VNSA-sold counterfeit fertilizers in China, Ukraine, and Italy have done serious environmental damage, sickened local farmers, and ruined their crops.[51] Schaeffler, the German ball bearings manufacturer, has launched an anticounterfeiting campaign after forty tons of Chinese counterfeit versions of their parts turned up across Europe, endangering larger manufacturing installations as well as the company's reputation.[52]

Brand-name clothing and shoes, produced in the Global South under regimes with little legal prohibition against trademark misuse, make effective fundraising items. Brothers Saïd and Chérif Kouachi, who executed the 2015 attack on the *Charlie Hebdo* offices in Paris, funded their living expenses and the operation by selling fake Nike sneakers they imported from China. In the Molenbeek neighborhood of Brussels, a number of foreign fighters raised their travel money to get to Syria by hawking T-shirts and jeans.[53] With the resources to do this on a larger scale, a VNSA can import and distribute hundreds of thousands of items, as followers of Sheik Omar Abdel-Rahman did in the lead-up to the 1996 Atlanta Olympics, concentrating on souvenirs for tourists with the distinctive logos of the event.[54] In Los Angeles, raids in the garment district turned up counterfeit designer denim and sneakers in warehouses used by Hezbollah- and al-Qaeda-affiliated personnel, packaged for sale.[55]

Any VNSA that invests in a computer and DVD burner to distribute its propaganda has an easy next step to pirating music, movies, and software. Bored consumers frustrated with their access to globalized popular culture

An assortment of counterfeit goods seized by Immigration and Customs Enforcement agents in partnership with the National Intellectual Property Rights Coordination Center. *Photograph by Paul Caffrey (2010), U.S. Immigrations and Customs Enforcement, Defense Visual Information Distribution Service*

have few reservations about getting what they want expeditiously. The equipment is available off the shelf, and duplication requires no advanced skills, just patience and a distribution channel. Areas already known for their nonexistent regulation, like the TBA of South America, have emerged as pirating centers, cranking out 20,000 DVDs a day. In the TBA, Lebanese diaspora members like Assad Ahmad Barakat, designated a "global terrorist" by the United States in 2004, and Ali Khalil Merhi own the factories and maintain connections to Hezbollah or to Sunni extremist groups like Jama'at-i Islami, but they also sell to secular cartels and gangs who distribute the products using trafficked people as the sales force and stocking them in ethnic shops and groceries.[56] Bootleg media is so pervasive that most forward operating bases in Iraq and Afghanistan had vendors selling DVDs to coalition service people with the blessings of the local military commanders.[57]

■ How VNSAs Dream of Electronic Fleecing

Frank Abagnale, the con man turned security expert of *Catch Me If You Can* fame, opens his talks on cybersecurity with a *New Yorker* cartoon: a frowning bank teller tells a masked robber, "You know, you can do this just as easily online."[58] Identity theft, account pilferage, blackmail, and fraud are, to many analysts, just new tools applied to old crimes, requiring online skills rather than a willingness to mug someone with a weapon.[59] Even if this is true, cybercrimes *feel* different, perhaps because computer technology is so ubiquitous and unavoidable in twenty-first-century life. While a person may feel they have some control over avoiding dark alleys where their wallet can be taken, finding out that a retailer lost their credit card info to a hacker leads to even more powerlessness and frustration, especially if banks see it as just the cost of doing business and no one is ever caught. VNSAs, which are often risk-tolerant early adapters of new technology in order to skirt regulation and gain an advantage, see the online world as the same sort of virtual place as ungoverned physical spaces, "with limited bank supervision, no anti–money laundering laws, ineffective law enforcement institutions and a culture of no-questions-asked bank secrecy," making it a rich source of financing for illicit actors plying old scams with innovative twists.[60]

Technology offers enormous advantages to an illicit actor. Pressing the "enter" key from anywhere in the world, a hacker can steal or infect a machine thousands of miles away, lowering the threshold of risk aversion.[61] Using relatively inexpensive hardware and software, some of it developed to help people in oppressive regimes hide their identities, a criminal can target thousands of addresses at a time for a fraction of what it would cost to approach each one separately. For a politically oriented VNSA that lacks the capacity, this is an obvious crossover opportunity with the criminal world, which offers "pay-as-you-go" collaboration. If even a handful of the phishing lures work, there's profit and almost no chance of identification or prosecution. Cyber operations, which depend on an acquirable intellectual skill set—not an industrial base, big conscriptable population, or expensive military equipment—are a formidable asymmetric tactic and equalizer. Even if a group is on the run, its members can retreat to a virtual battle space to recruit, raise money, and wreak havoc.

The difficulty in stopping or reducing cybercrimes lies in the original architecture of the internet, which its designers intended to be open and egalitarian, and which offer users the same access in a spirit of community and unfettered exchange of information and commerce. Unfortunately, this means that malicious users can take advantage of uncoordinated regulations and arbitrage their behavior—locating servers in countries that don't care if they host child porn or behind the diplomatic shields of state sponsors who expect a cut of the proceeds. Law enforcement and security agencies find it extremely difficult to work in concert across dozens of countries for cooperative investigation and prosecution, civil liberties advocates struggle to balance how to draw lines of acceptable freedom of action, and businesses want both the perks of global reach and the security of copyright and fraud protection. Some VNSAs have been so confident that they use websites hosted by U.S. companies or—like the Pakistan-based Lashkar-e-Taiba, which planned the 2008 attack on Mumbai online—route their communications through a Texas server because it is reliable and cheap.[62]

Another hazard of attempts to regulate the cyber world comes because laws move at the speed of legislatures and the courts and function at the level of knowledge possessed by the people in those positions of authority, often a generation older than the technology being constrained. Prosecutions can attempt to use existing laws against blackmail and fraud but even then stumble, as did Crown lawyers in the United Kingdom, whose presiding judge interrupted the 2006 trial of Younes Tsouli (charged with incitement to commit terrorism and £2.5 million of credit card fraud online) to complain, "The trouble is I don't understand the language. I really don't understand what a website is," requiring the prosecution to call a computer science professor to give a background tutorial.[63]

There is no doubt that state actors use cyberspace as a warfare domain and lend protection and expertise to their proxies. U.S. strategy documents are clear about the state of the "cool" war existing with China, Russia, North Korea, and Iran over their hacking, denial of service attacks, and information warfare campaigns, including those surrounding the 2016 presidential election. Department of Homeland Security documents even point to Russian laws, which compel firms doing business in the United States to share information and allow the Federal Security Services of the Russian Federation to use them as routes for cyber espionage.[64] VNSAs, unless they are carrying out a longer-term strategy on behalf of a sponsor, tend to be less interested in using cyberspace this way and more invested in using it to propagandize, create drama and uproar, or fundraise through criminal means.

As an example, both al-Qaeda and ISIS recruited for members with hacking skills, circulating an article titled "39 Ways to Serve and Participate in Jihad," which assured those uneasy about physical violence that "electronic jihad" was equally acceptable.[65] For those who joined, the organizations screened for online skills in their personnel files and pointed would-be joiners to online forums where they could improve their capabilities.[66] Junaid Hussain, an ISIS foreign fighter from the United Kingdom, was using his "hacker Rolodex" as leverage in his ideological disputes within the organization until his death in a 2015 drone strike.[67] Most of ISIS' overt activities have been taking control of and defacing websites belonging to Western governments and institutions, or hacking CENTCOM's Twitter account in 2014, but they also harnessed this capability to hack into databases and assemble "kill lists" and doxing information about military personnel, federal employees, and the experts at a New York nonprofit who had documented ISIS hacking.[68]

This level of hacking skill can be put to more lucrative use scraping thousands of accounts for credit card, bank account, and Social Security numbers, which can be used to buy desirable materials "for whatever Allah has made permissible" or sold for a profit.[69] Even an inexperienced hacker can find friendly and helpful spaces in the Dark Web, where vendors rent botnets in thirty-day increments, allowing the user to collect personally identifiable information from the infected computers.[70] With purloined credit card numbers and supporting PINs and addresses in hand, a VNSA can order online from mainstream retailers or, if in search of something more illicit, can tap into the same Dark Web marketplaces, "a Craigslist for militias," to buy everything from chemicals to a T-55 tank.[71]

The old-fashioned crime of blackmail is made easy by hacking as well. In 2015 website Ashley Madison, which offered subscribers connections to facilitate adulterous affairs, lost ten gigabytes of customer information to hackers, who dumped it on the Dark Web, after which extortionists started sending letters to spouses of subscribers demanding $2,500 in Bitcoin or risk public exposure.[72] In one of the most bizarre anecdotal examples of a VNSA hustling semi-licit material online, there's also a guy who went online looking for cheat codes for the video game *FIFA* and PayPal'd his way into a visit from a squad of Afripol detectives looking for what they described as a "Russian terrorist" planning an attack in Algeria.[73]

In an era of austerity and high customer expectations, many municipalities have turned to "e-governance" to manage the provision of city services like utility bills, trash pickup schedules, issuance of traffic camera tickets, and permitting applications. Often pitched as a cost-saving measure requiring fewer staff members, it can also be an anticorruption measure, ensuring transparent and equally applied fees and access. It is also an open door for hackers since automation has gone up but the computer skills needed to manage the system have drastically gone down. Smart cities are in the hands of people who put their passwords on Post-it notes stuck to their monitors.[74] Hackers hit more than forty U.S. cities in 2019, with ransoms for protected data ranging from $5.3 million to the smallest amount the city's insurance was willing to pay, leading local governments, school districts, and legal systems to scramble to implement security measures.[75] Because of their obligation to protect client privacy, law firms and health care offices are also unusually vulnerable to ransomware attacks on their cyber systems.[76]

One of the most concerning aspects of hacking is its application to access resources in the physical world. In 2019 Car2Go in Chicago, a service with which a user can gain access to a rented luxury vehicle via an electronically transmitted code, reported that as many as one hundred Mercedes-Benz sedans were missing from their stock. Several of the vehicles were "used for crimes" before being recovered.[77] For a VNSA, the potential advantages of hacking its way to a getaway car, courier transport, or vehicles that could be stripped and sold are worth incorporating into planning if the environment includes rental systems like this or unmanned storage facilities for trucks and cars. Self-driving cars, although a long way from street legality or operation, are a major security risk to watch for cybercrime in the form of theft or hijacking.

Based on the success of the LTTE seizing control of the Intelsat-12 communications satellite to broadcast their messages and the ease with which

"Anonymous"-affiliated hackers leaked data from the European Space Agency "for lulz," there is reason to fear that VNSAs can hijack space assets either to boost their own propaganda, disrupt enemy communications, or ransom control of the system for financial benefit.[78] Although militaries train to repulse hacking attacks and "red team" scenarios where a VNSA can seize control, it is a constant arms race with each side incentivized to develop new tools and defenses, with the potential that it could move into ransom threats based on credible kinetic threats—crashing an unmanned aircraft system where a VNSA could recover its armaments or retarget it or could steer satellites into one another or into debris. From 2003 to 2010 U.S. drone systems were unencrypted and vulnerable to a downloadable $26, likely Russian-Iranian developed software hack called SkyGrabber, so the sky is far from the limit for VNSA cyber/space piracy.[79]

■ Going Legit, Sort Of

Because the illicit economy is so closely linked with the licit one, most criminal activities have some openly practiced twin.[80] Someone moving things from a high-tax to a low-tax area may realize that they can arbitrage something from high-demand to low-demand regions with less risk and pay taxes on it, or a front company created to have cover to buy precursor chemicals at wholesale might end up making more money than the illicit reason it was created. This is something of a pattern for the Russian Mafia, which became linked with licit businesses as part of their extortion expertise. PeterStar, the telecommunications company, and Sberbank Rossii hired mob-infested security companies to collect debts for them, leading to the realization that being an executive for a commercial bank or controlling a regional telephone network was profit by "capital accumulation rather than coercion."[81]

Similarly, a VNSA may find that, denied services in the licit economy, it needs to create its own ecosystem of providers in order to function, and then discover that it works well and generates money from other clients. The Mujahideen Council of Indonesia started a publishing house and branched into video production to make propaganda but turned a profit on other media products.[82] Hamas and its charity arm, Holy Land Foundation, invested money in InfoCom, a Texas-based internet service provider that eventually hosted a licit–illicit mix of five hundred Arab websites, including those of Holy Land Foundation, Al-Jazeera, Muslim Students Association, the Palestinian University of the West Bank, and the country domain .ir (Iraq) and sold software and computers to Syria and Libya before being investigated and shut down in 2001 for violating U.S. export controls.[83]

The naval wing of the LTTE, the Sea Tigers, with enormous expertise from gun running, human trafficking, and drug smuggling, and a fleet of merchant ships with safe berths in friendly territory, branched out into legitimate shipping, the "Sea Pigeons." Customers willing to do business with an obvious VNSA front company also trusted that their cargoes would be well guarded and reach their final destination safely and efficiently because of that reputation and skill. Had the LTTE achieved their goal of a separatist state, this would have been a major asset in their economic infrastructure if expanded and turned entirely to legitimate use.[84]

A VNSA with spare cash can choose to inject it into businesses that will return a profit and function as a support mechanism for its recruiting and upkeep of members. Boko Haram's founder, Mohammed Yusuf, gained a following and built up a cadre of young men by offering microloans to start small personal-service companies like motorcycle taxis. In a society with little social mobility and limited capital, attractive jobs for youths with few nonagricultural skills made him a man worth listening to, and the startups generated back the investment into the organization's coffers.[85] The LTTE offered its diaspora small loans to set up businesses, expecting a cut of the proceeds via larger remittances. One of the most lucrative businesses was an entirely legal scheme to buy long-distance telephone cards in bulk and then sell them through Tamil-owned shops across the Global North.[86] While an al-Qaeda team under Fazul Abdullah Mohammed worked the Kenyan–Somali coast to plan attacks on Mombasa, they bankrolled a series of lobster fisherman.[87] That this is a worthwhile tactic suggests that countries who want to shut out VNSAs should look into providing microfinancing and opportunities for their underemployed and frustrated populations.

Perhaps the pinnacle of a business for VNSA benefit is a bar. If the organization's value system allows for the consumption of alcohol, the opportunities abound. It might begin with noticing, as the PIRA did, that small bank robberies and extortion netted far less and for more risk than the legitimate operation of the pubs and drinking clubs they leaned on for "donations."[88] These shebeens served beer extorted from breweries and provided a place to hang out, store materials, hold meetings (one club in Belfast was the Provo's preferred diplomatic reception spot, with parties for North Koreans, the Palestine Liberation Organization, the African National Congress, and Sandinistas and to celebrate the Russian invasion of Afghanistan), and literally "show the flag."[89] Accessorized with jukeboxes, slot machines, and cigarette vending from which the PIRA took a cut (and in which they sold untaxed cigarettes), the network could bring in more annually than the Irish Northern Aid Committee collected in America.[90] As cash businesses, bars have notoriously easy to cook books, which allowed both republicans and loyalists in Northern Ireland to run them in evasion of government supervision and with enormous profits from ferociously supportive clientele.[91]

Legitimate businesses with VNSA affiliation can benefit from what a legitimate market would term "vertical integration," or coordination of all of the stages of profit usually handled by separate entities.[92] In 1972, British intelligence tracked a PIRA firebombing campaign against Belfast city buses, assuming that it was solely a terror tactic against the government and meant to unsettle the population and destroy infrastructure.[93] It turned out that the PIRA had decided to buy into the taxi business, putting money "to work" via Sinn Féin's grants to entrepreneurs affiliated with the cause. Every step of operating the black cabs—renting the vehicle, fueling it, repairing it, and paying a tax on earnings—went into republican pockets, with the additional expectation that the cabs were on call to ferry people around anonymously and deliver crates of arms. The firebombs had also been to render the city's public transportation inoperable and drive passengers to the more expensive cabs, while taking $3 million a year out of the city's budget.[94] The Haqqani network in Afghanistan and Pakistan makes much of its money smuggling and taxing trucks along a vital route but also requires the drivers to patronize gas stations, repair shops, restaurants, and other services owned by relatives and allies, all of whom pay tributes out of the revenue.[95]

With enough liquid assets, the VNSA should consider investing in the international financial markets, a move that can yield larger profits and be—by being tangled so thoroughly with the functioning of the licit commercial world—extremely difficult for authorities to find, confiscate, or police. Beginning in the 1970s the Palestinian National Fund placed millions of dollars into Western stock markets, holding blue chip stocks, money market funds, and portfolios from mainstream companies.[96] Al-Qaeda bought shares, too, in a Swedish medical equipment firm, a chain of dairies in Denmark, and Norwegian paper mills as well as real estate across Africa and Central Asia.[97] The IRA both invested in and laundered money through the London Stock Exchange to the tune of £200 million, while the Japanese Yakuza opened brokerage accounts in Malaysia to buy U.S. Treasury bonds on the Hong Kong stock market.[98] Analysts believe that FARC, along with owning property and investing in businesses, bought shares on the Colombian stock market as a place to stash their wealth.[99]

These kinds of investments can be handled through a competent money launderer, but groups with security to control territory and with regional credibility may open their own banks. Hamas capitalized the Al-Aqsa Islamic Bank in 1997 and operated it until 2010 (part of the time in partnership with Citigroup, to evade sanctions), when U.S. Treasury actions finally made the bank too risky for other financial institutions to transact business.[100] Hezbollah, borrowing the historical term for the Islamic caliphate's treasury and tax collection department, has Bayt al-Mal (House of Money) as their financial services company, with branches across Lebanon. To arrange support packages for Hezbollah projects, especially construction, the bank uses the Yousser Company for Finance and Investments, and both Yousser and Bayt-al-Mal act as intermediaries between Hezbollah and mainstream banks.[101]

In a conflict or post-conflict zone, owning a construction business or physical infrastructure (airports, toll roads) is a very lucrative move, allowing a group to sweep in with repairs, sop up reconstruction contracts from nongovernmental organizations and aid packages, and employ large numbers of men with manual labor backgrounds as well as control vital local outlets to the rest of the world. The Russian mob's building firms muscled in on government contracts for major projects like the Moscow water system and a gas pipeline from Turkmenistan to Ukraine.[102] Within their territory, ISIS has possession of five major cement plants owned by a French company, with the capacity to produce materials with a retail value of $580 million a year, to sell or use in fortifying and building.[103] With underwriting from the Yousser Company, Hezbollah runs Jihad al-Bina (Effort for Reconstruction) to rebuild houses and erect bunkers and bases. After the July 2006 conflict with Israel, Hezbollah allocated $450 million to an accelerated construction program, with most of the funds channeled from Iran.[104] In Somalia, Mohamed Afrah Qanyare, commanding his own subclan militia, used its labor to develop an airstrip south of Mogadishu, from which he collects landing fees, while warlord Bashir Raghe bought into the El Ma'an seaport and used control of it to skim off the charcoal-importing business.[105]

Cells sent ahead to an area to prepare for an operation or to raise funds, like Hammoud in North Carolina, can be ordered to figure things out for themselves based on local conditions or told to just get regular jobs. Veterans of the fighting in Bosnia moved into Western Europe as al-Qaeda and supported themselves doing under-the-table plumbing, construction, and backyard car mechanic work. Operatives who can pass as white-collar workers might pick up no-show jobs, as did Muhammad Haydar Zammar, who recruited a number of the 9/11 hijackers and worked at Tatex Trading Company for a former Syrian intelligence commander and Muslim Brotherhood member, Muhammad Majid Said.[106] Lone wolf terrorist Michael Zehaf-Bibeau, who attacked the Ottawa War Memorial in 2014, supported himself in a series of high-paying jobs in the Alberta oil fields, finding that in a labor market desperate for workers willing to tolerate harsh conditions, even a "confessed crack addict with a criminal record" could keep getting hired.[107]

Finally, a VNSA has the option to operate businesses that, if the profits were not going to an illicit organization, would be regarded as entirely mainstream and legal. It might be for the good of the community, like the IRA's neighborhood co-op grocery, to employ local people and raise the organization's reputation as a patron or to generate revenue while reducing the chances that authorities will become suspicious of their activities.[108] During Osama bin Laden's time in Sudan, he invested in more than thirty-five companies, including a peanut farm, a tannery, apiaries, a bakery, and a furniture making company.[109] This was probably to curry favor with the impoverished government, which regarded this as a valuable job-creation program and seized the companies as assets after pressuring bin Laden to leave in 1996.[110] In a far more sophisticated economy, the Japanese terror cult Aum Shinrikyo had a full portfolio of high-tech subsidiaries, including computer dating agencies, yoga clubs, copy shops, and a popular doughnut chain.[111] ISIS's surviving leadership cadre has allegedly smuggled as much as $400 million across borders to hide it in legitimate businesses in Turkey, which forms a reserve and emergency retirement plan.[112]

As lucrative and advantageous as VNSAs find legitimate and legitimate-adjacent business to be, any endeavor that operates in the licit marketplace has to keep books, pay taxes, and conceal its connections from regular employees and neighbors. Audits and complaints from disgruntled customers to inspectors offer the authorities entrée to the wider organization, a tactic that gangs have used as a weapon against one another. Having money tied up in ongoing businesses also complicates attempts by VNSAs to demobilize or participate in cease-fire agreements, as some cadre has to remain active to liquidate or oversee the investment in an acceptable way (acceptable to both the survivors of the group and the government), a factor that continues to plague the Irish peace process—are disarmed republicans easing out gracefully or assembling a slush fund for a return to action? You'd be a fool to trust the pub books to inform that judgment.

4
HANDS-ON VIOLENCE

Extortion is a delicate thing, requiring a balance of credible threat and an understanding of how much can be extracted from a target without prompting them to go out of business or appeal to authorities for assistance. Loyalist militias in Northern Ireland refined the approach and the tasking to an art that provided them with a steady stream of income for decades. Not long after opening, a new shopkeeper could expect a visit from a pair of men, one young, one older, soliciting donations for loyalist prisoners and their families. The older of the pair is charming, with at least a couple of heart-tugging stories of hardworking wives struggling at home with a husband or son in a British prison, men who sacrificed so much to preserve the Protestant way of life in the neighborhood. The younger one wanders the aisles, handling stock, maybe dropping something small or bumping into the fixtures. As a merchant described, "I reached into the till and gave them 20, but they just looked at me and handed it back. It obviously wasn't enough. In the end, I just had to cough up" and hand over £50.[1] Of course, if the shopkeeper failed to take the hint, he'd discover some damage—broken windows, graffiti, slashed tires, and admit the need for "protection."[2]

The duo approach was carefully managed. The younger man was new to the Ulster Defence Association or Ulster Defence Force, in prime physical condition, and anxious to prove himself through physical intimidation and obviously willing to do violence. Inevitably, he'd be caught and do a stint in prison, where he would learn some new criminal skills and cultivate patience and self-control, emerging after five or ten years as the new senior partner, sent to supervise a young Turk and lean on the counter while giving a pointed look into the till.[3]

Protection rackets work best in a context where there is little trust in law enforcement or loyalty to the state (ironic, in the case of Northern Ireland's loyalist militias), so the victims of the scheme are reluctant to complain. This does mean that the extortionists have to step in and provide real protection from rival gangs, ideological enemies (like the PIRA), and local hooligans.[4] To maintain their credibility on the high street and status as protectors of the community, Ulster Defence Association enforcers were honor-bound to pursue a sixteen-year-old who stole from one of their protected stores, and "six of them danced all over him. They jumped on his head, jumped on his stomach, jumped on his legs ... ach, he was just black and blue."[5] Until 1994 the Department of Inland Revenue in the United Kingdom allowed shop owners to claim protection money as a legitimate "business expense," at a rate of 40 percent reimbursement, creating a cycle in which their own tax revenue went back into the pockets of intractable, violent nonstate actors and solidified their grip as an alternative government.[6]

■ ■ ■

Frequently, for a VNSA, violence *is* the answer. Having signaled that they're willing to use force, getting resources by just taking them can often be the most expedient, least risky avenue. The methods considered here overlap with the basic skill set of a group and can double as displays to convince their rivals and targets that they are a serious threat whose demands should be met.

■ Expropriation

Military personnel looting and foraging are hard to deter with prosecutions and strict rules of engagement for conventional forces. As will surface in

Sandy Row, Belfast. Loyalist militias in Northern Ireland lay claim to neighborhoods from which they expect to extract protection money and tributes as part of their financing strategy. *Photograph by Chris Yunker, personal collection (2005), courtesy Flickr*

chapter 10, Allied and Axis forces in World War II amassed gargantuan amounts of loot taken by official order, by individual soldiers, and by assorted profiteers.[7] Among VNSAs, pillaging is a major form of financing and supply. Taking from a subject population, though, is a gamble, creating hostility among people that a group might need to rely on for intelligence, skilled work, or political support. When given willingly, getting supplies from the locals is a bonding activity that requires sensitivity and good situational awareness, while foraging and taking can create a problem-causing "Ponzi scheme" of resentment and alienation. Areas that change hands between a VNSA and government troops experience cycles of looting so thorough that postwar revival and repopulation are stunted by people unconvinced that their work and investment will be safe.[8]

On the other hand, if the population to be expropriated is the enemy or a minority whose place in the VNSA's ideology makes it undeserving, or if the cause is in extremis, well, the snatching and grabbing will commence. Some Islamic violent extremist organizations look to thirteenth-century-scholar Ibn Taymiyya for permission to "seize an enemy's property during jihad," augmented by modern fatwas authorizing taking from non-Muslims and apostates, and from businesses engaged in forbidden or morally question-able things, although the property seized must go toward group needs and goals, not personal enrichment.[9] A similar discussion took place among right-wing extremists from the white-supremacist group known as the Order, who planned to rob a series of small businesses in the Pacific Northwest in the early 1980s but had a falling out between the religious and libertarian wings over whether a porn shop was a legitimate target.[10]

VNSAs inculcate in their members that they are not bound by ordinary rules and are entitled to things that they want and need for the group's plans. For motivated groups, especially those who operate on a model of allowing individual initiative, this can lead to a stupefying array of muggings and theft. One of the branches of *vor* Razhden Shulaya's operations in New York faked Department of Transportation paperwork and stole a tractor trailer of Kirkland brand peanut butter cups just because it was there and might be worth money if fenced.[11] Khalid Zerkani recruited Belgian would-be foreign fighters to steal tourists' luggage on the street, enabling so many trips he picked up the nickname "Papa Noel." Ahmed Ressam, who planned to bomb the Los Angeles Airport on New Year's Eve 1999, made enough stealing from tourists in Montreal to fund his living expenses.[12]

Civilians under VNSA control can be stripped of their personal posses-sions, although this probably creates far more enemies than it benefits the group. Not only is this an exhaustible resource, the grudges and hard feelings carry over generations. Castro's new Cuban government seized personal property, including artwork and jewelry, from the homes of wealthy exiles, keeping some for national museums but auctioning the rest for operational cash. The grandchildren of exiles are still blisteringly angry about it and help fuel the political embargo. Somali warlords sent their followers to loot so indiscriminately that they dug up the Italian bishop of Mogadishu's grave and took his gold teeth.[13] ISIS is especially comprehensive in their appropriation, taking "necklaces off women—earrings off their ears. They also went after livestock, furniture, cars," which they liquidated and sold off at a discount in "loot markets" to their favored fighters.[14]

Cars are an extremely useful item of movable loot. Taken from Global North cities, they can be stripped for parts, shipped in containers to Latin America or the Middle East and resold, or used as military assets. Project Mermaid, a 1998 police operation in Quebec, found that fifty-five high-end vehicles had been transported and sold by Hezbollah for $40,000 each, with the very best given as gifts to the group's leadership. In Fallujah, U.S. troops raiding a bomb factory in 2004 discovered that the next vehicle being prepared to blow was an SUV with Texas plates.[15] Stolen closer to home, some vehicles can be ransomed back using well-known go-betweens in the police and local gangs, "so regular that victims know where to go buy back their car when it's taken." Chechen VNSAs worked with Georgian drug addicts to accumulate individual "savings accounts" of eight to ten cars at a time, always in the process of being bartered or ransomed for steady income.[16] Cars reserved for operational use by ISIS, however, merited a special memo directed at the young men dazzled by stolen sports cars and luxury SUVs: they were property of the group, not for racing, showing off, or doing trick driving.[17]

Confiscating or assuming control over the real estate of dispossessed people is another lucrative asset for a VNSA. Records from Iraq and Syria document extensive cataloging and reassignment of the houses and business properties of minorities and enemies. This serves the purpose of literally replacing local society with people the group wants, rewiring the fabric of the community and rewarding followers in ways that cost the group very little other than bureaucratic paperwork. Any post-conflict settlement is likely to be enormously complicated by these transfers of ownership and settlement as current and potentially returned residents make claims. For ISIS, which believes itself to be a state, the Bayt al-Mal, or Muslim Financial House, functions as a legal entity with the jurisdiction to issue title to these spoils of war.[18]

When asked why he robbed banks, Depression-era celebrity Willie Sutton replied, "Because that's where the money is."[19] Depending on the local culture, the money might be in a bank, a post office, or a jewelry store, all of them useful targets for armed expropriation. The IRA found that hitting urban

Seized by Homeland Security Investigation's Miami Illicit Proceeds and Foreign Corruption Group, these eighty-one luxury vehicles titled to straw buyers for bad actors were on their way to Venezuela, with some of them—equipped with lights and sirens—destined for the Venezuelan National Police. *Photograph by Keith Gardner (2020), U.S. Immigration and Customs Enforcement, Defense Visual Information Distribution Service.*

banks and post offices was a way to "blood" troops and test their commitment to the cause while undermining public faith in the ability of the government to protect assets. Where the banks are insured, it is an especially proletarian virtue to dispossess the state of capital. During a heist carried out by the Baader-Meinhof Gang in Germany, one of the robbers assured a bystander, "Keep quiet and nothing will happen to you. After all, it's not your money."[20] In 1969 the government of Uruguay, attempting to cope with labor unrest and the Tupamaros guerrillas, made the mistake of forcing striking bank clerks back to work. The clerks promptly offered themselves as inside personnel for a series of bank robberies, in which the Tupamaros not only got cash but account books with evidence of public officials committing tax fraud and currency speculation.[21]

Taking advantage of the lack of surveillance cameras, barriers between the tellers and customers, and the length of police response time to rural Nigerian banks, Boko Haram, justifying their actions on the grounds that bank usury is un-Islamic, has robbed hundreds of small financial institutions.[22] ISIS blurs the line between robbing and looting the banks in its territory, emptying vaults in Mosul, Nineveh, Salah Din, and Al-Anbar and holding personal accounts hostage to force the return of professionals like doctors and engineers, whose skills they want to utilize.[23] To prevent ISIS from using these branches to form corresponding relationships with international banks and to stop the skim from deposits, the government of Iraq has cut these banks off entirely, rerouting salaries and pensions elsewhere.[24] The IRA regularly conducted bank robberies netting them a few thousand pounds at a time but in 2004 robbed the Northern Bank by kidnapping the families of two bank employees and coercing their cooperation. The resulting haul, possibly £50 million, may have been a significant factor in the IRA's subsequent disarmament and willingness to negotiate, having guaranteed a slush fund and retirement plan beyond their wildest dreams.[25]

The collateral damage of conflicts is sure to start the flow of nongovernmental organizations (NGOs) and humanitarian aid to the area, providing rich pickings for a VNSA to hijack, appropriate, and dole out as desired. U.S. doctrine recognizes that insurgents and guerrillas are likely to disguise their personnel as aid workers (something explicitly denied to conventional forces—this was a controversial part of a Colombian hostage rescue) and pilfer relief supplies for their own use.[26] The Khmer Rouge got its startup money rerouting aid meant for South Vietnam, seizing not just food and medicine but the trucks and equipment brought by aid workers.[27] Since the 1990s Somali militants have looted humanitarian supplies, charging access fees to NGOs and making off with 20–80 percent of shipments, which the aid organizations consider as an acceptable loss in order to serve populations in need. Al-Shabaab was getting $20,000 from the World Food Program as a "security fee" every six months, along with food aid.[28] ISIS took $300,000 worth of generators and a steady supply of food, which they redistributed to supporters and promoted on their social media, using pictures with visible logos from the donor agency.[29] For the Hutu, refugee camps funded by the

UN High Commissioner for Refugees were a convenient place for militants to regroup and rearm at someone else's expense.[30] Not sending aid is unthinkable, but paying a "tax" in supplies to known VNSAs raises ethical questions with sponsoring governments and charities and possibly prolongs conflicts by making resources available.[31]

Without a manufacturing base, and until they get enough funding to buy weapons, VNSAs need to scrounge them. ISIS "has proven itself a skillful battlefield scavenger," stockpiling vehicles, weapons, and equipment left behind by Iraqi Shia and Kurdish enemies, including T-55 and T-72 Russian tanks, Humvees, antiaircraft missiles, and antitank weapons. These have the disadvantage of lacking spare parts and probably needing repair but the immediate advantage of being tanks and missiles.[32] Enemy supplies in convoy or storage are fair game, with International Security Assistance Force–NATO trucks ambushed in the Khyber Pass by militants with detailed knowledge of their routes, license plate numbers, and cargo manifests, and with, in 2008, the Taliban hijacking trucks from Bagram containing helicopter parts.[33] In a horrifying near-miss, one thousand metric tons of yellowcake uranium were abandoned in 2011 as part of Libya's civil war and luckily came into the hands of rebels willing to negotiate with the United Nations for its supervision.[34]

Raids on armories, arms factories, and police stations with gun lockers are another way for a VNSA to acquire weapons as well as to underscore the inability of authorities to stand in their way. The Shining Path in Peru used mining dynamite to attack police substations and trade up for shotguns and assault rifles, while the Quebec Liberation Front targeted a lightly guarded stash of small arms at Ashbury College in Ottawa used to train military cadets.[35] The ETA in Spain had the advantage of operating in a region with industrial arms factories in Elgoibar and Eibar so they could launch raids on the production source. Right-wing VNSAs in the United States feel particularly entitled to take the weapons of their perceived oppressors, stealing explosives and weapons in a series of construction site robberies preceding the 1995 Oklahoma City bombing.[36]

Getting training from your opponent is especially satisfying since it offers insight into their tactics and relieves a VNSA of doing all the grunt work of forming recruits into functional field operatives. Irish Fenians openly embraced this in the 1860s, seeing emigrant service in the American Civil War as an investment that would pay off later in the form of men with musket training and small-unit tactical drill to be used to take the fight back to Ireland against the British.[37] Armies relying on conscription of disgruntled youths risk forming a pool of discharged veterans with just enough skills to be even more angry at the government, now with the weapons training to be useful to a VNSA, as shown in the use of U.S. military training in the doctrine of white supremacists by Bo Gritz post-Vietnam.[38] The presence of an Egyptian former army conscript in planning the Madrid 2004 bombing, using his explosives training, and the ISIS intake paperwork seeking volunteers with skills gained in the Saudi National Guard signal that some of the draftees were paying attention in class. Chechens, who resented being dragged into the Russian army, saw it as preparation for later conflict: "We were more diligent pupils. Because for the Russians, it was a matter of acquiring knowledge and diplomas, but for the Chechens it was a matter of survival."[39]

In Mexico and Latin America, cartels prize personnel they can peel off from the state security forces, in whom the country and U.S. antidrug programs have invested millions of dollars. Los Zetas leader Osiel Cárdenas specifically recruited his inner circle of bodyguards from the elite Groupo Aeromovil de Fuerzas, tapping into inside of knowledge of how to surveil and capture drug kingpins, which he used against enemies and to predict precisely what authorities would do to him. The rapid expansion of law enforcement in cartel-infested regions meant that background checks and screenings suffered, and alarming numbers of trained officers defected with their free policing training. In Guatemala, the Kaibiles, special operations forces created to fight communist insurgents in the jungle and trained with infamously brutal hazing, proved attractive to drug traffickers, who offered far better remuneration and fewer human rights impositions.[40]

Getting your enemy to pay you cash is even better. Spain faced a scandal when it became known that language education and cultural grants to the Herri Batasuna, a Basque political coalition, were going into the coffers of the ETA to fund the maintenance of a VNSA. UN workers, peacekeepers, and NGO personnel with Global North cash salaries and expense budgets can end up hiring translators, renting property, and employing people in ways that inject that cash right back into groups the newcomers are there to work against. A state may face the classic "bureaucratic-political choice of the lesser of two evils" in situations where—like the United States in 2002, paying Chechen guerrillas to hunt down al-Qaeda members or Afghan warlords to bounty hunt Taliban members—the strategic value of the targets justified giving money to obviously dangerous people.[41]

The speed and urgency with which the United States and its allies set up post-9/11 bases in Iraq and Afghanistan became a bonanza for local gangs, militias, and warlords, even internationally known middlemen like Victor Bout, who managed to get off a UN sanctions list targeting suppliers of Liberia's Charles Taylor by subcontracting with KBR and Halliburton.[42] U.S. law—10 USC § 2302—prohibits "providing funds to the enemy" and requires due diligence in contracting to insure that, even indirectly, money isn't leaking into the wrong hands. Audits of global war on terror spending, though, show that this prohibition may have been impossible to enforce, with a sample of three thousand contracts worth $106 billion losing 25 percent to insurgents and 15 percent to corruption.[43] In theater, Gen. David Petraeus noted that "contracting is commander's business, because a large amount of money is going into this space, and when you start to fund the insurgency yourself, you'd better get a handle on it."[44] Sen. Jeanne Shaheen (D-N.H.) reiterated this with outrage, "It's like we're subsidizing the people who are shooting at our soldiers."[45]

Physical control of territory allows a VNSA to exploit the resources located there, a factor addressed in chapter 8 regarding raw materials and commodities. ISIS's control of prime wheat- and barley-producing land and storage silos allows them to sell off agricultural goods for needed cash as well as to deny food to minorities like the Yazidi and dole out subsistence rations to their fighters and favored followers. This presents particular dangers because ISIS is not following up, as the Iraqi Ministry of Agriculture did, in providing the next year's seeds and support to ensure another growing season. Unlike oil or warehouses full of cash, silos of grain are not good targets for air strikes since destroying them would provoke a human disaster.[46]

Having a hand on the tap or the electrical switch is a useful money generator for VNSAs. In Syria, possession of the Tabqa (Euphrates) Dam allowed

ISIS not just to channel electricity to their own use but to charge the Assad regime in Syria for utilities in Aleppo. Distributing utilities is complicated significantly by the extensive previous looting of copper power lines, which al-Qaeda sold to brokers in Turkey for $17,000 a ton.[47] Access to clean water (or just better-quality water than that available) is a path to money for "water mafias" in urban slums, refugee camps, and rural villages without wells. To goose things along, a VNSA may destroy government water projects, siphon from existing pipes, or forcibly keep people away from riverbanks and ponds.

A group with short-term profit horizons or one that holds land or coastline they don't care about, can expropriate the location and use it for extremely lucrative waste dumping. In the Global North, strict environmental regulations make garbage handling and disposal of medical and toxic waste into a criminal bonanza. "Ecomafia" in Southern Italy put so much dioxin into the groundwater that poisons showed up in the mozzarella produced by local dairies, while Taiwanese gangsters repurpose pits at their gravel yards by dumping in trash (and, conveniently, bodies and evidence). Anyone with a truck and some burly workers can get into the scheme, and in 2008 it generated an estimated €20.8 billion, with the clandestine approval of businesses and local authorities who find it convenient.[48] "Dirty collar crime" reaches out of the Global North whenever possible; Lawrence Summers, then chief of the World Bank, advised that "a given amount of health-impairing pollution should be done in the country with the lowest cost, which will be the country with the lowest wages," like Somalia.[49] Under the 1989 Basel Convention, waste can be transferred from a signatory country to the developing world so long as both governments involved approve. The problem, of course, is that when a government or faction in control of territory agrees without actually representing the people who live there, they can be paid by governments and corporations to pollute territory that doesn't belong to them in the first place.[50]

■ Extortion and Revolutionary Taxes

Threatening people for money requires some skill and credibility but has low startup costs and relies on something most VNSAs have in abundance: scary muscle. Conflict areas usually have a pool of underemployed young men, but especially good candidates can be found in veterans' clubs and gyms, where they've already had some training in physical pursuits and discipline. The collapse of the Eastern Bloc in the 1990s left a lot of Olympic-caliber athletes unfunded and available for recruitment by local VNSAs who put their skill with boxing, wrestling, and martial arts to extortionate use.[51] In a country with legal controls on weapons, constituting your goons as a corporate entity may allow all kinds of advantages, as a Russian police commander suggested in 2002: "Why not just call your 'gang' a private security firm, purchase a license for weapons and provide 'protection' to your heart's content?"[52] Even more advantageous, a private firm can pay and equip better than the official authorities, luring talent and knowing they can outgun rivals. When not making the rounds of businesses, the group can be hired out as bodyguards and rabble rousers, who Nigerian politicians expect to take to rallies and voting sites.[53]

Revolutionary taxes can be collected on individual behavior, with ISIS employing scores of enforcers to fine people under their control for smoking, wearing pants that are too long or too short, sending children to school, withdrawing money from banks, or not tying their hair up properly. This has the added effect of keeping people off balance, afraid, and docile. The LTTE in Sri Lanka charges people to travel across their territory and to have diaspora access to their families. This kind of exploitation is nearly impossible to prevent from outside; a U.S. Treasury official explained that Mosul is "like areas of France under Nazi control in WWII . . . we are trying to minimize the effect on the average citizen-hostage."[54] Control of roads and geographic bottlenecks allows a VNSA to charge extortionate tolls on residents and commerce passing through. Afghan trucking, even for supplies going to coalition military troops, pays tribute—"the army is basically paying the Taliban not to shoot at them"[55]—up to $800 per vehicle. Al-Shabaab has checkpoints on the roads leading out of Somalia's major ports, squeezing "road taxes" out of drivers who have no other way to move their goods.[56]

The traditional target for extortion is small business operating on narrow margins and unable to leave or join forces with others to resist. The IRA and ETA sent polite letters demanding money on a payment plan, with distinctly uncivil follow-up—firebombs and tire irons. Cartels skim from entrepreneurs in their area of control, sometimes using the cash businesses like taco trucks

and bars as money laundering vehicles or forcing them to sell branded merchandise at an inflated price: CDs, T-shirts, logo-bearing alcohol. Squeezing
shopkeepers requires coordination between local VNSAs to be sure that only
one claims a particular business, providing actual protection from teenage
shoplifters and vandals and figuring out how not to kill the golden goose by
extracting too much. Extended reigns of extortion gangs can stunt whole
neighborhoods, deter investment, and prompt shopkeepers to leave entirely
or put off improving their physical location and equipment.

Multinational corporations have far deeper pockets than local businesses and can be a profitable target for extortion. If equitable distribution
of resources is a key plank in a VNSA's ideology, forcing an international
mining or oil drilling company to pay is a propaganda coup and a solid
financial source as the company can't relocate the resources, the resources
are probably in a hard-to-access region, and the company may still make so
much money they can pay and continue to profit. This is especially popular
when used against companies that generate few jobs for local people, or that
contribute conspicuously to corruption by paying off law enforcement and
the government. The danger of this is that sometimes the company is more
powerful than the VNSA and simply chooses to leave. Loyalists in Northern
Ireland learned that European construction companies working on community reconstruction projects would abandon a worksite rather than pay
extortion, angering the people who would have benefited from the hospital,
senior care home, or school. When the IRA got too grabby with brewers, a
coalition developed to refuse and take shelter in the power of cutting off the
whole beer supply. Coca-Cola in Altamirano, Mexico, refused to pay protection money to cartels and wrote off their closed distribution and bottling
center, while in Ukraine they hired their own highly paid militia to scare off
"partnership agreements" with *vor*.[57]

A sufficiently loathsome VNSA can blackmail companies and local governments using the legal system. Right-wing groups in the United States have
generated income by filing nuisance lawsuits against any entity with funds,
often using self-taught legal expertise and relying on persistence and obnoxious
behavior to get a payoff. Aum Shinrikyo perfected a system of locating a
prosperous city and announcing that it planned to open a compound there,

advancing plans until paid bribes to go elsewhere. Also in Japan, the Yakuza purchased shares in publicly traded companies, entitling representatives to attend shareholder meetings. Companies received notice that unless they paid extortion, Yakuza members would attend and reveal corporate secrets or just be threatening. This continued until enough companies started holding annual meetings on the same day to make the threat unworkable.[58]

Confident in their hold over an area, a VNSA may extort from other illicit actors. This has the effect of giving tacit approval, the ramifications of which should be considered in the context of the reputation and values of the group but can also give a lever by which things can be kept to an acceptable margin. "Violence management agency" is a productive way to think of balancing income against social order, as a VNSA may choose to allow the sale of club drugs to tourists but not hard drugs to school kids, or fine joy riders but break legs of reckless drivers who injure bystanders. This level of coordination also heads off conflict between lesser illicit actors and establishes the group as an authority. In some cases, like Hamas' management of smuggling tunnels, this degree of organization is vital to keeping needed consumer products moving into the economy through a limited point of access.[59]

The hazard of extorting revolutionary "taxes" is that eventually the victims come to expect commensurate government services. The Italian and Russian Mafias took hold in spaces where the government could not be trusted to intervene fairly in disputes or enforce contracts. Taking advantage of a state's weakness is a useful tool but increasingly obligates the VNSA to take on duties of a surrogate state. ISIS knowingly walked into this trap, laying out "Principles in the Administration of the Islamic State" in 2014 and announcing that "all the requirements to establish a state have been met," fulfilling the group's vision of itself as a restored caliphate. While being a state comes with benefits, including the "orientation of global governance . . . to favor the nation state," that decision took them overnight from one of the world's wealthiest VNSAs to holding the reins of a poverty-racked failed state.[60] Other VNSAs, like Boko Haram, cartels in Mexico, and al-Shabaab, risk similar problems, uninterested in developing the mechanisms to be a successful state—property rights, human capital-building education, stability, protection for investments, civil liberties—but on the hook to keep the lights on.[61]

■ Smuggling

Smuggling is the ultimate form of violent arbitrage. A group that is competent to manage its own logistics and has mapped the weaknesses of the enforcement landscape in which they operate can easily branch out from moving troops to moving expensive items or go from taxing illicit traffic to handling it themselves. The LTTE's fleet of ships could just as easily carry more than their military needs—alcohol, drugs, jewelry, and trafficked people were regular cargo by the mid-1970s.[62] This is a low-risk, high-reward enterprise aided by modern tools of GPS mapping, covert air strips, and vacuum-sealed bags delivering something that people on the receiving end want with sufficient urgency to pay more for it. An Austrian novel, *The Radetzky March* (1932), had its imperial officer protagonist marvel at the wheeler-dealers who followed the army around nineteenth-century Europe: "They had no shops, no names, no credit. But they did possess a miraculous instinct for any and all secret sources of money. They dealt in feathers for feather beds, in horsehair, in tobacco, in silver ingots, in jewels, in Chinese tea, in southern fruit, in fields and woodlands. Some of them even dealt in live human beings. They sent deserters from the Russian army to the United States and young peasant girls to Brazil and Argentina. Their hands were gifted in striking gold from gravel like sparks from flint."[63] And yet, life finds a way. A VNSA with women field operatives can use them to an advantage in smuggling, with the IRA hiding C-4 explosives in the fashionable platform sandals of their agents, Boko Haram taking advantage of the reluctance of conservative Muslims to search a veiled woman, and cartels packing cocaine-carrying minivans with screaming children and their harried mothers so that the border agent just wants to "get them out of his hair."[64] Packing illicit items in with feminine hygiene products works too.

VNSA smugglers occupy an unusual place among the perpetrators of violent crime, often celebrated as postwar heroes or Robin Hood figures. Part of this may be that smugglers aren't overtly trying to tear down the states through which they pass—they need them for their work to be worthwhile, and they're evading taxes and control, which most people have some sympathy for. Until something veers into the grotesque, like child sex trafficking, the gray area is unusually permissive.[65] The smugglers may be doing it patriotically, with the winked approval from a state under sanctions or an impoverished minority population or because the recipient of the taxes is not considered legitimate. Another feature is one that economist Bruce Yandle first named in 1983: bootleggers and Baptists—that is, forces lobbying to regulate a product can demand it from the position of moral prohibition (Baptists) while having shadow allies in the illicit economy who make more money if it stays banned (bootleggers).[66] This creates the strange situation of Americans embracing NASCAR, a sport born not in the prohibition of alcohol but in a region's community-supported efforts to not pay the hated "revenuers."[67]

Liminal zones are ideal for smuggling, spaces where overlapping or absent jurisdictions allow residents and smugglers to ignore laws with impunity and have easy access to safe havens. These can be created deliberately, like the autonomous tribal homeland of Bophuthatswana in South Africa, which allowed sweat shops for Taiwanese, Israeli, and South African companies in contravention of labor laws and environmental controls.[68] The infamous Tri-Border region at the intersection of Argentina, Brazil, Paraguay, and Uruguay is the result of the "common market of the South," or MERCOSUR, trade zone agreements from the early 1990s and quickly became a favorite of the Yakuza, Hezbollah, Triads, and Nigerian drug kingpins for avoiding taxes and law enforcement, as each country puts investigation and enforcement off on another when politically expedient or not worth the danger or backlash.[69] Sovereign indigenous reservations that overlap the U.S.-Canadian border and along the U.S.-Mexico border are smuggling zones, as are frontiers like the three hundred kilometers of the Chechen-Russian borderlands or the mountainous Kurdish region exploited by the PKK across Turkey, Syria, Iraq, and Iran.[70]

A VNSA with enough guns to cover its own needs can make a great deal of money getting those weapons to others who can pay. Before 1989 arms procurement was largely a tool of state sponsorship, with great Cold War powers doling out access to industry. The collapse of the Soviet Union flooded the market not just with the guns (and tanks and planes and submarines) that Russian military units were willing to sell to pay salaries; it also cut loose the Czech and Bulgarian state factories that were willing to sell to anyone with

Around the world, smugglers use astounding feats of engineering to get over, around, and under international borders. This tunnel in San Diego brought drugs on mini railcars across the U.S.-Mexico border. *Photograph by Ron Rogers (2011), U.S. Immigration and Customs Enforcement, Defense Visual Information Distribution Service*

hard currency.[71] The availability of AK-47s in the early 1990s was so wide that a gun that cost $3,000 in 1988 could be had for $500 in 1991, and the price fell even further as the guns recycled among conflicts in Africa and Central Asia.[72] In 2005 Hollywood filmmakers produced a thinly veiled biopic of Russian smuggler and gunrunner Victor Bout (*Lord of War*), and the prop masters found that when they tried to acquire mock guns to use while shooting in Eastern Europe, puzzled vendors insisted that real ones would be substantially cheaper. They also rented tanks, which had to be back by December 2004, since the owner needed "them back . . . because I'm selling them to Libya."[73] At about the same time, the U.S. government wanted to outfit Iraqi police and militias, and two Miami entrepreneurs gamed the online procurement system to buy from stashes held by gangsters and warlords in the Balkans and former Soviet republics, arranging their deals largely by phone.[74]

Through a 2013 Arms Trade Treaty, the United Nations requires signatories to adhere to standards for manufacturing, shipping, and transshipping weapons, including avoiding sending them to states where they will likely be used in contravention of human rights laws or to commit crimes, especially those that are gender-based or affect minorities in those regions. However, it is left up to the sending states to determine that risk, and even if they do deem it too dangerous, counterfeit end-use certificates are pretty easy to forge. European Union (EU) gun laws are stringent and carry significant penalties, but determined VNSAs can buy decommissioned confiscated weapons or smuggled ones on the Dark Web, as did the *Charlie Hebdo* attackers, whose illegal guns arrived in the regular mail.[75] In less-regulated regions, including the United States and Yemen, the Dark Web isn't necessary—Facebook, Whatsapp, and the Craigslist-like Armslist.com can handle small-volume purchases and shipping.[76] More quantity involves bigger sums of money and hassle in delivery, allowing Boko Haram to charge a premium to take its surplus from Nigeria to VNSAs in Chad, an inclusive package paying for guards, vehicles, and bribes for frontier customs inspectors.[77]

The previous chapter deals with the Hezbollah scheme to move cigarettes from one U.S. state to another to capitalize on the tax differential, but many VNSAs smuggle the cigarettes themselves into restricted areas, with the cooperation of the companies that manufacture them. It's really a perfect commodity for trafficking: costs little to make, addictive—but not so dangerous that it rates with hard drugs—lightweight, shelf-stable, and in branded packages with fanatical customer loyalty.[78] This kind of corporate legerdemain is nothing new: After 1948 Hilton and Coca-Cola figured out how to relabel items and cultivate business in Israel and its Arab neighbors, and Sony, realizing that tariffs put its televisions out of reach in Pakistan, turned a blind eye to smuggling and allowed official service and repair for obviously contraband ones.[79] During the 1980s and 1990s, RJ Reynolds chose a corporate strategy of building market share and making money by colluding with the PKK and the sanctioned government of Iraq (specifically Saddam Hussein's son Uday) to move their products. At a corporate meeting the company agreed "to formulate a joint plan of action to protect the industry from the scrutiny of the U.S. Congress" investigating cigarettes and organized crime links.[80]

The resulting plan was a super-deluxe tour of arbitrage and material support for terrorism: Using an international subsidiary, Japan Tobacco, cigarettes from North Carolina went to Puerto Rico (a U.S. territory under slightly different laws than a state), then to Gibraltar (a U.K. territory with Spanish links), then to Cyprus (a virtual carnival of laundering and illicit activities), and into the hands of Kurdish PKK operatives, who escorted the cargo into Iraq, where the deal was a "live and let live" convenience between Hussein and the ethnic group he most enjoyed persecuting.[81] It was the EU that eventually prosecuted RJ Reynolds in 2002, alleging a decade's worth of knowingly creating fraudulent documents, using shell companies, and violating sanctions, thereby providing known terrorist organizations with millions of dollars in funding.[82]

VNSAs also traffic people. People-smuggling can use the same routes as drugs and guns while providing an asset obliged to pay protection money, serve as contacts in a new place, or work in illicit and shady industries like sweatshops or unlicensed fishing trawlers. Depending on the complexity and distances, a VNSA might charge $5,000 (Syria to Denmark), $32,000 (Sri Lanka to Canada), or $2,500 (Mexico to United States) and expect a cash payoff or installments from the smuggled person and his or her family.[83] Although this can happen to men, it is much more common that trafficked women and children are meant for the coerced sex trade, which operates with ease online and in plain sight.[84] *Vor* Razhden Shulaya imported Eastern European women to New York, where his organization profited from their prostitution and used them as bait in an elaborate "badger game" of luring elderly men to hotels, where they could be robbed and blackmailed. The public health and social consequences of this to sending countries is devastating, with Moldova in a long-term population crisis caused by women, if they come back at all, suffering diminished reproductive capacity, high rates of alcoholism and drug use, and epidemics of domestic violence, abused children, and wrecked human capital.[85]

A specialty subset of human smuggling is VNSAs using people for the organ trade. Tight restrictions on organ transplant prioritization in the Global North has resulted in wild, unregulated medical spaces where VNSAs, working with amenable medical personnel, coerce "donors" or create cadavers for wealthy recipients. After the March 2005 tsunami in the Indian Ocean, gang-affiliated brokers haunted refugee camps looking for people desperate for money on behalf of customers in Mumbai hospitals. A special EU task force has been tracking VNSA organ sales from KLA officers who execute prisoners to harvest kidneys and to impoverished Moldovans recruited by gangsters.[86] In 2015 Iraqi ambassador to the United Nations Mohamed Ali Alhakim alleged, based on findings from mass graves in recaptured areas, that ISIS was executing prisoners for organs that were then smuggled to buyers in Saudi Arabia and Turkey, although much of this remains speculation without concrete proof.[87] It is well known that states do this with their prison populations—China most notoriously—and exclude their own transplant-seeking population in favor of those who can pay, raising ethical and humanitarian questions about arbitrage and the participation of the medical community and recipients (and their insurance companies) exploiting people to the benefit of VNSAs.[88]

■ Kidnapping

VNSAs have a variety of reasons for taking hostages. In an asymmetric conflict, a small group able to seize and hold people nominally under the protection of a powerful one is a useful way to humiliate an enemy and manipulate their policy, as the Quebec Liberation Front did in the 1970s, choosing targets to criticize U.S. imperialism and the inability of the Canadian government to stop them.[89] Holding hostages is a way to compel another group to allow access to a resource or an area and, for a VNSA on the way up, to establish themselves as capable and badass actors. Most likely, though, the group needs hostages valuable enough to trade for their own incarcerated personnel; as al-Qaeda leader Ayman al-Zawahiri explained, "We are seeking, with the help of Allah, to capture others and to incite Muslims to capture the citizens of the countries that are fighting Muslims in order to release our captives."[90] For extraordinarily valuable prisoners like pirate leader Mohamed Abdi Hassan, on trial in Brussels in 2013, his son (also a pirate) specifically sought out a Belgian hostage he could trade, knowing that Western governments can use extremely aggressive diplomacy to get what they want. A government official in Burkina Faso noted that "you would not believe the pressure that the West brings to bear on African countries" when their own people are at stake.[91]

Monetizing hostage taking is an easy transition. Most VNSAs find it to be ideologically justifiable: "Thanks to Allah, most of the battle costs, if not all, were paid through the spoils. Almost half the spoils came from hostages. Kidnapping hostages is an easy spoil, which I may describe as a profitable trade and a precious treasure," spelled out one al-Qaeda communiqué, while an extremist group in Pakistan sought a fatwa: "The holy warriors who detain a foreign soldier, journalist or worker have the right to ask for money or exchange him. Though we condemn kidnapping for ransom, but if it is meant for the promotion of the Islamic cause, then it's very much fair."[92] This is not unique to Islamic extremists, as VNSAs like FARC were so invested in the practice that they formalized the best techniques during their fifth conference in the 1970s, and the Basque ETA chalked up 858 abductees by the time they accepted a cease-fire agreement in 2011.[93]

For ideological reinforcement, kidnappings also probably follow a pattern established by the VNSA's enemy: secret police carrying off dissidents in unmarked vans, intimidation, threats to family and children. The Ba'athist security establishment regularly used disappearances, rape, and "institutionalized criminal activity" to terrorize others, so given the chance for payback, militias and al-Qaeda seized it. Kidnappings can express a group's displeasure at the presence of an extractive industry by targeting its executives, highlight the inappropriate behavior of foreign tourists in a religiously conservative country, or serve the purpose of scaring potential opponents and their relatives out of the area permanently through a brain drain of white-collar workers who have the connections to get out.

There's no question this is lucrative, usually netting a VNSA hundreds of thousands, if not millions, of dollars at a time, in cash. The United Nations estimated that ISIS raked in $35–45 million in ransoms just in 2014, while AQIM, operating in North Africa, averaged $20 million a year.[94] A group can choose to get one huge score from a deep-pocketed target—as the Montoneros (a Peronist guerrilla VNSA) extracted $60 million from the Argentinian Born family in the mid-1970s (along with a promise to put busts of Eva and Juan Perón in all the industrial dynasty's factories)—or a steady stream of local poohbahs good for half a million each from their businesses.[95] Nearly every conflict zone has visiting aid workers, foreign soldiers, journalists, and hapless tourists if the local economy doesn't provide available tycoon abductees and their loved ones.

Ransoms don't even need to come from the victim's family or home country. In 1986 a group of Nicaraguan Contras, the anti-Sandinista VNSA backed and trained by the United States, became dissatisfied by their resources and floated kidnapping and ransoming former U.S. ambassador Lewis Tambs and rogue Contra jefe Edén Pastora, but to cartels in Colombia who posted $1 million bounties for the men because of their antidrug efforts. Along with the money, the Contras believed that they could frame the Sandinistas and provoke the United States to carry out a direct retaliatory strike.[96] Chechen Islamist rebels engineered a bidding war for the four telecom workers (three from Britain, one from New Zealand) they captured in 1998, working between Granger Telecom, the New Zealand government, and a mysterious bidder who paid $4 million for them to be executed rather than released. After their murders, it turned out that the bidder was a Saudi magnate with a rival business interest in the region.[97]

Outsourcing the snatching part of kidnapping to local criminal gangs is a prudent decision if the VNSA who intends to use them doesn't want to develop the expertise themselves or divert resources to carry out operations. The resulting tangled alliance of criminal and political VNSAs are "sometimes lucrative criminal enterprises, sometimes brutal aspects of sectarian violence, and sometimes a tangled mixture of the two," with a group accepting victims from multiple gangs, sometimes only until they learn the tricks of that gang's kidnapping success for themselves.[98] This tie can be a useful force multiplier, as in the case of Mokhtar Belmokhtar, an AQIM commander who married into at least four Berber and Tuareg tribal communities and employed his in-laws' kidnapping and smuggling acumen beyond the operations of the AQIM.[99]

Criminal gangs who originally kidnap targets can double-dip by also being the negotiators and go-betweens used to retrieve them. Intermediaries expect 10–50 percent of the ransoms and are usually involved in the whole scheme from start to finish, as were a Philippine mayor and his son who "heroically" negotiated the release of journalists but were caught by an anti–money laundering investigation as having orchestrated the crime in the first place. Some local godfathers appear again and again as the go-betweens when aid workers disappear and tourists need to be ransomed, becoming a lucrative local image enhancer and financial sideline. This can become so murky that stand-alone criminal gangs use the reputation of an unaffiliated but fearsome VNSA to leverage larger ransoms, since it is nearly impossible for an outsider to know with whom a kidnapping is really being negotiated.

Doing kidnappings in-house requires specialized research and planning since indiscriminate hauls of people are unlikely to yield financial rewards greater than the hassle. A VNSA may, through former government officials or their own compilations, have access to a database of wealthy people via their tax records or personnel files from a regime.[100] Paid informants and disgruntled servants are good sources of targets worth kidnapping, as are raids on resorts patronized by foreign workers.[101] Those VNSAs that want to avoid foreign entanglements can narrow their specialization down to mid-level officials with enough wealth to pay ransoms but enough not to have a formidable security detail. Groups ranging from Boko Haram to the Taliban Movement in Pakistan formed "special kidnapping squads" or "commando squads" to train in achieving complicated and more lucrative abductions.[102]

When carried out effectively, kidnappings are an instant source of useful publicity. Some analysts believe that the 2013 attack on the Amenas gas plant in Algeria by al-Mourabitoun jihadists was for demonstration effect and recruiting. New members flock to a VNSA after a well-publicized abduction of an oil executive or the payment of a substantial ransom, with the new recruits expecting to share in the loot or be part of the next big payoff.[103] How the group treats its unwilling guests is a critical part of their branding, whether it is Somali pirates being sure to feed their victims well and treat them carefully to encourage the payment of ransoms rather than rescue attempts, or it is the opposite: brutal beheadings and torture meant to frighten families into payment and allow recruits to take out their aggressions on an enemy.[104] In a larger strategy, being known as a kidnapping site can drive away tourism and spur capital flight, allowing a group to further destabilize the area and provide examples of anticapitalist propaganda as well as demonstrate that the authorities have lost control.

Done poorly, kidnappings can backfire in ways that damage the organization irreparably. Abductions by the Basque separatist group ETA generated huge sums of money, but they also went wrong with deadly mistakes.

Miscalculating the amount a family could pay, the ETA executed Angel Berazadi, a Basque industrialist, to public outrage in 1976. It happened again in 1977, with the execution of Javier de Ybarra for nonpayment of ransom, tarnishing the ETA in the eyes of younger Basques, who saw them as grubby criminals rather than freedom fighters. In 1981 they made a powerful enemy by kidnapping Dr. Julio Iglesias Sr., the Spanish gynecologist and father of the Latin music superstar. With a vast platform, Julio Iglesias Jr. rallied his global fanbase to shame the ETA during the two weeks before a police rescue succeeded in freeing his father. By 1993 many in the Basque region were tired of the kidnappings and started wearing blue ribbons as a support for 1993 ETA kidnapping victim Iglesias Zamora; in "many ways it's the culmination of so many years in which dozens of Basque businessmen have suffered in solitude and silence."[105] Something similar happened to the IRA when the kidnapping of Don Tidey in 1983 ended with a shootout that killed an Irish Garda and an Irish Republic soldier, souring the public on IRA exploits. In a grittier father-son scenario, Colombian president Alvaro Uribe lost his dad to a botched FARC kidnapping in 1983, hardening his resolve and making his lifetime goal to destroy them.[106]

Kidnapping *people* is usually the modus operandi for a VNSA, but cherished pets and valuable livestock might pay off, although not always. In the late 1970s the Italian Red Brigade stole a horse that they believed to be priceless racing stock, demanding a large ransom. Not understanding the basic chicanery of the horse-racing business, they discovered that the owner insured the horse for far more than it was worth, refused to pay the ransom, and suggested that the terrorists just keep it. To support themselves, they had it butchered and ate it, but the neighborhood where they were hiding knew all about it and ridiculed them with "neighs." The IRA, with a headquarters near the Ballymoney Stud Farm in Curragh, thought it would be easy to kidnap Shergar, a thoroughbred Derby winner, for ransom. Only the participants know what happened next, but Shergar was never recovered; his owner, the Aga Khan, refused to pay, and high-strung, large animals with fragile limbs are hard to control and freak out around unfamiliar and violent handling.[107]

If a VNSA wants to destroy an area and its economy, endemic kidnappings are a useful tool, but if they're the IRA or ETA, with dreams of a secessionist or nationalist liberation, kidnapping as a financial tactic is destructive and unpopular with the local people. After his 1973 kidnapping by the IRA, Dr. Tiede Herrema, a Dutch industrialist, closed his factory, withdrawing 1,400 jobs from Limerick to public outcry. In Algeria the lucrative tourist routes to the Sahara have dried up as Western vacationers don't want to risk their lives, devastating the small agencies and businesses that service the travelers. In an attempt to measure the political economy of terrorism, researchers found a profound negative effect driven by kidnappings and attacks, although this quantification should not be a surprise.[108] Kidnapping too often, or too brutally, or sexually assaulting women abductees, or taking the wrong family's children can result in a whole community turning against the VNSA, backing the government or occupation troops, and offering crucial intelligence against the kidnappers, a mechanism key to getting the Sinjar Group out of Anbar in Iraq and FARC dislodged from Puerto Boyacá in Colombia.[109]

The international laws covering kidnapping for ransom emerged from the spate of hijackings and terrorist attacks of the 1970s, led by West Germany, which had been the site of the 1972 Olympics massacre. The International Convention Against the Taking of Hostages (1979) was followed by the International Convention for the Suppression of the Financing of Terrorism (2002), enjoining signatories to prosecute hostage takers and freeze and confiscate funds meant for the support of terrorism. The United Nations followed this with Resolution 1904 (2009), which confirms a ban on paying ransoms to any groups on the sanctions list but does not attach an enforcement or sanctions mechanism for those who violate it. At a U.S.-Algerian sponsored meeting of the Global Counterterrorism Forum in 2012, attendees issued the Algiers memorandum on best policies to manage hostage taking and ransoms. Subsequently, the G8 produced a 2013 statement: "We unequivocally reject the payment of ransoms to terrorists."[110]

The United States and United Kingdom have the most restrictive regulations covering negotiating and paying ransoms. Due to the long conflict in Northern Ireland, the U.K. Terrorism Act (2000) and Counterterrorism and Security Act (2015) explicitly ban the provision of funds to terrorists under any circumstances or being party to an arrangement that puts money into the hands of terrorists, with a very low threshold for prosecution, and the United

Kingdom has gone on record that they will prosecute insurance companies for paying ransom demands.[111] U.S. policy against paying ransoms is rooted in a 1970s conviction that to do so would alleviate responsibility from local governments, widen regional conflicts, and undermine political will, although the global war on terror has shifted this reasoning into a desire to deter hostage taking in the first place and deny bad actors a source of funding.[112] All of this hinges, however, on the willingness of the United States and United Kingdom to pursue and prosecute entities through which money flows to kidnappers, including examining the policy of shunting domestic kidnappings to the FBI as a matter not covered under the nonconcession rules and whether kidnappers in remote parts of the world know or care about the distinctions.[113]

Having a policy and following it in the face of traumatized families are two different things. Kidnappings place a government in a no-win situation: Denouncing concessions signals strength, but a beheaded captive makes this look heartless and negligent. The voting public likes the idea of a tough-talking stance but becomes invested in and sympathetic to an appealing hostage and a desperate family, especially if, like murdered abductee Edwin Dyer's brother proclaimed, "It seems Britain gives little importance to its citizens" and "a U.K. passport is essentially a death sentence."[114] Families agonize about what their loved ones would want them to do—advance the larger goals of why an NGO volunteer was in a war zone or put their safety first. Some hostages attract enormous followings, with support groups organized to pressure their captors to release them, raise money for ransoms, and lobby governments to intervene.[115] Ultimately, in 2015, after five years of ambiguity following the *Holder v. Humanitarian Law Project* ruling on material support for terrorism, the Obama administration officially announced that although U.S. policy remained one of nonconcession, families who chose to pay a ransom themselves would not be prosecuted.[116]

Other countries, although signatories to the international conventions, have found ways to pay for the return of their citizens. Captured al-Qaeda documents and revelations by captives show that European countries have developed elaborate systems of proxies, front organizations, and third-party diplomats to evade their own stated policies. "The Europeans have a lot to answer for . . . it's a completely two-faced policy. They pay ransoms and then deny any was paid," Vicki Huddleston, former deputy assistant secretary of defense for African affairs, complained. "It makes all our citizens vulnerable."[117] To facilitate the return of their citizens kidnapped at a music festival in Mali, the Swiss and German governments cloaked the payments in emergency humanitarian aid, delivered in bricks of Euros.[118] France prefers to work through its multinational companies with branches in the region, negotiating and funneling ransoms for prisoners in the Sahel through nuclear giant Areva, which has uranium mines in Mali and Niger. One of the abductees released this way had a celebratory meeting with President François Hollande. "He told me, looking me in the eye, 'France did not pay.'"[119]

A country without extensive in-country connections might lean on Qatar, which sees negotiating with VNSAs as a reputation-builder and has the business links to find the right points of contact and less concern that the money is development capital for terrorists. In 2013 Qatari officials worked with Cameroonian car dealer Alhaji Abdalla to free a tourist family from Boko Haram, paying $3.14 million, and found a hostage in Yemen using a $30 million lure. Yemen's foreign minister was not pleased, pointing out that before this windfall, al-Qaeda in the Arabian Peninsula was selling its guns to fund operations, but a private jet arriving with bags of cash "may have led to a disaster."[120]

Since the 1970s corporate responses have been available too. Lloyds of London began offering insurance policies complete with security advisers, negotiators, and extraction experts, signaling that having executives kidnapped was just the cost of doing business in the developing world. For an organization that already hires armed drivers and bodyguards, it isn't much of a stretch to have resources to book flights with pilots skilled in doing jungle drops of cash in canvas bags.[121] The hazard of this is calculating whether a nation in which the insurance company (or the policy holder) does business will fine or prosecute for violating no-concession policies as well as for having it known (through theft of records or announcement) that an organization that holds ransom insurance will generate a target list for a VNSA, as was common in Colombia.[122]

If the alternative is a high-risk military rescue, made even more hazardous by VNSA responses designed to kill the hostages at the first sign of approaching force, ransoms remain a defensible option for many countries.

Acknowledging that the money does fund terrorism and that the availability of ransoms creates an escalation of demands and targeting of citizens with amenable governments, a European ambassador pointed to prioritizing the well-being of its people. "It was a very difficult situation, but in the end, we are talking about human life."[123]

■ Piracy

VNSAs operating on a coast and with the expertise to conduct seaborne piracy have done so as soon as the opportunity has presented itself, with the "pests of mankind" appearing wherever there was cargo to steal and hostages to bargain with.[124] Bodies of water function as vast, ungoverned spaces where entrepreneurial and aggressive illicit groups can acquire spoils many times the cost of the expedition with relatively little risk and under circumstances that look advantageous next to the strict discipline of a military vessel or low wages on a fishing boat, for the same skills.[125] Although the focus here is on the well-documented twenty-first-century Somali pirate epidemic, piracy also flourishes in the oil-producing delta region of Nigeria, where youth gangs clash over cargoes of bunkered crude. The LTTE Sea Tigers were also opportunistic pirates with their armed fleet of smuggling vessels.[126]

Piracy as a viable economic sector emerged in Somalia in the 1990s as warlords armed with leftover weapons from regional conflicts staked out fishing territory for sponsors and then, when global fishing fleets responded by escalating to tactics like vacuums and dynamite, turned to imposing a "tax" on trawlers and toxic-waste dumping vessels.[127] The December 2004 tsunami devastated the coast of Puntland, making the risk of attacking large ships more palatable, given the lack of other economic opportunities and the dearth of other marketable skills.[128] Somalia's culture also rewards "warrior" norms, whether on land or sea, and many pirates see themselves as patriotic social bandits in the Robin Hood model: "We consider 'sea bandits' those who illegally fish in our seas and dump waste in our seas and carry weapons in our seas. . . . Think of us like a coast guard."[129]

Somali piracy is absolutely the work of violent nonstate actors, but it is unclear just how closely they have been tied into regional insurgencies like al-Shabaab and other manifestations of Islamic extremism. Some experts argue that the infusion of cash and employment for disgruntled men has actually kept out recruitment for violent extremist organizations. However, pragmatically speaking, each group has something the other wants—the pirates have ready cash, while al-Shabaab has battle-won expertise and weapons.[130] Translations of Osama bin Laden's captured archives in Abbottabad show that al-Qaeda instructed al-Shabaab to forge closer links to the pirates and "give their full attention to collecting ransom money and hijacking ships."[131] Somalia's network of clans provides overlap between pirates and al-Shabaab leadership, and there were reports in 2011 of a forced meeting in Harardhere after al-Shabaab kidnapped a number of pirates and coercively negotiated a "tax" payment on the ransoms collected.[132] For their part, some pirates have amped up their demands by threatening to turn over Western hostages to al-Shabaab, but this may be just for effect and leverage.

If a group of willing would-be pirates already has access to a boat, the cost of mounting a foray at sea in East Africa is about $500, plus $100 a day (plus cigarettes). An attack on a large, valuable ship requires several such boats, so the funding comes from previous profits, regional "godfathers," or, in a new innovation, local pirate stock exchanges, where relatively small contributions of cash, fuel, and equipment like binoculars and range finders or weapons buy a share in the potential ransom.[133] Like many financial arrangements between investors and very poor people executing the plans, the real bulk of the money goes into a "Mafia-like" system reaching back to more powerful VNSAs "who wore suits and had secretaries and went to offices in towering buildings" in Nairobi, Mombasa, or Boosaaso and risked very little other than seed money.[134]

Once pirates seize a vessel, negotiations become an international affair. The maritime insurance company, or the nation whose citizens are hostages, steps in to bargain. Lloyds of London and other underwriters add substantial "pirate surcharges" to their policies and carefully calculate the demands against the replacement value of a ship, its cargo, the life insurance payout on the crew, and the cost of each day's delay in the ship's itinerary.[135] Both insurance adjusters and pirates prepare for a standard period of about seventy days, during which the pirates make arrangements with local businesses to bring in restaurant food and reserve accommodations for the negotiators while subcontracting hostage supervision to clan relatives as a way to spread the wealth and give their

Somali pirates (Indian Ocean) allow a U.S. Navy wellness check on hostage crew members of the *MV Faina*. To make things more complicated, the ship is owned by a Ukrainian firm, flagged in Belize, and, on this run, was carrying Ukrainian military equipment. *Photograph by Petty Officer 2nd Class Jason Zalasky, U.S. Naval Forces Central Command/U.S. 5th Fleet, Defense Visual Information Distribution Service*

crews a rest period. The negotiators usually succeed in bringing outlandish demands down to $2–4 million for a commercial cargo ship and arranging for delivery of the cash, sometimes airdropped by Russian smugglers onto a dhow in the open ocean.[136] U.S. law forbids companies to provide material support to terrorism, and the policy of other countries prevents them from negotiating with kidnappers and terrorists, but the ransoms always seem to get paid through an opaque structure of third-country negotiators, shell companies, and vessels flagged to countries who have no such qualms.[137]

Where there are pirates, there are inevitably boom towns with economies distorted from the infusion of cash unsupported by a sustainable industry. Like seventeenth-century Port Royal, Jamaica, coastal towns in Puntland depend on pirates as customers for their boat repair docks, bars, shops, and clubs, charging the inflated rates tolerated by young men with cash in hand.[138] Philanthropically minded pirates might donate money to a local hospital or school but first build their parents a lavish house, purchase SUVs, and "throw the best parties" in a timeless bid for the attention of local women.[139] This is a locally legitimate means of social mobility, with the most skillful crew members using their reputations for specialty roles like navigation to demand bigger cuts and sit out ventures that don't please them.[140] Local elders are necessarily ambivalent about the situation, awash in a tidal wave of cash but aware that not only is it not cycling back into sustainable community investment, it is also inflating prices on commodities and preventing aid from reaching larger and more desperate swaths of the population.[141]

Enough ships escape being targets of piracy that owners and captains are willing to roll the dice and traverse the region, unwilling to add expensive detours or run at higher speeds that burn more fuel.[142] Piracy is a truly transnational crime, but instead of making suppression everyone's problem, the multitude of stakeholders introduces problems of responsibility and jurisdiction. American-Chinese and Chinese-Russian military patrols show a professional maritime coordination against pirates, but, beyond deterrence, the presence of major powers doesn't mean that any of them have standing or a legal framework to prosecute captured buccaneers, especially if the targeted ships fly flags of convenience.[143]

Some companies, estimated at 25 percent in 2013, prefer to introduce armed "ship riders," at a cost of about $40,000 per voyage. Crews are reluctant to have deadly weapons on board, and captains raise thorny problems about their obligations under the customary laws of the sea—the contractors may repulse a pirate wave and disable the attacking vessel, but the targeted ship is then required to render aid.[144] Ports in the region have strict regulations barring weapons from entering their territory, leading to the establishment of floating storage armories in international waters, where the ship guards check their arsenals in and out for use on the high seas. Since these aren't regulated at all, the armories themselves are potential targets for VNSAs.[145] Long-term, the solution to piracy in the Horn of Africa is transformative economic development offering jobs with the status and steady pay to make pirate raiding risky and unattractive, but this would do nothing to get the raiders off the bow today.[146]

5
DIASPORAS

Buying enough Timberland boots to outfit an army, it is worth asking for a discount, and, after some consideration, Marty Frankel's Discount Clothing in Brooklyn was happy to oblige. Their customer, Florin Krasniqi, was the cheerleader, fundraiser, and chief gunrunner for the nascent Kosovo Liberation Army (KLA), which formed in the late 1990s to defend Kosovo from Serbs and create a Greater Albania in the Balkans. Smuggled into the United States from the former Yugoslavia in 1988, Krasniqi gave up teaching high school math to embrace the American Dream—driving cabs, roofing, and then owning his own construction business, Triangle General Contractors. News from back home was increasingly grim, with marauding Serbs and the death of his cousin Adrian as the first KLA uniformed casualty in 1996.[1]

The small Albanian diaspora in the United States already had a New York–based newspaper, *Zeri i Kosoves* (Voice of Kosovo), and lobbying groups working to advocate for fellow Albanians in the aftermath of Yugoslavia's implosion, like the Albanian American Civic League and the Democratic League of Kosovo. Many among this diaspora made regular donations to the 3 percent fund as a tithe to support Ibrahim Rugova's government of Kosovo and the shadow educational system that kept students out from under Serbian institutions.[2] In 1998, though, Serb soldiers massacred an extended family with a son in the KLA, a triggering event that radicalized the most aggressive members of the diaspora, including Krasniqi. He became convinced that the KLA could take advantage of the breakdown of the Albanian government (because of a pyramid scheme and economic collapse) to acquire arms and military advantage and that waiting around for a peace agreement like the 1995 Dayton Accords that had ended the war in Bosnia would accomplish nothing for the Kosovars.[3]

Krasniqi knew enough about American politics to understand that he needed higher-profile lobbying and began donating to and attending local political events in the New York area. He hit a jackpot discovering Rep. Joe DioGuardi from Westchester, who, until he was in his forties, believed that he was Italian (and lived the Italian American culture with the enthusiasm of a politician always running for reelection). Turns out, he was Arbëreshë, descended from a small group of Albanian migrants to southern Italy. Embracing his newfound heritage, DioGuardi threw himself into amplifying the plight of "his people." Albanian American celebrities like Jim Belushi and Hollywood director Stan Dragoti turned out for rallies, propaganda campaigns, and donation drives.[4]

The money generated went into the Homeland Calling Fund, which was very casually run out of Krasniqi's construction office and used to purchase supplies for the KLA. Leaders of the KLA wanted cash, but "what the fuck do you need cash for? They said they were buying guns cheaper. Yeah, buying shitty guns. I'll bring you uniforms, radios, guns, food, everything. You can't bring thousands of young people over the border to fight and give them these crummy weapons to get killed with."[5] Treating the American East Coast as one big gun show, Krasniqi bought uniforms, walkie-talkies, anti-dog sonic devices, New York Police Department surplus body armor and .50 caliber sniper rifles, with ultra conservative dealers delighted to help once they established that the KLA was fighting "communism." For specialty items, Krasniqi even flew to Peshawar on the advice of an Albanian waiter he met on a fundraising trip to Alaska, which yielded $80 bargain

AK-47s but not the surface-to-air missiles he really wanted.[6] Technically, the Homeland Calling Fund was a nonprofit and thus tax deductible, so there was some pretense that this was all "humanitarian supplies," and Krasniqi romanticized the KLA as freedom fighters who carefully only killed hardened Serb "moustache" bad guys, but once the stuff arrived in-country, well, he didn't have much control over that.[7]

Getting things in-country required the help of the diaspora and a lot of winking by authorities who pretended to believe that Krasniqi really was running an elephant-hunting tour group whose itinerary required a stop in Tirana, Albania, so crates of sniper rifles had a perfectly reasonable cause to be on commercial flights as luggage. A friendly Albanian American flight line worker at a Midwest hub loaded cargo on the sly. Pilots on charter flights agreed that the excited young men in camo outfits were obviously aid workers and not would-be soldiers.[8]

These soldiers were part of what Krasniqi hoped would be the master propaganda stroke: the Atlantic Brigade. Homeland Calling recruited several hundred volunteers from the Albanian community—waiters, grad students, construction workers—to don uniforms and take an oath in a hotel parking lot to "free Kosovo!" as DioGuardi yelled encouragement on a bullhorn. Krasniqi never really expected them to go. "I did everything in my power not to have them sent to the front. It didn't matter whether they went or not, the important thing was that they showed up in uniform in Yonkers. With that alone they would have done their part."[9] Their six weeks in Kosovo's primitive conditions was shocking to them and their families, who besieged Krasniqi's office with complaints that they were cold, hungry, and homesick, but "did they think they were going to a party?"[10] The abrupt victory of the KLA in 1999 seemed like "something out of a movie," concluding with the Atlantic Brigade taking over an iconic Serbian-run hotel for a celebration that required British peacekeepers to break up, but the brigade had suffered serious injuries and the deaths of the three Bytyqi brothers, kidnapped and murdered by Serb antiterrorist troops.[11]

Reminiscing is popular at the Atlantic Brigade veterans' association in the Bronx, along with complaining that U.S. insurance won't cover prosthetics or continued treatment for war wounds.[12] Krasniqi used his money and construction expertise to invest in a hydroelectric dam and served as a deputy in the Kosovan legislative assembly from 2010 to 2014, but many Albanian Americans were disillusioned by the difficulty rebuilding and establishing a workable infrastructure when many KLA members wanted to concentrate on avenging themselves on Serbs. Post-9/11 and in the aftermath of the 2002 Beltway sniper attacks in the D.C. region, with his illusion of safety from terrorist violence in America shattered, Krasniqi himself admitted that "anything you need to run a small guerilla army, you can buy here in America . . . all the rifles which U.S. soldiers use in every war, you can buy them in a gun store or gun show," and it probably wasn't such a great idea.[13]

■ Leaving Home

People migrate for a whole spectrum of reasons—they're seeking better economic opportunity, fleeing religious or ethnic persecution, captured and trafficked to enslavement, forcibly ejected from a territory, or part of temporary cycles of employment and homecoming. "Diaspora," a Greek term for a scattering of seeds, is a useful way to think about the people dispersed from their point of origin but with resources and attachment enough to that place to influence things that happen there. In the context of VNSA financing, diasporas aren't just crucial to sustaining a conflict, using money and other assets unavailable in the conflict area; they're likely also a major factor in a VNSA initiating hostilities, knowing they have supporters, safe havens, and influence out of the reach of their enemies.

In general, outmigration happens first, with those who have the means to leave when trouble erupts, wealthy professional people with foreign bank accounts and connections who can reestablish themselves in a new place on favorable terms. Next come those able to work, the key young demographic on which most countries (and VNSAs) are built, in many cases hollowing out the economy and prospects for recovery. A crisis that goes on long enough will create a wave of the most helpless people as refugees, sending the elderly, widows, and orphans into exile. Because of this, diasporas can be far from monolithic, with stages of emigrants embracing drastically different visions for possible return, desires for change, and cultural values stretching over generations. It would be a serious mistake to lump together Cambodian exile supporters of the old monarchy with those who fled because they wanted democratic government, or to see the United Kingdom's Islamic population as something other than a vast mosaic of peoples from the globalized former British Empire.[14] These tensions can even spill over into conflicts between groups, as with pro-Castro and very much anti-Castro Cubans in Canada (or Miami).[15]

Despite these fractures, most diasporas in a new place begin to form mutual-aid societies, tapping into their social connections and shared backgrounds to provide humanitarian relief, jobs, and social services, especially if excluded from these by their host communities' bias in providing public goods. Participating in charitable activity is a socially acceptable way to display success as well as build political capital in the homeland and new location through supplying largesse when needed, for a new church, a hospital, or a cousin's lavish wedding. This network of patrons for good works can be used as a financing source for fringe groups with links to the more mainstream members, leveraging their mutual belonging and emphasizing their ties to memory of the ancestral territory.

Diasporas swiftly adopt technologies, which allows them to maintain contact with the homeland, from telegraphy to cell phones to jet travel. The availability of satellite TV stations and websites makes it possible to follow Latin American football, Turkish historical soap operas, and Balkan politics from an apartment in Queens, keeping alive an immediate relationship to events and people left behind.[16] A community will cluster around available physical centers, like an Eritrean Orthodox church or a Sikh gurdwara, or even an ethnic market, to organize language classes for their kids, participate in sports leagues and women's' auxiliaries, pick up a newspaper, or hear a speech from a visiting political figure.[17] The group will celebrate key cultural events like Saints Days, anniversaries of historical events (Tamil Martyr's Day), and holidays like the Iranian or Chinese New Year, sometimes seeing their culture become so mainstream that it is adopted by the host country and recognized with official celebrations like Columbus Day or St. Patrick's Day.[18] To maintain ties, a group can sponsor pilgrimages to important homeland sites or conduct tours for second-generation diaspora, and established members of the community can further institutionalize their presence and outlook by endowing ethnic studies programs like Sikh Studies at Hofstra or Basque Studies at Boise State University in Idaho.[19]

Where a diaspora doesn't exist naturally, a VNSA can try to create one. Quebecois separatists in the 1960s appealed to Charles de Gaulle's francophone cultural promotions and saw themselves in the same colonial position as the recently decolonized nations of West Africa, aggressively enough that Canadian prime minister Lester Pearson asked de Gaulle directly not to get involved in domestic Canadian politics.[20] Always in the shadow of the IRA's spectacular Irish Catholic diaspora, the loyalist Protestants attempted to create links to Scotch Irish settlers around the world, including South Africa and the United States.[21] Much more successfully, Osama bin Laden's observation that "in a world where the majority of refugees in the 21st century had become Muslims," recruiting and shaping a Wahabi diaspora through the alumni network of Afghan mujahideen, scholarships to madrassas, and cultivation of grievances in Global North minority communities paid off, an effort that ISIS has continued.[22]

African Americans, whose individual origins enslavement brutally erased, responded to Marcus Garvey's pan-Africanism in the 1920s. Outrage over the Italian invasion of Ethiopia in 1935 converted a number of volunteers into Spanish Civil War republicans, seeking another way to be antifascist and thus anti-Mussolini and pro-Haile Selassie.[23] Trying to tap into this same feeling of diaspora, Jonas Savimbi, the guerrilla leader of the National Union for the Total Independence of Angola (UNITA), hired D.C. lobbying firm Black, Manafort, Stone and Kelly in 1985. The public relations advisers then curated a carefully managed tour of America for Savimbi, who had renounced his previous affiliation with Marxist and Maoist ideology and was fighting a brutal civil war against the Russian- and Cuban-backed Angolan government. The purpose of this was to drum up support from African Americans, justifying Ronald Reagan's $15 million yearly Cold War aid to UNITA and smoothing over Savimbi's sponsorship by apartheid South Africa.[24] In what would be called "astroturfing" now, the firm created and funded more than a dozen organizations like Black Americans for a Free Angola and donated money to existing philanthropic groups. Professionally coached, groomed, and set up as a "freedom fighter" in a Nehru suit, Savimbi set out for the Deep South.[25]

Things started well, with Savimbi accepting the Medgar Evers Humanitarian Award from the civil rights hero's brother, Mayor Charles Evers of Fayette, Mississippi, but angry protesters forced the ceremony inside. Evers' widow, Myrlie, was firmly on the other side, organizing with Jesse Jackson, the Black Congressional Caucus, and the National Urban League to follow the tour, pointing out that Savimbi was doing South Africa's dirty work in Angola and that his tactics included crushing prisoners with heavy vehicles, smashing children's heads against trees, and burning women alive for witchcraft.[26] No amount of handing out scripts for chanting "Savimbi is a hero, Castro's a zero" was going to make this convincing to a created diaspora, especially not when Bill Cosby, on the country's most popular sitcom, had just named his fictional grandchildren Winnie and Nelson.[27]

When diasporas put down roots in a new location that allows them to gain citizenship, vote, and hold office, they quickly leverage the system to the benefit of their compatriots left behind. Famously, the Greek American lobby mobilizes any time feta and olive oil come under threat of U.S. tariffs, exercising economic power far out of proportion to their actual numbers.[28] Armenian Americans have made sure that foreign aid packages of more than a billion dollars have flowed into Yerevan since the breakup of the Soviet Union, a remarkable feat considering that U.S. interests are far more lucratively engaged in regional rival Azerbaijan's oil fields.[29] The 2020 U.S. National Defense Authorization Act contains a bizarre provision confirming belief in the legitimate position of the current Dalai Lama and sanctions, should the Chinese government attempt to name his successor, a diplomatic coup courtesy of the Tibetan diaspora and their powerful celebrity supporters.[30] Large and vocal ethnic populations in the United States demanded representation for their positions at the Treaty of Versailles, backing the creation of post–World War I Poland, Czechoslovakia, and independent Ireland, and woe betides any New York elected official who neglects the "3 I's": Israel, Italy, and Ireland.[31]

Freedom of the press and assembly in their new places of residence allow diasporas to organize rallies, protests, and solicitations for help. Kurds in the United Kingdom, Germany, and Canada denounced the 1999 capture of PKK chief Abdullah Öcalan on the sites of Turkish embassies and petitioned the European Council, European Parliament, and European Court of Human

Rights for political and legal relief.[32] EU protections for minorities like the Catalans and Basques, as well as legislation like Canada's Multiculturalism Act, ensure that there are venues for diasporic minorities to present their case.[33] Spokespeople for VNSAs and dissident political parties can far more safely spread their message and raise funds in the Global North than in Haiti, Colombia, or 1990s Croatia, particularly if the home country allows for diaspora voting and representation.[34]

■ The Bank of Exiles

Indian prime minister Rajiv Gandhi remarked that Indians working abroad were "a bank from which one could make withdrawals from time to time."[35] In many developing countries, remittances from economic migrants amount to more every year than country-to-country foreign aid, providing desperately needed hard currency and a cushion against the need for a government to step in with natural disaster relief. Regular transfers of money from workers abroad is so crucial that government policy exists to smooth the way, with Morocco subsidizing transfer fees, the Philippines offering duty-free shipping home up to $1,000, Mexico issuing bank-compliant IDs, and the InterAmerican Bank counting remittance income in evaluations of domestic personal and business loans.[36]

Remittance workers feel heavy obligations to send money home to their families: "You eat with your brother when he has money" is a Somali refrain about sharing resources. The obligation increases rather than diminishes when those left behind live in proximity to a VNSA that can demand "revolutionary tax" and extort family money. Abu Rami, living in Raqqa, Syria, under ISIS, showed a reporter the row of *hawala* kiosks allowed to operate in order to access money sent from abroad. "Every person who has a relative abroad gets help. My brother is in Lebanon. Every month he would send me $100, which is what he earns in two days."[37] Not sending money is unthinkable, but the money itself is fungible, able to be taken by a VNSA and relieving them of providing other services for the people they rule. Global North banks have largely ceased to transfer money to conflict regions, shying away from being tainted for material support of terrorism but pushing transfers to *hawala*, where lack of accessible records further obscure what is going on.

Among those remittance workers are many people who plan to return to their homelands, making their financial involvement with VNSAs more visceral and immediate. Western Europe, suffering from World War II demographic losses at the same time they were rebuilding industrial capacity, imported "guest workers" from their former colonies and the Near East. In Germany, Kurdish and Turkish migrants occupied a special, liminal status, encouraged to keep their culture in anticipation of going home. The PKK used networks of *Gastarbeiter* (guest worker) clubs to inculcate Kurdish nationalism, which exacerbated the sense of alienation when the workers not only didn't return in one generation but their children also faced assimilation and bias problems. This diaspora formed a rich vein for recruiting and fundraising. Something similar happened in France, where North African workers clustered in the outer *banlieue* splintered further away from aggressive efforts at French education and nationalism and toward radicalization as they soured on hopes of being included in the licit economy.[38] In Libya, Muammar Gaddafi regarded Palestinian guest workers as obligated to the Palestine Liberation Organization (PLO), for whom he officially deducted 5 percent of guest workers' salary, although his willingness to pass it on to PLO chairman Yasser Arafat depended on Gaddafi's particular whims. Muslim workers in the Gulf States, along with sending money to their families in Pakistan, India, and Bangladesh, donate to extremist VNSAs, also radicalized by their poor treatment at the hands of wealthy Sunnis who use them for construction, household labor, and military sustainment duties under exploitative conditions.[39]

Prosperous diasporas can organize significant financial contributions to their homelands. Beginning in the 1920s, Italian and Mexican village associations pooled money to build improvements in their hometowns, sponsoring schools, clinics, and water projects and sending frequent inspectors to check up on the progress of the work. One of the unanticipated by-products of this was a rising expectation that the homeland government provide more basic services and answer to audits and accountability in new, sometimes conflict-provoking ways.[40] Post-conflict regions can use the skills and financial resources of their diaspora by asking them to return to take political office, buy "diaspora bonds" for rebuilding infrastructure, or pay an income tax on their much higher wages abroad.[41] Since before the founding of the State of Israel, the Jewish diaspora has underwritten social services, welfare, and agricultural development on a massive scale.[42]

■ Long-Distance Violence

These diaspora movements are all well-intentioned, but they can fester dangerous ideas as well. Political scientist Benedict Anderson captured the concept of these "imagined communities" and "long-distance nationalism" in a conversation with a Sikh American friend whose Canadian coreligionists send money to buy guns for the Khalistan movement, keeping his sons secure in North America but cheering on insurgency elsewhere: "politics without responsibility or accountability."[43] Thousands of miles away, an uncompromising and romanticized attachment to a cause makes VNSA funding appeals and actions seem reasonable, even noble, since the car bomb won't go off on your street and the reprisals won't end up with your child dead. Singing songs about dying "for the freedom of the nation" is different when the participation is grounded in "rights over obligations, passive entitlements and the assertion of an interest in the public space without a daily presence."[44] Diasporas can be shockingly disconnected from the realities of a current conflict, seeing it through a lens of their grandparents' experience and an emphasis on backing action to make up for their lack of direct commitment.

Specific news from the homeland can galvanize even well-assimilated, prosperous diasporas into violent action or can spur larger donations to VNSAs. For Albanians, the February 1998 massacre of the family of a KLA commander by the Serb army triggered an outpouring of interest and support. In the Sikh diaspora, Operation Blue Star, the 1984 attack on the Golden Temple in Amritsar by India's military forces, radicalized cadres who set off to volunteer in Khalistani-affiliated VNSAs in Pakistan. Milan Herekol, who grew up in Melbourne as part of the Kurdish diaspora, reacted to Saddam Hussein's bombing of Halabja by joining the PKK in 1990.[45] Disproportionate suppression, like the Spanish government's use of the Grupos Antiterroristas de Liberacion to hunt ETA members in France, backfired on them and amped up diaspora support in the early 1980s. Denials of justice, like the Indian government's failure to prosecute people involved in the anti-Muslim Gujarat riots in 2002, stoke outrage and participation in the international diaspora affected.[46]

A diaspora may tolerate brutal activities in the homeland as part of their framing of conflict, but they can reach a critical breaking point when threatened themselves, either with physical danger or with embarrassment and social opprobrium in their new residence. The Armenian Secret Army for the Liberation of Armenia "deeply miscalculated" in 1983 what their supportive diaspora would bear and attacked the Turkish Airlines counter at Orly Airport in Paris. Wealthy donors could imagine themselves in that carnage, and it no longer felt right or just to participate.[47] The IRA carefully directed their violent activities away from their U.S. patrons and from American tourists in the Republic and Northern Ireland, allowing them to keep their romantic view of the organization intact. Boko Haram enjoyed a wide diaspora approval for their criticism of corruption and rejection of Western beliefs but squandered it with the highly publicized kidnapping of the Chibok schoolgirls in 2014.[48]

Diasporas tangled up with or victimized by illicit activity or suspected of being complicit are extremely hard to police in their new place of residence. If they come from a situation that taught them to rely on one another and distrust the authorities, they may be reluctant to summon help when extorted by a VNSA. The community might have a language and structure impenetrable to outsiders, as investigators found when trying to track money laundering through a network of Hasidic Jewish yeshivas—the FBI's hired translator felt guilty and tipped off one of the rabbis.[49] The Vietnamese émigré community in East Germany remained isolated, with even the Stasi secret police hindered in attempting to surveil and break up their cigarette smuggling because of a lack of connection and language skills.[50]

A diaspora group can be useful to a VNSA for intelligence and cover. Although fictionalized, the film *Argo* realistically cautioned about the information-gathering Iranian diaspora inside the United States in the late 1970s: "The Khomaniacs are fruit loops, but they have cousins selling eight tracks and prayer rugs on La Brea."[51] Conversely, a diaspora's participation in law enforcement, the diplomatic corps, and military service is a huge asset for their new nations. Getting people to join, though, usually takes time, as trust develops and second-generation members of the community see these jobs as viable careers, although they may never entirely have the approval of their group for siding with powerful outsiders. In the United Kingdom, a push by MI6 and the police to recruit from diverse populations foundered on Project Champion, the installation of cameras in majority Muslim areas, provoking protests and feelings that the government's desire for inclusion was exploitative rather than sincere. Having connections with an "in" to a diaspora community can be crucial to resolving crises like the 2007 kidnapping of British embassy staff in Ethiopia, but building and maintaining the links is delicate and easily destroyed by a single misstep.[52]

Community policing and recruitment of diaspora members has to happen long before they're needed, and with an underlying respect for the community's culture, which involves concerted efforts and substantial resources in training and time spent building trust. Departments don't prioritize this against other demands or push back on having to "have meetings with anti-government groups" when the response from a diaspora community is not cooperative and compliant. Self-styled counterterrorism experts billed local police departments for post-9/11 seminars on Islamic culture that did far more harm than good and sent people out into the field believing that long beards equaled "radicalization" or that Muslims kneeling in a parking lot to pray were a threat.[53] British efforts to translate their "hearts and minds" campaign in Northern Ireland into something allies could replicate in Afghanistan stumbled on these same problems—public outreach had to be without expectations of immediate aid, people were right to assume their information was being collected as intelligence, and the concept of a "strategic corporal," whose low-level mistake resounded with serious repercussions, was just as relevant at a meet-and-greet as a neighborhood armed patrol.[54]

Assimilating a diaspora, especially when a large group arrives on a short timescale in response to conflict or crisis, requires a whole-of-government commitment and intentionality. Successful programs include language support, educational provisions, housing that is not isolated or segregated, access to jobs valued by the receiving community, and openness to cultural practices the diaspora group holds dear, whether religion or dress conventions. The host population may resent opportunities presented to newcomers or feel threatened by the presence of job competitors or groups of young people, especially from backgrounds they've seen painted in media as terrorists and criminals. Threading the needle of being responsive to constituents' genuine concerns while not alienating already disoriented and displaced people is a task for which few governments allot sufficient resources or achieve critical mass of buy-in. Any failure, like the radicalization of one teenage boy, or community reaction to an attack on the other side of the world sets back the whole process from all sides.[55]

▪ The LTTE

Portuguese, Dutch, and British colonial rule of Sri Lanka stoked tensions between the majority Buddhist Sinhalese population and the Tamils, whose Hinduism and conversion of some to Christianity set them apart. Tamils dominated the civil service and white-collar work, causing resentments that flared after the island became independent in 1948. Tamils organized protests against government policies imposing Sinhalese language use, quotas limiting jobs in academia and licensed professions, and escalating harassment by law enforcement. Armed Tamil groups emerged in the early 1970s, with the Liberation Tigers of Tamil Eelam (LTTE) eventually predominating. Brutal suppression followed, igniting a violent conflict that displaced 700,000 people and sent waves of refugees to British Commonwealth countries and Western Europe, where their professional qualifications and language skills translated into valued jobs in the British National Health Service and bureaucracies.[56] With more than a quarter of the Tamils in the world living outside of Sri Lanka, the LTTE began organizing them as a diaspora fundraising mechanism; the LTTE so successfully reminded this diaspora of the ongoing humiliations and depredations of Sinhalese majority rule that by the mid-1990s they could pull $12 million Canadian dollars a year from that population alone.[57]

The LTTE used diaspora Hindu temples as an organizing platform, spinning off youth organizations, dance troupes, language classes, and cricket teams. Tamil-language newspapers, websites, radio programs, and satellite TV pushed propaganda vehicles like the film *Mother of War* (1994) and promoted fund drives.[58] At a rally on Heroes Day in Toronto's Queen's Park, representatives of the LTTE sold flags, recordings of war ballads, and videos and featured testimonies from mothers of martyrs and performances from local children's temple dance classes. Explicitly linking Tamil romanticized mythology and martyrdom has made it more palatable for the diaspora to fund violence, seeing the deaths as a redemption and necessity.[59]

Tamil protest, London 2017. Tamils flying the LTTE flag protest the continuing conflict with the Sinhalese-majority government in Sri Lanka, demonstrating the power of an engaged and organized diaspora. *Courtesy Alamy*

In the thinking of the LTTE, this obligation on the part of the diaspora for the guerrillas' hardship and sacrifice has entitled them to a share of the revenue generated away from the homeland, and for those contributions that didn't come voluntarily, they set up a ruthless and systematic structure of collection and extortion. Representatives carefully cataloged diaspora members, issuing personal identification numbers (PIN) to those who paid regular contributions and linking them in a database to relatives remaining behind in Sri Lanka. It was obvious that the relatives were hostages, and any Tamil who wished to travel back home would encounter checkpoints checking the PINs and threatening "problems" if payment was in arrears.[60] The LTTE also had business trafficking refugees into Global North countries, expecting them to run tribute-paying businesses and conduct the collection portion of their extortion schemes, veering into threats, stalking, and violence, if necessary.[61] Victims of these actions were afraid to interact with the Canadian and British authorities, who lacked entrée to the community and had few translators available who weren't active members of the LTTE.[62]

Tamils in their new homes quickly formed powerful voting blocs and realized that, in regions with concentrations of their community, they had members of parliament (MPs) to represent their interests at the national level, hitting the jackpot with a legislator from Toronto, Bill Graham, who became minister of foreign affairs in 2002 and put the Sri Lankan Civil War on Canada's policy agenda. Tamil organizations have legal recognition, publish voter guides recommending candidates with favorable views, and accept grants from the Canadian government to conduct social programs and crime prevention studies.[63] British constituents place similar lobbying pressure on their MPs, organizing the "key campaign" to "unlock the concentration camps in Sri Lanka."[64]

The 9/11 attacks, though, were a critical point of departure for many diaspora Tamils. Countries that had permitted fundraising and LTTE propaganda listed the organization as terrorist, causing donors to weigh their risks of being prosecuted for material support. Instead they increasingly channeled money to home village associations for community projects and to responses for the 2004 tsunami using the sophisticated and highly developed fundraising apparatus, including radio telethons and rallies, to deliver relief.[65] This sea change in attitude, and in reducing the diaspora's role as a bank, helped to force the LTTE into negotiations.[66]

■ The ETA

The Basque people of the Pyrenees mountain region are one of the most unusual ethnic minorities in Europe. It's possible that they are the descendants of the prehistoric cave painters of Lascaux, and their language is a rare pre-Indo-European survivor. Basque history is studded with resistance heroes—against the Celts, Romans, Goths, Charlemagne, and Islamic invaders. As the kingdom of Navarre, the Basque Country sat between France and Spain's centralizing early modern monarchies, wringing "*fueros*," or concessions of rights, out of both.[67] Basque soldiers and navigators were key to the fifteenth-century voyages of exploration by Spain and Portugal, beginning a vast diaspora in the Americas. Like their nationalist parallels in nineteenth-century Ireland, Basque scholars promoted the preservation of the language, cultural traditions, and romanticized history as a defense against being swallowed by a modernizing and industrializing Spain and campaigned for regional autonomy.[68] These political goals were on the brink of success, with autonomy granted by the republican government of Spain in October 1936 but extinguished (along with the Republic) by Francisco Franco's victory in the Spanish Civil War.[69]

Franco and the nationalist government of Spain saw the Basques, like the Catalan people, as obstacles to their program of hardline conservatism and authoritarian dictatorship. During the Spanish Civil War, Franco and the Falange Española Tradicionalista allowed German and Italian fascist allies to test weapons and tactics, destroying the Basque market town of Guernica, and considered republican Basques to be enemies, seizing their property, interning them as political prisoners, and ferociously repressing their language. Franco relocated workers to factories in the region as an attempt to dilute Basque culture. A government-in-exile operated in France, and Basque members of the resistance hoped that the United States and its allies would continue to be antifascist and turn on Franco.[70] Unfortunately, Franco made a more useful Cold War ally than an enemy, especially with his willingness to allow the use of Rota as a naval base.[71]

Seeing themselves as comrades of other nationalist groups like the Welsh, Breton, and Irish separatists of the 1960s, the ETA also legitimized their violent resistance in the context of Franz Fanon's theories of decolonization and the oppression of the developing world. Their orientation gave them links to other VNSAs like the IRA and Fatah but shut out non-Basque recruitment and forced them to turn to blackmail, kidnapping, and robbery for financial support.[72] Their first attack in 1961, bombing trains carrying Falange veterans to a memorial in San Sebastián, became emblematic of the high level of violence the ETA was willing to use against the Spanish state and those they believed collaborated against the Basque people.[73] Franco had no compunction about jailing, torturing, and executing ETA members in response, culminating in the 1970 Burgos trials of sixteen defendants, including two women and two Catholic priests, resulting in nine death sentences.[74]

The Burgos trials were a catalyzing event for the surprisingly large Basque diaspora. Across the border in France, there was no love for Franco, who had supported the Organisation Armée Secrète in Algeria. French Basques welcomed their cousins with open arms, supplies, and safe haven, including training camps. The French refused extradition requests, waved people through the border, indulged rallies in front of the Spanish embassy protesting the Burgos sentences, and functioned as a practical "rearguard, our logical staging area." In solidarity, other Western European nations threatened to withdraw their diplomatic staffs, possibly more about the death penalty than the ETA, but the threats worked, with commutation of the sentences and massive fundraising in a "Home for Christmas" campaign in 1976–77 to provide for prisoners' families and medical aid in jail. Two executions in 1975 brought out another wave of protests and giving, with Swedish prime minister Olof Palme leading public donations in Stockholm.[75]

In the Western Hemisphere, things were a little more complicated. The FBI recruited Basques to help them look for fascists in South America during World War II but abandoned those efforts by the early 1950s. The Catholic Church was staunchly anticommunist, preaching against the ETA and opposition to Franco and shutting down Basque-language parishes. Peronist Argentina and its right-wing neighbors were no place to be outspoken about minority rights, with only anticlerical Mexico allowing the ETA to operate an official delegation and request asylum on political grounds.[76] Instead the diaspora concentrated on less political events, celebrating "Fatherland Day" in conjunction with Easter Sunday, raising money for cultural programs via "Sheepherder's Balls," and endowing academic programs in the late 1960s, although passing the hat for distressed relatives in the homeland was never forbidden.[77] The Burgos trials, though, brought these private concerns into the public eyes—prominent Basques in Idaho, Nevada, and Oregon, including Sen. Pete Cenarrusa (whose son had been on a student exchange in Spain in 1970) sponsored official resolutions in state legislatures condemning Franco's government. The "Brothers All" organization stood up in Boise and openly raised money for ETA prisoners, lobbying the U.S. government to intervene.[78]

Basques around the world celebrated Franco's death in 1975, and the ETA took credit for promoting democracy by having assassinated his likely successor, Adm. Luis Carrero Blanco. The new socialist government, though, unexpectedly launched a brutal counterstrike against the ETA, empowering their own VNSA, the Grupos Antiterroristas de Liberacion, to kidnap and murder ETA members and sympathizers, even across the border in France.[79] This had a bifurcated effect on the diaspora. In France, the deaths of twenty-seven people, some of whom had nothing to do with the ETA at all, finally wore out the group's welcome, when Prime Minister François Mitterrand, spooked by Islamist VNSA attacks in Paris and pressured by President Jacques Chirac, closed the border and rounded up known ETA members. The French, as expressed by a shopkeeper in Saint-Jean-de-Luz, had had enough: "We think it is horrible that they are killing the Spanish refugees, but that's not our problem . . . we're sick of all this trouble, and it would be better if they left."[80] The Spanish government's blatant break with democratic norms while operating a death squad, though, galvanized the ETA and the more distant diaspora, extending their support for another two decades.

As with other diasporas, 9/11 exposed the tension of this situation. The ETA's kidnappings, bombings, and street violence drove business and tourism away from the Basque Country and aggravated the local population.[81] Spanish constitutional reform and EU cultural outreach were moving Basque political parties into mainstream participation, and support for language and identity ensured that forced assimilation would not be pursued. When George W. Bush's administration designated the ETA, along with the IRA and others, as "terrorists" in the wake of 9/11, Idaho Basques stepped in again, sponsoring a legislative memorial praising Basque self-determination. The Spanish government took this as a "gratuitously unfriendly gesture," prompting the State Department to intervene and direct the legislature to specifically condemn the ETA.[82] The ETA was still conducting violent operations in 2004 when an Islamic VNSA bombed the Madrid train station and was enough of a threat that they were viable suspects in the attack.[83] With the approval of the European Court of Human Rights, the Spanish authorities shut down the ETA's political branch and media outlets that had doxed businesses refusing to pay extortion, drawing angry responses from the American diaspora.[84]

The eventual cease-fire (2010) and dissolution (2018) of the ETA is one of the great success stories of a VNSA. While they never achieved independence, they have autonomous status within a liberal democracy, cultural protections, and a dedicated diaspora. The diaspora, though, has a curiously sanitized and historical view of the Basque culture, highlighting the sports, dancing, cooking, and expertise as explorers and mariners and sidestepping the messy complications of the Spanish Civil War and the ETA.[85] In fact, like the Tamils in Canada, they're more comfortable with a conservative view of the homeland, rather than the burgeoning high-tech industry, Guggenheim Museum, and participation in the European Union, and they're mortified when, thanks to EU grants, Basque-region politicians offer community centers in Idaho and Nevada generous funding to buy computers and cultural materials, reversing the traditional relationship.[86]

▪ Al-Shabaab

Large numbers of Somali emigrants began arriving in the Global North in the mid-1990s in response to civil war in the Horn of Africa, and started forming a large diaspora in the suburbs of Nairobi, Kenya. One of the largest concentrations is in the Minneapolis–St. Paul region of Minnesota, especially in high-density housing like the Skyline Towers. By 2000 the community had sufficient numbers and resources to convert an old church into the Masjid Al-Ansar mosque and operate self-help organizations and community centers.[87] From the snowy Midwest, Somali Americans sent money and expertise to the Islamic Courts Union (ICU), a functional government in their homeland, whose success offered hope in public order, the safety of their clans, and the possibility of returning. When, in December 2006, Ethiopia invaded and overthrew the ICU, the Somali diaspora reeled in shock and humiliation from their traditional enemy. With U.S. intelligence support, Ethiopia wanted to reclaim territory lost to Somalia and restore the Transitional Federal Government of Somalia.[88]

   Al-Shabaab, which grew from a Sharia court militia, stayed on to fight the Ethiopians and their American backers while the government fled to Eritrea. The diaspora felt lost and betrayed, with only al-Shabaab doing anything to resist. "All they were doing is fighting the Ethiopians. People didn't see any danger in that."[89] Resisting foreign domination seemed like the best way back to the lost stability and unity of the ICU, and the external enemy, rather than problems inside of Somalia, offered a reason for the collapse of their hopes. Fundraisers for al-Shabaab were already active in Kenya, making it a center for opposition groups and a safe haven, and some American diaspora members sent donations to connections there.[90] By 2007, though, the fundraisers were asking directly, and the community's teenage boys were packing their bags as foreign fighters.

Law enforcement and social services agonize about what makes young men susceptible to radicalization. Their parents, often single mothers who were traumatized by the emigration process themselves, have to work, leaving the kids struggling with assimilation. There are English as a Second Language classes in St. Paul, but starting with phonics like a small child is humiliating. One foreign fighter articulated his motivation as going to a place where he "would be able to live, pray, act, dress and be a Muslim without anyone yelling at me, calling me names, refusing me jobs or apartments."[91] Many Somalis report police harassment and derogatory treatment for their dress, religion, and customs.[92] Meanwhile, al-Shabaab is online, available in chatrooms, streaming videos, and hosting websites. An angry, lonely teenager who feels powerless can plug into a global movement and hear someone who looks like him proclaim "if you guys only knew how much fun we have over here—this is the real Disneyland. You need to come here and join us!" Once interested, "jihadihobbyists" face challenges from recruiters to sacrifice and send money, prove their faith with acts of public support, and, eventually, come to fight.[93] At least twenty of them left to become foreign fighters, slipping off from school or runs to the laundromat, only to discover that the cool thing al-Shabaab wants them to do is be a suicide bomber.[94]

For those who aren't desirable as foreign fighters, or who want to claim status in the diaspora community, fundraising is a path to prominence and influence. Basaaly Moalin, who "tries to outshine others in supporting the home region," also liked to be the authority on "on matters ranging from politics to health to the best way to cook spaghetti" and confidently assured people that donations were the same thing as traditional *zakat* charitable giving.[95] These senior members of the community tell youths that they aren't wanted in their new country, that they can never really fit in, and that the only answer is to devote themselves to al-Shabaab to redeem their honor as Somalis and members of their extended clans. This is powerful leverage with little effective countermessaging.[96]

In Rochester, Minnesota, two women, Amina Farah Ali and Hawo Mohamed Hassan, tapped into the diaspora contingent of Somali women, aggressively raising funds for al-Shabaab door to door in their neighborhood and on the phone, eventually collecting $8,608, which they sent using *hawalas* under false names. At first they asked for donations for the needy, but then began stating outright that the money was for "violent jihad." On one teleconference they hosted, a member of al-Shabaab's women's department harangued participants that "it was not the time to help the poor and needy in Somalia; rather, the priority was to give to the mujahidin."[97] Both received lengthy sentences in 2013 for conspiracy to support a terror group and lying to investigators.[98]

Prosecutions like these, and of the handful of returned foreign fighters, dampened diaspora support, as did al-Shabaab's brutal methods. Maintaining the narrative that al-Shabaab was upholding Somali national pride while joining with al-Qaeda and ISIS was increasingly impossible, as one fundraiser pled with a donor. "Well, that has its problems, but Abdulkadir, let's look at it from another angle—they are the ones who are firing the most bullets at the enemy."[99] The diaspora didn't buy it.

Even without direct donations, authorities and the diaspora worry that money still finds its way to al-Shabaab. With a full 14 percent of Somalis living outside of their homeland, the expectation that the diaspora support those left behind makes for powerful pressure to send regular transfers for community projects, family crises, and the support of parents and siblings. Al-Shabaab operatives have announced that they are entitled to a larger than normal *zakat*—10 percent—and they collect it on behalf of the community on traditional holidays, rather than allowing clans to dole it out as charity as they see fit. Additionally, they take a cut of businesses, livestock, and personal possessions so that money sent home is fungible in some way and can be taken for violent purposes.[100]

Hawalas, a money transfer system, is the most effective way to send funds to rural regions of Somalia but raises suspicions with Western authorities that a banking method without formalized written records is especially vulnerable to VNSA exploitation. The closure of Al-Barakat, a dominant remittance handler, in 2001 caused major disruption to the Somali economy, and the diaspora scrambled to find local alternatives. Global North banks, especially those in the United Kingdom and United States, shied away from handling accounts with *hawaladars*, afraid of being hit with material support charges or having accounts frozen and finding regulatory compliance too costly to bother for a specialty group of customers. Eventually this became so pressing that the Somali American diaspora sought help from their congressional delegation in the Midwest, leading to the 2014 passage of the Money Remittances Improvement Act.[101]

Law enforcement continues to find it challenging to engage with the Somali diaspora. Few members have been recruited to fill the ranks, and among non-Somalis, language capabilities are scarce. Programs meant to keep Somali youths out of gangs, modeled on lessons learned from the Hmong diaspora's emigration to Minnesota, pivoted aggressively to counterterrorism, leading many Somalis to distrust the sincerity of the engagement—was it to help them or to infiltrate their community for persecution? Experts, including the Minneapolis deputy police chief, who wrote a thesis about Somali American community outreach for the Naval Postgraduate School, identified serious problems: distrust of law enforcement, the undocumented status of some members of the diaspora, culture clash, and disengagement with U.S. politics and laws.[102] None of these have easy or fast fixes. So far the most effective deradicalization and deterrent has been peers from within the community taking the sugar-coating off VNSAs, like pointing out the fundamental uncoolness of being manipulated or underlining, "You were eating McDonalds; you don't know how to fight, dude. You're not gonna help. As opposed to if you learn something . . . then you can go back and help your people."[103]

It is hard to convince the diaspora when Minnesota locals taunt their kids at school for being "terrorists," their elders get harassed by security agents at the airport, and former senator Norm Coleman labeled the state "land of 10,000 terrorists."[104] Generally, the election of a diaspora member to public office signals a mainstreaming and acceptance in a new location, but the Somali Americans' most visible leader is Rep. Ilhan Omar, a favorite target of right-wing criticism and invective, including death threats serious enough to warrant prosecution.[105]

■ The IRA

Irish Americans may be the quintessential diaspora success story for assimilation and acquisition of political and social influence. Protestant

Irish participated in the British colonial experiment in the North American colonies, establishing links that brought Theobald Wolfe Tone to America as a refugee in 1795, but the critical mass of Irish people arrived in response to the devastating potato famine of the 1840s.[106] Their presence enabled the American Industrial Revolution, built the transcontinental railroad, and filled out the armies of the Mexican American War and American Civil War. Powerful and effective political machines delivered Irish votes in key states like New York, Massachusetts, and Pennsylvania throughout the nineteenth century, bolstered by cultural institutions like the Ancient Order of Hibernians, Gaelic Athletic Association, and Gaelic-speaking parishes of the Catholic Church. If Fenians used U.S. military training to invade Canada, well, it served the British right for refusing to back the federal government in the Civil War.[107] Irish Americans cast the 1916 Easter Rising in explicit comparisons to the American Revolution and lobbied to save the life of Eamon de Valera, whose American mother and dual nationality spared him from the firing squad. Subsequently, the new Irish Republic sold the diaspora more than $6 million in bonds.[108]

As "The Troubles" spun up in the mid-1960s, the United States had five times (44 million or 19 percent of the U.S. population) as many people of Irish descent as existed in the Republic and Northern Ireland. There were still some hard feelings over Ireland's neutrality in World War II, but that resentment was being eroded by the enduring idealization of Ireland as the lush setting of *The Quiet Man* (1952) and American visions of heroic partnership with freedom-loving people.[109] Michael Flannery, an archconservative member of the old (1920s) IRA North Tipperary Brigade stood up the Irish Northern Aid Committee (NORAID) in 1969, holding fundraisers, building political connections, securing American support, and funneling millions of dollars a year back to the IRA's treasury via the Bank of Boston. Flannery's stock statement when asked if the money was really going to support the families of prisoners was that "our job is to get the money and send it to the people over there. What they use it for is up to them. We attach no strings."[110]

A big part of operating in America was getting access to weapons. George Harrison, the primary gunrunner until 1981, went to a small shop in Yonkers, New York, which eventually sold him more than $1 million in guns. Other operatives toured Midwest gun shows, while Gerry McGeough drove around

Florida in a recreational vehicle with a woman he met in a bar, using her ID to purchase dozens of assault rifles with cash. This is how the IRA got its beloved ArmaLite AR-15s and later M-16s and smuggled them across the Atlantic via sympathetic dockers and members of the U.S. Merchant Marine.[111] Both Harrison and Flannery were arrested in 1981 as part of an FBI sting, but their trials turned into circuses, with Harrison decrying the indictment that he had been accused of only "aiding and abetting" for six months when in truth he had "supplied arms to the rebels in Northern Ireland for a quarter of a century."[112] Defense lawyers argued that the men were freedom fighters, "resisting British oppression" and working with the CIA "on US government business."[113] The CIA could not confirm or deny, which led the jury to acquit and the court clerk to raise his fists in the air and start shouting, "IRA all the way!"[114] The FBI agents who engineered the sting and the arrests were disgusted, but the FBI wasn't exactly free of Irish American influence and had ignored the problem all through the 1970s.[115]

NORAID loved big gestures like this showing the degree to which it operated with impunity in America. In 1981 a federal court forced them to disclose under the Foreign Agents Registration Act, with the PIRA as the recipient of record, although they continued to insist it was for humanitarian relief of prisoners and their families.[116] They held public fundraising dinners, headlined by actor Richard Harris—"you talk about Russians in Afghanistan. If those were Russian troops in Northern Ireland, the U.S. would consider the IRA freedom fighters"[117]—author Len Deighton, and the head of the Longshoreman's Union, Teddy Gleason.[118] Their publicity director, Martin Galvin, a New York City civil servant, gave incendiary speeches in Belfast praising the torture death of a British army private, got banned from traveling there, and immediately snuck back in and forced the Royal Ulster Constabulary to try to drag him off the speaker's dais.[119] The highlight of NORAID's year, though, was using its influence over the nominating clubs to have the grand marshal of the New York City St. Patrick's Day parade be one of their own: Michael Flannery in a triumphant return from his trial acquittal in 1983, followed by Michael O'Rourke in 1984, despite the fact that he was under arrest in a New York City jail for making mortars for use against the British army.[120]

Graffiti in South Boston makes explicit the relationship between the Irish American diaspora and their financial support of NORAID and Sinn Féin (and the IRA).
Courtesy Alamy

NORAID membership overlapped with other groups in America, like the Emerald League, all of which were encouraged to raise money. Musical evenings at pubs were a good place to pass the hat, but there was always a discreet "Derry can" on the bar for donations. Dinner dances affiliated with building trade unions reinforced Irish identity and offered charity bazaars selling crafts made by IRA prisoners, Irish linens, and musical recordings. Sports leagues promoted male bonding and added pressure to belong to the group through outward demonstrations of loyalty. Catholic parishes held raffles, although at one their new Polish priest disapproved and shut it down, prompting a call by parishioners to the cops, who arrived to announce their own Irish surnames and demand to buy tickets.[121] Police and fire companies were especially generous and prominent in IRA support, raising money to send their marching bands to participate in IRA public funerals.[122] One of the ugliest aspects of this was the conscious stoking of racial tensions in encouraging working-class Irish Americans to "save their heritage" at a time when their job sites and unions were being joined by a more diverse membership of African American and Latino tradespeople.[123]

One of the most bizarre aspects of the IRA–Irish American love affair was the utter disconnect of the organization's stated goals and the American understanding of them. The IRA and Sinn Féin made no secret that they had an unabashedly socialist program (Marxist when it came to the Provos) of reunification of the whole island, hostility to the Republic, nationalization of industry, and the end to personal ownership of productive property "such as a large farm or a large factory."[124] Bernadette Devlin, an Irish Socialist Party MP, toured America in 1969, met with Black Panthers, and made no secret that she was pregnant out of wedlock. Irish Americans balked, and the IRA subsequently produced spokespeople and fundraisers in the mold Americans wanted—conservative, patriarchal, and Catholic. Italian political analyst Loretta Napoleoni, staying with a very traditional clan in Boston as a Fulbright student, pointed out the gap between a mysterious fellow guest (an IRA bag man) and the family's behavior, only to be shushed. "We are Irish. They are our people."[125] Into the 1990s, many American NORAID supporters believed that the "real" Ireland they campaigned for was antiabortion, fiscally conservative, and English-language first, with one supporter melting down on learning that LGBTQ marchers participated in St. Patrick's Day parades while another proclaimed, "Ireland has gone to the dogs . . . I don't know what they think they are up to."[126]

Meanwhile, the IRA had no problem allying itself with other separatist groups in Europe, like the ETA; Breton, Corsican, Welsh, and Catalan nationalists; and organizations that Americans loathed. The IRA explicitly supported the African National Congress, the PLO (murals liked to show IRA and PLO members holding aloft a rocket launcher under the title "One Struggle"), the SWAPO Party of Namibia, and Castro's regime in Cuba. For guns, the IRA was willing to make deals with the FARC in Colombia and seek help from Gaddafi in Libya.[127] The rank and file of the IRA didn't like being held hostage to NORAID's respectability politics either, responding to America's bombing of Libya in 1986 with a spate of West Belfast graffiti: "FUCK NORAID!"[128]

The willful blindness was enabled by careful management of American feelings. The IRA bought guns on American soil and robbed an armory in conjunction with organized crime groups, but these transgressions didn't muss the hair of ordinary people. Although some IRA planners complained that they "fought with one hand tied behind [their] back," they left alone targets in London where American tourists might be collateral damage, never conducted attacks on U.S. soil, and even actively hid their political orientation by producing a drastically toned-down version of Sinn Féin newspapers omitting socialist and Marxist rhetoric.[129] In return, American money flowed and, with few exceptions, the IRA looked like freedom fighters in popular culture. In 1978 an IRA fundraiser turned up on an episode of *Colombo*, his crime being killing an arms dealer for cheating the cause—not for being in the United States and providing material support for terrorism. In 1997 Brad Pitt played an exceptionally sympathetic IRA operative hiding in the home of a New York Police Department officer (Harrison Ford, of course) who develops a father-son bond with him in *The Devil's Own*. To catch a world-class assassin before he can kill the First Lady, Americans had to beg the assistance of an imprisoned IRA man, Declan Joseph Mulqueen (Richard Gere) in *The Jackal* (1997).[130]

American support tended to jump in response to traumatic events, which the IRA would publicize, like British soldiers wrecking homes during searches for weapons along the Falls Road in Belfast in 1970, the death of hunger striker Bobby Sands in 1981, or Operation Flavius in 1988, in which the British military tracked and killed three IRA operatives, one of them a woman, in Gibraltar.[131] Starting in 1983 NORAID sponsored tours of Northern Ireland for Americans, housing them with the families of prisoners and taking them to places where they would most likely be hassled by the Royal Ulster Constabulary or see British military personnel. Helpful Irish researchers would assist American visitors in finding ancestral farms and take them to pubs full of IRA veterans to hear appealing war stories.[132]

Things began to shift slowly in the diaspora, starting with President Ronald Reagan's relationship with British prime minister Margaret Thatcher, one in which the president wouldn't indulge attacks on his ally but encouraged her to make concessions leading to a hopeful address to a joint meeting of

Congress and the 1985 Anglo-Irish agreement. Reagan's own Tipperary family history helped lend authority within the Irish American community and, in Thatcher's words, "put us on side with the Americans."[133] The Anglo-Irish agreement established the International Fund for Ireland, which invested in cross-community development and provided an alternative place for donors to send money. This in turn allowed previous initiatives to finally get real traction, like the Irish National Caucus's promotion of the MacBride Principles, drafted by New York City comptroller Harrison Goldin and aimed at getting multinational corporations doing business in Northern Ireland to promise equal treatment for Catholics and Protestants in hiring, salaries, and promotions.[134]

Celebrities who had been wary of speaking out against the IRA came forward in the late 1980s, especially in response to the 1987 Enniskillen bombing (Poppy Day massacre), most prominently singer Bono's denunciation at a U2 concert in Denver. "Where's the glory in bombing a Remembrance Day parade of old-age pensioners, their medals taken out and polished up for the day?"[135] Richard Harris, disgusted by the violence, had started getting death threats and was fed up. Perhaps most crucially, the most powerful Irish American politicians, the "Four Horsemen" (Speaker of the House Tip O'Neill, Sen. Daniel Patrick Moynihan, Sen. Edward Kennedy, and New York governor Hugh Carey) were ready to apply leverage.[136]

Bill Clinton, whose administration was grappling with the post–Cold War world, threaded the needle between needing the Irish American vote for his policies and not alienating Great Britain by throwing his influence into brokering a peace agreement. Economic opportunities stemming from the European Union allowed Catholics in the Republic to access credit, work, and study in Europe and to build an identity as Europeans, all of which undermined the IRA's appeal. Sinn Féin was allowed to open an office in D.C. in 1994, with donations going exclusively for political purposes. Clinton's appointment of Jean Kennedy Smith (JFK's sister) as ambassador to Ireland pleased the diaspora and signaled how important it was, while "not once would Clinton allow room for terrorism in Northern Ireland, as summed up by his reproach of the IRA on his 1995 Belfast tour: 'You are the past, your day is over.'"[137] Violating the 1994 cease-fire they'd agreed to, the IRA chose to detonate a car bomb in London's Canary Wharf days after Clinton's visit, prompting the United States to bring out the hammer—a ban on Sinn Féin's fundraising privileges, which stung enough to work and helped push toward the 1998 Good Friday agreement.[138]

Then 9/11 shattered the American insulation from terrorist attacks. The British government pointed out that, despite the United States being a "staunch opponent of terrorism," the IRA, Sinn Féin and their offshoots had been indulged on American soil for decades.[139] Executive Order 13224, meant to disrupt terror financing, explicitly blocks not just loyalist Irish groups but all assets of the IRA and its splinters.[140] Rep. Peter King abruptly halted his twice-a-year tours of Belfast and announced that he had "cooled on Ireland," blaming the Irish people themselves for "knee jerk anti-Americanism" for protesting the invasions of Iraq and Afghanistan and "begrudgery . . . and resentment towards Americans." Instead, he was all aboard for counterterrorism in the Middle East and was embraced by the Bush administration. Irish American politicians "turned to the stick" when it came to adherence to the Good Friday agreement, and the links with the IRA were severed.[141] In 2013, when the Chechen Tsarnaev brothers, Tamerlan and Dzhokhar, bombed the Boston Marathon, harsher voices in the British intelligence community reiterated that Boston had been the epicenter of NORAID and that "it is easy to support a war when you can romanticize the conflict from a distance, telling yourself it's all about your cultural heritage, especially when you don't have to live with the consequences of bombs."[142]

The romance with Ireland is far from done, though. President Joseph Biden, who has maintained ties to Ireland and his ancestral roots in Ballina, County Mayo, delighted the Irish press when he revealed in January 2020 that he would be keeping the Secret Service code name he used while vice president: Celtic.[143]

6
DONORS AND SPONSORS

Justice Sotomayor: "Under the definition of this statute, teaching these members to play the harmonica would be unlawful?"

Justice Scalia: "Well, Hamid Hatah and his harmonica quartet might tour the country and make a lot of money, right?"[1]

In the 2009 term of the United States Supreme Court, the justices heard *Holder v. The Humanitarian Law Project*, a case that began in March 1998 and wound its way through the courts, encompassing the collapse of one of the groups involved and the addition of the Patriot Act to the legal structure governing material support to terrorism. The Humanitarian Law Project (HLP), founded in 1985, works to promote conflict resolution through training in international human rights laws and techniques for advocacy in internal venues like the United Nations. The HLP and its president, lawyer and activist Ralph Fertig, believed strongly that successes like the end of apartheid in South Africa and the Oslo Peace Accords offered a model to bring extremist groups to nonviolent negotiation.[2] Alarmed by the implications of the 1994 and 1996 material support statutes to their work with the Kurds and

Tamils, including unavoidable contact with the PKK and LTTE, the HLP and a coalition of human rights groups brought suit on the grounds that the existing law violated their First and Fifth Amendment rights (freedom of speech and association), winning in California but encountering federal appeals up to the Supreme Court.[3]

In 1994 Congress passed 18 U.S. Code 2239A (Providing Material Support to Terrorists), prohibiting material support or resources to designated foreign terrorist organizations (FTO) knowing or intending that they be used for carrying out terrorism. After the Oklahoma City bombing in 1996, this law was amended to prohibit any material support to an FTO, regardless of how it was to be used, a response to concerns about VNSAs using humanitarian aid as a cover for fundraising.[4] Muddying the water, though, was the exclusion of "medicine and religious materials," and varying interpretations of what, precisely, constituted "training, expert advice or assistance." This and the broadening of the definitions in the Patriot Act after 9/11 to one in which donations violate the law if the donor knows that the organization might use the resources to commit terrorism, or that the organization has been designated as a FTO, led the HLP to file the case.[5] In contrast, Australian and Canadian law stops at the point that material support aids a FTO in committing terrorist acts, while at the far end of the scale, law in the United Arab Emirates had no restrictions on financial interaction with FTOs until 2004 because their government saw financial services or donors as having "no more agency or responsibility than any other service, as if the flight school for 9/11 hijackers would be considered supporters of terrorism for offering lessons."[6]

Questioning by justices showed a clear break between the liberal and conservative wings of the court on what they considered material support. The HLP's aim of getting groups to embrace negotiation and petition, which Fertig and his colleagues saw as the foundation of Western liberal tradition, struck conservatives as just a method by which a VNSA can stall, recover from losses, manipulate, and undermine rule of law by participating in it in bad faith. As in the exchange above, Justices Sotomayor and Scalia asked if it would count if someone set up chairs at a meeting or showed people in the FTO's area of operation how to apply for disaster aid. The underlying concern was and is that all resources are, in the hands of a VNSA, fungible: Any help given to them is help they don't have to pay for another way, freeing up more for violence. This is especially prominent in arguments about medical care—excluded by statute—in which any fighter treated by Doctors without Borders is a fighter whose upkeep the VNSA now doesn't have to bear, but who the sworn medical profession can't refuse to treat. Does this apply to other professions like the law (even the worst are entitled to representation) and providers of humanitarian relief?

Another issue raised was the wild inconsistency of what VNSAs made the FTO list: the African National Congress was designated that way until 2008, although it had been on the ballot in South Africa since 1994. The IRA wasn't placed there until the summer of 2001, for reasons discussed at length in chapter 5, and the LTTE had collapsed by 2009, before the case reached the court. As we've seen, groups have hired lobbying firms to woo American political support with the express object of evading listing as an FTO. Proponents of the law argued that the court should follow Congress's judgment about the dangerousness of a particular VNSA and allow the administration the tool of listing a group as part of the relationship between the United States and the group's target, as in the case of the PKK and Turkey, but other allies like the United Kingdom and Spain have been frustrated with State Department decisions about which groups make the list.[7]

Ultimately, the Court found 6-3 in favor of the government's position, upholding the material support law as written. Since then it has been used to prosecute people like Ali Asad Chandia, a Pakistani American teacher from Maryland who was alleged to have visited a Lashkar-e-Taiba office while in Pakistan for his brother's wedding and provided computer access and shipping assistance (including purchasing 50,000 paintballs) for Mohammed Ajmal Khan during Khan's visit to the United States. Chandia, by knowing Khan was a member of a FTO, broke the law no matter what was in the shipped boxes.[8] This has had a chilling effect on NGOs, which are caught between VNSAs who demand bribes to operate and the threat of U.S. prosecution. People retain their First Amendment rights to join or have contact with a VNSA but are enjoined from doing anything that furthers the aims of the group, a needle's eye that allows for enormous leeway in prosecutorial discretion—useful against Chandia but unlikely to be used against Jimmy Carter monitoring elections in Gaza after meeting with Hezbollah and Hamas candidates, or Rudy Giuliani speaking in support of the Iranian opposition group Mujahideen Khalq, or a family paying a ransom.[9]

Solicitor General Elena Kagan, who, ironically, would join the liberal wing of the Court shortly after the Holder decision was announced in 2010, summed up the government's case: "Hezbollah builds bombs. Hezbollah also builds houses. What Congress decided was when you help Hezbollah build homes, you are also helping Hezbollah build bombs."[10]

▪ Individual Giving and Crowdfunding

VNSAs take great care with their marketing and branding, whether to attract donors, frighten rivals, or convince a global audience that their cause is righteous or tolerable. During the 1967–70 Nigerian Civil War, Biafrans hired public relations firms and mobilized global support in sophisticated ways that ran circles around the government, teaching VNSAs that they needed the same tools, charismatic and savvy figureheads, and slick presentations as the ones used by businesses and increasingly professional electoral campaigns.[11] A level of traditional media participation also legitimizes an organization, which is why Hamas prints a glossy magazine, *Filastin al-Muslimah*, which looks at home on an elegant coffee table next to *Grazia* or *Edgar* lifestyle publications.[12]

Groups with websites have an even cheaper and more agile form of communication, especially if VNSAs invest in making them available in multiple languages and tailored for their desired audience. The plethora of Hamas sites show a deliberate and thoughtful approach: the English site avoids extremist language and focuses on analysis of current events, the Russian site has a heavy dose of anti-Semitic content, the Turkish language one stresses the affinity of the Palestinian and Turkish people, and the Urdu version leans into comparisons of the Nakba and the partition of India and Pakistan. FARC and individual Chechen militias maintain pages that propagandize their side of conflicts, providing material banned by censors and showing the organization in the most heroic light. Some of the VNSA websites even have "kid's pages," designed for children and complete with games and activities.[13] Sophisticated media managers will offer access to journalists, taking them on tours of bombed-out neighborhoods and inside training camps and setting up interviews with sympathetic victims. An organization that makes its raw footage available through a Creative Commons license can actively solicit help from supporters to edit it in compelling forms themselves and distribute it through social media, curated for the specific tastes of an influencer's followers.[14]

Talk to someone in law enforcement, and odds are they have a favorite recent "dumb criminal" story about how a gang member bragged on Twitter or Instagram about committing a felony. Cartel members and VNSAs like MS-13 regularly post music videos of murder scenes, showing off obviously illegal weaponry and eulogy retrospectives of the careers of their members, which police and prosecutors regularly use as evidence. From the perspective of a bystander, these are astoundingly foolish, but for membership recruiting and displaying machismo and bravado, they're extremely effective. All the graffiti tagging, posing with gold-plated guns, songs about decapitation, and Los Zetas banners hung on a freeway overpass with a phone number for recruiting is building the brand, even if a couple of members are sacrificed to jail for it.[15]

When the brand appeals strongly enough, "angel investors" can emerge and bankroll a VNSA through personal wealth. Hozh-Ahmed Nukhaev, former deputy prime minister of Chechnya and alleged Mafia godfather, used his fortune to start the Transcaucasian Energy Consortium and the Caucasian Common Market holding company, and to invest in St. Petersburg car factory LogoVAZ and a publishing house, all to funnel money into Chechen *boeviki* (resistance fighters).[16] Boko Haram collected large donations from several Nigerian regional politicians like Commissioner for Religious Affairs Alhaji Buji Foi and Sen. Ali Ndume in Borno state, both of whom openly sympathized with the cause.[17] Alt-right VNSAs acquire rich donors, such as Robert and Rebekah Mercer and Robert J. Shillman, willing to fund their mostly respectable front-facing branches like Breitbart, Project Veritas, and the English Defense League.[18]

Wealthy Muslim investors subsidize VNSAs, a pattern that began with the funding of the Afghan mujahideen and solidified in the 1990s with support for Bosnian militias. Mustafa Ahmed al-Hasnawi sent the 9/11 hijackers operational funds, as did Princess Haifa al-Faisal, whose stipend to "the allegedly needy family" of Omar al-Bayoumi ended up in the hands of Khaled al-Mihdhar and Nawaf al-Hazmi, who attacked the Pentagon on September 11, 2001.[19] Well-to-do Kuwaitis and Qataris publicized their gifts to Syrian militias, posting social media photos of cars and jewelry sold to donate, although donors to the Islamic State were more discreet in their generosity.[20]

VNSAs can appeal to international supporters by selling them branded merchandise broadcasting their message as well as collecting money from bumper stickers, newsletters, t-shirts, videos, and handicrafts. The Sol Peru committee in Europe peddled posters and buttons reading "Yankee Go Home!" to support Shining Path, while the 32 County Sovereignty Movement opened an internet storefront to merchandise the IRA and its splinters, linking with Amazon until November 2000.[21] Right-wing hate groups arbitrage their website server locations to take advantage of permissive laws, hosting sites that sell a bewildering array of promotional items, from body jewelry to clothing to publications with the Third Reich Books imprint. A popular clothing brand, Thor Steinar—so closely associated with neo-Nazis that it is banned in parts of Germany and several soccer stadiums in Europe—is still in lucrative operation but was bought out by International Brands General Trading (a Dubai-based holding company) in 2008, and CEO Mohammed M. Aweidah now profits from the sale of skinhead clothing.[22] Where allowed, VNSAs hold concerts, conferences, and summits, like Atomwaffen's 2018 "Death Valley Hate Camp" in Las Vegas or the U.K. neo-Nazi group Blood and Honor's regular schedule of musical events at their Lincolnshire compound, all of which generate money and host vendors.[23] Japanese terror cult Aum Shinrikyo was astoundingly comprehensive in its fleecing of members, charging for everything from pamphlets to the opportunity to drink the founder's blood and bathwater.[24]

One of the most insidious of the products sold by VNSAs are downloads of video games, which not only raise funds for the group but also propagandize their message and desensitize players to the dehumanization of their targets.[25] Hezbollah's version is *Special Force* (2003) and its sequel is *The Kept Promise*, which puts a player into the thirty-three days of the Second Lebanon War (2006) against the Israel Defense Forces, killing settlers and shooting rockets at towns. In 2003 the initial run sold out 100,000 units immediately. Neo-Nazis have a variety of downloads, including *Border Patrol*, *N Hunt*, *ZOG's Nightmare* (a knockoff version of *Escape from Castle Wolfenstein*), and *KZ*

Beloved by neo-Nazis, clothing brand Thor Steinar operated a retail outlet in Saxony that it named Brevik, claiming that it was only accidental that it was close to the name of Norwegian mass murderer Anders Breivik. This hoodie's logo translates to "Good hunting!" Pictured is a German right-wing protester wearing a Thor Steinar hoodie, Rostock (2012). *Photograph by Daniel Reinhardt, courtesy Alamy*

Manager Millennium.[26] Free demos lure interested players, who then pay and get more immersed in "the 'positive' aspects of joining a radical group," encouraged to use defamatory language and rewarded for considering the targets of the game as nothing more than objects to destroy.[27] A new game promoted by pan-European VNSA *Generation Identity*, still on the sales and digital distribution system Steam as of September 2020, allows players to act as Kyle Rittenhouse and murder Black Lives Matter protesters as a first-person-style shooter.[28]

Although to my knowledge not yet used by a VNSA, a state can employ international intellectual property rights to generate large sums of money for its own use. Alberto Korda, a Cuban photographer, captured the famous image of Che Guevara in 1960 but did not pursue or receive copyright protection for its ubiquitous use—Korda and Castro did not believe in the Berne Convention, especially if those reproducing the image did so in the cause of social justice and revolution. However, when Smirnoff Vodka used the photo in an ad campaign, Korda sued and donated the substantial settlement to the Cuban health care system. Similarly, the government, at the encouragement of Raul Castro, packaged and monetized the artistic resources of Cuba to send groups like the Buena Vista Social Club out on hugely popular world tours beginning in 1996. The revenue generated was a crucial support in an economy reeling from the loss of Soviet subsidy. It isn't inconceivable that a VNSA with members who owned valuable copyright could reap the financial windfalls and collect them from a friendly jurisdiction.[29]

A VNSA significantly dependent on donors is a group that has the infuriating task of humoring and indulging those donors. On one hand, the group may have to forgo attacking otherwise useful targets so as to not upset squeamish deep pockets, obeying the social norms of people who don't live in a conflict zone and pulling their punches about the harsher edges of their ideology or plans for post-conflict power.[30] On the other hand, donors might be impatient to see results, even if they risk the group's operational security and overall strategy. Hamas and Palestinian Islamic Jihad compete for the same pool of donors, and each has conducted attacks to demonstrate to their funding base that they are more "hawkish" and thus more worthy than the other. Kuwaiti donors to anti-Assad militias in Syria competed among themselves to show that "their brigade" had been in the most difficult battles and lost the most people to martyrdom, a display of vanity that enraged commanders in the field and cost fighters their lives for no tactical gains.[31] This string pulling prevented militias from effectively joining forces in coordinated efforts and backfired as one effusive donor insisted on not just visiting his militia in the field but immediately tweeting the exact location of their position.[32]

Innovative VNSA fundraisers borrow from the successful packaging of sponsorship as a "parasocial" relationship—think of the emotional bond cultivated by an organization between the needy child sponsored in a developing country and a donor, or an especially pathetic-looking shelter dog whose updates you get every month.[33] Anna Sandalova, founder of Help the Army of Ukraine, in raising money to equip militias in Crimea, deliberately highlights specific donors' contributions in social media posts, as people love spotting "their hat" or "their watch" on a fighter, or footage from "their drone" dropping explosives on Russian trenches. Stressing that "whoever equips one who is fighting for the sake of Allah is like one who fights himself," a Gaza militia offered donors the ability to sponsor individual items, like a sniper rifle, grenade launcher, or body armor, and (like all fundraisers who print programs with tiers of donors) publicized the names of people in special "silver" and "gold" status to spur social competition for recognition.[34]

A variation of this, enabled by technology, is the use of crowdfunding platforms like GoFundMe and Kickstarter. This form of financing has opportunities for laundering money but, when genuinely offered to potential supporters, brings in cash independently as well.[35] Groups fundraising from a diaspora have long understood the power of naming things after donors, offering a kind of "ownership" and encouraging protectiveness toward that named playground, hospital ward, or library collection. Online crowdfunding offers that advantage but on a global scale, recognizing much smaller amounts of money. The 2012 JOBS Act, meant to encourage "access to the public capital markets for emerging growth companies," relaxed regulatory requirements for investment solicitation and disclosure by the organization asking for funds, opening the door not just to microfinancing local projects but to international illicit ones.[36]

Mainstream platforms like GoFundMe and Kickstarter can and sometimes will remove solicitations that cross a corporate line of acceptability. In 2012 Kickstarter investigated and suspended two men, an American journalist and a Libyan songwriter, for raising money to travel to Syria to make an inspirational movie about the anti-Assad resistance, a project that skirted too close to VNSA propaganda for Kickstarter's lawyers.[37] Following the 2017 Charlottesville Far Right rally, GoFundMe, Kickstarter, Patreon, and YouCaring removed accounts associated with the movement, but replacements Hatreon and GoyFundMe sprang up, along with less inflammatory but less picky platforms like GiveSendGo and individual web pages with PayPal links. Hatreon was pulling in $25,000 a month until PayPal and Apple/Google Pay blocked their transactions for violating terms of service.[38] For the less high-tech, VNSAs with access to traditional media like television and radio hold old-school variety show telethons, as the LTTE did on its Canadian Tamil station and Hezbollah continues to do through Al-Manar broadcasting.[39]

In the mid-1990s the Zapatista movement of southern Mexico had so successfully marketed itself that it was fielding genuine offers of corporate sponsorship. With 70 percent name recognition in Mexico, public relations professionals marveled that Subcomandante Marcos was "gay in San Francisco, black in South Africa, an Asian in Europe, a Chicano in San Ysidro, an anarchist in Spain, a Palestinian in Israel, a pacifist in Bosnia, a housewife alone on a Saturday night in any neighborhood in Mexico"—achieving peak projected global cool.[40] Celebrities, including Oliver Stone, who conspicuously skipped the 1996 Oscars to pay court, swarmed Chiapas, followed by representatives from fashion house Benetton, who offered to be the rebels' official outfitters in return for appearing in ads. The group, which had declared war on the Mexican government in 1994 and denounced multinational corporate neoliberalism, considered the deal but eventually gave a diplomatic answer: "Companeros, we have decided it is not suitable to wear sweaters in the jungle."[41] Benetton ran a season of ads with models in rebel chic and camouflage anyway.[42]

This seems like a joke, but because of the drastically different view of VNSAs held around the world, corporate sponsorship is lucrative and likely to increase. Sometimes it is an obvious quid pro quo, like the $25 million "donation" to the Taliban paid by gas company Unocal for advantage in a pipeline contract, but Muslim-owned companies producing Mecca-Cola in France and Zamzam bottling (which took over Coca-Cola's Iranian facilities in 1979) advertise that they give 10 percent to Palestinian causes, including Hamas and Hezbollah.[43] Conservative U.S. churches and their outreach foundations underwrite violent antigay gangs in Uganda and Russia and promote their political wings. Pat Robertson, enamored of Charles Taylor's regime in Liberia, threw his religious organization's clout behind the Liberian mining venture Freedom Gold, Ltd. and touted it as an investment for good Baptists.[44]

On a far more positive note, actor George Clooney uses the income stream from one set of advertisements, Nespresso, to fund a satellite that monitors the border between North and South Sudan to provide early warning for aggression. Sudanese dictator Omar al-Bashir, accused of war crimes against the southern minority, lashed out at Clooney for spying on him and asked how he'd feel with cameras following everywhere. Clooney's response: "Welcome to my life, Mr. War Criminal!" Individual actors with money can donate an intelligence, surveillance, and reconnaissance network with side endorsement work. Nike's global commitment to promoting football player Colin Kaepernick in the face of American boycotts is an interesting signal that companies, when they see potential widespread appeal in a cause, may offer substantial financial support even if it is politically targeted or seen as a VNSA by authorities in its own region.[45]

■ Foreign Fighters

"If you are carrying a lot of money, then do not hide it in your bag or in the pockets of your backpack, as they will go through everything and such actions will cause them to suspect you. If you are really going for a vacation in Turkey, then why are you hiding your money?" So goes the advice to volunteers headed for Syria as foreign fighters, along with tips about asking the European airport security guards about their recent holidays as small talk while waiting. Would-be jihadis read blogs urging them to escalate their support activities, from donating in the Global North to donating themselves, bringing their talents and whatever money and equipment they can carry into a transnational fight for the survival of their community.[46] Europol estimated that 3,000–5,000 EU nationals were in Syria and Iraq in 2015, with higher numbers coming from the Gulf States and North Africa in the wake of the Arab Spring.[47]

The American-sponsored Afghan resistance to Soviet invasion created one of the world's most durable and dangerous pools of foreign fighters. Those who survived the 1980s spread out around the globe, joining insurgencies in Chechnya, the Philippines, Bosnia, Indonesia, and Turkey.[48] Battle-hardened and doctrinaire, jihadist volunteers in Chechnya drove the conflict there from tribal fighting over control of the Caucasus into a larger ideological war for Salafi Islam, a change that alienated some of the leaders: "We do not need them, they will give us a lot of trouble—but we won't be able to stop them."[49] Without ties to the local population, the foreign fighters were willing to be far more violent and escalate actions against the Russian military since reprisals had little to do with them.[50]

New recruits, even those without conscript service in the military, might bring other useful skills: Intake documents collected by ISIS's bureaucracy identified volunteers like a Tunisian named Muhammed S., who had studied

Brandishing their passports, foreign fighter volunteers for ISIS hold a press conference to declare their allegiance to the caliphate, Anbar Province, Iraq (2016). *Courtesy Alamy*

chemistry and physics and had experience with animal diseases like anthrax and bubonic plague. Another had been trained in Germany as a chemist and engineer, while an engraver highly skilled in counterfeiting died in a sniper attack before turning out anything useful, much to the frustration of his superiors.[51] Less tangibly, these volunteers are ideal stars of YouTube videos, useful to show the transnational appeal of the cause, enthusiastic about taking part in activities that repel the local population, like a 2014 stoning in al-Raqqa, or tuned in to what will motivate more fighters back in the Global North, like Denis Cuspert (a.k.a. Deso Dogg and Abu Talha al-Almani), a Ghanian-German rapper who converted to Islam and traveled to Syria as a foreign fighter. His *nasheeds*, or battle hymns, quickly became the soundtrack to propaganda videos, and his charisma was such that the group scored a moral victory when he seduced the FBI translator assigned to monitor him over Skype.[52] Authorities particularly fear that these fighters' most dangerous resource is their ability to return to the Global North to act as recruiters, sleeper agents, or attackers, although a group would be smart to calculate the effect of attacks on a diaspora population and the potential backlash.[53]

Foreign fighters are expected to bring money with them, even acting as cash couriers from contacts in their home countries, and to contribute continuing funds they receive from student bursaries and social welfare payments. Volunteers from wealthy Saudi families are especially sought after, since they have a reputation for arriving with ready money and generous allowances, but for those without family resources, blogs offer instructions on getting consumer loans, selling personal property, and asking for donations from friends and relatives before departing.[54] Whenever possible, the newcomers are instructed to bring useful Western goods, particularly dual-use technologies like night vision goggles, camping gear, watches, and computers, which would be redistributed for military use. The trick is to keep naive volunteers from losing what they're carrying to the border smugglers and criminals necessary to get them into the region.[55]

This naiveté may make foreign fighters more trouble than they're worth. Although warned that their time won't be all "brothers doing forward rolls, flips, etc." because such cool tricks are "completely worthless and irrelevant on the battlefield when bullets are flying," many foreign volunteers to VNSAs expect the luxuries of home, including chocolate, Axe body spray, and Red Bull, and to immediately be given fun jobs, not assigned the scut work of low-ranking military recruits, like cleaning toilets.[56] They often expect deference and continual acknowledgment as heroes while displaying "wild enthusiasm with a lack of knowledge" about the religion, the political realities of the cause, and the local mores, sowing resentment with longer-serving colleagues. One French volunteer quickly got fed up with ISIS's ban on smoking and flounced back home.[57] In a VNSA that needs cohesion, dealing with rogue "Gucci soldiers" posting whatever they want on social media, including complaints of homesickness, whining about the conditions, and glorification of unauthorized violence, is a risky tactic.[58] In the same personnel files that highlight useful catches like chemists, engineers and programmers, there are even more marked "lazy," "undecided," and "needs monitoring."[59]

■ Doing unto Others

Charities, because they occupy a place of respect with the public and tap into cultural expectations of giving, can be harnessed in a variety of scams and covers for VNSAs. The most basic are like the frauds described in chapter 3, with would-be funders passing themselves off as representatives of a genuine U.K. nonprofit, Muslim Aid, and collecting donations during Ramadan on the street in Birmingham in separate incidents in 2012 and 2013. The real charity suffered damage to its reputation from being associated with funds sent to Somalia and Pakistan for VNSA use and saw a sizable drop in donations from an angry public.[60]

Far more money passes through formally incorporated nonprofits, either through the co-option of the organization for VNSA purposes or by the actions of individual employees to divert funding for illicit purposes. Although this happens across the religious and political spectrum, with the LTTE using a network of Hindu temples in Canada and Western Europe and identarian movements leveraging the tax advantages allowed to NGOs to accumulate money, the Islamic mandate of *zakat* has been entwined with charities in ways that complicate record keeping and administration. As a religious obligation, Muslims are expected to donate 2.5 percent of their income to charity, and in majority-Muslim countries with no income tax, there is no mechanism for tracking what is donated or to whom, but intense social pressure exists to comply. Additionally, donations should be given anonymously in order not to shame the recipient, a condition that provides cover for obfuscation. In a wealthy nation like Saudi Arabia, this flow of money adds up to millions of dollars a year.[61]

To return to our 2020 version of the fictional Jack Ryan, he continues to plead with his boss to pay attention to a new threat, insisting that the bosses wished they had paid attention the first time they heard the name "bin Laden" twenty years ago.[62] Setting aside Jack's amnesia, the bosses were paying attention as far back as the mid-1980s, when the CIA found not just Pakistan's Inter-Services Intelligence (ISI) but Islamic charities useful for shoveling money toward the mujahideen in Afghanistan. Along with the American money, the Afghan cause picked up donations from a world of coreligionists awash in oil profits and funneled their way by more than twenty organizations set up by Saudi intelligence.[63] One of the central groups was bin Laden and Sheikh Abdullah Azzam's "services bureau" in Peshawar to aid arriving foreign fighters, but the "golden chain" expanded to, among many others, the Muslim World League, the Benevolence International Foundation, and the Qatar Charitable Society.[64]

Not only did the CIA and U.S. government know about this, but they also encouraged it. Charles Cogan, the CIA chief for South Asia, recognized the potential problem—"the long range aims of the mujahedeen were wholly incompatible with the aims of a Western nation"[65]—but found the temporary alliance convenient. Secretary of Defense Caspar Weinberger held his nose to "not very nice people" because "we had this terrible problem of making choices."[66] Once the PR machine kicked into gear, the rebels were the equal of "the civil rights leaders who led American blacks to equality that society had denied them. The Sakharovs who have held up the flame of freedom in the Soviet Union. The tattered Vietnamese refugees who put to sea in leaky boats."[67] Embedded reporters enthused about the ragtag heroes and a whole string of Hollywood productions painted them as freedom fighters and sympathetic corollaries to American revolutionary patriots.[68] With the blessing of U.S. authorities, the charity cash rolled out to Afghan militias and established patterns of giving that had become habit by the time the dust settled in the Khyber Pass and the conflict moved on to Bosnia.[69]

In 1992 the slow response of the Global North to the persecution of Muslims in the former Yugoslavia sparked these ostensibly charitable organizations into action. Benevolence International was back in the game, advertising openly as a "trustworthy hand for the support of both mujahedeen and refugees" in Bosnia, while the new Third World Relief Agency, built on bin Laden contacts from the Afghan war, shifted smoothly from community development contacts to hiring Victor Bout to fly in guns from Sudan.[70] The Bosnians didn't necessarily want the Afghan-veteran fighters who came along with the guns and aid, but that was the price of outside support and access to the network of suppliers and smugglers. The aftereffects of this were profound—Col. Abdul Manaf Kasmuri, the Malaysian head of the UN peacekeeping operation, was radicalized by the deaths of Muslims in safe havens and retired to do aid work with the al-Qaeda-affiliated charity Koperasi Belia Islam; Reda Seyam developed into a talented propagandist, producing "Martyrs of Bosnia" for al-Qaeda then emigrating to Indonesia to do the public relations work for the cause; and the honorary consul of Kuwait in Milan was using his office in Italy to host and organize not just humanitarian aid for the Balkans but recruits for al-Qaeda training camps in Afghanistan who later carried out the 1998 embassy bombings in Kenya and Tanzania.[71] After 9/11 Benevolence International in the United States became a target of terror financing investigations, and its director defended himself against charges that he had diverted charitable funds to Bosnian and Chechen fighters by pointing to the long history of the Americans encouraging him to do just that.[72]

Charities provide outstanding cover for the movement of useful supplies and enjoy protections under the Geneva Conventions' provisions for humanitarian support that shield VNSA activity. In egregious contravention of the rules, the United Nations found that the Sudanese government painted chartered Antonov-26 planes in UN livery to deliver arms to the Janjaweed in Darfur. In harder to police forms, blogs advise foreign fighters going to Chechnya and Syria to build fictitious histories of investigating humanitarian opportunities, identify themselves to airport or border security as aid workers, and hitch rides with charity-run convoys. This is reiterated by their families, who avoid the stigma of being associated with foreign fighters by insisting that they are doing good works.

Even more so, they're a conduit for money. Al-Qaeda had the most extensive network, including branches of the Global Relief Foundation, Al Wafa, Benevolence International, al-Haramain, the International Islamic Relief Organization, and Revival of Islamic Heritage Society. The Holy Land Foundation and Qur'anic Literacy Institute were tied to Hamas, while the Palestinian Islamic Jihad used the Islamic Concern Project and the World and Islam Studies Enterprise to filter money their way.[73] Boko Haram in Nigeria has been the recipient of aid from the Islamic World Society and, allegedly, Al-Muntada al-Islami Trust.[74] At its height, the LTTE had its own network of NGOs, including the Tamils Rehabilitation Organisation and International Medical Health Organization/Tamil Health Organization, which outfitted the group's field hospitals and medical units.[75]

Collective agreement on how to regulate and monitor charities is a minefield of differing expectations of what humanitarian organizations do, the responsibility of a state to supervise them, and the customs and social context of the sponsoring society, with the additional fraught complication that elites are almost always involved as patrons and administrators of nonprofits. The United States allows wide latitude in the IRS registration of 501(c)(3) organizations because of the extent to which such groups supply large parts of the social welfare system, from adoption agencies to food banks.[76] States add another layer of regulation and may make the articles of incorporation available to the public through auspices, but, in general, charities that don't draw attention to themselves with garish financial misconduct don't get audited unless the government is investigating them specifically, as they did after 9/11.

Japan, which doesn't have a robust system of NGOs for humanitarian work because of its comprehensive state structure, found itself hamstrung in attempting to control Aum Shinrikyo because of the way the VNSA positioned itself as a religion. Under Japan's post–World War II constitution, the American-dictated separation of church and state allowed the organization to abuse the legal system extensively until the 2004 application of Financial Action Task Force suggestions on prevention of terrorism.[77] Canada's long wrangle with the LTTE led to the Charity Commission being shifted under a joint supervision by the Minister of National Revenue and the Minister of National Security, a signal that charities were a component of terrorist financing.[78] Great Britain's NGOs' answer was the government's Charity Commission, which has long trusted the socially elite patrons of organizations to keep them on the straight and narrow. Since the 2000 Terrorism Act and further regulation in 2005, 2006, and 2008, however, suspicions that any funds go to terrorism or the "glorification of terrorism" must be reported to the Home Office and Treasury.[79] Germany, sensitive to claims of persecution by religious groups, exempted faith-based NGOs from charity regulation until 2001, when Security Packages I and II dramatically changed their privileges and banned Kalifatstaat, al-Aqsa, and the Islamic Liberation Party for inciting violence and anti-Semitism in 2001.[80]

What makes this exponentially more difficult to manage is that VNSAs do genuine humanitarian activity in places and with people who have no other resources. A VNSA's approach to charity is part of their larger political strategy, although most don't take the tack of Shining Path: preventing any improvement in the lives of the peasants in order to speed the population toward revolution.[81]

As discussed in chapter 4, collecting "revolutionary taxes" obligates a VNSA to provide state services in ways that can impoverish and stress the organization's abilities, but engaging in charity allows them to choose how much to engage and how to aim their efforts as an implicit criticism of the failure of the state they oppose or whose laws they evade to take care of their citizens, especially if an ethnic or religious minority receives little or no help from the government.

Criminal VNSAs regularly put on large community celebrations, hold festival days, host huge weddings with distribution of goodies to the public, build churches, sponsor hospital wards, and build homes in slums, building social capital and loyalty among local people who may well be called upon to shield them from detection by the authorities. It is inexpensive to make an individual personally grateful and loyal by providing a generator when the state can't keep the power on, rebuilding a house razed by the enemy, paying a student's exam fees, getting a family medical care, and making whole damages by fighting or accidents, like the house that was "hit by mujahedeen cars."[82] For a little more, a VNSA can support the whole community, which loyalist militias in Northern Ireland did when they bought milk from distressed dairies during the Workers' Strike of 1974 (which the Ulster Defence Association had organized) and then opened outlets to needy families. The fearsome Japanese Yakuza turned out to have ground-level knowledge of the neighborhoods they prowled, proving critical in the response to the 1995 earthquake and 2011 tsunami, delivering food, water, and blankets and organizing emergency housing in their real estate holdings.[83] The 2020 COVID-19 crisis brought out similar social services from the world's most dangerous VNSAs: Brazilian gangs enforce social distancing and curfews in favelas, cartels offer aid packages to keep businesses open, and the Taliban has sent health teams into rural villages to explain mask usage and deliver food packages.[84]

VNSAs are often the only people who can get into remote regions after a flood, earthquake, or fire, or who have the smuggling connections to move supplies in challenging terrain. The failure of the Nicaraguan government to respond to the 1975 Managua earthquake was an open door for the Sandinistas, as was the October 2005 earthquake in Kashmir for Lashkar-i-Taiba.[85] For conservative societies, representatives who follow strict seclusion of women and local mores may be the only aid acceptable to the victims, a quandary that places Global North women's organizations in the position of delivering critical assistance through VNSAs like the Taliban. In 2013 Ansar al-Sharia from Libya swept into flood-ravaged rural Sudan with aid flights delivered by volunteers with logo'd uniforms and halal food parcels.[86]

The aid, of course, comes with strings; as an Israeli counterterrorism official said, "In the territories, there are no free lunches: Those who receive help from the Islamic associations pay with support for Hamas."[87] A group can see charity as an obligation to the people they claim to represent but also extract maximum utility from it. They can be as exclusionary and discriminatory in distributing aid as the government they oppose, targeting those most likely to support them with votes or actions. The house rebuilt by a VNSA is likely to have illicit material hidden in the attic. Sponsoring scouting groups or schools is a vital social service as well as access to a vulnerable population that can be cultivated from an early age to be socialized to the group's goals and available for recruitment. Those, too, are useful campuses, as a Palestinian security chief discovered 32 kg of Hamas explosives buried in a Nablus kindergarten playground built by the group and used as a storage facility.[88]

Untangling VNSA social services from the population that depends on them is risky and difficult. The people have few other options to meet their basic needs and will feel betrayed and anxious without an adequate replacement in everyday life. Many of the programs provide as much stabilization—dowries for young women, jobs for idle young men, programs for unsupervised children—as the VNSA's activities destabilize the community. A government attempting to undermine a VNSA can attempt to displace these services, which the Uruguayan state accomplished against the Marxist Tupamaro guerrillas in the 1970s. Morocco has experimented with neighborhood policing stations to make the state and its assistance immediately visible to radicalized neighborhoods, although this walks a fine line of being oppressive and additional resented surveillance. The overall aim should be to replace the VNSA's social capital in the area with that of the state, although this can be a hard sell in the DDR process to "reward" recently rebellious or oppositional populations with the same services enjoyed by the "loyal" population.

■ State Sponsorship

Among the many fascinating documents included in Wikileaks was a memo written by the CIA's "Red Cell" of "out of the box thinkers" in February 2010. Their provocative musing was this: *What if the United States was perceived as sponsoring and exporting terrorism?* That other countries and many U.S. citizens believed this absolutely to be the case throughout the Cold War seems to have fallen off the Red Cell's radar, even with a pair of Benedictine nuns jailed in the summer of 2001 for protesting the training of Latin American death squads at Fort Benning's School of the Americas (Georgia). The memo seems to acknowledge that the United States was a state sponsor but worries about the implications of being accurately seen that way in a post-9/11 world where "evil terrorists rather than political gamesmanship" hold sway.[89]

The political gamesmanship of sponsoring VNSAs is nothing new: France continually spun up Jacobites in Scotland and Ireland to throw a wrench into any war fought with the British in the eighteenth century, Mussolini was encouraging the Croat Ustasha in the 1920s, and Germany twice tried to ally with the IRA as a back door into the United Kingdom during the World Wars. The Cold War, though, was the golden age of Manichean state sponsorship, as the United States, the Soviet Union, and China, along with their allies, bankrolled dozens of opposing guerrilla groups, terrorist splinters, and rogue separatist movements and provided training, arms, and advising. Some of the intervention was direct, sponsoring the overthrow of governments likely to nationalize corporate assets, but after the Vietnam War American sponsorship shifted to the use of less obvious proxies happy to gain stature with a Great Power and maybe get some of their own goals satisfied in the bargain. The bipolar world made it a given that for every Soviet aid to the Afghan government, the United States would balance it with support (with long lasting consequences) to the rebel mujahideen.

The 1990s spelled the end of the Cold War gravy train as democratic states reckoned with their citizens' protests and disapproval of proxy behavior without the shield of anticommunist rhetoric and the Soviet successor states reckoned with an economy that couldn't keep propping up Cuba or Angola. Removing the Cold War lenses made the fighting far more complicated and confusing—no longer us versus them, more this group fighting for religious reasons versus this group that wants access to a commodity versus a state dominated by one ethnic group. The limitations in place enforced by Great Power sponsors were gone, as was the steady flow of money and guns, which VNSAs rushed to replace with their own entrepreneurial activity, access to the post–Cold War flood of surplus, and new second-tier sponsors like Libya, North Korea, Iran, and Syria. Oh, and some of the old game masters, too.

The disadvantages of state sponsorship are substantial. A VNSA answers to them in a distinctly subordinate capacity and can be cut off at any time the sponsor chooses, like a child on an allowance. A sponsoring nation has its own reasons for writing checks: It wants to be seen as a regional hegemon, so controlling the local temperature dial through VNSAs is useful; it wants to be the focus of the global population of that religion or ethnic group, so backing "brothers and sisters fighting for freedom" elsewhere is good status signaling, as Russia has set itself up as a shield for cultural Western civilization against Islam; VNSAs are cat's paws to achieve things festering in the state's historical baggage, like Syria's and Turkey's fixation on Euphrates River water rights; VNSAs and their personnel can be strategically sacrificed as pawns to get concessions and rewards from Great Powers in negotiations or deployed as an easily disavowed asymmetric weapon against a rival. A very skillful state might cultivate some VNSAs and then solicit counterterrorism funds to build up its army and intelligence services in the cause of suppressing them. All of this, rightfully, can lead to the VNSA itself being seen by its members and constituents as flunkies or stooges of the sponsor, a charge that enemies will be quick to use to undermine it and may motivate the VNSA to bite the hands that fed them.

In the 1970s Pakistan's ISI agency was a minor department with a budget of just a couple million dollars. Its officers and Pakistan's martial president, Gen. Muhammad Zia-ul-Haq, saw an opportunity in the Soviet–Afghan War to build it into a powerhouse.[90] The United States was happy to have the ISI managing the distribution of weapons and money to the mujahideen and didn't look too closely when a large chunk of these stayed in the ISI's hands, although in 1988 an American auditing team was en route when the storage camp where the ISI claimed to be holding resources exploded in a giant fireball. The pilferage was covered and the evidence incinerated.[91] These weapons went to hand-picked Islamist warlords the ISI believed would be a thorn in the side of India in Kashmir while avoiding stirring up Pashtun nationalism in Pakistan.[92] After Zia's death, the civilian government of Benazir Bhutto wanted its own armed proxy to counter the ISI's and identified the Taliban as the way to have Afghanistan under a pro-Pakistan influence rather than pro-Russian, -Indian, or -Iranian, in the process creating and providing for a bevy of VNSAs, including Lashkar-i-Taiba, who remain only vaguely under Islamabad's control.[93]

The biggest advantage of a state sponsor, though, is the cash flow. Nations have resources that dwarf independent fundraising efforts of a VNSA and can supply steady amounts predictably, allowing the group to focus on operations and training rather than scrounging. Attracting a state-level sponsor signals legitimacy and stability to other potential supporters, an asymmetrical alliance system like the one the PLO leveraged throughout the 1970s–80s to gain recognition as the de facto government for Palestinians. The post–Cold War world also allows for some shopping around by the weaker party. If there are too many conditions about respecting human rights or strings for the kind of victory that is allowed, a VNSA can deal with China, a sponsor more interested in getting access to a deep-water port or exclusive contracts for a commodity.

Aside from money, states have access to things that VNSAs do not. They can issue passports, as Venezuela does for Hezbollah and FARC personnel;[94] they have seats at the United Nations, World Bank, and other international organizations where they can advocate for the group to place sanctions on their oppressors or get them a place in treaty negotiations, as Chechen sympathizers did against Russia;[95] or even intervene directly with military force when pushed, like China's invasion of Vietnam in support of the Khmer Rouge or when the Iranians lob missiles at Iraq as cover for the Kurds.[96] A state placed on the United States' list of those "not cooperating fully" with counterterrorism really doesn't have to play along if they're willing to shrug off public condemnation or use other advantages like strategic location, crucial bases, or resource control of existing alliance obligations. Frustrated officials place critical partners Saudi Arabia, Qatar, Greece, Pakistan, and Turkey in the mental box of "frenemy" for their indulgence and support of VNSAs.

A country willing to buck international disapproval to sponsor a VNSA is also likely to be amenable to sheltering them; providing training camps and a safe retreat to rest, receive medical attention, and regroup; or just refusing to extradite or identify personnel who have fled there. Cuba was famously the destination of 1970s hijackings and fugitive radicals from the United States and Canada, while Venezuela and Saudi Arabia allowed FARC and al-Qaeda members to "live freely" on their soil.[97] A sovereign safe haven makes it exponentially harder to deliver a knockout blow to a VNSA or to assassinate their leader without escalating conflict with the sponsor and its allies, even if the sponsor claims a defense that they are incapable of ousting the dangerous group from a remote or under-governed territory within their borders.[98] Not all liminal regions are good though. Despite an invitation from Hassan al-Turabi for Osama bin Laden to use Sudan as a safe haven, the reality of the country's infrastructure and poor human capital resources made it a nightmare compared to better digs in Kenya and ultimately in Afghanistan, where bin Laden could reliably plug in a fax machine.[99]

Sovereign states are allowed to buy the printing presses used to make currency, a gift that North Korea shares with some of its proxies and criminal partners, and they have financial structures that can launder large amounts of money through a central bank or national industry.[100] State sponsors can provide weapons and supplies straight from the factory, with appropriate end-use certificates and trainers available to make sure VNSA personnel are able to use them effectively—perhaps the Chinese cannons and radar systems seized on an LTTE boat in 2007, which can normally only be obtained with "proper permission from a government."[101] National-level intelligence services can share information, talent scout, and make introductions to useful experts, and may even use their own diplomatically protected personnel to conduct dry runs of operations, which may have been what Iran's embassy guards in New York were doing in 2004 when apprehended photographing bridges and tunnels.[102]

Domestic pressure to support coreligionists and ethnic links motivates some state sponsorship of VNSA, as does placating refugee populations within a government's borders. It might be in the form of Gaddafi setting himself up as the "godfather" of Pan-Arab Nationalism, or China furnishing ethnic Han VNSAs inside of Myanmar with weapons and money. In the 1970s Lebanon allowed the PLO safe haven rather than agitate the powerful Palestinian community against their fragile government structure, and Uganda found it more expedient to aim refugee Tutsis toward the Rwandan Patriotic Front, which they fed and subsidized, than to have them interfere in domestic Ugandan affairs.[103] Indira Gandhi tasked India's Research and Analysis Wing to train the LTTE in order to conciliate ethnic Tamils in southern India, although the surprising subsequent success of the LTTE against the Sri Lankan authorities encouraged an uncomfortable surge in Tamil Nadu nationalism, prompting a withdrawal of help and a reversal of sponsorship in 1987.[104]

Some sponsorship arrangements are more "the enemy of my enemy is my friend" than anything else. Greece and Armenia have long offered sanctuary to the PKK as a way to antagonize Turkey.[105] In 1947 the Soviet Union sent Czech-made guns to the Haganah not because the Soviet Union had any interest in an independent Israel—Stalinist Russia was viciously anti-Semitic—but because they really wanted to destabilize the British presence in the Middle East.[106] Regional rivals sponsor equal and opposite VNSAs entirely for the purpose of making their neighbors bleed and tying up their militaries: Iran-Iraq, Eritrea-Ethiopia, Uganda-Sudan, and India-Pakistan all invest in keeping their frontiers disrupted and local powers leveled out.[107] One of the most bizarre cases of this was the largesse of Gaddafi, who sought revenge for British involvement in the American bombing of Tripoli in 1986 by donating a gigantic amount of money and weapons (ten tons of AK-47s, Semtex, Sam-7 missiles, RPGs, and hundreds of thousands of rounds of ammunition—enough that they were still using it in the late 1990s) to the IRA. He then also gave money to the Northern Irish loyalists on the vast misunderstanding that they were also against the British government.[108]

Both sides in the sponsorship relationship have to be prepared for the rules to change abruptly. The end of the Cold War shifted the landscape, but so does a country's effort to clean up its act and get international rehabilitation, like Libya—they handed over the Lockerbie bombers in 1999 and kicked out the Abu Nidal Organization.[109] Pakistan clamped down on its proxies in Kashmir after 9/11 rather than have the United States see it as a terrorism supporter, and it reaped the benefits of $3 billion in relief and a waiver on American restrictions on giving aid to governments that came to power in military coups.[110] Cuba scaled back its financial support to the National Liberation Army in Colombia but continues to offer medical aid and diplomatic consultation on treaties, changing the terms of its sponsorship. Saudi Arabia's tolerance for al-Qaeda came to a screeching halt in 2003 with attacks on Saudi soil, while the PKK had to forgo Syrian and Iranian aid as those nations' harsh abuse of their Kurdish minorities alienated the diaspora that the PKK depended on for support.[111]

VNSAs with a burgeoning treasury can be sponsors themselves. Al-Qaeda's model of disbursing "seed money" to affiliates who are then expected to develop their own financing streams has been instrumental in expanding the "brand" across the globe, but it also carries the risk that groups operating under their banner undertake attacks unauthorized by and detrimental to overall strategy. As with any large organization, the balance between not micromanaging day-to-day business and keeping coherence in goals is an ongoing challenge, especially because the original core leadership has little leverage to discipline franchises once the seed money is spent. It is simpler to just pay other VNSAs for their expertise as a way of injecting cash into political fellow travelers, as FARC did with ETA mortar experts, the IRA, and Japanese Red Army urban warfare specialists.[112] In a couple of cases the VNSA was more financially stable than a recognized nation, leading the PLO to advance the new Nicaraguan government $12 million in 1981, and al-Qaeda to fund Sudan's development projects in the 1990s.[113]

■ Legal Liabilities of State Sponsorship

The end of the Cold War changed not just the funding landscape but also the willingness of countries to act against state sponsors. The shock of 9/11 shook loose harsher commentary from people like George W. Bush's ambassador to the United Nations, John Negroponte. "We may find our self-defense requires further actions with respect to other organizations and states."[114] Although she later walked it back, Secretary of State Condoleezza Rice threatened Lebanon about freezing Hezbollah accounts that their "very survival depended on such compliance."[115] This was tough talk, as was President Bush's promise that state sponsors "will not do business with the United States of America."[116] Turns out, it is a lot harder to put those threats into action.

A handful of states are willing to take swift and retaliatory action against other states for their aggressive moves as well as their sponsorship of VNSAs.

In January 2021 South Korea immediately froze $7 billion in Iranian assets after the Iranian navy seized the *Hankuk Chemi*, a tanker in the Strait of Hormuz, giving them tremendous leverage in negotiating for its safe return. India's Cold Start doctrine was formulated as a proactive and deterrent plan aimed at making sure Pakistan knows that sponsored VNSA strikes will be met with action teams and air attacks sped into Pakistan to destroy training camps.[117]

The Israelis started physically hitting at banks in Lebanon, using old-school tradecraft to plant viruses in their computer system or, more directly, using air targeting to destroy records and cash deposits belonging to Hamas and Hezbollah. In partnership with the civil rights organization Shurat HaDin, which took inspiration from the Southern Poverty Law Center's suits against the Ku Klux Klan, the Mossad sued Deutsche Bank for damages because they handled Iranian accounts. Harnessing the power of contingency fees, they sparked a kind of legal "gold rush," assisting lawyers in Israel and the United States to launch suits against deep-pocketed business entities doing transactions with countries on the state sponsor list.[118]

Suing in a U.S. court because a state sponsor uses a bank with a branch in New York is possible but runs into complicated legal issues of foreign policy. States refrained from suing one another, preferring to take claims—like the U.S. government's demands for monetary damages from Britain for building Confederate ships in the Civil War—to arbitration rather than courts. Additionally, states also discouraged their citizens from suing other countries. After World War II, this absolute immunity seemed unworkable in the face of communist governments operating commercial entities like airlines and banks, so the United States updated its laws to define "restrictive immunity," in the 1976 Foreign Sovereign Immunity Act, which places the onus of deciding whether any U.S. person or the state can sue a sovereign entity on the judiciary rather than the State Department.[119] VNSAs' acts of terrorism in the 1980s challenged this legal state of affairs, with the family of Leon Klinghoffer, murdered in the *Achille Lauro* hijacking, suing the PLO to attach assets the group held in the United States. Settled in 1996 out of court for an undisclosed amount, the case was the harbinger of demands for more accountability by VNSAs and their sponsors.[120]

In February 1996 the Cuban air force shot down two civilian aircraft carrying members of a charity group, Brothers to the Rescue, killing four. Joined by families of the victims of the Libyan-sponsored Lockerbie bombing (1988) and the family of Alisa Flatow, who died in a suicide bombing carried out in Gaza by the Islamic Jihad Movement (1995), the survivors lobbied Congress not just to tighten sanctions on Cuba but to add an amendment to their package of laws responding to the Oklahoma City bombing. The result, named the Flatow Amendment, altered the Foreign Sovereign Immunity Act to say that state sponsors of terrorism "shall be liable to a U.S. national . . . for personal injury or death caused by acts of that party."[121] The United Nations subsequently used the 1999 Convention for the Suppression of Terrorism Financing to call on states to take responsibility for private actors in their territory, specifically demanding that Sudan and Libya suppress VNSAs.[122]

American plaintiffs, sometimes advised by Shurat HaDin, have consistently brought suit ever since, including *Flatow v. Islamic Republic of Iran*, *Kilburn v. Islamic Republic of Iran*, *Estates of Ungar v. Palestinian Authority*, and *Linde v. Arab Bank*.[123] A collective lawsuit by the victims of the 9/11 attacks against Saudi citizens and institutions foundered on a U.S. District Court ruling that several of the defendants had sovereign immunity because their activities took place while acting in an official capacity. In 2016 Congress passed, over Obama's veto, the Justice Against Sponsors of Terrorism Act, bolstering the ability of Americans to launch civil suits against foreign states. The administration's reason for vetoing the bill was the complication introduced to rehabilitating rogue states by an outstanding judgment, which turned out to be the case with negotiating Sudan's removal from the terrorism-sponsor list.[124] Some of these cases settled out of court, but many have struggled to collect the large judgments. Frozen accounts from which judgments could be extracted are also claimed by adherents of governments before the one that sponsored the VNSA, like the pre-1979 Iranian regime, and plaintiffs from multiple cases try to attach the same funds. The U.S. government has offered to pay some of the judgments, but for victims, getting acknowledgment of their loss from the party responsible is a major motivator for their cases. In one ongoing dispute, plaintiffs have tried to seize antiquities from ancient

Persia held in the University of Chicago's Oriental Institute because they are also claimed by the Iranian government as cultural treasures.[125]

What should be a powerful tool for the U.S. government to exert leverage on state sponsors of terrorism—placing them under economic sanctions—quickly runs into domestic trouble. Lobbyists swarm to find loopholes to get their products and industries spared under the humanitarian and medical exemptions, leading to completely ludicrous situations like issuing a license for the export of Jolly Time popcorn to Iran and Sudan because it "has fiber, which are useful to the digestive system." Wrigley's gum, nutritional supplements for sanctioned countries' athletic teams, and hot sauce have found their own equally ridiculous justifications, although a former Treasury official warned that "when you create loopholes like this that you can drive a Mack truck through, you are giving countries something for nothing, and they just laugh in their teeth."[126]

7
MOVING
THE MONEY

How much is a *World of Warcraft* magic sword worth in the real world? If nongamers have thought about this at all, it is probably in the context of a plot point in the sitcom *The Big Bang Theory* in which Sheldon acquires the "sword of Azeroth" and promptly abandons his colleagues in the game to list it on eBay. A lot of middle schoolers can explain money laundering at length because it is a narrative arc in the film *Ralph Breaks the Internet*. U.S. federal court, though, has a hard time keeping up with innovations like washing illicit funds via Linden Dollars, loot boxes, and *Counterstrike: Global Offensive* container keys.[1]

For gamers, in-game currency has been a feature of online interaction for decades, with games like *Second Life*, *World of Warcraft*, and *Ultima Online* allowing players to use fiat currencies to purchase units of exchange within the game. Consistent engagement and skilled play are rewarded in "questing"-type games with valuable items like swords, armor, or magic spells that can be given, traded, and sold (in the game, but also in real life). Since many players want to level up their skills by investing money rather than time, entrepreneurs emerged.[2] Within *EVE Online*, an outer space trade strategy game, a player established what became a virtual investment bank, accumulating $170,000 before absconding with it.[3] The player chat rooms, with thousands of participants, are an available space for making friends but also for political dissidents discussing plans and illicit transactions, which grow in parallel to the overt trading and selling of characters, digital magic spells, and online fashion accessories.[4]

Because players can be located around the world and function anonymously until authorities present the game company with a warrant, using in-game currency and objects for money laundering is extremely easy: a VNSA purchases $500,000 in virtual things, sells those things, and cashes out, all in the space of a couple of hours. No banks were involved, no suspicious transactions reports filed, and no tax records kept.[5] If a forum isn't available within the game, players and would-be launderers can take their transactions to a third party like eBay or "gold exchangers." Valve, the developer for the *Counterstrike* game, had to completely shut down trading in container keys after discovering that "nearly all" the transactions were money laundering and fraud.[6] In 2018 South Korean police intercepted $38 million being moved by gangs through games into China.[7]

Depending on the jurisdiction where the servers sit, this kind of transaction may not even be a crime. An individual company may institute policies to cap daily trades or ban players for buying and selling but won't know of violations of those policies unless they put resources toward investigating and policing it. For games with microtransactions, like *Fortnite* or *Candy Crush*, the company's income stems from hooking "whales" who get so involved that they spend real money on "digital hats," while 95 percent of other players use the free version, so there is no incentive for them to deploy an algorithm that cuts into their profits and discourages buying.[8] A British Fraud Advisory panel issued a recommendation that "there is nothing virtual about online crime; it is all too real. It is time the government took it seriously," saying that *Second Life* is a "parallel universe with almost no external rule of law, no enforced banking regulations or compliance, no policing and no governmental oversight."[9] The ungovernable tribal regions of massively multiplayer online role-playing games remain fertile fields for money laundering.

■ ■ ■

In the first century AD, Vespasian, a very practical-minded Roman Emperor, mandated a tax on the urine collected from public toilets. Since this was a valuable resource, used in tanning, fulling, and bleaching processes, the emperor wanted the state to get a cut. His son Titus was squeamish and noted the disgusting origins of the money, only to have his father hold up a gold coin and ask if he was offended by the smell. Titus laughed and shook his head, to which Vespasian replied, "Pecunia non olet"—money doesn't stink.[10] Money is the tool, but where it comes from and what is done with it includes crimes a VNSA probably wants to conceal by moving it away from the group, mixing it in with a confusing amount of money in the licit economy, and then placing it where it can be used conveniently. This can happen through a variety of methods.[11]

People in the legitimate market have been concealing their income from state tax collection for millennia, but the modern advent of centralized bureaucracy and law enforcement have made money tracking a tool used against VNSAs. In 1931, unable to nab mobster Al Capone another way, the FBI prosecuted him successfully for tax evasion, causing gangsters with more impulse control like Meyer Lansky to pioneer new ways to obscure their cash flows—casinos, offshore havens, interbank transfers, and cash businesses— rather than the clumsy and incriminating method of keeping double sets of books.[12] While focused on organized crime, "money laundering" prosecutions expanded to politics with investigation of Richard Nixon's Committee to Re-Elect the President hiding donations and allowing anonymity in 1973.[13] This structure of training and legal orientation shattered after 9/11, when governments directed their anti–money laundering teams to go after terrorist money and prevent it from arriving for use rather than tracking criminal money to punish the activities that generated it.[14]

On one end of the Makarenko spectrum, a mobster wants to enjoy his villa in the sun, confident that he has plausible explanations for the income that do not lead to drugs, prostitution, and extortion but to a chain of successful bars and a lucrative garbage hauling route.[15] At the other end, a nationalist group planning a car bombing needs to be able to get funds to buy materials in a Global North country without leading cops right to their apartment. In between, a VNSA needs a safe place to stash excess donations, convert marked bills from a kidnapping or bank robbery into usable currency, or assistance in getting assets in or out of an area under sanctions.

Our big forces, globalization and sovereignty, come into play immediately. Rapid globalization transformed the financial industry from one in which it was possible to manage cash flow by choosing banks in remote locations to ensure the longest "float" possible before a paper check's value could be withdrawn from an account to one in which the push of a button transfers money from New York to the Cayman Islands. Internet access, mobile phones, digital currency, standardized banking systems, corresponding relationships between institutions, and credit cards all create such enormous "noise" that money laundering hides in plain sight, rarely caught and even less often prosecuted.[16] In what turned out to be a little too pointed metaphor, the Federal Reserve Bank in New York tried to lock its door during their 9/11 evacuation only to find that there was no external way to do so: money movement never sleeps and determined people can find those pockets of arbitrage where a financial institution is willing to deal. Long starburst patterns of laundering will pass through multiple locations where the legitimate authorities decide to tolerate it (one of Joe Cahill's favorite paths for IRA money was Dublin-London-Istanbul-Luxemburg-Antwerp-Marbella-Isle of Man-Oslo-Frankfurt-Antigua), and pressure applied to blacklist or spotlight a sovereign territory for being especially good at it just acts as free advertising.[17] A country with other influence or leverage can simply refuse to apply anti–money laundering agreements or to apply them selectively.[18]

In the last decade, the cost for laundering money has settled at about 20–30 percent of the total, with additional fees for complicated transactions.[19] Some organizations like al-Qaeda bragged that, like Osama bin Laden himself, they had sophisticated understanding of the weaknesses of Western financial networks, "as they are aware of the lines in their hands."[20] Hezbollah operates its own in-house laundry, charging other groups a fee but offering access to their legitimate Western Union franchises.[21] A VNSA willing to pay and to put up with the eccentricities of their laundryman can easily find outside professionals to handle the details. Skilled money movers with diverse illicit clientele—say, a Hell's Angels chapter in Quebec and the Autodefensas Unidas de Colombia in Colombia—can manipulate the assets of the criminal and ideological networks for best obfuscation and access to the money.[22]

■ Dealing with Money

Whether swimming in pools of money or rolling around on coins, Scrooge McDuck's style seems luxurious and fun, but paper and metal currency is inconvenient and nasty. One million $1 bills weighs a ton, and even if you can get those bills converted into $100 bills, that is still twenty-two pounds of stinky, germy, and flammable disadvantage.[23] U.S. marijuana producers have found that out the hard way, operating legally at the state level but, because of federal laws like the Racketeer Influenced Corrupt Organizations statute, unable to put their profits into banks. Instead they have to put 24/7 security on secret warehouses full of small bills. COVID-19 travel restrictions put a huge crimp in the practiced cash conversion routines of VNSAs, with couriers working for India's mob bosses grounded and unable to get to the United Arab Emirates with their gold and cash and with cartels impatient to clear out counting houses in Los Angeles bursting at the seams with weighted and shrink-wrapped bills.[24] Shortly after 9/11, two Yemenis attempted to get through security at Kennedy Airport with $180,000 in disorganized small bills and checks stuffed in with boxes of jarred honey. This is clearly not the way to go, triggering as many security protocols as possible.[25]

Obviously, cash is vulnerable to thieves, Mother Nature, and enemies who know where you're storing it. One of the partners of Air America became frustrated laundering cocaine cash in the 1980s and instead buried it in his Florida backyard only to find that, when he needed to dig it up to buy a new plane, it smelled like rot and vomit, even after going through a couple of *real* wash cycles. Bundles of cash stuffed into ceilings can be casualties of house fires. Cops find it in washing machines, freezers, and closets.[26] FARC soldiers buried caches of what they couldn't launder, but the jungle ate a lot of it, some of it was discovered by outsiders, and a couple of times the digging party got high and forgot where it was.[27] Under the Military Commissions Act of 2009, the United States bombs known storage facilities with ISIS cash because it is an object that "effectively contributes to the war-fighting or war

As part of the campaign against ISIS, coalition forces targeted "finance centers," blowing up stockpiles of cash in order to degrade the group's capability to pay salaries and acquire necessary supplies. *Inherent Resolve Graphic (2016), combined Joint Task Force–Operation Inherent Resolve, Defense Visual Information Distribution Service.*

sustaining capability of an opposing force."[28] Operation Point Blank, since beginning in 2016, has destroyed $500–800 million through airstrikes across Iraq and Syria.[29]

When it works smoothly, counting houses organize cash into packages that can be moved without triggering suspicious activity reports (SAR) or declarations at customs inspections. A group with access to transportation might just plow the bundles into a container for trans-Pacific shipping or load it on a private plane, especially for flights to countries that don't ask about currency coming in.[30] Otherwise, the first step is to consolidate into the largest possible bills, or into instruments like cashier's checks below the limit requiring a SAR. In Europe, law enforcement lobbied effectively to have the largest denomination of the Euro in circulation reduced to a one hundred, after discovering that 90 percent of five hundred denomination bills were being used by VNSAs.[31] At airports, smuggling "smurfs" walk through with money in their flight crew carry-ons, taped to their bodies, swallowed like cocaine packets in condoms, and stuffed down their underwear. VNSAs with connections recruit people least likely to be searched—women, people with scary looking injuries, clergy, celebrities.[32] Trucks cross borders with cash taped in wheel wells, hidden under false floors, or in bags disguised as sacks of rice or coffee beans.[33] In 2006 Palestinian prime minister Ismail Haniyeh expected to be able to use diplomatic immunity to move a truck with donated money (largely from Iran) from Egypt and across Israel to Gaza. Israeli border officials refused to admit the truck, and Haniyeh and his entourage could hand-carry only what was in their personal possessions. Of the $35 million in the truck, only $4 million could be stuffed in luggage and pockets and dragged over the line.[34]

Most VNSAs have volunteers willing to be electronic smurfs too. A cartel might charitably open accounts with a minimum deposit and then expect hundreds of people to dutifully deposit cash delivered to them by a circuit-driving cash courier; on a prearranged signal, their local branch would send that money to a larger account under cartel control. The fear of retaliation keeps smurf hands off the cartel's money, and, once in a large lump, it can be sent to an offshore haven. Since this is relatively low risk, it is an ideal use of ancillary members of VNSAs—families, girlfriends, retired personnel.

The next time you're in a Walmart or Target, have a look at the prepaid cards available at the checkout. It's going to piss off the people behind you, but you can convert handfuls of small bills into $500 Visa gift cards without anyone batting an eye, and once you've got them, they can go across borders in a purse or have their numbers used on the internet by absolutely anyone. Before gift cards were available, VNSAs began using prepaid cards as a strategy by having personnel buy insurance policies and then cash them out for a discounted lump sum (in the form of a check from the company), then overpaying credit cards, which would issue a refund when the total hit a particular mark. Blockbuster invented the first gift card in 1994, changing the landscape of money laundering dramatically.[35]

On one hand, banks promoted reloadable cards as a safe alternative to remittance payments for Latin America; on the other hand, these are really great for illicit activity. Colombian traffickers moved $7 million to Medellin in three months in 2006 using smurfs in Philadelphia. Tammy Black, an Ohio Department of Motor Vehicles employee, was being paid in stacks of $10 phone cards to issue fake IDs for criminal groups. In 2017 a Washington transit police officer tried to use Google Play gift cards to send money to ISIS—his only mistake being having an FBI informant as his connection.[36] PayPal has been in trouble for this, too, allowing accounts in Cuba, Sudan, Turkey, and Iran to sell (literally) pieces of paper with scribbles on them for inflated prices on eBay, paid by launderers in the United States and Europe moving money through their accounts.[37]

VNSAs with access to a casino and willing to pay taxes (or wanting documentation of where the money came from) have an easy laundering mechanism in the form of betting chips. A few hours invested in wandering around the casino floor, drinking complimentary cocktails, and losing a small amount entitles a gambler to cash out with a W-2G form. Technically, W-2Gs are for wins of at least $600 when the payout is three hundred times the amount of your wager, but this is rarely checked. An additional layer of protection comes from choosing casinos on sovereign indigenous land, which operate under their own agreements with the state and federal government.[38] A variation of this is to buy out lottery winners and holders of valuable horse-racing bets, offering them tax-free cash on the spot.[39] Online and offshore gambling are even more convenient if a group has money in an electronic form.[40]

Another possibility is to engage in under- or overvaluing imported goods in a scheme usually labeled a "Black Market Peso Exchange." Rather than sending cash south of the border, a VNSA holding, say, $1 million in cash will have a confederate in the place they wish the money to land to pay out in local currency. Meanwhile, the VNSA will order goods in the sending country and export them to the confederate, who sells them and recoups the money. This can be jiggered with fraudulent valuation to explain influxes of cash and get around price controls, and it can be augmented by government funds if there are tax breaks or bonuses promoting trade (Argentina paid one VNSA $130 million in export incentives). These exchanges can have a deleterious effect on the local economy where the products get dumped on the receiving end, undermining local production and industry.[41]

Some countries have been willing to hold money for VNSAs in the form of issuing bearer bonds in order to get hard currency. Sri Lanka, India, Pakistan, and the United States (until the Tax Equity and Fiscal Responsibility Act of 1982) were happy to sell bearer securities anonymously, redeemable after a set amount of time by anyone in possession of them. A variation of this, "whitener bonds," requires the buyer to declare their identity and pays less interest, but the country issuing it won't reveal the source and, once it matures, the money is entirely clean, like an official "money amnesty."[42]

■ Just Ask the Bank

For every press release touting how enthused a bank is to be partnering in patriotic compliance with anti–money laundering legislation, there's a wealth manager who gets paid on commission and is resentful that the institution is paying millions in compliance efforts to *turn customers away*. Some of the resulting behavior by wealth managers and the banks was passive-aggressive, like filing thousands of SAR reports and clogging the system in an act of punctilious acquiescence; other behavior was more overt, like the Broadway National Bank in New York City where the guard would alert the smurfs lined up in the lobby to scatter when the cops came around.[43] The incentive structure of bonuses and commissions have led many account managers to reclassify customers from high risk to low, claim ignorance of easily Googleable information (like "recently indicted as a gangster"), make up backgrounds for the rich Russian "whales," and talk themselves around to the idea that "illicit proceeds had been invested in licit industry, so it was legitimate income now."[44]

Since 2010 major mainstream banks (Wachovia, Barclays, ING, Credit Suisse, HSBC, and Deutsche Bank—not their individual employees) have been fined for knowingly laundering gargantuan sums of money for illicit actors, including drug cartels. Sen. Carl Levin, in response to bank pushback on "know your customer" laws, marveled that a bank told his staff "that 'these are bad people.' If the bank thinks that they are bad people, why are they seeking them as customers of the bank? . . . It appears that the bank DOES know its clients, but what it knows is that the client is BAD."[45] And profitable.

HSBC allowed the Sinaloa and Norte del Valle cartels to launder $7 billion between 2000 and 2008, allowing cash deliveries in specially designed boxes made by the cartel to fit into bank teller windows; the bank found nothing suspicious enough about it to file SAR reports and set aside a fund of $700 million for potential fines (the eventual fine in 2012 was $1.9 billion), although they "clawed back" bonuses for their senior executives (not their compliance officer, who resigned) out of the deal with prosecutors.[46] Wachovia, meanwhile, got caught when drug dogs at the Miami-Opa Locka Executive Airport in Florida found drugs on a plane in 2006, leading to a vast laundering flow through the bank's accounts—$4.7 billion in bulk cash and $378 billion in corresponding transfers from Mexican *casa de cambio* (currency exchange) institutions. During the investigation Wells Fargo acquired Wachovia, knowing a fine was coming, and in 2010 happily paid $160 million, which was only about 2 percent of the profit from facilitating a brutal drug war.[47]

As grim as this is, Antonio Maria Costa, head of the UN's Office on Drugs and Crime, suggested that the giant slush fund of drug money resting in bank vaults in 2008 was "capitalism's global savings account" and had, by being available and liquid, propped up the financial system as other assets cratered, thereby saving the stability of the global economic system. No fools, many of the VNSAs used their advantageous position to buy up valuable assets like real estate, shares in utilities, and even chunks of national debt, intertwining them irrevocably with the licit economy in a position of enormous leverage.[48]

From 1972 to 1991, the Bank of Credit and Commerce International (BCCI) was every VNSA's friendly banker, by design. Its Pakistani founder, Agha Hasan Abedi, started the United Bank Limited in 1959; until its nationalization in 1974, it specialized in assisting Pakistan's wealthy in hiding their financial assets.[49] In partnership with the sheik of Abu Dhabi, he set up his own seizure-proof multinational, with out-of-reach branches in banking havens like Luxembourg and protection from a constellation of autocratic heads of state whose money he massaged. One subordinate remembered Abedi's motto: "The only laws that are permanent are the laws of nature. Everything else is flexible. We can always work in and around the laws. The laws change."[50] BCCI carefully probed new markets, finding cooperative corresponding partners and influential politicians to invite onto new supervisory boards and, when it acquired banks in the United States, hiring presidential counselor Clark Clifford to be chair of its First American Bankshares.[51]

Abedi and his bank executives would do anything for their influential clients, from finding Manuel Noriega's college-age daughter a part-time job at their Miami branch to maintaining a prostitution recruitment branch for VIP entertainment in the Gulf. It hired Kissinger and Associates as consultants, donated money to Jimmy Carter's charity foundations, and developed a Rolodex of any luxury service its customers might want.[52] Even more protection came from being the preferred "fixer" for the CIA and British intelligence services, handling Iran–Contra money for the National Security Council, helping the Syrians buy Silkworm missiles from China, managing the Afghan rebel slush fund, financing Pakistan's nuclear program, and brokering deals in which Saudi Arabia acquired Israeli guidance systems. The terrorist Abu Nidal group, the Medellin cartel, Samuel Doe of Liberia, and Bangladesh's military dictator Hussain Muhammad Ershad were also clients.[53]

The fun came to an end in 1991, when the British government instigated an audit, Operation Sandstorm, which leaked to the public. U.S. regulators had been pulling at threads in the bank's bizarre, freewheeling structure since 1986, but the Sandstorm report kicked public outrage into gear, leading to a congressional investigation that revealed even more entanglement of the government with Abedi and BCCI: Sen. Orrin Hatch's impassioned floor defense of the bank was easy to link to his request that it approve a $10 million loan to his friend, Houston businessman Monzer Hourani.[54] The bank's liquidators paid a $10 million fine to the U.S. Treasury and forfeited its American assets, with almost all the major players escaping into retirement, including Abedi, who returned to Pakistan, which refused to extradite him until his death in 1995.

Prosecutors have recently begun to take advantage of provisions in material support for terrorism statutes to freeze accounts that have run through the New York financial market. Being a major center of the financial world gives U.S. law extraterritorial jurisdiction whenever money, even in electronic form, touches American shores. This leverage has been useful in getting records from financial institutions whose home branches have more restrictive privacy laws, and in cutting off access to resources, but the globalized flow of money has a serious downside. A U.S. bank that itself practices good anti–money laundering controls doesn't necessarily have to vet its "corresponding" relationships and can transfer money in from, say, bin Laden's Al-Shamal Islamic Bank in Khartoum, which was a link to Citibank, American Express, and ING. A really suspicious-looking bank in Afghanistan might not be able to get a relationship with a major U.S. or British institution, but all they need is one link to a bank with lower standards who already has one.[55]

■ Know Your Customer

In the 1990s, particularly in the context of the war on drugs and welfare reform, the United States promoted the acquisition of formal bank accounts through legislation like the Community Reinvestment Act (1997), requiring financial institutions to offer credit everywhere they operate branches, not just in wealthy areas. This, in tandem with proposed 1998 regulations requiring banks to "know your customer" (KYC), was meant to reduce untracked transactions and offer alternative forms of financial mobility for households of low socioeconomic status. However, a coalition of broad-spectrum opposition, including civil liberties advocates, banks who didn't want the extra burden, and anti-immigration lobbyists who wanted to refuse accounts to undocumented people, lobbied the Treasury to change course, and shortly before 9/11 the KYC proposal was scrapped.[56]

However, as the 9/11 hijackers had successfully opened regular bank accounts and used them with the helpful advice of the SunTrust tellers, the sweeping package of financial controls included in the Patriot Act imposed much more stringent requirements. This did not result in inclusion plus banks knowing their customers; it instead became a convenient reason for banks to evade dealing with small-balance accounts, deny complicated identification situations, and set penalties high enough to drive troublesome accounts off to "the usurious practices of money transfer companies, check cashers and payday lenders."[57]

Being unbanked is very expensive. Without an account, transactions like receiving a social welfare payment, paying utility bills, or even being paid by an employer become a time-consuming hassle of traveling to a check-cashing storefront, paying high service fees, buying money orders, and getting payday loans for small amounts in emergencies. This inconvenience and friction increase in the developing world, where the trip to deposit proceeds from a harvest may involve a multiday bus trip, with the increased potential for robbery or extortion. Depending on global location, people may be unbanked because the financial institutions don't want to bother with branches in dangerous or impoverished locations, they are undocumented and can't meet the KYC rules for identification, they may be illiterate, their balances are too low to meet minimums, they have insecure housing, or they had poor experiences with banks that crashed or treated them insultingly.[58]

The Financial Action Task Force estimated in 2012 that more than half of the world's adult population lacked access to modern financial services, constituting a significant and dangerous opportunity for loan sharks, organized crime, and corruption as well as making it more difficult for people to climb out of poverty. In the United States, as of 2017, 6.5 percent of households were unbanked entirely, but overall 25 percent were "underbanked"—reliant on pawnshops, payday loan programs, and expensive "second chance" accounts at institutions like Woodforest National Bank (the kiosks in the front of many Walmarts). In all cases, women are the most likely to be shut out of financial services.[59]

Technology has solved part of the problem through mobile phones, which completely bypass the infrastructure of phone lines to provide coverage and access for billions of people. In East Africa, 86 percent of Kenyans have used m-payments (M-Pesa), which make small-value electronic transfers using cell phones. Retailers who sell phone network time can also register to be money agents, taking in cash and issuing M-Pesa credits, which can be transferred by customers to a creditor and redeemed by another participating retailer. The fees are small, the retailers far more numerous than traditional banks, and the technology is familiar to the majority of the population, moving more than $1 billion monthly.[60] This has materially improved the economic lives of the people who use it and transformed the financial landscape of the developing world, although, as with all globalizations, it can be used just as easily by VNSAs to move money anonymously. Retaining some ability to track transactions requires that, at some level, governments and institutions know who the people are in the transaction so that the paths authorities most want people to use and incentivize with protections (like FDIC insurance) require a standardized identification.[61]

Paying social welfare benefits like pensions and food subsidies, which are done with in-person disbursal or a system of mailed checks, is hugely inefficient, expensive to staff, and subject to theft and delays in places where remote delivery and nonstandard addresses are involved. Brazil found that when it tied their Bolsa Família (Family Allowance) payments to electronic benefit cards, their costs to administer the program dropped from 14.7 percent of the value of the benefit to 2.6 percent, with a substantial reduction in leakage and fraud.[62] Entrepreneurs in India have been working to harness their tech sector to remedy the problem that less than half of the $60 billion in social programs distributed every year reaches its intended recipients and is instead drawn off by middlemen and corrupt administrators. Hundreds of millions of people have no formal identification, can't open bank accounts or start cell phone service, and are vulnerable to having their benefits stolen or extorted. Since 2009, using competing corporate vendors operating mobile field stations, India's government has been collecting biometric information (iris scan, fingerprints, and facial photos), on the basis of which people are issued a twelve-digit "Aadhaar" (which means "platform" or "foundation" in twenty-two languages used in India) number tied to a massive central database, from which they can apply for benefits, bank access, and passports. For the very poor, enrollment in the system automatically opens them a no-frills account at the national bank.[63]

Nandan Nilekani, the tech mogul behind the Aadhaar program, frames it in terms of citizens accessing their "rights, entitlements and duties," and holding the state accountable for delivery, but the rollout and system haven't been without pushback and problems. Biometric data is hard to harvest from people whose lifetime of manual labor has worn away their fingerprints, who don't know their year of birth, and whose names can be written multiple ways. Pregnancy can alter the subtle patterns in the eye, and women (especially if their in-laws are hovering nearby) are reluctant to look at a camera for facial scans.[64] Distributing money rather than food supplies has alarmed the contractors who could count on selling bulk commodities to the state for distribution, people have panicked when they didn't know how to contact Aadhaar to correct mistakes, and questions remain about what could happen if the database is hacked. Minorities fear that being identifiable in a government system will make them easy to cut out of social benefits, or a target for violence, a concern that looms large when Hindu nationalist politicians fire up their rhetoric.[65] Russian dissidents, including Garry Kasparov, claim that Putin's strict anti–money laundering and identification laws aren't for keeping the books straight but a tool for persecuting opponents, whose assets can be found and seized and their ID used for surveillance and control.[66]

Like our Baptists and bootleggers from chapter 4, there are also always lobbying groups who want the system to remain set up in a way that benefits them. In the United States, tax time is far more complicated than it needs to be because a powerful lobby representing tax return preparers needs people to pay for assistance.[67] Who wouldn't want poor people to have small-scale bank accounts and access to low-interest emergency lending? Organized lobbies representing credit cards (and the states where the laws favor them, like South Dakota and Delaware), payday lenders, pawnshops, and title loans jump in to repel reforms that might break their hold on pocketbooks, even when these changes increase transparency and fall in line with Patriot Act financial regulation.[68] Enrolling people with state-issued ID can be difficult when they are members of a marginalized group who lack traditional documentation (born at home because hospitals were segregated, records burned or lost in relocation or disasters, etc.), and this is compounded when a desire to exclude them from political participation exceeds the state's wishes for bureaucratic control.

Sweden offers an opposite view of the potential of a cashless, advanced economy. With excellent broadband coverage and a population comfortable using technology as well as an already existing transparent tax system, going virtual (even to pay for public toilets) is seen as a way to achieve efficiency, cut down on muggings and store robberies, and reduce opportunities for corruption and exploitation of people being paid under the table.[69] Children as young as seven can be issued debit cards with parents as cosigners and with low limits, and the police tout that there has been a sharp reduction in bank robberies, from 210 in 2008 to just 2 in 2018 (it's well known there's no cash in the drawer). The pushback has come from senior citizens uncomfortable with being online, and from advocates for emigrants and people with disabilities, and questions have been raised by Swedish defense planners about the possibility of "Om krisen eller kriget kommer" (if crisis or war comes), being the targets of a cyberattack or a shutdown of the electrical grid.[70]

■ *Hawalas*

Every human society that has engaged in long-distance travel and trade has developed some form of informal value-transfer system to avoid hauling currency or valuables that could be stolen, lost at sea, or damaged in transit. This might take the form of merchants using Phoenician temples around the Mediterranean as banks, or the *hawala* (Middle East), *hundi* (Pakistan and Bangladesh), Fei-chien (China), Phoei kuan (Thailand), Hui (Vietnamese), or Padala (Philippines) networks for moving money. This works especially well among a religious or ethnic group with solid bonds of relationship and shared ethical standards, recognizable in medieval Europe as the Lombard and Jewish family bankers in major trade cities. This trust over distance is strong enough to move the value of money without moving the money itself, an ultimate kind of safety and convenience. During World War II, *hawaladars* in India assisted British intelligence in identifying Axis agents while supplying covert financial inflows to Allied agents in remote regions of Burma and Japanese-occupied Southeast Asia. In the postwar world, these systems—absolutely the norm in their home regions—followed the diasporas of globalization and became the methods of safely and cheaply sending remittances home.[71]

How does it work? A Sri Lankan Tamil wants to send money to her village from Toronto and goes to a friendly local market, where there's a kiosk next to the Bollywood rental movie racks. She gives the *hawaladar* $100 plus a small commission and receives a code word, often the random name of an animal, to send to her mother via a cell phone call. Meanwhile, the *hawaladar* calls or faxes his connection in that area and updates him on the balance sheet. When the sender's mother arrives, she uses the animal codeword as her identification, receives the money, and goes away with cash in less than a couple of hours. Over time the two ends of the network will balance out their ledgers, perhaps with people in Sri Lanka sending money to students abroad or in the form of over-invoiced local goods sold in the market or through a hub bank in Singapore or Dubai, but it all works out, far more securely, quickly, and cheaply than a Western commercial sender, even in the aftermath of a tsunami.[72] This level of trust is possible through rigorous self-policing of the trustworthiness of *hawaladars*—they're quick to throw out a cousin whose khat addiction imperils their reputation for probity or anyone who breeches confidentiality about who receives money. This has the additional advantage of being accessible, since it is a known trustworthy and religiously or ethnically related service, to women in conservative societies who would not go to a public bank or post office.[73]

NGOs work through *hawalas*, as do millions of ordinary people for whom they function innocuously. Western militaries have accepted that this is a safe way to pay translators and informants and to reach into remote areas without transporting conspicuous cash. The problem is, just like cartels and armed groups employ Global North–regulated banks, VNSAs find *hawalas* useful, too. Investigations tracking back funding for busted jihadist cells in Spain and guerrillas in Kashmir find that the money passed through *hawaladars*, and heroin dealers use Fei-chien networks in China alongside workers sending home money from worksites in Africa.[74]

Immediately after 9/11, as part of the U.S. government's Operation Green Quest, the Treasury targeted Somalia's largest money transfer network, Al-Barakat, although one official admitted, "This is not normally the way we would have done things. . . . We needed to make a splash. We needed to designate now and sort it out later."[75] Acting on intelligence from Hussein Farrah Aidid, son of the warlord whose militia caused the *Black Hawk Down* incident in 1993, who was interested in getting out of exile in Eritrea (and, not coincidentally, owed Al-Barakat $40,000), the United States believed the network was a conduit for al-Qaeda funds. Unaware of the crucial role the company played in Somalia's economic stability, officials shut it down abruptly by blacklisting it as "the quartermasters of terror," suggesting that Somalis just go use Western Union.[76] The wreckage was immediate and drastic, as the Somalia diaspora received word that their families were starving without remittances, local banks refused to work with them, and *hawaladars* received hostile interrogations from law enforcement. In Somalia, the company laid off hundreds of workers, amplifying the disorder and despair that al-Shabaab was ready to leverage.[77]

Most of us have *hawala*-like trust arrangements, even if we don't think of them that way. There's always a friend who can be trusted to pick up something for you at the store and is paid back in some lawn mowing next month, or a relative in a college-age nephew's town who can advance some emergency money and expect to get repaid by mom and dad. *Hawalas* suffered from being suddenly "discovered" in the wake of 9/11 as an opaque, exotic, and "underground" system without the kind of documentation investigators expected to find.[78] It didn't help that bin Laden boasted that *hawalas* were one of the three financial systems available to him, leading to "exposés" by local reporters who amped up their anxiety at visiting "shabby, smoky, dark and illegal places" that didn't look like Global North bank lobbies.[79] A U.S. Treasury official sent to investigate found a much less threatening reality. "Folks agreed that they did 'know their customers' and . . . much of the time what the business they facilitated included. . . . That said, everyone I spoke with did admit that facilitating terror (and other illicit activity for that matter) was not a good thing and that they did want to find solutions that they could shove out of this business but do so in a way that still retained their access to the larger pool of funds."[80]

This solution may take the form of requiring *hawaladars* to register with a national bank, as in the Netherlands and United Arab Emirates, and to keep records more recognizably "bank" and maintain a verified log of customers, as required in Canada. What won't work is treating them with hostile suspicion, requiring bonds or capitalization that is out of scale to the enterprise, or shutting them down. The aim is to build some "safer path," to get needed remittance money into spaces the formalized banking system can't or won't go while allowing for documentation and deterring illicit use. Pushed out of *hawalas*, VNSAs will find another way but leave the stabilizing mechanisms and useful networks in place.

■ Islamic Banking

One alternative to *hawalas* for rural Islamic populations reluctant to do business with a Global North bank or microfinance NGO is the emerging sector of Sharia-compliant finance. Begun in Egypt in the 1960s, Islamic banking combines the technology and record-keeping of Western institutions with the religious ethics of Islamic law, operating under a profit-and-loss-sharing model rather than generating income from interest.[81] For Africa or Asia's unbanked, this may be a way to offer access to investment money while reducing the suspicions that illicit funds are moving through value-transfer systems, and it provides resource-rich areas of the Islamic world stable mechanisms to build infrastructure and good governance in the developing world.[82]

Because Islamic law forbids interest and sees profiting from others' lack as a serious ethical lapse, the bank approaches working with customers in a roundabout way. Someone wanting to buy a truck for work will partner with the bank after showing a business plan, the bank will buy the truck, and the person who wanted it will pay in installments with an added convenience fee. But how this is different from the car loans or mortgages from the local credit union? In the case of a house or a vehicle, not much, although any late fees in this system go to charity, and the bank will not penalize a client in financial distress. The real difference is in investment in larger concerns, like starting up a restaurant or other small business—the bank is a partner, not just a source of funding, and they take great care not to acquire what a Western bank would term a "toxic asset," like houses to flip or common cash-business laundering vehicles, or to allow a business to slide into mismanagement when they have the power to step in and provide stability and expertise. Sharing in the more modest rate of return makes the bank viable.[83]

Some economists point to the resilience of the Islamic banking sector during the 2008 recession as evidence that the more cautious, hands-on approach to financial development works well in the Global South. The market is attractive enough that some major Western financial institutions like HSBC offer Sharia-compliant products as part of their portfolio, although a devout believer may prefer a stand-alone bank with its correspondent relationship to convenient international links and without what they'd see as unethical obligations and practices. For finding a middle ground between completely opaque *hawala* networks and the freewheeling Western-style banking system, this is certainly worth trying.

■ Cryptocurrency

The digitally networked world has allowed for the creation of entirely virtual currencies meant to serve as an unregulated and denationalized alternative to fiat currencies and tangible commodities like gold. Some, like Liberty Reserve

(2006–13), have already come and gone, but Bitcoin, which was created in 2008, has persisted and emerged as a popular form for illicit transactions. Bitcoins, which are either purchased or generated by users participating in "mining" or using their computer to verify the transactions of others, are held in online wallets; when used for transactions, those exchanges are recorded irrevocably in ledgers. The wallets do not require users to provide personally identifiable information, offering the advantage of seeming anonymity. Advocates point to the use of Bitcoin by dissidents who perhaps receive support without interference from an oppressive government, but it is far more common that Bitcoin is used on the Deep Web or in organized marketplaces like Silk Road to purchase illicit materials—guns, drugs, porn.[84]

VNSAs are definitely moving money this way, and it especially appeals to right-wing organizations with a strong libertarian bent. After losing access to PayPal and credit card companies in 2017, the neo-Nazi Daily Stormer site started requesting donations in Bitcoin and other virtual currencies, followed by Stormfront, Atomwaffen, Defend Europa, and individual alt-right celebrities/internet trolls Andrew Auernheimer and Christopher Cantwell. The week before the January 6, 2021, attacks on the U.S. Capitol, twenty-two individuals associated with the Far Right received $500,000 in Bitcoin transfers from a patron, Laurent Bachelier (a.k.a. Pankkake), in France.[85] Bitcoin appeals to ISIS financiers for different reasons: it can be done by its internet-savvy supporters in the Global North, it isn't tied to an enemy nation, and it might serve as a currency until its own plan for gold dinars is viable.[86] Hackers affiliated with ISIS demanded Bitcoin ransoms for stolen data; in 2017 Zoobia Shahnaz, a New York resident radicalized during volunteer work in Jordan, raised and dispatched $62,000 to ISIS using Bitcoin.[87] Theoretically, as long as one sovereign country is willing to exchange its currency for Bitcoin, this is a viable mechanism, but it is far easier to work in the Global North than a war zone in Syria. Someone has to go to an exchange location to get physical currency or take delivery of items ordered, and this is much more of a hassle than *hawalas* and other existing means.[88]

Bitcoin presents some other hazards. Transactions are irrevocable, so groups that change their plans, get scammed, or are hacked have no recourse. There's no password reset, so a VNSA has to share access to its wallet among multiple designated key financial personnel. In a sector with unexpected and violent leadership turnover, this poses significant risks. Quadriga, a Canadian cryptocurrency exchange, lost access to $250 million when its founder (and the only one with the key) died in India on his honeymoon.[89] Other account holders have simply forgotten their logins, lost them when a girlfriend rebooted the laptop, or been victimized by thieves.[90] Areas that invest in Bitcoin "farms" because of their access to cheap electricity risk their grid's stability as the servers draw excessive amounts of power to function. Chinese-run farms in Iran caused rolling blackouts in early 2021, causing a different kind of national security problem for countries willing to host them.[91]

Anonymity isn't guaranteed, either. There's no personally identifiable information, but unless someone has been remarkably disciplined in purchases, the ledgers, which are available and open, can show patterns of behavior leading back to customers definitively enough that courts accept such patterns as evidence. Narrow it down to one person, and his or her whole criminal transaction history is all laid out in the ledgers. In the arms race that is cryptography, services have popped up promising to obscure this purchase history while others develop data analysis programs to uncover it.

Human factors enter into it, too. Douglas Jackson, founder of E-gold, was hardcore for personal privacy right up until violating other peoples' privacy was a chance to save himself and his investments by helping the FBI in 2005. Some cryptocurrency wallet companies, like Coinbase, refuse to do business with known neo-Nazis or those who send money to affiliated accounts, while GhostSec, an offshoot of the hacker group Anonymous, is dedicated to hunting for ISIS-related transactions.[92] On the other side of the (virtual) coin, activists interested in preserving art and antiquities would like to develop blockchain ledgers for the ownership provenance of valuable items, establishing incontrovertible proof of who has what.[93]

■ Laundering through Things

In the immediate wake of 9/11, calls for anti–money laundering regulation were strong and broad, but this quickly faded as lobby after lobby—representing real estate agents, auction houses, art dealers, accountants, car dealers, and hedge fund managers—asked (and mostly got) exemptions that ended

Sixty-five million dollars in cash, discovered by law enforcement as part of an investigation of Los Angeles fashion industry companies participating in a trade-based money laundering operation for Mexican drug cartels, Los Angeles (2014). *U.S. Immigration and Customs Enforcement, Defense Visual Information Distribution Service*

up falling on traditional banks. Because of this, VNSAs have continued to move their money through a variety of loosely regulated large purchases and businesses. Ideally, as sleazy lawyer Saul Goodman explains in *Breaking Bad*, the best way to move money is through a "local institution, looked upon with favor by the Chamber of Commerce, the Better Business Bureau," one that handles a lot of cash and deals in a licit product whose value is wildly variable or subjective.[94] Because they don't actually have to make money, they can indulge a VNSA leader's artistic side, sponsor a member's rap recording career or monetize a hobby.[95]

Unlike board feet of standard lumber or grosses of iron pipe of a particular grade, the best laundering materials can be plausibly valued at the extreme end of comparable items. Cars and car lots are a favorite for just that reason—there's a Blue Book value and then there's the negotiated price with salt coating, leather bucket seats, adjustment for in-house financing, lost ground with aggressive salesperson, and the couple of thousand dollars in intangible cool. Most car dealers don't have to answer to anti–money laundering regulators, so some, as in Germany, offer a discount for paying in cash on the spot.[96] Movies are cool and incur inflated services under a Byzantine system of accounting that require legions of entertainment accounts and litigators, factors which made the industry attractive to Riza Aziz, the stepson of Malaysian prime minister Najib Razak, who ran millions from the nation's sovereign wealth fund through the production of, ironically, *The Wolf of Wall Street* (2013), while the Greek guerrilla VNSA 17N hid funds by investing in the decidedly less glamorous *Still Looking for Morphine* (2001). Hezbollah double-taps its propaganda asset, Al-Manar Television, to pad the expenses of an ongoing broadcast operation.[97]

Terrifying Los Zetas chief Miguel Trevino had a brilliant laundering operation going in Texas and Oklahoma for several years: quarter horses. Setting his younger brother, a bricklayer with a clean jacket and a lifelong dream of horse training, up with a bankroll, Trevino took advantage of a number of ideal conditions. The value of racing stock is highly subjective, can change on a single veterinary report, and involves endless investment in upkeep; the market in 2010 was one in which wealthy white hobbyists were pinched by drought and unlikely to question big spenders; and the market operates in a closed social circle of arcane expertise and social influencers.[98] When they named the horses things like "Number One Cartel," fellow trainers thought it was a joke, and auction houses getting big commissions didn't blink at the jacked-up prices and the shaky straw purchasers. Things only fell apart in the $1 million a month laundering plan when horse-loving brother Jose actually intended to breed and train winners, surfacing in 2010 with a stunning victory in a Ruidoso, New Mexico, race and claiming a large purse with public fanfare.[99]

Real estate can take a variety of useful forms for a VNSA. A cartel buying ranch land or forest justifies all kinds of expenses in labor and upkeep while allowing access to areas where drugs can be processed or key routes through which things can be smuggled. Spree purchases of condemned houses in urban centers serve as waystations for human trafficking. These can grant a leader status as a local caballero with political leverage or establish useful residency for legal purposes. At the high end, purchases of mansions and apartments in global centers like London, New York, and Vancouver are safe retreats for VNSA members who fear threats to themselves and their families or fear confiscation of their wealth. Use a shell company to buy a place in the Global North with solid property rights, park a couple of college-age relatives in it to maintain tax breaks and residency, and you've got an appreciating asset and personal fallback location.[100] The secondary effects are not subtle: cartel "narco-ranches" tear up ecosystems and do environmental damage that governments and activists are powerless to stop, and the straw purchasing of housing stock by nonresident owners is a major contributing factor to housing shortages and the unaffordability of the world's major cities.[101]

■ Offshore Banks and Shells

The tiny Principality of Monaco, reveling in its casino revenue, was probably the first deliberate tax haven, repealing personal income tax in 1869 and generously extending residency to visitors. The world wars spooked people into wanting safe places to stash their resources—and revealed that a lot of small countries like Liechtenstein or former colonies like Bermuda had little to build from except decent infrastructure and exposure to Global North–style business. Realizing that tourism wasn't enough, these countries' one big advantage was the "right to write their own laws," to their own benefit.[102] Sir James Mitchell, prime minister of St. Vincent and the Grenadines, was frank about it: "Harmful tax competition has nothing to do with drug money or money laundering. We're doing nothing that is illegal or immoral. Tax competition is really about whose treasury gets the money."[103] Being the next popular offshore haven is an arms race, with sovereign territories sweetening the deal by adding a drop-off service at the end of the airport runway (Anguilla), underwriting laws allowing companies to hold a huge untaxed "hedge" if they self-insure (Isle of Man), allowing incorporation in Cyrillic and Chinese characters (Tuvalu), or promising immunity from asset seizure or prosecution if the initial investment was $10 million (Seychelles).[104]

A by-product of offshore companies is the ability to register ships under the flag of a country with desirably lax tax regulations, safety standards, or employment procedures. Panama was a pioneer in this, flagging ships in the early twentieth century and officially making the registry for all Standard Oil tankers in 1919. Until 1941, the United States reregistered a large number of commercial ships there to supply Britain without technically violating neutrality. Other countries got into this lucrative business, including Liberia (whose registry was set up by Shell Oil and operates from New York, even during Liberia's civil war), Cyprus, Luxembourg (which is landlocked), and Honduras.[105] A similar registry exists for airplanes for the same reason, which Victor Bout and other smugglers, including the LTTE Sea Pigeons, exploit with abandon.[106]

Answering to a country that overtly does not care about responsibility for the operation of the ships and planes means that it can be captained by someone who wouldn't qualify for a license elsewhere, the crew can be treated like indentured servants and confined, and, if it is a cruise ship, crimes committed onboard against passengers—including rape—are extremely difficult to investigate and prosecute.[107] Recent questions about flags of convenience surfaced during debates over COVID-19 stimulus packages for the beleaguered tourist industry, with the eventual bill limiting funds to ships registered in the United States and leading to a tax investigation by the state of Michigan, which has lost a large chunk of revenue because former secretary of education Betsy DeVos' yacht is registered in the Cayman Islands but docked in the Great Lakes.[108]

Until people are adversely affected by a shell company—like the parents who found out that the amusement park where an unsafe ride decapitated their child held insurance run from the Cayman Islands and was legally untouchable—most regard them with indulgence and don't connect them with undermining the tax base or being used by a VNSA, just a clever way to evade the IRS or Inland Revenue.[109] Tax advisers to even the modestly well-off know how to set up domestic corporate registrations in friendly states to hide money in a divorce, pay a minimum amount of tax, or benefit from incentives for a particular industry. It's easy to go more exotic and farther offshore, as Australian researchers found out when they tested whether providers would ask for ID or question suspicious incorporation plans.[110] Companies have no reason to curtail offshore incorporation since they can use it to commit fraud in eco-certification and carbon-trading schemes, defer payments of export duties to a shell, or cheat their outside shareholders, like Enron and Parmalat.[111] Microsoft learned that Ireland's much-beloved protection for the income of writers and artists could, legally speaking, cover software and moved their overseas distribution there in 2005.[112]

Being a tax haven has a profound effect on the society. VIPs, including representatives of the Big 4 accounting firms, live in isolated compounds, defiant of local laws and indulging in other criminal acts, including prostitution, drugs, and child trafficking, which corrode the fabric of the small population. Reformers and critics are quickly shunned, with the standard answer to questions of propriety being, "There's always a boat in the morning."[113] A number of havens sell their passports, affording VNSAs non-extradition safe spaces as well as a new and dangerous wrinkle: These sovereign nations are, in order to get a free global diplomatic corps, allowing new passport holders from Russia, China, and substate criminal organizations to represent them and use the diplomatic bags to transport goods in a way that cannot be opened or searched.[114] Looking at it another way, an offshore haven has outsourced its foreign policy, its votes at the United Nations, and its diplomatic privileges to the highest bidder.

Reforming or curtailing the activities of offshore havens faces significant obstacles. People, especially people with resources to lobby their political representatives, enjoy having the ability to control whether they pay taxes. State clandestine services use shell companies and offshore banks to funnel money to their operations and don't want to lose the depot function they serve. Countries dependent on jobs and income from banks and shell companies might be treated as though these financial products are coca and offered a "crop substitution program," although it would be unpalatable to most countries able to sponsor such an effort and just drive illicit activity to the next haven.[115] Sweden and Norway have demonstrated that having a public tax register showing beneficial shares, wealthy people, and their positions in trusts and accounts and ownership of shares and bonds generates more in tax revenue than the bureaucracy costs to regulate it, but it was only in 2020 that the United States legislated a requirement (part of the National Defense Authorization Act) to ban anonymous shell companies. It's far from a panacea: The registry isn't public, just with the Treasury, and is limited to those incorporated in a U.S. state.[116]

■ Grand Corruption

Most kleptocracies, whether VNSAs or in official power, have exit strategies. Like Ozymandias, the foundations will crumble, the peasants will get enraged, the failsons will piss off the wrong family, or the multinational company paying the oil leases will get fed up with the human rights abuses and its effect on their public relations. Having a nicely feathered nest somewhere with nice beaches, rule of law, sophisticated medical facilities, Swiss accounts, and a plane ready to carry the national gold reserve off into exile is the best plan for surviving (or sending the most competent son) to return in triumph another day.[117]

Many of my military students have been deployed to Africa or Southeast Asia and come back struck by the vast disparity of the resources (cobalt, oil, diamonds) that groups there are fighting over and the extremely low standard of living for the majority of the population. It's easy to get sucked into simplistic arguments spun off from Jared Diamond's book *Guns, Germs, and Steel* that there's just something lacking in the people who live there, some genetic or cultural character flaw, so no matter how much Global North aid goes south, things just fester.[118] The numbers tell a staggeringly different story: For every $1 of aid, the Global North gets back $10 illegally in capital flow, resources, and money looted from the public treasuries of developing countries and their citizens and stashed away in banks and expensive real estate. World Bank estimates a loss of $20–40 billion every year, or a 25 percent loss of Africa's gross domestic product, with increased inefficiencies from bribes and poor infrastructure.[119]

Toleration of open corruption and stripping of assets, "eating the sweat" of the people, infests a whole society, building resentment, undermining belief in democracy, and breaking down public goods like education and medical care.[120] This is prime VNSA territory, operating between an indifferent state and a desperate people. ISIS reveled in the Panama Papers exposé, tweeting, "Arab tyrants stole the wealth of the Muslims and allied themselves with the infidels against Muslims." Driving past ornate palaces every day in Tunisia enraged a taxi driver into the belief that only a return to austere and harsh religious reform would accomplish anything. Boko Haram fighters in DDR programs recall with white-hot rage having to pay bribes to get into school or seeing their sisters pimped out to get favorable judgments in court cases.[121] This kind of experience is what psychologists describe as a moral injury, traumatic events that violate a person's deeply held values.[122]

How did things get this way? During the Cold War, the answer was security. Franklin Roosevelt's attitude to strongman Anastasio Somoza in Nicaragua was that "he's a son of a bitch, but he's *our* son of a bitch."[123] Being the only competent and pro-Western military in a region, standing firm against communism, overthrowing a left-leaning government, or preventing resources from being nationalized bought a lot of indulgence and propped up a horrifying cast of torturers, dictators, and grotesques. Allowing them to skim off resources was a reward for leading rebel armies and creating a nice slush fund to fend off coups and keep wealth out of the hands of any challengers or potential successors.

With the end of the Cold War new governments were left hamstrung by old deals, like Mobutu Sese Seko selling off future contracts for the Congo's mines, and Baby Doc Duvalier having dismantled Haiti's rail system for scrap and pocketed the money.[124] The new ticket to steal was controlling vital resources. The United States, which had closed its embassy in Equatorial Guinea in 1995 over human rights violations by the Obiang presidential family, reopened it in 2002 when the country tapped new oil wells and it became a viable alternative to OPEC sources. In 2006 the ruling family of Congo-Brazzaville came to New York to renegotiate their debt with the World Bank but partied so conspicuously at the Waldorf Astoria that Paul Wolfowitz, speaking as president of World Bank, wanted to stop the deal. Quickly, France organized a defense among francophone countries, arguing that it was vital to "stay engaged with stakeholders," which bank staff angrily translated as "continue to give money to crooks."[125]

After the first Gulf war, Saddam Hussein and his family understood that they would lose any subsequent conventional conflict. They began preparing for exile and a guerrilla comeback by looting $10 billion from the Oil for Food program, smuggling cigarettes and kickbacks and using what half brother

Barzan al-Tikriti didn't run to Swiss banks to create weapons caches around the country. Saddam himself didn't survive to benefit from these preparations, but the training and resources established through grand corruption fueled former regime elements and their militias in Al-Anbar and then Syria.[126]

Jonas Savimbi, unhappy with his share of the take in a newly elected government, restarted the Angolan civil war in 1994 with his $4 billion in hoarded diamond money. Grand corruption by disgruntled elites bankrolled anti-Mobutu and anti-Kabila rebels in the Democratic Republic of the Congo and the Revolutionary United Front in Sierra Leone.[127] Second bananas can get in on the act and plan for their promotions, like various Kim relatives in North Korea, the children of Gen. Sani Abacha of Nigeria, intelligence chief Vladimiro Montesinos of Peru, or Prime Minister Pavlo Lazarenko of Ukraine. Even if the efforts fail, dying in bed with a luxury view is far better than a jail cell, as the Shah of Iran, Mobutu, and Ferdinand Marcos experienced.[128]

With a few exceptions, this mindboggling amount of money is not buried in a dusty hole in the ground. It's in banks located in Global North countries with strong rule of law and bank secrecy norms, where helpful asset managers record that Gabon's president, Omar Bongo, is "self-made because of position. Country is oil producer" and take as a given that a regime relative with a $200,000 a year civil-service appointment obviously came by the millions honestly. When pressed, the bank will refuse to repatriate funds and shield transactions from legal scrutiny. These portfolios are staggering, with one individual often holding more than the total external debt of the nation it was stolen from, aided by cheerful private bankers who shuffle accounts across shell companies and consider that they've done enough due diligence. In 2006 a congressional committee asked executives at Citibank to freeze and examine wire transactions from the Obiangs to various luxury goods dealers and banks but were told that "identifying, freezing and investigating these transfers would generate too much work for its anti-money laundering staff."[129]

Most of the time, new regimes lack the international pull, expertise, and resources to pursue recovering looted assets or don't want to risk antagonizing the people who stole them into attempting a dangerous comeback.[130] In the aftermath of the Arab Spring, Swiss banks proved unusually willing to freeze assets, followed by the British government's hold on real estate and accounts. Some of the absconded officials, like Hosni Mubarak's confidant Hussein Salem, have cut deals for amnesty abroad in return for giving back portions of their haul, while Qatar brokered the return of money to Egypt from a Lebanese bank in return for a right of first refusal buying some of the repatriated assets. The World Bank trains investigators under its Stolen Asset Recovery Initiative, but some success has been experienced by freelance lawyers working on contingency and expecting a cut of the money found and recovered. One of these freelancers, Mohamed Shaban, found that a £10 million mansion in London owned by Saadi Gaddafi via a British Virgin Islands shell company was up for grabs because, in the chaos of regime change, the Gaddafis failed to pay a $500 renewal fee, leaving the shell company without jurisdiction to protect it.[131]

The U.S. Department of Justice's Kleptocracy Asset Recovery Initiative, launched in 2010, assisted in the return of $480 million to the people of Nigeria from accounts held by the Sani Abacha family: $115 million to Kazakhstan, $28 million to South Korea as a result of bribery stings, and $22 million for Peru. The most striking success, however, was in reaching an agreement in 2014 with Equatorial Guinea for the forfeiture of one of the Obaing sons' Malibu mansion, sports cars, and assorted collectibles. including "six Michael Jackson Neverland Ranch Life Sized Statues" and a Jackson sequined glove. Real estate is easy to resell, but six Michael Jackson statues?[132] The hazard of repatriating money, though, is making sure it doesn't just go back into elite pockets. The Philippine government, after years of litigation, got back $624 million from the Marcos' Swiss accounts but promptly plowed the money into projects riddled with corruption. Attempts to lessen Angola's national debt through refinancing continue to enrich its former ruling family, whose entourage takes cuts from handling parts of the restructuring.[133]

Jack Blum, a former special counsel to the U.S. Senate Relations Committee, offered a sweeping Occam's razor in the interest of national security: "Bribery and theft would end if the international community agreed to find and repatriate the money. . . . The impact of such a coordinated campaign would be immeasurable; every other corrupt official on the continent would worry that his ill-gotten gains were no longer safe."[134] The release of the Panama Papers, revealing that Western leaders, including British prime minister David

Cameron, were neck-deep in shell companies themselves, highlighted that creditor countries use aid withholding and austerity provisions in International Monetary Fund loans to enforce good governance while actively benefiting from features that promote and sustain bad governance. Making politically exposed people keep their wealth within reach of their own regulators is a good lever for responsible behavior, which could be further pushed by Global North legislation like requiring public disclosure of beneficial ownership or tighter issuance of U.S. EB-5 investor visas.[135]

More optimistic people would like to use carrots instead of sticks. The internet offers anonymous portals to report officials who take bribes, like Bangalore's IPaidaBribe.com, which also allows citizen spotters to praise offices that did not ask for a bribe. In Bogotá, carefully calibrated public theater performances organized by the mayor employed mimes to harass and mock traffic violators who were accustomed to paying bribes to avoid fines. The Mo Ibrahim Prize, donated by the Sudanese founder of telecom giant Celtel, rewards African heads of state with the largest annual cash award in the world ($5 million over ten years, then $200,000 yearly for life) if they retire and support a peaceful democratic transition of power. All these efforts work toward a broad reshaping of norms aiming at financial transparency and replacing personal profit with an ethic of public service.[136]

8
COMMODITIES

Business really took off after *Titanic*. The "Heart of the Ocean" gem isn't really a blue diamond, it's tanzanite. The beautiful precious stone, discovered in 1967, exists only in a five-mile patch of ground in northern Tanzania.[1] In the 1990s professional marketers began promoting tanzanite aggressively, especially in the United States, inventing a mythology in which Masai tribes people believed it to be the creation of the gods via a lightning strike and sentimentalizing it as a special tribute to new mothers—which, translated into the American market, meant "push presents" to reward a woman for enduring childbirth. This boosted sales on home shopping networks and in cruise ship gift shops, making it a commodity embraced by middle America.[2]

While the American buying public was reeling from 9/11, journalists Robert Block and Daniel Pearl published an exposé alleging that al-Qaeda was acquiring tanzanite and moving the stones to Dubai in order to fund their operations and launder money, with the transactions taking place at a radicalized mosque in Mererani. Daniel Pearl's subsequent kidnapping and murder by al-Qaeda members added gravity to this peripheral story, and alarm spread among retailers.[3] QVC, Walmart, Zales, and Tiffany & Co. had already canceled orders and suspended sales ahead of the 2001 Christmas season, cutting off 80 percent of the global market for the gem, with severe economic consequences for miners and dealers in Tanzania.[4] By February 2002, lawyers representing the families of 9/11 victims sued in federal court, seeking to force STS Jewels and the Tanzanite Mineral Dealers' Association to stop trading in the commodity and to turn over all profits from previous sales to a supervised compensation fund, plus $1 billion in compensatory damages.[5]

The government of Tanzania, afraid of losing the needed revenue, immediately started working with U.S. distributors to formulate an agreement patterned on the Kimberley Process negotiated two years earlier to certify diamonds. The resulting Tucson Tanzanite Protocol requires the government to license and issue identification to tanzanite miners and to ensure "transparency and accountability in the supply chain" as well as "warranties . . . to be required of exporters and all those in the downstream chain of commerce." While this imposed order on the market, it also forced individual miners into compliance with a state monopoly, without which they couldn't sell their uncertified and undocumented finds.[6] The plan worked, consumers forgot about the al-Qaeda panic, and, today only, a 14k gold tanzanite and diamond oval cut ring can be yours for three easy payments of $341.67.

■ The Resource Curse?

Surely a recently decolonized nation with oil wells or a diamond funnel must be in want of nothing. Angola, Sierra Leone, Liberia, Congo-Brazzaville, Democratic Republic of the Congo—all of them have dazzling natural resources but have staggered politically as failed states, unable to turn their mineral wealth into consistently functional governments. By the 1970s, development economists started labeling this dilemma the "resource curse" or, as in a 1977 *Economist* article about the discovery of North Sea oil, "the Dutch Disease": a country in possession of a valuable commodity will suffer inflation of its currency, which damages any other exportable production, and will neglect other industry.[7] This "blessing" can then spiral out into other damaging habits, like high unemployment even in the resource extraction sector (because the jobs go to foreigners), boom and bust cycles of spending and austerity, and lack of even reinvestment in diversification and social welfare. Longitudinal studies of national economies point to stability and internal cohesion coming from trade and exports of manufactured goods, while the opposite stem from commodities, which tend to produce poverty and political instability or, as Zambian president Kenneth Kaunda described it, the "curse of being born with a copper spoon in our mouths."[8]

The most dangerous temptation is corruption: A government that sees the resources as patrimonial or belonging to the ruling family or ethnic group is likely to keep them to themselves and their cronies. Multinational companies mining or drilling are happy to assist in stashing the proceeds of whoever is going to allow them the freest access, with the result that economic inequality balloons, rapid modernization undermines traditional forms of social control, and a few get rich while the rest get left behind. An instantly wealthy state may have desperate requirements that can be fulfilled with the proceeds of the bonanza, but these needs are too often carried out with no-bid contracts to outsiders, unsustainable infrastructure investments, and parachuted in without the domestic social or bureaucratic support necessary to maintain them. A leader who can essentially grant wishes and is accountable to nothing but a Global North mining company is at high risk for opposition and instability.

Along with corruption, vulnerabilities keep raining down. Many commodities like oil and rare earth minerals are tied to volatile price fluctuations on the world market. A state relying on consistent income from its natural bounty can get caught out by crashes in the value of their exports and on the hook for payments to bondholders and domestic creditors. Humanitarian relief agencies respond to hurricanes and earthquakes but not the equally disruptive problems caused by price shocks, so the usual remedy is International Monetary Fund or World Bank programs that demand drastic austerity cuts to already shaky social services, pensions, and bureaucracy. Without a domestic check on how the bonanza is handled—the ability to audit the income, assess the commodity, and provide public scrutiny of how the revenue is spent—the state has lost crucial leverage in negotiating with buyers and lost control even of the basic knowledge of how much is being produced. A traditional source of state legitimacy is the ability of a government to extract tax revenue from its population in a social contract that most people support. Being a "rentier" state lets the government out of needing to be accountable to its citizens, who may enjoy some of the benefits of the boom times but have nothing and no lever of power when the bust arrives.

A government that fears dissent might endow its secret police and military with independent funding in perpetuity from the commodity. The Indonesian military draws most of its budget from timber contracts on land it controls as well as from long-term oil, gas, and mineral leases. Since the late 1960s the Chilean military received 10 percent of Codelco's copper export revenue, a move set up by the Eduardo Frei government "to have an automatic appropriation rather than having to debate and justify the full military budget every year."[9] This creates an extraordinarily dangerous problem: armed people who, no matter the regime, have no budgetary check on their activities and complete autonomy from an elected legislature, the courts, and executive supervision. A monopoly of force like this, once established, is extremely difficult to force back into the bottle and can operate as a kingmaker, placing in power whoever lets them do as they please.

This process isn't exclusive to the developing world. I had a front row seat to the Bakken Formation fracking boom in North Dakota, and the parallels were striking. The satirical site *The Onion* ran a piece framing the story as if writing about a Global South petrostate, with the alarming detail that they had their own nuclear missiles and Western counties full of religious extremists, "as [Governor] Hoeven is using the nuclear program as a bargaining chip to gain badly needed economic benefits for his state. Hardly at the forefront of technology, in other aspects North Dakota has a largely rural population and a child poverty rate of 14%."[10] Meant as parody, it wasn't all that far off—the one-party state allowed extractive industry to carry off the proceeds without plans to do development with the tax revenue, demanding that companies construct infrastructure to carry the oil trucks or any supporting services for the itinerant workers who brought with them all the negative accessories of mostly male boomtowns. Peaking in 2012 and dropping downhill with lowered demand, the state is holding the bag on bonded projects, dumps of waste material, abandoned "man camps," and social problems. In this case, federal aid in the form of the EPA and FBI stepped in, and the nuclear "potholes" owned by the U.S. Air Force were never in dispute, but the temptations of a resource windfall are too much for even Global North areas.[11]

In 1998 economists Paul Collier and Anke Hoeffler put into print what development experts had long suspected, that dependence on a commodity ups the risk of violent conflict for a country, especially if the resource tips over 26 percent of the gross domestic product. With the additional factors of available diasporas, neighboring state sponsors, and a recent history of civil war, the fracas is just a spark away.[12] There are contributing factors, like where the resource is located and whether it is easily "lootable" or requires major expertise and infrastructure to remove, but overall, the resource curse seems to predispose a state to trouble unless carefully managed. Collier and his various collaborators have grouped these conflicts under the famous dichotomy "greed or grievance," a term later expanded to "need, greed, or creed" by subsequent scholarship.[13]

Greed is the easiest narrative to see. Rebel leaders snatching and grabbing an alluvial diamond field or an oil refinery is something that policymakers want to respond to, painting the VNSA as illegitimate in their self-aggrandizing aims, as bandits and criminals who can be defeated without concessions. Certainly, some of the conflicts are driven by VNSAs whose aims are to replace the existing patronage networks and place at the trough with themselves, and whose orientation is remediating their sense of "relative deprivation" versus the opulent leaders they see.[14] The greed motivation, though, papers over the complexity of wicked problems in favor of blaming political chaos on moneygrubbing rebels. Without the sharp bifurcation of cold war ideology, grievances are messy and sometimes intractable. Reporters and researchers who do their investigations based in a capitol city can miss the depth of the fractures in a state as well as the subtle differences among ethnic groups, political factions, and peripheral resentments. The grievance can be from a resource region against a far-off administrative center, especially if the elite are of a different religion or tribe, against an exploitative multinational company that pollutes the river and has the collusion of the authorities, perhaps a whole region that feels able to secede and go it alone on the basis of their resource base, or purely belief-based as a state tries to institute a national education system or dominant religion and real offense is taken.

Regardless of whether greed or grievance gets a conflict rolling, having a resource commodity within reach certainly fuels its continuation. A manufacturing facility can relocate if the conflict becomes too disruptive, but a commodity is location-specific, allowing an otherwise rural and poor population to overcome the problems of starting up a VNSA and enter a fight with a chance against a state entity. No matter how deep in the jungle, isolated in the mountains or hidden in desert caves, a VNSA with diamonds to pay for rocket-propelled grenades will find eager brokers ready to deliver, forge end-use certificates, launder the proceeds, and obscure the methods by which the gems came out of the ground, especially if the commodity is one that can't be easily tracked to the source. By 1995 the Revolutionary United Front (RUF) in Sierra Leone controlled assets worth more than $200 million a year, fighting a government that could only access $60 million to pay troops and finance its defense. This kind of deep pocket allows a VNSA to out-compete a state for recruitment, sustain operations over a long conflict, and even cause disruption that makes the commodity they control more valuable on the world market. Like other conflicts we've seen, this ability to continue and to accumulate assets can change the orientation of the VNSA from grievance to continuing an insurgency or civil war as a "satisfactory way of life."[15]

The form of commodity and how it is processed make a big difference in the way a VNSA organizes itself to use it as financing and affects how it treats the population around it (for whom it may be claiming to fight). A resource that is findable and accessible to unskilled diggers or raiders, like an oil pipeline or alluvial diamonds that can be found with a water sifter, gives rise to VNSAs that have rapidly changing leadership structures since any officer with ambition can brutalize a group of civilians and soldiers to pan for gems or steal truckloads of crude and challenge a leader. An offshore platform or something requiring deep-shaft mining by a company with extractive tools puts money into the hands of a figurehead who is the conduit to outside support and insulated from both his subordinates and needing to interact with the locals, although VNSAs in retreat have found that the population they ignored when raking in the multinational contracts is unforgiving and uninterested when their assistance is needed.

Those corporate contracts take the form of the charmingly named "booty futures," which VNSAs can use as unofficial war bonds for their activities. Laurent-Désiré Kabila bragged that rebellion in Zaire is easy; even a VNSA in a weak position can march on the capital with $10,000 and a satellite phone, hire some cheap soldiers to keep the group afloat, and speed-dial companies and weapons dealers. At least five VNSAs in Africa did this between 1989 and 2004, throwing gasoline on conflicts that might have otherwise fizzled out.[16] During the Nigerian Civil War, it was an open secret that Banque Rothschild was running a line of credit for Biafra, based on the promise of oil futures, while Katanga separatists in the Congo in 1960 received aid from the Belgian mining company Union Manière du Haut-Katanga in exchange for exclusive access. More recently, Charles Taylor extorted millions from U.K. African Mining Consortium Ltd. and France's Société Lorraine de Laminage Continu (Sollac), which wanted iron ore from an area he controlled on the Liberian–Guinea border.[17] Companies in the Global North, shielded by distance, rarely have to deal with the VNSAs they fund, although the Houston headquarters of oil company Unocal ordered their secretaries to dress modestly on the days Taliban representatives arrived to negotiate in 1996.[18] The Panama Papers have revealed the snarl of commitments into which winning rebels have dragged down their states, mortgaging vital commodities decades in advance to pay for AK-47s dropped on a battlefield decades ago, and the extent to which this has been a regular business practice for extractive industries.

The company that Kabila called on his satellite phone, American Mineral Fields of Canada, underwrote his victory, but he then either couldn't or wouldn't enforce the deal he made for mining rights. Corporate policy that encompasses "booty futures" is prepared for this eventuality—firms doing business in the Global South this way have identified a special niche, being willing to go into conflict zones where there are few competitors and reaping the bargains, even setting up deals to be purchased by larger companies who require clean hands and don't want to know too much about how the concessions were secured. Under threat that the deal would be abrogated or the mines nationalized, a company can hire its very own VNSA, a private military company (PMC), to secure the facility or overthrow the VNSA that overthrew the government and install someone more friendly.

In the 1990s the most infamous of these PMCs was Executive Outcomes, which recruited from the recently downsized South African secret police and border guards, known for their brutality and creativity with sanction evasion and dissident suppression (in the Civil Cooperation Bureau, no less), but the field teemed with recently redundant KGB officers, angry cold warriors, and a variety of eccentric oddballs and expat mercenaries, even Gurkhas. Quickly dug into the illicit economy of the region, the PMCs were in demand by NGOs and visiting VIPs as bodyguards and as partners in a whole spectrum of ventures that could consider the buy-in the equivalent of protection money. Obviously, these guys answered to no one but their employer's bottom line, and often—unsupervised in the peripheries of the Global South—not even that.

Possession of resources makes ending conflicts more difficult since a government military has to drive the VNSA completely out of the area where it is or prevent the profitable export of the yield. Neighbors who benefit from the export probably won't help cut it off, and rebels dependent on the commodity will have arranged their own assets around holding and protecting it. Peace settlements, like that in Sierra Leone, may have to include rebel leaders in the new government: Foday Sankoh, chief of the RUF, demanded a cabinet-level job as Minister of Mines in 1999, which would have allowed him to reignite hostilities any time he didn't get his way. The government chose to enlist help from the United Kingdom and a coalition of neighbors, the Economic Community of West African State Monitoring Group, to defeat RUF more conclusively. "Rewarding" VNSAs by buying them out or off to get them to the negotiating table can be politically fraught and deeply unpopular with the survivors of their brutality but is critical to permanently disarming and reorienting them as productive participants in the country's political process.

Cleanup from resource-funded wars can be expensive and extensive. Death squads of young people need to be demilitarized and put to work, rebel leverage over the resource needs to be untangled from national finances, and PMCs must be pried out of local businesses and sent home. Countries have to build a sense of shared purpose and identity, justifying shared access to the payout from resources, which can be hard if there are long-standing cleavages of ethnic and religious persecution and exclusion. VNSAs probably didn't follow safety or environmental rules while maximizing output from their commodity source, so years of toxic waste cleanup, replanting of forests, or restocking of fisheries might be necessary with funding from the United Nations or humanitarian groups. One of the most productive moves is to diversify the economy, building but not depending entirely on a commodity. Uganda's post-conflict promotion of coffee opened up the haulage industry, and government supervision broke the hold a corrupt cartel had over the industry, allowing other applications, like small farm production, to market their goods competitively.[19]

If a post-conflict administration can achieve buy-in, wealth sharing may be an answer to prevent a resurgence of the VNSA. In Papua New Guinea and Timor-Leste, resource wealth goes into a sovereign wealth fund, which calculates long-term sustainability of the windfall moneys and pays out investments in infrastructure, social welfare, and building human capital, all meant to cushion shocks in the commodities market and spread around the benefits. This was similar to the approach taken by Gov. Jay Hammond in establishing Alaska's permanent fund in 1982, which gives residents a stake in the petroleum generated.[20] These payments, which some countries tie to desirable behavior, like sending children to school or cooperating with public health initiatives, put cash into the economy at ground level, spurring local businesses and allowing people to make meaningful decisions about their spending. The government, meanwhile, develops a tax base, which builds the kind of citizenship that hopefully avoids civil wars.

Not many Global South countries have the technical expertise or startup capital to handle the resources entirely on their own, so they remain dependent on companies that had a hand in the conflict. Few profit-motivated firms will be joyful at the prospect of disavowing booty futures or committing to transparent reporting of revenue but can be pushed in that direction by Global North regulation like the United Kingdom's Extractive Industry Transparency Initiative and the Publish What You Pay campaign against corruption. Registers of beneficial ownership cut through layers of shell companies and subsidiaries, but corporate entities have to be held accountable by both shareholders willing to profit less and national jurisdictions willing to enforce standards and withdraw the benefits of national residence if the firm plays arbitrage to find a location where they're allowed to continue to act as they like. In an interesting development, the International Criminal Court is likely to expand criminal culpability from the Nuremburg case of IG Farben to wider corporate responsibility for genocide and war crimes.[21]

■ Blood Diamonds

Diamonds are probably the world's most perfect smuggled commodity. Months of output fits into the false bottom of a briefcase, there's a global structure of distribution and grading, and for the foreseeable future, a corporate monopoly manages the overall supply to maintain a demand and relatively constant price. Unless subjected to extensive chemical testing, a cut, polished, and mounted diamond is almost impossible to track back to its source, allowing VNSAs to mix their supply with stones from other supply chains. Diamonds don't alert sniffer dogs in airports, and they are processed in centers like Antwerp, where the local government has little interest in prosecuting crimes that took place on the other side of the world.[22] VNSAs can force people under their control to pan diamonds out of a river or only dabble in the trade to move money from a conflict zone to a Swiss bank, secure that—more than any other commodity—diamonds are, in the words of a former De Beers chair, "less susceptible to dangers from UN sanctions."[23]

VNSAs with access to the source can use them to fund their activities directly. The RUF in Sierra Leone had safe haven over the border in Liberia because Samuel Taylor fully expected the RUF to seize diamond fields from which he'd get a generous share. In the aftermath of Mobutu's government in the Democratic Republic of the Congo, invading troops from Uganda and Rwanda made deals with local rebels to leave them in control in return for diamonds. Jonas Savimbi's UNITA in Angola turned to looting diamond-producing regions once Cold War subsidies dried up in 1990 and bought new friends in the heads of state of Burkina Faso, Togo, and Zaire.[24] The VNSA is probably only getting 10 percent of the diamonds' value on the global market, but they just don't care—there are always more. Arms dealers like Victor Bout started bringing along a certified gemologist to make estimates of the handfuls of stones offered from sacks or safes, once indulging the whim of

Congolese warlord Jean-Pierre Bemba, who dispatched a flight crew with a fistful of diamonds just to bring him cold beer.[25]

Even without a VNSA, diamonds in an alluvial field are a resource curse. Anyone with a $15 shaker screen and a shovel can try their luck, creating a corrosive social order where fortune makes instant wealth and undermines traditional deference and control. Sierra Leone had struggled to control and tax their diamond fields before the civil war, but efforts foundered on their inability to know what was coming out of the ground and where it was going—in 1988, official diamond exports were $22,000 while diamond merchants in the Global North were buying many times that.[26] This obvious government weakness was a siren song to rebels there and in the Congo, who had ample demonstrations of the inability of the authorities to control its own territory. Once a conflict is under way, the VNSA can extort diamonds mined by prospectors or use their monopoly of force to coerce local people to do it for them, beheading and maiming the disobedient and driving off anyone who won't comply. A few diamonds at a time, this added up to an estimated $25–125 million every year for the RUF.[27]

Diamonds in a funnel—that is, requiring deep-shaft mining and expensive equipment—can be used by a VNSA but usually require a deal with a corporation to handle the expert engineering and operational funds. Extraction companies, sometimes with their own PMCs, kept the production churning, isolating their executives and management in safe enclaves and paying the rebels or the government, or both, to smooth the way. Regardless of the company that did the mining, 85 percent of all diamonds are sold to De Beers, a monopoly established by Cecil Rhodes in 1888. Headquartered in London, De Beers' power was such that it had no qualms about fronting for the apartheid South African government through its banks, ignoring the U.S. Justice Department's investigation of price fixing by just withdrawing all but three employees from American soil, and operating a "no questions asked" sourcing policy when UNITA turned up with gems.[28]

Once sold, diamonds make very useful laundering mechanisms for moving money. This is such a well-understood tactic that in 1940, when the Nazis swept through Belgium, British intelligence subsidized the transplant of the diamond brokering industry from Antwerp to Palestine, where they busily used the system throughout World War II (as did the Stern Gang and Irgun). In West Africa, a Lebanese Shia diaspora has been handling diamonds since the 1970s, and Hezbollah has tapped into the network at their convenience, with personnel moving back and forth from Sierra Leone to Beirut engaging in licit and VNSA-backed business. In 1999, after the Clinton administration froze millions of dollars in Taliban assets in Global North banks, al-Qaeda began transferring money from dollars into diamonds as a hedge against seizure.[29] Even though the network is Shia, diamond brokers were willing to do trades with Sunni al-Qaeda operatives, and in May 2003 Charles Taylor of Liberia not only welcomed but harbored members of the VNSA who came to use Lebanese middlemen to buy leftover surface-to-air missiles with gems.[30]

In the late 1990s rumors of these financial mechanisms and exposés by NGOs like Global Witness sparked interest in regulation of the diamond market. In the United States a bipartisan bill in the House of Representatives, written by Frank Wolf (R-Va.) and Tony Hall (D-Ohio) after a fact-finding trip to West Africa, languished in Congress until 9/11 and more substantial reports that al-Qaeda was hustling diamonds, despite the 2000 Fowler Report issued by the United Nations.[31] De Beers judged that they needed to cooperate lest they face harsher measures and engaged in the negotiations that produced the Kimberley Process in 2002. Producing countries must label and certify stones, guarantee that they are not financing VNSAs, and exclude nonsignatories from their trade to avoid mixing in illicit gems. Monitoring authorities mandated tamper-proof transport cases, national legislatures wrote statutes with penalties for failing to abide by the rules, and statistics were kept of exports.[32]

The Kimberley Process, though, is far from perfect. Zimbabwe, which is a signatory, uses diamonds as an unbudgeted and off-the-books financing stream for their military and secret police, who violently seized fields in the Marange region in 2008, murdering hundreds of artisanal miners in the process. Large companies used the process as justification for crackdowns on rivals and small-scale miners, forcing them into deals to the advantage of the firm, and have done nothing about the other ugly features of the industry—child labor, safety problems, and coerced workers—so long as the money isn't obviously going to a VNSA.[33] De Beers, meanwhile, had a path through which they could offload their huge stockpile of diamonds as "clean" even though, inevitably, most of them were previously acquired conflict diamonds from Liberia, Sierra Leone, and Angola.[34]

Consumers, when they aren't millennials killing the fine jewelry industry, seem to have forgotten the Blood Diamonds campaigns and trust the Kimberley Process to deliver "clean" engagement rings and aggressively marketed "eternity rings" and "chocolate diamonds" in addition to the wedding traditions marketing departments created in the 1930s. De Beers stood up the "Peace Diamonds" initiative in partnership with NGOs like Catholic Relief Services to put diamond profits back into communities where the gems originate and encourage "peace and prosperity," but Global Witness dropped out as a cosponsor in 2011 after DeBeers continued to buy from Zimbabwe.[35] An alternate model exists in the experience of Botswana, which, from the first identification of its diamond mines shortly after independence from Britain, considered the mines a public good, carving out shrewd deals with De Beers (including demanding two seats on the board of directors) and plowing the money into health care and education. It's a matter of national pride and identity that Botswana's first president outwitted the mining companies and turned a resource curse into the catapult into prosperity.[36]

▪ Black Gold, Texas Tea

Possessing petroleum became a strategic national asset in the mid-nineteenth century, accelerating into a necessity for modern warfare and developed economies by the first decades of the twentieth. A labor-intensive industry, one tank of gasoline equals the 24/7 labor of one hundred people for a month, and in the early twenty-first century, methods to get at the most remote reservoirs in the ground cost a barrel of fuel for every five retrieved. Despite this cost, oil doesn't go bad; has multiple uses, including in the plastics and artificial fertilizer industry; and will be soaked up somewhere in the global economy no matter how bloody the extraction. Most of the time, oil is the province of a nation-state and large corporations like titan Standard Oil, with vertical monopolies on every stage of its discovery, extraction, and distribution.[37] As discussed with other commodities, an oil discovery has the dangerous potential to warp the society and economy around dependence on a single, volatile commodity, linking a state to boom and bust cycles, corruption, and detachment from other kinds of development and accountability to its citizens. State failure to handle oil revenue in a way perceived as fair can spark civil war, as it did in Biafra, or it can briefly enable the promise of radical economic justice made by a dictator like Gaddafi in Libya, or it can set up the catastrophic state collapse of Venezuela over three generations of "corruption, mismanagement, and an inability to effectively sow the seeds of oil wealth for future generations."[38]

Oil within the reach of a VNSA is a powerful financial tool—to export, extort, smuggle, resell, or leverage for outside sponsorship—although it comes with significant disadvantages as a payment mechanism. The Kurds of Northern Iraq owe their autonomy to oil fields but can't control the export process because of the necessity of sending the oil through pipelines owned by the Iraqi state, curtailing both the revenue and their decision-making. Chechen militia leaders with literal backyard oil wells sold their crude to Russian enemy commanders, who had already bargained away their official draw of Ministry of Defense fuel to pay enough salary to keep their troops loyal so that Chechens were enabling their own opposition.[39] Irregular armed groups in post-Gaddafi Libya hold tiny petro-fiefs but lack the organizational power or logistics capabilities of the National Oil Corporation and get what they can from smuggling to Mediterranean ports. Most dangerously, a VNSA that makes moves on oil territory in the expectation that a weak state can't stop them may well bring on the attention of a Great Power that can, or an angry company with its own mercenaries.[40]

ISIS, keenly cognizant of the value of petroleum, targeted oil fields for conquest, reaping a commodity asset as well as denying it to the state they took it from. Absorbing them as VNSA property allowed them to collect staggering amounts of money, as much as $300–500 million a year, making them likely the wealthiest terrorist group in the world.[41] ISIS, though, has a couple of obstacles, including the decision to set themselves up as a state and provide commensurate services, without the national-level connections and trade relationships with buyers. To be valuable to anyone but an internal market, oil has to be refined and then transported for export. Modular refineries are aerial targets, backyard refineries put out low-quality product, and buyers

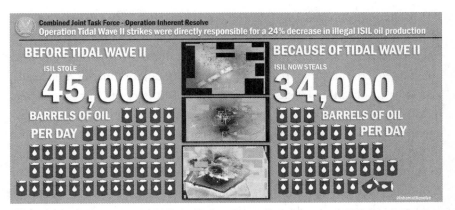

As part of Operation Inherent Resolve, coalition forces targeted ISIS oil production and trafficking in an effort to reduce the financial resources of the organization. *Photograph by Tidal Wave II, Syria (2016), Combined Joint Task Force–Operation Inherent Resolve, Defense Visual Information Distribution Service*

who know they have the upper hand pay a fraction of the global market price. Or, as a commentator snarked, without the big refinery at Basra, "then ISIS are just Palestinians."[42]

Oil drilling is a skilled-labor specialty, requiring access to an inventory of spare parts and specialized repair tools. Captured ISIS documents show long laundry lists of tasks from the Oil and Gas Division, including both regular maintenance and the repair jobs from malfunctions and damage from air strikes. Early in the conflict, ISIS commanders coerced petroleum engineers and their families to stay by promising them protection, higher wages, and special access·to food, but they can't always deliver on these incentives to stay on the job.[43] Some of the mature fields, like Syria's al-Omar, require water injection to maximize the extraction of oil, but the workers left under ISIS have resorted to primitive measures that yield far less crude and risk contaminating both the oil and water involved in the process. The parts for specific rigs, which would ordinarily be flown in from a manufacturer, have to be acquired through smuggling and long delays, and at the price demanded by the company taking the risk of doing business with them.

Like its cash warehousing, ISIS's oil reserve makes an attractive target. The coalition air targeting named Operation Tidal Wave II, after discussions of the risks to civilians forced to work in the fields or drive convoy trucks, by June 2016 targeted the entire supply chain, from the modular refineries, well heads, and streams of tanker trucks to even the ISIS Ministry of Oil headquarters in Mosul. The oil keeps flowing, but leaflet warnings to truckers can discourage them from taking the risks, and the trucks destroyed are expensive and difficult to replace. Air superiority allowed the United States and its allies to significantly degrade ISIS oil production, with follow-on effects to their economy and ability to maintain pretensions of being a state.[44]

During the long decade of sanctions between the Gulf wars, the Saddam Hussein regime and its senior leaders cultivated and protected a network of smugglers—everything from cigarettes to oil—which never went away. Tied into traditional tribal routes, these smuggling patterns were easily reactivated for a profitable product, sometimes under the same leadership as during the 1990s. Border guards expected bribes as part of illicit patronage, young people saw smuggling as an apprenticeship to more lucrative forms of criminal activity, and refinery workers long perfected means by which paperwork got "lost" or weights of trucks just never worked out right on the logs. Even under the threat of death from above, people were willing to drive trucks, lead mule trains, or dig underground pipelines for a small profit gained by moving ISIS oil across borders in what intelligence officials termed "ant trading."[45] These opportunities aren't just for ISIS: criminal gangs within Iraq take advantage of the artificially low domestic price of gas to cross the border into Iran, where eager buyers snap up the bargain.[46] Smuggling makes even stranger bedfellows than Iraq and Iran, as the Kurdish Peshmerga depends on taking a cut of oil passing through to hold down their own fuel expenses, even though they know they're subsidizing the very militias and gangs that they're fighting.[47]

A VNSA doesn't have to have access to the oil wells, just the pipeline or the routes the tanker convoy travels. In Nigeria's delta region, where drilling has fouled the traditional fishing industry and left a generation of underemployed young men idle, "bunkering" from pipelines drains as much as 10–15 percent of daily production. Some of this is done under the ideological banner of protest against the big companies and their abandonment of the people who live in the delta, but a lot of it slides along the scale to purely criminal activity.[48] Small-time gangs are capable of messily tapping a pipeline, but those with local political protection (usually in return for using their intimidation and force at rallies and polling places) can employ skillful former oil company technicians and get enough money to fund their weapons purchases and a flashy lifestyle. Many of the participants, whether they're engaging in violence to force Dutch Shell or Chevron to put money back into their communities and clean up the frequent oil spills or are in it for the cash and approval of a regional "godfather," believe that the oil belongs to them in the first place, not the government that sold contracts to foreign industry.

In Colombia, since the oil boom of the 1980s the National Liberation Army (ELN) has treated pipelines "like an ATM . . . they learned to milk the cow without killing it."[49] The necessity of transporting petroleum from the interior to the coastline exposes hundreds of miles of pipeline to attacks, and extortion and requires maintenance that puts company employees where they can be kidnapped for ransom. The ELN was a victim of its own success in this endeavor. They did get the companies to put money into communities and forced the government to adopt the 1994 National Law of Royalties, which directs oil revenue into development projects, but they did it in ways that generated little additional political capital for their own operations.[50] FARC, looking to diversify from drug funding, also attacked pipelines and refineries, collecting millions in extorted protection payments. The government, meanwhile, had to levy a special tax of $1 a barrel to pay to secure oil infrastructure at the same time the companies were paying off the VNSAs, an irony that ELN and FARC highlighted with gusto.[51]

Because they and their employees are vulnerable to extortion and pilfering, oil companies prefer, even at higher costs, to put their terminals and refineries offshore, out of the reach of VNSA attacks. This is the root of a whole different menu of problems. Detached entirely from the origins of the commodity, the company doesn't need any local employees or pretense of reinvestment in the community, which can rev up resentment and secessionist ideas. Instead, the government holding agreements with the company reaps the benefits, including siphoning off money, as former president Pascal Lissouba of the Democratic Republic of the Congo did in 1997 to fund his private militias against Denis Sassou Nguesso (who was getting money from French firm Elf Aquitaine). This is a prime source of grand corruption slush funds allowing leaders to subvert elections, buy their own VNSAs, and return to power if ejected. The International Monetary Fund estimated that in 2001 alone, $1 billion disappeared from Angolan government accounts because of graft, which puts any attempt at administration further and further in the red to creditors as the country continues to get high-interest loans against their guaranteed oil revenue.[52]

Oil futures have figured in the government of Chad since the 1970s, with President François Tombalbaye overthrown in 1975 after losing French military support by allowing a U.S. company to prospect for oil in the southern Doba fields. Subsequent administrations under Hissène Habré and Idriss Déby juggled competing offers from French and American companies, backed by their government's military commitments, creating squabbling VNSA militias, a corrupt military, an authoritarian human rights disaster, and an economic chaos catastrophic for Chad's residents.[53] In 2000 the World Bank proposed a loan for a Chad-Cameroon pipeline, with the condition that 72 percent of the profits from oil export go into a sovereign wealth fund required to put the revenue into infrastructure and social welfare. This was considered especially crucial as the fields were expected to produce at peak for only thirty years, offering a limited window to accomplish positive development and establish a sustainable, diversified economy. Decrying the available wealth as "crumbs," Déby forced a renegotiation in 2006, then rushed repayment of the loan in 2008 so he could cease to abide by the conditions.[54]

■ Nature, Red in Tooth and Claw

While I was working on this project, I happened to be in the Dallas–Fort Worth airport wandering around between flights and noticed a big hallway display of items seized by the U.S. Fish and Wildlife Service and impounded under customs regulations against the import of endangered species. There were ostrich eggs, snake skins, ivory, furs, feathers, powdered rhino horn, and other exotic pieces of poached animals. A fellow traveler wandered up next to me, became engrossed in the leather items and asked, "Do you know what shop these are at? I want one of those belts." VNSAs in control of, or with access to, regions with desirable wildlife have a lucrative source of income from hunting—an activity that not only replicates the firearms, fighting, and stalking skills that armed actors enjoy and need to practice in their downtime but also has lower penalties than many other crimes and responds to an elite demand signal.

During the period of decolonization wars in the 1960s and 1970s, the apartheid regime in South Africa saw poaching and ivory dealing as well as trafficking in rhino horn, exotic timber, and other wildlife products as a convenient way to pay for their VNSA subordinates like the Mozambican National Resistance (RENAMO) and UNITA as well as create a logistical hub that could double as paths for other sanctions-busting commodities they wanted.[55] This may have begun with units like the Selous Scouts salvaging ivory from elephants killed by minefields, but it quickly grew to be the recommended side work of counterinsurgents in Mozambique, Angola, and Rhodesia, keeping them busy and allowing them to range out across borders and into national parks. This had the additional benefit of destabilizing neighboring areas and magnifying the impression that the region was in violent chaos.

In Angola, especially as Cold War funding declined in the early 1990s, Savimbi turned to looting the areas without diamonds or oil—but rife with elephants and rhinos. Already in the 1980s UNITA-controlled regions lost 60,000–100,000 elephants, sent through a Portuguese company, Frama Inter-Training, to South Africa. One military adviser reported a young captain reporting to his commander: "Are you aware that there are hundreds of boxes of ivory in our store? Because I went there to get ammunition and all I could find is ivory. I couldn't find any ammunition, just ivory."[56] On the other side in Angola, Cuban forces were poaching, too, led by Gen. Arnaldo Ochoa Sanchez, who ran afoul of the Castros for having been a little too successful in accumulating a resource stash and was executed in 1989.[57] To the east of South Africa, the apartheid government's sponsored VNSA in Mozambique, RENAMO, was busy generating up to $13 million a year in ivory, from people trading with them for scarce supplies, their own hunting, and Zimbabwean game wardens and military units who justified their presence in the area by blaming depredations on RENAMO guerrillas.[58]

This level of lucrative trade continues at the hands of contemporary VNSAs, who multitask not just harvesting tusks and horns but also feeding their

Anti-poaching training, Gabon, 2018. Gabonese Eco-Guards orient U.S. Army team members during a partner force counter–illicit trafficking course in Loango National Park, Gabon. *Photograph by Chief Petty Officer John Hageman, Southern European Task Force Africa, Defense Visual Information Distribution Service*

soldiers on bushmeat and using the carcasses and dead game wardens to terrorize the local population and claim territory.[59] In East Africa, investigators for the Elephant Action League and Somali informants allege that al-Shabaab is both charging an "ivory tax" on trafficking through their territory and organizing units to cross into Kenya to raid game parks.[60] It remains a point of contention how much al-Shabaab might be getting from this resource exploitation, but their control of ports and the porous border with Kenya, leading to a diaspora network, makes it possible for them to profit enough to underwrite attacks like that in 2013 on the Westgate Mall in Nairobi.[61] Escapees from the Lord's Resistance Army in Uganda report that the group shoots elephants for meat and ivory, with witnesses naming Joseph Kony as instructing them to send the tusks to him to be used to purchase radios and medical supplies.[62] To the north, Janjaweed militias in Darfur have ridden hundreds of miles to poach in national parks in Uganda and Kenya, most likely with the approval and support of the North Sudanese military, with the ivory and horn turning in up Khartoum markets and in the hands of Asian traders.[63]

Africa is far from the only location that VNSAs poach to generate revenue. In Southeast Asia, Karen rebels in Myanmar like the Democratic Karen Buddhist Army and the New Mon State Party trade in tigers and endangered corals and sea cucumbers. Secessionist guerrillas, the Bodo Security Force in Assam, swing between enforcing protectionist policies in Manas National Park and trafficking in it themselves, depending on the degree of public pressure, while the National Socialist Council of Nagaland and Islamist groups in northeast India have regular deals with wealthy Gulf buyers to sell both houbara bustards and the falcons used to hunt them. Bangladesh's Muslim community forms a convenient commercial network orienting the traffic to the Middle East rather than China because, for supporters of the militias, "It's become God's work. A friend in common at a local mosque [in West Bengal] passed me a message saying representatives working for two militia groups in Bangladesh wanted a meet in a madrassah in Siliguri."[64]

VNSAs don't need to be politically motivated to traffic in poaching. Many of the criminal syndicates moving skins, horns, and tusks are in it purely for the money, as part of a portfolio of smuggled goods moving in similar and overlapping patterns. Criminals don't usually do the poaching themselves, instead relying on desperately poor people to take the risk and do the actual hunting and butchery, earning perhaps $600 for elephant tusks that will be sold for $3,000 per kilogram in Hong Kong. In Gabon, subsistence hunters might be paid as little as a bag of salt for a pair of tusks.[65] In most countries, wildlife exploitation carries far lighter penalties than drugs or weapons smuggling, making it a "soft option," where most of the risk can be displaced onto the lowest rungs of the operation.[66] Where legal hunting exists, criminals find ways to exploit the loopholes, like the Vietnamese gang that in 2012 enlisted young women sex workers to pose as "hunters" and pay a fee to shoot rhinos, which would then be butchered by hired professionals.[67] Ironically, the harder the push to message that criminal poaching is leading to extinction, the more valuable the wildlife becomes, with some gangs holding stockpiles in anticipation of price increases with scarcity.[68]

Underpaid and alienated state officials work in league with VNSAs too. Fighting in Congo's national parks, the uniformed national army slaughters wildlife while fighting its guerrilla enemies; the North Sudan military, supplied by Iran with identifiable ammunition, kills elephants for profit; and gamekeepers have taken bribes to allow poachers in or to kill the animals themselves.[69] The United States has a hand in training and underwriting armies with infamous reputations for poaching, including the Congolese, South Sudanese, and Ugandan forces, which have used helicopters to instigate mass slaughters in Garamba National Park. The chief ranger of the area, Mr. Onyango, was stunned by the carcasses of twenty-two elephants shot from helicopters and butchered. "They were good shots, very good shots. They even shot babies—why? It was like they came here to destroy everything."[70]

Armed antipoaching units, especially those made up of women, like the Black Mamba Anti-Poaching Unit of Kruger National Park in South Africa, get a big positive reaction in class and enjoy international reputations as badasses. Viewing this from the Global North, it's satisfying to think of elephants and rhinos having their own revenge hit squads, but the situation is far more complicated. "Green militarization" or "fortress conservation" began in the 1980s, with organizations like the World Wildlife Federation and national parks drawing on the same pool of regional mercenaries as the roaming VNSAs, with ex-commandos giving heartfelt interviews about finding in animals a cause "greater than themselves," which still gave them tacit permission to shoot people. PMCs unemployed by the end of the Cold War found ready employment from NGOs who prioritized the animals over the context of the problem and exercised about as much supervision as their corporate employers. Framing all poachers as terrorists and criminals makes shoot-to-kill policies palatable and justifies further destabilizing responses.

Countries with limited resources welcome military modernization donated or underwritten in the name of conservation since the training, aircraft, firearms, and night-vision scopes can be just as easily used by conventional forces to conduct operations. Not only do some of these militaries, like Uganda's and Congo's, use improved equipment to poach for themselves, the weapons injected into an unstable situation can also spark an arms race between poachers and gamekeepers or simply get lost and stolen, resurfacing in the hands of VNSAs. Donors to Global North conservation charities aren't thinking about the second- and third-order effects of their willingness to support militarization of game wardens and are often surprised that the receiving government has political plans for the upgraded hardware and expertise. The emotional pull of protecting well-known and loved animals like elephants and lions from terrorism allows NGOs to remain relevant and draw donors, pitting "innocent" creatures against evil threats, especially bolstered by films like Kathryn Bigelow's *Last Days* (2014).[71] Countries and individual gamekeepers have taken the license to shoot to kill as an opening to engage in the removal of troublesome populations from the land, or to engage in long-running feuds, with permission from their donors to prioritize the animal resource over people in ways that eerily echo other resource fights over diamonds and oil.[72]

Complicating the antipoaching militarization further is the way in which this mission forms the core of some of the national forces' identities. In the 1970s Botswana, which had been cultivating a stable economy from diamonds and big game tourism, was the neighbor of multiple decolonization wars, most of which wanted to slop over and through their borders. They founded a defense force in 1977 but kept things low-key and avoided a mythology of national liberation and revolution, fearing cold war intervention and spillover. In June 1985 South African troops brazenly invaded in pursuit of African National Congress personnel, humiliating the Botswanan government. On the advice of the president's son, Ian Khama, a general in the Botswana Defence Force, they oriented their buildup of personnel and equipment in line with aggressive antipoaching, including calling home guerrilla trackers working for the South African military and building a secret base that, as it was not overtly a regional security measure, was left alone.[73]

In 2013 Botswana took an even harder line on poaching, instituting a shoot-to-kill policy justified to "send a clear message . . . if you want to come poach in Botswana, one of the possibilities is that you may not go back to your country alive."[74] This garnered immediate pushback from human rights groups and neighboring countries, whose nationals were among the dead interlopers, leading to a stand-down of armed antipoaching units in 2018.[75] The country is keenly aware of the role that endangered elephants play in

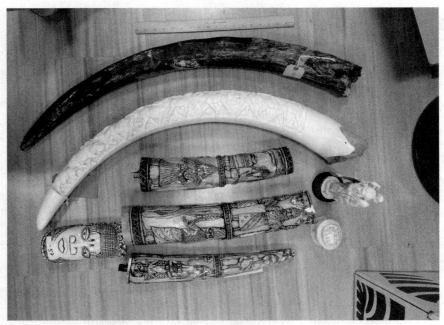

Ivory items seized by the U.S. Fish and Wildlife Service, destined to be crushed publicly so that they cannot be subsequently sold. Critics argue that this reduction in the amount of ivory actually drives up prices and encourages more poaching and trafficking. *Photograph by U.S. Fish and Wildlife Service (2015), courtesy Flickr*

their tourist revenue as well as the advantages of having the central identity of their military be protective and depoliticized, so the ongoing debate on use of force is likely to remain a priority in civilian–military relations.[76]

This is not to say that VNSAs aren't trafficking in endangered creatures and doing immense damage to the natural environment, undermining the tourist economy and ecological diversity of the places they poach. The problem is that the issue is place-specific and requires engagement with the root causes of the activities like subsistence poverty and instability, consumer demand and access, climate change and political alienation as well as balancing local autonomy and long-range ecological planning. That this may involve selling hunting licenses for trophy hunting a rebounded population, removing animals that destroy crops or allowing for export of stocks of animal products by one country and not another that causes arbitrage exploitation, and cross-border smuggling that defeats the purpose of the regulations in the first place. Establishment of game reserves for ecotourism can disrupt traditional means of support for a population, with little replacement, making poaching a lucrative source of income touching the whole community in the absence of other options, a phenomenon that occurred when the United States established its own national parks like Yellowstone and the Adirondacks in the early twentieth century.[77]

■ Other Valuable Commodities

In a restrictive environment, a VNSA will exploit almost any commodity available in the area it controls as long as there is a buyer and the international means to move the goods from the source to a point at which they can be exchanged for something the VNSA wants—guns, currency, drugs. Like other materials we've discussed, it is likely that the group, and ultimately the workers digging it up, fishing it out, or cutting it down, gets a fraction of the retail value while providing the labor and suffering the long-term environmental degradation that comes from expeditious mining, clear-cutting timber, overfishing, and other exploitation in pursuit of illicit funds.

VNSAs with possession of a gold mine or alluvial deposits in rivers will inevitably turn to them as funding sources. In Colombia and Peru, illegal gold mining by cartels and FARC may have started to yield more than cocaine production, with a seizure of just one FARC stash from Vichada worth $3.4 million. As with other commodities, a VNSA can put their own personnel to extraction work or use their monopoly of force to skim off "taxes" from the miners and panners who do the labor. Around 2010, major Mexican cartels, including Los Zetas, Sinaloa, and the Knights Templar, expanded into extortion of miners, quickly moving to control the production and export of refined gold.[78] North Korea, anxious to strip anything of value from its territory, sends citizens out to rivers and streams with sand sifters, rewarding them with access to special stores with consumer goods. Of course, the gold belongs to the government; it just gets one in the door with the right to purchase a TV or sewing machine with currency.[79]

Gold is the currency of most traditional societies, exchanged as dowries, security for loans, inherited property for women, and transported as jewelry as well as ingots and coins. Outlaw regimes like the Taliban and al-Qaeda found it useful to offer rewards, like 10,000 grams of gold for the assassination of American diplomat Paul Bremer in an untraceable form recognized by their potential agents. In the United States, the right-wing VNSA Posse Comitatus values gold for its separation from governments the group refuses to recognize, so much so that they set up a series of barter houses to assist members in making anonymous transactions based on stored bullion.[80] Regimes afraid of confiscation of their funds, like the Taliban in retreat to Pakistan, or apartheid South Africa under sanction, even 1980s Peru, fearing that their foreign assets abroad would be seized to pay national debts, convert cash to gold and smuggle it to safe holding areas at home or in trustworthy middleman countries where it is a normal means of exchange.[81]

Because of its high value and anonymity, gold is a perfect vehicle for smuggling and laundering. Al-Qaeda manuals offered instructions on carrying gold in vests, recommending that good couriers handle $500,000, or eighty pounds, at a time. Customs inspectors have found gold cast into machine parts, belt buckles, license plates, and bolts spray-painted black and disguised with grease. Some VNSAs have their refineries case gold in small bars with rounded edges, to avoid snagging bags and allowing them to be hidden on and in the human body.[82] Cartels find scrap gold to be a convenient trade-based laundry, having their personnel with cash in the United States buy jewelry, even at an inflated price, from pawnshops and sellers, then melt that down into bars and sell the "clean" gold for currency in the United States, Mexico, or elsewhere in Latin America.[83]

Gems like emeralds, lapis lazuli, Burmese rubies, and jade are useful to VNSAs, with the illegal mining of semiprecious stones earning $500 million in 2013. Afghanistan's Northern Alliance, without outside sponsors, kept itself in guns during the 1990s selling $40–60 million in lapis lazuli a year, while the Taliban's control of the Swat District gave them a steady supply of high-quality emeralds.[84] The Khmer Rouge, once the Chinese cut off their funding, depended on areas with ruby mining, sold through Thai brokers, a practice continued by the Kachin Independence Organization in Burma, which leveraged the political influence of brokers and the Dawei Princess Company to get concessions from the government.[85]

Greater corporate pressure is in play when the commodity at stake is a rare metal like coltan, which is vital to the manufacture of cell phones, computers, cameras, and personal electronics via tantalum capacitors. Coltan, like the conflict minerals cassiterite and wolframite, formed part of the financing of rebel groups in central Africa, including Rwanda and the Democratic Republic of the Congo. The price of coltan soared from $30 a pound to more than $300 in the early 2000s because of the exponential expansion of capacitor production and the inventory done by major manufacturers of existing stocks. A troop of Rwandan soldiers who captured a coltan mine in Kasese, a Ugandan area on the border of eastern Congo in 2001, charged a company $1 million a month, paid to the rebel group the Congolese Assembly for Democracy. Rare earth metals remain critical to the manufacture of desirable consumer items by the most powerful companies in the Global North, which require new ore despite aggressive recycling and reclamation programs.[86]

Rural VNSAs may have access to lootable timber, which has a ready market and rarely causes buyers to look closely into its origins. A few soldiers with chainsaws or axes can produce a load of wood they can sell locally or, if a rare product like rosewood, olive, or ebony, to a wholesaler or manufacturer. Illegal logging has significant overlap with agricultural drug production as growers clear-cut fields for coca, poppies, or marijuana, and it is common for addicts to forage in protected forests for valuable commodities like gall, burl, and rare specimens. The unfortunate by-products of deforestation, including loss of erosion control, fires, landslides, and flooding, usually aren't in the calculations of a group hungry for quick cash, leaving the area they control even less stable than before. In Somalia, al-Shabaab cuts down old-growth trees to make charcoal shipped out of the ports they control, disadvantaging the herders who need the shade and the water retention for their animals, causing desperate migration to find forage.[87]

Russian organized crime groups dominate the timber trade in Siberia, in league with corrupt officials, and maintain a grip encompassing more than a third of logging operations. Equipped with low-noise saws and GPS tagging, illegal cutters range into the forests that house endangered Siberian tigers,

U.S. Army personnel intercept Taliban-smuggled timber on the last leg of its route to Pakistan's furniture industry, Konar Province, Afghanistan (2009). *U.S. Army*

harvesting rare Korean pine, oak, and linden and chasing off rivals and game wardens with guns. Loads of timber leave Vladivostok for Chinese factories, aided by Mafia goons who were paid to squeeze out small Japanese firms and by a Russian *vor* known as "Winnie the Pooh" who allegedly murdered a Nakhodka port manager. The ecological effect is severe, confounding Anatoly Lebedev, a former KGB agent turned activist who fears that "the forests seem fine, but they're actually dead. They're taking the most valuable species, which are key to maintaining the ecosystem. It's a disgrace."[88]

In West Africa, Charles Taylor and Samuel Doe treated Liberian forests as a personal bankroll for their armed supporters, finding Middle Eastern companies through the Lebanese diaspora that weren't bothered by sanctions and environmental controls. Leonid Minin, a godfather in the Ukrainian Mafia, set up Exotic Tropical Timber Enterprises with Taylor's blessing, so long as he also supplied arms to both Taylor's men and the RUF units allowed to take safe haven on the Liberian side of the border. Meanwhile, a shell company, Bong Bank, run by Taylor's brother, skimmed off forestry royalties into personal accounts.[89] Although prosecutions for resource exploitation are rare, the depredations of timber magnate and gunrunner Guus Kouwenhoven in 1990s Liberia were so egregious that the Dutch government arrested and prosecuted him, a convoluted process during which he fled to South Africa and was sentenced in absentia in 2017 to a nineteen-year term for arms trafficking and war crimes. He remains unextraditable as of 2021.[90]

Almost anything of value has been sold by a VNSA at one time or another. North Korea expects people to collect rare wild mushrooms, clams, and wild ginger roots in a program euphemistically called "loyalty foreign dollars," with the bounty headed for the same Chinese medicinal markets as the Nepalese caterpillar fungus Ophiocordyceps sinensis, harvested by the Maoist insurgency there, which is so lucrative that possession of the valleys where it grows dictates their battle strategy. Guerrillas in El Salvador extorted money from coffee plantations, while in Nicaragua the Contras destroyed plantations the Sandinista regime used for funding their own military units.[91] Marble and chromite from Afghanistan, Somali frankincense, and phosphate mined in Anbar Province in Iraq have all enriched the treasuries of the VNSAs in possession of their location.[92] Perhaps the strangest is gum arabic, the ingredient that keeps carbonated drinks from separating and that coats candy and pharmaceuticals for easy chewing and swallowing. While in exile in Sudan, Osama bin Laden bought a company holding 80 percent of the world's supply. The Clinton administration's 1998 sanctions package, accompanied by cruise missiles in response to the African embassy bombings, ended up excluding gum arabic at the insistence of American manufacturers who feared that Taba Investment Company would sell the stockpile to French companies.[93]

9
DRUGS

Neo-Nazis love meth. Selling it. Producing it. Taking it. If there's a heritage drug for the Far Right, it's methamphetamine. Smith/Klein first synthesized a Benzedrine inhaler for asthma in 1932, but much like Ritalin now, students in the 1930s found it to be a handy binge-study aid. Its effect on alertness and focus came to the attention of militaries, particularly the air forces, who saw it as a way to keep their pilots awake for long-haul missions.[1] Original-recipe Nazis deplored most drug use as degenerate and punished users harshly as lazy and weak, but meth was different. Pervitin (meth's brand name in Germany) was no escapist pleasure but imbued a "vigorous urge to work" and "excellent working capacity and mood!"[2] One German commander assessed the effect as "everyone fresh and cheerful" but added a few hours later, "double vision and seeing colors."[3] Quickly nicknamed "tank chocolate" and "pilot salt," it was handed out by medical officers and sent in care packages from home. Even better, unlike other drugs requiring agricultural products from overseas, meth could be made by the domestic chemical industry.[4] Certainly Germany was not the only World War II military fueling its mobility with meth—fascism and ultramilitarism entwined so closely with the drug that, in postwar Japan, hustling the leftover government stockpile catapulted the Yakuza back to the top of organized crime.[5]

Modern skinheads have a sentimental attachment, "like a black leather glove on an outstretched hand." It renders users immune to pain and exhaustion but without the loss of control like alcohol, and it hypes up aggression. "I get so drunk before a football game they don't let me in. If I take a line of crystal, they don't notice a thing" was the endorsement from a German hooligan.[6] Since the early 1980s the neo-Nazi subculture in Los Angeles has made and sold meth as a financing vehicle since it can be produced with a small investment of skilled labor and instructions found on the internet.[7] True to their roots, the National Democratic Party of Germany in Saxony warns their members against dirty, foreign meth "cooked up in Czech kitchens and then illegally sold in Asian markets."[8]

The German federal government is very concerned about the linkage of skinheads and meth trafficking, especially a mail order business in Thuringia and concert consumption surrounding metal bands as well as the funds generated going into violent activities and attacks against vulnerable populations.[9] In the United States, attempts to police skinheads in the 1980s put incarcerated members of loosely organized gangs in contact with the much harder-core Aryan Brotherhood motorcycle clubs, creating a network for production and distribution as well as escalating the ideological rhetoric and setting them in competition with ethnic rivals like MS-13.[10] U.S. policy and law enforcement have been quick to identify the meth trade as a national security threat, with Gov. Kathleen Sebelius' plans for Kansas explicitly naming a convergence of meth and terrorism as a national security issue worthy of federal funding, and with George W. Bush linking the Combat Methamphetamine Epidemic Act with the renewal of the Patriot Act.[11] However, the United States has shied away from naming right-wing groups as domestic terrorists or treating them with the same gravity as cocaine-dealing cartels and urban crack distributors, although a new 2020 Department of Homeland Security threat assessment categorizes white supremacists as the "most persistent and lethal threat" to the United States.[12]

■ Just Say No?

For VNSAs outside of areas where drug production is a traditional and long-standing part of the agricultural economy, the decision to make drugs part of the funding stream is a calculated risk. In most of the Global North drugs are a law enforcement priority, with personnel and prosecutors devoted to tracking trafficking and money put toward counternarcotics. Drugs draw attention from the authorities and undermine the claims of ideologically based groups to be protecting their communities from malicious oppressors. Drug trafficking runs the risk of alienating a conservative diaspora support network and destabilizing the hierarchy of the group itself. From post-conflict oral histories and amnesty declarations, we know about the discussions within the IRA, which was suspicious of members drinking too much and becoming loose-tongued and careless, and extended that distaste to hard drugs and their sales. They also feared the lure of easy money, as low-level members conducting extortion realized that robbing dealers yielded less money than dealing and skimming off cash for themselves.[13] Stepping over that line changes the orientation of the organization, which loses the moral high ground against rivals who do sell drugs and obligates them to behaviors and risks that may impede the ideological goals of the VNSA.

In 1984 Catholic bishops in Spain issued a pastoral letter rebuking the Basque group ETA for trafficking drugs in the conservative region they claimed to be defending from Madrid and its decadence and oppression. The ETA's response was to adopt a harsh stance, punishing dealers with vigilante justice and proclaiming that drugs eroded the political consciousness of Basque youth, a move that allowed them to position themselves as local enforcers of proper behavior in place of the state.[14] The IRA and its splinters took to kneecapping dealers who sold drugs in Catholic neighborhoods but threaded the funding needle by allowing soft and club drugs they could justify as being sold to outsiders and having less harmful effects than heroin and cocaine. Marijuana and ecstasy, as well as hosting the "raves" at which they were consumed, were a nice little earner for IRA properties, without the sleazy connotation of harder substances, and were parallel to their interest in the alcohol business. In the late 1990s Sinn Féin politicians began running on "fervent anti-drugs" platforms that, as funding needs decreased, would create pressure to give up the trade entirely.[15]

If possible, a VNSA can get money from drugs while framing the activity as harming their enemies rather than their communities. In the mid-1980s Hezbollah sought and obtained a fatwa that permitted them to be involved in trafficking for their cause, as they "are making these drugs for Satan-America and the Jews. If we cannot kill them with guns, we will kill them with drugs."[16] Painting an opponent as decadent and as bringing on their own destruction through innate flaws is a powerful propaganda tool, and one we'll see several VNSAs use in response to pressure to stop drug production. No one is making Global North people shoot heroin, so if their selfishness and lack of self-control puts guns into the hands of righteous martyrs in Lebanon, who's to say that isn't a divine design?[17] Why stop?

Even if this compartmentalization isn't possible, the sheer amount of money available from drugs as a commodity is sufficient motivation for VNSAs to take the risk. Groups that violently reject the authority of a state and have the numbers or control of a safe haven are better positioned to benefit, as are those who know that they have a tolerant diaspora network or existing routes from which drugs could be an additional bonus. Major defeats or existential threats to the group's survival may also override caution and push a group's leadership to embrace drugs to recover or as a last throw of the dice in the face of loss of a sponsor or drastic change in world circumstances.

There may be another reason for a VNSA to get their funding for drugs without worrying as much about the risk: Controlled substances and state intelligence services have enjoyed a deeply entwined relationship for as long as both have existed, whether it is czarist spies in Russian taverns, or the post–World War II Japanese government allowing the Yakuza to have their military stockpile of meth in exchange for intimidating communist parties. In 1960s Marseilles, French intelligence was more afraid of unions among the dockworkers than heroin dealing by the Corsican Mafia, so they formed a partnership that built the infamous "French Connection" exporting narcotics to Popeye Doyle's (the fictional version of real cop Eddie Egan) New York. On the other side of the world, the South Vietnamese Ngo Dinh Diem regime attempted a harsh crackdown on vice only to realize that cooperation with drugs, pimps, and mobsters gave them an anti–Viet Cong informer in every block of Saigon. The 1960s Mossad, in need of funding for its covert operations, allowed Bedouin allies to move hashish from Lebanon through Israel for a cut and shared intelligence.[18] The CIA and its Office of Strategic Services forerunner, having set the stage with their World War II links to organized crime, didn't blink before using exiled Cuban drug chiefs in their campaign against Castro, nor was it a surprise that Pablo Escobar and the Medellín cartel formed a vital link in the financing and supply chain supporting the Contras in Nicaragua.[19]

VNSAs that don't produce drugs themselves make their money on the markup as the commodity changes hands from the source to the point that it reaches retail dealers, with the illegality and risk creating arbitrage along the way from areas where the supplier may offer insurance policies for confiscated shipments to locations where law enforcement do the confiscating. The drugs are already illegal at the receiving end, so a sanctions regime is pointless. The same conditions that supply recruits for a VNSA—young, underemployed people, many of them with few employable skills—make for a useful and highly efficient trafficking network of drivers, packing crews, building guards, lookouts, and expendable couriers. The globalized logistics revolution makes it possible to move drugs in standardized containers compatible with commonplace warehouse equipment, using opportunistic, flexible organization that would be the envy of the most ruthless corporate cost-cutter as they alter routes and techniques in response to increased surveillance, unfavorable political demands, or simply a better deal moving through another island's harbor. Just as quickly as consumers adapt to Skype, Xboxes, and chat rooms—not to mention Dark Net or organized forums like Silk Road—drug traffickers adopt them as sales venues.[20]

VNSAs with useful infiltration of a sovereign country have an advantage in hosting drug routes, using influence over border security, airspace permissions, use of national carriers, and even access to passports and diplomatic bags. In countries like Guinea-Bissau, Senegal, or Cape Verde, the drug money reinforces the "winners" from other kinds of corruption, creating an entrenched elite with income to spend on cars, the construction of new McMansions, their own offshore accounts, and nouveau riche treats like European wines.

Predictably, none of this finds its way into a tax base or sustainable develop-ment.[21] Descent into a fully criminalized black hole, though, is bad news and often prompts a change in route: "Corruption-corroded, coup-prone nations" without trustworthy property and banking laws or decent infrastructure and with so much turmoil that they attract outside intervention are just too much risk.[22] Almost as good are regions under the control of an amenable VNSA, like the north of Sri Lanka occupied by the LTTE, or the areas of the Sahara (especially convenient for clandestine air traffic) in the functional possession of tribal groups affiliated with AQIM or Tuareg rebels.[23] The landscape itself may create a functional area of control, like that enjoyed by the PKK, whose smuggling network across the mountains encompasses areas of Iran, Iraq, Syria, and Turkey claimed by Kurds, who have experience navigating the passes to their advantage in concealment and difficulty in pursuit.[24]

A willing (or trafficked in and coerced) diaspora makes for a useful dis-tribution network in a receiving Global North country. The PKK, with a three-generation Kurdish diaspora in Western Europe, used their secondary army of young, underemployed men to move heroin, at one point supplying an estimated 80 percent of the drug sold in Paris.[25] The LTTE used its people in Canada and Switzerland, often under threat of violence, to sell heroin from their connections in the Golden Triangle of Southeast Asia and via a managerial diaspora in Thailand. The cocaine networks in West Africa came into being with the organization of Hezbollah agents among the Lebanese Shia diaspora there for the diamond industry, connected to those in the Latin American population we've already encountered in the Tri-Border Area.[26] Where a diaspora doesn't already exist, a VNSA can cultivate one, with Nigerian and Ghanaian drug traffickers building a system of drug-swallowing couriers among the population of African students attending Global North universities who weren't getting enough in nationally sponsored bursaries to pay their living expenses.[27]

In the early 1970s, Welsh marijuana smuggler Howard Marks advised the IRA that "if you can smuggle arms, you can smuggle drugs."[28] Drugs are, after all, high value, can be broken down into small units for shipment, are generally shelf-stable, and require no special handling if sealed in bags. Estab-lished lines of transportation, from knowing friendly boat owners to having reliable spotters with binoculars watching the entry lanes at the US–Mexico border for inspection patterns, aid any kind of illicit movement of goods. The structure of a VNSA features existing links to crooked officials, pools of available drivers, and a flexible and dispersed network of cells whose knowledge of the overall operation can be compartmentalized from one another—and, if they don't want to do the end-user retailing themselves, they likely have links to distributors who are willing and able. At every point the "V" in the VNSA can be employed by experienced armed people to guard shipments, intimidate obstacles, and chase off competitors, an advantage that the group may eventually consider less a distraction from their ideological goals than a chance to keep their personnel sharp and busy.

When this comes together, as it did in the 2004 Madrid bombings, even a small amount of drug-trafficking money can enable devastating carnage. Without aid from al-Qaeda, just encouragement and instructions that the attack should occur in Spain before the general election, the small cell of six men organized a route moving hashish and the party drug ecstasy from Morocco into Europe. Practical knowledge as dealers made it easy for them to find safe houses, buy prepaid phones, and co-opt the infrastructure of a drug trafficking group for ideological purposes. The Spanish police were monitoring them for cannabis sales, which was significantly lower priority than heroin or cocaine, but didn't suspect that they'd trade sixty-six pounds of it for explosives or use that dynamite to murder 191 people, all for an operational cost of about $50,000.[29]

■ Suspicious Baggies

VNSAs without an agricultural base can make their own drugs for distribution, thanks to synthetic chemical processes. LSD, first synthesized in 1938, became the focus of the 1960s "hippie mafia," a group that wanted to evangelize psychedelic drug use for spiritual purposes but whose funding for the experiment led them into trafficking hashish from Afghanistan and then into distribution deals with biker gangs, most notoriously the Hell's Angels. Organizing as the Brotherhood of Eternal Love, they reaped the (at least temporary) benefits of being a church. The Japanese cult Aum Shinrikyo replicated this advantage, producing high-quality LSD for sale and religious use in their laboratories as a parallel effort to their poison gas experiments while claiming religious exemptions from taxes and normal government supervision. By the 1990s law enforcement estimated that half of the global supply of LSD was coming from Aum Shinrikyo.[30]

Methamphetamine manufacture is not just the choice of neo-Nazis but of any VNSA with connections to get precursor chemicals and the expertise to carry out the chemical process. North Korea is ideally positioned to do both, branching out into meth after devastating droughts crippled their agriculturally based opium trade. As a sovereign nation, they can acquire ingredients at industrial scale, and they have professional laboratories and trained scientists who can be assigned to cook. In 1998 Thai customs inspectors stopped a huge shipment of ephedrine from India, which North Korea's medical department had ordered under the guise of allergy treatment but was eventually forced to let go as a compassionate necessity. Of course, there was no hay fever epidemic needing "enough ephedrine to last 100 years," just the shopping list for meth.[31] Once ready, the drugs move out on state-owned transport, including military vessels and the diplomatic bags of their embassy staff.[32] In the absence of ephedrine, the North Koreans are experimenting with benzene-based precursors, which they can extract from fuel aid offered as humanitarian assistance. Similarly, in Myanmar, when the United Wa State Army was pushed out of territory it used to grow poppies, it shifted production to meth, which could be done with no land needed except a location for a cooking laboratory.[33]

Criminal gangs' largest challenge in engaging in meth sales is almost always finding ways to get the chemical components, sending smurfs to buy cold medicine until state restrictions put pills behind locked cabinet doors at Walgreens, then buying from VNSA-connected businesses in Mexico, China, India, and Lebanon (Lebanese connections usually spell Hezbollah involvement). One such relationship is that of Zhenli Ye Gon, a Chinese businessman who provided precursor chemicals to a Mexican cartel that, seeing the future, was branching out from cocaine. The confluence of interests was so lucrative that Zhenli was able to indulge a gambling habit so extensive that, after he lost $72 million in Las Vegas, the casino bought him a Rolls-Royce as a consolation gift. Meth empires, like other criminal enterprises, develop distribution channels, money laundering, and logistics via other businesses, often legitimate-looking ones. Lori Arnold (actor Tom Arnold's sister) ran Midwest drug production from Ottumwa, Iowa, solving transport and money moving problems by setting up a high-volume car dealership.[34]

Hezbollah and ISIS make money on a dangerous and adulterated chemical cousin of meth, Captagon, produced in Lebanon and Syria. The original drug formulation, fenethylline, was developed in the 1960s by a German company and used for attention deficit hyperactivity disorder until superseded by Ritalin and banned for harmful side effects by the 1980s. Because of illicit Balkan manufacturing in the 1990s, it persisted as a euphoria-generating party drug, especially in Saudi Arabia and the Gulf states, where its forbidden nature jacks up the price from a few cents to produce to $10–15 a pill. Factories with pill pressing (or candy shaping) machines crank out ersatz versions, using whatever ingredients they can source, any mixture of available caffeine, quinine, amphetamines, and vitamins, colored to look like the original versions. The lack of quality control or concern about the components creates "exactly the kind of drug you would not want to mix together with a bunch of terrorists."[35] Customs seizures in Saudi Arabia and the United Arab Emirates, even in Camorra drug stashes in Italy, turn up shipments of hundreds of thousands of Captagon tablets, sometimes in the luggage of VIPs, all adding up to consistent profits of $200 million a year. Short on cash, ISIS has paid its personnel in Captagon, expecting them to retail it and collect the profit as their wages.[36]

Along with the money, unfettered access to Captagon offers ISIS a tool to render their fighters impervious to fatigue, pain, cold, and boredom, the bane of all field assignments. Reports state that ISIS fighters can "battle commandos for over 50 hours with no food or sleep," are "zombielike," can "go into a fight without caring if [they] lived or died," and "keep going even in the rain."[37] Interviews with captured ISIS fighters suggest that users take Captagon to overcome hesitancy to fight or to engage in taboo activities like beheading, and they are promised that the drug will allow them to resist interrogation and torture or complete a suicide mission. Most of what they're called on to do doesn't require critical thinking or following complex instructions, so being numb and high for pennies on a substance that their version of Islam allows is not at all a disadvantage.[38]

VNSAs are also involved in the fentanyl market and in the broader opioid crisis. As pharmaceutical companies engaged in questionable marketing practices to promote high-dose painkillers, criminal gangs saw an opportunity to acquire pills for people who couldn't get them through medical prescriptions as well as people who developed a tolerance and wanted far more than their prescriptions allowed. This took the form of co-opting doctors to run pill mills, writing prescriptions to literal busloads of smurfs who were allowed to keep a few pills but obliged to turn over the rest to the gang for sale. Russian *vor* Razhden Shulaya, as one of his many schemes, had goons selling OxyContin on the street in Brooklyn after blackmailing a Manhattan physician into overprescribing.[39] Fentanyl, a synthetic designed for hard-core pain relief, including palliative cancer care, became the replacement of choice once Oxy-Contin didn't dull senses anymore. Cartels saw a robust market opportunity and began producing fentanyl with Chinese chemicals, taking advantage of gaps in enforcement, like search dogs not being trained to find it until 2017.[40]

Fentanyl's illicit users defied the usual categorization of addicts as deviants. The opioid crisis has infiltrated blue-collar America as legitimate doctors offered relief, albeit in excessive and highly addictive form, to broken down bodies, all with the respectability of a hometown doctor and scripts filled at Walmart. When things spiraled beyond that, the dealing was suburban, and even available by mail. Silk Road and other Dark Web sellers listed fentanyl for sale, complete with customer reviews and reliability ratings, even suggesting that buyers have the drugs shipped regular U.S. mail, separating soccer parent addicts from the unpleasantness of cartel operations and, from the seller's point of view, streamlining logistics and making it unnecessary to fight for physical territory. Where this becomes especially dangerous is that illicit fentanyl is imported in pure form and is then cut by VNSA dealers who have no idea what they're doing. Dose to dose, an addict gets drastically different amounts of the drug, making overdoses common and frequently fatal. Increasingly, public health authorities, law enforcement, and the military look at the stream of fentanyl from China, direct or through cartels, as a national security threat, perhaps even "gray zone" warfare against the population. Even if sanctions and an enforcement regime can cut off the synthetic supply, cartels are ready with a traditional alternative: there's always black tar heroin.[41]

In East Africa, khat, or qat, is a traditional botanical stimulant ingested by chewing leaves from a native shrub, yielding an alkaloid similar to amphetamine. In majority Muslim areas, where the consumption of alcohol is forbidden, khat is an easily available recreational drug. Al-Shabaab discovered that it was not only extremely useful for combatants—with its stimulant and constipation side effects—but began trafficking it to their Somali diaspora in Kenya for a revenue stream.[42] Unlike other drugs covered in this chapter, khat has never made the leap to mainstream use as it is shipped and used in the form of fresh leaves, which have to be air freighted to distant users and is chewed like betel nuts, staining the mouth and producing copious amounts of saliva, which is distasteful to outside observers. Khat addiction, though, is a serious problem for former combatants and has been included in successful DDR programs since reckless behavior rooted in khat abuse is a significant enough social disqualifier to figure in the trustworthiness evaluations of hawala networks, but PTSD management and traditional use stabilize the community of users.[43]

Marijuana is a case of an agricultural product, under a prohibition regime, turned into a far more powerful and marketable commodity. Cannabis, in the form of joints, edibles, and processed into hashish, is an Old World agricultural crop grown widely and found in the wild. Because it was an illicit substance in many places (and a religious and socially acceptable one in others), VNSAs got into cultivation and distribution as a revenue source. A high-profile prohibition campaign linking the drug, famously, to "reefer madness," corruption of teenagers, and unpatriotic politics with a strong racist streak made it a prime target of federal law enforcement. To be sure, escalated embargo made it worth more to VNSAs who trafficked in cannabis extensively, from the IRA to anti-Castro group Omega 7. Most spectacularly, the Lebanese Civil War made the rich Bekaa Valley a prime growing location for PLO and Hezbollah-affiliated groups, driving out fruit and vegetable production (a problem for food supply even now) and producing 4.3 tons of Lebanese Gold (worth $12 million a year) throughout the 1980s.[44]

The heightened risk incentivized a botanical transformation. VNSAs invested in improving cannabis, using genetic expertise to breed strains that had drastically higher THC content, had a broader growing zone, and eventually would flourish in hydroponic indoor grow houses and have identifiable flavor and effect profiles marketed with catchy brand names. These new varieties could be sold at higher prices, making it worthwhile to stand up grow operations.[45] VNSAs across the spectrum of motivations produce and traffic this high-quality cannabis, using indoor grow operations, fields hidden in forests with good air cover, and, in countries where it is a traditional product, out in the open.[46]

In the United States, state-level legalization of cannabis has created a wide-ranging arbitrage across state lines because the federal government continues to classify it as a strictly controlled substance. Despite the presence of legal dispensaries, federal prosecutors can not only pursue people directly involved in the trade, under the Racketeer Influenced Corrupt Organizations Act, they can go after anyone with any connection at all—the real estate agent who helped set up the purchase of the facility, the marketing consultant who designed the packaging, and any federally insured financial institution that handles the money. This exposes a highly professionalized, billion-dollar business sector to VNSA influence at every level of their operations, creating an especially dangerous situation where warehouses full of cash have to be guarded by a private army of security people. The current situation, mixing the worst aspect of bootlegger and Baptists regulatory lobbying, state tax revenue, VNSA influence and highly valuable assets, is riper for exploitation along its whole supply chain than if it was entirely illicit.[47] Full federal legalization may solve that problem in the near term, but, as always, VNSAs have contingency plans and can refocus on harder drugs, branch out into side products like avocados from agricultural land near their drug growing operations, or, like gangsters after the repeal of Prohibition, embrace ways to exploit a legal industry for their own advantage.[48]

▪ Far and Wide, in a Scarlet Tide, the Poppy's Bonfire Spread

Poppies are beautiful, easy to grow, and, since at least 500 BCE in the Neolithic Mediterranean, people have been selectively breeding them to produce a sap used for medicinal and ritual purposes.[49] The flowers are extremely hardy, love warm, dry climates, and are highly drought resistant, making them a crop of choice in challenging regions where little else grows reliably. Getting the sap is labor intensive, with harvesters using sharp, small knives to cut slits into the seed pods after they bloom, then returning up to seven times to scrape off the resulting sap. This yield, dried, is a potent narcotic, shelf-stable, and easy to transport, even more so if processed further.[50] In the form of opium, this was a panacea perfectly suited to premodern life: In affordable, available small quantities with a context of traditional use, it relieves the indignities of life, like the chronic fatigue of peasant farmers, boredom, anxiety, colic in children, and diarrhea from tainted water sources. As a moneymaker for the early global corporations like the British East India Company, opium poppies grown in northern India on an industrial scale and distributed worldwide opened the possibilities of large-scale recreational use and abuse as well as formed the foundations of the company's fortunes. Attempts at rejection or regulation of the opium trade met with armed opposition from the Global North, including a war fought in nineteenth-century China largely to force the imperial government to allow European and American merchants free rein.[51]

Morphine, extracted in 1804, became the pain reliever of choice in nineteenth-century medical practice, so easily available that it became a public health plague among veterans of the American Civil War and Europe's *levée en masse* conflicts. Heroin, ironically, came about in 1874 through chemical experiments to find a more powerful but nonaddictive substitute for morphine (surprise!). Seeing the danger, many Global North countries placed morphine and heroin under regulation and pushed opium out of its place on the ingredients list of mainstream household remedies. Making it illicit outside of medical use didn't slow down the rate of addiction or the attraction of recreational use, so the demand continued, and the poppies flourished in Southeast Asia, India, Pakistan, and Iran after World War II. The presence of eradication-minded Communist Chinese troops in Yunnan Province, a key opium-producing region, drove Nationalist guerrillas and drug cultivation over the border into Laos, Thailand, and Burma in the late 1940s.[52] In 1955 the shah of Iran, disgusted by the poor quality of military conscripts because of chronic opium use, banned its production and enforced the edict with harsh measures by the secret police. With that source cut off, traffickers turned next door to Afghanistan.[53]

Because ease in transport, especially on aircraft, is a paramount concern for smuggling, much of the processing now takes place in the growing regions. To make morphine base, which is "low bulk and low smell," the accumulated and dried poppy sap goes to a central collection point, where someone following basic instructions can dump the opium into an oil drum of hot water, add ordinary lime to precipitate out waste, then filter through cloth. The resulting material goes into a second oil drum with hot water and ammonia (easily obtainable from fertilizer), where it forms into chunks and sinks to the bottom of the drum. Once fished out and dried, the weight is reduced by 90 percent.[54] The next step, making heroin, requires a real chemist and the acquisition of acetic anhydride. In the twenty-first century, this is easily available from Chinese exporters and makes its way into Afghanistan hidden in carpets and trucked across borders. Depending on the market destination, the morphine base may be processed multiple times for purity. At this stage mistakes involve ether as a by-product, so labs are dangerous and prone to explosions.[55]

In the postwar Southeast Asian Golden Triangle of opium production, the establishment–narcotrafficking partnership was alive and well. Thai military officers who had been assigned to tribal Shan areas during World War II revived links to local warlords, got into the opium business, and raised a war chest that supported their 1947 coup. The French colonial government of Vietnam and its Service de documentation extérieure et du contre-espionnage, which had unsuccessfully attempted to police production and consumption earlier, turned to narcotics to fund expensive intelligence operations and acquire surplus guns from China, vertically integrating the entire narcotics trade from growing fields to Saigon's opium dens, even back to France via the Corsican Mafia. Ed Lansdale, working for the CIA, reported this but was both warned off embarrassing a friendly government and deterred from interfering with a revenue stream that the CIA itself would embrace after replacing the French intelligence service in Southeast Asia. Drug money meant independence from Washington, D.C., directives, and set up Burmese warlords, as one of them, Gen. Tuan Shi-wen explained: "To fight you must have an army, and an army must have guns, and to buy guns you must have money. In these mountains, the only money is opium."[56]

In Myanmar, the drug business long outlasted the Cold War, arming hill country warlords into the twenty-first century. The government of Ne Win attempted to curtail this, but its collapse in 1988 allowed the trade to flourish in the chaos, producing so much that the 1993 crop "could satisfy the world's known demand" for opium. Some of the guerrillas lost their ideological opposition to the government in Rangoon, focusing on survival and wealth through drugs, a situation which opened the United Wa State Army and Shan leaders like Khun Sa to government persuasion in 2005. Given regional autonomy and financial incentives and left to continue drug dealing, they were willing to sign on to a peace agreement by 2013. In some cases, as their population turned to other jobs, the VNSAs switched to nonagricultural drugs like meth, which need fewer people to make but still bring in the cash.[57]

When the 1979 Soviet invasion of Afghanistan and overthrow of the Iranian shah disrupted the regular routes of narcotics trafficking for Pakistani VNSAs, drug lords turned to the LTTE in Sri Lanka to bypass the region and ship drugs to Europe and Canada via the Tamil diaspora. In some cases the trafficking route ran through Eastern Europe, where the governments tolerated smuggling since the drugs were meant for Western consumers, poisoning themselves with capitalist decadence.[58] By the late 1980s, though, the political turmoil in Myanmar and Tamils living in Thailand offered a better scenario: Burmese producers supplied the heroin, LTTE ships (including a mini submarine) carried it for distribution, and most of the risk was offloaded onto street-level retailers.[59]

Meanwhile, in Afghanistan, the Soviet invasion changed the cultivation of poppies from a sideline to a survival mechanism. Failing to win over the Afghan population, Soviet forces began ranging out from areas under their control to obliterate the agricultural infrastructure, destroying irrigation systems and displacing rural farmers who fled over the border to refugee camps in Pakistan. Those who remained had to find a cash crop that would grow in the ravaged landscape, while those seething and grieving their losses in a camp in Peshawar were eager recruits for anti-Soviet jihad.[60] Far away in Washington, D.C., President Carter's adviser on drug policy, Dr. David F. Musto, saw a stark side effect looming and begged the administration to avoid tolerating narcotics as a rebel funding source. "I told the council that we were going into Afghanistan to support the opium growers in their rebellion against the Soviets. Shouldn't we try to avoid what we had done in Laos?" Instead, deaths from drugs in New York jumped by 77 percent in 1980 as cheap heroin flowed out and guns flowed in.[61]

Fields of heroin-producing poppies flourish in Afghanistan, defying drought and eradication efforts, Marjah, Afghanistan (2012). *Photograph by Sgt. Michael Snody, Defense Imagery Management Operations Center/U.S. Marine Corps, permission via Defense Visual Information Distribution Service*

Once the Afghan mujahideen got American-supplied surface-to-air missiles, the Soviets could no longer conduct aerial eradication of crops, leaving the countryside too devastated for a return to previous crops but perfect for poppies. Pakistan's intelligence arm, ISI, built their power fronting distribution of arms and supplies while taking Afghan-grown drugs back over the border to Karachi, where the National Logistics Cell, a company owned by Pakistan's military, took over as transport. The Haqqani network of truckers used by the CIA in Afghanistan dug in as a regional criminal enterprise thanks to narcotics trafficking and was powerful enough to launch attacks against the U.S. Embassy in Kabul in 2011. Leading resistance figures like Gulbuddin Hekmatyar, Mullah Nasim Akhundzada, and Ismat Muslim kept their followers by distributing loot gained by trading for drugs and built loyalty delivering consumer goods like TVs and vehicles, even establishing clinics and schools with the excess income. The U.S. Drug Enforcement Administration (DEA) had a skeleton staff in Pakistan in the 1980s, all of whom were keenly aware of this system, and they resented the CIA's protection of "brave freedom fighters" who were the source of their agency's primary problem.[62]

Mujahideen groups received fatwas encouraging them to sell drugs "to fight our holy war against Russian nonbelievers," despite Koranic injunctions not to use or produce drugs. To get Russian conscripts hooked, agents "donated" packets of heroin labeled "Crumble the Kremlin" and "Smoke Russia Away" by throwing them over the fence into Russian military compounds. Quickly addicted, Russian troops cannibalized their equipment to buy more and used the needles from their medic kits to shoot up, and morale plummeted while the CIA applauded: "One tiny mosquito can drive a bear crazy."[63] The KGB, though, saw the possibilities in harnessing the traffic into Soviet territory to fund their own operations and corrupt Westerners, especially American troops living on bases in Europe.[64] The social consequences of this strategy were horrendous, with a plague of addiction among youths and the empowerment of Chechen gangs and *vor* kingpins who would emerge from the wreckage of the state with full treasuries and connections.[65] As the Russians pulled out in 1989, the poppy fields increased, absorbing returned refugee labor and enriching warlords, while the CIA created a counternarcotics center, presumably to monitor the VNSAs they'd partnered with during the Cold War.[66]

Beginning in 1994 the victorious Taliban, which took over the government in Kabul in 1996, forbade the consumption of narcotics as part of their regime of religious austerity, along with destroying vineyards so that no one could make alcohol and brutally punishing addicts. However, they didn't stop the production of narcotics, even exempting women from their work prohibitions so they could take part in the labor-intensive cultivation process, because the Taliban levied a lucrative 20 percent tax. Their strict sense of discipline and intolerance of corruption actually organized sectors of the trade more efficiently. Mullah Omar allowed Osama bin Laden, who had returned to Afghanistan from Sudan in 1996, to turn the Afghan national airline, Ariana, into a "narco-terror charter service," moving heroin, rare timber, and weapons across Central Asia and the Gulf, with profits shared with jihadi groups in Chechnya and Uzbekistan.[67] Peasant farmers were allowed to pay taxes and barter with "golf ball-sized" lumps of morphine base, and Taliban commanders interrogated their Northern Alliance enemy prisoners with heroin-laced hash.[68] In July 2000 the Taliban issued an order banning the cultivation of opium, possibly as a bid for recognition beyond Pakistan, the United Arab Emirates, and Saudi Arabia and to counter their horrific human rights record.[69] Global North drug enforcement agencies welcomed this turnaround, but more cynical observers noticed that by cutting the supply, the Taliban drastically increased the value of the stockpile they possessed while trying to rehabilitate their image.[70]

Of course, poppy growers hated the prohibition. Subsidies did nothing to implement sustainable replacement crops, so farmers fell into grinding, catastrophic poverty while brutal public punishments alienated people from the Taliban. By the spring of 2001 farmers were openly defying the ban in Nangarhar Province and a governor warned that "implementation of the ban for a second year would require many people to be killed and others to face starvation."[71] When U.S. forces invaded in October 2001, they joined with aggrieved Northern Alliance warlords angry at losing the opium income and Pashtun populations who reported later that anti-Taliban leaders promised them they could return to growing poppies immediately. At least temporarily, the Taliban cut its own throat and sent Afghans over to the side of U.S. intervention.[72] As early as 2003 they and al-Qaeda were back at it, as satellites tracked cargoes of Afghan heroin being loaded on ships in Karachi, and a load worth $3 million was seized by the U.S. Navy boarding dhows in the Persian Gulf, guarded by known al-Qaeda members. Using the revenue, Taliban fighters were reestablishing control over Pashtun villages.[73]

In 2005 the Taliban reversed their ban, and opium production under their aegis had an estimated value of $2.5 billion, more than half Afghanistan's total domestic product. Because by then the United States and NATO allies had themselves undertaken an aggressive eradication and antidrug campaign, the Taliban positioned itself as the friend and protector of opium cultivators, offering small loans to get farming restarted, distributing fliers with a number to call if eradication was under way, and winning the support of the ancillary industries—trucking, restaurants, guest houses, and fuel stations servicing the trafficking. One village in Kandahar, firmly back in the Taliban camp, got wise to a counternarcotics officer posing as an opium dealer and turned him in to the local Taliban commander, who then used the officer as bait to lure the Afghan National police into an ambush, achieving multiple goals for themselves with the enthusiastic approval of the community.[74] The Taliban created a finance committee, to which regional commanders send a "money guy," working out a system where poppy-poor areas subsidized poppy-rich ones, making it possible to pay fighters $150 a month in a place where local police officers might get $60.[75] Estimates are that the Taliban today derives about 30–60 percent of their annual budget from opium, although this may come at the cost of tolerating less ideologically motivated members and committing to holding territory on the basis of its opium productivity rather than defensibility.[76]

American and coalition eradication programs ran into the same reaction as the Taliban did. Back in 1990 just one interaction was a harbinger of the trouble to come: Mullah Nasim, a warlord in Helmand Province, agreed to end drug production in exchange for $2 million from USAID. He went ahead, only to learn that the U.S. government, bound by laws not to make deals with drug traffickers, revoked the entire agreement. His neighboring warlord, who owned a refining laboratory, assassinated him and put in a replacement who got the poppy supply going again. Nothing had changed twenty years later. Like many crop-subsidy programs, paying people not to grow things caused farmers to acquire more land in order to claim to not be growing more crops. Some farmers destroyed their poppies, only to learn that the money had run out and they would receive nothing. Others took the money and didn't burn the crops since there was little monitoring for compliance. Entirely rational farmers couldn't see sustainable jobs being implemented and refused eradication payments, while DDR programs shuffled ex-combatants into an economic sector "rural crop option," with no actual jobs.[77] Many of the coalition planners entrusted with the eradication program had so little local cultural knowledge or understanding of farming that they were characterized as having "read *Kite Runner* on [the] plane"; as a result, "the Afghans took them to the cleaners."[78] It's also likely that eradication created a Darwinian process in which the strongest and most resilient drug operations strengthened their hand and used programs to rat out rivals and consolidate control.[79]

The coalition military genuinely tried to deeply invest in pursuing policies that would make their operations safer and more effective; as a British officer said, "The guys have been out there, building relationships with local people that bring in crucial intelligence and keep us safe. If the same guys start kicking down doors and reporting on ordinary people who are just trying to earn a living in difficult circumstances, then they are not going to see us as friends anymore."[80] Gen. Benjamin Freakley halted DEA and Afghan counternarcotics operations in Eastern Afghanistan in 2006, followed by a refusal by the commander of the 101st Airborne to destroy crops unless they had proof that the farmers had been compensated. Others warned that Afghanistan was a drastically different place than Colombia, where cocaine eradication had been a successful element of Plan Colombia, and that sending in DynCorp employees to slash and burn made more enemies than friends.[81] The Commander's Emergency Response Program authorized local units to sponsor and put money toward alternative projects, including attempts to grow market garden crops for sale in Kabul; ship pomegranates to Russia in cold storage donated by India; and build roads, irrigation projects, and bakeries, but many foundered on profits eaten up by bribes and the inability to generate revenue more reliably than with poppies.[82]

Part of the problem is that nothing is a better economic alternative than poppies. Poppies won't fail in a drought, the labor-intensive nature of poppy agriculture absorbs large numbers of low-skilled people, and creditors are willing to lend seeds and startup money for the poppy economy but not for riskier projects with longer time to recoup costs. In a desperately poor society where failure means selling off daughters as child brides, losing the sure thing of a poppy crop is unthinkable and terrifying. Wheat, fruit trees, black cumin—they suck up more water, take years to fully produce, and only need forty hours of work to harvest rather than the 350 per hectare for poppies.[83] Real crop substitution programs would have to be embedded in a full sector reform including sustainable, available credit; banks the rural people trust more than sticking chunks of opium sap under their beds; other jobs for itinerant farmhands; land tenure for sharecroppers; and other long-term change. Instead there are fearful, starving people with nothing to lose; as a grower challenged an eradication team, "Why don't you just shoot us now? If you cut down my fields, we'll all die anyway."[84]

The other big problem is that the opium economy is so deeply entwined with the power structure. Warlords who make the most effective anti-insurgent partners and intelligence sources are themselves major drug producers and will cease to cooperate if "we suddenly start trashing their poppy crops and burning their opium warehouses."[85] Within the Afghan government, people with long-term involvement in the drug trade have been given influential positions to keep their support and loyalty, including making Mohammad Daud Daud, a man who dispatched the Afghan army to fight Tajiks in order to keep control of a trafficking route, the minister of counter narcotics. Another appointment went to Izzatullah Wasifi, whose 1980s Las Vegas arrest for trying to sell $2 million in heroin to an undercover cop must have been valuable experience in preparation for being Afghan "drug czar."[86] In a larger regional threat picture, the Pakistani intelligence division, ISI, continues to draw a large part of its operational budget from trafficked narcotics, with a substantial portion of profits directed to supporting their VNSA allies in Kashmir, a lever that makes them less accountable to politicians in Islamabad and more willing to be generous with their sponsored proxies.[87]

■ Marching Powder

Coca is another ancient, hardy plant native to the Andes Mountains. Peasants in the region have been chewing the leaves with alkaline lime powder as a stimulant for at least eight thousand years, especially to sustain them while doing work at high altitudes. Although the plants dislike the cold, they thrive in humid, tropical conditions where other plants struggle and, once established, live for up to forty years and yield harvests up to four times a year. The Spanish conquistadors and their accompanying Catholic priests tried to ban coca but realized that it was key to maintaining their coerced labor force in the silver mines and relented, banning only its presence in religious ritual.[88] Global North consumers enjoyed extracts of the leaves in "coca wine," health tonics, and other over-the-counter stimulants, but in 1859 German chemist Albert Niemann isolated the chief alkaloid, cocaine. This far more powerful drug became a desirable cultivated export, farmed in Java by Dutch colonists and the Japanese in Taiwan. These Pacific ventures collapsed during World War II, and the cocaine trade shifted back to the plant's origins, with Colombia quickly taking the lead in growing, processing, and exporting across the Western Hemisphere by the early 1970s.[89]

Coca production is land and labor intensive. Expanding the growing region has taken the plant from its original habitat and into fields cleared using slash-and-burn tactics, where it quickly depletes the thin soil base. This creates areas where, without serious remediation, nothing else can be grown and erosion makes mudslides and floods much more likely. Processing the leaves begins by soaking them in kerosene or gasoline, often stolen or extorted from oil companies. In the crudest versions, just crushing these soaked leaves underfoot in a ditch will yield a paste that is 75 percent cocaine while leaving behind contaminated soil, water, and flammable pools of waste. For purer product, the paste is mixed by a chemist with precursor chemicals like ether and acetone, then dried and packaged as powder.[90] One hectare of cocaine production generates two metric tons of chemical waste products, which producers usually just leave behind.[91]

The most obvious VNSAs using cocaine as a funding mechanism are cartels, which operate as large transnational criminal enterprises, vertically connecting the production, transport, and wholesaling of drugs. Cartels' interest in politics tends to be limited to those actions that intimidate the government in whose jurisdiction they operate, but they tend to be intensely conservative, patriotic in their own peculiar way, and primarily interested in the money generated. During the 1970s a handful of centralized, hierarchical cartels, including the Medellín, headed by Pablo Escobar from Colombia, dominated the cocaine trade and served as an "aggressive competitor" to the state. Their power was bolstered by coercing the Colombian diaspora in North America, even using relatives left behind as hostages. Kingpins like Escobar indulged in flamboyant lifestyles, importing hippos to live in the local river (where they remain an invasive pest) and openly funding schools, clinics, and housing projects, all of which bought him tremendous goodwill even in the face of the cartels' blistering violence toward rivals and bystanders.[92]

Under threat of extradition, a demand by the United States on the Colombian government, the cartels unleashed terrorist violence against judges, legislators, and law enforcement, eventually bringing on a crisis that destroyed them.[93]

During this golden age of the kingpin cartel, Medellín, Cali, and other giants had a friendly haven in Panama, where Manuel Noriega and the banks laundered hundreds of millions in drug money and served as a transit hub. Noriega was also a U.S. asset in the 1980s, allowing support for the Nicaraguan Contras to funnel through Panama, fueled by funds generated with cartel cocaine. The cartels themselves had no trouble attracting a rogues' gallery of assassins, enforcers, and goons, including European neo-Nazis.[94] In response to the waning tolerance for these organizations in the early 1990s—a product of Cold War sponsorship withdrawal that ended Noriega's administration—the DEA initiated a new strategy of decapitating the major cartels. Escobar, José Santacruz Londoño, brothers Gilberto and Miguel Rodríguez Orejuela, and others faced arrest, extradition, and confiscation of their wealth. While this solved one problem, it created another as smaller, more flexibly organized replacements rushed into the vacuum left by the collapse of the titans. This spilled over into violent turf wars in New York, a spike in the price of cocaine, the rise of Mexican drug-trafficking organizations, and important tertiary effects destabilizing the Shining Path's funding in Peru.[95]

The opportunistic replacement cartels were a new evolution of drug VNSA: less hierarchical, operating more like a networked business with decentralized operations, diversified into licit businesses, and more interested in co-opting the governmental structure than threatening them into compliance. Colombian cartels, pressured by the kingpin decapitation strategy, shifted their smuggling routes from the Caribbean into Mexico and paid their traffickers in cocaine. At the same point in the mid-1990s, the North American Free Trade Agreement (NAFTA) made cross-border trade—licit and illicit—far easier, incentivizing VNSAs in Mexico to step up from one link in the Colombian's logistics operations to running the show themselves. Farmers displaced by NAFTA's cheap, American-subsidized produce were available for drug agricultural cultivation as well as recruitable as VNSA members.[96] Dangerously savvy survivors of the Colombian cartels were available with their vital middle-management skills, transforming drug trafficking with the corporate accounting, efficiency metrics, and global logistics chops to retool shipments in order to (literally) fly under the radar of law enforcement and even offer their associates a "robust and surprisingly reliable system of credit . . . no different from Wal-Mart or Sears."[97]

Cartels, though, do muster far more militarized security than Walmart and Sears. The proliferation and availability of weapons and sophisticated equipment, along with the ability of the VNSAs to lure trained professionals away from state-sponsored military and law enforcement organizations, allows cartels to field armed personnel with the same skills of their establishment opponents. Their communications systems are encrypted and relayed along remote and camouflaged signal stations and antennae powered by solar panels, a "criminalized infrastructure" far better than that used by their pursuers, and they can track the Colombian armed forces' planes and ships more accurately than their officers can. Adept at the full spectrum of military activity, these cartel soldiers have crossed the barrier from "the gangsterism of traditional narco hit men to paramilitary terrorism with guerrilla tactics."[98]

These successor cartels have drastically expanded their shipping networks, exploring new markets in the early 2000s when, astoundingly, they found the North American cocaine market saturated to the point that prices had declined. Better deals could be found selling in Europe, so they arranged smuggling routes via air legs to West Africa, then across the Mediterranean and deep into western and central Europe, partnering with local gangs in Poland, the Czech Republic, and the Netherlands.[99] For convenience and market access, these cartels will link up with established VNSA-friendly institutions, introduced to the Hezbollah-affiliated Lebanese Canadian Bank by members of the Shi'ite diaspora in Latin America. Using this connection, Ayman Joumaa, a Colombian Lebanese citizen and skilled global "fixer," shipped 85,000 kilos of cocaine and laundered $850 million for the Mexican Los Zetas via the bank and a variety of Middle Eastern front companies.[100]

Cartel logistics assume a percentage of the product will be lost to confiscation, theft, and damage, but their supply chain management is breathtakingly sophisticated and effective. Harnessing globalized transport, they move cocaine in light aircraft, cargo planes, container shipping, and maritime vessels from fighting boats to fiberglass "go-fast" speedboats. In an effort to evade U.S. Coast Guard and U.S. Navy tracking, some cartels invested in mini submarines, even attempting to buy a real, decommissioned Russian submarine in the 1990s for $5 million.[101] Taking advantage of the flood of trucks incentivized by NAFTA, cartels pack cocaine in every conceivable cargo loaded on tractor-trailers, including sealed in cans of chiles (El Chapo bought a cannery to produce "Comrade Jalapeños!" brand); dissolved and impregnated in sheets of cardboard; hidden in upholstered furniture, wheel wells, false dashboards, stinking cargoes of rotting fish (judging correctly that inspectors would not dig in); and carried in the personal luggage of drivers. Paid "hawks" watch the inspection lanes for shift changes and patterns, a sinister twist on licit "logistics consultants" hired to increase efficiency and bring down loss metrics.[102] Cartels are endlessly inventive getting product over obstacles, using the highest tech available in the form of drones to "2,500 year-old technology" like catapults, tunnels, and sandbag bridges across the Colorado River.[103]

Most of the time cartels, being in an illicit economic sector, don't have recourse to courts to enforce business agreements. What they do have is stunning, terrifying violence. In 2006, in a cross-pollination with jihadi videos, cartels began beheading their victims, sometimes filming the execution and torture for added effect and repeat propaganda availability.[104] This theatrical death-dealing and targeted assassination is carried out by specialists, *sicarios*, who may work for more than one organization and who have an army of spotters, errand boys, and tipsters.[105] The ability to reach anyone, anywhere, as well as that person's friends, family, and neighbors, has jacked the death toll up into tens of thousands and prompted the mass resignations of local government officials, law enforcement, and corporate executives in major branches of Coca-Cola and Pepsi in one town.[106] Journalists, whether employees of traditional media or independent bloggers, have been intimidated and murdered for attempting to cover cartel violence.[107] This heavy hand allows cartels to create their own reality and control perceptions of their actions.

Often they want that perception to be genial. Like other VNSAs offering social services, cartels are big donors to local projects that suit them. Co-opting the reputation and high status of the Catholic Church, cartels sponsor lavish weddings, funerals, and festivals for their personnel and bystanders, and they have even convinced some of the clergy to declare that their cash

Smuggling "go-fast boat," carrying 90 kg of cocaine and 2,150 lb. of marijuana, intercepted by the U.S. Coast Guard in the eastern Pacific Ocean, 2021. *U.S. Coast Guard Pacific Area, permission via Defense Visual Information Distribution Service*

donations have been spiritually cleansed by being put toward good works like the construction of chapels, rehab centers, and schools. Officially, the Church hierarchy repudiates the cartels, but one priest explained, "Where not even the government has funds to spend, drug traffickers carry out projects that mean a great deal to the community. I'm not justifying them, I'm just saying how things are."[108] The cartel La Familia, drawing on evangelical Protestant rather than Catholic Christianity, built a similar regime of self-help, family values, and community discipline, increasing their influence over the population they need to control to operate freely.[109]

A big part of this image is built on lavish and conspicuous consumption. Cartel soldiers may have a short life that ends beheaded in an oil drum, but for the time they lived, they had the finest liquor, sports cars, alligator boots, and doting, beautiful arm candy. The lifestyle resonates with long-standing folk memory of heroes noted for their cleverness, defiance, and ability to snooker gringos. Their preferred brands quickly become mainstream fashion in the form of cheaper knockoffs, like Ralph Lauren big pony shirts and trucks with stylized silver wolves airbrushed on the sides.[110] While alive, they can force public deference to their motorcades and to the whims of their girlfriends, and after they're gone, they can have narcocorridos sung about them, despite doomed attempts by the government to censor and ban songs that glorify cartel business.[111] Cartels are masters of propaganda, documenting their activities on social media as well as literally staking out public space in the form of banners bragging about their territory and offering a phone number to call for job recruitment. This is all highly competent, sophisticated information warfare for a VNSA whose goal is wealth.

Economic analysis of the cocaine trade usually points out that the entire illicit industry does not pay taxes, but they probably invest more in paying bribes to government officials in order to conduct their business unmolested. This is one of the destructive facets of illicit commodity financing: Revenue generated does nothing to build the location where it takes place through public goods. Instead the money pours into luxury goods like cars that speed down unpaved streets, and into ensuring that rule of law will only apply to cartels when it benefits them, not when they endanger public order or the social fabric. This corrupt system stretches from local police up to cartels funding the campaigns of national-level office holders, who are expected to return full service to the cartels when they win. When the International Monetary Fund and other reform packages demanded that debtor countries like Peru, Colombia, and Mexico privatize state industries, this cozy cartel–political relationship allowed illicit organizations with cash to buy crucial infrastructure, invest in high-profile companies, and, in the case of Colombia, buy a giant chunk of the national debt at an advantageous rate. At one point there was a rumor, likely true, that cartel chiefs had offered to forgive the national debt if extradition were to be permanently abandoned as policy. One observer offered that "deviant globalization isn't a sideshow. It is the show."[112] Even when the connection isn't that open, cartels have used their state levers to act against rivals, cooperating with the police or the army to eliminate a competitor and secure their own access to the market.

One of the most insidious ways that cocaine barons have embedded themselves in government is through becoming substantial landowners. Tragically, some of this became possible because of well-intentioned land reforms that mapped and guaranteed property rights for indigenous farmers, doing cadastral registration of land that had been held in traditional forms but not recognized by the national government. While the reform was intended to make it possible for owners to get capital and benefit from land improvements, it instead identified available land for cartel personnel to coerce farmers into selling. This is a great vehicle for money laundering but also gives the owner control of crucial routes through the area, agricultural land for growing coca plants (or diversifying into other valuable commodities like avocados), and leverage in local political affairs. It is not a surprise that the new owners are far less invested in using the land responsibly, engaging in slash-and-burn clearing to prepare to plant coca bushes, and ignoring erosion control and other conservation practices that affect soil, animal habitats, and continued growing viability.

The FARC was the outgrowth of a decade of conflict known as La Violencia (1948–58) for its widespread and extremely high death toll as liberals and conservatives fought for political power, with most of the victims peasants and rural workers. Part of the National Front agreement ending the war was a program of expanded agribusinesses that further squeezed and displaced the peasants, who formed self-defense groups, some of which adopted communist ideology. At the height of the Cold War, this sparked concern from the United States, which sent a "special survey team" from Fort Bragg, North Carolina, in 1962, advising the Colombian government to begin a harsh counterinsurgency campaign, Plan Lazo, against these groups. In May 1964 these COIN forces attacked Marquetalia, a communist enclave operating as an autonomous region, with overwhelming force against one thousand peasants, only forty-eight of whom were armed. The forty-eight escaped into the hills, with Marquetalia as the founding, iconic event of the FARC in 1966.[113] Throughout the 1970s FARC persisted in rural areas but struggled to finance itself through extortion of landowners. In 1977 narcos began encroaching on FARC territory, pressuring peasants to grow and process coca, and prompting the revolutionary leadership to reconsider their ideological ban on drugs as a "greedy, capitalist enterprise." Through a formal decision in 1982, FARC decided to collect revolutionary taxes from the coca business and extend protection to peasants from exploitation by the cocaleros, creating what one Colombian politician described as a Frankenstein monster: "It has a revolutionary beard, its pockets are stuffed like a drug dealer, and it has the soul of a terrorist."[114]

Through the 1980s FARC moved into the drug business link by link, taxing the traffickers, charging tolls on roads and airstrips, taking a piece of gasoline sales, and eventually controlling the growers and wholesaling coca paste itself, processing it in their own refineries. Any time the cartels, armed Far-Right VNSAs like the Autodefensas Unidas de Colombia/United Self-Defense Forces of Colombia (AUC), or the government encroached with land purchases, eradication plans, or intimidation, their actions drove the peasants into the grip of FARC.[115] The decapitation or "kingpin" strategy benefited FARC as well, allowing them to pick and choose among surviving trafficking organizations for maximum profit. By the 1990s drugs—just one of the package of funding mechanisms including kidnapping, extortion, and oil theft—had become important enough to dictate geographical movement, with FARC garrisoning forces and choosing expansion based on utility to the coca business rather than defensibility.[116]

This windfall from drug money allowed FARC to survive the end of the Cold War without concern for sponsorship loss and to purchase enormous armories of weapons, support a standing force of 18,000 fighters, and even operate their own staff college for doctrinal training.[117] The money allows for further specialization, including highly trained units doing demolitions, sappers, and engineering; targeted assaults; and directed fire support as well as a political branch leveraging armed clientism—identifying promising politicians and then investing in their campaigns until they achieve office useful to FARC's ideological goals. None of this is cheap, but collecting standardized fees like $15.70 per kilo of coca paste adds up to an estimated $150–400 million a year, allowing the group to stockpile resources as a reserve.[118]

The group remained acutely conscious that drugs challenged their ideological foundations, so they balanced it with the role of a surrogate state: providing public good–like schools, clinics, and roads, with strict discipline over their personnel and systems for handling and distributing the money, achieving the status of providing law and order, and mediation in lieu of a functional government court system in rural areas.[119] A rigid central committee redistributed funds from high-producing areas to poorer ones and went so far as to forbid the trappings of *cocaleros*—no gold chains on FARC personnel, and those confiscated off the chests of rogue soldiers went to make medals for obedient ones. FARC only wanted volunteers but expected those who did to give up comfortable lifestyles for the austerity of the jungle, acquiring no riches for themselves or their families, and they enforced this with harsh punishment for those who strayed, including executions as a lesson for others about pilfering, desertion, and corruption.[120]

By the late 1990s, though, cracks began to show. Their longtime leader Jacobo Arenas died, replaced by members of the secretariat less opposed to the drug business and who immediately cultivated closer relationships with cartels FARC supplied with product. The group became less concerned with protecting the peasant farmers than with coercing them into quotas, terrorizing disobedient communities with bombings and fields of landmines, and increasingly discrediting themselves with former sympathizers in the cities. Independent commanders began to be seen as neglecting to share their drug income while comrades in underfunded units starved to death, and hostages reported that the young fighters holding them captive were more interested in drinking brandy than understanding the basic ideology they claimed to represent. Dr. Thomas Hargrave, questioning his guards, found that most of them were illiterate and had never heard of Marx but were extremely familiar with drug money. Offered a large land reserve as part of peace talks in 1999, FARC went all in on cocaine.[121]

The United States had been sending assistance to the Colombian police since the early 1990s, but in 1999 the Clinton administration and the Colombian government entered into a vastly expanded operation, dubbed Plan Colombia, for multiyear aggressive coca eradication and military advising and intervention. In its original form, it concentrated on addressing the issues ideologically motivating FARC—income inequality, alienation from the land, deeply rooted social violence—but in American hands it shifted almost exclusively to elimination of drug trafficking.[122] This changed further after 9/11, when the Bush administration placed FARC, ELN, and AUC (a right-wing drug militia) on the official list of terrorist organizations, allowing for melding of counternarcotics and counterterrorism operations. When asked about the displacement of ideological reforms, President Alvaro Uribe told a reporter, "To fund a social policy, you need resources, and without security you cannot get resources."[123]

This came at a high cost for the people of Colombia. Clinton waived most of the provisions of the Leahy amendments, which forbid foreign aid to organizations with poor human rights records, but the plan assumed that U.S. military advisers would be a more convincing force for restraint than NGOs, as "third world military men were more likely to listen to American officers who briefed them about human rights as a tool of counterinsurgency than to civilians who talked abstractly about universal principles of justice."[124] Instead the Colombian army used right-wing militias to carry out human rights violations and stay on the good side of U.S. sponsors while FARC responded by going on a coke-funded buying spree of higher-powered weapons. The price of cocaine in the Global North didn't go up, indicating no lessening of supply, but the body count steadily rose.[125]

A major part of Plan Colombia was an escalation of aerial spraying and crop eradication. The 2003 *International Narcotics Control Strategy Report* reflected the belief that "the closer we can attack the source, the greater the likelihood of halting the flow of drugs altogether. . . . Theoretically, with no drug crops to harvest, no cocaine or heroin could enter the distribution chain."[126] In practical terms, this meant U.S. DynCorp contractors in helicopters spraying Roundup herbicide over the jungle, affecting not just coca plants but people, animals, and other crops.[127] Predictably, farmers hated this and developed evasion strategies, hiding coca plants under foliage, covering the leaves with sugarcane syrup to protect it from absorbing the chemicals, or pruning them to force new growth. Some farmers just moved farther into FARC-controlled territory for protection. Since the loss of coca produced a crisis of credit, starvation, and dislocation, FARC leveraged this in its propaganda, putting up billboards—"Plan Colombia: Los gringos ponen las armas, Colombia pone los muertos" (The gringos bring the weapons, Colombia supplies the dead)—and offering bounties for anyone who shot down the helicopters. Since this spraying affected more than just FARC cocaine, criminally oriented cartels began sharing intelligence and resources with FARC to drive off the sprayers.[128]

This wicked problem continued for the next fifteen years, with FARC working with cartels, which also worked with right-wing militias, who worked with the military to suppress FARC, and all the permutations in between. After a spike in violence in 2010–11, the Colombian public and political establishment became more interested in a peace settlement, tired of the private military forces, kidnapping, botched rescues by the police and armed forces, and social and economic disruption. After significant land reform promises, the loss of support from the Chavez regime in Venezuela, and political compromises that would transition FARC into a political party eligible for elections (much like the IRA and Sinn Féin), FARC agreed to a cease-fire in 2016.[129] The overall peace deal has been complex and was initially rejected narrowly by a national plebiscite in 2016. A revised agreement, approved by parliament, went through in November 2016. Some of the sticking points involve money—where did FARC put its millions, and is it available for reparations to victims, national infrastructure, and environmental damage? What can demilitarized career FARC personnel do for jobs? Removing FARC as a major coca player created a vacuum for new cartels to fill in order to service the continued demand, so who is moving paste through the jungle now? Somebody will.[130]

In a parallel to FARC in Colombia, Sendero Luminoso (SL, or Shining Path), a brutal Maoist insurgency in Peru, emerged in the 1970s as a response to long-term neglect of rural areas and increasing poverty and crises cascading from demographic pressure, land exhaustion, prejudice against Quechua-speaking people, and disappointment that reforms launched by the Juan Velasco government mostly benefited coastal elites and overlooked the highlands. Some of the group's key early recruits were the educated children of highland peasants who expected to return from college and take up posts as teachers but instead found grinding poverty and personal tragedies at the hands of public service mismanagement. Shining Path doctrine against corruption resonated with pleas in an early 1980s community survey: "Here, they've forgotten us. There's no help. They're killing the poor people."[131] This original orientation predisposed SL against drugs as exploitative and anti-Marxist, along with other vices like prostitution and alcohol abuse, and their hard line on resourcing limited their acquisition to dangerous and costly raids on police stations for guns and ammunition. Expansion, especially to urban areas, and independence from a foreign sponsor would require a better cash source.[132]

SL found its answer in the Upper Huallaga Valley, to which they retreated after military defeats in the early 1980s. The *cocaleros* there were no friends of revolution, an example of a conservative, religious, criminally minded VNSA uninterested in drawing attention or rocking the boat in ways that endangered their income from cocaine. Matters shifted dramatically after SL murdered the mayor of Tingo Maria, to which the government responded by placing the area under a repressive state of emergency that harassed the *cocaleros* as much as the insurgents. Showing that they were willing and capable of fighting off eradication teams and shielding the farmers from the army and the police, the cocaine traffickers increasingly came to bargain with SL leaders, even finding that the revolutionaries drove a harder, more consistent deal for the peasants. In turn, SL charged access fees for airstrips and revolutionary "taxes" on the cocaine, and tapped into trafficker contacts for better weapons on which to spend their cash.[133] Their ideological justification for this shift in attitude was that the United States was responsible for its own consumption problem, and that the response of the Peruvian government—brutal repression of peasants—was "*hambreador*" (making people hungry) and that they were "against genocide and against [coca] eradication."[134]

Thus began a horrific and destructive dance between the government and the SL insurgents: A new army commander, like Gen. Alberto Arciniega, would be sent to suppress the SL but left to draw his funding from drug trafficking so that he'd run into opposition not just from SL but from the local police and U.S. antidrug policymakers. Then a president like Alan García might attempt development projects and try to hold the military to human rights rules only to see them sabotaged violently by the SL, with the angry military standing by shrugging and pointing to their tied hands. When the United States sent aid, it was to the police, exacerbating tensions with the army, which resented the influx of money and attention. At one point, in March 1989, SL attacked a police station in Uchiza. Through the night, the besieged police commander pled for assistance from military units based minutes away by helicopter but received no response. SL killed everyone in the station and took complete control of the town. Rumors abounded that the military released SL prisoners in order to keep conflict going and justify their presence in lucrative positions.[135]

The steady stream of coke money allowed SL to outlast the end of the Cold War, but it also made them more confident in their ideological austerity, imposing unpopular and brutal compliance with their collectivization and moral edicts on the farmers. Without needing to listen to local people for their support, they dealt harshly with the traffickers and with dissent. This opened the door for the government to attempt another round of development projects focused on the highlands, including health clinics, schools, roads, and irrigation. In the early 1990s Colombia was becoming the competitive source for cocaine, aided by a plant fungus that devoured 30 percent of the Huallaga Valley crop—a setback that SL couldn't blame on the government or eradication programs. Cocaine leaving Peru was being intercepted through interdiction of the air leg of the transport, not eradication. Fed up with SL ideology and no longer in need of protection, peasants were encouraged to form armed groups, *rondas*, to chase off the insurgents. Although SL splinters still exist as of 2021, subsequent Peruvian administrations have regained control and reduced them to a shadow of their former power, especially as they've lost FARC as an over-the-border ally.[136]

Crop substitution programs for cocaine run into the same complications as those offered for opium: very few products offer the guaranteed return of coca bushes, complete with continuing loans and processing support (mules, seeds, gasoline, generators) from traffickers. In 1990, when the United States offered Bolivia, Peru, and Venezuela $1.5 billion in a five-year crop substitution program, the governments pointed out that as long as the United States was generating demand, no amount of money could entice farmers to do something less certain to be profitable.[137] Propaganda aimed at guilting cocaine producers into other avenues because of the harm wrought by their product inevitably backfires as farmers see no reason to care that Global North addicts take drugs, other than that they get a small fraction of the money generated in the process.

Alternative crops like bananas, pineapple, and citrus fruits require investment in infrastructure to get the produce to market before spoilage, a challenge in areas with poor roads, and more stable crops like coffee and cacao take several years to start producing, requiring a sponsor to support a project long-term before seeing any profits. In worst cases, farmers became frustrated and returned to coca, which, if discovered, would disqualify them from future programs. In the best case, boutique programs in areas especially suited to coffee and cacao, like San Martin, can put out a luxury product marketed as fair trade and an alternative to cocaine production, securing a niche market. This, of course, won't work for all areas or if more communities compete for the dollars of reform-minded chocolate lovers at Whole Foods.[138] Reform packages with the possibility of success must include long-term guarantees of income at a level that allows for social mobility and savings, land tenure and rule-of-law stabilization, and provision of social services on a level that competes with those provided by traffickers, who find it easy to staff a clinic or hire a couple of school teachers from their profits. Reduced demand in the form of legalization of cocaine is extremely unlikely in any administration, and even if it happened, cartels would diversify their extortive hold on agricultural production to keep their income and status, even if avocados and lemons are licit and less profitable.[139]

As a source of VNSA revenue, drugs are one of the most intractable, wicked problems. Estimates suggest that 95 percent of the world's drugs come from conflict zones, allowing groups to fund their operations without resorting to a sponsor, giving them a commodity barterable around the world for anything they need, and offering them the advantageous position of protecting vulnerable rural people from oppressive, livelihood-eradicating authorities.[140] The long-running entanglement of intelligence services with drug trafficking makes it extremely difficult to break down established production systems and logistical routes, even when they pass into entirely VNSA hands, but it is more likely that many of those hands still work in the agencies and governments tasked with stopping the flow of controlled substances and depend on the income to run operations. Even a crisis like 9/11—when Bush explicitly linked drugs to terrorism financing, saying "if you quit drugs, you join the fight against terror"—failed to budge consumers who were far more interested in their addictions than in national defense strategy or counterterrorism policy.[141]

Intermixing counterterrorism and counternarcotics, always an uncomfortable twining of military and law enforcement resources, raises further questions of how blurred legal lines of posse comitatus and jurisdiction are, not to mention agencies making the case to keep an expensive technology, say, the Over-the-Horizon Backscatter radar network, designed to track Soviet bombers but maintained as a way to find drug couriers.[142] Finally, even when pushed out of agricultural land or away from trafficking routes, a VNSA with a speculator willing to be a source of chemicals can make synthetic drugs in a shack with a handful of people, even staying a few steps ahead of the authorities by choosing to formulate variations a few molecules off from whatever the most recent legislation makes illicit. With that in hand, the arms dealers will make a house call and get the group back on its feet.

10
ART AND ANTIQUITIES

Even though the cultural property lawyer he consulted advised him not to do it, Steve Green really wanted those clay tablets. And the Dead Sea Scroll fragments. And the Egyptian antiquities. The pieces were all meant for the Museum of the Bible in Washington, D.C., long a cherished project of Green's, meant to underscore his evangelical Christian faith and funded by his chain of craft stores, Hobby Lobby, "consistent with the company's mission and passion for the Bible." Between 2009 and 2012 Green and the museum acquired more than 40,000 objects, ranging from papyri, tablets, coins, and mummies to manuscript fragments.[1] Scholars had begun raising concerns about not just the provenance of the artifacts the museum was showing off but also their treatment—unwrapping mummies to look for biblical texts on the papyrus is not acceptable practice. The biggest problem was that a lot of it had been looted or was fake; was in contravention of directives of the UN Educational, Scientific and Cultural Organization (UNESCO) and of U.S. law; and was very likely to have put money into the hands of terrorists.[2]

One of the thousands of artifacts purchased by Steve Green and Hobby Lobby, smuggled into the United States in crates labeled "tile samples." *Photograph by Keith Gardner (2018), U.S. Immigration and Customs Enforcement, permission via Defense Visual Information Distribution Service*

In July 2010 Green and a consultant traveled to the United Arab Emirates to examine a trove of small clay tablets, which the sellers "spread out on the floor before him, arranged in layers on a coffee table, and packed loosely in cardboard boxes with little or no protective material."[3] One seller explained that the pieces had been "legally acquired in the 1960s" and had been in family collections in Israel, Mississippi, and Washington, D.C.[4] It was a bargain, $2 million for the lot. Hobby Lobby's corporate lawyers asked one of the leading cultural property litigators, Patty Gerstenblith, to comment, and she tried to dissuade them: "I would regard the acquisition of any artifact likely from Iraq . . . as carrying considerable risk . . . an improper declaration of country of origin can also lead to seizure and forfeiture of the object."[5]

Undeterred, Green executed the sale in December 2010 and agreed to wire $1.6 million split across seven bank accounts and arranged to have the shipment of 5,500 objects labeled as "tile samples" from Turkey or Israel, valued at $300, and addressed to the company's Oklahoma business offices as if they were product samples. Customs intercepted five of the shipments and alerted the FBI, which began an investigation because of the boom in looting surrounding the Arab Spring.[6] Four years later a federal court reached an agreement with Green and Hobby Lobby for the company (not Green personally) to pay a $3 million fine and hand over the objects. Meanwhile, the money Green had originally paid for the objects sailed off to middlemen whose links reached back to looters working for Saddam Hussein's regime, al-Qaeda, and local VNSAs. "Anyone who purchases an antiquity without being 100 percent sure it is a legitimate piece is risking funding organized criminals, armed insurgents and even terrorist networks," cautioned Tess Davis of the Antiquities Coalition.[7]

Despite the settlement, including guarantees that the museum would adopt new acquisitions standards and submit quarterly reports to the court on any cultural property purchases, the museum's prior deals continue to haunt them. Sixteen of the Dead Sea Scroll fragments the museum bought have proven to be forgeries, mostly likely made of ancient leather sandals. Rather than conserving long-lost treasures, the museum and Green had been bamboozled.[8] Then, in fall 2019, Oxford University revealed that an investigation of fragments missing from their Oxyrhynchus Papyri Project traced eleven pieces to Professor Dirk Obbink, who had stolen them from the collections and sold them to the Green family.[9] Most recently, the museum has agreed to terms with the Egyptian government for the return of five thousand antiquities—funeral masks, heads of statues, coffins, and manuscripts in Coptic and Greek—illegally excavated by grave robbers. Mr. Green attributes these misunderstandings to his "naiveté" in collecting.[10]

■ War Trophies

Since the first defeated tribe had something worth carrying off, victorious violent actors have likely considered valuables their right by conquest, either repurposing the loot for their own use or, as far back as the twelfth century BCE, displaying it as trophies, demonstrating their superiority to toppled foreign gods and displaced rulers.[11] Romans became accustomed to seeing captured stuff as part of public triumphs, and the personal possession of tasteful and unusual items became a hallmark of sophistication, although finger-wagging lawyers and moralists warned that too much plunder made areas more difficult to govern for the next Roman official and were just excessive and unnecessary.[12] Early Christians, especially once they attained imperial power, sought out pagan trophies to downgrade, as Constantine used porphyry marble columns stripped from temples in his cistern system but incorporated "found" trophies into more luxurious pieces of religious artwork when his mother, Helena, discovered the True Cross and crucifixion nails on a pilgrimage to Jerusalem. Carrying off shiny things, whether they had talismanic value or not, became standard in Global North ancient and medieval warfare, with generals' fortunes made in the pillaging. Efforts were made, particularly at the urging of the Catholic Church, to constrain the looting and harm to civilians of the same faith, but the admonition rarely stuck.

Renaissance appreciation of artwork didn't slow down the stealing, like the epic 1527 Sack of Rome, but it did make the snatchers more conscious that they were holding works of genius, not just things that could be melted down. Having a "name" work was prestigious, and nobles constructed their palaces to offer display space as a measure of their power and ability to command the force to take them.[13] Colonization was "plunder in the form of entrepreneurship," as conquistadors, settlers, and traders began to take as their due that trophies from indigenous people were conversation starters, the foundations of family fortunes, and absolutely the prerogative of the powerful. Early-modern military scholars advised rational application of force and restraint—after all, coalitions shift, and today's foe may be tomorrow's friend—but the collections of enemy rulers were sought out and carried off, as in Christina of Sweden's 1648 instructions to her generals to "take good care to send me the library and works of art there [Prague], for you know that they are the only things for which I care."[14] The Grand Tour, in which British and American gentlemen traveled Europe to sow wild oats and pick up trendy art as souvenirs, cemented the belief that buyers and finders were obviously the keepers.

In 1794, as the French armies of the Revolution swept through the Austrian Netherlands, the Committee of Public Safety in Paris established a commission of trade and supply to find and export artwork and religious items of value back to their treasury. Napoleon Bonaparte perfected this system, adding a more cultural gloss, instructing that because of the new, enlightened regime, works of genius should be in their true home (Paris), setting up the Louvre to receive the trophies. Famously, he recruited and assigned antiquarians and experts to accompany the armies, sending Jacques-Pierre Tinet on the Italian campaigns and Dominique Vivant Denon to Egypt, where troops found the Rosetta Stone.[15] Unusually, though, Napoleon and his empire met defeat in 1815 at the hands of victors who not only wanted their cultural treasures back, they also wanted to set norms prohibiting the possibility of that kind of humiliation of a Western sovereign nation, even sending troops to the Louvre to repossess collections.[16]

Franz Lieber, a veteran of the Napoleonic conflicts as a young man in Prussia, moved to the United States in 1827 and became a respected jurist, tasked by Abraham Lincoln to formulate laws of war for the federal army fighting the Civil War. The resulting "Lieber Code," or General Orders 100, required ethical treatment of prisoners, forbade rape, and instructed that artworks and property of charitable, educational, and scientific institutions should be left out of seizure and shielded from wanton destruction. These things could ultimately be taken as punishment but not destroyed. Although not always followed, this code became familiar in Europe and would be included in the subsequent Geneva Convention of 1859 and Brussels declaration of 1874.[17]

The prohibitions, though, were aimed at the Global North, not Great Power armies as they fought indigenous people elsewhere, with, for example, the French sacking Korea in 1866 and the British carrying off most of the treasures of the Old Summer Palace in Beijing in 1860, Ethiopia in 1868, Ahanti in 1874, and Benin in 1897, with lots of engagements in between as the scramble for Africa and competition in Southeast Asia unleashed imperialism across the globe. A country house drawing room wasn't complete without an eye-catching pagan idol, some rugs, and a tiger skin marking the owner as well-traveled and powerful. Even when it didn't come at the point of a bayonet, Global North looting by missionaries and archaeologists looking for antiquities stripped Egypt and the Ottoman Middle East of tens of thousands of items as enthusiastic scholars searched for biblical cities and ancient Greek proofs of the Trojan War.[18] Many European archaeologists, both amateurs and professionals, were often doing double duty as employees of companies or as intelligence agents of Great Powers, where their surveying, sketching, and language skills were invaluable sources of information.

Multilateral agreements signed as the Hague Conventions of 1899 and 1907 further clarified rules about weapons, prisoner treatment, and pillage and established courts to arbitrate misconduct. However, the beginning of World War I broke the procedures for commencement of hostilities, and transgressions spiraled out from there, with poison gas used on the battlefield and widespread destruction of cultural institutions, including the German military burning Louvain, Belgium, and its university in 1914. Postwar regulation discussed at the Versailles conference and other venues attempted to codify new problems like aerial bombardment, the role of museums as neutral institutions, marking cultural property as being militarily off limits as targets, and British mandate governance in the Middle East enforcing long-ignored Ottoman prohibitions on antiquities trafficking.[19] Meanwhile, the new Soviet state was plundering Orthodox churches and confiscating the former properties of the czarist aristocracy to fund their operations, carefully inventorying them as part of the State Treasury for the Storage of Valuables and selling pieces to foreign collectors or trading them for German arms.[20]

Any belief that Great Powers would abide by the Hague Convention was shattered by the early 1930s as the Nazi Third Reich started Aryanizing property, including art collections; Russian, Italian, and German troops pillaged Ethiopia and Spain; and the Japanese Imperial military took what they wanted from Southeast Asia. World War II was a continual churn of countries attempting to shield and hide their cultural assets from destruction, with the British packing off the National Gallery to a secret mine in Wales, and aggressive combing for and confiscation of property—cultural as well as industrial—was a policy of Nazi officials and Soviet "trophy hunting brigades" in Eastern Europe and Germany. Since many of the areas of active fighting encompassed cultural heritage treasures like the medieval monastery Monte Cassino, Renaissance bridges, palaces used as military headquarters, and whole ancient cities—Rome negotiated to be an Open City—things got ugly, fast. The British and American military fielded a special unit of "Monuments Men" in an attempt to locate and protect items in an effort we'll discuss later in this chapter, but individual soldiers stuffed things into their pockets, from church altar pieces to pages from medieval manuscripts and the Hessian crown jewels, some of which have emerged from Midwest attics only in the twenty-first century.[21]

Post–World War II repatriation was a mess, complicated by shifted borders; genocide; Swiss banking secrecy; Soviet refusal to return things they took from Nazi stashes of stolen goods; the disappearance of "Yamashita's gold," a trove of loot assembled by the Japanese army in Malaya (maybe into the hands of Ferdinand Marcos); and the necessity in Cold War Europe of not agitating key countries like West Germany, Austria, and Italy. The 1954 Hague Convention for the Protection of Cultural Property in the Event of an Armed Conflict, a UN effort, set out that the destruction of cultural heritage was a loss to the entire global community and, thus, the responsibility of all. Signatories were expected to plan during peacetime for the careful labeling and conservation of cultural property, but the United States refused to ratify until 1994, citing the inability to both meet that obligation and invoke nuclear deterrence.[22] In the meantime, the Khmer Rouge stripped Cambodia of cultural works to sell for support, 1990s fighting in the former Yugoslavia deliberately targeted the treasures of enemy populations, and museums faced a rising backlash of post-colonial nations demanding repatriation of pieces under these regulations.[23]

The Hague Declaration and the 1970 UNESCO Convention recognize an intangible harm that comes from the destruction and looting of a people's cultural property. Humiliating a group by undermining their identity and seizing or defacing the objects in which their history or religion are reflected is usually part of genocides, meant to erase the group's claims to an area, devalue their accomplishments, and show their powerlessness. The 1860 looting of the Summer Palace was an explicit punishment of the Chinese court by Western armies for defiance of their authority; this remains deeply resented today. The Hague indictment against Slobodan Milosevic included his efforts to conduct "cultural cleansing" as well as ethnic erasure for the deliberate destruction of Muslim sites.[24] ISIS's explicit goal in obliterating sites is to repudiate national identity built on shared pre-Islamic history and "annihilate the local sense of belonging and the collective sense of memory among local communities."[25]

Eighteenth-century theorists, especially in opposition to the seizure of their cultural property by Napoleon's troops, had argued that context of objects mattered, that something's use by the people who lived with it added value and meaning, and that a sculpture or tapestry meant for a particular location lost something when removed from that setting. Even if it doesn't lead to the work's destruction, violent confiscation and removal changes something fundamental about it as well as the people who lose it, making it more difficult to resume life after conflict and causing people to be willing to risk their lives to preserve it. Again and again, citizens in Afghanistan, Egypt, Libya, Syria, and Mali have shown themselves capable of and motivated to undertake dangerous and self-sacrificing plans to shelter and protect their cultural heritage.[26] A group's cultural patrimony is a key element of who they are, what art they will produce, and how they understand who they are and represent that identity to others, making it especially heinous when their cultural heritage is ripped away from them and used to fund their oppression.

During World War II, the increased use of aerial bombing and the deliberate collection and confiscation of cultural treasures accelerated the need to place institutional limits on behavior toward cultural property. Accused by Italian government propaganda of destroying the Roman city of Cyrenaica in North Africa, the British responded by joining with the American military to locate expertise within the ranks of their forces—archaeologists, art historians, architects, artists, and engineers—to form a unit dispatched to locate and protect these valuable objects. The Monuments Men (and women) undertook dangerous operations that enabled the return of thousands of priceless works, enhancing the credibility of the postwar Allies in seeking to enforce the 1954 Hague Declaration.[27] In 1996 professional organizations in the fields of library, archives, museums, and monuments formed the International Committee of the Blue Shield to systematize markings and cataloging of potentially endangered objects and to conduct training for conservators and museum staff ahead of problems. In 2016 UNESCO created the Blue Helmets of Culture, a task force to be deployed to conflict zones.[28]

The most successful interventions rely on relationships and preparations made far in advance of potential disasters, making it difficult to justify funding and prioritization in developing countries whose pressing needs for human security aid are obvious first choices when allotting scarce time and resources. Whether in Peru or Syria, the programs have to be organic and involve the full participation of local experts and the current professionals responsible for the cultural property rather than a Global North rescue squad sweeping in because objects that interest them are in danger. Long-term investment in training programs, contingency planning, and money set aside for immediate response are not glamorous, but they have the best chance of overcoming suspicions that the foreign experts are just there to snatch treasures or locate targets and offer agency to the people who have the closest connection to the property in danger.

Because of the presence and efforts of cultural property protection experts like Corine Wegener and Dr. Laurie Rush, best practices have been included in U.S. military doctrine, including the Stability Operations manual and the Arts, Monuments and Archives Guide from Civil Affairs. Troops in the field have found that, despite initial frustration that these guidelines would get in the way of their plans, meeting obligations to protect cultural property turns out to be a force multiplier and improves relations with local people. Laying out the footprint of a base expansion to avoid archaeological sites, not billeting people or putting recreation centers in sacred sites, and noticing that HESCO barriers were being filled with clay shards all limited irreparable destruction to priceless and irreplaceable heritage items.[29] Dr. Rush's widely promoted playing cards, distributed to soldiers in Iraq, offered tips on protecting and identifying art and antiquities and proved useful and popular. An attitude of "stuff happens," like former Secretary of Defense Donald Rumsfeld's reaction to Iraqis looting the Iraqi National Museum in 2003, filters into hard-to-repair disrespect and disregard for the people and their culture and undermines efforts to keep cultural property out of the hands of VNSAs likely to destroy or sell it to raise funds. The opposite—interactions that are mutually interested and respectful—make stability more likely, the population more prone to sharing information, and VNSAs shut out of sources of information and power.[30]

Like almost everything else in this book, though, cultural property protection is rarely easy or straightforward. Some regimes, like that of Saddam Hussein, co-opt the historical past to aggrandize their own authority. Hussein showcased reconstructions of Babylonian antiquities so outlandishly that experts labeled it "Disneyland for Despots," and he identified so closely with the

UNESCO's Culture and Emergencies Section produced cultural property protection cards for global use in order to encourage respectful and responsible actions when emergencies and conflicts take place in the world's cultural heritage sites. The cards in this photo urge players to look for the Blue and Red Shield, denoting sites under Protection and Enhanced Protection. *Photograph by Emma Cunliffe (2020), courtesy Blue Shield International*

mythological hero Gilgamesh that he produced his own ghostwritten fan-fiction novel, *Zabibah and the King*, which Iraqis saw as propaganda. Archaeology and the preservation of antiquities that a government uses as evidence for their claim on land, or to burnish their version of discovery or possession, can be hated by other groups who live there and may end up as targets when conflict erupts. Trying to preserve or return an artifact that has been weaponized and propagandized is politically fraught. Things become even more complicated when conflict is framed as a "clash of civilizations," in which the barbarity of the opponent is shown by their disregard for cultural property, as in the Taliban's destruction of the Bamiyan Buddhas in 2001. The Afghan diaspora community leaned heavily on this to call for intervention, while other Muslims labeled this a cynical button pushed with Global North people when pointing out crimes against humans had failed. For our purposes, keeping artworks and antiquities out of VNSA hands so that they can't use them for financing is a useful goal, but where that denial of money fits with complex and nuanced prioritization of political and humanitarian problems will never be clear.

When artifacts can be recovered, like those confiscated from Hobby Lobby and the Green family, or they've been relocated under extreme circumstances from a war zone, safe havens can be established for their preservation until they can be returned. During the Spanish Civil War, the Republican government shipped art from the Museo Nacional del Prado in Madrid to a museum in Geneva, Switzerland, for safekeeping, and many treasures from the National Museum in Kabul were transferred to the Afghanistan Museum in Bubendorf, Switzerland, in 2001.[31] Britain, France, Switzerland, Lebanon, and the United States all passed legislation for funding and exemptions to sanctions (to allow legal importation) and set up storage under the supervision of museum professionals. This, too, gets sticky since someone has to decide when and under what circumstances things can be sent back, and to what governing authority. Can the safe-haven institutions ask for reimbursement or advantageous loans in return for having taken care of the property? What if the region remains in the hands of VNSAs who will destroy or sell off anything returned to them? To what degree should the safe-haven experts have access to the items for their own scanning, cataloging, and work without approval of their original owners? Even the noblest intentions to shield artifacts from harm can become tangled in legal, political, and ethical quandaries.

■ Digging for Dollars

"I would like to see some helicopters flying over those sites, and some bullets fired at the looters. I think you have to kill some people to stop this."[32] At a conference in London, this kind of thinking, familiar in antipoaching strategies, is easy—if breathtakingly callous—to say. The sheer scale of looting in conflict areas, driven by continuing demand from buyers, is frustrating and threatens to obliterate the work of generations of archaeologists and their crews. Modern archaeology doesn't study just the jewels and aesthetically pleasing items but also the dropped seeds, scat, and arrangements of a settlement's garbage pile, so sites strip-mined for the most sellable objects lose the rest of the information available from a systematic analysis.[33] Looters may also deliberately deface or obscure the sites they mine in order to cover excavation or just to be malicious, leaving things they're not interested in uncovered and vulnerable in crater holes and unsecured shafts.[34] Because there is no modern record of looted objects before they come out of the ground, smugglers can label most of them generically as "Mediterranean" or "Andean" to avoid sanctions and can use aids like bulldozers and online programs like Skype and WhatsApp to retail their finds.[35] Damage done during periods of conflict exacerbates problems in peacetime, deterring lucrative tourism and investment by research teams and not employing the skilled crews who support professional excavation projects.[36]

A "coping economy" of looting may be short sighted, but it also meets the needs of people with few other resources. Living next to fields with sellable things in them when children are starving and there aren't other options is difficult to refuse. Subsistence diggers interviewed often expressed regret or say they knew it was illegal or damaging but, not surprisingly, prioritize their survival.[37] In large areas of the American Southwest, long local traditions of hunting for pots to sell to tourists or to collectors make it difficult to socialize changing norms in archaeology rather than regarding "fields [as] full of pottery we can dig up whenever we're broke."[38] Like other valuable resources, people in possession of territory can also see it as belonging to them rather than a far-off centralized state or antiquities authority, like a diamond mine or an oil field but with the added connection to their religion or ethnic heritage. Seeing themselves as legitimate heirs to the makers of the artifacts, people living on islands in the Bering Sea justify digging by saying the "artifacts are regarded as gifts left by the ancestors, that, if they allow themselves to be found, are meant for use in today's world."[39] Latin American "heucheros" view items as seeds buried by ancestors, to be harvested now for their benefit.[40] Whatever the motivations of the diggers at the source, selling artifacts almost always involves crossing paths with the illicit economy and an organized VNSA, which can control any or all levels of the process, from coerced digging to smuggling or marketing abroad.[41]

Organized gangs of thieves already entwined with drug and arms smuggling are adept at acquiring and moving artifacts, using violence and the connections they already have. In the Ivory Coast a gang took advantage of conflict surrounding the 2011 presidential election to raid the National Museum, making off with $6 million in ceremonial objects, while in Mali the leading traffickers of guns and cocaine just as easily move cultural property into Europe as an additional moneymaker.[42] Similarly, drug routes from South and Central America are useful for the movement of pre-Colombian antiquities, dug up under the supervision of a tightly organized "Mafia-like consortium," alongside bales of marijuana. In 1993 Cambodian bandits armed with hand grenades and a rocket launcher left over from the country's occupation by Vietnam blew open a warehouse at the Angkor Wat conservation center and hauled away religious statues. Meth dealers in the southwest United States have found it productive to use addicts for this task, whose tolerance for repetitive digging "makes them the perfect, tireless looting workforce."[43]

In Italy the "scratch and win" culture of the *tombaroli* (grave robbers), who illegally excavate for antiquities, has long been bound up with the Mafia. Some of the crews are highly skilled, with generational expertise in predicting where to dig and equipped with "mechanical diggers" and ground-penetrating radar, while others are goons of the local Mafia chief, conscripted as a shovel-bearing workforce to indulge a genteel illicit hobby. Antiquities found in Italy's soil and off its coastline belong to the state, going back to a 1939 archaeological law, so every step of the process is illegal, from farmers not reporting diggers, to middlemen paying flat fees and threatening diggers with tips, to police and mafiosi using international connections to sell the loot. Few *tombaroli* or their godfather sponsors care much past identifying objects of precious metals and high resale value, destroying tombs to get to the contents, even breaking fingers off skeletons to get at rings.[44]

In the armed conflict following Cyprus' independence in 1960, Greek and Turkish VNSAs have looted the island's rich archaeological heritage for money, although they cloak it in the rhetoric of saving their particular group's history and protecting it in the name of patriotism. Ottoman governors, followed by British administrators and American ambassadors, indulged widespread relic hunting up to independence, normalizing private sales to collectors, and massive transfers of artifacts to museums in the United States and Britain. During the fighting, the Turkish (Cypriot) Resistance Organization, backed by the Turkish Special Warfare Department, enlisted the aid of Turkish heroin smugglers to move looted treasures from enclaves surrounded by Greek Cypriot paramilitaries answering to the government. The Greeks, meanwhile, winked at sales to private collectors in order to "rescue" items, even allowing dealers to interact with Turkish enclaves and pay "taxes" to their VNSAs. All of this, of course, jumbled the archaeological records, underpinned each side's historical narrative, and allowed both to blame the other for looting. In some cases, "Greek Cypriot archaeologists have blamed Turkish Cypriots for crimes committed by both Turkish Cypriots and Greek Cypriots, which were funded by Greek Cypriots, who were supported by the Greek Cypriot administration."[45]

During the Khmer Rouge's regime of terror in Cambodia, ancient temples were fair game for both destruction in the name of ideology and looting by wealthy art collectors who paid the government for the privilege. One of many, Douglas Latchford, who amassed more than one thousand Khmer objects, worked through armed gangs and Thai brokers, deliberately fabricating provenances and even physically altering the pieces to disguise their origins. The post-1998 Cambodian government has aggressively investigated and prosecuted looters, in conjunction with UNESCO, using self-published books that Latchford assembled, which one scholar assessed as "pretty much the inventory of the missing cultural patrimony of Cambodia."[46] Museums to which Latchford donated pieces, including the Metropolitan Museum of Art in New York, have returned them as looted property of the Cambodian government, and in 2019 federal prosecutors in New York initiated prosecution for trafficking. Latchford defended his actions as rescuing art from being "shot up for target practice by the Khmer Rouge" or left to rot in the jungle. Latchford died, still unextradited, in Thailand in 2020, but his daughter agreed to repatriate the entire stash, evaluated at $50 million, to the Cambodian National Museum.[47]

The wave of Arab Spring uprisings provided cover for gangs and militias to loot cultural property across North Africa. In Libya, unguarded Greek and Roman tombs swarmed with organized crews stripping them to load onto Chinese-flagged ships bound for ports like Gioia Tauro in southern Italy, where Camorra and 'Ndrangheta trade them for weapons and then clean, package, and sell the artifacts at huge markup. The surviving site guards, outgunned and overwhelmed, reported gangs with GPS and fleets of four-wheelers, even fighting one another for choice pickings.[48] In Egypt, where control of antiquities is a huge part of the tourism industry and pride in national heritage, looters swept through, leaving obvious holes in archaeological sites and brokering selections of goods to Global North buyers who had them shipped to the duty-free zone of the Zurich airport. After 2012 the listings for Egyptian antiquities in Sotheby's catalogs topped $13 million a year, reflecting the surge in pillaging and making it nearly impossible to wink and see the items as plausibly "good faith" purchases.[49]

Al-Qaeda's serious interest in antiquities as a funding source seems to have developed in the late 1990s, when Mohammed Atta, later a key leader in the 9/11 attacks, approached professors at the University of Göttingen in Germany to ask if there was a market for Afghan artifacts.[50] Under sanctions, Iraq's museums and archaeological sites were drastically underfunded; Saddam Hussein placed looters under death penalty charges and used cultural treasures himself to raise money. In the south, where his authority had frayed the most, organized crime VNSAs were already moving on underdefended sites.[51] The end of the regime opened the door to widespread pillaging of the National Museum in Baghdad as well as abandoned sites across Iraq. Some communities took proactive steps, issuing religious fatwas against looting at the request of Archaeology Inspector Abdulamir Hamdani, but grand-scale digging, complete with floodlights, vendors selling cigarettes to looters, and on-site brokers, continued.[52]

Coalition troops began capturing insurgents with caches of arms as well as antiquities, connecting the looting to VNSA financing streams and making it more difficult to offer amnesty programs that might allow threats to go free in exchange for the return of objects.[53] Although the outstanding Italian carabinieri specializing in heritage crimes deployed to Iraq in support of protection efforts, the large area and determined looters continue to stymie thinly stretched efforts to stop them and getting large numbers of artifacts into the art market, with "spikes in supposed legal imports perfectly correlated with the breakdown in law and order."[54] In Afghanistan, the Haqqani network, linked to al-Qaeda and the Taliban, moves smuggled antiquities along with everything else, sometimes paying tolls to even more and different VNSAs at checkpoints.[55] Matthew Bogdanos, the rare prosecutor and military officer with training in the classics and art history, served as a key investigator of the 2003 National Museum thefts while on active duty as a Marine, then turned to the ongoing despoliation of heritage sites. His conclusion is sad but realistic: "Given the bloodshed, it is a pretty tough sell to ask people to care about a bunch of old rocks with funny writing. Finding the political will to divert resources to saving cultural artifacts, no matter how precious, seems like cutting funding for the police and fire department in order to expand the public library."[56]

■ ISIS: Art Apocalypse Right Now

The Islamic state certainly didn't pioneer the use of archaeological looting as a funding source. Al-Qaeda and the Taliban, as well as opportunistic criminal gangs, ravaged Iraqi and Afghan sites, while Syrian diggers had been operating for decades, evading Assad's laws against cultural property exploitation. The erosion of authority allowed established and organized criminals to come out of the shadows and steal with impunity, along with Iraqi crews who bring their tools and experience to prospect for valuables and a whole spectrum of political militias looking for money.[57] Syrian regime forces occupying Apamea and Ebla were active in looting themselves and allowed diggers to operate and appear in YouTube videos hauling grave reliefs out of Palmyra on trucks. Al-Nusra and the Free Syrian Army have their own arrangements with "associations of diggers," although a spokesman for the Free Syrian Army explained, "Sure, there are people who loot, but they work alone. If that's how they buy weapons to fight, we can't control them; it's a revolution."[58]

Like its taxation of any other resource in its territory, ISIS began by requiring anyone excavating artifacts to pay one-fifth of any treasure found buried in the ground, based on a ninth-century Islamic legal interpretation. This branched out into selling digging permits for a schedule of fees, all of which was recorded by the ISIS bureaucracy on spreadsheets that were later captured and analyzed.[59] Co-opting the expertise of local mapmakers, archaeology crews, and locals with construction equipment, the group enforces its cut with a brutal hand, whipping a smuggler in Palmyra who attempted to cheat them of a fee and kidnapping the child of an excavator who refused to cooperate.[60] Other people in occupied territory pick up a shovel to feed their families and survive, or, as one commentator described, have hope, although "not a hope of a better world or a hope for eventual freedom. This hope is hope in an ISIS regime, a way to rationalize subservience."[61]

Possession of thousands of archaeological sites, including Palmyra and Nimrud, offered more funding possibilities than just taxing freelancers and collecting tolls from smugglers. Dealing with people who found particularly rich troves, ISIS realized that it could pay them low settlements and then resell the entire batch, using their established channels for other smuggling routes into Turkey.[62] Establishing an "archaeological administration" as part of the Diwan al-Rikaz (Department of Precious Resources), eerily paralleling the licit and scholarly departments overseeing cultural heritage, ISIS sells shovels and metal detectors and rents heavy excavators, tracking the proceeds and organizing mass removals, like the theft of books from the Mosul Museum.[63] Although ISIS gets a fraction of the eventual retail sales price, the revenue stream was sufficiently important that in 2014 the governing council decided to remove the man in charge of the antiquities branch of the Diwan al-Rikaz, characterized in captured documents as "a simpleton who can't manage the division," and replace him with Abu Sayyaf, also head of the oil smuggling operation, showing the useful relationship of these funding streams.[64]

ISIS destroys a lot too. Some of this stems from their ideological disdain for pre-Islamic cultures and a desire to obliterate any identity that is not theirs, but the intense reactions to their propagandized obliteration of museum pieces has a sinister secondary effect. While they circulate YouTube videos of sledge-hammering statues, they're also capitalizing on fear to raise the prices and motivate sellers to give up the artifacts they decide to sell lest they be destroyed. Buyers are more likely to think that they're "saving" things and to be willing to pay a premium to do it, snatching precious objects from villains. It's an extremely effective use of weaponizing their hold on the sites and troves of archaeological material—increase demand by ramping up the threat to destroy while satisfying their iconoclast supporters with carefully chosen acts of defacement.[65]

Those highly motivated customers are easier to reach than ever. Existing networks of dealers in Middle Eastern antiquities have folded the illicit objects into their regular supply chain, overlooking the flawed links, so that an iconic Syrian object, widely photographed there in situ, could turn up in a London gallery window. Large dealers have the capacity to hold illicit items in their safe warehouses for years, releasing them on the market once sanctions have waned and damage incurred in their excavation has been managed.[66] Smaller and even more portable things like cylinder seals, coins, and votive statues leave Syria's battlefields in pockets and turn up on eBay and Facebook labeled as generically sourced "the Bible lands" and "Middle Eastern," a claim that is extremely difficult to police or disprove.[67] The jump in auction listings and online trades reflects a widespread evasion of UN sanctions against the movement and sale of these "blood antiquities" as well as the tolerance that the collecting community has for allowing it to happen, even encouraging it via online groups that offer advice on dating, cleaning, and marketing the individual pieces.[68]

Coalition forces have targeted ISIS's money and oil supplies but have reasons to be far more cautious when dealing with archaeology sites. Burning cash and destroying a tanker truck are exponentially different from a warehouse filled with clay tablets or looters digging on a grid in the desert. Pilots have targeted some of the large equipment, like excavators, but can't do much against people with shovels and are understandably reluctant to do so. Because the directors of the Department of Precious Resources are defying a UN Security Council Resolution condemning the trafficking of antiquities, captured or surrendered ISIS personnel may be tried, as Serbian and Malian war criminals have been, for cultural offenses at The Hague, but it is less likely because Syria is not a signatory of the Rome Statute. In 2016 the U.S. Department of Justice filed, and received, a blanket civil complaint request based in the Patriot Act's counterterror finance provisions to confiscate all antiquities held by ISIS, although what this covered and where they are remains out of reach and not necessarily the purview of the United States.[69]

Adding to the problem, the global shelter-in-place under way in 2020 because of the COVID-19 pandemic has left archaeological sites unprotected since it is even harder to justify personnel to guard them when human needs are so pressing. Meanwhile, in May 2020 one online group specializing in Middle Eastern antiquities gained 120,000 new members, a signal that looters aren't staying home and hobbyists are enjoying an expanded lockdown activity.[70]

■ Museums and the VNSA Ecosystem

If the popular perception of art thieves is Thomas Crown in a sexy turtleneck, the reality is much grubbier. Some of the thefts are individuals with a grievance, like the pensioner who made off with the National Gallery in London's Francisco Goya portrait of the Duke of Wellington, incensed that his TV license fee had gone up, or a nationalist unable to bear that the *Mona Lisa* was in French hands rather than Italian. Most are more sinister, commissioned or carried out for profit, with some of the most effective backed and fenced by VNSAs. Rose Dugdale, an English debutante who converted to the IRA, used her inside knowledge as the daughter of a Lloyd's of London insurance executive to rob first her own family's art collection (1972), then Russborough House in Ireland (1974), hoping to bargain the paintings for IRA prisoners and cash ransoms. Irish crime boss Martin Cahill robbed the same collection in 1986, more for mob profit than ideology, although he turned to a militia on the opposite side of the sectarian divide (the Protestant Ulster Volunteer Force) in an attempt to launder them.[71] Whitey Bulger, the infamous Boston gangster, remains the leading suspect in the burglary of the Isabella Stewart Gardner museum in 1990, although it is unclear whether this was tied to the IRA as well or purely for mob cash-building.[72]

Stately homes, churches, and small museums have priceless items and lack the sophisticated security systems and budget for guards needed to deter thefts.[73] Mafia members hit southern Italian chapels for Renaissance artwork, including a Caravaggio nativity scene taken from Palermo in 1969, and have teased its possible survival and location as a bargaining chip in negotiations with police ever since.[74] Libraries and archives that balance making their treasures available to researchers and providing security are open to canny thieves who slice folios from books and walk out with manuscripts bearing valuable names. Artworks whose materials hold intrinsic value are good theft targets, and laundering means breaking them down, like the two tons of bronze in Henry Moore's *Reclining Nude*, stolen from an outdoor sculpture garden in Hertfordshire in 2005 and sold for scrap, or the solid gold toilet, titled *America*, ripped out of the wall at its installation in Blenheim Palace in 2019.[75]

While museums and art dealers are sometimes the targets of thieves, they're also part of the VNSA ecosystem as the receivers of stolen property. By the mid-twentieth century, many countries legislated policies nationalizing treasures (mineral rights and antiquities) found in the ground, from giving a national museum first right of refusal to outright ownership. As part of their postcolonial assertion of independence, several Global South countries began to lodge suits for the return of antiquities under these laws. Even though it would only cover items taken out of the country illicitly after the law, the pillage had been so extensive that cases existed that met qualifications. The U.S. law used, ironically, was the National Stolen Property Act (1934), which was meant to counter early twentieth-century car theft across state lines and to punish the transportation of goods worth more than $5,000 knowing that they were illegally obtained. The first case, *U.S. v. Hollinshed* (1974), addressed the return of pre-Colombian objects smuggled out of Guatemala to California, with the concealment, bribes, and secrecy so obvious that the court had no problem determining that the Mayan stele should go home. The second, *U.S. v. McClain* (1977), dealt with items taken from Mexico in contravention of their 1972 anti-exportation law.[76] Critics of the decisions argued that it was not up to the United States to enforce the cultural patrimony laws of other countries, especially if those laws contradict the U.S. conception of private property.[77]

The United States has also joined the Convention on Cultural Property Implementation Act in 1983, applying the rules of the 1970 UNESCO Convention on the Means of Prohibiting and Preventing the Illicit Import, Export and Transfer of Ownership of Cultural Property. In some cases, this structure has supported the repatriation of a moon rock to Honduras, since Honduran law required specific alienation by act of Congress to export patrimonial materials, but in others, like the suit filed by a church for the return of a stolen mosaic in the possession of a dealer in Indiana, the court fees were so high that even though they won, the Cypriot Orthodox Church had to give up the piece anyway.[78] Iraq legislated Antiquities and Heritage Law Number 55 in 2002, under which ISIS's looted artifacts might be returned, although Syria is not a participant in the legal mechanisms by which this could happen for antiquities taken from inside its borders. An additional complication is that the United States might have to enforce the confiscations of a country like Cuba, which, under its own laws, seized the property of class enemies and those who fled the island after 1959.[79]

A giant discrepancy in Global North legal attitudes toward stolen property facilitates arbitrage in the illicit art market. In the Anglosphere, laws follow the concept of *nemo dat quod non habet* (no one gives what they do not have), which means that a thief cannot convey fair title to a stolen item, no matter how far back the theft or how many times it has changed hands in between. A buyer has no defense in ignorance of bad title, and the item can be confiscated and returned to its bona fide owner. British law softens this by putting the burden of establishing bad title on the prosecution and by (until 1995) tolerating bizarre loopholes like the medieval Bermondsey Market, at which anyone buying an object there obtains legal title, whatever the object's background.[80] In sharp contrast, continental European law—most notoriously, Swiss interpretation of it—recognizes title so long as the buyer purchased it in "good faith," even if the background was not investigated and the circumstances are overtly shady.[81] This has surfaced most strikingly in Holocaust restitution cases, where the circumstances by which the artwork changed hands was obviously coercive and documented with even casual research but can be trumped by a gallery or museum pointing to their own willfully blind ignorance of how a priceless portrait collection might have been transferred in 1943. The postwar Allied occupation authorities had good intentions in following the recommendations of the Monuments Men for restoring works to their owners but instead quickly defaulted to making things simple by placing them in national museums rather than tracking down surviving heirs.[82]

Suits by origin countries to retrieve their patrimony have exposed the complicity of venerable institutions in artifact trafficking. Many museums have accepted donations from wealthy patrons on the condition that they don't investigate the provenance of the items, and they issue the donors a hefty tax deduction, a sort of "no questions asked, no information given" system. Because these transactions receive a tax break, the public underwriting this has an additional interest in whether the items have come from something that violated the law or benefited a VNSA. Leading legal authority Patty Gerstenblith suggests that "if a museum accepts a gift . . . to which the museum is not receiving title, then the museum is receiving nothing of value and the American public is subsidizing the trade in undocumented artifacts. The IRS should be taking into consideration the certainty of title in determining whether to permit . . . a deduction."[83]

Academic collections contain donations like the University College London's Aramaic incantation bowls, which had been looted from Iraq during the first Gulf War, a fact that the institution suppressed until the relevant papers turned up on Wikileaks. Likewise, in 2000 Cornell University gladly accepted 1,679 cuneiform tablets from collector Jonathan Rosen, although it was likely they had been looted during the same chaos in 1991 Iraq. Dartmouth, meanwhile, had the Afo-A-Kom, a sacred royal artifact from Cameroon. A former Peace Corps volunteer recognized it as having been stolen in 1966 and began organizing pressure to return it. Shelby White and Leon Levy gave $200 million to New York University to set up a center for ancient studies but ran into protests from professors who pointed out that their personal collection was more than 90 percent unprovenanced, pointing to illicit acquisition. The last case is unusual in that scholars are often reluctant to point out unethical practices for fear of being blackballed in the museum and antiquities community.[84]

In 2008 the Association of Art Museum Directors revised their guidelines on acquisitions from stating that a museum must "not knowingly" accept illicitly acquired objects to stating that a museum has a responsibility to research an object's provenance, showing that, at a minimum, the object was outside its country of origin before 1970.[85] This new policy, however, is voluntary, enforced by cultural norms, and does nothing for the legal kicking and obfuscating done by museums to avoid returning Holocaust-looted art to surviving families or other previously acquired controversial items.[86] The Boston Museum of Fine Arts trumpeted its 1969 acquisition of a Raphael as part of its one-hundredth anniversary celebrations, claiming it came from a

Swiss private collection. Italian police investigations showed it being illegally purchased in Genoa and smuggled out of Italy against their exportation rules. The Boston MFA did it again in 2012, accepting the Benin Bronzes as a gift from a collector who purchased them in the 1970s, although the Nigerian government asserts that they were stolen in 1897 as part of the looting by British soldiers following the Benin massacre.[87] The New York Metropolitan Museum of Art followed its policy of demanding a ten-year documented pedigree, in line with its director Philippe de Montebello's belief that "the context in which an artifact is found is virtually meaningless," and, by 2013, making antiquities stolen from the Baghdad Museum entirely acceptable for acquisition. Unlike New York University, without protest, the Met did take Shelby White and Leon Levy's money, establishing the Court for Hellenistic and Roman Antiquities in 2007.[88] Another couple, building a collection for their sponsored museum in Jerusalem, justified illicit collecting by saying, "You're right. It's stolen. But we didn't steal it. We didn't encourage it to be stolen. On the contrary, we have collected it from all over the world and brought it back to Jerusalem."[89]

The J. Paul Getty Museum in Los Angeles is one of the most infamous in illicit collecting. Getty's original acquisitions took place as an adjunct to his strong-arm oil and gas contracts around the world, and the institution established to house them (and provide a tax deduction) continued the tradition through the decisions of director Jiří Frel, who leveraged the Getty's $1.2 billion endowment to wheel and deal. "He would sneak things into the museum at night. . . . He came from the Soviet bloc, and that was just a way of life for him."[90] Later policy constrained the Getty to acquire only items documented prior to 1995, but they almost immediately broke the rule to get three hundred Mediterranean pieces, 85 percent of which had no provenance. The Getty curators solved this problem by manufacturing documentation with its own catalogs from a loaned collection. On other occasions they bought from well-known shady dealer Giacomo Medici, with curator Marion True discussing with him where the *tombaroli* dug them up. Using True to fire a shot across the bow of museums, the Italian government prosecuted her for trafficking in antiquities, a complicated suit which eventually ran out of time in the court system, letting her walk free, but serving as a cautionary tale for others. True echoed familiar justifications: "The art is on the market. We don't know where it comes from. And until we know where it comes from, it's better off in a museum collection."[91]

Voices claiming that illicitly acquired works are better off in the safety of a Global North museum are particularly loud and often speak from positions of authority as curators and institutional directors that "antiquities are the cultural property of all mankind." This overlooks that in asymmetrical conflict, nowhere is really secure—the Mafia set off a car bomb outside the Uffizi Gallery in Florence in 1993, killing six people and significantly damaging three paintings, as a protest against aggressive Italian prosecution of mob leaders.[92] Repatriation can be complicated, though—do objects go back to a deposed royal family or to the national museum of the regime that unseated them? Do religious artifacts belong to that faith's hierarchy or to the people created it, even if they have converted to another belief system? Forced migration and diasporas create competing claims for valuables between the people who now live in its area of discovery and the people who have been dislocated from it. Active conflict adds an additional degree of difficulty: the Crimean Scythian Gold collection, on tour in Europe when Russia annexed the Crimea and its home museum in early 2014, remained in Amsterdam until courts could assign ownership to things claimed by Russia and by the Ukraine, deciding in favor of the Ukrainian claims in October 2021.[93]

When institutions are willing to cooperate, positive outcomes are possible. Museums and governments making the claim may be amenable to long-term loan agreements or exchange programs benefiting both parties. Nearly all heritage institutions agree that tourism and broad exposure to cultural styles and creative works are tools for understanding and better relationships but also want recognition of colonial history, financial benefits of their artistic heritage, and the ability to tell their story, sometimes incorporating this into the display with the objects. Appreciation of artifacts has moved beyond just aesthetic enjoyment of the very best shiny objects, so rotating collections to bring out of storage pieces that illuminate the culture of their makers has done no damage to museum attendance or educational programs. No galleries have empty cases after returning objects, and some have even learned that, by cooperating, they can reunite broken sets and appreciate them in new ways.

When agreements can be reached, it signals that illicit trafficking in art and antiquities is not an accepted cultural and professional norm, and the people whose culture the work comes from are worthy of respect and consideration, defusing a common VNSA ideological grievance.

■ Art Washing

Experts believe that the illicit art trade is generating $3 billion to $6 billion a year, functioning as a revenue generator for VNSAs as well as a convenient form of money laundering and tax evasion, a contention backed up by the unfolding revelations from leaks like the Panama Papers. The art world is ideal for criminal enterprises for a whole laundry list of advantages: Unlike real estate and banking, it requires no state-issued licensing or authorization to participate as an expert; the demand in the wealthy circles of buyers is constant and liquid; aside from the base value of the materials in a work, art is almost entirely subjective in valuation and poorly understood by laypeople; and the elite nature of the transactions offers an unregulated space where gangsters, terrorists, and cartel heavies can take on a veneer (Vermeer?) of respectability.

In the 1960s, as the art world gained more coverage in mainstream media and Picasso and Cezanne canvases broke highly publicized sales records, VNSAs began stealing them. It makes a lot of sense, since the media immediately announces that a painting worth X amount of money has been taken, allowing the possessor of the work to have an independently verified statement of worth. In circulation in the illicit economy, a stolen canvas can change hands for years, serving as collateral for drug deals (usually at 7 to 10 percent of the publicized value), taking up little space, and offering some pride and smug amusement at holding it to spite authorities and insurance companies. When Martin Cahill stole paintings from Russborough House in Ireland, a Vermeer ended up in Antwerp being used by the Mafia for cocaine deals, while a seventeenth-century Gabriël Metsu landed in Turkey. One expert described a transaction as, "I need a kilo of coke quickly, I haven't got cash, but I have a painting supposedly worth a couple of million. I can swap it or offer you a share in it until I get rid of it at a very serious price."[94]

For laundering money, artwork is convenient and "easier to transport across international boundaries than cash, and . . . a lot more difficult for law enforcement officials to trace than the flow of money."[95] Pablo Escobar enjoyed a collection of French impressionist canvases he assembled to use for moving cash, while Brazilian embezzler Edemar Cid Ferreira put $8 million of his ill-gotten funds into a Jean-Michel Basquiat painting, which he walked through Kennedy Airport with an appraisal in hand, fraudulently listing the work as worth $100. Shell company purchasers and a whole spectrum of willing experts can doctor the values, provenance, and insurance coverage to tailor the price for whatever purpose is required. Similar methods can be used to dodge taxes, introducing the possibility of buying and selling a piece between a shell company and a real one, which can hold it as an investment, insure it for an inflated price, and then arrange for it to be "stolen" or donate it for a jacked-up value. The J. Paul Getty Museum was, in fact, created as a tax shelter for the oil tycoon's collection, and early curators eagerly extended this opportunity to other wealthy collectors in order to build the catalog.

Clients in the art world expect discretion, and auction houses, which don't fall under the Bank Secrecy Act, are left to organize their own "know your customer" and anti–money laundering monitoring guidelines in an industry that takes it as a given that anonymous phone bidders can pay cash and that catalog listings are discreetly massaged so that no one has to know the dynasty has fallen on hard times and needs to raise some cash out of the portrait collection. Galleries and museums have a high tolerance for exchanges, loans, and donations with eccentric conditions applied, and they prioritize their clients' privacy over government regulation lest they lose lucrative commissions to a competitor who won't pry. Aiding all of this is a network of "freeport" warehouses that exist in legal free trade zones and into which valuable art can disappear, housed in climate-controlled security outside the Geneva airport, an industrial park in Delaware, or in storage facilities in Luxemburg, Monaco, Singapore, or Beijing. Because these exist as extraterritorial transactions, there are no taxes, no records are kept, and art may stay crated up for decades but legally change ownership dozens of times inside the building.

Where this becomes really dangerous is when it offers a means for organizations and people under sanctions to evade legal controls on their financial activities. In 2014 the Obama administration placed the Rotenberg brothers, Arkady and Boris, and Arkady's son, Igor, on a blacklist of Russian oligarchs involved in the annexation of Crimea via their construction company and gas pipeline. Visa and MasterCard followed U.S. instructions and stopped transactions with the Rotenbergs' bank, the European Union seized property in Italy, and the trio were on the 2017 Countering America's Adversaries through Sanctions Act. Deterred from easier paths of moving money, they've turned to the art market, purchasing $18 million in works and using Boris' Finnish passport to evade restrictions. Using shell companies and employees, often women, they've put an additional $91 million through Sotheby's and Christies' auction houses. This behavior was so flagrant that a Senate committee investigated, with its chair, Sen. Robert Portman, stating that "it is shocking that U.S. banking regulations don't currently apply to multi-million dollar art transactions and we cannot let that continue."[96]

■ Behind Closed Doors

Like some of the other mechanisms used to move money and generate an income stream (horse racing, tax havens, yachts flagged to Panama, etc.), the art world is shielded from law enforcement scrutiny and regulation partly because many of its participants are wealthy people with immense social capital and connections. In 2003 a lobby group formed, the American Council for Cultural Policy, to pressure the Bush administration into loosening the laws controlling the importation and sale of Iraqi artifacts so that members could have first crack at the best items.[97] The norms in the field governing ethics are heavily influenced by donors like Leon Pomerance, who set up fellowships and awards within the Archaeological Institute of America, even providing the paper that the organization's magazine was printed on as part of his donations. Frederick Schultz Jr., convicted of trafficking Egyptian artifacts, had been an outspoken critic of export restrictions from his position as president of the National Association of Dealers in Antique, Oriental and Primitive Art and operated at the center of an elite Manhattan social circle. By insisting on maintaining gentlemen's agreements rather than transparent records, illicit transactions continued under a veneer of prestige and respectability. Buyers felt confident enough to include illicit purchases in photo spreads of their lovely homes, and junior researchers or curators who might blow the whistle or complain can count on not receiving fellowships or access necessary to participate in the field.

Nouveau riche collectors, or those who want to offload any risk to others, can call on the services of the same kind of fixers other illicit commodities employ, only with a far more publicly acceptable face than international gunrunners. These are classy people "who can speak seven languages, have university degrees and are highly intelligent," and—like Jonathan Tokeley-Parry (convicted in 1997 for smuggling antiquities out of Egypt)—wearing the right regimental tie, invited to the right clubs, and with a prestigious degree.[98] These "Janus figures" carefully manage the process of "knowing what not to know" and manage the risks, playing up the thrill of possession and hunt for discovery, which includes the illicit nature of many of the transactions as a feature, not a bug.[99] The danger is definitely there; as one London art dealer cautioned: "The people in Hong Kong don't tell you about the provenance because the people who smuggle goods out of China are not people you want to talk about. . . . They just say that you don't ask those kinds of questions. That's the way . . . to end up in the harbor."[100]

Key to this is a shared narrative that antiquities and art trafficking is a victimless crime. The traffickers obviously are nice people who are continuing activities done publicly by their friends and relatives, who are also nice people who "like wonderful things" and cultivate a deliberate blindness to why or how regulations and norms have changed. They're rescuing "orphan" objects from countries and people who can't possibly appreciate them and giving them the setting and attention they deserve. This takes a particularly nasty turn when collectors vilify countries of origin as undeserving, poor cultural resource managers, corrupt and, as one New York collector pejoratively explained about repatriation demands, "the Italians always wail, right? That's part of the national character."[101]

Arbitrage operates aggressively, with dealers and collectors seeking out jurisdictions with advantageous rules. Finding an amphora off the coast of Turkey versus the Israeli coast carries vastly different obligations to report the find to authorities, but the object itself, divorced from its context, can be labeled with the easier export scenario. The Cayman Islands, ever willing to please, allows any goods stored there to become the legal, titled property of the possessor after only seven days, after which the goods can go anywhere.[102] Experienced participants in the market know even more tricks: disguising

an illicit export as a modern forgery, breaking up a known piece into fragments and having expert craftsmen reconstruct it elsewhere, auction houses
allowing a shady object to be sold to the person who consigned it for sale, thus
generating a provenance, dealers carefully coaching sellers to "remember" it
came from a family collection, or even finding a plausibly aristocratic person
to claim it had been at their ancestral manse for generations (for a small fee).
The real Wild West in art trafficking takes place at "fairs" in Maastricht,
the Netherlands, or Basel, Switzerland, where private sales take place in an
unrecorded and lightly regulated way—pretty much the gun shows of the
art world.[103]

Many collectors behave like the Hobby Lobby dynasty, determined to
believe they have stumbled on artifacts fortuitously discovered only recently
and available to them through the generosity and good business sense of the
dealer, even when the circumstances are suspicious and the suspension of
disbelief nearly herculean. Noah Charney, of the Association for Research into
Crimes against Art, offers extremely basic guidelines: Tamp down wishful
thinking that the very piece you want is somehow available legally to you
and demand a substantial set of documentation of where the work has been,
who owned it, and under what circumstances it was sold. The potential buyer
needs to scrutinize the provided paper trail carefully, with their own lawyers
and advisers asking realistic questions about where the money is going and
paying attention to red flags like wiring money to multiple accounts, disguising
shipments as something else to evade customs, or participating in title transfers
through third-party countries. In some fields, volunteer crowdsourcing groups
exist to research auction catalogs and databases like Interpol's ID-Art app,
the Art Loss Register, and Red Lists from the Council of Museums.[104]

For smaller purchases, there's no need for an international cultural property
lawyer, but it is smart to ask questions of sellers. Internet dealers can be located
anywhere and make their money selling a volume of small items rather than
big scores of a single painting or tablet. One investigator asked an eBay seller
about an amphora and received a hostile "it has been in North America for
a very long time, far before any laws or whatever mumbo jumbo you are
trying to lay on me and demanding who and what and where I am and export
laws."[105] Yes, this one seems suspicious.[106] eBay Germany and Switzerland have

put hard limits on sales, including those of Nazi paraphernalia, and require antiquities to meet substantial proof of legality and provenance before listing, independently monitored for compliance in Germany by the government's Landesdenkmalpflege (Monuments Protection Authority). Other countries can demand and achieve these kinds of controls as a start to eroding the mainstream acceptability of artifact trafficking.

Until the 1970s police and insurance investigators lumped art and artifacts with consumer property like furniture, microwaves, and cameras in stolen property reports, making no special efforts to recover them beyond pawn shop and fence checks, where things usually turned up. Interest in art crimes coincided with some of the greatest obstacles to investigating them—global shipping, the internet, drug money, and aggressive transnational criminal organizations. Caught in this, few national police forces and almost no local ones could justify specialized training for personnel or carrying an "art squad" when there were crimes against people and more mainstream thefts of cars and robberies of banks. Some art-rich countries have established partnerships among the police, customs, and foreign offices, like France's Central Office for the Fight against Trafficking in Cultural Goods (Office Central de lutte contre le traffic des Biens Culturels), which develops career-long contacts in criminal networks like the art dealers who use the Clignancourt flea market in Paris. Norway entrusted the investigation of the theft of Edvard Munch's famous *Scream* in 2004 to its organized crime and economic and environmental crime officers in Økokrim, which also handles the defacement of monuments and damage to wildlife sites, only a handful of cases a year. Denmark and the Netherlands have no art-dedicated officers at all, assigning incidents on a case-by-case basis, which means starting from scratch and developing contacts in this closed world of auctions houses, museums, dealers, and collectors, although under pressure from Parliament, Dutch police have invested in a database for art crimes and three staff positions to manage it.[107]

In the United Kingdom, Scotland Yard established an art and antiques unit in the late 1960s but disbanded it, only to stand up successors in the mid-1980s but lose investigators to the point of dissolution when personnel were seconded into big cases like the 2005 London bombings and the 2017 Grenfell fire. With minimal staffing, the Met Police team manages the London

Stolen Art Database but struggles, like managers of other attempts to create comprehensive catalogs of the world's cultural property, to integrate it with other systems and make it accessible.[108] The FBI set up an art crimes team in 2004, with specially trained agents and prosecutors, but it remains small and must constantly defend itself with metrics of art recovered. New York County's district attorney, Cyrus Vance Jr., authorized Matthew Bogdanos to start an art prosecution squad, responding to ISIS trafficking and the potential for using New York's vast claims to jurisdictions as leverage as the hub of the global financial network, but aligning the stars of a champion with a legal and art background who can sell political spending on cultural property protection is rare.[109]

One powerful exception is Italy's commitment to policing and investigating crimes against its cultural patrimony, shown in the 1969 establishment of the Carabinieri Command for the Protection of Cultural Heritage, a branch of the military gendarmerie with branches dealing with archaeological sites, antiquities trafficking, forgery, and museum thefts and with emergency expertise in stabilizing valuables during natural disasters and conflict. They began computerizing their records in 1980 as the database LEONARDO and now include an app with which volunteers can spot potentially stolen works and report them in an innovative crowdsourcing approach to policing. Carabinieri personnel are famous for being on vacation and spotting stolen paintings in gallery windows or exhibit catalogs, and for tracing voluntarily returned property like items picked up by tourists at restricted dig sites and special circumstances, such as the family who bought a stolen Gaugin because museum thieves abandoned it on a train, and the rail company had a lost-and-found sale. Personnel have deployed to Iraq and Afghanistan to guard sites and train conservators, and the unit runs capacity-building programs in Latin America to introduce law enforcement to illicit trafficking prevention tools, even drafting suggested legislation.[110]

Technology makes it easier than ever to scan and make high-resolution photographs of even 3-D print replicas of cultural heritage artifacts. The complication is that merging databases around the world requires massive investment of time and expertise, and some agreed-upon sync of method, whether barcodes, RFID chips, or some other ID. Also acting against the potential of centralized record keeping are powerful stakeholders who want to keep their illicitly acquired art secret, don't want their parts of a broken-up collection identified and reunited as a whole, and don't want to embarrass or scare off influential and wealthy donors by revealing shady provenances. A database that includes the text of tablets would boost accessibility to global scholars and enhance the prestige of legally owned artifacts used in research. The potential, though, is enormous not just for repatriating items and finding their missing parts but also for using art trafficking to follow routes used for guns, drugs, and human trafficking, using items surfacing on the market as an early warning of conflict in particular regions and perhaps even leveraging knowledge from prosecuting VNSAs for art crimes into actionable intelligence for use against them by other forces, rather than being the little posh brother of operations to go after more violent and typical VNSA activities.

11
SETTLING
ACCOUNTS

Spring semester 2012, Joseph Kony was everywhere . . . and nowhere. On the rural Minnesota campus where I was teaching history and security studies, undergraduates diligently put up hundreds of fliers with his picture and the slogan "Make him famous!" Intrigued, I tracked this back to the local organizers, who had become interested via a viral YouTube video produced by an NGO, Invisible Children, which encouraged viewers to publicize Kony and the atrocities of the Lord's Resistance Army (LRA) in Uganda, and to purchase "action kits," bracelets, T-shirts, and other merchandise. After celebrities like Oprah Winfrey, Rihanna, Angelina Jolie, and Justin Bieber amplified it, the piece had 9 million views in a matter of days, 112 million by the end of the month.[1]

There was no denying that undergraduates who had previously expressed no interest in East Africa were revved up, and I admit that I shamelessly took advantage of this for classroom purposes, filling in background on the political history of the region and the LRA. The problem was that all the enthusiasm was spinning a gear that didn't mesh with anything else. The

Despite flashy media coverage and widespread Global North youth engagement, the Kony 2012 campaign had few tangible courses of action and fizzled out without Joseph Kony's capture or the suppression of the Lord's Resistance Army in Uganda. Dublin (2012). *Photograph by William Murphy, courtesy Flickr*

campaign urged participants to lobby for military intervention, but in terms of what a twenty-year-old in the upper Midwest could do to thwart the LRA, an email to a political office fell short of satisfying. The LRA made its money pillaging and extorting Ugandans and selling poached elephant tusks to pay for weapons, things that Global North activists couldn't do much about other than not buy ivory.[2] Lobbying did produce a congressional resolution reiterating a previous authorization of force in 2009, and pressure for the African Union to send troops, but neither action succeeded in catching Kony, who remains at large.[3]

NGOs and long-experienced activists criticized the project as "poornography" and "slacktivism," simplifying deep-rooted and complex issues into T-shirt slogans for Global North teenagers, for whom force is the go-to tool of intervention and a savior mentality. Measured on awareness raised, the Kony 2012 campaign was a success, but it asked people to do things they were already comfortable with: wearing "cause" bracelets, donating money, showing up to public rallies where there was no police presence or chance of harm. It hadn't asked anyone to pay more for an item, stop using something, investigate the source of a commodity, or change any everyday habits. As a blip, it encapsulates the problems of attempting to halt VNSAs and their money generation through individual choices, no matter how well-intentioned, and the obstacles to global action.[4]

■ Red Flags and Red Tape

One of the fundamental problems of VNSA finance is that VNSAs are *very* motivated. Whether their goal is wealth generation or a burning need to buy weapons to advance an ideological revolution, groups have members committed enough to risk their lives for it. In researching for this book, I encountered plenty of analyses from the security realm that ended with some pithy bullet-point recommendations, most of which boiled down to

- make it illegal,
- enforce existing laws against it,
- or tell VNSAs what they're doing is bad.

Well, sure, no problem!

There are plenty of international and national laws that aim at investigating, prosecuting, and preventing VNSA financing. At the international level, the United Nations has been issuing agreements meant to curtail VNSAs for decades. The 1988 Vienna Convention, or the Convention against Illicit Traffic in Narcotic Drugs and Psychotropic Substances, included substantial anti–money laundering standards, which were adopted by most of the convention's signatories as their own anti–money laundering statutes, although the orientation of this as a tool in the drug war framed most anti–money laundering efforts as a law enforcement and organized crime problem.[5] Al-Qaeda's bombings of U.S. embassies in Africa prompted the Clinton administration to become more interested in seeing terrorism and transnational crime as intertwined and fed through overlapping financial sources.

This push resulted in the UNSCR 1267, sanctioning and freezing the assets of the Taliban, and the 1999 International Convention for the Suppression of the Financing of Terrorism, which required signatories to establish legislation criminalizing terrorist financing and regulating financial mechanisms within their sovereign states.[6] On 9/11, only a handful of countries had signed the agreement, but bandwagon interest jumped in the aftermath of the attacks, although the "carrot" of funds to help with implementation and technical assistance has never been fully disbursed.[7] A countertransnational crime convention followed in 2000 as the Palermo Convention (the UN Convention against Transnational Organized Crime and the Protocols Thereto), dealing with human trafficking, arms dealing. and smuggling, but the bifurcation of terrorism and crime continued, and the United States was primarily interested in terrorism.[8] Other UN conventions exist about specific VNSA acts, like hijacking, kidnapping for ransom, and piracy, but their implementation gets hung up on disputed definitions of what individual nations believe to be terrorism and crime and the degree to which they agree to cooperate.

Other international organizations exist to monitor illicit financing, including the Organisation for Economic Cooperation and Development (OECD), founded in 1961 among primarily Global North states but expanded in the twenty-first century to Latin America. Its discussion of anti–money laundering regulations and tax regime transparency hit a snag in 2003, when congressional Republicans voted to cut U.S. funding to the group (amounting to 25 percent of OECD's budget) because, while they were happy to pursue the prosecution of terrorists, they weren't so keen on pushing for people to pay taxes.[9] In 1989 the G7 nations established the Financial Action Task Force (FATF) in Paris, offering recommendations on banking secrecy laws and guided self-assessments of national banking systems and rolling out a "naming and shaming" list. However, the FATF has no enforcement abilities, and its blacklist, ironically, was taken as an advertisement as the best places to launder and hide funds.[10] The Egmont Group, a meeting for government agencies covering financial functions, formed in Paris in 1995 and succeeded in getting forty countries to stand up financial intelligence units, which the Egmont Group supports with advice and standardization of financial intelligence, but compliance is entirely voluntary.[11]

The U.S. legal system has been interested in using financial enforcement against organized crime and drugs since Al Capone went to Alcatraz for tax evasion. The big moves, part of Nixon's war on drugs, were the Bank Secrecy Act of 1970, which required suspicious transaction reports (which resentful banks promptly overdid, submitting so many that most rotted in a warehouse), and the Racketeer Influenced Corrupt Organizations statute, which allowed prosecution of racketeering offenses and confiscation of ill-gotten gains.[12] These were meant as weapons against Mafia-style VNSAs like the Gambino crime family and the Hells Angels Motorcycle Club, so when an intrepid IRS investigator used the law in Operation Tradewinds (1972) to investigate the Bahamian Castle Bank and Trust—uncovering financial chicanery by Hugh Hefner, Tony Curtis, Richard Nixon, and Nixon's adviser Bebe Rebozo as well as CIA-affiliated anti-Castro groups—the appointed IRS commissioner ruled him out of bounds and crushed the case.[13] In 1977 the International Emergency Economic Powers Act (IEEPA) gave the president the ability to declare a national emergency in response to a foreign threat, then block and freeze the assets of that threat—used by Carter against Iran and Clinton against Colombian drug traffickers.[14] Ronald Reagan's war on drugs yielded the 1986 Money Laundering Control Act, which made laundering a crime if the money was the product of tax evasion, fraud, theft, or trafficking and instructed the Treasury Department to establish bilateral international agreements for information sharing.[15]

In addition to U.S. interest in international law about terrorist financing, U.S. legislation focused on finding terrorist financing had been spurred by the 1998 African embassy bombings (and, on the domestic front, the Oklahoma City bombing), and the Clinton administration had applied the IEEPA to bin Laden and al-Qaeda and set up the Committee on Transnational Threats, headed by Jonathan Winer, who had investigated both the Bank of Credit and Commerce International and the Contras.[16] Unfortunately, the IEEPA only allows the Office of Foreign Asset Control to go after U.S. entities aiding a group on the blacklist, and bin Laden had moved his money from Sudan to Afghanistan. Republicans in Congress, led by Sen. Phil Gramm (R-Ga.), vociferously resisted banking reform that Sen. Carl Levin (D-Mich.) had been pushing for two years, bragging that they had "killed the Clinton administration anti–money laundering legislation" on the grounds that it violated privacy.[17]

The attacks on 9/11 changed this dramatically. President George W. Bush appeared at a press conference on September 24, 2001, and announced, flanked by Secretary of the Treasury Paul O'Neill (previously an opponent of banking reform), that the United States would follow FATF guidelines, fold Levin's failed legislation into the Patriot Act, and "will lead by example. We will work with the world against terrorism. Money is the life-blood of terrorist operations. Today, we're asking the world to stop payment."[18] Secretary of Defense Donald Rumsfeld chimed in that "the uniforms of this conflict will be bankers' pinstripes and programmers' grunge just as assuredly as desert camouflage."[19] Congress passed the Patriot Act, which included sweeping measures for identifying and seizing the assets of organizations deemed to be terrorist threats, the Customs Service embarked on Operation Green Quest to track terrorist financing as the lead in a multiagency investigative unit, and the Office of Foreign Asset Control got a special subdivision as the Foreign Terrorist Asset Tracking Center.[20]

Swinging a huge bureaucracy with a wide spectrum of stakeholders and lobbying groups into action is harder than declaring war on terrorists' account books. Counterterrorism financing units stood up by the Clinton administration had only been half staffed by 9/11, and agencies scrambled to establish information-sharing protocols and centralized collection responsibilities. Friction emerged immediately about each group's legal jurisdiction in the domestic and international sphere, with a larger strategic conflict immediately apparent: The CIA wanted to follow the trail of money and keep the option of using illicit channels to fund their assets, the State Department wanted to avoid diplomatic embarrassments at what investigations would inevitably find, and the FBI wanted to freeze and confiscate. Over time the United States has set up coordinating offices such as the FBI's Terrorist Financing Operations Section and the Policy Coordinating Committee on Terrorism Financing. The 2009 Afghan Threat Finance Cell unites Treasury, CIA, FBI, and DEA efforts, but the fundamental differences in mission, approach, and desired goals remain a significant challenge. Meanwhile, critics of the Patriot Act emerged at all points of the political spectrum, from civil liberties advocates criticizing the legislation's empowerment of the police to expand civil forfeiture without due process to the lobbying groups representing luxury real estate, private wealth management, and escrow agents for private jet sales wheedling exemptions to transaction reporting in order to protect their clients. Because of these complications, some of the most successful prosecutions in the aftermath of 9/11 used old-school Capone-style strategies like investigating Benevolence International offices in the United States for sloppy tax filings.

Other Global North countries have encountered similar clashes. Great Britain's counterterrorism financing laws prior to 9/11 had been focused on their greatest threat, the IRA, and these tailored legal tools applied largely in Northern Ireland, where the government had different regulatory powers than in the rest of Britain. The 2000 Terrorism Act sponsored by the Labour government, partly in recognition that its pressure on the developing world to comply with FATF recommendations would be bolstered if they followed them too, added significant scope and executive powers, alarming civil liberties activists as well as lobbyists for London's very powerful financial institutions, who saw these new regulations, including seizure, forfeiture, and appeals processes, as constraining the global flow of capital. After 9/11 Great Britain escalated their regulatory regime with further provisions of the Anti-Terrorism Crime and Security Act of 2001, seen as the "most draconian peacetime legislation in over a century"; the 2002 Proceeds of Crime Act; and the 2010 Terrorist Asset Freezing Act, all criticized as conflicting with EU Human Rights provisions.[21] Flowing in the other direction, British bankers and other interested parties decried new EU tax avoidance and financial transparency initiatives as a hindrance to their business and to traditional client privacy. Some analysts point to organized resistance to the implementation of these EU measures as a significant element of Brexit support.

Just these examples point to a primary difficulty identified at the start of this book: People who want to move money for illicit purposes will arbitrage regulations and find the combination of laws, loopholes, and winks to do so. Effective curtailment of VNSA money involves synchronized and cooperative legislation, investigation, and enforcement within the administration of a country and then also with those of allies and partners. Because so much of the global financial system flows through London and New York, the United

Kingdom and United States were able, after 9/11, to force compliance with their new regulations by extending jurisdiction to any corresponding bank or transaction that touched their (virtual) soil. However, getting buy-in to terrorism financing as a collective security problem is not so simple: Developing countries resent bearing the heavy costs of compliance, especially if their own economy has been damaged by VNSA actions, or they see the new regulations as a form of protectionism, bigotry toward their ethnic or religious majority, or attacks on their ability to determine their own sovereign rights.[22] Even more problematic, members of the cooperative group need to have confidence sharing information with one another and believe that corrupt officials and systems won't endanger and negate their efforts.

This isn't completely impossible—the Counter-ISIL Financing Group, consisting of twenty-six countries, including the United States, Saudi Arabia, and Italy, was set up in 2015 to coordinate efforts to block oil sales, money transfers, and ISIS's export of support to other VNSAs. The hazard is being willing to put up with members of the group denying problems with their own practices for the sake of overall unity and recognizing that deep-seated institutional values, like the Saudi approach to *zakat* and charity donation, will never sync up with secular expectations of reporting nonprofit accounts. Similarly, the Israeli Harpoon team encountered resistance when reporting its findings to the European Union's financial regulators—it wasn't worth the political fight to categorize Hezbollah fundraising as terrorism rather than charity, and bank privacy traditions necessitated ceasing and desisting pursuit through European financial institutions. As it stands, no group or institution has oversight of the global financial system, nor can anyone mandate or enforce compliance with UN Security Council resolutions or information standardization, nor do anything about the pockets of rogue offshore states who exist to facilitate shady transactions.

States that want to make headway in counter-VNSA financing have to make commitments to harmonizing legal frameworks that bifurcate criminal and terrorist actions when they overlap, better facilitate communication and cultural cooperation among their own government departments, fund and assign sufficient personnel with the right technical expertise, demand that action-oriented agents treat wonky accountant experts as full members of the team, set the example of prosecuting their own elites under existing statutes for corruption, and extend generous financial support so that developing countries can cultivate this orientation of their system as well. Slaps on the wrist for Wachovia laundering cartel money, conspicuous violations of the Sarbanes-Oxley Act and the Hatch Act, toleration of shell purchases of real estate, and other markers of Global North indulgence do little to encourage cooperation in places where doing so means real sacrifices and dangerous disruption.[23] Assisting this is a culture rewarding and protecting a robust whistleblower system and a legally shielded investigative press, so that revelations like the Panama Papers can translate into real reforms rather than titillated excitement in the tabloids and then government silence or embarrassment.[24]

■ Consumer Demand

The overall tone of this book is pessimistic, so it is worth considering that, occasionally, curtailment of the demand side of a source of VNSA financing can change the strategic landscape just enough to bring a VNSA to the negotiating table, push them into more easily managed (or licit) industries, or undermine their public support. In efforts to change that dynamic, successful campaigns have shared methods with other behavior-changing information campaigns and advertising—and some of them have wrought significant change in norms and acceptable social parameters in ways that shift VNSA activities in tandem. The goal in most of these circumstances is to create openings rather than expect to completely suppress an undesirable behavior, especially since prohibition and heightened awareness of the illicit nature of something can, perversely, make it more attractive and raise the amount of money available.

In 1989 Salvadoran right-wing militia members, trained by the United States and funded by El Salvador's government to conduct counterinsurgency operations against its leftist opponents, murdered six Catholic priests, their housekeeper, and her daughter. Appalled Catholic social justice activists in the United States, many with backgrounds in the labor movement and in organizing consumer protests around boycotts of Gallo wine in the 1980s, sprang into action. Organizers researched how the Salvadoran government funded their VNSA allies and discovered that they were pulling money from

STOP FUNDING
THE DEATH SQUADS

BOYCOTT
SALVADORAN COFFEE

The White Hand ("Mano Blanco") is the feared signature of the Salvadoran Death Squads.
The hand above is from a photo of the front door of a slain peasant organizer
in Chalatenango Province.

FOR MORE INFORMATION CONTACT NEIGHBOR TO NEIGHBOR: 1-800-366-8289

Neighbor 2 Neighbor flyer, 1990. Activists organized a successful boycott targeting Folgers coffee, which undercut financing of Salvadoran death squads and lent corporate support to a negotiated end to the civil war in El Salvador. *Personal collection of Jeff Smith, courtesy Grand Rapids People's History Project* coffee plantations that sold beans to Folgers (owned by Proctor & Gamble), Kraft General Foods, and Nestlé.

The resulting boycott, the Neighbor 2 Neighbor campaign, was skillfully executed using networks of Catholic social influencers and community organizers to target a product for which there were alternatives and to tap a powerful constituency of white-collar, well-to-do consumers. Organizers distributed posters to hang next to the break-room coffee pot, threatened broader boycotts of other corporate products, and sponsored a public service announcement (PSA) on local TV stations showing a cup of coffee running over with blood. The movement got a boost when Robbie Gamble, one of the corporate heirs, used his status to force shareholders to hear about the potential damage to the company's reputation in being associated with death squads. In the face of $200 million lost in export revenue over 1989–92, the Salvadoran government issued protests against infringement of their "right to free trade," but in the end the big companies leaned on El Salvador to participate in a negotiated end to their civil war.[25]

In a parallel movement, antiapartheid activists pressured companies, pension plans, university endowment fund holdings, and banks to divest themselves of investments in South Africa, and boycotted artists and firms who conducted business there. Consolidated Gold Fields, one of the country's prominent mining firms, brokered secret talks between the late-apartheid South African government and representatives of the African National Congress, concerned with their public image as well as the prospect of a violent transition of power that might endanger their assets.[26] IKEA, which has staked a lot of its image on being environmentally conscious, responded to pressure by Global Witness and other NGOs and developed a system of timber source certification that would help it avoid putting money into the hands of VNSAs exploiting conflict-zone forests as well as give them a publicity boost. This worked as a lever on the Khmer Rouge in Cambodia when Thailand helped to enforce a logging ban, but it had little effect in Liberia.[27] Consumer boycott campaigns may have an advantage in low-cost access to social media campaigns but must be carefully calibrated against a target with an identifiable supply chain that cares about its public image and against which altered consumer choices make a difference. A campaign against a giant oil company that doesn't care if people think they're warm and fuzzy is not likely to affect a VNSA gang's access to ransom money and guns in the Niger delta. Opponents of boycotts argue that a reduction in consumer demands harms already harried people in conflict zones by reducing their income.

Celebrity appeals can be extremely powerful. Singer Bono's public announcement that supporting the IRA wasn't romantic, cool, or morally defensible had a real effect on the diaspora's willingness to keep the money coming and played a role in the public shift toward pushing the IRA toward negotiations. George Clooney's presence at protests in support of South Sudan's independence gave the cause much more coverage than it would have otherwise received, backed by continuing commitment to funding a counter-VNSA-monitoring intelligence, surveillance, and reconnaissance system. In 2006 the film *Blood Diamond*, with the enthusiastic support of star Leonardo DiCaprio, leveraged its publicity tour to stump for the Kimberley Process in an attempt to reduce the use of diamonds as a funding mechanism by West African VNSAs. These efforts had traction for closely matching the audience with real leverage, whether long-term interest in the Irish Troubles or someone who was considering buying an engagement ring and took cues from DiCaprio. Good candidates for talking down VNSAs are the same sort of people who have done the talking up—diaspora success stories, former users of a commodity with a determined following, influencers who can change a fashion in a subculture. On the other hand, Oprah Winfrey's interest in Kony may have generated millions of YouTube views but didn't translate into action, and neither did #bringbackourgirls to pressure Boko Haram to stop kidnapping for ransom. Celebrities who do PSAs for their own publicity, without a deep connection to the cause or an audience that can do anything about it, are a blip in the publicity noise, sometimes even becoming a joke for the disconnect between their message and their own behavior or fluctuating popularity.

Expanded into a fully uncool backfire, public information campaigns to change undesirable behavior can actually reinforce the desire to participate in illicit activity. Concerned with the financial loss to counterfeiting and piracy, the recording industry, movie studios, and software companies launched extensive and deeply ineffective media blitzes against freeloading consumers of their products. They probably should have seen this coming. In the 1970s the British Phonographic Industry attempted to shame bootleg recordings with the slogan "Home Taping Is Killing the Music Industry," only to encounter fans devoted to the parasocial relationships of exchanging special underground recordings also exchanging and wearing T-shirts with the slogan, adding "And it's fun!"[28] Among the programs aimed at young people using Napster, buying illicitly reproduced DVDs, and downloading expensive cable TV shows using file sharing were PSAs starring Arnold Schwarzenegger and Jackie Chan smashing ersatz watches and chasing fake purse ninjas, a Scholastic Weekly Reader series for fifth through seventh graders with "Lucky" and "Flo" sniffing out counterfeits with Customs Service K-9s, a Boy Scout badge on "Respect Copyrights," and the British "Knock-off Nigel" shaming file sharing as "uncool."[29] Aside from this being precisely the wrong way to approach jaded tweens, many of the consumers of counterfeit products felt entitled to partake and resentful that wealthy stars like Arnold and prosperous and unethical corporations were trying to thwart them. In the quarantine year 2020, frustrated viewers and readers enthusiastically and publicly defended pirated media, despite pleas from favorite authors and musicians explaining their actual incomes.[30] Correspondingly, knock-off Gucci sunglasses, Nike shirts, and Adidas sneakers—even when identified as supporting VNSAs—enjoy widespread acceptability as purchases.[31]

Along with information campaigns, demand for commonly trafficked items may be reduced though the provision of less harmful substitutes. Part, but not all, of the demand for wildlife products like rhino horn and Nepalese caterpillars is because of the expansion of traditional Chinese medicine into areas of influence along the One Belt, One Road initiative and in regions of Chinese investment in Africa. Leading universities in China have conducted official studies demonstrating no medicinal benefits of these wildlife commodities for virility, cancer treatments, or blood pressure control but urging workers in Chinese-run projects to seek relief with donkey skins and herbal infusions rather than providing evidence-based medical care that is more efficient and cost-effective for their employers. In this case of medicinal demand, debate centers around differing strategies of continuing to try to discredit the validity of powdered rhino horn for hangovers and impotence or diluting the market with artificially produced replacements that are virtually indistinguishable from the keratin in the real thing. Conservation activists fear that encouraging the use of endangered ingredients at all just enables poachers and smugglers to continue the slaughter for illicit markets.

Cultural heritage professionals are often the first to acknowledge and understand why collectors want to own a piece of the past since many of them got their own start after picking up a Minié ball at Gettysburg or buying a fragment of the Berlin Wall. Satisfying that craving for connection to a meaningful past without putting money into the pockets of VNSA looters might take the form of projects like a browser extension that rates online collectible sellers based on their provenance documentation, allowing for a quick evaluation of the sellers' sourcing and the risk of buying a trafficked object. Taking things even further, some projects attempt to connect the past with the people living among those heritage objects and offer Global North consumers handicrafts and artwork inspired by the originals in ways that support the licit economy, especially women's collectives and stabilization efforts for employment, reconstruction, and deradicalization.

The biggest challenge is when consumers want a thing *because* it is rare, titillatingly illicit, and a marker of conspicuous consumption. This is certainly the case with ivory, which is highly prized by nouveau riche buyers in Asia, who plug into a millennia of elite traditions in displaying items made from tusks.[32] Status items are powerful things, and one of the drivers of ivory consumption is a desire to be seen as "arrived," admired, and part of the establishment by others who view the carved statue in the home or who receive it as a business gift and think more highly of the giver. Knowing where to buy it, having the money and connections to do so, and making sure others see it all signal that the person involved is powerful. Because of this—for ivory as well as other prestige items that VNSAs peddle—knowing that consumption of the items funds dangerous organizations isn't really a negative. Changing minds is much more likely to come from an influencer within that social system deciding (like John F. Kennedy's inaugural hatlessness, or Clark Gable sans undershirt, or Elvis Presley getting the polio vaccine, or Billie Eilish being a vegan) that ivory is an undesirable gift, or old-fashioned, or cruel.[33] Using the message of cruelty might be the most promising way to change minds, as surveys discovered that more than 50 percent of Asian consumers thought that elephant tusks and rhino horns fall off the animals and grow back, a grisly misunderstanding that offers an opening to peel off consumers who have empathy for the animals.[34]

There will continue to be a hard core of consumers who want to participate in economic activity that helps VNSAs, but there are social science models for how enormously popular norms change under pressure. Students are always shocked when I show them some of the responses to early anti–drunk driving campaigns by Mothers Against Drunk Driving: How dare these pushy, meddling women constrain the freedom of the open road! Dueling isn't cool anymore, and neither are mink stoles accepted middle-class fashion accessories. Millennials have figured out how to straddle traditional expectations with diamond engagement rings made with synthetics, sidestepping the "blood diamonds" and saving money. "Norm entrepreneurs" have successfully changed widespread and accepted practices in relatively short spaces of time, often by combining social influencers with intimations that the activity is becoming too widespread and accessible to the masses and, thus, diluted and tainted (this ends up being the case with original items *too often* counterfeited).[35] Giving to a Kosovar scholarship fund rather than a fund that buys guns and body armor is a social norms transition that makes a real difference in the behavior of VNSAs while conveying similar social prestige. Breaking down the patina of glamour around Mafia extortion helps raise the expectation that this is not acceptable neighborhood behavior. The norm of public tax registers showing who owns beneficial shares or laws requiring public pension funds to rate companies held in the portfolio for environmental compliance all move the needle toward blocking VNSA access to convenient money and tolerated means of moving it around.

Like drug legalization, this is a process of triangulating what a majority of people will accept as additional financial or behavior modification before turning to illicit sources (for example, how high should a cigarette tax be to collect money to mitigate public health effects while not driving more people to get bootleg ones?), the interest of the state to control negative effects through enforcement and taxation, and the toleration for those effects. This process definitely shifts over time, as with drunk driving, public smoking, and state-level marijuana acceptance. HBO, for example, adapted to widespread pirating of *Game of Thrones* by offering a stand-alone streaming service, knowing that it could never entirely prevent illegal downloading but would get enough money from willing consumers to make it worthwhile. This kind of moderated approach has a decent chance of undermining many VNSA revenue sources if applied patiently and consistently, with modifications as social norms adapt. The hazard is the need to respond to "moral eyesores" like human trafficking immediately and for excellent reasons other than just cutting off dirty money.

■ Worth the Squeeze?

Counter-VNSA financing is a lot of hassle. It involves long-term commitment of scarce expertise and resources for investigations that may not pay off in preventing an attack or for the confiscation of mountains of cocaine and shiploads of weapons. It swims upstream in the modern globalization of capital flows and demands that coalitions of sovereign nations work together to prevent illicit actors from venue-shopping the most advantageous place to conduct their financial activities, often to the detriment of their economic advantages. Overall, it's a continual and grinding war of attrition, degrading VNSA resources rather than ever scoring a decisive defeat, making it hard to promote as a "victory" or justify in popular political discourse as organizations fight for budgets. Tracking down VNSA resources may mean some bizarre bureaucratic bedfellows to understand hazardous waste disposal, abalone poaching, insurance fraud, art smuggling, or the inner workings of a diaspora cultural association. Government civil service has to compete for the forensic accountants, tax law attorneys, and cyber hackers who could make more money in private-sector (and illicit) application of their valuable skills, and has to engage in a constant regulatory arms race with VNSA innovation and highly motivated interest groups of the Baptist and bootleggers dynamic.

In the wake of a "lone wolf" attack, counter-VNSA financing looks particularly useless for prevention since someone like Anders Breivik can pull off horrendous carnage without making financial waves visible to antiterrorism personnel, only providing a trail for tracking after the tragedy.[36] So what does success look like in counter-VNSA financing? From this survey of methods,

I'd suggest that positive outcomes might include eroding the donor base and mainstream tolerance of a VNSA's presence; offering intelligence on the priorities, operational parameters, and networked connections of a group; injecting friction and conflict into the workings of the organization; degrading the means available to carry out attacks and sustain the group; and, whenever possible, using financial resources to locate VNSA operations and members.

Actions taken—whether prosecuting or discrediting a VNSA or making it difficult to move money—that cut into the donor base of a group can have cumulative effects. Within a social group, reducing the acceptability of putting cash in a Derry can at the bar or counting donations to a Syrian militia as *zakat* can add up to serious reduction in financial resources. State-level pressure for another nation to disengage as a sponsor or safe haven can trigger enormous shifts in the VNSA landscape, as occurred at the end of the Cold War. Targets of extortions, offered reliable police protection and community rejection of VNSA exploitation, can dry up funding. In a similar vein, pressuring companies not to buy a commodity from a VNSA-controlled source can undercut reasons to hang on to those production areas—forests, mines, or oil pipeline—and make the return on operations disadvantageous. Legalization of a controlled/illicit substance and taxation at a rate the consumers will accept is another pathway states can adopt in competition with VNSAs for donor money. Reciprocally, squeezing other forms of the group's support may force them to parasitize their donors more aggressively, leading to a loss of support, as happened when ETA demands in the Basque country became too much to endure.[37]

Where a VNSA gets its money and where it chooses to invest resources offer key insights into the inner workings of the organization. U.S. military doctrine points out that while violence is the most visible aspect of insurgent groups, there's a whole iceberg of sustainment, recruitment, and logistics that offers hooks to engaging them and can ultimately be more important than their loudest bids for attention. As an intelligence function, understanding the accounts gives clues to what sort of structure the VNSA uses—hierarchy, a flat network, seed money to subsequently autonomous actors—and to how they prioritize their activities. Knowing that a group has moved on Makarenko's spectrum from ideological to criminal is critical to planning responses and countering the group's appeal. If they've dug in where they can roll in drug money, continuing offers of recognition of their religious demands are likely to fail. Getting a look at the group's use of money is akin to profiling an individual suspect by combing through their wallet—very few are able to disguise their values and most pressing concerns by throwing money away in extraneous spending.

VNSAs are at their most vulnerable when they reach out for expertise beyond their committed membership. A group that entrusts its financial dealings, including acquisitions, money laundering, or sales of commodities, to a freelance "fixer" has not just connected itself to a disparate collection of other dangerous rogues; it has taken on the risk of all those rogues and their experts being surveilled and pressured by authorities. The career of Monzer al-Kassar offers a cautionary tale of a fixer who simultaneously did deals for VNSAs and National Security Council staff member Lt. Col. Oliver North and exploited a full-spectrum roster of contacts to live unmolested in Marbella, Spain, until he was tempted to sell arms to two Guatemalans claiming to be buyers for FARC. Turns out, they were DEA informants, and forty years of playing one group off against another came crashing down in 2008, with everyone's tolerance for Kassar's convenient services expended and secrets revealed.[38] Using the overlapping space in the VNSA Venn diagram is a handy tool for prying loose information and weaknesses and sowing discord between groups that might otherwise cooperate or coexist, as well as for removing high-level enablers like Victor Bout or Kassar from their lucrative and destructive engagements (although this will remove them from the intelligence service's Rolodex as well). A VNSA that relies on an affiliated group to sell its drugs, plant its bombs, or conduct its surveillance is vulnerable to the lowest-ranking goon letting things slip to plea bargain, especially if authorities are in a mood to forgive petty crime in exchange for information on terrorism or insurgency.

The real danger is that intelligence gained from seeing into a network of networks, or into one group, is just insight into that one group. As we saw earlier in this book, each VNSA arrives at a financing package dependent on its unique circumstances at the time—what is available to it, what its needs are, what resources are located in its stronghold, what skills are held among its members (LTTE was an early adopter of online communications and fundraising because of the unusually high number of computer industry workers among the diaspora), and what parameters of activities are acceptable to their ideology and constituents. This package, like a fingerprint, is extremely useful in analyzing what a VNSA wants, what it might do, and what can be done to maneuver it out of the violence and into obsolescence or participation as a legitimate political group. If the worst happens, financial clues are often the first and most concrete leads tracking back to surviving members of an operational cell, especially if authorities fear that the cell has a series of attacks planned.

Pinching a VNSA budget is an opportunity to sow discord within the group. Tracking how ISIS and AQIM were using the internet to recruit foreign fighters and ask for donations allowed the U.S. military to reverse engineer access to the networks being used and sabotage them in ways that, following message traffic, prompted VNSA personnel to criticize and insult their information technology people. Just like a licit workplace, ticking off tech support is a terrible idea, especially since some of the key workers were volunteers from the diaspora who were out of reach of the group's discipline and able to quit in pique or spill secrets to the authorities. More directly, losing money forces a group to make economies, whether cutting social services and having to explain to their recipients why the food boxes aren't coming, stopping salaries, or reducing the quality of supplies—always a move dangerous to morale. Unless these cuts can be explained and felt across the whole organization, this is a recipe for accusations of embezzlement (especially if the leadership or Global North representatives live comparatively luxuriously) and fights over who should be prioritized, and it endangers the participation of people who volunteered to be suicide bombers after being assured that their families would receive pensions and financial rewards. Reduction in spending signals weakness in a marketplace of violence in which VNSAs compete for recruits, supporters, and sources of income. We know from captured documents that cutbacks result in snippy attitudes, like "we've been receiving only half salaries for five months. What is your reaction or response to this?"[39]

With the caveat and reminder that operations don't cost a large amount in proportion to sustainment, VNSAs whose budgets have been reduced have to make hard decisions about maintaining their capabilities. In some cases, there's a clear pattern that more money means more attacks, with al-Qaeda in Iraq consistently increasing by one attack for every $2,700 sent by the central leadership to sectors.[40] Mustafa Abu al-Yazid, an al-Qaeda financing chief, put it starkly: "There are hundreds wishing to carry out martyrdom-seeking operations, but they can't find the funds to equip themselves. So funding is the mainstay of jihad."[41] The 1993 World Trade Center bombers complained that their limited budget constrained the size of the bomb that they built, and said they would have put cyanide in the explosives if they'd had the resources to do so, increasing the death toll and destruction.[42] In 2006 Philippine police announced that the Abu Sayyaf group had an extensive bombing campaign planned, but that it was foiled by a shortage of funding for each operation.[43] Cutting costs may mean reducing bribes paid and increasing the risk of visibility or vulnerability to law enforcement or shuttering specialized functions and requiring experts to shut down training camps or cyber operations to pick up a gun and go to the front lines if recruiting ebbs. Some hard-pressed groups sell off assets like vehicles and stockpiles of weapons. Studies of VNSA innovations suggest that groups with limited funding take fewer chances in trying new things and stick to tried-and-true tactics that authorities already know about rather than investing in something that might fail or have unexpected consequences. We should avoid a simplistic conception that cutting the money will translate to fewer attacks, but stanching funds does kneecap the group's plans and force internal reckonings that may provide openings for engagement and suppression.

Financial analysis is a tool for tracking where a group might be as well as one of the indicators that they may be planning larger operations. In 2002 the al-Qaeda attack on the MV *Limberg* oil tanker in the Gulf of Aden was preceded by a substantial transfer of $2 million to accounts in Yemen, where the planning and training by Abd al-Rahim al-Nashiri took place.[44] More unorthodox modes of examination, like German and Italian police sifting for renters paying landlords in cash, yielded Red Brigade and Baader-Meinhof members' hiding places.[45] Interest in new regions, movement of personnel tracked by their spending, or unusual patterns, like foreign fighters from the United Kingdom using ATMs in areas of Turkey bordering Syria, are data points that offer a fuller picture of what a group might be doing. Tracking the movement of commodities, especially those identifiable by origin, whether elephant tusks or Palmyra-looted artifacts, is an indicator that a group is active there. In a wider conflict picture, scholars suggest that tracking the sudden appearance of cultural artifacts or liquidated possessions of an area's elite is a harbinger of conflict about to erupt as they prepare to flee or as a VNSA begins exploiting the lowest-hanging fruit for ready cash.

Groups that have been backed into a corner financially are extremely dangerous. Still in need of support, they may change targets or explore easier pickings in a new sector or location. Even if they are on the road to transitioning into a political party or standing down their operations, they may feel compelled to display their continued viability or hedge their bets by attracting diversified sponsors with a show of strength. This may take the form of their most reliable and simplest tool—a car bomb or a suicide attack, which make splashy, high-casualty events that attract attention. If a process succeeds in subduing a VNSA, understanding the illicit financial networks they leave behind is key to stabilizing the vacuum they cause. Their area of operations and the people with whom they interacted have become acclimated to whatever resource management the group used and are likely to continue it using the established routes for selling diamonds or bunkered oil, continuing to loot cuneiform tablets, stepping into extortion routes, and challenging the authorities for control of checkpoints and border crossings with lucrative bribe potential. Any expeditionary police force, peacekeepers, or new government has to take into account the continuing ramifications of an illicit system with proven advantages and offer something as good as or better to get people away from perpetuating it.

■ Summing Up

The bad news is that VNSAs will always be more motivated and agile at finding illicit means of support than establishment authorities will be at finding ways of detecting, preventing, and prosecuting them for it. Arbitrage will make it possible for a determined group to locate virtual or physical space in which they can operate with as few constraints as possible. It is feasible to reduce those opportunities or make the friction involved a deterrent to the group, but full suppression is extremely unlikely. The pursuit of VNSA dirty money is a continual exercise in chopping off hydra heads, hopefully at the speed of replacement growth, in an environment where competition for scarce security resources makes attrition hard to justify.

Even more frustrating and alarming is the problem that many of the vehicles used by VNSAs to generate, move, and hide their funds are also in the toolboxes of governments, militaries, and intelligence services, not to mention beloved and expected privileges of elite members of society who very much want to continue paying minimal taxes, hiding assets from divorce lawyers, putting cash into escape hatch real estate, and peeling off commodity profits into untouchable offshore accounts. It's extremely difficult, if not impossible, to separate "ISIS terrorist dirty money" from "Russian oligarch grand corruption dirty money" from "angry libertarian car dealer in Texas dirty money" because they all use the same network. The pull of illicit money is so enormous that mainstream firms like Wachovia and Wells Fargo didn't blink before handling cartel money, venerable museums accept shady donations in exchange for tax breaks, and the prospect of being cut off from opportunities to shield wealth seems to have been critical to propagandizing support for Brexit.

Changing the landscape for groups that we really don't want—VNSAs whose behavior is abhorrent, scary, and coercive—means changing the whole financial landscape. This is the good news . . . maybe? In the last six months of writing this manuscript, the 2020 National Defense Authorization Act made headway in forcing states to allow investigators to dig into shell company ownership, and local laws have been curtailing real estate purchases meant for money laundering. In the United Kingdom, tools like unexplained wealth orders allow law enforcement to demand explanations for origins of money passing through their system, and the European Union has made headway wearing down the bank secrecy laws that have traditionally shielded dirty money from supervision. Slowly, there's been agreement on some procedures to repatriate grand corruption money back to its source, as in the case of Libya's riches stashed by the Gaddafi children, but no overall refusal of or scrutiny of money flowing from suspicious sources—a privilege of globalized capitalism and regular practice for multinational business.

Many reforms that aren't directly targeted at VNSAs have the secondary effect of making dirty money harder to get, move, and hide—a well-assimilated

Somali American teenager in St. Paul with an afterschool program is less likely to be sending money to al-Shabaab via a chatroom solicitation; getting people's bank accounts and IDs in accessible, trusted, and convenient forms cuts down on the use of *hawalas* and unmonitored, exploitative financial networks; expecting high standards for provenance and collecting ethics raises the profile of cultural institutions and discourages the sale of looted artwork; robust and sustainable social welfare programs allow the state to compete with VNSAs in offering charity services; good partnerships with the communities around international archaeological digs and game reserves add initiative to protect those resources when they're threatened; and highly regarded, culturally sensitive policing offers chances to shut extortive VNSAs out of diaspora networks.

Just as even a small amount of funding can enable a VNSA to launch something negative, in the Sisyphean task of counter-VNSA work, small successes chip away at the underlying grievances and criminal opportunities too. Mopping up dirty money is not just a whole-of-government but a whole-of-financial- and social-system project, balancing collective security and sovereign rights, regulation and arbitrage, and personal freedom with cultural norms to arrive at some point where good governance is patriotism, and VNSAs have to work too hard to pay.

NOTES

Chapter 1. Show Me the Money

1. Michael Freeman, "The Sources of Terrorist Financing: Theory and Typology," *Studies in Conflict and Terrorism* 34, no. 6 (2011): 462.
2. Freeman, "Sources of Terrorist Financing," 462; Nora Bensahel, "A Coalition of Coalitions: International Cooperation against Terrorism," *Studies in Conflict and Terrorism* 29, no. 1 (January 2006): 37; Michael Jonsson and Svante Cornell, "Countering Terrorist Financing," *Georgetown Journal of International Affairs* 8, no. 1 (2007): 74; and Javier Jordán, Fernando M. Mañas, and Nicola Horsburgh, "Strengths and Weaknesses of Grassroot Jihadist Networks," *Studies in Conflict and Terrorism* 31, no. 1 (January 2008): 30.
3. Dina Temple-Raston, "How Much Does a Terrorist Attack Cost?," *NPR*, June 25, 2014.
4. Temple-Raston, "How Much." See also Joshua Geltzer, "Taking Hand-Outs or Going It Alone," *Studies in Conflict and Terrorism* 34, no. 2 (January 2011): 145.
5. Maura Conway, "Terrorism and the Internet: New Media—New Threat?," *Parliamentary Affairs* 59, no. 2 (April 2006): 303.
6. John Robb, *Brave New War: The Next Stage of Terrorism and the End of Globalization* (Hoboken, N.J.: Wiley, 2007), 135.
7. Zachary Abuza, "Funding Terrorism in Southeast Asia: The Financial Network of Al Qaeda and Jemaah Islamiya," *Contemporary Southeast Asia* 25, no. 2 (August 2003): 172; Robb, *Brave New War*, 6; and Todd Sandler, "Collective Action and Transnational Terrorism," *World Economy* 26, no. 6 (June 2003): 780.
8. Laura Donohue, "Anti-Terrorist Finance in the United Kingdom and United States," *Michigan Journal of International Law* 27, no. 2 (2006): 325.
9. Graham Myres, "Investing in the Market of Violence: Toward a Micro-Theory of Terrorist Financing," *Studies in Conflict and Terrorism* 35 (2012): 698.
10. Steve Kiser, *Financing Terror: An Analysis and Simulation for Affecting Al Qaeda's Financial Infrastructure* (Santa Monica, Calif.: RAND, 2005), 32.

11. Tolga Koker and Carlos Yordán, "Microfinancing Terrorism: A Study in al Qaeda Financing Strategy," in *State of Corruption, State of Chaos: The Terror of Political Malfeasance*, ed. Michaelene Cox (Lanham, Md.: Lexington, 2008), 172; Celina Realuyo, *"Following the Money Trail" to Combat Terrorism, Crime, and Corruption in the Americas* (Washington, D.C.: Wilson Center, August 2017), 5; and FATF, "Emerging Terrorist Financing Risks" (Paris: FATF, October 2015), 13.

12. Austin Long, "Whack-a-Mole or Coup de Grace? Institutionalization and Leadership Targeting in Iraq and Afghanistan," *Security Studies* 23, no. 3 (2014): 471.

13. Freeman, "Sources of Terrorist Financing," 463.

14. Adam Dolnik, *Understanding Terrorist Innovation: Technology, Tactics and Global Trends* (London: Routledge, 2007), 75.

15. Kevin Desouza and Tobin Hensgen, "Connectivity among Terrorist Groups," *Studies in Conflict and Terrorism* 30, no. 7 (2007): 598.

16. David Petraeus and James Mattis, *Counterinsurgency*, FM3-24/FMFM 3-24 (Washington, D.C.: Headquarters, Department of the Army, June 16, 2006), 17.

17. Douglas Philippone, "Hezbollah" (master's thesis, Naval Postgraduate School, 2008), 32.

18. John Daly, "LTTE," *Asian Tribune*, June 14, 2007.

19. Dolnik, *Understanding Terrorist Innovation*, 63.

20. Juan Gomez, "A Financial Profile of the Terrorism of Al-Qaeda and Its Affiliates," *Perspectives on Terrorism* 4, no. 4 (October 2010): 5.

21. C. J. Chivers and David Rohde, "Turning Out Guerrillas and Terrorists to Wage a Holy War," *New York Times*, March 18, 2002; and "Tapes Show al Qaeda Trained for Urban Jihad on West," *CNN*, August 21, 2002.

22. Mark Hamm, *Crimes Committed by Terrorist Groups: Theory, Research and Prevention*, report prepared for the Department of Justice, June 1, 2005, 82.

23. Arabinda Acharya, Syed Adnan Ali Shah Bukhari, and Sadia Sulaiman, "Making Money in the Mayhem: Funding Taliban Insurrection in the Tribal Areas of Pakistan," *Studies in Conflict and Terrorism* 32, no. 2 (February 2009): 95.

24. James Forest, ed., *Teaching Terror: Strategic and Tactical Learning in the Terrorist World* (Lanham, Md.: Rowman and Littlefield, 2006), 212; and David Cohen, "Remarks of Under Secretary for Terrorism and Financial Intelligence David S. Cohen at the Carnegie Endowment for International Peace, 'Attacking ISIL's Financial Foundation,'" U.S. Department of the Treasury, October 23, 2014, https://www.treasury.gov/press-center/press-releases/Pages/jl2672.aspx.

25. Michael Kenney, "'Dumb' Yet Deadly," *Studies in Conflict and Terrorism* 33, no. 10 (October 2010): 915.

26. Kenney, "'Dumb' Yet Deadly," 924.

27. Andrew Silke, ed., *Routledge Handbook of Terrorism and Counter-Terrorism* (London: Routledge, 2019), 202.

28. Forest, *Teaching Terror*, 178.

29. Kenney, "'Dumb' Yet Deadly," 918.

30. Martin Ewi and Uyo Salifu, "Money Talks: A Key Reason Youths Join Boko Haram," Policy Brief 98, Institute for Security Studies, February 2017, p. 6.

31. Carla Humud, Robert Pirog, and Liana Rosen, *Islamic State Financing and U.S. Policy Approaches* (Washington, D.C.: CRS, April 10, 2015), 13.

32. Sarah Benali, "ISIS Entices Youth with High Salaries," *Forbes*, September 22, 2014.

33. Andrew Silke, "In Defense of the Realm," *Studies in Conflict and Terrorism* 21 (1998): 336.

34. Patrick B. Johnston, Mona Alami, Colin P. Clarke, and Howard J. Shatz, *Return and Expand? The Finances and Prospects of the Islamic State after the Caliphate* (Santa Monica, Calif.: RAND, 2019), xiv, https://doi.org/10.7249/RR3046; and Roland Marchal, "The Rise of a Jihadi Movement in a Country at War" (Paris: CNRS SciencesPo, March 2011), 65.

35. Brian Fishman, Jacob Shapiro, Joseph Felter, Peter Bergen, and Vahid Brown, *Bombers, Bank Accounts, and Bleedout: Al-Qa'ida's Road In and Out of Iraq* (West Point, N.Y.: Combating Terrorism Center, 2008), 10.

36. Shaylih Muehlmann, *When I Wear My Alligator Boots: Narco-Culture in the U.S.-Mexico Borderlands* (Berkeley: University of California Press, 2014), 159.

37. Stewart Patrick, *Weak Links: Fragile States, Global Threats, and International Security* (Oxford: Oxford University Press, 2011), 120.

38. James Adams, *The Financing of Terror* (New York: Simon and Schuster, 1986), 145.

39. Philip M. Seib and Dana M. Janbek, *Global Terrorism and New Media: The Post-Al Qaeda Generation* (New York: Routledge, 2011), 32.

40. Borzou Daragahi and Erika Solomon, "Fuelling ISIS, Inc.," *Financial Times*, September 21, 2014.

41. Simon Cottee, "Why It's So Hard to Stop ISIS Propaganda," *Atlantic*, March 2, 2015.

42. Jack Guy, "Colombia's 'Cocaine Hippos' Must Be Culled, Scientists Say," *CNN*, January 19, 2021; Cottee, "Why It's So Hard to Stop ISIS Propaganda"; Mark Townsend, "Inside the Islamic State's Capital," *Guardian*, November 30, 2014; and Eric Hobsbawm, *Bandits* (New York: Dell, 1969), 15.

43. Muhammad al-'Ubaydi, Nelly Lahoud, Daniel Milton, and Bryan Price, *The Group That Calls Itself a State: Understanding the Evolution and Challenges of the Islamic State* (West Point, N.Y.: Combating Terrorism Center, December 2014), 49.

44. James B. Love, *Hezbollah: Social Services as a Source of Power* (Hurlburt Field, Fla.: Joint Special Operations University Press, 2010), 21; Fuat Salih Sahin, "Case Studies in Terrorism-Drug Connection: The Kurdistan Workers' Party,

the Liberation Tigers of Tamil Eelam, and the Shining Path" (master's thesis, University of North Texas, 2001), 22; and Daly, "LTTE."

45. Reuven Erlich and Yoram Kahati, *Hezbollah as a Case Study of the Battle for Hearts and Minds* (Ramat Hasharon: Intelligence and Terrorism Information Center, June 2007), 3.

46. H. Richard Friman and Peter Andreas, eds., *The Illicit Global Economy and State Power* (Lanham, Md.: Rowman and Littlefield, 1999), 38.

47. John Horgan and Max Taylor, "Playing the 'Green Card,' Part 1," *Terrorism and Political Violence* 11, no. 2 (Summer 1999): 6.

48. Erlich and Kahati, *Hezbollah as a Case Study*, 16; and Neil DeVotta, "The Liberation Tigers of Tamil EELAM," *Asian Survey* 49, no. 6 (2009): 1035.

49. Adams, *Financing of Terror*, 165; and Horgan and Taylor, "Playing the 'Green Card,' Part 1," 7.

50. Franklin Foer, "Paul Manafort, American Hustler," *Atlantic*, March 2018.

51. Dolnik, *Understanding Terrorist Innovation*, 114.

52. Morten Boas, "Guns, Money and Prayers: AQIM's Blueprint for Securing Control of Northern Mali," *CTC Sentinel* 7, no. 4 (April 2014): 4.

53. Namrata Goswami, Robert A. Norton, and Gregory Weaver, *ISIS 2.0: South and Southeast Asia Opportunities and Vulnerabilities* (Hurlburt Field, Fla.: Joint Special Operations University Press, 2018), 36; and Frédéric Lemieux and Fernanda Prates, "Entrepreneurial Terrorism: Financial Strategies, Business Opportunities, and Ethical Issues," *Police Practice and Research* 12, no. 5 (2011): 369.

54. Katherine Petrich, "Al-Shabaab's Mata Hari Network," *War on the Rocks* (blog), August 14, 2018.

55. W. A. Tupman, "Ten Myths about Terrorist Financing," *Journal of Money Laundering Control* 12, no. 2 (2009): 307.

56. Hamm, *Crimes Committed by Terrorist Groups*, 56; Matthew Levitt, "The Political Economy of Middle East Terrorism," *Middle East Review of International Affairs* 6, no. 4 (December 2002): 49; and Jacob Shapiro and David Siegel, "Underfunding in Terrorist Organizations," *International Studies Quarterly* 51, no. 2 (2007): 405.

57. Steven Levitt and Sudhir Venkatesh, "An Economic Analysis of a Drug-Selling Gang's Finances," *Quarterly Journal of Economics* 115, no. 3 (August 2000): 762; Myres, "Investing in the Market of Violence," 696; Jacob Shapiro and David Siegel, "Moral Hazard, Discipline and the Management of Terrorist Organizations," *World Politics* 64, no. 1 (2012): 47.

58. Michael Freeman, *Financing Terrorism: Case Studies* (Burlington, Vt.: Ashgate, 2011), 171.

59. Rukmini Callimachi, "$0.60 for Cake," Associated Press, December 30, 2013; and Sebastian Rotella, "Al Qaeda Crosses the Ts in 'Terrorist,'" *Los Angeles Times*, April 16, 2008.

60. Ray Fisman and Tim Sullivan, *The Org: The Underlying Logic of the Office* (Princeton, N.J.: Princeton University Press, 2013), 265; and Rotella, "Al Qaeda Crosses the Ts in 'Terrorist.'"

61. Jeanne K. Giraldo and Harold A. Trinkunas, eds., *Terrorism Financing and State Responses: A Comparative Perspective* (Stanford, Calif.: Stanford University Press, 2007), 67; Fishman et al., *Bombers, Bank Accounts, and Bleedout*, 78; and Rohan Gunaratna, *Inside Al-Qaeda: Global Network of Terror* (New York: Berkeley Books, 2003), 44.

62. Timothy Wittig, *Understanding Terrorist Finance* (New York: Palgrave MacMillan, 2011), 94.

63. Alexander Wendt, "Anarchy Is What States Make of It," *International Organization* 46, no. 2 (1992): 391.

64. Myres, "Investing in the Market of Violence," 703.

65. R. T. Naylor, "The Insurgent Economy," *Crime, Law and Social Change* 20, no. 1 (1993): 13.

66. Craig Whitlock, "Afghan Insurgents' Diverse Funding Sources Pose Challenges," *Washington Post*, September 27, 2009; and Benjamin Bahney, Howard J. Shatz, Carroll Ganier, Renny McPherson, and Barbara Sude, *An Economic Analysis of the Financial Records of Al-Qa'ida in Iraq* (Santa Monica, Calif.: RAND, 2010), 2.

67. Freeman, *Financing Terrorism*, 10; and Freeman, "Sources of Terrorist Financing," 463.

68. Freeman, *Financing Terrorism*, 11; and Freeman, "Sources of Terrorist Financing," 464.

Chapter 2. Crossing the Streams

1. Reis Thebault, "Iranian Agents Once Plotted to Kill the Saudi Ambassador," *Washington Post*, January 4, 2020; and Peter Finn, "Notorious Iranian Militant Has a Connection to Alleged Assassination Plot," *Washington Post*, October 14, 2011.

2. Peter Finn, "Man in Iran-Backed Plot to Kill Saudi Ambassador Gets 25 Years," *Washington Post*, May 30, 2013; and Finn, "Notorious Iranian Militant."

3. Michael Miklaucic and Jacqueline Brewer, eds., *Convergence: Illicit Networks and National Security in the Age of Globalization* (Washington, D.C.: National Defense University Press, 2013), 71.

4. Finn, "Notorious Iranian Militant"; Andrea Villa, "Combatting Narcoterrorism," *University of Miami National Security and Armed Conflict Law Review* 6 (2015): 126; and A. Aaron Weisburd, "Whatever Happened to the A-Team of Terrorism?," George Washington University, Homeland Security Policy Institute, February 23, 2012, 1.

5. Joby Warrick, "Investigators Initially Doubted Plot Had Iran Ties," *Washington Post*, October 12, 2011; and Weisburd, "Whatever Happened to the A-Team."

6. Villa, "Combatting Narcoterrorism," 133.

7. Finn, "Notorious Iranian Militant"; Weisburd, "Whatever Happened to the A-Team," 4; and Warrick, "Investigators Initially Doubted Plot."

8. Finn, "Man in Iran-Backed Plot"; and John Rollins and Liana Wyler, *Terrorism and Transnational Crime: Foreign Policy Issues for Congress* (Washington, D.C.: Congressional Research Service, June 11, 2013), 13.

9. CNN Wire Staff, "Man Accused in Iranian Plot Is More 'Mr. Bean than 007'," *CNN*, October 14, 2011.

10. David Zucker, dir., *The Naked Gun: From the Files of Police Squad!* (Los Angeles: Paramount Pictures, 1988).

11. Steven Bender, "Sight, Sound, and Stereotype," *Oregon Law Review* 81 (2002): 1158.

12. Bilal Saab and Alexandra Taylor, "Criminality and Armed Groups," *Studies in Conflict and Terrorism* 32, no. 6 (May 28, 2009): 457; Ronald Crelinsten, "The Discourse and Practice of Counter-Terrorism in Liberal Democracies," *Australian Journal of Politics and History* 44, no. 3 (1998): 398; and Richard Hofstadter, "The Paranoid Style in American Politics," *Harper's Magazine*, November 1964.

13. Annette Hubschle, "From Theory to Practice: Exploring the Organised Crime-Terror Nexus in Sub-Saharan Africa," *Perspectives on Terrorism* 5, no. 3/4 (September 2011): 93; and David Kilcullen, *The Accidental Guerilla: Fighting Small Wars in the Midst of a Big One* (Oxford: Oxford University Press, 2009), 21.

14. Thomas Friedman, *The Lexus and the Olive Tree: Understanding Globalization* (New York: Farrar, Straus and Giroux, 1999).

15. Thomas Friedman, "Big Mac I," *New York Times*, December 8, 1996.

16. Thomas Friedman, "Big Mac II," *New York Times*, December 11, 1996; and "Special McDonald's Menu Items," lovefood.com, accessed December 23, 2020, https://www.lovefood.com/galleries/60910/special-mcdonalds-menu-items-from-around-the-world.

17. James McDonald, "The Cultural Effects of the Narcoeconomy in Rural Mexico," *Journal of International and Global Studies* 1, no. 1 (November 2009): 1–29; Edward Luce, "The End of the Golden Arches Doctrine," *Financial Times*, May 10, 2015; and George Abungu, "Illicit Trafficking and Destruction of Cultural Property in Africa," *Journal of Art Crime* 15 (Spring 2016): 35.

18. Peter Andreas, "Illicit International Political Economy," *Review of International Political Economy* 11, no. 3 (2004): 646.

19. Maggie Wong, "An Acquired Taste?," *CNN*, December 22, 2020.

20. John Robb, "Brave New War: The Next Stage of Terrorism and the End of Globalization," in *Deviant Globalization: Black Market Economy in the 21st Century*,

ed. Nils Gilman, Jesse Goldhammer, and Steven Weber (New York: Continuum, 2011), 25.

21. Riley Post and Jeffrey Peterson, *Unconventional Economics: Operational Economics in Unconventional Warfare* (MacDill Air Force Base, Fla.: Joint Special Operations University Press, 2016), 45; André Standing, *Transnational Organized Crime and the Palermo Convention: A Reality Check* (New York: International Peace Institute, December 2010), 8; and Philippe Le Billon, "The Political Ecology of War," *Political Geography* 20, no. 5 (2001): 577.

22. Timothy Wittig, *Understanding Terrorist Finance* (New York: Palgrave MacMillan, 2011), 56; R. T. Naylor, *Wages of Crime: Black Markets, Illegal Finance, and the Underworld Economy* (Ithaca, N.Y.: Cornell University Press, 2004), 3; and John Robb, "The Open-Source War," *New York Times*, October 15, 2005.

23. Margaret Crahan and Alberto Vourvoulias-Bush, eds., *The City and the World: New York's Global Future* (New York: Council on Foreign Relations Press, 1997), 82; Phil Williams, "The Nature of Drug Trafficking Networks," *Current History* 97, no. 618 (1998): 156; and Nils Gilman, Jesse Goldhammer, and Steven Weber, Conclusion to *Deviant Globalization: Black Market Economy in the 21st Century* (New York: Continuum, 2011), 273.

24. Harry Yarger, *SOF and a Theory of Modern Terrorism* (MacDill Air Force Base, Fla.: Joint Special Operations University Press, 2016), 11.

25. Mitchel Roth and Murat Sever, "The Kurdish Workers Party as Criminal Syndicate," *Studies in Conflict and Terrorism* 30, no. 10 (2007): 903; Jarret Brachman, *The War Within: A Look inside al-Qaeda's Undoing* (MacDill Air Force Base, Fla.: Joint Special Operations University Press, 2016), 9; and Hubschle, "From Theory to Practice," 84.

26. Tamara Makarenko, "The Crime-Terror Continuum," *Global Crime* 6, no. 1 (February 2004): 129–45.

27. Joseph Celeski, *Policing and Law Enforcement in COIN—the Thick Blue Line*, JSOU Report 09-2, Joint Special Operations University, February 2009, 21; Chester Oehme III, "Terrorists, Insurgents, and Criminals—Growing Nexus?," *Studies in Conflict and Terrorism* 31, no. 1 (January 2008): 90; and Roth and Sever, "The Kurdish Workers Party," 902.

28. Makarenko, "The Crime-Terror Continuum," 138; and Paul Kan, "Dark International Relations: When Crime Is the DIME,'" *War Room* (blog), July 24, 2019.

29. Alex Schmid, ed., *Forum on Crime and Society*, vol. 4 (New York: United Nations, 2005), 12; John B. Alexander, *Convergence: Special Operations Forces and Civilian Law Enforcement*, JSOU Report 10-6, Joint Special Operations University, July 2010, p. 41.

30. Rukmini Callimachi and Lorenzo Tondo, "Scaling Up a Drug Trade," *New York Times*, September 13, 2016; and Tamara Makarenko, "Europe's Crime-Terror

Nexus: Links between Terrorist and Organised Crime Groups in the European Union," Report for Directorate-General for International Policies, European Union, 2012, http://www.europarl.europa.eu/document/activities/cont/201211 /20121127ATT56707/20121127ATT56707EN.pdf, p. 23.

31. Louise Shelley, "A Tangled Web," *War on the Rocks* (blog), November 15, 2018; and Austin Long, "Whack-a-Mole or Coup de Grace? Institutionalization and Leadership Targeting in Iraq and Afghanistan," *Security Studies* 23, no. 3 (2014): 492.

32. Frank Perri and Richard Brody, "The Dark Triad," *Journal of Money Laundering Control* 14, no. 1 (2011): 49; James Cockayne and Adam Lupel, eds., *Peace Operations and Organized Crime: Enemies or Allies?* (London: Routledge, 2011), 6; and Reece Walters, "Dirty Collar Crime and the Environment," in *Proceedings of Crime, Justice and Social Democracy: An International Conference* (Queensland, Australia: Queensland Institute of Technology, 2012), 107.

33. Makarenko, "The Crime-Terror Continuum," 134.

34. Chris Dishman, "Terrorism, Crime, and Transformation," *Studies in Conflict and Terrorism* 24, no. 1 (January 2001): 55; and Louise I. Shelley and John T. Picarelli, "Methods and Motives: Exploring Links between Transnational Organized Crime and International Terrorism," *Trends in Organized Crime* 9, no. 2 (December 2005): 55.

35. U.S. Department of the Army, *Urban Operations: Field Manual 3-06* (Washington, D.C.: Department of the Army, 2006), 65.

36. Russell D. Howard and Colleen Traughber, *The Nexus of Extremism and Trafficking: Scourge of the World or So Much Hype?* (MacDill Air Force Base, Fla.: Joint Special Operations University Press, 2013), 44; Anton Blok, *The Mafia of a Sicilian Village* (New York: Harper and Row, 1974), 191; and Peter Andreas, *Killer High: A History of War in Six Drugs* (Oxford: Oxford University Press, 2020), 158.

37. R. T. Naylor, *Patriots and Profiteers: Economic Warfare, Embargo Busting, and State-Sponsored Crime* (Montreal: McGill-Queen's University Press, 2008), 186.

38. Andrew Silke, ed., *Routledge Handbook of Terrorism and Counter-Terrorism* (London: Routledge, 2019), 200; H. Richard Friman and Peter Andreas, eds., *The Illicit Global Economy and State Power* (Lanham, Md.: Rowman and Littlefield, 1999), 188; and Raymond Baker, *Capitalism's Achilles Heel: Dirty Money and How to Renew the Free-Market System* (Hoboken, N.J.: Wiley and Sons, 2005), 114.

39. Robert I. Friedman, *Red Mafiya: How the Russian Mob Has Invaded America* (Boston: Little, Brown, 2000), 112; Garrett M. Graff, "A Vor Never Sleeps," *Longreads*, June 2018, https://longreads.com/2018/06/04/a-vor-never-sleeps/; and Shelley, "A Tangled Web."

40. Phil Williams, *Criminals, Militias, and Insurgents: Organized in Iraq* (Carlisle, Pa.: Strategic Studies Institute, 2009), 34; Paul Rexton Kan, *Drug Trafficking and International Security* (Lanham, Md.: Rowman and Littlefield, 2016), 49; and Eric J. Hobsbawm, *Bandits* (New York: Dell, 1969), 26.

41. Ignacio Sanchez-Cuenca, "The Dynamics of Nationalist Terrorism: ETA and the IRA," *Terrorism and Political Violence* 19, no. 3 (2007): 297; and Hobsbawm, *Bandits*, 70.

42. W. A. Tupman, "Where Has All the Money Gone? The IRA as a Profit-Making Concern," *Journal of Money Laundering Control* 1, no. 4 (April 1998): 309; Jim Cusak and Max Taylor, "Resurgence of a Terrorist Organisation," *Terrorism and Political Violence* 5, no. 3 (Autumn 1993): 2; and John Horgan and Max Taylor, "Playing the 'Green Card,' Part 2," *Terrorism and Political Violence* 15, no. 2 (Summer 2003): 52.

43. Howard Meehan, "Terrorism, Diasporas and Permissive Threat Environments" (master's thesis, Naval Postgraduate School, 2004), 21.

44. Horgan and Taylor, "Playing the 'Green Card,' Part 2," 14; see also Michael Freeman, *Financing Terrorism: Case Studies* (Burlington, Vt.: Ashgate, 2011), 174.

45. Horgan and Taylor, "Playing the 'Green Card,' Part 2," 24. See also Paul Miller, "Financial Vulnerabilities in Terror Organizations" (elective course paper, Air War College, Maxwell Air Force Base: November 2018).

46. Dishman, "Terrorism, Crime, and Transformation," 47; and Hobsbawm, *Bandits*, 39.

47. Horgan and Taylor, "Playing the 'Green Card,' Part 2," 10; see also Connor Simpson, "Al Qaeda Are Strict about Keeping Track of Their Receipts," *Atlantic*, December 29, 2013.

48. Horgan and Taylor, "Playing the 'Green Card,' Part 2," 51; Cusak and Taylor, "Resurgence of a Terrorist Organisation," 10; and Freeman, *Financing Terrorism*, 178.

49. Isabel Woodford and M. L. R. Smith, "The Political Economy of the Provos: Inside the Finances of the Provisional IRA—A Revision," *Studies in Conflict and Terrorism* 41, no. 3 (2018): 227; and Tupman, "Where Has All the Money Gone?," 305.

50. Jacob Shapiro and David Siegel, "Underfunding in Terrorist Organizations," *International Studies Quarterly* 51, no. 2 (2007): 411.

51. Thanassis Cambanis, "The Man Who Madoff with Hezbollah's Money," *Think-Progress*, September 17, 2009; and Nitsana Darshan-Leitner and Samuel Katz, *Harpoon Inside the Covert War against Terrorism's Money Masters* (New York: Hachette, 2017), 173.

52. Louise Richardson, ed., *The Roots of Terrorism* (New York: Routledge, 2006), 93.
53. Committee on Armed Services, House of Representatives, *Tracking and Disrupting Terrorist Financial Networks: A Potential Model for Interagency Success?*, H.A.S.C. No. 111-20 (Washington, D.C.: Government Printing Office, March 11, 2009), 30; and Cusak and Taylor, "Resurgence of a Terrorist Organisation," 9.
54. Paul Watson and Sidhartha Barua, "Worlds of Extremism and Crime Collide in Indian Jail," *Los Angeles Times*, February 8, 2002.
55. David Keen, *The Economic Functions of Violence in Civil Wars* (Oxford: Oxford University Press, 1998), 12; Martin Ewi and Uyo Salifu, "Money Talks: A Key Reason Youths Join Boko Haram," Policy Brief 98, Institute for Security Studies, February 2017, p. 4; and Justine A. Rosenthal, "For-Profit Terrorism: The Rise of Armed Entrepreneurs," *Studies in Conflict and Terrorism* 31, no. 6 (2008): 482.
56. Michael Desch, ed., *Soldiers in Cities: Military Operations on Urban Terrain* (Carlisle Barracks, Pa.: Strategic Studies Institute, 2001), 71; see also Uros Komlenovic, "State and Mafia in Yugoslavia," *East European Constitutional Review* 6, no. 4 (Fall 1997): 73.
57. Mary Kaldor, *New and Old Wars: Organized Violence in a Global Era* (Stanford, Calif.: Stanford University Press, 2012), 113; see also Angelina Stanojoska, "The Connection between Terrorism and Organized Crime: Narcoterrorism and the Other Hybrids," paper presented at the Combating Terrorism: International Standards and Legislation conference, Banja Luka, Republic of Srpska, March 2011, p. 2; and Heiko Nitzschke and Kaysie Studdard, "The Legacies of War Economies: Challenges and Options for Peacemaking and Peacebuilding," *International Peacekeeping* 12, no. 2 (2005): 225.
58. Alex Schmid, *Revisiting the Relationship between International Terrorism and Transnational Organised Crime 22 Years Later* (The Hague: International Centre for Counter-Terrorism, August 2018), 20.
59. Sudhir Venkatesh, "The Financial Activity of a Modern American Street Gang," in *Looking at Crime from the Street Level: Plenary Papers of the 1999 Conference on Criminal Justice Research and Evaluation*, ed. Sudhir Venkatesh, Richard Curtis, and Charles H. Ramsey (Washington, D.C.: National Institute of Justice, 1999), 7; and Rajan Basra and Peter Neumann, "Criminal Pasts, Terrorist Futures," *Perspectives on Terrorism* 10, no. 6 (2016): 29.
60. Makarenko, "The Crime-Terror Continuum," 133; Celina B. Realuyo, *"Following the Money Trail" to Combat Terrorism, Crime, and Corruption in the Americas* (Washington, D.C.: Wilson Center, August 2017), 3; and Colin P. Clarke, "An Overview of Current Trends in Terrorism and Illicit Finance," Testimony presented before the House Financial Services Committee, Subcommittee on Terrorism and Illicit Finance, September 7, 2018, https://www.rand.org/content/dam/rand/pubs/testimonies/CT400/CT498/RAND_CT498.pdf, 6.

61. Silke, *Routledge Handbook of Terrorism and Counter-Terrorism*, 201; and Allan Jones A. Salem, "Nexus of Crime and Terrorism: The Case of the Abu Sayyaf Group" (master's thesis, Naval Postgraduate School, 2016), 16.

62. Svante Cornell, "Narcotics and Armed Conflict," *Studies in Conflict and Terrorism* 30, no. 3 (April 2007): 212.

63. Sudhir Venkatesh and Steven Levitt, "Are We a Family or a Business?," *Theory and Society* 29, no. 4 (August 2000): 458; and Sudhir Venkatesh, *Off the Books* (Cambridge, Mass.: Harvard University Press, 2006), 66.

64. James Adams, *The Financing of Terror* (New York: Simon and Schuster, 1986), 94; and Eric Sass, "The Massive Bank Robbery That Lasted a Week," *Mental Floss*, July 12, 2011.

65. Dishman, "Terrorism, Crime, and Transformation," 54; and Jeffrey Robinson, *The Laundrymen: Inside Money Laundering, the World's Third Largest Business* (New York: Arcade, 1996), 68.

66. Michael Miklaucic, "Convergence," lecture, Marshall Center, July 11, 2019.

67. Makarenko, "The Crime-Terror Continuum," 131; and Javier Jordan, Fernando M. Manas, and Nicola Horsburgh, "Strengths and Weaknesses of Grassroot Jihadist Networks," *Studies in Conflict and Terrorism* 31, no. 1 (January 2008): 33.

68. Charlie Savage, Eric Schmitt, Nicholas Fandos, and Adam Goldman, "Trump Got Written Briefing in February on Possible Russian Bounties, Officials Say," *New York Times*, June 29, 2020; and Charlie Savage, Mujib Mashal, Rukmini Callimachi, Eric Schmitt, and Adam Goldman, "Suspicions of Russian Bounties Were Bolstered by Data on Financial Transfers," *New York Times*, June 30, 2020.

69. Amy C. Collins, *The Need for a Specific Law against Domestic Terrorism*, GW Program on Extremism, George Washington University, September 2020.

70. John Picarelli, "Osama Bin Corleone? Vito the Jackal?," *Terrorism and Political Violence* 24, no. 2 (2012): 183; and Liana W. Rosen, John W. Rollins, June S. Beittel, and Clare Ribando Seelke, *Designating Mexican Drug Cartels as Foreign Terrorists* (Washington, D.C.: Congressional Research Service, December 6, 2019), 3.

71. Christian Parenti, *Tropic of Chaos: Climate Change and the New Geography of Violence* (New York: Nation Books, 2011), 36; and Naylor, *Patriots and Profiteers*, xvi.

72. Naylor, *Patriots and Profiteers*, 347; and Salkic, quoted in Peter Andreas, *Blue Helmets and Black Markets: The Business of Survival in the Siege of Sarajevo* (Ithaca, N.Y.: Cornell University Press, 2008), 122.

73. Mimi Yagoub, "What the FARC's Elusive Finances Mean for Peace," *InSight Crime*, April 20, 2016.

74. Karen Ballentine and Heiko Nitzschke, *The Political Economy of Civil War and Conflict Transformation* (Berlin: Berghof Center, 2005), 19; and Nitzschke and Studdard, "The Legacies of War Economies," 228.

75. Kaldor, *New and Old Wars*, 149; see also Jean-Paul Azam, David L. Bevan, Paul Collier, Stefan Dercon, Jan Willem Gunning, and Sanjay Pradhan, *Some Economic Consequences of the Transition from Civil War to Peace* (New York: World Bank, December 1994), 10.

76. Jesse Driscoll, "Commitment Problems or Bidding Wars?," *Journal of Conflict Resolution* 56, no. 1 (2012): 121; and Hobsbawm, *Bandits*, 78.

77. Phil Williams and Vanda Felbab-Brown, *Drug Trafficking, Violence, and Instability* (Carlisle Barracks, Pa.: Strategic Studies Institute, 2012), 76; see also Azam et al., *Some Economic Consequences*, 44.

78. Duncan Wilson, "A Dilemma for Burundi's War Veterans," *Guardian*, September 29, 2011.

79. John Sullivan and Robert Bunker, "Third Generation Gang Studies," *Journal of Gang Research* 14, no. 4 (Summer 2007): 3.

80. Graff, "A Vor Never Sleeps"; Stergios Skaperdas, "The Political Economy of Organized Crime: Providing Protections When the State Does Not," *Economics of Governance* 2 (2001): 175; and Robb, "Brave New War," 92.

81. Paul Rexton Kan, *Drug Trafficking and International Security* (Lanham, Md.: Rowman and Littlefield, 2016), 138; Gretchen Peters, *Seeds of Terror: The Taliban, The ISI and the New Opium Wars* (New York: St. Martin's Press, 2009), 17; Cornell, "Narcotics and Armed Conflict," 211; and Matthew Levitt, "Untangling the Terror Web," *SAIS Review of International Affairs* 24, no. 1 (2004): 34.

82. John McTiernan, dir., *Die Hard* (Los Angeles: Twentieth Century Fox, 1988). See also Naylor, *Wages of Crime*, 56.

83. Prospero, "Would the World Be a Better Place if James Bond Had Never Existed?," *Economist*, October 28, 2015.

84. Adams, *The Financing of Terror*, 252.

Chapter 3. Crime

1. Jeffrey Goldberg, "In the Party of God II," *New Yorker*, October 28, 2002; and Tom Diaz and Barbara Newman, *Lightning Out of Lebanon* (New York: Presidio, 2005), 178.

2. Louise Shelley and Sharon Melzer, "The Nexus of Organized Crime and Terrorism," *International Journal of Comparative and Applied Criminal Justice* 32, no. 1 (2008): 53; and Diaz and Newman, *Lightning Out of Lebanon*, 82.

3. Frank Perri and Richard Brody, "The Dark Triad," *Journal of Money Laundering Control* 14, no. 1 (2011): 50; and William Billingslea, "Illicit Cigarette Trafficking and the Funding of Terrorism," *Police Chief* 71, no. 2 (2004).

4. Sari Horwitz, "Cigarette Smuggling Linked to Terrorism," *Washington Post*, June 8, 2004.

5. Petrus C. van Duyne, Klaus von Lampe, and Nokos Passas, eds., *Upperworld and Underworld in Cross-Border Crime* (Nijmegen, The Netherlands: Wolf Legal, 2003), 149.

6. Diaz and Newman, *Lightning Out of Lebanon*, 217; and Billingslea, "Illicit Cigarette Trafficking."

7. R. T. Naylor, *Wages of Crime: Black Markets, Illegal Finance, and the Underworld Economy* (Ithaca, N.Y.: Cornell University Press, 2004), 325.

8. C. Wright Mills and Alan Wolfe, *The Power Elite* (New York: Oxford University Press, 2000), 95.

9. For the "Know Your Neighborhood," tool, click on the "Explore your zip code" button on the ESRI website, under "Discover the Power of Data," accessed February 14, 2022, https://www.esri.com/en-us/arcgis/products/data/.

10. Magnus Ranstorp, "Microfinancing the Caliphate: How the Islamic State Is Unlocking the Assets of European Recruits," *CTC Sentinel* 9, no. 5 (May 2016): 13.

11. John Horgan and Max Taylor, "Playing the 'Green Card,' Part 1," *Terrorism and Political Violence* 11, no. 2 (Summer 1999): 1.

12. James Adams, *The Financing of Terror* (New York: Simon and Schuster, 1986), 157; and Laura Donohue, "Anti-Terrorist Finance in the United Kingdom and United States," *Michigan Journal of International Law* 27, no. 2 (2006), 318.

13. Graham Turbiville, *Private Security Infrastructure Abroad* (Hurlburt Field, Fla.: JSOU Press, 2007), 40.

14. FATF, *Emerging Terrorist Financing Risks* (Paris: FATF, October 2015), 25; and Jason Blazakis and Conner Freeman, "How Hate Groups Abuse the Tax Code," *Talking Points Memo*, October 15, 2019.

15. "Counterfeit Goods: Easy Cash for Criminals and Terrorists," Testimony before the Homeland Security and Governmental Affairs Committee Hearing, U.S. Senate, May 25, 2005; Phil Williams, "Crime, Illicit Markets, and Money Laundering," in *Managing Global Issues: Lessons Learned*, ed. P. J. Simmons and Chantal de Jonge Oudraat (Washington, D.C.: Carnegie Endowment for International Peace, 2001), 115; and Maura Conway, "Terrorism and the Internet: New Media—New Threat?," *Parliamentary Affairs* 59, no. 2 (April 2006): 294.

16. Richard Barrett, "Preventing the Financing of Terrorism," *Case Western Reserve Journal of International Law* 44, no. 3 (2012): 724; Zeynep Ece, Svetlana Nikoloska, and Ivica Simonovski, "Methods, Trends and Future Challenges in Financing of Terrorism," in *Security Concepts and Policies* (Skopje, Macedonia: ISC, 2017), 114; and Erica Alini, "The Meticulous Planning of the Oslo Massacre," *Macleans*, July 28, 2011.

17. Elisabeth Braw, "The Non-Halal Ways Potential Jihadists Are Funding Their Work," *Foreign Affairs*, October 25, 2015; Rajan Basra and Peter Neumann,

"Criminal Pasts, Terrorist Futures," *Perspectives on Terrorism* 10, no. 6 (2016): 35; and Ranstorp, "Microfinancing the Caliphate," 13.

18. Perri and Brody, "The Dark Triad," 53; and William Gaines and Andrew Martin, "Terror-Funding Probe Touches Suburban Group," *Chicago Tribune*, September 8, 1998.

19. Michael Freeman, *Financing Terrorism: Case Studies* (Burlington: Ashgate, 2011), 177; and Donohue, "Anti-Terrorist Finance," 321.

20. Garrett Graff, "A Vor Never Sleeps," *Longreads*, June 2018, https://longreads.com/2018/06/04/a-vor-never-sleeps/; and FATF, *Emerging Terrorist Financing Risks*, 18.

21. Bard O'Neill, *Insurgency and Terrorism: Inside Modern Revolutionary Warfare* (Washington, D.C.: Potomac, 2005), 17; and Perri and Brody, "The Dark Triad," 55.

22. Graff, "A Vor Never Sleeps."

23. John A. Cassara, *Trade-Based Money Laundering: The Next Frontier in International Money Laundering Enforcement* (Hoboken, N.J.: Wiley, 2016), 67.

24. Turbiville, *Private Security Infrastructure Abroad*, 31; and Adam Dolnik, *Understanding Terrorist Innovation: Technology, Tactics and Global Trends* (London: Routledge, 2007), 75.

25. Ece et al., "Methods, Trends and Future Challenges," 113; FATF, *Emerging Terrorist Financing Risks*, 27; and Ranstorp, "Microfinancing the Caliphate," 13.

26. Isabel Woodford and M. L. R. Smith, "The Political Economy of the Provos: Inside the Finances of the Provisional IRA—A Revision," *Studies in Conflict and Terrorism* 41, no. 3 (2018): 221; and W. A. Tupman, "Where Has All the Money Gone? The IRA as a Profit-Making Concern," *Journal of Money Laundering Control* 1, no. 4 (April 1998): 310.

27. Richard Paxton, "Where Money Laundering Hides in America," *Medium*, April 7, 2016.

28. Jeff Baillon, "Whistleblower Reported Daycare Fraud," *Fox 9*, May 14, 2018.

29. Matt Sepic, "Somali-American Child Care Providers Push Back on Reports of Fraud," *Minnesota Public Radio News*, May 21, 2018; Ibrahim Hirsi, "What You Need to Know about Somali Money Transfers," *MinnPost*, May 23, 2018; and Riham Feshir, "Four Twin Cities Day Care Centers Raided for Fraud," *Minnesota Public Radio News*, September 29, 2015.

30. Patrick Blannin, "Sources, Methods and Utilisation," *Counter Terrorist Trends and Analyses* 9, no. 5 (2017): 20.

31. Anneli Botha, Martin Ewi, Uyo Salifu, and Mahdi Abdile, *Understanding Nigerian Citizens' Perspectives on Boko Haram* (Pretoria: Institute for Security Studies, 2017), 57.

32. Jean-Loup Richet, "Laundering Money Online: A Review of Cybercriminals Methods," white paper, UN Office on Drugs and Crime, June 1, 2013, p. 17.

33. Aunshul Rege, "What's Love Got to Do with It?," *International Journal of Cyber Criminology* 3, no. 2 (2009): 498; Harvey Glickman, "The Nigerian '419' Advance Fee Scams," *Canadian Journal of African Studies* 39, no. 3 (2005): 475; and Jenna Burrell, "Problematic Empowerment," *Information Technologies and International Development* 4, no. 4 (2008): 23.

34. Catherine Herridge, "ISIS Accused of Selling Fake PPE Online to Finance Terrorism," *CBS News*, August 13, 2020.

35. Mark Hamm, *Crimes Committed by Terrorist Groups: Theory, Research and Prevention*, report prepared for the Department of Justice, June 1, 2005, p. 191.

36. James Love, *Hezbollah: Social Services as a Source of Power* (Hurlburt Field, Fla.: JSOU, 2010), 28; and Douglas Farah, *Blood from Stones: The Secret Financial Network of Terror* (New York: Broadway Books, 2004), 166.

37. Graff, "A Vor Never Sleeps"; and Andrew Adams, "Money Laundering and TNOC" (lecture, Marshall Center, July 2019).

38. Brendan Koerner, "Russians Engineer a Brilliant Slot Machine Cheat," *Wired*, February 6, 2017.

39. R. T. Naylor, *Patriots and Profiteers: Economic Warfare, Embargo Busting, and State-Sponsored Crime* (Montreal: McGill-Queen's University Press, 2008), 30; and Sheena Chestnut, "The 'Sopranos State'?" (honors thesis, Stanford University, 2005), 19.

40. John K. Cooley, *Currency Wars: How Forged Money Is the New Weapon of Mass Destruction* (New York: Skyhorse, 2008), 288; and Naylor, *Wages of Crime*, 58.

41. Cooley, *Currency Wars*, 43; Anthony Spaeth, "Kim's Rackets," *Time*, June 9, 2003; and Bruce E. Bechtol Jr., "North Korean Illicit Activities and Sanctions: A National Security Dilemma," *Cornell International Law Journal* 51 (2018): 64.

42. Cooley, *Currency Wars*, 34; and Nitsana Darshan-Leitner and Samuel M. Katz, *Harpoon: Inside the Covert War against Terrorism's Money Masters* (New York: Hachette, 2017), 114.

43. Paul Clare, *Racketeering in Northern Ireland: A New Version of the Patriot Game* (Chicago: University of Illinois, 1989), 24; and Donohue, "Anti-Terrorist Finance," 321.

44. Mackenzie Institute, "Funding Terror: The Liberation of Tigers of Tamil Eelam and Their Criminal Activities in Canada and the Western World," *Mackenzie Institute*, December 26, 1995, https://mackenzieinstitute.com/1995/12/funding -terror-the-liberation-tigers-of-tamil-eelam-and-their-criminal-activities -in-canada-and-the-western-world/; and Mitchel Roth and Murat Sever, "The Kurdish Workers Party as Criminal Syndicate," *Studies in Conflict and Terrorism* 30, no. 10 (2007): 912.

45. Hamm, *Crimes Committed by Terrorist Groups*, 149; and Siobhan O'Neil, *Terrorist Precursor Crimes: Issues and Options for Congress* (Washington, D.C.: Congressional Research Service, May 24, 2007), 12.

46. Mackenzie Institute, *Funding Terror*; John Picarelli, "Osama Bin Corleone? Vito the Jackal?," *Terrorism and Political Violence* 24, no. 2 (2012): 187; and Naylor, *Wages of Crime*, 58.

47. Peter Aldhous, "Line of Fire," *Nature* 434, no. 134 (March 9, 2005); and Boaz Ganor and Miri Wernli, "The Infiltration of Terrorist Organizations into the Pharmaceutical Industry," *Studies in Conflict and Terrorism* 36, no. 9 (September 1, 2013): 703.

48. Ariel Solomon and Benjamin Weinthal, "Hezbollah Maintains Complex Network of Front Companies Trading in Counterfeit Medicine," *Jerusalem Post*, August 1, 2013; James J. F. Forest, ed., *Teaching Terror: Strategic and Tactical Learning in the Terrorist World* (Lanham, Md.: Rowman and Littlefield, 2006), 51; and Douglas T. Cannon, "War through Pharmaceuticals: How Terrorist Organizations Are Turning to Counterfeit Medicine to Fund Their Illicit Activity," *Case Western Reserve Journal of International Law* 47, no. 1 (2015): 373.

49. Michael Pollan, "The Way We Live Now," *New York Times Magazine*, September 12, 1999.

50. Channing May, *Transnational Crime and the Developing World* (Washington, D.C.: Global Financial Integrity, March 2017), 47.

51. Alan Zimmerman and Peggy Chaudhry, *The Economics of Counterfeit Trade* (Berlin: Springer, 2009), 11.

52. Phil Taylor, "Schaeffler Scraps 26m Tonnes of Fake Bearings," *Securing Industry*, July 9, 2013.

53. Stephanie Wash and Candace Smith, "Authorities Say Sale of Counterfeit Sneakers Can Lead to Terrorist Financing," *ABC News*, September 7, 2017; and May, *Transnational Crime*, 50.

54. Farah, *Blood from Stones*, 168; and Hamm, *Crimes Committed by Terrorist Groups*, 148.

55. Nimrod Raphaeli, "Financing of Terrorism: Sources, Methods, and Channels," *Terrorism and Political Violence* 15, no. 4 (2003): 75.

56. Blanca Madani, "Hezbollah's Global Finance Network: The Triple Frontier," *Middle East Intelligence Bulletin* 4, no. 1 (January 2002); Howard Meehan, "Terrorism, Diasporas and Permissive Threat Environments" (master's thesis, Naval Postgraduate School, 2004), 28; and Sylvia Longmire, "Legalizing Marijuana Won't Kill the Mexican Drug Cartels," *New York Times*, June 18, 2011.

57. Gregory F. Treverton, Carl Matthies, Karla J. Cunningham, Jeremiah Goulka, Greg Ridgeway, and Anny Wong, *Film Piracy, Organized Crime, and Terrorism* (Santa Monica, Calif.: RAND, 2009), 144.

58. Frank Abagnale and Ori Eisen, "Follow the Money: The Link between Passwords and Terrorism" (RSA conference, San Francisco, February 24, 2020).

59. Blythe Bowman, "Transnational Crimes against Culture: Looting at Archaeological Sites and the 'Grey' Market in Antiquities," *Journal of Contemporary Criminal Justice* 24, no. 3 (August 2008): 236; and van Duyne et al., *Upperworld*, 19.

60. Stephen Landman, "Funding Bin Laden's Avatar," *William Mitchell Law Review* 35 (2009): 5166.

61. Joseph L. Votel, Christina Bembenek, Charles Han, Jeffrey Mouton, and Amanda Spencer, "#Virtual Caliphate: Defending ISIL on the Battlefield Is Not Enough," Center for a New American Security, January 12, 2017; Brian Petit, *Chechen Use of the Internet in the Russo-Chechen Conflict* (Ft. Leavenworth, Kan.: Command and General Staff College, 2003), 19; and David Alberts and Daniel Papp, eds., *Information Age Anthology* (Washington, D.C.: Center for Advanced Concepts and Technology, 2001), 318.

62. Michael Jacobson, "Terrorist Financing and the Internet," *Studies in Conflict and Terrorism* 33, no. 4 (April 2010): 359.

63. Association of Chief Police Officers, "Younes Tsouli," https://preventforfeand training.org.uk/wp-content/uploads/2017/09/Copy-of-Case_study_Younes_ Tsouli.pdf, 2.

64. Edward Luce, "The End of the Golden Arches Doctrine," *Financial Times*, May 10, 2015; Bryan Hurd, "Cyber Landscape" (lecture, Marshall Center, July 15, 2019); Louise I. Shelley and John T. Picarelli, "Methods and Motives: Exploring Links between Transnational Organized Crime and International Terrorism," *Trends in Organized Crime* 9, no. 2 (December 2005): 49; and Department of Homeland Security, *Homeland Threat Assessment* (Washington, D.C.: Department of Homeland Security, October 2020), https://www.dhs.gov/sites/default /files/publications/2020_10_06_homeland-threat-assessment.pdf, p. 8.

65. Votel et al., "#Virtual Caliphate."

66. Jacobson, "Terrorist Financing and the Internet," 357.

67. Daniel Milton, Julia Lodoen, Ryan O'Farrell, and Seth Loertscher, "Newly Released ISIS Files: learning from the Islamic State's Long-Version Personnel Form," *CTC Sentinel* 12, no. 9 (October 2019): 18; Aymenn Al-Tamimi, "Archive of Islamic State Administrative Documents," January 11, 2016, http://www .aymennjawad.org/2016/01/archive-of-islamic-state-administrative-documents-1; and Laith Alkhouri, Alex Kassirer, and Allison Nixon, *Hacking for ISIS: The Emergent Cyber Threat Landscape* (New York: Flashpoint, April 2016), 23.

68. Audrey Alexander and Bennett Clifford, "Doxing and Defacements," *CTC Sentinel* 12, no. 4 (April 2019): 26; Hurd, "Cyber"; Nicholas Sambaluk, ed., *Conflict in the 21st Century: The Impact of Cyber Warfare, Social Media, and Technology* (Santa Barbara, Calif.: ABC-Clio, 2019), 23; Kyle Swenson, "She Seemed like a Normal

Web-Savvy Teen," *Washington Post*, March 21, 2019; and Audrey Kurth Cronin, "Behind the Curve," *International Security* 27, no. 3 (January 1, 2003): 48.

69. Brian Krebs, "Terrorism's Hook into Your Inbox," *Washington Post*, July 5, 2007; and Alkhouri et al., *Hacking for ISIS*, 14.

70. Arndt Sinn, "Organized Crime 3.0" (lecture, Marshall Center, July 18, 2019); Paul Rexton Kan, *Drug Trafficking and International Security* (Lanham, Md.: Rowman and Littlefield, 2016), 177; and Zachary K. Goldman, Ellie Maruyama, Elizabeth Rosenberg, Edoardo Saravalle, and Julia Solomon-Strauss, *Terrorist Use of Virtual Currencies* (Washington, D.C.: Center for a New American Security, May 3, 2017), 26.

71. Killian McCarthy, ed., *The Money Laundering Market: Regulating the Criminal Economy* (Newcastle upon Tyne, U.K.: Agenda, 2018), 185; and Adam Rawnsley, Eric Woods, and Christiaan Triebert, "The Messaging App Fueling Syria's Insurgency," *Foreign Policy*, November 6, 2017.

72. Matt Egan, "What Is the Dark Web," *Tech Advisor*, October 25, 2019.

73. "saidaninour," "TIFU by Buying Game Cheats from a Terrorist, Who Then Got Me Arrested and Forced to Marry My GF," Reddit, July 3, 2020.

74. Kevin Collier, "Texas Working to Recover from Ransomware," *CNN*, August 20, 2019; Margaret Crahan and Alberto Vourvoulias-Bush, eds., *The City and the World: New York's Global Future* (New York: Council on Foreign Relations, 1997), 55; and Robert I. Rotberg, *The Corruption Cure: How Citizens and Leaders Can Combat Graft* (Princeton, N.J.: Princeton University Press, 2017), 260.

75. Samantha Raphelson, "Town Avoids Paying Massive $5 Million Ransom in Cyberattack," *NPR*, September 6, 2019; and Joie Tyrrell, "Rockville Centre Pays Almost $100G to Hackers," *Newsday*, August 24, 2019.

76. Sambaluk, *Conflict in the 21st Century*, 77.

77. Adi Robertson, "16 People Arrested for Allegedly Stealing 100 Car2Go Luxury Cars," *The Verge*, April 17, 2019.

78. John Daly, "LTTE," *Asian Tribune*, June 14, 2007; and Darlene Storm, "Attackers Hack European Space Agency," *Computerworld*, December 14, 2015.

79. Jessica D'Ambrosio, "Space Aggressors Jam AF, Allies' Systems," *U.S. Air Force*, February 13, 2017; "Satellite Hack Raises Security Questions," *CNET*, January 2, 2002; and Noah Sachtman, "Pentagon Spy: Terrorists Ready to Launch Satellite Strikes by 2020," *Wired*, May 25, 2008.

80. Nils Gilman, Jesse Goldhammer, and Steven Weber, Introduction to *Deviant Globalization: Black Market Economy in the 21st Century* (New York: Continuum, 2011), 13.

81. Vadim Volkov, *Violent Entrepreneurs: The Use of Force in the Making of Russian Capitalism* (Ithaca, N.Y.: Cornell University Press, 2002), 123.

82. Zachary Abuza, "Funding Terrorism in Southeast Asia: The Financial Network of Al Qaeda and Jemaah Islamiya," *Contemporary Southeast Asia* 25, no. 2 (August 2003): 183.

83. Jacobson, "Terrorist Financing," 358.

84. Mike Bourne, "The Proliferation of Small Arms and Light Weapons," in *New Threats and New Actors in International Security*, ed. Elke Krahmann (New York: Palgrave MacMillan, 2005), 170; Phil Williams, "Transnational Criminal Enterprises, Conflict, and Instability," in *Turbulent Peace: The Challenges of Managing International Conflict*, ed. Pamela R. Aall, Chester Crocker, and Fen Osler Hampson (Washington, D.C.: USIP, 2001), 104; and Fuat Salih Sahin, "Case Studies in Terrorism-Drug Connection: The Kurdistan Workers' Party, the Liberation Tigers of Tamil Eelam, and the Shining Path" (master's thesis, University of North Texas, 2001), 65.

85. Abdulmajeed Bello, "Boko Haram," *International Journal of Management and Social Sciences Research* 2, no. 2 (February 2013): 69; and Botha et al., *Understanding Nigerian Citizens' Perspectives*, 39.

86. Robert Bunker, ed., *Non-State Threats and Future Wars* (New York: Routledge, 2012), 113; and Shanaka Jayasekara, "LTTE Fundraising and Money Transfer Operations" (paper presented at the International Conference on Countering Terrorism, Colombo, Sri Lanka, October 18–20, 2007), 7.

87. Annette Hubschle, *Unholy Alliance? Assessing the Links between Organised Criminals and Terrorists in Southern Africa* (Cape Town: Institute for Security Studies, October 2004), 9.

88. Stefano Caneppele and Francesco Calderoni, eds., *Organized Crime, Corruption and Crime Prevention* (Cham: Springer International, 2014), 270.

89. Clare, *Racketeering in Northern Ireland*, 21; and Donohue, "Anti-Terrorist Finance," 317.

90. Bruce Zagaris, "Protecting the Rule of Law from Assault in the War against Drugs and Narco-Terrorism," *Nova Law Review* 15, no. 2 (1991): 706; and Adams, *The Financing of Terror*, 179.

91. Andrew Silke, "Drink, Drugs, and Rock 'n' Roll," *Studies in Conflict and Terrorism* 23 (2000): 108; John Horgan and Max Taylor, "Playing the 'Green Card,' Part 2," *Terrorism and Political Violence* 15, no. 2 (Summer 2003): 14.

92. Adams, *The Financing of Terror*, 174.

93. *Joint Publication 3-24: Counterinsurgency* (Washington, D.C.: Department of Defense, April 25, 2018), 123.

94. Woodford and Smith, "The Political Economy of the Provos," 220; Donohue, "Anti-Terrorist Finance," 317; and Horgan and Taylor, "Playing the 'Green Card,' Part 2," 11.

95. Gretchen Peters, *Haqqani Network Financing: The Evolution of an Industry* (West Point, N.Y.: Combating Terrorism Center, 2012), 53.

96. Adams, *The Financing of Terror*, 199.

97. Steve Kiser, *Financing Terror: An Analysis and Simulation for Affecting Al Qaeda's Financial Infrastructure* (Santa Monica, Calif.: RAND, 2005), 79.

98. Jeffrey Robinson, *The Laundrymen: Inside Money Laundering, the World's Third Largest Business* (New York: Arcade, 1996), 259.

99. Mimi Yagoub, "What the FARC's Elusive Finances Mean for Peace," *InSight Crime*, April 20, 2016.

100. Joshua Geltzer, "Taking Hand-Outs or Going It Alone," *Studies in Conflict and Terrorism* 34, no. 2 (January 2011): 147.

101. Martin Rudner, "Hizbullah Terrorism Finance: Fund-Raising and Money-Laundering," *Studies in Conflict and Terrorism* 33, no. 8 (July 15, 2010): 702.

102. Volkov, *Violent Entrepreneurs*, 124.

103. Jean-Charles Brisard and Damien Martinez, *Islamic State: The Economy-Based Terrorist Funding* (Toronto: Thompson Reuters, October 2014), 8.

104. Rudner, "Hizbullah Terrorism Finance," 704.

105. Klejda Mulaj, ed., *Violent Non-State Actors in World Politics* (New York: Columbia University Press, 2010), 354.

106. Matthew Levitt, "The Political Economy of Middle East Terrorism," *Middle East Review of International Affairs* 6, no. 4 (December 2002): 52.

107. Geoffrey Morgan, "How Did Ottawa Shooter Michael Zehaf-Bibeau Get Work in the Oil Patch?," *Financial Post*, October 28, 2014.

108. Adams, *The Financing of Terror*, 175; Caneppele and Calderoni, *Organized Crime*, 199; and Michaela Martin and Hussein Solomon, "Islamic State: Understanding the Nature of the Beast and Its Funding," *Contemporary Review of the Middle East* 4, no. 1 (2017): 23.

109. Michael Freeman, "The Sources of Terrorist Financing: Theory and Typology," *Studies in Conflict and Terrorism* 34, no. 6 (2011): 469.

110. Tolga Koker and Carlos Yordán, "Microfinancing Terrorism: A Study in al Qaeda Financing Strategy," in *State of Corruption, State of Chaos: The Terror of Political Malfeasance*, ed. Michaelene Cox (Lanham, Md.: Lexington, 2008), 170; and John Roth, Douglas Greenburg, and Serena Wille, *National Commission on Terrorist Attacks upon the United States*, Monograph on Terrorist Financing, Staff Report to the Commission (Washington, D.C.: GPO, 2002), 20.

111. Dolnik, *Understanding Terrorist Innovation*, 74; and Brian A. Jackson, John C. Baker, and Peter Chalk, *Aptitude for Destruction*, vol. 2, *Case Studies of Organizational Learning in Five Terrorist Groups* (Santa Monica, Calif.: RAND, 2005), 28.

112. Colin P. Clarke, "An Overview of Current Trends in Terrorism and Illicit Finance," Testimony presented before the House Financial Services Committee, Subcommittee on Terrorism and Illicit Finance, September 7, 2018, https://www.rand.org /content/dam/rand/pubs/testimonies/CT400/CT498/RAND_CT498.pdf, p. 1.

Chapter 4. Hands-on Violence

1. Andrew Silke, "In Defense of the Realm," *Studies in Conflict and Terrorism* 21 (1998): 339.

2. Sudhir Alladi Venkatesh, *Off the Books: The Underground Economy of the Urban Poor* (Cambridge, Mass.: Harvard University Press, 2006), 304.

3. Silke, "In Defense of the Realm," 352; and Steven Levitt and Sudhir Venkatesh, "An Economic Analysis of a Drug-Selling Gang's Finances," *Quarterly Journal of Economics* 115, no. 3 (August 2000): 758.

4. Kai Konrad and Stergios Skaperdas, "Extortion," *Economica* 65, no. 260 (November 1998): 461.

5. James Adams, *The Financing of Terror* (New York: Simon and Schuster, 1986), 173; Silke, "In Defense of the Realm," 348; and Paul K. Clare, *Racketeering in Northern Ireland: A New Version of the Patriot Game* (Chicago: University of Illinois, 1989), 4.

6. Michael Freeman, "The Sources of Terrorist Financing: Theory and Typology," *Studies in Conflict and Terrorism* 34, no. 6 (2011): 467.

7. R. T. Naylor, *Wages of Crime: Black Markets, Illegal Finance, and the Underworld Economy* (Ithaca, N.Y.: Cornell University Press, 2004), 198; and R. T. Naylor, *Patriots and Profiteers: Economic Warfare, Embargo Busting, and State-Sponsored Crime* (Montreal: McGill-Queen's University Press, 2008), 31.

8. Mary Kaldor, *New and Old Wars: Organized Violence in a Global Era* (Stanford, Calif.: Stanford University Press, 2012), 112; and Hanan G. Jacoby, Guo Li, and Scott Rozelle, "Hazards of Expropriation: Tenure Insecurity and Investment in Rural China," *American Economic Review* 92, no. 5 (December 2002): 1420.

9. Mitchel Roth and Murat Sever, "The Kurdish Workers Party as Criminal Syndicate," *Studies in Conflict and Terrorism* 30, no. 10 (2007): 904; Bruce Hoffman, RAND Corporation, and National Security Research Division, *The Radicalization of Diasporas and Terrorism: A Joint Conference by the RAND Corporation and the Center for Security Studies* (Santa Monica, Calif.: RAND, 2007), 44; Jeanne Giraldo and Harold Trinkunas, eds., *Terrorism Financing and State Responses: A Comparative Perspective* (Stanford, Calif.: Stanford University Press, 2007), 210; and Aymenn Al-Tamimi, "Archive of Islamic State Administrative Documents," January 27, 2015, http://www.aymennjawad.org/2015/01 /archive-of-islamic-state-administrative-documents.

10. Mark Hamm, *Crimes Committed by Terrorist Groups: Theory, Research and Prevention*, report prepared for the Department of Justice, June 1, 2005, 147.

11. Garrett Graff, "A Vor Never Sleeps," *Longreads*, June 2018, https://longreads .com/2018/06/04/a-vor-never-sleeps/; and Andrew Adams, "Money Laundering and TNOC" (lecture, Marshall Center, July 2019).

12. Magnus Ranstorp, "Microfinancing the Caliphate: How the Islamic State Is Unlocking the Assets of European Recruits," *CTC Sentinel* 9, no. 5 (May 2016): 12; Freeman, "The Sources of Terrorist Financing," 467; and "Counterfeit Goods: Easy Cash for Criminals and Terrorists," Testimony before the Homeland Security and Governmental Affairs Committee Hearing, U.S. Senate, May 25, 2005.

13. Sarah Cascone, "Reclaiming Seized Cuban Art Will Be Difficult," *Artnet News*, January 8, 2015; and Richard H. Schultz Jr. and Andrea J. Dew, *Insurgents, Terrorists, and Militias: The Warriors of Contemporary Combat* (New York: Columbia University Press, 2006), 58.

14. Janine Di Giovanni, Leah McGrath Goodman, and Damien Sharkov, "How Does ISIS Fund Its Reign of Terror?," *Newsweek*, November 6, 2014; Erika Solomon and Sam Jones, "ISIS Inc.," *Assyrian International News Agency*, December 15, 2015; and Stefan Heißner, Peter R. Neumann, John Holland-McCowan, and Rajan Basra, *Caliphate in Decline: An Estimate of Islamic State's Financial Fortunes* (London: International Centre for the Study of Radicalisation and Political Violence, King's College London, 2017), 12.

15. Stewart Bell, *Cold Terror: How Canada Nurtures and Exports Terrorism around the World* (Toronto: Wiley, 2004), 95; and Phil Williams, *Criminals, Militias, and Insurgents: Organized in Iraq* (Carlisle, Pa.: Strategic Studies Institute, 2009), 178.

16. Lennox Samuels, "Al Qaeda in Iraq Ramps Up Its Racketeering," *Newsweek*, May 20, 2008; Williams, *Criminals, Militias, and Insurgents*, 181; and Timothy Wittig, *Understanding Terrorist Finance* (New York: Palgrave MacMillan, 2011), 13.

17. Al-Tamimi, "Archive of Islamic State."

18. Graciela Singer, "ISIS's War on Cultural Heritage and Memory," *Museodata*, June 2015; Nawzat Shamdeen, "Money-Making Plots," *Niquash*, September 10, 2014; and Mariam Karouny, "In Northeast Syria, Islamic State Builds a Government," *Reuters*, September 4, 2014.

19. "Willie Sutton," Federal Bureau of Investigation, accessed February 18, 2020, https://www.fbi.gov/history/famous-cases/willie-sutton.

20. W. A. Tupman, "Where Has All the Money Gone? The IRA as a Profit-Making Concern," *Journal of Money Laundering Control* 1, no. 4 (April 1998): 305; Hamm, *Crimes Committed by Terrorist Groups*, 199; and Naylor, *Wages of Crime*, 60.

21. Naylor, *Wages of Crime*, 60.

22. Marc-Antoine de Montclos, ed., *Boko Haram: Islamism, Politics, Security and the State in Nigeria*, vol. 2 (Nairobi: African Studies Centre, 2014), 148; Jason Rock,

"The Funding of Boko Haram and Nigeria's Actions to Stop It" (master's thesis, Naval Postgraduate School, 2016), 43; and David Doukhan, *Who Are You, Boko Haram?* (Herzliya, Isr.: International Institute for Counter-Terrorism, December 12, 2012), 8.

23. Patrick B. Johnston, Mona Alami, Colin P. Clarke, and Howard J. Shatz, *Return and Expand? The Finances and Prospects for the Islamic State after the Caliphate* (Santa Monica, Calif.: RAND, 2019), 1; Onur Burcak Belli, Andrea Böhm, Alexander Bühler, Kerstin Kohlenberg, Stefan Meining, Yassin Musharbash, Mark Schieritz, et al., "The Business of the Caliph," *Zeit Online*, December 3, 2014; and FATF, *Emerging Terrorist Financing Risks* (Paris: FATF, October 2015), 14.

24. "Remarks of Deputy Assistant Secretary for Terrorist Financing Jennifer Fowler at the Washington Institute for Near East Policy on the U.S. Efforts to Counter the Financing of ISIL" (press release, U.S. Department of the Treasury, February 2, 2015).

25. Darwin Templeton, "The Provos Got So Much Cash from Northern Bank Heist They Could Not Handle It," *Belfast Telegraph*, December 15, 2014; and Laura K. Donohue, "Anti-Terrorist Finance in the United Kingdom and United States," *Michigan Journal of International Law* 27, no. 2 (2006): 310.

26. U.S. Department of the Army, *Urban Operations: Field Manual 3-06* (Washington, D.C.: Department of the Army, 2006), 57.

27. Naylor, *Wages of Crime*, 51; and Nathan Nunn and Nancy Qian, "U.S. Food Aid and Civil Conflict," *American Economic Review* 104, no. 6 (2014): 1634.

28. Schultz and Dew, *Insurgents, Terrorists, and Militias*, 97; Graham Turbiville, Josh Meservey, and James Forest, *Countering the Al-Shabaab Insurgency in Somalia: Lessons for U.S. Special Operations Forces*, Report 14-1 (MacDill Air Force Base, Fla.: Joint Special Operations University, 2014), 12; and Nunn and Qian, "U.S. Food Aid," 1634.

29. Maria Abi-Habib, "Islamic State Poaches International Aid for Syria," *Wall Street Journal*, November 17, 2014; and Julian Pecquet, "Congress Demands Review after Islamic State Aid Theft," *Al-Monitor*, February 12, 2015.

30. Alexander Cooley and James Ron, "The NGO Scramble," *International Security* 27, no. 1 (Summer 2002): 29.

31. Béatrice Pouligny, *Peace Operations Seen from Below: UN Missions and Local People* (Bloomfield, Conn.: Kumarian Press, 2006), 203; Shawn Flanagan, "Nonprofit Service Provision by Insurgent Organizations," *Studies in Conflict and Terrorism* 31 (2008): 511; and Philippe Le Billon, Jake Sherman, and Marica Hartwell, *Controlling Resource Flows to Civil Wars: A Review and Analysis of Current Policies and Legal Instruments* (paper for the International Peace Academy "Economic Agendas in Civil Wars" project conference, Bellagio, Italy, May 20–24, 2002), 31.

32. James Fromson and Steven Simon, "ISIS: The Dubious Paradise of Apocalypse Now," *Survival* 57, no. 3 (May 11, 2015): 5; W. Andrew Terrill, "Understanding the Strengths and Vulnerabilities of ISIS," *Parameters* 44, no. 3 (Autumn 2014): 18; and Roland Marchal, *The Rise of a Jihadi Movement in a Country at War* (Paris: CNRS SciencesPo, March 2011), 65.

33. Arabinda Acharya, Syed Adnan Ali Shah Bukhari, and Sadia Sulaiman, "Making Money in the Mayhem: Funding Taliban Insurrection in the Tribal Areas of Pakistan," *Studies in Conflict and Terrorism* 32, no. 2 (February 2009): 102.

34. Richard Spencer, "Dumped in the Desert," *Telegraph*, September 25, 2011; and Joshua D. Foss, "Plutonium and Picasso: A Typology of Nuclear and Fine Art Smuggling," *InterAgency Journal* 8, no. 2 (2017): 37.

35. Román Ortiz, "Insurgent Strategies in the Post-Cold War: The Case of the Revolutionary Armed Forces of Colombia," *Studies in Conflict and Terrorism* 25, no. 2 (2002): 129; Daniel Fitz-Simons, "Sendero Luminoso," *Parameters* 33, no. 2 (Summer 1993): 65; Alain Carrier, *The Quebec Liberation Front (FLQ) as an Insurgency* (Fort Leavenworth, Kan.: School of Advanced Military Studies, U.S. Army Command and General Staff College, 2009), 31; and Sean Maloney, "A 'Mere Rustle of Leaves'," *Canadian Military Journal* 1, no. 2 (Summer 2000): 73.

36. Robert P. Clark, *The Basque Insurgency: ETA, 1952–1980* (Madison: University of Wisconsin Press, 1984), 224; Bard E. O'Neill, *Insurgency and Terrorism: Inside Modern Revolutionary Warfare* (Washington, D.C.: Potomac, 2005), 16; and Hamm, *Crimes Committed by Terrorist Groups*, 9.

37. Yossi Shain, ed., *Governments-in-Exile in Contemporary World Politics* (New York: Routledge, 1991), 207; and Hazel Smith and Paul Stares, eds., *Diasporas in Conflict: Peace-Makers or Peace-Wreckers?* (New York: UN University Press, 2007), 221.

38. Eli Berman and David Laitin, *Hard Targets: Theory and Evidence on Suicide Attacks* (working paper 11740, National Bureau of Economic Research, November 2005), 5; and James Forest, ed., *Teaching Terror: Strategic and Tactical Learning in the Terrorist World* (Lanham, Md.: Rowman and Littlefield, 2006), 265.

39. Adam Dolnik, *Understanding Terrorist Innovation: Technology, Tactics and Global Trends* (London: Routledge, 2007), 124; see also Lawrence Wright, "The Terror Web," *New Yorker*, July 25, 2004; and Brian Dodwell, Daniel Milton, and Don Rassler, *The Caliphate's Global Workforce: An Inside Look at the Islamic State's Foreign Fighter Paper Trail* (West Point, N.Y.: Combating Terrorism Center, April 18, 2016), 32.

40. Lisa Campbell, "Los Zetas: An Operational Assessment," *Small Wars and Insurgencies* 21, no. 1 (2010): 56; Paul Rexton Kan, *Drug Trafficking and International Security* (Lanham, Md.: Rowman and Littlefield, 2016), 54; and Graham Turbiville,

"Firefights, Raids, and Assassinations: Tactical Forms of Cartel Violence and Their Underpinnings," *Small Wars and Insurgencies* 21, no. 1 (2010): 129.

41. Jonathan Goodhand, "Frontiers and Wars: The Opium Economy in Afghanistan," *Journal of Agrarian Change* 5, no. 2 (April 2005): 203; and Wittig, *Understanding Terrorist Finance*, 23.

42. Matt Potter, *Outlaws, Inc.* (New York: Bloomsbury, 2011), 132; John Daly, "Part II: The Deadly Convenience of Victor Bout," Center for Security Studies, June 24, 2008; and "Trapping the Lord of War," *Spiegel Online*, October 6, 2010.

43. David Petraeus and James Mattis, *Counterinsurgency*, FM3-24/FMFM 3-24 (Washington, D.C.: Headquarters, Department of the Army, June 16, 2006), 218; and Gert Berthold, "Lessons Learned Interview," *Washington Post*, October 6, 2015, 5.

44. Berthold, "Lessons Learned Interview," 3.

45. Matthew Rosenberg, "Afghan Companies with Insurgent Ties Still Receive U.S. Contracts," *New York Times*, November 12, 2013.

46. Maggie Fick, "Islamic State Uses Grain to Tighten Grip," Reuters, September 30, 2014; Riley Post and Jeffrey Peterson, *Unconventional Economics: Operational Economics in Unconventional Warfare* (MacDill Air Force Base, Fla.: Joint Special Operations University, 2016), 57; Hadi Jaafar and Eckart Woertz, "Agriculture as a Funding Source of ISIS," *Food Policy* 64 (2016): 23; and Muhammad al-'Ubaydi, Nelly Lahoud, Daniel Milton, and Bryan Price, *The Group That Calls Itself a State* (West Point, N.Y.: Combating Terrorism Center, December 2014), 72.

47. UNODC, *Addressing Organized Crime and Drug Trafficking in Iraq: Report of the UNODC Fact Finding Mission* (Vienna: UN Office on Drugs and Crime, August 25, 2003), 13.

48. Michelle Tsai, "Why the Mafia Loves Garbage," *Slate*, January 11, 2008; Monica Massari and Paola Monzini, "Dirty Business in Italy," *Global Crime* 6, no. 3/4 (August 2004): 289; Alessio D'Amato and Mariangela Zoli, "Illegal Waste Disposal in the Time of the Mafia," *Journal of Environmental Planning and Management* 55, no. 5 (2012): 648; and Reece Walters, "Dirty Collar Crime and the Environment," in *Proceedings of Crime, Justice and Social Democracy: An International Conference* (Queensland, Australia: Queensland Institute of Technology, 2012), 106.

49. Quoted in Jim Vallette, "Larry Summers' War against the Earth," *Counterpunch* June 15, 1999, https://www.counterpunch.org/1999/06/15/larry-summers-war-against-the-earth/.

50. James Ferguson, *Global Shadows: Africa in the Neoliberal World Order* (Durham, N.C.: Duke University Press, 2006), 70; Debora MacKenzie, "Toxic Waste Adds to Somalia's Woes," *NewScientist*, September 19, 1992; and Stephen Anning and M. L. R. Smith, "The Accidental Pirate," *Parameters* 42, no. 2 (Summer 2012): 37.

51. Alexander Kupatadze, "Organized Crime before and after the Tulip Revolution," *Central Asian Survey* 27, no. 3/4 (December 2008): 281; Vadim Volkov, *Violent Entrepreneurs: The Use of Force in the Making of Russian Capitalism* (Ithaca, N.Y.: Cornell University Press, 2002), 12; and Graham Turbiville, *Private Security Infrastructure Abroad* (Hurlburt Field, Fla.: JSOU Press, 2007), 13.

52. Turbiville, *Private Security Infrastructure Abroad*, 6.

53. Sarah Chayes, *Thieves of State: Why Corruptions Threatens Global Security* (New York: Norton, 2015), 125.

54. Solomon and Jones, "ISIS Inc."; see also Damian Paletta and Adam Entous, "Militants in Iraq Siphon State Pay," *Wall Street Journal*, March 23, 2015; Johnston et al., *Return and Expand?*, 79; Al-Tamimi, "Archive of Islamic State"; and Anna-Lotta Aijala, "How Is ISIS Funded?" (Tallinn University of Technology, 2016).

55. Aram Roston, "How the US Army Protects Its Trucks," *Guardian*, November 13, 2009.

56. Richard Barrett, *The Islamic State* (New York: The Soufan Group, November 2014), 53; Mitchell Prothero, "Islamic State Issues Fake Tax Receipts to Keep Trade Flowing," *McClatchy DC Bureau*, September 3, 2014; and Itziar Aguirre, "Financial Self-Sufficiency Fuels Terrorist Climate," *Global Risk Insights*, February 16, 2016.

57. Silke, "In Defense of the Realm," 346; Adams, *The Financing of Terror*, 178; Kate Linthicum, "Inside the Bloody Cartel War for Mexico's Multi-Billion-Dollar Avocado Industry," *Los Angeles Times*, November 21, 2019; and Potter, *Outlaws, Inc.*, 26.

58. Dolnik, *Understanding Terrorist Innovation*, 49; K. B. Olson, "Aum Shinrikyo: Once and Future Threat?," *Emerging Infectious Diseases* 5, no. 4 (1999): 515; and Stergios Skaperdas, "The Political Economy of Organized Crime: Providing Protections When the State Does Not," *Economics of Governance* 2 (2001): 177.

59. Volkov, *Violent Entrepreneurs*, 64; Andrew Silke, "Drink, Drugs, and Rock 'n' Roll," *Studies in Conflict and Terrorism* 23 (2000): 113; Levitt and Venkatesh, "An Economic Analysis," 765; and Terrance Lichtenwald and Frank Perri, "Terrorist Use of Smuggling Tunnels," *International Journal of Criminology and Sociology* 2 (2013): 214.

60. Dov Lynch, *Engaging Eurasia's Separatist States: Unresolved Conflicts and de Facto States* (Washington, D.C.: U.S. Institute of Peace Press, 2004), 17; see also al-ʿUbaydi et al., *The Group That Calls Itself a State*, 3; and Johnston et al., *Return*, 25.

61. Peter Weber, "Who's Financing Boko Haram?," *The Week*, May 12, 2014; Indira Lakshmanan, "Mafia Meets the IRS," *Bloomberg Business*, June 10, 2015; Jamie Hansen-Lewis and Jacob Shapiro, "Understanding the Daesh Economy," *Perspectives on Terrorism* 9, no. 4 (2015); and Eli Berman and Jacob Shapiro, "Why ISIL Will Fail on Its Own," *Politico*, November 29, 2015.

62. Ajith Wickramasekara, "Transnational Organized Crime and New Terrorism in Sri Lanka" (master's thesis, Naval Postgraduate School, 2017), 55; and Eric Hobsbawm, *Bandits* (New York: Dell, 1969), 16.

63. Joseph Roth, *The Radetzky March*, trans. Joachim Neugroschel (New York: Overlook, 2002), 192.

64. Stefan Cassella, "Terrorism and the Financial Sector," *Journal of Money Laundering Control* 7, no. 3 (Winter 2004): 281; Rock, "The Funding of Boko Haram," 25; and Howard Campbell, "Female Drug Smugglers on the U.S.-Mexico Border," *Anthropological Quarterly* 81, no. 1 (2008): 255.

65. Alan L. Karras, *Smuggling: Contraband and Corruption in World History* (Lanham, Md.: Rowman and Littlefield, 2010), 21.

66. Bruce Yandle, "Bootleggers and Baptists: The Education of a Regulatory Economist," *Regulation* 7, no. 3 (January 1983): 13; Bruce Yandle, "Bootleggers and Baptists in Retrospect," *Regulation* 22, no. 3 (1999): 5; and Bruce Yandle, Joseph Rotondi, Andrew P. Morriss, and Andrew Dorchak "Bootleggers, Baptists, and Televangelists: Regulating Tobacco by Litigation," *University of Illinois Law Review*, 2008, 1231.

67. David T. Courtwright, *Forces of Habit: Drugs and the Making of the Modern World* (Cambridge, Mass.: Harvard University Press, 2001), 160.

68. R. T. Naylor, *Economic Warfare: Sanctions, Embargo Busting, and Their Human Cost* (Boston: Northeastern University Press, 1999), 169.

69. Ana Sverdlick, "Terrorists and Organized Crime Entrepreneurs in the 'Triple Frontier,'" *Trends in Organized Crime* 9, no. 2 (Winter 2005): 84; and John P. Sullivan, "Future Conflict: Criminal Insurgencies, Gangs and Intelligence," in *Deviant Globalization: Black Market Economy in the 21st Century*, ed. Nils Gilman, Jesse Goldhammer, and Steven Weber (New York: Continuum, 2011), 252.

70. Raymond William Baker, *Capitalism's Achilles Heel: Dirty Money and How to Renew the Free-Market System* (Hoboken, N.J.: Wiley, 2005), 199; Robert J. Bunker, ed., *Non-State Threats and Future Wars* (New York: Routledge, 2012), 35; Courtney Hunt, dir., *Frozen River* (New York: Cohen Media Group, 2008); Roth and Sever, "The Kurdish Workers Party," 906; and Paul Collier, V. L. Elliott, Håvard Hegre, Anke Hoeffler, Marta Reynol-Querol, and Nicholas Sambanis, *Breaking the Conflict Trap: Civil War and Development Policy* (Washington D.C.: World Bank, 2003), 78.

71. Naylor, *Wages of Crime*, 91; John Daly, "Part 1: The Deadly Convenience of Victor Bout" (Zurich: ETH, June 24, 2008), 2; and Christian Parenti, *Tropic of Chaos: Climate Change and the New Geography of Violence* (New York: Nation Books, 2011), 94.

72. Jeffrey Boutwell and Michael Klare, eds., *Light Weapons and Civil Conflict: Controlling the Tools of Violence* (Lanham, Md.: Rowman and Littlefield, 1999),

55; and Amado de Andrés, *West Africa under Attack: Drugs, Organized Crime and Terrorism as the New Threats to Global Security,* UNISCI Discussion Papers, no. 16 (January 2008), 8.

73. Will Ashton, "Why 'Lord of War' Starring Nicolas Cage Bought 3,000 Real Guns Instead of Props," *Cinemablend,* May 23, 2019; see also "Director Finds Real Guns Cheaper than Props," *NZ Herald,* September 6, 2012.

74. Guy Lawson, "'War Dogs' True Story: How Two American Kids Became Big-Time Weapons Traders," *Rolling Stone,* March 16, 2011.

75. Matthew Bolton, Eiko Elize Sakamoto, and Hugh Griffiths, "Globalization and the Kalashnikov: Public–Private Networks in the Trafficking and Control of Small Arms," *Global Policy* 3, no. 1 (January 2012): 3; Beatrice Berton, "The Dark Side of the Web: ISIL's One-Stop Shop?," European Union Institute for Security Studies, June 2015, p. 2; and Channing May, *Transnational Crime and the Developing World* (Washington, D.C.: GFI, March 2017), 16.

76. Christopher Mele, "Facebook Banned Gun Sales," *New York Times,* July 21, 2016; and May, *Transnational Crime,* 18.

77. Anneli Botha, Martin Ewi, Uyo Salifu, and Mahdi Adbile, *Understanding Nigerian Citizens' Perspectives on Boko Haram* (Pretoria: ISS, 2017), 67; Rock, "The Funding of Boko Haram," 24; and Peter McCabe and William Mendel, eds., *SOF Role in Combating Transnational Organized Crime* (MacDill Air Force Base, Fla.: Joint Special Operations University, 2016), 150.

78. Courtwright, *Forces of Habit,* 100; Martine Stead, Laura Jones, Graeme Docherty, Brendan Gough, Marilyn Antoniak, and Ann McNeill, "'No-One Actually Goes to a Shop and Buys Them Do They?': Attitudes and Behaviors Regarding Illicit Tobacco in a Multiply Disadvantaged Community in England," *Addiction* 108, no. 12 (2013): 2212–19; and Tracey A. Basler, "Cigarettes, Smuggling, and Terror: The European Community v. RJ Reynolds," *Chicago-Kent Journal of International and Comparative Law* 4, no. 1 (2004): 4.

79. Naylor, *Patriots and Profiteers,* 108; Loretta Napoleoni, *Modern Jihad: Tracing the Dollars behind the Terror Networks* (London: Pluto Press, 2003), 196; and Loretta Napoleoni, "The New Economy of Terror," *OpenDemocracy,* January 26, 2005, https://www.opendemocracy.net/en/article_2321jsp/.

80. Basler, "Cigarettes, Smuggling, and Terror," 9.

81. Louise Shelley and Sharon Melzer, "The Nexus of Organized Crime and Terrorism," *International Journal of Comparative and Applied Criminal Justice* 32, no. 1 (2008): 50; Basler, "Cigarettes, Smuggling, and Terror," 6; and Kyle Orton, *The Forgotten Foreign Fighters: The PKK in Syria* (London: Henry Jackson Society, August 17, 2017), http://henryjacksonsociety.org/wp-content/uploads/2017/08/3053-PYD-Foreign-Fighter-Project-1.pdf, p. 15.

82. Shelley and Melzer, "The Nexus of Organized Crime and Terrorism," 49; Basler, "Cigarettes, Smuggling, and Terror," 8; and William Billingslea, "Illicit Cigarette Trafficking and the Funding of Terrorism," *Police Chief* 71, no. 2 (2004).

83. Freeman, "The Sources of Terrorist Financing," 467; Campbell, "Los Zetas," 68; Daniel Byman, Peter Chalk, Bruce Hoffman, William Rosenau, and David Brannan, *Trends in Outside Support for Insurgent Movements* (Santa Monica, Calif.: RAND, 2001), 52; and Matt Herbert, "Partisans, Profiteers, and Criminals: Syria's Illicit Economy," *Fletcher Forum of World Affairs* 38, no. 1 (Winter 2014): 78.

84. Richard DiGiacomo, "Prostitution as a Possible Funding Mechanism for Terrorism" (master's thesis, Naval Postgraduate School, 2010), 20.

85. Sean Flynn, "The Sex Trade," in *Deviant Globalization: Black Market Economy in the 21st Century*, ed. Nils Gilman, Jesse Goldhammer, and Steven Weber (New York: Continuum, 2011), 63; Nils Gilman, Jesse Goldhammer, and Steven Weber, eds., Introduction to *Deviant Globalization: Black Market Economy in the 21st Century* (New York: Continuum, 2011), 3; and Adams, "Money Laundering and TNOC."

86. May, *Transnational Crime*, 32; and Nancy Scheper-Hughes, "Parts Unknown," *Ethnography* 5, no. 1 (2004): 49.

87. Aijala, "How Is ISIS Funded?," 21; May, *Transnational Crime*," 33; and Michaela Martin and Hussein Solomon, "Islamic State: Understanding the Nature of the Beast and Its Funding," *Contemporary Review of the Middle East* 4, no. 1 (2017): 39.

88. Becky Brickwood, "Forced Organ Harvesting: 'One of the Worst Mass Atrocities of This Century,'" *Health Europa*, January 30, 2020; and Dan Even, "Ex-Mossad Chief Meir Dagan Back in Israel after Liver Transplant," *Haaretz*, October 28, 2012.

89. Brian Michael Jenkins, "A 50-Year-Old Terrorist Innovation Is Still Creating Life-and-Death Dramas," *RAND Blog*, September 25, 2019; Seth Loertscher and Daniel Milton, *Held Hostage: Analyses of Kidnapping across Time and among Jihadist Organizations* (West Point, N.Y.: Combating Terrorism Center, December 2015), 45; and David A. Charters, "The Amateur Revolutionaries: A Reassessment of the FLQ," *Terrorism and Political Violence* 9, no. 1 (March 1, 1997): 142.

90. "Al Qaeda's Zawahri Calls for Kidnap of Westerners," Reuters, October 27, 2012; Wolfram Lacher, *Organized Crime and Conflict in the Sahel-Sahara Region*, Carnegie Papers, Middle East (Washington, D.C.: Carnegie Endowment, September 2012), 15; and Jacob Zenn, "Boko Haram and the Kidnapping of the Chibok Schoolgirls," *CTC Sentinel* 7, no. 5 (May 2014): 1.

91. Loertscher and Milton, *Held Hostage*, 53; and David Andrew Weinberg, "Terrorist Financing: Kidnapping, Antiquities Trafficking, and Private Donations," Hearing

before the House Committee on Foreign Affairs, Subcommittee on Terrorism, Nonproliferation, and Trade, November 17, 2015, https://docs.house.gov/meetings /FA/FA18/20151117/104202/HHRG-114-FA18-Wstate-WeinbergD-20151117.pdf, p. 8.

92. Nasser al-Wuhaushi, "Al Qaeda Letter on the Importance of Kidnapping Revenue," Associated Press, August 6, 2012; and Arshi Saleem Hashmi and Muhammad Saqib, "Terror Financing and Growth of Terrorist Groups: A Case Study of Tehrik-e-Taliban Pakistan," *NDU Journal* (Pakistan), 2017, 75.

93. Jon-Paul Maddaloni, *An Analysis of the FARC in Colombia: Breaking the Frame of FM 3-24* (Fort Leavenworth, Kan.: School of Advanced Military Studies, 2009), 11; and Andrew Silke, ed., *Routledge Handbook of Terrorism and Counter-Terrorism* (London: Routledge, 2019), 593.

94. Carla E. Humud, Robert L. Pirog, and Liana W. Rosen, *Islamic State Financing and U.S. Policy Approaches* (Washington, D.C.: Congressional Research Service, April 10, 2015), 10; Barrett, *The Islamic State*, 53; and Aguirre, "Financial Self-Sufficiency."

95. Alex Schmid, *Revisiting the Relationship between International Terrorism and Transnational Organised Crime 22 Years Later* (The Hague: International Centre for Counter-Terrorism, August 2018), 12; and Paul Watson and Sidhartha Barua, "Worlds of Extremism and Crime Collide in Indian Jail," *Los Angeles Times*, February 8, 2002.

96. Naylor, *Wages of Crime*, 75; and Mark Prendergast, "Murder Plot Allegations under Inquiry," *South Florida Sun Sentinel*, May 18, 1986.

97. Alex Schmid, ed., *Forum on Crime and Society*, vol. 4 (Vienna: UNODC, 2004), 48; Napoleoni, *Modern Jihad*, 170.

98. Williams, *Criminals, Militias, and Insurgents*, 107. See also Lacher, *Organized Crime and Conflict*, 17; and Alvaro de Souza Pinheiro, *Narcoterrorism in Latin America: A Brazilian Perspective* (Hurlburt Field, Fla.: JSOU Press, 2006), 52.

99. Chester Oehme III, "Terrorists, Insurgents, and Criminals—Growing Nexus?," *Studies in Conflict and Terrorism* 31, no. 1 (January 2008): 86; and "Profile: Mokhtar Belmokhtar," *BBC News*, June 15, 2015.

100. Al-'Ubaydi et al., *The Group That Calls Itself a State*, 74.

101. Jean-Charles Brisard, "Terrorism Financing in North Africa," in *Terrorism Threats in North Africa from a NATO Perspective*, ed. J. Tomolya and L. D. White (Fairfax, Va.: IOS Press, 2015), 3; and Weber, "Who's Financing Boko Haram?"

102. Hashmi and Saqib, "Terror Financing," 75; and Jacob Zenn, "Leadership Analysis of Boko Haram and Ansaru in Nigeria," *CTC Sentinel* 7, no. 2 (February 2014): 27.

103. Erik Alda and Joseph Sala, "Links between Terrorism, Organized Crime and Crime," *Stability* 3, no. 1 (2014): 2; Justine Rosenthal, "For-Profit Terrorism:

The Rise of Armed Entrepreneurs," *Studies in Conflict and Terrorism* 31, no. 6 (2008): 487; and Ian Bannon and Paul Collier, eds., *Natural Resources and Violent Conflict: Options and Actions* (Washington, D.C.: World Bank, 2003), 6.

104. Molly Dunigan, Dick Hoffmann, Peter Chalk, Brian Nichiporuk, and Paul deLuca, *Characterizing and Exploring the Implications of Maritime Irregular Warfare* (Santa Monica, Calif.: RAND, 2012), 114; and Steven T. Zech and Zane M. Kelly, "Off with Their Heads: The Islamic State and Civilian Beheadings," *Journal of Terrorism Research* 6, no. 2 (May 2015).

105. Joseba Zulaika, *Basque Violence: Metaphor and Sacrament* (Reno: University of Nevada Press, 1988), 87; Clark, *The Basque Insurgency*, 101; Jose Gurriaran, "ETA Announces End to 40 Years of Extortion," *Inter Press Service*, April 29, 2011; and Ciaran Giles, "ETA Kidnapping Backfires," Associated Press, October 5, 1993.

106. Michael Jonsson and Svante Cornell, "Countering Terrorist Financing," *Georgetown Journal of International Affairs* 8, no. 1 (2007): 70; and Mark Moyar, Hector Pagan, and Wil R. Griego, *Persistent Engagement in Colombia* (MacDill Air Force Base, Fla.: Joint Special Operations University, 2014), 43.

107. Adams, *The Financing of Terror*, 205; and John Horgan and Max Taylor, "Playing the 'Green Card,' Part 1," *Terrorism and Political Violence* 11, no. 2 (Summer 1999): 11.

108. Donohue, "Anti-Terrorist Finance," 320; Aomar Ouali and Paul Schemm, "Algeria Crisis Strangling Sahara Tourism," Associated Press, January 30, 2013; and Fernanda Llussa and Jose Tavares, "The Economics of Terrorism," *Economics of Peace and Security Journal* 2, no. 1 (2007): 63.

109. Brian Fishman, Jacob Shapiro, Joseph Felter, Peter Bergen, and Vahid Brown, *Bombers, Bank Accounts, and Bleedout: al-Qa'ida's Road in and Out of Iraq* (West Point, N.Y.: Combating Terrorism Center, 2008), 70; and Francisco Gutiérrez Sanín, *Criminal Rebels? A Discussion of War and Criminality from the Colombian Experience* (London: London School of Economics and Political Science, 2003), 10.

110. Brisard, "Terrorism Financing in North Africa," 38; Weinberg, "Terrorist Financing," 7; and "Remarks of Deputy Assistant Secretary Fowler."

111. Yvonne M. Dutton, "Kidnap and Terrorism Financing," in *Palgrave Handbook of Criminal and Terrorism Financing Law*, ed. Colin King, Clive Walker, and Jimmy Gurulé, 1141–66 (London: Palgrave MacMillan, 2018), 1157; and FATF, *Financing of the Terrorist Organization Islamic State in Iraq and the Levant* (Paris: FATF, 2015), 27.

112. Brian Michael Jenkins, *Does the U.S. No-Concessions Policy Deter Kidnappings of Americans?* (Santa Monica, Calif.: RAND, 2018), 5; David Cohen, "Remarks

of Under Secretary for Terrorism and Financial Intelligence David S. Cohen at the Carnegie Endowment for International Peace, 'Attacking ISIL's Financial Foundation,'" U.S. Department of the Treasury, October 23, 2014, https://www .treasury.gov/press-center/press-releases/Pages/jl2672.aspx; and Allan Jones A. Salem, "Nexus of Crime and Terrorism: The Case of the Abu Sayyaf Group" (master's thesis, Naval Postgraduate School, 2016), 138.

113. Lawrence Rutkowski, Bruce G. Paulsen, and Jonathan D. Stoian, "Mugged Twice? Payment of Ransom on the High Seas," *American University Law Review* 59, no. 5 (June 2010): 1429; and Ellie Maruyama and Kelsey Hallahan, "Following the Money: A Primer on Terrorist Financing," Center for a New American Security, June 9, 2017, https://www.cnas.org/publications/reports/following-the-money-1.

114. Rukmini Callimachi, "Paying Ransoms, Europe Bankrolls Qaeda Terror," *New York Times*, July 29, 2014; see also Adams, *The Financing of Terror*, 210.

115. Jonathan Holmes, "Islamic State Hostage Ransom Demands Often Met by European Governments," *ABC News*, June 8, 2015; and Maureen Orth, "Inside Colombia's Hostage War," *Vanity Fair*, November 2008.

116. Dutton, "Kidnap and Terrorism Financing," 1155; and Jenkins, *Does the U.S. No-Concessions Policy Deter Kidnappings of Americans?*, 9.

117. Callimachi, "Paying Ransoms"; see also Holmes, "Islamic State Hostage Ransom."

118. Weinberg, "Terrorist Financing," 8; Lacher, *Organized Crime and Conflict*, 9; and Callimachi, "Paying Ransoms."

119. Holmes, "Islamic State Hostage Ransom"; see also Di Giovanni et al., "How Does ISIS Fund"; and Aurel Croissant and Daniel Barlow, "Following the Money Trail," *Studies in Conflict and Terrorism* 30, no. 2 (2007): 135.

120. Weinberg, "Terrorist Financing"; see also Belli et al., "The Business of the Caliph"; and Jacob Zenn, "Boko Haram," *CTC Sentinel* 7, no. 10 (October 2014): 8.

121. Potter, *Outlaws, Inc.*, 209; and Christopher Kinsey, *Corporate Soldiers and International Security: The Rise of Private Military Companies* (London: Routledge, 2006), 50.

122. Collier et al., *Breaking the Conflict Trap*, 9; Bannon and Collier, *Natural Resources*, 6; and John B. Alexander, *Convergence: Special Operations Forces and Civilian Law Enforcement*, JSOU Report 10-6, Joint Special Operations University, July 2010, 42.

123. Callimachi, "Paying Ransoms"; see also Rock, "The Funding of Boko Haram," 42; and Aijala, "How Is ISIS Funded," 35.

124. Karras, *Smuggling*, 41.

125. Adam Young and Mark Valencia, "Conflation of Piracy and Terrorism in Southeast Asia," *Contemporary Southeast Asia* 25, no. 2 (August 2003): 274; and Peter T. Leeson, "An-*arrgh*-chy: The Law and Economics of Pirate Organization," *Journal of Political Economy* 115, no. 6 (December 2007): 1069.

126. Augustine Ikelegbe, "The Economy of Conflict in the Oil Rich Niger Delta Region of Nigeria," *Nordic Journal of African Studies* 14, no. 2 (2005): 228; and Dunigan et al., *Characterizing and Exploring the Implications*, 100.

127. James Cockayne and Adam Lupel, eds., *Peace Operations and Organized Crime: Enemies or Allies?* (London: Routledge, 2011), 91.

128. Annette Hübschle, "From Theory to Practice: Exploring the Organised Crime-Terror Nexus in Sub-Saharan Africa," *Perspectives on Terrorism* 5, no. 3/4 (September 2011): 90; and Adjoa Anyimadu, "Somalia: Moving Beyond Piracy?," *Chatham House Expert Comment*, May 7, 2013.

129. Jeffery Gettleman, "The Pirates Have Seized the Ship," *GQ*, February 1, 2009. On "warrior" norms, see Anning and Smith, "The Accidental Pirate," 36.

130. Valter Vilkko, "Al-Shabaab: From External Support to Internal Extraction" (research paper, Department of Peace and Conflict Research, Uppsala University, March 2011), 23; and Jonathan Saul and Camila Reed, "Shabaab-Somali Pirate Links Growing," Reuters, October 20, 2011.

131. Loertscher and Milton, *Held Hostage*, 52.

132. David Shinn, "Rise of Piracy and Other Maritime Insecurity in Somalia" (paper presented at the Maritime Piracy Summit, Virginia, September 22, 2009); Bronwyn Bruton, "In the Quicksands of Somalia," *Foreign Affairs* 88, no. 6 (2009): 82; and Turbiville et al., *Countering the Al-Shabaab Insurgency*, 14.

133. Dunigan et al., *Characterizing and Exploring*, 113; Gettleman, "The Pirates Have Seized the Ship"; and Mohamed Ahmed, "Somali Sea Gangs Lure Investors at Pirate Lair," Reuters, December 1, 2009.

134. Gettleman, "The Pirates Have Seized the Ship." See also Klejda Mulaj, ed., *Violent Non-State Actors in World Politics* (New York: Columbia University Press, 2010), 357.

135. Potter, *Outlaws, Inc.*, 211; and John Alexander, *Piracy: The Best Business Model Available* (MacDill Air Force Base, Fla.: JSOU Press, 2013), 33.

136. James Kraska, "Freakonomics of Maritime Piracy," *Brown Journal of World Affairs* 16, no. 2 (Summer 2010): 115.

137. Alexander, *Piracy*, 36; and Shinn, "Rise of Piracy."

138. Anning and Smith, "The Accidental Pirate," 31.

139. Ahmed, "Somali Sea Gangs"; and Gettleman, "The Pirates Have Seized the Ship."

140. Kraska, "Freakonomics," 115; Cockayne and Lupel, *Peace Operations*, 91; and Pouligny, *Peace Operations*, 61.

141. Anning and Smith, "The Accidental Pirate," 30; and Mark Nance and Anja Jakobi, "Laundering Pirates?," *Journal of International Criminal Justice* 10, no. 4 (2012): 862.

142. Shinn, "Rise of Piracy."

143. Rutkowski et al., "Mugged Twice?," 1427.

144. Anyimadu, "Somalia."
145. Alexander, *Piracy*, 42.
146. Nance and Jakobi, "Laundering Pirates?," 875.

Chapter 5. Diasporas

1. Joelle Demmers, "New Wars and Diasporas," *Peace, Conflict and Development* 11 (2007): 11; and Klaartje Quirijns, dir., *The Brooklyn Connection* (Quebec: Films Transit International, 2005).
2. Maria Koinova, *Conditions and Timing of Moderate and Radical Diaspora Mobilization: Evidence from Conflict-Generated Diasporas*, working paper no. 9, Project on Global Migration and Transnational Politics, Center for Global Studies (George Mason University, October 2009), 5; and Stacy Sullivan, *Be Not Afraid for You Have Sons in America: How a Brooklyn Roofer Helped Lure the U.S. into the Kosovo War* (New York: St. Martin's Press, 2004), 76.
3. Sullivan, *Be Not Afraid*, 5; and Koinova, *Conditions and Timing*, 6.
4. Sullivan, *Be Not Afraid*, 168; and Quirijns, *The Brooklyn Connection*.
5. Paul Hockenos, *Homeland Calling: Exile Patriotism and the Balkan Wars* (Ithaca, N.Y.: Cornell University Press, 2003), 254.
6. Quirijns, *The Brooklyn Connection*; and Sullivan, *Be Not Afraid*, 155.
7. Sullivan, *Be Not Afraid*, 6.
8. Sullivan, *Be Not Afraid*, 216; and Quirijns, *The Brooklyn Connection*.
9. Hockenos, *Homeland Calling*, 241.
10. Hockenos, *Homeland Calling*, 242; and Sullivan, *Be Not Afraid*, 256.
11. Hockenos, *Homeland Calling*, 261.
12. New York Daily News, "Kosovo Carries Costs but No Regrets for N.Y. Volunteers," *Baltimore Sun*, June 25, 1999.
13. Quirijns, *The Brooklyn Connection*; see also Sullivan, *Be Not Afraid*, 313.
14. Doron Zimmermann and William Rosenau, eds., *The Radicalization of Diasporas and Terrorism* (Zürich: ETH Zürich, Center for Security Studies, 2009), 18; Peggy Levitt, "Social Remittances: Migration Driven Local-Level Forms of Cultural Diffusion," *International Migration Review* 32, no. 4 (Winter 1998): 6; and Hazel Smith and Paul Stares, eds., *Diasporas in Conflict: Peace-Makers or Peace-Wreckers?* (New York: United Nations University Press, 2007), 261.
15. Stewart Bell, *Cold Terror: How Canada Nurtures and Exports Terrorism around the World* (Toronto: Wiley, 2004), 5; and Daniel Byman, Peter Chalk, Bruce Hoffman, William Rosenau, and David Brannan, *Trends in Outside Support for Insurgent Movements* (Santa Monica, Calif.: RAND, 2001), 61.
16. Ingrid Therwath, *Cyber-Hindutva: Hindu Nationalism, the Diaspora and the Web* (Paris: Projet e-Diasporas Atlas, 2012), 8; Ted Robert Gurr, "Minorities

and Nationalists: Managing Ethnopolitical Conflict in the New Century," in *Turbulent Peace: The Challenges of Managing International Conflict*, ed. Chester A. Crocker, Fen Osler Hampson, and Pamela R. Aall (Washington, D.C.: United States Institute of Peace Press, 2001), 167; and Kachig Toloyan, "Rethinking Diasporas: Stateless Power in the Transnational Moment," *Diaspora* 5, no. 1 (Spring 1996): 29.

17. Yossi Shain, ed., *Governments-in-Exile in Contemporary World Politics* (New York: Routledge, 1991), 176; C. Christine Fair, "Diaspora Involvement in Insurgencies," *Nationalism and Ethnic Politics* 11, no. 1 (2005): 132; and Fiona Adamson, "Globalisation, Transnational Political Mobilisation, and Networks of Violence," *Cambridge Review of International Affairs* 18, no. 1 (2005): 40.

18. C. Christine Fair, *Urban Battlefields of South Asia: Lessons Learned from Sri Lanka, India, and Pakistan* (Santa Monica, Calif.: RAND, 2004), 76; Terrence Lyons, "Engaging Diasporas to Promote Conflict Resolution: Transforming Hawks into Doves" (George Mason University, April 2004), 8; and Dan Fletcher, "A Brief History of Columbus Day," *Time*, October 12, 2009.

19. "Basque Studies," Basque Studies at Boise State University, accessed June 15, 2020, https://www.boisestate.edu/basquestudies/; and Toloyan, "Rethinking Diasporas," 17.

20. Frank Wilson, "French-Canadian Separatism," *Western Political Quarterly* 20, no. 1 (March 1, 1967): 129; and William Safran, "Diasporas in Modern Societies: Myths of Homeland and Return," *Diaspora* 1, no. 1 (Spring 1991): 93.

21. James G. Leyburn, *Scotch-Irish: A Social History* (Chapel Hill: University of North Carolina Press, 1989); James H. Webb, *Born Fighting: How the Scots-Irish Shaped America* (New York: Broadway, 2005); and James Naughtie, "IRA Probe Yields Arms Cache," *Washington Post*, July 30, 1981; R. T. Naylor, *Patriots and Profiteers: Economic Warfare, Embargo Busting, and State-Sponsored Crime* (Montreal: McGill-Queen's University Press, 2008), 158.

22. John Braithwaite, "Pre-Empting Terrorism," *Current Issues in Criminal Justice* 17, no. 1 (July 2005): 104; see also Philip M. Seib and Dana M. Janbek, *Global Terrorism and New Media: The Post-al Qaeda Generation* (New York: Routledge, 2011), 3; and Cerwyn Moore and Paul Tumelty, "Foreign Fighters and the Case of Chechnya," *Studies in Conflict and Terrorism* 31 (2008): 425.

23. Nir Arielli, *From Byron to Bin Laden: A History of Foreign War Volunteers* (Cambridge, Mass.: Harvard University Press, 2018), 72.

24. Prexy Nesbitt, "Terminators, Crusaders and Gladiators: Western (Private and Public) Support for Renamo and Unita," *Review of African Political Economy* 15, no. 43 (November 1, 1988): 114; and Franklin Foer, "Paul Manafort, American Hustler," *Atlantic*, March 2018.

25. James Brooke, "Blacks in U.S. Are Lobbied by Angolans," *New York Times*, October 3, 1988; and Linda Heywood, "Unita and Ethnic Nationalism in Angola," *Journal of Modern African Studies* 27, no. 1 (1989): 64.

26. Klejda Mulaj, ed., *Violent Non-State Actors in World Politics* (New York: Columbia University Press, 2010), 305; Brooke, "Blacks in U.S."; and Nesbitt, "Terminators, Crusaders and Gladiators," 116.

27. Timothy Johns, "Laughing Off Apartheid," *Journal of Narrative Theory* 39, no. 2 (2009): 229.

28. Linda Basch, Nina Glick Schiller, and Cristina Szanton Blanc, *Nations Unbound: Transnational Projects, Postcolonial Predicaments, and Deterritorialized Nation-States* (Langhorne, Pa.: Gordon and Breach, 1994), 51; Safran, "Diasporas in Modern Societies," 93; and Nick Kampouris, "Greek Feta Receives Exemption from Proposed US Tariffs on EU Products," *Greek Reporter*, April 11, 2019.

29. Koinova, *Conditions and Timing*, 5; Maria Koinova, "Diasporas and Secessionist Conflicts: Mobilization of the Albanian, Armenian, and Chechen Diasporas," *Ethnic and Racial Studies* 34, no. 2 (February 2011): 347; and Smith and Stares, *Diasporas in Conflict*, 122.

30. Paul O'Donnell, "How the Dalai Lama's Reincarnation Ended up in Congress's $900 Billion Relief Bill," *Washington Post*, January 2, 2021.

31. Basch et al., *Nations Unbound*, 24; Safran, "Diasporas in Modern Societies," 85; and Margaret Crahan and Alberto Vourvoulias-Bush, eds., *The City and the World: New York's Global Future* (New York: Council on Foreign Relations, 1997), 22.

32. Susan Olzak, "Does Globalization Breed Ethnic Discontent?," *Journal of Conflict Resolution* 55, no. 1 (2011): 6; Bahar Baser and Ashok Swain, "Stateless Diaspora Groups and Their Repertoire of Nationalist Activism," *Journal of International Relations* 8, no. 1 (2010): 53; and Päivi Pirkkalainen and Mahdi Abdile, *The Diaspora-Conflict-Peace-Nexus: A Literature Review*, working paper no. 1, Diaspeace (Brussels: European Commission, March 2009), 28.

33. Kalyani Thurairajah, "The Shadows of Terrorism," *Canadian Ethnic Studies* 43, no. 1 (2011): 130.

34. Crahan and Vourvoulias-Bush, *The City and the World*, 111; Charles Ricks, *Preserving Sovereignty in a Borderless World* (MacDill Air Force Base, Fla.: Joint Special Operations University, 2017), 17; and Lyons, "Engaging Diasporas," 2.

35. Michele Wucker, "Remittances: The Perpetual Migration Machine," *World Policy Journal* 21, no. 2 (2004): 43.

36. Basch et al., *Nations Unbound*, 3; and Bruce Zagaris, "The Merging of the Anti-Money Laundering and Counter-Terrorism Financial Enforcement Regimes after September 11, 2001," *Berkeley Journal of International Law* 22, no. 1 (2004): 146.

37. Erika Solomon and Sam Jones, "ISIS Inc.," *Assyrian International News Agency*, December 15, 2015; see also Josh Richardson, "The Somali Diaspora," *CTC Sentinel* 4, no. 7 (July 2011): 13; and Wucker, "Remittances," 37.

38. Abdel Soliman, "The Relationship between International Terrorism and Terrorism in North Africa," in *Terrorist Threats in North Africa from a NATO Perspective*, ed. J. Tomolya and L. D. White (Fairfax, Va.: IOS Press, 2015), 95.

39. James Adams, *The Financing of Terror* (New York: Simon and Schuster, 1986), 97; and Stephen Tankel, *The Indian Jihadist Movement: Evolution and Dynamics* (Washington, D.C.: National Defense University Press, July 2014), 19.

40. Crahan and Vourvoulias-Bush, *The City and the World*, 119; and Peggy Levitt and Deepak Lamba-Nieves, "Social Remittances Revisited," *Journal of Ethnic and Migration Studies* 37, no. 1 (January 2011): 18.

41. Paul Collier, V. L. Elliott, Håvard Hegre, Anke Hoeffler, Marta Reynal-Querol, and Nicholas Sambanis, *Breaking the Conflict Trap: Civil War and Development Policy* (Washington, D.C.: World Bank, 2003), 162; Michele Wucker, "The Perpetual Migration Machine and Political Power," *World Policy Journal* 21, no. 3 (2004): 44; and Jagdish Bhagwati, "Borders beyond Control," *Foreign Affairs* 82, no. 1 (2003): 101.

42. Gabriel Sheffer, "Ethno-National Diasporas and Security," *Survival* 36, no. 1 (Spring 1994): 71; Jeffrey Robinson, *The Laundrymen: Inside Money Laundering, the World's Third Largest Business* (New York: Arcade, 1996), 215; and Arielli, *From Byron to Bin Laden*, 67.

43. Benedict Anderson, *Long-Distance Nationalism: World Capitalism and the Rise of Identity Politics* (Amsterdam: Centre for Asian Studies, 1992), 11.

44. Lyons, "Engaging Diasporas," 10; see also Toloyan, "Rethinking Diasporas."

45. Koinova, "Diasporas and Secessionist Conflicts," 348; Fair, "Diaspora Involvement in Insurgencies," 129; and Arielli, *From Byron to Bin Laden*, 107.

46. Javier Argomaniz and Alberto Vidal-Diez, "Examining Deterrence and Backlash Effects in Counter-Terrorism," *Terrorism and Political Violence* 27, no. 1 (2014): 166; and Ryan Clarke, *Lashkar-i-Taiba: The Fallacy of Subservient Proxies and the Future of Islamist Terrorism in India* (Carlisle, Pa.: Strategic Studies Institute, 2010), 61.

47. Luis de la Calle and Ignacio Sanchez-Cuenca, "Killing and Voting in the Basque Country," *Terrorism and Political Violence* 25, no. 1 (2013): 95; and Laura Dugan, Julie Y. Huang, Gary LaFree, and Clark McCauley, "Sudden Desistance from Terrorism: The Armenian Secret Army for the Liberation of Armenia and the Justice Commandos of the Armenian Genocide," *Dynamics of Asymmetric Conflict* 1, no. 3 (2008): 245.

48. Ignacio Sànchez-Cuenca, "The Dynamics of Nationalist Terrorism: ETA and the IRA," *Terrorism and Political Violence* 19, no. 3 (2007): 300; and Michaela Martin

and Hussein Solomon, "Islamic State: Understanding the Nature of the Beast and Its Funding," *Contemporary Review of the Middle East* 4, no. 1 (2017): 25.

49. Victor Asal, H. Brinton Milward, and Eric W. Schoon, "When Terrorists Go Bad: Analyzing Terrorist Organizations' Involvement in Drug Smuggling," *International Studies Quarterly* 59, no. 1 (March 2015): 204; R. T. Naylor, *Wages of Crime: Black Markets, Illegal Finance, and the Underworld Economy* (Ithaca, N.Y.: Cornell University Press, 2004), 158.

50. Crahan and Vourvoulias-Bush, *The City and the World*, 71; and Petrus van Duyne, Klaus von Lampe, and Nokos Passas, eds., *Upperworld and Underworld in Cross-Border Crime* (Nijmegen, the Netherlands: Wolf Legal, 2003), 157.

51. Ben Affleck, dir., *Argo* (Los Angeles, Warner Brothers, 2012).

52. Imran Awan and Brian Blakemore, eds., *Policing Cyber Hate, Cyber Threats and Cyber Terrorism* (Burlington, Vt.: Ashgate, 2012), 28; Feargal Cochrane, Bahar Baser, and Ashok Swain, "Home Thoughts from Abroad," *Studies in Conflict and Terrorism* 32, no. 8 (2009): 683; and William J. Lahneman, *Impact of Diaspora Communities on National and Global Politics*, Report on Survey of the Literature (College Park, Md.: University of Maryland, June 5, 2005), 32.

53. David Schanzer, Charles Kurzman, Jessica Toliver, and Elizabeth Miller, *The Challenge and Promise of Using Community Policing Strategies to Prevent Violent Extremism* (Durham, N.C.: Triangle Center, January 2016), 31; and Brian Michael Jenkins, *No Path to Glory: Deterring Homegrown Terrorism* (Santa Monica, Calif.: RAND, May 26, 2010), 9.

54. Thomas H. Henriksen, *What Really Happened in Northern Ireland's Counterinsurgency* (Hurlburt Field, Fla.: JSOU Press, 2008), 43; Michael Price, *Community Outreach or Intelligence Gathering?* (New York: Brennan Center, January 2015), 2; and Charles Krulak, "The Strategic Corporal: Leadership in the Three-Block War," *Leatherneck*, January 1999, 5.

55. Ashley Powers, "The Teen Jihadist of Suburban Maryland," *Washington Post*, February 8, 2021; Laura Hammond, Mustafa Awad, Ali Ibrahim Dagane, Peter Hansen, Cindy Horst, Ken Menkhaus, and Lynette Obare, *Cash and Compassion: The Role of the Somali Diaspora in Relief, Development and Peacebuilding*, Report of a Study Commissioned by UNDP Somalia (New York: UN Development Program, 2011), 15; Bruce Hoffman, RAND Corporation, and National Security Research Division, *The Radicalization of Diasporas and Terrorism: A Joint Conference by the RAND Corporation and the Center for Security Studies* (Santa Monica, Calif.: RAND, 2007), 24; and Oliver Bullough, "Beslan Meets Columbine," *New York Times*, April 19, 2013.

56. Oivind Fuglerud, *Life on the Outside: The Tamil Diaspora and Long-Distance Nationalism* (London: Pluto Press, 1999), 31; Baser and Swain, "Stateless Diaspora

Groups," 49; and Wolfram Zunzer, *Diaspora Communities and Civil Conflict Transformation* (Berlin: Berghof Center, September 2004), 21.

57. Mackenzie Institute, "Funding Terror: The Liberation Tigers of Tamil Eelam and Their Criminal Activities in Canada and the Western World," *The Mackenzie Institute*, December 26, 1995; Jo Becker, *Funding the "Final War": LTTE Intimidation and Extortion in the Tamil Diaspora* (New York: Human Rights Watch, 2006), 11; and Neil DeVotta, "The Liberation Tigers of Tamil EELAM," *Asian Survey* 49, no. 6 (2009): 1027.

58. Zunzer, *Diaspora Communities*, 19; Shanaka Jayasekara, "LTTE Fundraising and Money Transfer Operations" (paper presented at the International Conference on Countering Terrorism, Colombo, Sri Lanka, October 18–20, 2007), 6; and Fuglerud, *Life on the Outside*, 164.

59. Victor Asal, Brian Nussbaum, and D. William Harrington, "Terrorism as Transnational Advocacy: An Organizational and Tactical Examination," *Studies in Conflict and Terrorism* 30, no. 1 (2007): 31; Fuglerud, *Life on the Outside*, 53; and Byman et al., *Trends in Outside Support*, 45.

60. Jayasekara, "LTTE Fundraising," 8; and Becker, *Funding the "Final War,"* 27.

61. Graham Myres, "Investing in the Market of Violence: Toward a Micro-Theory of Terrorist Financing," *Studies in Conflict and Terrorism* 35 (2012): 705; Fair, *Urban Battlefields*, 31; and Peter Chalk, "The Tigers Abroad: How the LTTE Diaspora Supports the Conflict in Sri Lanka," *Georgetown Journal of International Affairs* 9, no. 2 (Summer/Fall 2008): 102.

62. Becker, *Funding the "Final War,"* 4.

63. Jennifer Hyndman, "Aid, Conflict and Migration: The Canada–Sri Lanka Connection," *Canadian Geographer* 47, no. 3 (2003): 261; Becker, *Funding the "Final War,"* 43; and R. Cheran, "Diaspora Circulation and Transnationalism as Agents for Change in the Post Conflict Zones of Sri Lanka" (policy paper submitted to the Berghof Foundation for Conflict Management, Berlin, 2003), 10.

64. Baser and Swain, "Stateless Diaspora Groups," 54.

65. Collier et al., *Breaking the Conflict Trap*, 75; Sharryn J. Aiken and Rudhramoorthy Cheran, "The Impact of International Informal Banking on Canada: A Case Study of Tamil Transnational Money Transfer Networks (Undiyal), Canada/ Sri Lanka," Law Commission of Canada, Government of Canada Publications (Spring 2005), 13; and Baser and Swain, "Stateless Diaspora Groups," 55.

66. Cochrane et al., "Home Thoughts," 698.

67. Joseba Zulaika, *Basque Violence: Metaphor and Sacrament* (Reno: University of Nevada Press, 1988), 5; and Robert P. Clark, *The Basque Insurgency: ETA, 1952–1980* (Madison: University of Wisconsin Press, 1984), 13.

68. William Douglass, "Basque Immigration in the United States," *BOGA: Basque Studies Consortium Journal* 1, no. 1 (October 2013): 2; and Diego Muro,

"Nationalism and Nostalgia: The Case of Radical Basque Nationalism," *Nations and Nationalism* 11, no. 4 (2005): 576.

69. Zulaika, *Basque Violence*, 19; and Clark, *The Basque Insurgency*, 14.

70. William Douglass and Joseba Zulaika, "On the Interpretation of Terrorist Violence," *Comparative Studies in Society and History* 32, no. 2 (April 1990): 244; Zulaika, *Basque Violence*, 19; and Julienne Gage, "A Basque Terrorist Organization Has Disarmed," *Public Radio International*, May 15, 2018.

71. Muro, "Nationalism and Nostalgia," 579.

72. Clark, *The Basque Insurgency*, 69; Douglass and Zulaika, "On the Interpretation," 245.

73. Jose Gurriaran, "ETA Announces End to 40 Years of Extortion," *Inter Press Service*, April 29, 2011; and Carlos Barros, "An Intervention Analysis of Terrorism," *Defence and Peace Economics* 14, no. 6 (2003): 402.

74. Omar Encarnación, "Democracy and Dirty Wars in Spain," *Human Rights Quarterly* 29, no. 4 (November 2007): 960.

75. Paddy Woodworth, *Dirty War, Clean Hands: ETA, the GAL and Spanish Democracy* (Cork: Cork University Press, 2001), 68; Clark, *The Basque Insurgency*, 229; and Fernando Reinares, "Exit from Terrorism," *Terrorism and Political Violence* 23, no. 5 (2011): 787.

76. Gloria Totoricaguena, "Comparing the Basque Diaspora: Ethnonationalism, Transnationalism and Identity Maintenance in Argentina, Australia, Belgium, Peru, the United States of America, and Uruguay" (Ph.D. diss., London School of Economics and Political Science, 2000), 127; and Gloria Totoricaguena Egurrola, "Church of the Good Shepherd, Boise, Idaho, USA," December 2002, accessed June 23, 2020, http://www.euskonews.eus/0190zbk/kosmo19001en.html; and Ramon Miro, *Organized Crime and Terrorist Activity in Mexico, 1999–2002* (Washington, D.C.: Library of Congress, February 2003), 47.

77. Douglass, "Basque Immigration," 13; "Aberri Eguna 2012," *A Basque in Boise*, April 5, 2012; and the website of the Basque Studies College of Liberal Arts, University of Nevada, Reno, accessed June 15, 2020, https://www.unr.edu/basque -studies.

78. Totoricaguena, "Comparing the Basque Diaspora," 128; Pete T. Cenarrusa Papers, 1937–2008, Archives West, Orbis Cascade Alliance, accessed September 20, 2020, http://archiveswest.orbiscascade.org/ark:/80444/xv58386; and Gloria Totoricagüena, "Pete T. Cenarrusa," *Euskonews and Media*, March 18, 2003.

79. Argomaniz and Vidal-Diez, "Examining Deterrence," 176; Rogelio Alonso, "Why Do Terrorists Stop?," *Studies in Conflict and Terrorism* 34, no. 9 (September 2011): 700; and Carlos Barros and Luis Gil-Alana, *A Note on the Effectiveness of National Anti-Terrorist Policies* (Pamplona: Universidad de Navarra, October 2009), 7.

80. Woodworth, *Dirty War*, 95; see also William S. Shepard, "The ETA: Spain Fights Europe's Last Active Terrorist Group," *Mediterranean Quarterly* 13, no. 1 (Winter 2002): 60; Robert Slater and Michael Stohl, eds., *Current Perspectives on International Terrorism* (New York: St. Martin's Press, 1988), 57; Julen Zabalo and Mikel Saratxo, "ETA Ceasefire: Armed Struggle vs. Political Practice in Basque Nationalism," *Ethnicities* 15, no. 3 (2015): 372.

81. Alberto Abadie and Javier Gardeazabal, "The Economic Costs of Conflict: A Case Study of the Basque Country," *American Economic Review* 93, no. 1 (March 2003): 113.

82. Bob Fick, "Idaho Compromises with Bush Administration on Basque Resolution," *Billings Gazette*, March 11, 2002; "Idaho Basque Resolution Sends Waves to White House and Spain," *Deseret News*, March 16, 2002; and Pedro J. Oiarzabal, "'We Love You': The Basque Government's Post-Franco Discourse on the Basque Diaspora," *Sancho El Sabio* 26 (2007): 114.

83. Ignacio Lago and Jose Ramon Montero, *The 2004 Election in Spain: Terrorism, Accountability, and Voting* (Barcelona: Institut de Ciències Polítiques i Socials, 2006), 3.

84. Giles Tremlett, "Fourth Estate—Or Fifth Column," *Guardian*, March 3, 2003; Karlos Zurutuza, "Cracking Down on Spain's Basque Media," *Al-Jazeera*, May 17, 2015; Katy Moeller, "Martxelo Otamendi, A Basque with Idaho Ties, Faces Terror Trial," *Idaho Statesman*, December 15, 2009; and Javier Martin-Pena and Susan Opotow, "The Legitimization of Political Violence," *Peace and Conflict* 17, no. 2 (2011): 138.

85. Jay Jones, "Basking in Basque Culture," *Los Angeles Times*, May 27, 2011; Totoricaguena, "Comparing the Basque Diaspora," 57; and "Abertzaleak—Patriots: Sacrifice and Honor," *The Basque Museum and Cultural Center* (blog), accessed July 19, 2020, https://basquemuseum.eus/see/past-exhibits/abertzaleak-patriots-sacrifice-honor/.

86. Oiarzabal, "'We Love You'," 102; Kimberlee Kruesi, "Idaho's Jaialdi Festival Celebrates Basque Culture," *KBOI*, July 28, 2015; and M. Bryce Ternet, *A Basque Story: A Novel* (Baltimore: Publish America, 2010).

87. Mattathias Schwartz, "How to Catch a Terrorist," *New Yorker*, January 19, 2015; and Dennis Jensen, "Enhancing Homeland Security Efforts by Building Strong Relationships between the Muslim Community and Local Law Enforcement" (master's thesis, Naval Postgraduate School, 2006), 67.

88. Ken Menkhaus, "Violent Islamic Extremism: Al-Shabaab Recruitment in America," Hearing before the Committee on Homeland Security and Governmental Affairs, U.S. Senate (March 11, 2009), 3; Valter Vilkko, "Al-Shabaab: From External Support to Internal Extraction" (research paper, Department of

Peace and Conflict Research, Uppsala University, March 2011), 7; and Jeffrey Jones, "Countering Islamic Radicalization" (master's thesis, Naval Postgraduate School, 2010), 1.

89. Schwartz, "How to Catch a Terrorist."

90. Peter Gastrow, *Termites at Work: A Report on Transnational Organized Crime and State Erosion in Kenya: Comprehensive Research Findings* (New York: International Peace Institute, 2011), 12; and Ken Menkhaus, "Al-Shabaab and Social Media: A Double-Edged Sword," *Brown Journal of World Affairs* 20, no. 2 (Spring/Summer 2014): 312.

91. Jones, "Countering Islamic Radicalization," 53.

92. Dina Temple-Raston, "FBI Sheds Light on Missing Somali-Americans," *NPR*, March 11, 2009; and Sasha Aslanian and Laura Yuen, "Online Tools May Have Been Used to Recruit Young Somalis," *MPR News*, March 6, 2009.

93. Paul Joosse, Sandra M. Bucerius, and Sara K. Thompson, "Narratives and Counternarratives: Somali-Canadians on Recruitment as Foreign Fighters to Al-Shabaab," *British Journal of Criminology* 55, no. 4 (2015): 820; see also Roland Marchal, *The Rise of a Jihadi Movement in a Country at War* (Paris: CNRS SciencesPo, March 2011), 45; and Daniel Agbiboa, "Terrorism without Borders," *Journal of Terrorism Research* 5, no. 1 (February 2014): 30.

94. Michelle Norris and Dina Temple-Raston, "New Charges in Somali Terror Case," *NPR*, November 23, 2009; Randall Mikkelsen, "Somali-Americans Recruited as 'Cannon Fodder,'" Reuters, March 11, 2009; and David Shinn, "Somalia's New Government and the Challenge of Al-Shabab," *CTC Sentinel*, no. 2 (March 2009): 2.

95. Schwartz, "How to Catch a Terrorist."

96. Esther, "Denmark: Financing Terrorism in Somalia," *Islam in Europe* (blog), January 11, 2010, http://islamineurope.blogspot.com/2010/01/denmark-financing -terrorism-in-somalia.html; and Timothy Wittig, *Understanding Terrorist Finance* (New York: Palgrave MacMillan, 2011), 119.

97. Pioneer Press, "12 Minnesota Residents Charged with Aiding Terrorists in Somalia Linked to Al-Qaeda," *Pioneer Press*, August 4, 2010.

98. Faith Karimi, "2 Minnesota Women Sentenced for Funding Somali Militants," *CNN*, May 17, 2013.

99. Schwartz, "How to Catch a Terrorist"; see also Muhyadin Roble, "Al-Shabaab Razes Somali Forests to Finance Jihad," Jamestown Foundation Terrorism Monitor, November 18, 2010; and Ken Menkhaus, "Al-Shabab's Capabilities Post-Westgate," *CTC Sentinel* 7, no. 2 (February 2014): 4.

100. Anna Lindley, "Between 'Dirty Money' and 'Development Capital'," *African Affairs* 108, no. 433 (2009): 527; Menkhaus, "Violent Islamic Extremism," 10;

and Thomas Maguire, "Kenya's 'War on Poaching'," in *Militarised Responses to Transnational Organised Crime: The War on Crime*, ed. Tuesday Reitano, Lucia Bird Ruiz-Benitez de Lugo, and Sasha Jesperson (Cham: Palgrave Macmillan, 2018), 36.

101. "Ellison, Paulsen, Duffy Applaud Passage of Money Remittances Improvement Act" (Office of Representative Keith Ellison, May 8, 2014); Bronwyn Bruton, "In the Quicksands of Somalia," *Foreign Affairs* 88, no. 6 (2009): 94; and Jamila Trindle, "Bank Crackdown Threatens Remittances to Somalia," *Foreign Policy*, January 30, 2015.

102. Jensen, "Enhancing Homeland Security Efforts."

103. Joosse et al., "Narratives and Counternarratives," 822; see also Dina Temple-Raston, "Minneapolis Unveiling Plan to Counter Recruiting by ISIS," *NPR*, September 9, 2015.

104. Temple-Raston, "Minneapolis Unveiling Plan." See also Ron Nixon, "Minnesota T.S.A. Manager Says He Was Told to Target Somali-Americans," *New York Times*, April 27, 2016.

105. Ed Shanahan, "Man Who Threatened to 'Put a Bullet' in Rep. Omar Pleads Guilty," *New York Times*, November 19, 2019; and William Cummings, "Ilhan Omar Says Trump Tweet Caused Spike in Death Threats," *USA Today*, April 14, 2019.

106. Michael Pollan, *The Botany of Desire: A Plant's-Eye View of the World* (New York: Random House, 2001), 229; and Wucker, "The Perpetual Migration Machine," 42.

107. Shain, *Governments-in-Exile*, 206; Cochrane et al., "Home Thoughts," 688; and Joseph O'Grady, "An Irish Policy Born in the U.S.A.," *Foreign Affairs* 75, no. 3 (June 1996): 2.

108. Michael McKinley, "Lavish Generosity: The American Dimension of International Support for the Provisional Irish Republican Army 1968–1983," *Conflict Quarterly*, Spring 1987, 22; Henriksen, *What Really Happened*, 26; and Andrew Silke, ed., *Routledge Handbook of Terrorism and Counter-Terrorism* (London: Routledge, 2019), 196.

109. Andrew Mumford, "Intelligence Wars: Ireland and Afghanistan—The American Experience," *Civil Wars* 7, no. 4 (Winter 2005): 379; Timothy Collins, "The IRA" (master's thesis, Defense Intelligence College, 1986), 18; and Zack Boyd, "Irish-American Nationalism: From the Kennedy Administration to the Clinton Administration" (honors thesis, University of Alaska Fairbanks, 2009), 12.

110. McKinley, "Lavish Generosity," 28; see also Robinson, *The Laundrymen*, 260; and Daniel Byman, *Deadly Connections: States That Sponsor Terrorism* (Cambridge: Cambridge University Press, 2005), 246.

111. Daniel Byman, "Passive Sponsors of Terrorism," *Survival* 47, no. 4 (Winter 2005): 130; "Gunrunner Admits Supplying Arms for Quarter-Century," Associated Press, December 17, 1985; and Peter Taylor, "The IRA and Sinn Fein," *Frontline*, 1997.

112. "Gunrunner Admits Supplying Arms."

113. Ivan Little, "IRA Gun Runner Hosted Martin McGuinness in New York Home," *Belfast Telegraph*, September 24, 2019.

114. Little, "IRA Gun Runner"; see also T. K. Jones, "Irish Troubles, American Money," *Washington Post*, March 22, 1987.

115. Byman, *Deadly Connections*, 249.

116. Jones, "Irish Troubles"; and Wittig, *Understanding Terrorist Finance*, 151.

117. "Richard Harris Says IRA Has a Just Cause," *Ocala Star-Banner*, January 24, 1984.

118. Michael McKinley, "The Irish Republican Army and Terror International," in *Contemporary Research on Terrorism*, ed. Paul Wilkinson and Alisdair Stewart (Aberdeen: Aberdeen University Press, 1987), 209.

119. Michael Ryan, "America's Leading IRA Supporter, Martin Galvin, Says He 'Understands' Why Terrorists Targeted Mrs. Thatcher," *People*, November 5, 1994; and Tyler Marshall, "American Defies Ban and Attends IRA Services," *Los Angeles Times*, August 10, 1985.

120. Raymond James Raymond, "Irish America and Northern Ireland," *World Today* 39, no. 10 (October 1983): 407; and Adams, *The Financing of Terror*, 138.

121. Paul K. Clare, *Racketeering in Northern Ireland: A New Version of the Patriot Game* (Chicago: University of Illinois, 1989), 19; McKinley, "Lavish Generosity," 26; Danielle Zach, "Transnational Insurgency: Irish America, the IRA, and Northern Ireland's Troubles" (conference paper, CUNY Graduate Center, Politics and Protest Workshop, December 1, 2016), 39; and Collins, "The IRA," 20.

122. "New York Police Band Members March with IRA Supporters," Associated Press, August 31, 1985.

123. Zach, "Transnational Insurgency," 19.

124. McKinley, "Lavish Generosity," 36; Collins, "The IRA," 13; Jones, "Irish Trouble."

125. Loretta Napoleoni, *Modern Jihad: Tracing the Dollars behind the Terror Networks* (London: Pluto Press, 2003), 29. See also McKinley, "The Irish Republican Army," 205; Adams, *The Financing of Terror*, 141.

126. Feargal Cochrane, "Irish-America, the End of the IRA's Armed Struggle and the Utility of 'Soft Power,'" *Journal of Peace Research* 44, no. 2 (March 2007): 223; see also Anderson, *Long-Distance Nationalism*, 14; and Ed Moloney, "Rep. King and the IRA," *New York Sun*, June 22, 2005.

127. Adrian Guelke, "Irish Republican Terrorism," *Studies in Conflict and Terrorism* 40, no. 7 (2017): 564; Andrew Mumford, "Covert Peacemaking: Clandestine

Negotiation and Backchannels with the Provisional IRA during the Early 'Troubles,' 1972–76," *Journal of Imperial and Commonwealth History* 39, no. 4 (November 2011): 645; and Matthew Hart, *The Irish Game: A True Story of Crime and Art* (New York: Walker, 2004), 81.

128. Clare, *Racketeering in Northern Ireland*, 3.

129. Sanchez-Cuenca, "The Dynamics of Nationalist Terrorism," 300; see also Anne Applebaum, "The Discreet Charm of the Terrorist Cause," *Washington Post*, August 3, 2005; de la Calle and Sanchez-Cuenca, "Killing and Voting," 96; Wittig, *Understanding Terrorist Finance*, 70; and Philip Noyce, dir., *Patriot Games* (Burbank, Calif.: Paramount Pictures, 1992).

130. Leo Penn, dir., *Colombo*, season 7, episode 5, "The Conspirators," aired May 13, 1978, on NBC; Alan Pakula, dir., *The Devil's Own* (Burbank, Calif.: Columbia Pictures, 1997); and Michael Caton-Jones, dir., *The Jackal* (Burbank, Calif.: Universal Pictures, 1997).

131. Michael Desch, ed., *Soldiers in Cities: Military Operations on Urban Terrain* (Carlisle, Pa.: Strategic Studies Institute, 2001), 106; McKinley, "Lavish Generosity," 27; Taylor, "The IRA and Sinn Fein"; and Joseph Treaster, "Man in Queens Accused of Plot to Arm IRA," *New York Times*, October 2, 1981.

132. Zach, "Transnational Insurgency," 24; Ryan, "America's Leading IRA Supporter"; and Moloney, "Rep. King and the IRA."

133. Conor O'Clery, "Reagan in the White House Leaned on Thatcher to Reach Historic Agreement," *Irish Times*, November 6, 2015.

134. Cochrane et al., "Home Thoughts," 689; and Boyd, "Irish-American Nationalism," 22.

135. Hardeep Phull, "How Bono Went Head-to-Head with the IRA," *New York Post*, June 28, 2017; see also "Richard Harris Ducking IRA 'Bombs,'" *Gettysburg Times*, November 25, 1988.

136. Raymond, "Irish America," 408; and Boyd, "Irish-American Nationalism," 19.

137. Mumford, "Intelligence Wars," 389.

138. Ricks, *Preserving Sovereignty*, 22; and O'Grady, "An Irish Policy," 4.

139. Byman et al., *Trends in Outside Support*, 129; see also Zach, "Transnational Insurgency," 1.

140. Laura Donohue, "Anti-Terrorist Finance in the United Kingdom and United States," *Michigan Journal of International Law* 27, no. 2 (2006): 324; and Valpy FitzGerald, "Global Financial Information, Compliance Incentives and Conflict Funding" (Finance and Trade Policy Research Centre, University of Oxford, 2003), 13.

141. Cochrane et al., "Home Thoughts," 695.

142. "NORAID Supporters Must Examine Their Consciences over IRA Support," *Security News Desk*, May 16, 2015; see also Moloney, "Rep. King and the IRA."

143. LUB098, "President-Elect Joe Biden Will Use 'Celtic' as Secret Service Code-name," *Celtic Star*, November 8, 2020, https://thecelticstar.com/president-elect-joe-biden-will-use-celtic-as-secret-service-codename/.

Chapter 6. Donors and Sponsors

1. "Teaching Terrorists to Play the Harmonica," *Foreign Policy*, February 26, 2010.
2. Aaron Tuley, "Holder v. Humanitarian Law Project," *Indiana Law Review* 49 (2016): 588; Georgia Wralstad Ulmschneider and James Lutz, "Terrorism Analysis and Holder v. Humanitarian Law Project," *Terrorism and Political Violence* 31, no. 4 (July 4, 2019): 806; and William Aceves, "Litigating the Arab-Israeli Conflict in U.S. Courts," *Case Western Reserve Journal of International Law* 43, no. 1 (2010): 321.
3. David Savage, "Supreme Court Upholds Law against Advising Terrorists," *Los Angeles Times*, June 22, 2010; and "The Supreme Court 2009 Term," *Harvard Law Review* 124, no. 1 (November 2010): 260.
4. Tuley, "Holder v. Humanitarian Law Project," 583; Wadie Said, "Humanitarian Law Project and the Supreme Court's Construction of Terrorism," *Brigham Young University Law Review* 2011, no. 5 (2011): 1487; and Marjorie Heins, "The Supreme Court and Political Speech in the 21st Century," *Albany Law Review* 76 (2013): 576.
5. Sara Pantuliano and Samir Elhawary, "Counter-Terrorism and Humanitarian Action," Overseas Development Institute, October 17, 2011; Heins, "The Supreme Court," 582; and "The Supreme Court 2009 Term," 261.
6. Timothy Wittig, *Understanding Terrorist Finance* (New York: Palgrave MacMillan, 2011), 78; see also Kate Mackintosh and Patrick Duplat, *Study of the Impact of Donor Counter-Terrorism Measures on Principled Humanitarian Action* (New York: United Nations, July 2013), 46.
7. Nora Bensahel, "A Coalition of Coalitions: International Cooperation against Terrorism," *Studies in Conflict and Terrorism* 29, no. 1 (January 2006): 38; Valpy FitzGerald, "Global Financial Information, Compliance Incentives and Conflict Funding" (Finance and Trade Policy Research Centre, University of Oxford, 2003), 12; Anne Clunan, "The Fight against Terrorist Financing," *Political Science Quarterly* 121, no. 4 (2006): 574; and Paul Bremer, *Countering the Changing Threat of International Terrorism: Report from the National Commission on Terrorism: Pursuant to Public Law 277* (Washington, D.C.: National Commission on Terrorism, June 2000).
8. Innokenty Pyetranker, "Sharing Translations or Supporting Terror?," *American University National Security Law Brief* 2, no. 2 (2012): 39.
9. Elizabeth Bloodgood and Joannie Tremblay-Boire, "International NGOs and National Regulation in an Age of Terrorism" (paper presented at the Annual

Conference of the International Studies Association, New York, February 15–18, 2009), 12; Jimmy Gurulé and Sabina Danek, "The Failure to Prosecute ISIS's Foreign Financiers under the Material Support Statute," in *The Palgrave Handbook of Criminal and Terrorism Financing Law*, ed. Colin King, Clive Walker, and Jimmy Gurulé (London: Palgrave MacMillan, 2018), 1017; and David Cole, "Reform Material Support Laws for Terrorists," *New York Times*, January 2, 2001.

10. "Teaching Terrorists."

11. Clifford Bob, *The Marketing of Rebellion: Insurgents, Media, and International Activism* (Cambridge: Cambridge University Press, 2005), 25.

12. Tomer Mozes and Gabriel Weimann, "The E-Marketing Strategy of Hamas," *Studies in Conflict and Terrorism* 33, no. 3 (February 3, 2010): 213.

13. Mozes and Weimann, "The E-Marketing Strategy," 216; Kenneth Geers, "Cyberspace and the Changing Nature of Warfare," Keynote speech (Tallinn, Estonia: Cyber Defence Centre, 2008), 5; Paul Saskiewicz, "The Revolutionary Armed Forces of Colombia—People's Army (FARC-EP): Marxist-Leninist Insurgency or Criminal Enterprise" (master's thesis, Naval Postgraduate School, 2005), 99; and Andrew Selepak, "Skinhead Super Mario Brothers: An Examination of Racist and Violent Games on White Supremacist Web Sites," *Journal of Criminal Justice and Popular Culture* 17, no. 1 (2010): 9.

14. FATF, "Emerging Terrorist Financing Risks" (Paris: FATF, October 2015), 26f; Will Ward, "Social Media in the Gaza Conflict," *Arab Media and Society*, January 2009, 3; and Haroro Ingram, "What Analysis of the Islamic State's Messaging Keeps Missing," *Washington Post*, October 14, 2015.

15. Sarah Womer and Robert Bunker, "Sureños Gangs and Mexican Cartel Use of Social Networking Sites," *Small Wars and Insurgencies* 21, no. 1 (2010): 85; and Scott Decker and David Pyrooz, "Gangs, Terrorism and Radicalization," *Journal of Strategic Security* 4, no. 4 (2011): 160.

16. Robert Windrem, "Who's Funding ISIS?," *NBC News*, September 21, 2014; and Wittig, *Understanding Terrorist Finance*, 9.

17. David Doukhan, *Who Are You, Boko Haram?* (Herzliya: International Institute for Counter-Terrorism, December 12, 2012), 9; and Jason Rock, "The Funding of Boko Haram and Nigeria's Actions to Stop It" (master's thesis, Naval Postgraduate School, 2016), 21.

18. Tom Keatinge, Florence Keen, and Kayla Izenman, "Fundraising for Right-Wing Extremist Movements," *RUSI Journal* 164, no. 2 (2019): 21.

19. Carol Berger, "Bosnian Muslims Turn to Kuwait for Money," *Christian Science Monitor*, January 28, 1993; Nimrod Raphaeli, "Financing of Terrorism: Sources, Methods, and Channels," *Terrorism and Political Violence* 15, no. 4 (2003): 72; and Matthew A. Levitt, "The Political Economy of Middle East Terrorism," *Middle East Review of International Affairs* 6, no. 4 (December 2002): 51.

20. Elizabeth Dickinson, *Playing with Fire: Why Private Gulf Financing for Syria's Extremist Rebels Risks Igniting Sectarian Conflict at Home* (Washington, D.C.: Brookings Institution, December 2013), 12; and Riley Post and Jeffrey Peterson, *Unconventional Economics: Operational Economics in Unconventional Warfare* (MacDill Air Force Base, Fla.: Joint Special Operations University Press, 2016), 62.

21. Maura Conway, "Terrorism and the Internet: New Media—New Threat?," *Parliamentary Affairs* 59, no. 2 (February 2006): 293; and Tim Rumbough, "Explosive Information: How the Internet Can Help Terrorists," *Journal of Information Ethics* 12, no. 2 (October 1, 2003), 16.

22. *White Supremacy Extremism: The Transnational Rise of the Violent White Supremacist Movement*, The Soufan Center, September 27, 2019, https://thesoufancenter.org/wp-content/uploads/2019/09/Report-by-The-Soufan-Center-White-Supremacy-Extremism-The-Transnational-Rise-of-The-Violent-White-Supremacist-Movement.pdf, p. 20; and Raphael Cohen-Almagor, "Taking North American White Supremacist Groups Seriously," *International Journal for Crime, Justice and Social Democracy* 7, no. 2 (2018): 44.

23. Ashley A. Mattheis, "Shieldmaidens of Whiteness: (Alt)Maternalism and Women Recruiting for the Far/Alt-Right," *Journal for Deradicalization* 17 (Winter 2018): 129; Seth G. Jones, Catrina Doxsee, and Nicholas Harrington, "The Escalating Terrorism Problem in the United States," *CSIS Briefs*, June 2020, p. 6; and Keatinge et al., "Fundraising," 19.

24. Daniel A. Metraux, "Religious Terrorism in Japan: The Fatal Appeal of Aum Shinrikyo," *Asian Survey* 35, no. 12 (1995): 1142; and K. B. Olson, "Aum Shinrikyo: Once and Future Threat?," *Emerging Infectious Diseases* 5, no. 4 (1999): 514.

25. Selepak, "Skinhead Super Mario Brothers," 13.

26. Reuven Erlich and Yoram Kahati, *Hezbollah as a Case Study of the Battle for Hearts and Minds* (Ramat Hasharon: Intelligence and Terrorism Information Center, June 2007), 87; and Philip M. Seib and Dana M. Janbek, *Global Terrorism and New Media: The Post–Al Qaeda Generation* (New York: Routledge, 2011), 68.

27. Selepak, "Skinhead Super Mario Brothers," 3.

28. Cohen-Almagor, "Taking North American White Supremacist Groups Seriously," 42; and Joshua Fisher-Birch, "The Emerging Threat of Extremist-Made Video Games," *Counter Extremism Project*, September 16, 2020.

29. Michael J. Casey, *Che's Afterlife: The Legacy of an Image* (New York: Vintage, 2009), 309; and Ariana Hernández-Reguant, "Copyrighting Che: Art and Authorship under Cuban Late Socialism," *Public Culture* 16, no. 1 (January 1, 2004): 3.

30. Graham Myres, "Investing in the Market of Violence: Toward a Micro-Theory of Terrorist Financing," *Studies in Conflict and Terrorism* 35 (2012): 702; Bruno

Dominici, "Anti-Mafia Operations in Italy" (lecture, Marshall Center, July 17, 2019); and Graeme Wood, "What ISIS Really Wants," *Atlantic*, March 2015.

31. Michael Freeman, "The Sources of Terrorist Financing: Theory and Typology," *Studies in Conflict and Terrorism* 34, no. 6 (2011): 471; and Dickinson, *Playing with Fire*, 13.

32. Dickinson, *Playing with Fire*, 12.

33. Geah Pressrove and Carol Pardun, "Relationship between Personal Technology Use and the Donor/Volunteer: A Parasocial Approach," *Journal of Promotion Management* 22, no. 1 (January 2, 2016): 140.

34. David Patrikarakos, *War in 140 Characters: How Social Media Is Reshaping Conflict in the Twenty-First Century* (New York: Basic Books, 2017), 107; "Salafi-Jihadis Conduct Online 'Equip Us' Campaign," Cyber and Jihad Lab, December 16, 2015; and Tom Keatinge, "The Importance of Financing in Enabling and Sustaining the Conflict in Syria," *Perspectives on Terrorism* 8, no. 4 (2014): 56.

35. Colin Bucksey, dir., *Breaking Bad*, season 2, episode 12, "Phoenix," aired May 24, 2009, on AMC; Killian McCarthy, ed., *The Money Laundering Market: Regulating the Criminal Economy* (Newcastle upon Tyne, U.K.: Agenda, 2018), 97; and Zachary Robock, "The Risk of Money Laundering through Crowdfunding: A Funding Portal's Guide to Compliance and Crime Fighting," *Michigan Business and Entrepreneurial Law Review* 4, no. 1 (2014): 114.

36. Alexander Sokolov, "Russian Political Crowdfunding," *Demokratizatsiya* 23, no. 2 (Spring 2015): 121; and Robock, "The Risk of Money Laundering," 114.

37. Spencer Ackerman, "New Kickstarter Pitch: 'Join the Syrian Uprising,'" *Arizona State University Center for Strategic Communication*, August 21, 2012.

38. Sarah Hauer and Natalie Brophy, "A Texas Legal Foundation Is Planning to Help Defend Kyle Rittenhouse," *Milwaukee Journal Sentinel*, August 27, 2020; Keatinge et al., "Fundraising," 20; and *White Supremacy Extremism*, 22.

39. Maurice Greenberg, Mallory Factor, William F. Wechsler, and Lee S. Wolosky, *Update on the Global Campaign against Terrorist Financing: Second Report of an Independent Task Force on Terrorist Financing* (Washington, D.C.: Council on Foreign Relations, June 15, 2004), 33.

40. Jerry W. Knudson, "Rebellion in Chiapas: Insurrection by Internet and Public Relations," *Media, Culture and Society* 20, no. 3 (July 1, 1998): 511.

41. James Ferguson, *Global Shadows: Africa in the Neoliberal World Order* (Durham, N.C.: Duke University Press, 2006), 107.

42. Victor Perera, "Waiting for Subcomandante Marcos," *Los Angeles Times*, April 21, 1996; Mark Fineman, "Zapatistas in Transition from Fighting to Fashion," *Los Angeles Times*, April 21, 1996; and Trina Kleist, "Chiapas Rebels Say Oliver Stone to Skip Oscars to Meet with Them," Associated Press, March 24, 1996.

43. Jonathan Benthall and Jerome Bellion-Jourdan, *The Charitable Crescent: Politics of Aid in the Muslim World* (London: I. B. Taurus, 2003); Louise Richardson, ed., *The Roots of Terrorism* (New York: Routledge, 2006), 165; and Alex Schmid, ed., *Forum on Crime and Society*, vol. 4 (New York: United Nations, 2005), 52.

44. Kristen Cheney, "Locating Neocolonialism, 'Tradition,' and Human Rights in Uganda's 'Gay Death Penalty,'" *African Studies Review* 55, no. 2 (2012): 84; Omar Encarnación, "The Troubled Rise of Gay Rights Diplomacy," *Current History* 115, no. 777 (January 2016): 22; Douglas Farah, *Blood from Stones: The Secret Financial Network of Terror* (New York: Broadway, 2004), 27; and Colbert King, "Pat Robertson and His Business Buddies," *Washington Post*, November 10, 2001.

45. Sam Moore, "George Clooney's Nespresso Adverts Helped Fund a Satellite," *NME*, November 29, 2019; and Amy Kittlestrom, "In Spite of Boycotts, Nike's New Colin Kaepernick Ad Campaign Will Be a Winner," *Washington Post*, September 9, 2018.

46. Abu Sa'eed Al-Britani, "Hijrah Advice Part 7: Security Measures," *Untitled* (blog), August 30, 2015, https://balquois124.tumblr.com/post/128836217964 /hijrah-advice-part-7-security-measures; Nir Arielli, *From Byron to Bin Laden: A History of Foreign War Volunteers* (Cambridge, Mass.: Harvard University Press, 2018), 70; and Jennifer Fowler, "Remarks of Deputy Assistant Secretary for Terrorist Financing Jennifer Fowler at the Washington Institute for Near East Policy on U.S. Efforts to Counter the Financing of ISIL," U.S. Department of the Treasury, February 2, 2015.

47. Elisabeth Braw, "The Non-Halal Ways Potential Jihadists Are Funding Their Work," *Foreign Affairs*, October 25, 2015; Eckart Woertz, "How Long Will ISIS Last Economically?," *Notes Internacionals CIDOB*, no. 98 (October 2014): 3; and Peter Bergen, Brian Fishman, and John P. Abizaid, *Bombers, Bank Accounts, and Bleedout: al-Qa'ida's Road In and Out of Iraq* (West Point, N.Y.: Combating Terrorism Center, 2008), 6.

48. B. Raman, "Counter-Terrorism: India-China-Russia Cooperation," *China Report* 40, no. 2 (2004): 162; Evan F. Kohlmann, *The Role of Islamic Charities in International Terrorist Recruitment and Financing* (Copenhagen: Danish Institute for International Studies, 2006), 5; and R. T. Naylor, *Economic Warfare: Sanctions, Embargo Busting, and Their Human Cost* (Boston: Northeastern University Press, 1999), 88.

49. Lorenzo Vidino, "How Chechnya Became a Breeding Ground for Terror," *Middle East Quarterly* 12, no. 3 (Summer 2005): 57.

50. Andrew Silke, ed., *Routledge Handbook of Terrorism and Counter-Terrorism* (London: Routledge, 2019), 210.

51. Muhammad al-'Ubaydi, Nelly Lahoud, Daniel Milton, and Bryan Price, *The Group That Calls Itself a State: Understanding the Evolution and Challenges of the Islamic State* (West Point, N.Y.: Combating Terrorism Center, December 2014), 75; Brian Dodwell, Daniel Milton, and Don Rassler, *The Caliphate's Global Workforce: An Inside Look at the Islamic State's Foreign Fighter Paper Trail* (West Point, N.Y.: Combating Terrorism Center, April 18, 2016), 26; and Harald Doornbos and Jenan Moussa, "The Islamic State's Terror Laptop of Doom," *Foreign Policy,* August 28, 2014.

52. Spencer Ackerman, "There's No Turning Back," *Wired,* April 4, 2013; al-'Ubaydi et al., *The Group That Calls Itself a State,* 88; Jessica Stern and J. M. Berger, "ISIS and the Foreign-Fighter Phenomenon," *Atlantic,* March 8, 2015; and Scott Glover, "The FBI Translator Who Went Rogue and Married an ISIS Terrorist," *CNN,* May 1, 2017.

53. Kristin M. Bakke, "Help Wanted? The Mixed Record of Foreign Fighters in Domestic Insurgencies," *International Security* 38, no. 4 (Spring 2014): 151; Barak Mendelsohn, "Foreign Fighters: Recent Trends," *Orbis* 55, no. 2 (2011): 197; and Guido Steinberg, *A Chechen Al-Qaeda? Caucasian Groups Further Internationalise the Syrian Struggle* (Berlin: Deutsches Institut, 2014), 8.

54. Duncan DeVille and Daniel Pearson, "Responding to Money Transfers by Foreign Terrorist Fighters," in *Palgrave Handbook of Criminal and Terrorism Financing Law,* ed. Colin King, Clive Walker, and Jimmy Gurulé (London: Palgrave MacMillan, 2018), 1071; Tolga Koker and Carlos L Yordán, "Microfinancing Terrorism: A Study in al Qaeda Financing Strategy," in *State of Corruption, State of Chaos: The Terror of Political Malfeasance,* ed. Michaelene D. Cox (Lanham, Md.: Lexington, 2008), 168; and FATF, "Emerging Terrorist Financing Risks," 24.

55. "ISI Border Sector Income, Expense, Equipment, and Personnel Report" NMEC-2007-657676, Combating Terrorism Center, https://ctc.usma.edu/harmony -program/isi-border-sector-income-expense-equipment-and-personnel-report- original-language-2/; "Border Sector 1 Financial Status and Valuable Distribu- tion Report" NMEC-2007-657998, Combating Terrorism Center, https://ctc .usma.edu/harmony-program/border-sector-1-financial-status-and-valuable -distribution-report-original-language-2/; and Meir Amit Center, "Updated Security Recommendations Issued by ISIS to Operatives Traveling to Syria," *Israeli Intelligence Heritage and Commemoration Center,* March 23, 2015.

56. Al-Britani, "Hijrah Advice Part 7"; see also Christopher Jones, "How Much Money Is ISIS Making from Antiquities Looting?," *Gates of Nineveh,* January 12, 2016; and "I Cleaned Toilets While in ISIS," *Times of India,* November 30, 2014.

57. Stern and Berger, "ISIS and the Foreign Fighter"; see also Kyle Orton, *The Forgot- ten Foreign Fighters: The PKK in Syria* (London: Henry Jackson Society, 2017), 125;

and Peter Andreas, *Killer High: A History of War in Six Drugs* (Oxford: Oxford University Press, 2020), 100.

58. Jamie Hansen-Lewis and Jacob N. Shapiro, "Understanding the Daesh Economy," *Perspectives on Terrorism* 9, no. 4 (2015); and Jeanine de Roy van Zuijdewijn and Edwin Bakker, *Returning Western Foreign Fighters: The Case of Afghanistan, Bosnia, and Somalia* (The Hague: International Centre for Counter-Terrorism, 2014), 5.

59. Martin Chulov, "How an Arrest in Iraq Revealed ISIS's \$2bn Jihadist Network," *Guardian*, June 15, 2014.

60. Clive Walker, "Terrorism Financing and the Governance of Charities," in *Palgrave Handbook of Criminal and Terrorism Financing Law*, ed. Colin King, Clive Walker, and Jimmy Gurulé (London: Palgrave MacMillan, 2018), 1087; Rodger Shanahan, *Charities and Terrorism: Lessons from the Syrian Crisis* (Sydney: Lowy Institute for International Policy, March 14, 2018); *UK National Risk Assessment of Money Laundering and Terrorist Financing* (London: HM Treasury, October 2015), 94; and Dominic Casciani, "The Joker Who Wanted to Be a Bomber," *BBC News*, February 21, 2013.

61. Laura Donohue, "Anti-Terrorist Finance in the United Kingdom and United States," *Michigan Journal of International Law* 27, no. 2 (2006): 428; Raphaeli, "Financing of Terrorism," 62; Loretta Napoleoni, *Modern Jihad: Tracing the Dollars behind the Terror Networks* (London: Pluto Press, 2003), 123; and Koker and Yordán, "Microfinancing Terrorism," 168.

62. Morton Tyldum, dir., *Tom Clancy's Jack Ryan*, pilot (Amazon Prime, August 31, 2018).

63. Zachary Abuza, "Funding Terrorism in Southeast Asia: The Financial Network of Al Qaeda and Jemaah Islamiya," *Contemporary Southeast Asia* 25, no. 2 (August 2003): 170; "The Iceberg beneath the Charity," *Economist*, March 13, 2003, 67; and Benthall and Bellion-Jourdan, *The Charitable Crescent*, 71.

64. Koker and Yordán, "Microfinancing Terrorism," 170; Mark Basile, "Going to the Source: Why Al Qaeda's Financial Network Is Likely to Withstand the Current War on Terrorist Financing," *Studies in Conflict and Terrorism* 27, no. 3 (June 2004): 173; and Arielli, *From Byron to Bin Laden*, 58.

65. Andrew Mumford, "Intelligence Wars: Ireland and Afghanistan—The American Experience," *Civil Wars* 7, no. 4 (Winter 2005): 386.

66. David Gibbs, "Forgotten Coverage of Afghan 'Freedom Fighters'," *Extra!*, February 2002.

67. Gibbs, "Forgotten Coverage."

68. Mary Walsh, "Mission: Afghanistan," *Columbia Journalism Review* 28, no. 5 (January 1990): 32; Peter MacDonald, dir., *Rambo III* (Los Angeles: Carolco

Pictures, 1988); and Kevin Reynolds, dir., *The Beast of War* (Hollywood, Calif.: A&M Films, 1988); and John Glen, dir., *The Living Daylights* (London: Eon Productions, 1987).

69. R. T. Naylor, *Wages of Crime: Black Markets, Illegal Finance, and the Underworld Economy* (Ithaca, N.Y.: Cornell University Press, 2004), 292; and Jeanne K. Giraldo and Harold A. Trinkunas, eds., *Terrorism Financing and State Responses: A Comparative Perspective* (Stanford, Calif.: Stanford University Press, 2007), 113.

70. Kohlmann, *The Role of Islamic Charities*, 11; see also John Pomfret, "How Bosnia's Muslims Dodged Arms Embargo," *Washington Post*, September 22, 1996; and Benthall and Bellion-Jourdan, *The Charitable Crescent*, 145.

71. Abuza, "Funding Terrorism," 182; and Lucy Komisar, "Shareholders in the Bank of Terror?," *Salon*, March 16, 2002.

72. Naylor, *Wages of Crime*, 322.

73. Juan Gomez, "A Financial Profile of the Terrorism of Al-Qaeda and Its Affiliates," *Perspectives on Terrorism* 4, no. 4 (October 2010), 10; Levitt, "The Political Economy," 56; and Freeman, "The Sources of Terrorist Financing," 470.

74. Daniel Agbiboa, "Terrorism without Borders," *Journal of Terrorism Research* 5, no. 1 (February 2014): 7; and Abdulmajeed Bello, "Boko Haram," *International Journal of Management and Social Sciences Research* 2, no. 2 (February 2013): 70.

75. Kyle Beardsley and Brian McQuinn, "Rebel Groups as Predatory Organizations," *Journal of Conflict Resolution* 53, no. 4 (2009): 640; and Shanaka Jayasekara, "LTTE Fundraising and Money Transfer Operations" (paper presented at the International Conference on Countering Terrorism, Colombo, Sri Lanka, October 18–20, 2007), 5.

76. Fausto Martin DeSanctis, *Money Laundering through Art: A Criminal Justice Perspective* (New York: Springer, 2013), 64.

77. Bloodgood and Tremblay-Boire, "International NGOs" (2009), 19; Elizabeth Bloodgood and Joannie Tremblay-Boire, "International NGOs and National Regulation in an Age of Terrorism," *Voluntas* 22 (2011), 162; and Brian A. Jackson and John C. Baker, *Aptitude for Destruction*, vol. 2, *Organizational Learning in Terrorist Groups and Its Implications for Combating Terrorim* (Santa Monica, Calif.: RAND Corporation, 2005), 16.

78. Bloodgood and Tremblay-Boire, "International NGOs and National Regulation" (2011), 160.

79. Bloodgood and Tremblay-Boire, "International NGOs and National Regulation" (2011), 157; and Bloodgood and Tremblay-Boire, "International" (2009), 15.

80. Bloodgood and Tremblay-Boire, "International NGOs and National Regulation" (2011), 166.

81. Benthall and Bellion-Jourdan, *The Charitable Crescent*, 4; and Shawn Flanagan, "Charity as Resistance: Connections between Charity, Contentious Politics, and Terror," *Studies in Conflict and Terrorism* 29, no. 7 (2006): 646.

82. James J. Forest, *Confronting the Terrorism of Boko Haram in Nigeria* (MacDill Air Force Base, Fla.: Joint Special Operations University Press, 2012), 51; Post and Peterson, *Unconventional Economics*, 21; "Notebook Entries Containing Expense Accounts, Distribution of Payments and Handwritten Notes Containing Daily Reports and Personnel Lists Found in a Cache Near Al Tuzliyah, Al-Anbar on 16 Jan 07" (Combating Terrorism Center, West Point, 2007), https://ctc.usma .edu/wp-content/uploads/2014/12/MNFA-2007-000564-Trans.pdf; and Rukmini Callimachi, "\$0.60 for Cake," Associated Press, December 30, 2013.

83. John Horgan and Max Taylor, "Playing the 'Green Card,' Part 2," *Terrorism and Political Violence* 15, no. 2 (Summer 2003): 54; H. Richard Friman and Peter Andreas, eds., *The Illicit Global Economy and State Power* (Lanham, Md.: Rowman and Littlefield, 1999), 36; and Terril Jones, "Yakuza among First with Relief Supplies in Japan," Reuters, March 25, 2011.

84. Sam Mullins, *Assessing the Impact of the COVID-19 Pandemic on Terrorism and Counter-Terrorism* (Honolulu: Asia-Pacific Center, August 2020), 6; and Kevin Sieff, Susannah George, and Kareem Fahim, "Now Joining the Fight against Coronavirus: The World's Armed Rebels, Drug Cartels and Gangs," *Washington Post*, April 14, 2020.

85. Post and Peterson, *Unconventional Economics*, 21; Matt Potter, *Outlaws, Inc.* (New York: Bloomsbury, 2011), 8; and Ryan Clarke, *Lashkar-i-Taiba: The Fallacy of Subservient Proxies and the Future of Islamist Terrorism in India* (Carlisle, Pa.: Strategic Studies Institute, 2010), 32.

86. Emile van der Does de Willebois, *Nonprofit Organizations and the Combatting of Terrorism Financing: A Proportionate Response* (Washington, D.C.: World Bank, 2010), 27; Duke Law International Human Rights Clinic and Women Peacemakers Program, *Tightening the Purse Strings: What Countering Terrorism Financing Costs Gender Equality and Security* (Durham, N.C.: Duke University, March 2017); and Aaron Zelin, "When Jihadists Learn How to Help," *Washington Post*, May 7, 2014.

87. Quoted in Matthew Levitt, "Teaching Terror: How Hamas Radicalizes Palestinian Society," paper presented at the Roots of Terror: Understanding the Evolving Threat of Terrorism conference, February 12, 2007, https://www.washingtoninstitute.org /pdf/view/7782/en, p. 2.

88. James B. Love, *Hezbollah: Social Services as a Source of Power* (Hurlburt Field, Fla.: JSOU Press, 2010), 25; Shawn Flanagan, "Nonprofit Service Provision by Insurgent Organizations," *Studies in Conflict and Terrorism* 31 (2008): 508; Erlich

and Kahati, *Hezbollah as a Case Study*, 71; and Matthew Levitt, *Hamas: Politics, Charity, and Terrorism in the Service of Jihad* (New Haven, Conn.: Yale University Press, 2006), 97.

89. The Free Library, "What If Foreigners See the United States as an 'Exporter of Terrorism'?," CIA Secret Memo, February 5, 2010, https://www.thefreelibrary .com/%22What+If+Foreigners+See+the+United+States+as+an+%27Exporter +of...-a0235673139; Ken Dilanian, "'Secret' CIA Memo on WikiLeaks Is Not Very Revelatory," *Los Angeles Times*, August 25, 2010; David L. Altheide, "Consuming Terrorism," *Symbolic Interaction* 27, no. 3 (Summer 2004): 290; and Laurie Goodstein, "Sibling Nuns Will Go to Prison for Protesting at U.S. Military School," *New York Times*, June 24, 2001.

90. Alfred McCoy, *The Politics of Heroin: CIA Complicity in the Global Drug Trade* (Chicago: Lawrence Hill, 1991), 449.

91. Naylor, *Economic Warfare*, 87; Giraldo and Trinkunas, *Terrorism Financing*, 112; and Mumford, "Intelligence Wars," 386.

92. Giraldo and Trinkunas, *Terrorism Financing*, 107; and Yossi Shain, ed., *Governments-in-Exile in Contemporary World Politics* (New York: Routledge, 1991), 79.

93. Giraldo and Trinkunas, *Terrorism Financing*, 97; Raman, "Counter-Terrorism," 161; and Vanda Felbab-Brown, *Shooting Up: Counterinsurgency and the War on Drugs* (Washington, D.C.: Brookings Institution Press, 2010), 122.

94. Scott Zamost, Drew Griffin, Kay Guerrero, and Rafael Romo, "Venezuela May Have Given Passports to People with Ties to Terrorism," *CNN*, February 14, 2017; and Emanuele Ottolenghi and John Hannah, "In Venezuela's Toxic Brew: Failed Narco-State Meets Iran-Backed Terrorism," *Foreign Policy*, March 23, 2017.

95. Daniel Byman, *Deadly Connections: States That Sponsor Terrorism* (Cambridge: Cambridge University Press, 2005), 61; and Bard E. O'Neill, *Insurgency and Terrorism: Inside Modern Revolutionary Warfare* (Washington, D.C.: Potomac, 2005), 143.

96. O'Neill, *Insurgency and Terrorism*, 145.

97. Ethan A. Nadelmann, "Global Prohibition Regimes: The Evolution of Norms in International Society," *International Organization* 44, no. 4 (Autumn 1990): 502; Miroslav Nincic, *Renegade Regimes: Confronting Deviant Behavior in World Politics* (New York: Columbia University Press, 2005), 55; Angel Rabasa, John Gordon IV, Peter Chalk, Audra K. Grant, K. Scott McMahon, Stephanie Pezard, Caroline R. Milne, David Ucko, and S. Rebecca Zimmerman, *From Insurgency to Stability*, vol. 2, *Insights from Selected Case Studies* (Santa Monica, Calif.: RAND, 2011), 50; Vera Eccarius-Kelly, "Surreptitious Lifelines: A Structural Analysis of the FARC and the PKK," *Terrorism and Political Violence* 24, no. 2 (April 1, 2012): 249; and Greenberg et al., *Update on the Global Campaign*, 26.

98. Byman, *Deadly Connections*, 68; and Daniel Byman, Peter Chalk, Bruce Hoffman, William Rosenau, and David Brannan, *Trends in Outside Support for Insurgent Movements* (Santa Monica, Calif.: RAND, 2001), 85.

99. Darryle J. Grimes, "The Financial War on Terrorism: Grading U.S. Strategy for Combating the Financing of Terrorism" (master's thesis, Norfolk, Va.: Joint Advanced Warfighting School, 2006), 10; Stewart Patrick, *Weak Links: Fragile States, Global Threats, and International Security* (Oxford: Oxford University Press, 2011), 95; and Charles Wallace II, "Airpower against 'Irregular' Adversaries: How Terrorist Insurgent, and Guerrilla Forces Have Attempted to Negate Airstrikes" (thesis, Maxwell Air Force Base, Ala.: School of Advanced Air and Space Studies, 2006), 65.

100. Post and Peterson, *Unconventional Economics*, 46.

101. Molly Dunigan, Dick Hoffmann, Peter Chalk, Brian Nichiporuk, and Paul DeLuca, *Characterizing and Exploring the Implications of Maritime Irregular Warfare* (Santa Monica, Calif.: RAND, 2012), 103; see also R. T. Naylor, "The Rise of the Modern Arms Black Market and the Fall of Supply-Side Control," in *Society under Siege*, ed. Virginia Gamba (Pretoria: Halfway House, 1997), 48.

102. Rachael Revesz, "Saudi Arabia Government 'Funded Dry Run' for 9/11," *Independent*, September 10, 2017; and Barry Schneider, Jerrold Post and Michael Kindt, *The World's Most Threatening Terrorist Networks and Criminal Gangs* (New York: Palgrave Macmillan, 2014), 85.

103. Nincic, *Renegade Regimes*, 77; Michael Jonsson, Elliot Brennan, and Christopher O'Hara, "Financing War or Facilitating Peace? The Impact of Rebel Drug Trafficking on Peace Negotiations in Colombia and Myanmnar," *Studies in Conflict and Terrorism* 39, no. 6 (June 2, 2016): 548; and Byman et al., *Trends in Outside Support*, 35.

104. C. Christine Fair, *Urban Battlefields of South Asia: Lessons Learned from Sri Lanka, India, and Pakistan* (Santa Monica, Calif.: RAND, 2004), 35; and Silke, *Routledge Handbook of Terrorism*, 341.

105. Anıl Karaca, "Disrupting Terrorist Networks: An Analysis of the PKK Terrorist Organization" (master's thesis, Monterrey, Calif.: Naval Postgraduate School, 2010), 46.

106. Alex P. Schmid, *Soviet Military Interventions since 1945: With a Summary in Russian* (New Brunswick, N.J.: Transaction, 1985), 76.

107. Clarke, *Lashkar-i-Taiba*, 42; Paul Collier, V. L. Elliott, Håvard Hegre, Anke Hoeffler, Marta Reynol-Querol, and Nicholas Sambanis, *Breaking the Conflict Trap: Civil War and Development Policy* (Washington, D.C.: World Bank, 2003), 74; and Niklas Karlén, "Turning off the Taps: The Termination of State Sponsorship," *Terrorism and Political Violence* 31 no. 4 (2019): 736.

108. Isabel Woodford and M. L. R. Smith, "The Political Economy of the Provos: Inside the Finances of the Provisional IRA—A Revision," *Studies in Conflict and Terrorism* 41, no. 3 (2018): 229; and Peter Taylor, "The IRA and Sinn Fein," *Frontline*, 1997.

109. Nincic, *Renegade Regimes*, 65; and Byman, *Deadly Connections*, 77.

110. Byman, *Deadly Connections*, 183.

111. Michael Freeman, *Financing Terrorism: Case Studies* (Burlington, Vt.: Ashgate, 2011), 219; Orton, *The Forgotten Foreign Fighters*, 19; and Gomez, "A Financial Profile," 9.

112. Román Ortiz, "Insurgent Strategies in the Post-Cold War: The Case of the Revolutionary Armed Forces of Colombia," *Studies in Conflict and Terrorism* 25, no. 2 (2002): 139; and Saskiewicz, "The Revolutionary Armed Forces of Colombia," 81.

113. James Adams, *The Financing of Terror* (New York: Simon and Schuster, 1986), 120; and John Robb, *Brave New War: The Next Stage of Terrorism and the End of Globalization* (Hoboken, N.J.: Wiley, 2007), 50.

114. Ken Booth and Timothy Dunne, eds., *Worlds in Collision: Terror and the Future of Global Order* (New York: Palgrave MacMillan, 2002), 124.

115. Giraldo and Trinkunas, *Terrorism Financing*, 330.

116. Basile, "Going to the Source," 182.

117. Simon Denyer, Min Joo Kim, and Erin Cunningham, "Iran Denies Its Seizure of South Korean Tanker Is Hostage-Taking," *Washington Post*, January 5, 2021; and Haider Mullick, *Pakistan's Security Paradox* (Hurlburt Field, Fla.: JSOU, 2009), 57.

118. Joshua Geltzer, "Taking Hand-Outs or Going It Alone," *Studies in Conflict and Terrorism* 34, no. 2 (January 2011): 154; and Nitsana Darshan-Leitner and Samuel Katz, *Harpoon: Inside the Covert War against Terrorism's Money Masters* (New York: Hachette, 2017), 214.

119. Joseph Keller, "The Flatow Amendment and State-Sponsored Terrorism," *Seattle University Law Review* 28 (2005): 1029.

120. David Kamien, ed., *McGraw-Hill Homeland Security Handbook* (New York: McGraw-Hill, 2012), 135.

121. Ruthanne Deutsch, "Suing State-Sponsors of Terrorism under the Foreign Sovereign Immunities Act," *International Lawyer* 38, no. 4 (2004): 892; see also Bernard H. Oxman and Stephen J. Schnably, "Foreign Sovereign Immunities Act—Denial of Immunity for Extrajudicial Killing—Cuban Liability for Shooting down Civil Aircraft—Punitive Damages—Retroactive Application of Statute Recognizing Cause of Action for Human Rights Violations," *American Journal of International Law* 92, no. 4 (1998): 769; and Keller, "The Flatow Amendment," 1031.

122. Ilias Bantekas, "The International Law of Terrorist Financing," *American Journal of International Law* 97, no. 2 (2003): 316; and Clunan, "The Fight against Terrorist Financing," 576.

123. Keller, "The Flatow Amendment," 1040; Aceves, "Litigating the Arab-Israeli Conflict," 319; and Lizangela A. Romylos, "Legal Measures to Combat the Trafficking of Antiquities That Serve to Finance Terrorism" (Ph.D. diss., South Africa: North-West University, 2016), 36.

124. Keller, "The Flatow Amendment," 1051; and John Hudson and Max Bearak, "Trump Says He Will Take Sudan off List of State Sponsors of Terrorism," *Washington Post*, October 19, 2020.

125. Jennifer Kreder and Kimberly Degraaf, "Museums in the Crosshairs: Unintended Consequences of the War on Terror," *Washington University Global Studies Law Review* 10, no. 2 (January 2011): 247; and Barry Meier, "Antiquities and Politics Intersect in a Lawsuit," *New York Times*, March 29, 2006.

126. Jo Becker, "U.S. Has Approved Billions in Business with Blacklisted Nations," *New York Times*, December 23, 2010. See also Steve Kiser, *Financing Terror: An Analysis and Simulation to Affect Al Qaeda's Financial Infrastructure* (Santa Monica, Calif.: RAND, 2005), 110.

Chapter 7. Moving the Money

1. Mark Cendrowski, dir., *The Big Bang Theory*, season 1, episode 3, "The Fuzzy Boots Corollary" (Burbank, Calif.: Warner Brothers, 2007); Phil Johnston and Rich Moore, dir., *Ralph Breaks the Internet* (Burbank, Calif.: Walt Disney Pictures, 2018); and Victor Tangermann, "Criminals Are Using Video Game Loot Boxes to Launder Money," *Futurism*, October 29, 2019.

2. Julian Dibbell, *Play Money: Or, How I Quit My Day Job and Made Millions Trading Virtual Loot* (New York: Basic Books, 2007); Michael P. Bombace, "Blazing Trails: A New Way Forward for Virtual Currencies and Money Laundering," *Journal of Virtual Worlds Research* 6, no. 3 (September 2013): 5; and Kim-Kwang Raymond Choo and Russell G. Smith, "Criminal Exploitation of Online Systems by Organised Crime Groups," *Asian Criminology* 3 (2008): 49.

3. Daniela Rosette, "The Application of Real World Rules to Banks in Online Games and Virtual Worlds," *University of Miami Business Law Review* 16 (2008): 284.

4. Clare Chambers-Jones, "Money Laundering in a Virtual World," in *Palgrave Handbook of Criminal and Terrorism Financing Law*, ed. Colin King, Clive Walker, and Jimmy Gurulé (London: Palgrave MacMillan, 2018), 172; Killian McCarthy, ed., *The Money Laundering Market: Regulating the Criminal Economy* (Newcastle upon Tyne, U.K.: Agenda, 2018), 94; and Angela Irwin and Jill Slay, "Detecting Money Laundering and Terrorism Financing Activity in Second Life and World

of Warcraft," in *Proceedings of the 1st International Cyber Resilience Conference* (Perth, Western Australia: Edith Cowan University, August 23, 2010), 4.

5. Rosette, "The Application of Real World Rules," 291.

6. Matthew Gault, "'Nearly All' Counter-Strike Microtransactions Are Being Used for Money Laundering," *Vice*, October 29, 2019; Zachary Baker, "Gaming the System: Money Laundering through Microtransactions and In-Game Currencies," *Journal of Law and International Affairs at Penn State Law*, February 28, 2020; Jean-Loup Richet, "Laundering Money Online: A Review of Cybercriminals' Methods," white paper, UN Office on Drugs and Crime, June 1, 2013, p. 11; and Steven Messner, "How Microtransactions and In-Game Currencies Can Be Used to Launder Money," *PC Gamer*, April 13, 2018.

7. Jennifer Carole, "In-Game Currency and Goods Used for Money Laundering, Part 2," *Bromium*, March 20, 2018.

8. Mike Rose, "Chasing the Whale: Examining the Ethics of Free-to-Play Games," *Gamasutra*, July 9, 2013; and Messner, "How Microtransactions."

9. Irwin and Slay, "Detecting Money Laundering," 5.

10. McCarthy, *The Money Laundering Market*, 46.

11. McCarthy, *The Money Laundering Market*, 15; and Zaiton Hamin, Normah Binti Omar, and Was Rosalili, "Airing Dirty Laundry: Reforming the Anti-Money Laundering and Anti-Terrorism Financing Regime in Malaysia," *Global Jurist* 16, no. 1 (2016): 130.

12. Eleni Tsingou, "Targeting Money Laundering: Global Approach or Diffusion of Authority?," in *New Threats and New Actors in International Security*, ed. Elke Krahmann (New York: Palgrave-McMillan, 2005), 92; Alfred W. McCoy, *The Politics of Heroin: CIA Complicity in the Global Drug Trade* (Chicago: Lawrence Hill, 1991), 40; and Jeffrey Robinson, *The Laundrymen: Inside Money Laundering, the World's Third Largest Business* (New York: Arcade, 1996), 5.

13. Robinson, *The Laundrymen*, 6.

14. Nicholas Ryder, ed., *White Collar Crime and Risk: Financial Crime, Corruption and the Financial Crisis* (London: Palgrave MacMillan, 2018), 333; Eric Gouvin, "Bringing out the Big Guns: The USA Patriot Act, Money Laundering, and the War on Terrorism," *Baylor Law Review* 55 (2003): 962; David Aufhauser, "Terrorist Financing: Foxes Run to Ground," *Journal of Money Laundering Control* 6, no. 4 (Spring 2003): 301; and Steve Kiser, *Financing Terror: An Analysis and Simulation for Affecting al Qaeda's Financial Infrastructure* (Santa Monica, Calif.: RAND, 2005), 3.

15. William Vlcek, "A Leviathan Rejuvenated: Surveillance, Money Laundering, and the War on Terror," *International Journal of Politics, Culture and Society* 20, no. 1–4 (September 2008): 25; and Tito Moreira, "A Two-Period Model of Money Laundering and Organized Crime," *Economic Bulletin* 11, no. 3 (2007): 2.

16. Aaron Brantly, "Financing Terror Bit by Bit," *CTC Sentinel* 7, no. 10 (October 2014): 2; Sidney Weintraub, "Disrupting the Financing of Terrorism," *Washington Quarterly* 25, no. 1 (2002): 54; Ken Booth and Timothy Dunne, eds., *Worlds in Collision: Terror and the Future of Global Order* (New York: Palgrave MacMillan, 2002), 76; and Richet, "Laundering Money Online," 6.

17. Aufhauser, "Terrorist Financing," 302; John Arquilla and David Ronfeldt, *In Athena's Camp: Preparing for Conflict in the Information Age* (Santa Monica, Calif.: RAND, 1997), 305; Donato Masciandaro, ed., *Global Financial Crime: Terrorism, Money Laundering, and Off-Shore Centers* (Burlington, Vt.: Ashgate, 2004), 100; and Matthew Hart, *The Irish Game: A True Story of Crime and Art* (New York: Walker, 2004), 145.

18. Maurice Greenberg, Mallory Factor, William F. Wechsler, and Lee S. Wolosky, *Update on the Global Campaign against Terrorist Financing: Second Report of an Independent Task Force on Terrorist Financing* (Washington, D.C.: Council on Foreign Relations, June 15, 2004), 25.

19. Jeanne Giraldo and Harold Trinkunas, eds., *Terrorism Financing and State Responses: A Comparative Perspective* (Stanford, Calif.: Stanford University Press, 2007), 69; and Alex Schmid, ed., *Forum on Crime and Society*, vol. 4 (New York: United Nations, 2005), 54.

20. Kiser, *Financing Terror*, 62.

21. James B. Love, *Hezbollah: Social Services as a Source of Power* (Hurlburt Field, Fla.: JSOU Press, 2010), 30.

22. Peter McCabe, ed., *Countering Transregional Terrorism* (MacDill Air Force Base, Fla.: Joint Special Operations University, 2018), 147; R. T. Naylor, "The Rise of the Modern Arms Black Market and the Fall of Supply-Side Control," in *Society under Siege: Crime, Violence, and Illegal Weapons*, ed. Virginia Gamba-Stonehouse (Pretoria: Halfway House, Institute for Security Studies, 1997), 60; and FATF, "Emerging Terrorist Financing Risks" (Paris: FATF, October 2015), 14.

23. Celina B. Realuyo, *"Following the Money Trail" to Combat Terrorism, Crime, and Corruption in the Americas* (Washington, D.C.: Wilson Center, August 2017), 7.

24. Yuki Noguchi, "Bags of Cash, Armed Guards and Wary Banks," *NPR*, April 10, 2019; "India Gold Smuggling Case Sparks Political Row," *BBC News*, July 8, 2020; and Matthew Ormseth, "Dirty Money Piling up in L.A. as Coronavirus Cripples International Money Laundering," *Los Angeles Times*, April 29, 2020.

25. John Kane and April Wall, "Identifying the Links between White-Collar Crime and Terrorism" (National White Collar Crime Center, September 2004), 14; and Jim Freer, "FIU Study: Honey Trade Launders Al-Qaeda Cash," *South Florida Business Journal*, October 26, 2001.

26. R. T. Naylor, *Wages of Crime: Black Markets, Illegal Finance, and the Underworld Economy* (Ithaca, N.Y.: Cornell University Press, 2004); Tara John, "Man

Suspected of Money Laundering after $400,000 Found in Washing Machine," *CNN*, November 23, 2018; and Gabrielle Fonrouge, "Firefighters Battling Brooklyn Home Blaze Discover Heaps of Hidden Cash," *New York Post*, September 24, 2020.

27. International Crisis Group, *War and Drugs in Colombia* (Brussels: International Crisis Group, January 27, 2005), 26; "Diez Años de La 'Maldita' Guaca Millonaria," *El Espectador*, April 12, 2013; and Michael Freeman, *Financing Terrorism: Case Studies* (Burlington, Vt.: Ashgate, 2011), 207.

28. Kenneth Watkin, "Targeting 'Islamic State' Oil Facilities," *International Law Studies* 90 (2014): 503.

29. Conor Gaffey, "Up to $800 Million of ISIS Cash Has Been Destroyed," *Newsweek*, April 27, 2016; Patrick B. Johnston, Mona Alami, Colin P. Clarke, and Howard J. Shatz, *Return and Expand? The Finances and Prospects of the Islamic State after the Caliphate* (Santa Monica, Calif.: RAND, 2019), 53; and Conservative Outfitters, "US Airstrike Destroying ISIS Cash Stockpile in Iraq," YouTube, January 17, 2016, https://www.youtube.com/watch?v=TJUlBr5k2RU&ab_channel=ConservativeOutfitters.

30. Anna Fifield, "He Ran North Korea's Secret Moneymaking Operation," *Washington Post*, July 13, 2017; Matt Potter, *Outlaws, Inc.* (New York: Bloomsbury, 2011); Masciandaro, *Global Financial Crime*, 78; and William Wechsler, "Follow the Money," *Foreign Affairs* 80, no. 4 (August 2001): 42.

31. Paul Bauer and Rhoda Ullmann, "Understanding the Wash Cycle," Federal Reserve Bank of Cleveland, September 15, 2000, p. 1; Roberto Saviano, "Where the Mob Keeps Its Money," *New York Times*, August 25, 2012; Michele Riccardi and Michael Levi, "Cash, Crime and Anti-Money Laundering," in *Palgrave Handbook of Criminal and Terrorism Financing Law*, ed. Colin King, Clive Walker, and Jimmy Gurulé (London: Palgrave MacMillan, 2018), 151; and Naylor, *Wages of Crime*, 155.

32. Lateshia Beachum, "Four Flight Attendants Arrested for Smuggling Thousands of Dollars," *Washington Post*, October 23, 2019; Robinson, *The Laundrymen*, 80; Janine Di Giovanni, "A Jihad of Her Own," *Newsweek*, March 4, 2014; Shaylih Muehlmann, *When I Wear My Alligator Boots: Narco-Culture in the U.S.-Mexico Borderlands* (Berkeley: University of California Press, 2014), 153; and Naylor, *Wages of Crime*, 149.

33. Patrick Keefe, "How a Mexican Drug Cartel Makes Its Billions," *New York Times*, June 15, 2012; and Margaret Crahan and Alberto Vourvoulias-Bush, eds., *The City and the World: New York's Global Future* (New York: Council on Foreign Relations, 1997), 75.

34. Greg Myre, "Hamas Leader Barred from Bringing Money to Gaza," *San Francisco Chronicle*, December 15, 2006.

35. Rose Eveleth, "The Gift Card Was Invented by Blockbuster in 1994," *Smithsonian Magazine*, December 23, 2013; and Paul Reuter and Edwin Truman, *Chasing Dirty Money: The Fight against Money Laundering* (Washington, D.C.: Institute for International Economics, 2004), 29.

36. Michele Wucker, "Remittances: The Perpetual Migration Machine," *World Policy Journal* 21, no. 2 (2004): 42; Realuyo, *"Following the Money Trail,"* 11; Choo and Smith, "Criminal Exploitation," 46; and Zachary K. Goldman, Ellie Maruyama, Elizabeth Rosenberg, Edoardo Saravalle, and Julia Solomon-Strauss, *Terrorist Use of Virtual Currencies: Containing the Potential Threat* (Washington, D.C.: Center for a New American Security, 2017), 18.

37. Choo and Smith, "Criminal Exploitation," 48; Goldman and CNAS, *Terrorist Use of Virtual Currencies*, 20.

38. Garrett Graff, "A Vor Never Sleeps," *Longreads*, June 2018, https://longreads .com/2018/06/04/a-vor-never-sleeps/; Jose Pagliery, "Trump's Casino Was a Money Laundering Concern," *CNN*, May 22, 2017; Heather Petrovich, "Circumventing State Consumer Protection Laws," *North Carolina Law Review* 91, no. 1 (2012): 329; and David Mackenzie, dir., *Hell or High Water* (Los Angeles: CBS Films, 2016).

39. Robinson, *The Laundrymen*, 41; and Reuter and Truman, *Chasing Dirty Money*, 29.

40. Peter Lilley, *Dirty Dealing: The Untold Truth about Global Money Laundering, International Crime and Terrorism* (London: Kogan Page, 2009), 97; Victor Colorado, "The Uncomfortable Link between Smartphones and the Rise in Gambling," *Quartz Africa*, November 24, 2019; and Jeff Morganteen, "Online Gambling Will Fuel Terrorism, Organized Crime," *CNBC*, February 12, 2014.

41. John Zdanowicz, "Trade-Based Money Laundering and Terrorist Financing," *Review of Law and Economics* 5, no. 2 (2009): 859; and John Cassera, *Trade-Based Money Laundering: The Next Frontier in International Money Laundering Enforcement* (Hoboken, N.J.: Wiley, 2016), 37.

42. Naylor, *Wages of Crime*, 280; and Shahbaz Rana, "State Bank to Discontinue Issuance of Rs40,000 Bonds," *Express Tribune*, February 13, 2019.

43. McCarthy, *The Money Laundering Market*, 42; and Reuter and Truman, *Chasing Dirty Money*, 108.

44. J. C. Sharman, *The Despot's Guide to Wealth Management: On the International Campaign against Grand Corruption* (Ithaca, N.Y.: Cornell University Press, 2017), 137; see also Shina Keene, *Operationalizing Counter Threat Finance Strategies* (Carlisle, Pa.: Strategic Studies Institute, 2014), 27; Richard Behar, "Billionaire Heir Helly Nahmad's Art Gallery Raided," *Forbes*, April 16, 2013; and Ken Silverstein, *Narco-A-Lago: Money Laundering at the Trump Ocean Club Panama* (London: Global Witness, November 2017), 15.

45. Lilley, *Dirty Dealing*, 56; see also McCarthy, *The Money Laundering Market*, 37; and Saviano, "Where the Mob Keeps Its Money."

46. Saviano, "Where the Mob Keeps Its Money"; Agustino Fontevecchia, "HSBC Helped Terrorists, Iran, Mexican Drug Cartels Launder Money," *Forbes*, July 16, 2012; Matt Taibbi, "Outrageous HSBC Settlement Proves the Drug War Is a Joke," *Rolling Stone*, December 13, 2012; and Realuyo, *"Following the Money Trail,"* 6.

47. Ed Vulliamy, "How a Big US Bank Laundered Billions from Mexico's Murderous Drug Gangs," *Guardian*, April 2, 2011; Pascal Fletcher, "Wachovia Pays $160 Million to Settle Drug Money Probe," Reuters, March 17, 2010; Saviano, "Where the Mob Keeps Its Money"; and Ed Vulliamy, "Western Banks 'Reaping Billions from Colombian Cocaine Trade,'" *Guardian*, June 2, 2012.

48. Muehlmann, *When I Wear*, 148; and Jay Jenkins, "Did Drug Cartels Save the Global Financial System?," *Motley Fool*, October 15, 2018.

49. R. T. Naylor, *Patriots and Profiteers: Economic Warfare, Embargo Busting, and State-Sponsored Crime* (Montreal: McGill-Queen's University Press, 2008), 71.

50. John Kerry and Hank Brown, *The BCCI Affair: A Report to the Committee on Foreign Relations,* U.S. Senate, 102nd Congress, 2nd session, December 1992, https://irp.fas.org/congress/1992_rpt/bcci/, p. 49.

51. Kerry and Brown, *BCCI Affair*, 5.

52. Kerry and Brown, *BCCI Affair*, 70.

53. Kerry and Brown, *BCCI Affair*, 66; and Robinson, *The Laundrymen*, 59; and John Braithwaite, "Pre-Empting Terrorism," *Current Issues in Criminal Justice* 17, no. 1 (July 2005): 105.

54. Dean Baquet and Jeff Gerth, "Lawmaker's Defense of B.C.C.I. Went Beyond Speech in Senate," *New York Times*, August 26, 1992.

55. Lawrence Freedman, ed., *Superterrorism: Policy Responses* (Malden, Mass.: Blackwell, 2002), 61; Masciandaro, *Global Financial Crime*, 25; Mark Basile, "Going to the Source: Why Al Qaeda's Financial Network Is Likely to Withstand the Current War on Terrorist Financing," *Studies in Conflict and Terrorism* 27, no. 3 (June 2004): 178; and Mary Beth Goodman and Trevor Sutton, "To Stem the Flow of Illicit Drugs from Afghanistan, Follow the Money," *Center for American Progress*, March 17, 2015.

56. Sudhir Alladi Venkatesh, *Off the Books: The Underground Economy of the Urban Poor* (Cambridge, Mass.: Harvard University Press, 2006), 96; Abdullah Shehu, "Promoting Financial Inclusion for Effective Anti-Money Laundering," *Crime, Law and Social Change* 57, no. 3 (April 2012): 309; and Bruce Zagaris, "The Merging of the Anti-Money Laundering and Counter-Terrorism Financial Enforcement Regimes after September 11, 2001," *Berkeley Journal of International Law* 22, no. 1 (2004): 128.

57. Marike de Goede, "Hawala Discourses and the War on Terror Finance," *Environment and Planning B* 21 (2003): 522; see also Ilias Bantekas, "The International Law of Terrorist Financing," *American Journal of International Law* 97, no. 2 (2003): 321; Gouvin, "Bringing out the Big Guns," 970; and Alan Gelb, *Balancing Financial Integrity with Financial Inclusion* (Washington, D.C.: CGD, February 2016), 3.

58. Marva Williams, "Community-Bank Partnerships Creating Opportunities for the Unbanked," *Reinvestment Alert*, no. 15 (June 2000): 2; Richard Paxton, "It's Not That Easy to KYC," *Medium*, November 5, 2015; Louis de Koker, "Aligning Anti-Money Laundering, Combating of Financing of Terror and Financial Inclusion," *Journal of Financial Crime* 18, no. 4 (2011): 365; Gelb, *Balancing Financial Integrity*, 9; and FATF, "Anti-Money Laundering and Terrorist Financing Measures and Financial Inclusion" (Paris: FATF, November 2017), 6.

59. Shehu, "Promoting Financial Inclusion," 306; Dan Leibsohn, "A Non-Predatory Financial Services Program for the Unbanked and Underbanked: A New, Encompassing Strategy," *Community Development Finance*, July 31, 2019, http://communitydevelopmentfinance.org/2019/advocacy/a-non-predatory-financial-services-program-for-the-unbanked-and-underbanked-a-new-encompassing-strategy/; and Duke Law International Human Rights Clinic and Women Peacemakers Program, *Tightening the Purse Strings: What Countering Terrorism Financing Costs Gender Equality and Security* (Durham, N.C.: Duke University, March 2017), 39.

60. Goldman and CNAS, *Terrorist Financing*, 13; Richet, "Laundering Money Online," 17; and John Cassara, "Mobile Payments, Smurfs and Emerging Threats," *SAS*, accessed August 4, 2020, https://www.sas.com/en_us/insights/articles/risk-fraud/mobile-payments-smurfs-emerging-threats.html.

61. Kristopher M. Rengert and Sherrie L. W. Rhine, "Bank Efforts to Serve Unbanked and Underbanked Customers," *Qualitative Research Report, Economic Inclusion.gov* (Washington D.C.: FDIC, 2016), 8; Cassara, "Mobile Payments"; Irwin and Slay, "Money Laundering and Terrorism Financing," 52.

62. Todd Moss, *Oil to Cash: Fighting the Resource Curse through Cash Transfers* (Washington, D.C.: Center for Global Development, 2011), 14.

63. John Daugman, "600 Million Citizens of India are Now Enrolled with Biometric ID," *SPIE Newsroom*, May 7, 2014; Ian Parker, "The I.D. Man," *New Yorker*, September 26, 2011; and Ursula Rao and Graham Greenleaf, "Subverting ID from Above and Below," *Surveillance and Society* 11, no. 3 (2013): 288.

64. Parker, "The I.D. Man"; and Rao and Greenleaf, "Subverting ID," 294.

65. Anuraj Soni and Reena Duggal, "Reducing Risk in KYC for Large Indian Banks," *International Journal of Computer Applications* 97, no. 9 (July 2014): 50;

U. Ramanathan, "Considering Social Implications of Biometric Registration," *IEEE Technology and Society Magazine* 34, no. 1 (March 2015): 12; and Rahul Bhatia, "How India's Welfare Revolution Is Starving Citizens," *New Yorker*, May 16, 2018.

66. Alexandra Orlova, "Russia's Anti-Money Laundering Regime," *Journal of Money Laundering Control* 11, no. 3 (2008): 225.

67. Justin Elliot and Paul Kirl, "Inside TurboTax's 20-Year Fight to Stop Americans from Filing Their Taxes for Free," *ProPublica*, October 17, 2019.

68. Steven Graves and Christopher Peterson, "Usury Law and the Christian Right," *Catholic University Law Review* 57, no. 3 (2008): 647.

69. Tom Heberlein, "I'm an American Living in Sweden," *Vox*, April 8, 2016; Liz Alderman, "Sweden's Push to Get Rid of Cash," *New York Times*, November 21, 2018; Susan Fourtane, "How to Live in the World's First Cashless Society," *Interesting Engineering*, February 20, 2019; Maddy Savage, "Sweden's Cashless Experiment," *NPR*, February 11, 2019; and Harry de Quetteville, "What Can We Learn from Sweden, the Ultimate Cashless Society?," *Telegraph*, October 10, 2019.

70. Fourtane, "How to Live"; Alderman, "Sweden's Push"; and de Quetteville, "What Can We Learn?"

71. Naylor, *Wages of Crime*, 236; James Cockayne and Liat Shetret, *Capitalizing on Trust: Harnessing Somali Remittances for Counterterrorism, Human Rights and State Building* (Washington, D.C.: Center on Global Counterterrorism Cooperation, 2012), 12; and N. S. Jamwal, "*Hawala*—The Invisible Financing System of Terrorism," *Strategic Analysis* 26, no. 2 (2002): 182.

72. de Goede, "Hawala Discourses," 514; Tatiana Klemar and Sonja Cindori, "Hawala's Appeal in Terrorism Financing," in *Security Concepts and Policies: New Generation of Risks and Threats*, ed. Marjan Gjurovski (Skopje, Macedonia: International Scientific Conference Security Concepts and Policies, 2017), 123; and Emily Schaeffer, "Remittances and Reputations in Hawala Money-Transfer Systems," *Journal of Private Enterprise* 24, no. 1 (2008): 99.

73. Giraldo and Trinkunas, *Terrorism Financing*, 68; and Anna Lindley, "Between 'Dirty Money' and 'Development Capital'," *African Affairs* 108, no. 433 (2009): 525.

74. Stephen Tankel, *The Indian Jihadist Movement: Evolution and Dynamics* (Washington, D.C.: National Defense University Press, 2014), 21; Magnus Ranstorp, "Microfinancing the Caliphate: How the Islamic State Is Unlocking the Assets of European Recruits," *CTC Sentinel* 9, no. 5 (May 2016): 14; and Klemar and Cindori, "Hawala's Appeal," 126.

75. de Goede, "Hawala Discourses," 523.

76. Khalid Medani, "Financing Terrorism or Survival? Informal Finance and State Collapse in Somalia and the US War on Terrorism," *MERIP*, no. 223 (Summer 2002); Eliza Griswold, *The Tenth Parallel: Parallel Dispatches from the Fault Line*

between Christianity and Islam (New York: Farrar, Strauss and Giroux, 2010), 154; and Naylor, *Wages of Crime*, 319.

77. R. Cheran and Sharryn Aiken, "The Impact of International Informal Banking on Canada: A Case Study of Tamil Transnational Money Transfer Networks (Undiyal), Canada/Sri Lanka" (working paper, York University, Ottawa, Ontario, Law Commission of Canada, Spring 2005), 8; Rupa Shenoy, "U.S. Somalis Lose Only Means of Sending Cash Home," *NPR*, December 17, 2011; Sam Dillon with Donald McNeil Jr., "A Nation Challenged: The Legal Front; Spain Sets Hurdle for Extraditions," *New York Times*, April 13, 2002; and Marin Strmecki, "Lessons Learned Interview," *Washington Post*, October 19, 2015, https:// www.washingtonpost.com/graphics/2019/investigations/afghanistan-papers /documents-database/?document=background_ll_01_xx_xx_10192015.

78. John Oseth, "Combatting Terrorism," *Parameters* 15, no. 1 (1984): 70; Jude McCulloch and Sharon Pickering, "Suppressing the Financing of Terrorism," *British Journal of Criminology* 45, no. 4 (2005): 479; and Roger Ballard, "Hawala Transformed: Remittance-Driven Transnational Networks in the Post-Imperial Economic Order" (paper, University of Manchester, 2004), 25.

79. de Goede, "Hawala Discourses," 515; see also Basile, "Going to the Source," 174; and David M. Cook and Timothy Smith, "The Battle for Money Transfers: The Allure of PayPal and Western Union over Familial Remittance Networks," *Journal of Information Warfare* 10, no. 1 (2011): 31.

80. Daniel Adam Hancock, "The Olive Branch and the Hammer: A Strategic Analysis of Hawala in the Financial War on Terrorism" (master's thesis, Naval Postgraduate School, March 2008) 43.

81. Richard Shelby, "Money Laundering and Terror Financing Issues in the Middle East," Hearing before the Committee on Banking, Housing and Urban Affairs, U.S. Senate, July 13, 2005; Sarah Rundell, "Africa: A New Frontier for Islamic Banking," *Raconteur*, March 26, 2018; and Mohammed Akacem and Lynde Gilliam, "Principles of Islamic Banking: Debt versus Equity Financing," *Middle East Policy Council* 9, no. 1 (Spring 2002).

82. Basile, "Going to the Source," 175; Bill Rammell, "The Financial War against Terrorism: The Contribution of Islamic Banking," *RUSI Journal*, June 2003, 74; and Julio C. Colón, "Choice of Law and Islamic Finance," *Texas International Law Journal* 46 (2011): 412.

83. Christine Walsh, "Ethics: Inherent in Islamic Finance through Shari'a Law," *Fordham Journal of Corporate and Financial Law* 12, no. 4 (2007): 760; and Jerry Useem, "Banking on Allah," *CNN Money*, June 10, 2002.

84. Goldman and CNAS, *Terrorist Financing*, 26; Nikita Malik, "How Criminals and Terrorists Use Cryptocurrency," *Forbes*, August 31, 2018; John Bohannon,

"Why Criminals Can't Hide Behind Bitcoin," *Science*, March 9, 2016; and Brantly, "Financing Terror," 3.

85. *White Supremacy Extremism: The Transnational Rise of the Violent White Supremacist Movement*, The Soufan Center, September 27, 2019, https://thesoufancenter.org/wp-content/uploads/2019/09/Report-by-The-Soufan-Center-White-Supremacy-Extremism-The-Transnational-Rise-of-The-Violent-White-Supremacist-Movement.pdf, p. 23; Tom Keatinge, Florence Keen, and Kayla Izenman, "Fundraising for Right-Wing Extremist Movements," *The RUSI Journal* 164, no. 2 (2019): 22; Jordan Pearson, "Can the Bitcoin Community Stop Neo-Nazis?," *Vice*, August 18, 2017; and "Large Bitcoin Payment Made to Far-Right Individuals before U.S. Capitol Attack: Report," Reuters, January 14, 2021.

86. Irwin and Slay, "Detecting Money Laundering," 69; Katie A. Paul, "Ancient Artifacts vs. Digital Artifacts: New Tools for Unmasking the Sale of Illicit Antiquities on the Dark Web," *Arts* 7, no. 2 (March 2018): 3; and Lewis Sanders IV, "Bitcoin: Islamic State's Online Currency Venture," *DW.com*, September 20, 2015.

87. Nicholas Ryder, "Counter-Terrorist Financing, Cryptoassets, Social Media Platforms, and Suspicious Activity Reports: A Step into the Regulatory Unknown" (paper presented at the Centre for Financial and Corporate Integrity, Coventry University, March 2019); and Harriet Alexander, "New York Woman Charged with Sending $85,000 in Bitcoin to Support ISIL," *Telegraph*, December 14, 2017.

88. David Manheim, Patrick B. Johnston, Joshua Baron, and Cynthia Dion-Schwarz, "Are Terrorists Using Cryptocurrencies?," *RAND Blog*, April 21, 2017; Jonathan Chester, "How Questions about Terrorism Challenge Bitcoin Startups," *Forbes*, December 14, 2015; and Miriam Berger, "Massive Blackouts Have Hit Iran," *Washington Post*, January 16, 2021.

89. Goldman and CNAS, *Terrorist Use of Virtual Currencies*, 15; Karen Zraick, "Crypto-Exchange Says It Can't Pay Investors Because Its C.E.O. Died," *New York Times*, February 5, 2019; and Aaron Mak, "How Weird Is It That a Company Lost Hundreds of Millions in Cryptocurrency Because Its CEO Died?," *Slate Magazine*, December 18, 2019.

90. Nathaniel Popper, "Lost Passwords Lock Millionaires Out of Their Bitcoin Fortunes," *New York Times*, January 12, 2021.

91. Berger, "Massive Blackouts."

92. Brantly, "Financing Terror," 5; P. H. Madore, "GhostSec: ISIS Has Bitcoin Wallet Worth $3 Million," *Crypto Coins News*, November 16, 2015; and Goldman and CNAS, *Terrorist Use of Virtual Currencies*, 22.

93. Paul, "Ancient Artifacts," 9; and Chris Cooper, "Blockchain and the Battle for 'Blood Antiquities'," *DCEBrief*, September 26, 2016.

94. Michael Slovis, dir., *Breaking Bad*, season 3, episode 9, "Kafkaesque," aired May 16, 2010 (Culver City, Calif.: Sony Pictures Television, 2010).

95. *Estimating Illicit Financial Flows Resulting from Drug Trafficking and Other Transnational Organized Crimes*, Research Report (New York: UNODC, August 31, 2011), 146; and Realuyo, *"Following the Money Trail,"* 9.

96. Riccardi and Levi, "Cash, Crime and Anti-Money Laundering," 147; Alfredo Corchado, "Mexico's Zetas Gang Buys Businesses along Border," *Dallas Morning News*, December 6, 2009; and Richard Paxton, "Used Cars, Drug Dealers and Money Laundering," *Medium*, July 21, 2016.

97. Adam Dolnik, *Understanding Terrorist Innovation: Technology, Tactics and Global Trends* (London: Routledge, 2007), 142; Sharon Tan and Richard Paddock, "'Wolf of Wall Street' Producer, Riza Aziz, Is Charged," *New York Times*, July 4, 2019; and Martin Rudner, "Hizbullah Terrorism Finance: Fund-Raising and Money-Laundering," *Studies in Conflict and Terrorism* 33, no. 8 (July 15, 2010): 705.

98. Melissa Del Bosque, *Bloodlines: The True Story of a Drug Cartel, the FBI, and the Battle for a Horse-Racing Dynasty* (New York: Harper Collins, 2017), 195; Ginger Thompson, "A Drug Family in the Winner's Circle," *New York Times*, June 13, 2012; and Joe Tone, *Bones: Brothers, Horses, Cartels, and the Borderland Dream* (New York: Penguin Random House, 2018).

99. Richard Paxton, "Where Money Laundering Hides in America," *Medium*, April 7, 2016; Del Bosque, *Bloodlines*, 195; and Thompson, "A Drug Family."

100. Louise Story and Stephanie Saul, "Stream of Foreign Wealth Flows to Elite New York Real Estate," *New York Times*, February 7, 2015; "Britain's New Anti-Corruption Tool Is Proving Useful—in Certain Cases," *Economist*, October 10, 2020; and Lawrence Trautman, "Following the Money: Lessons from the Panama Papers, Part 1: Tip of the Iceberg," *Pennsylvania State Law Review* 121, no. 3 (2017): 816.

101. Gouvin, "Bringing out the Big Guns," 980; Sam Cooper, "Canada Proposes National Money Laundering Task Force," *Global News*, March 19, 2019; and Kendra McSweeney, Nazih Richani, Zoe Pearson, Jennifer Devine, and David J. Wrathall, "Why Do Narcos Invest in Rural Land?," *Journal of Latin American Geography* 16, no. 2 (June 2017): 17.

102. Josh Allen, "How Decolonisation Helped Create Tax Havens," *Past and Present*, November 2, 2020; John Waszak, "The Obstacles to Suppressing Radical Islamic Terrorist Financing," *Case Western Reserve Journal of International Law* 36 (2004): 702; and Ronen Palan, Christian Chavagneux, and Richard Murphy, *Tax Havens: How Globalization Really Works* (Ithaca, N.Y.: Cornell University Press, 2010), 159.

103. Masciandaro, *Global Financial Game*, 22.

104. Robinson, *The Laundrymen*, 178; Palan et al., *Tax Havens*, 97; and Wechsler, "Follow the Money," 42.

105. Jake Bernstein, *The Laundromat: Inside the Panama Papers Investigation of Illicit Money Networks and the Global Elite* (New York: Picador, 2018), 10; Palan et al., *Tax Havens*, 2; Jonathan M. Winer, *Illicit Finance and Global Conflict* (Oslo: Fafo Institute, March 2002), 27; and Naylor, *Patriots and Profiteers*, 145.

106. Douglas Farah and Stephen Braun, *Merchant of Death: Money, Guns, Planes, and the Man Who Makes War Possible* (Hoboken, N.J.: Wiley, 2007), 40; "Flying Anything to Anybody," *The Economist*, December 20, 2008; and Daniel Byman, "Passive Sponsors of Terrorism," *Survival* 47, no. 4 (Winter 2005): 119.

107. R. T. Naylor, *Economic Warfare: Sanctions, Embargo Busting, and Their Human Cost* (Boston: Northeastern University Press, 1999), 213; and Bernstein, *The Laundromat*, 101.

108. Maria Aspan, "No Bailouts for Bermuda and Liberia," *Fortune*, March 27, 2020; and Grant Hermes, "Nonpartisan Watchdog Group Raises Questions about $40m Yacht Tied to DeVos Family," *WDIV Detroit*, October 10, 2020.

109. Seth Porges and Chris Charles Scott III, dir., *Class Action Park* (Shreveport, La.: Perennial Media/HBO Max, 2020); and Bernstein, *The Laundromat*, 183.

110. M. Michelle Gallant, "Tax and Terrorism: A New Partnership," *Journal of Financial Crime* 14, no. 4 (2007): 455; Stephen Lee, "Billionaires Stashing Funds in South Dakota Trusts," *Pierre Capital Journal*, May 11, 2020; Del Bosque, *Bloodlines*, 379; and Bastian Obermayer and Frederik Obermaier, *The Panama Papers: Breaking the Story of How the Rich and Powerful Hide Their Money* (London: OneWorld, 2016), 311.

111. James O'Donovan, Hannes F. Wagner, and Stefan Zeume, "The Value of Offshore Secrets: Evidence from the Panama Papers," *Review of Financial Studies* 32, no. 11 (November 1, 2019): 4124; and Channing May, *Transnational Crime and the Developing World* (Washington, D.C.: Global Financial Integrity, March 2017), 73.

112. Palan et al., *Tax Havens*, 145.

113. Palan et al., *Tax Havens*, 187; Bernstein, *The Laundromat*, 23; and Brigitte Unger and Gregory Rawlings, "Competing for Criminal Money," *Global Business and Economics Review* 10, no. 3 (2008): 349.

114. Bernstein, *The Laundromat*, 276; Naylor, *Wages of Crime*, 150; and "Chinese with Grenada Diplomatic Passports," *New Today (Granada)*, September 12, 2020.

115. McCarthy, *The Money Laundering Market*, 51; Bernstein, *The Laundromat*, 69; and Naylor, *Wages of Crime*, 195.

116. Obermayer and Obermaier, *The Panama Papers*, 307; Jeanne Whalen, "Congress Bans Anonymous Shell Companies," *Washington Post*, December 11, 2020; and

Spencer Woodman, "US Lawmakers Move to End Anonymous Shell Companies in National Defense Spending Bill," *International Consortium of Investigative Journalists*, November 25, 2020.

117. Robert I. Rotberg, *The Corruption Cure: How Citizens and Leaders Can Combat Graft* (Princeton, N.J.: Princeton University Press, 2017), 26; Sarah Chayes, *Thieves of State: Why Corruption Threatens Global Security* (New York: Norton, 2015), 74; and Christian Parenti, *Tropic of Chaos: Climate Change and the New Geography of Violence* (New York: Nation Books, 2011), 63.

118. Jared M. Diamond, *Guns, Germs, and Steel: The Fates of Human Societies* (New York: Norton, 2017).

119. Raymond Baker and Eva Joly, "Illicit Money: Can It Be Stopped?," in *Deviant Globalization: Black Market Economy in the 21st Century*, ed. Nils Gilman, Jesse Goldhammer, and Steven Weber (New York: Continuum, 2011), 236; Gretta Fenner Zinkernagel, Charles Monieith, and Pedro Gomes Pereira, eds., *Emerging Trends in Asset Recovery* (Bern: Peter Lang, 2013), 118; Paul Collier, V. L. Elliott, Håvard Hegre, Anke Hoeffler, Marta Reynal-Querol, and Nicholas Sambins, *Breaking the Conflict Trap: Civil War and Development Policy* (Washington D.C.: World Bank, 2003), 15; and Rotberg, *The Corruption Cure*, 8.

120. Nicholas Shaxson, "Oil, Corruption and the Resource Curse," *International Affairs* 83, no. 6 (2007): 1126; James Ferguson, *Global Shadows: Africa in the Neoliberal World Order* (Durham, N.C.: Duke University Press, 2006), 76; and Ndiva Kofele-Kale, "Only Fools Who Send Hyenas to Roast Meat for Them," *Florida A&M University Law Review* 9 (Fall 2013): 36.

121. Dave Allen, Will Cafferky, Abdallah Hendawy, Jordache Horn, Karolina MacLachlan, Stefanie Nijssen, and Eleonore Vidal de la Blache, *The Big Spin: Corruption and the Growth of Violent Extremism* (London: Transparency International, February 2017), 17; Philippe Le Billon, Jake Sherman, and Marica Hartwell, *Controlling Resource Flows to Civil Wars: A Review and Analysis of Current Policies and Legal Instruments* (paper for the International Peace Academy "Economic Agendas in Civil Wars" project conference, Bellagio, Italy, May 20–24, 2002), 27; and Sarah Chayes, "Corruption and Terrorism: The Causal Link" (Carnegie Endowment, May 12, 2016).

122. Brandon J. Griffin, Natalie Purcell, Kristine Burkman, Brett T. Litz, Craig J. Bryan, Martha Schmitz, Claudia Villierme, Jessica Walsh, and Shira Maguen, "Moral Injury: An Integrative Review," *Journal of Traumatic Stress* 32, no. 3 (June 2019): 350–62.

123. Sharman, *The Despot's Guide*, 18.

124. Ray Fisman and Miriam A. Golden, *Corruption: What Everyone Needs to Know* (Oxford: Oxford University Press, 2017), 59; and Sharman, *The Despot's Guide*, 27.

125. Sharman, *The Despot's Guide*, 17; and Zinkernagel et al., *Emerging Trends*, 131.

126. Baker and Joly, "Illicit Money," 237; Richard H. Schultz Jr. and Andrea J. Dew, *Insurgents, Terrorists, and Militias: The Warriors of Contemporary Combat* (New York: Columbia University Press, 2006), 241; "Saddam Regime Funds Financing Iraq Insurgency," *CNN*, October 22, 2004; and John Robb, *Brave New War: The Next Stage of Terrorism and the End of Globalization* (Hoboken, N.J.: Wiley, 2007), 44.

127. Collier et al., *Breaking the Conflict Trap*, 73; and Kenneth Omeje, "The Diaspora and Domestic Insurgencies in Africa," *African Sociological Review* 11, no. 2 (2007): 100.

128. Bruce E. Bechtol Jr., "North Korean Illicit Activities and Sanctions: A National Security Dilemma," *Cornell International Law Journal* 51 (2018): 61; Kenneth Vogel, "Paul Manafort's Wild and Lucrative Philippine Adventure," *Politico Magazine*, June 10, 2016; Farah and Braun, *Merchant of Death*, 22; and Baker and Joly, "Illicit Money," 233.

129. Andy Kroll, "Lawyers, Guns and Money," *Mother Jones*, February 4, 2010; see also Kofele-Kale, "Only Fools," 37; Sandra Barnes, "Global Flows," *African Studies Review* 48, no. 1 (2005): 5; Silverstein, "Narco-A-Lago," 25; and Laura Strickler, "We Found $1 Billion in Sackler Family Wire Transfers," *NBC News*, September 14, 2019.

130. Zinkernagel et al., *Emerging Trends*, 52; and Sharman, *The Despot's Guide*, 157.

131. Paul Peachey, "UK 'Loses' Nearly £1 Billion of Frozen Libyan Funds," *National*, December 17, 2019; Sharman, *The Despot's Guide*, 143; and "Making a Hash of Finding the Cash," *Economist*, May 11, 2013. 2011.

132. Trautman, "Following the Money," 855; Sharman, *The Despot's Guide*, 77; and Joseph Wheatley, "Counter-Threat Finance" (lecture, Marshall Center, July 29, 2019).

133. Zinkernagel et al., *Emerging Trends*, 323; BBC Panorama Team, "Africa's Richest Woman 'Ripped Off Her Country,'" *BBC News*, January 19, 2020; and Story and Saul, "Stream of Foreign Wealth."

134. Jack Blum, Foreword to *Economic Warfare: Sanctions, Embargo Busting, and Their Human Cost*, by R. T. Naylor (Boston: Northeastern University Press, 1999), vii.

135. Mark Fenwick and Erik P. M. Vermeulen, *Disclosure of Beneficial Ownership after the Panama Papers* (Washington, D.C.: World Bank, 2016), 9; Cynthia Arnson and I. William Zartman, eds., *Rethinking the Economics of War: The Intersection of Need, Creed, and Greed* (Baltimore: Johns Hopkins University Press, 2005), 245; Jenik Radon and Mahima Achuthan, "Beneficial Ownership Disclosure," *Journal of International Affairs* 70, no. 2 (Summer 2017): 97; and Ben Judah and

Nate Sibley, "The West Is Open for Dirty Business," *Foreign Policy*, October 5, 2019.

136. Trautman, "Following the Money," 861; Fisman and Golden, *Corruption*, 259; Halif Sarki, "The Mo Ibrahim Prize," ISS Africa, October 26, 2009; "Ibrahim Prize for Achievement in African Leadership," Mo Ibrahim Foundation, accessed December 23, 2020, http://mo.ibrahim.foundation/prize; and Rotberg, *The Corruption Cure*, 38.

Chapter 8. Commodities

1. Robert Block and Daniel Pearl, "Underground Trade," *Wall Street Journal*, November 16, 2001; and R. T. Naylor, *Wages of Crime: Black Markets, Illegal Finance, and the Underworld Economy* (Ithaca, N.Y.: Cornell University Press, 2004), 312.

2. Katherine Donahue, "Tanzanite: Commodity Fiction or Commodity Nightmare?," in *Between the Plough and the Pick: Informal, Artisanal and Small-Scale Mining in the Contemporary World*, ed. Kuntala Lahiri-Dutt (Canberra: Australian National University Press, 2018), 73.

3. Glenn Simpson and Robert Block, "Diary Offers More on Tanzanite, Al Qaeda Link," *Wall Street Journal*, January 24, 2002; Block and Pearl, "Underground"; and Douglas Farah, "The Role of Conflict Diamonds and Failed States in the Terrorist Financial Structure," *RUSI Monitor* 3, no. 3 (November 14, 2007).

4. Eric Gouvin, "Bringing Out the Big Guns: The USA Patriot Act, Money Laundering, and the War on Terrorism," *Baylor Law Review* 55 (2003): 980; Annette Hubschle, *Unholy Alliance? Assessing the Links between Organised Criminals and Terrorists in Southern Africa* (Cape Town: Institute for Security Studies, October 2004), 9; and Ann Zimmerman, "Zale Corp. to Resume Tanzanite-Jewelry Sales," *Wall Street Journal*, May 7, 2002.

5. Donahue, "Tanzanite," 71; and Jerry Markon, "Gemstone Dealers Named in Suit over Sept. 11," *Wall Street Journal*, February 15, 2002.

6. Donahue, "Tanzanite," 71; and Zimmerman, "Zale Corp."

7. Michael Ross, "Booty Futures" (working paper, University of California, Los Angeles, May 6, 2005), 3; Owen Barder, "A Policymakers' Guide to Dutch Disease" (working paper, number 91, Washington, D.C.: Center for Global Development, July 2006), 4; and Macartan Humphreys, "Natural Resource, Conflict, and Conflict Resolution" (paper prepared for the Santa Fe Institute / Javeriana University "Obstacles to Robust Negotiated Settlements" workshop, Bogota, Colombia, May 29–31, 2003), 6.

8. Jenik Radon and Mahima Achuthan, "Beneficial Ownership Disclosure," *Journal of International Affairs* 70, no. 2 (Summer 2017): 86; Michael Ross, "Natural

Resources and Civil War: An Overview" (paper submitted for review to *World Bank Research Observer*, August 15, 2003), 5; Jonathan Winer, *Illicit Finance and Global Conflict* (Oslo: Fafo Institute, March 2002), 9; and Ray Fisman and Miriam A. Golden, *Corruption: What Everyone Needs to Know* (Oxford: Oxford University Press, 2017), 113.

9. Ian Bannon and Paul Collier, eds., *Natural Resources and Violent Conflict: Options and Actions* (Washington, D.C.: World Bank, 2003), 58.

10. Lenovo, "North Dakota Found to Be Harboring Nuclear Missiles," *Onion*, February 5, 2003.

11. Stephen Brown and Mine Yücel, *The Shale Gas and Tight Oil Boom: U.S. States' Economic Gains and Vulnerabilities* (New York: Council on Foreign Relations, October 2013); Bret A. Weber, Julia Geigle, and Carenlee Barkdull, "Rural North Dakota's Oil Boom and Its Impact on Social Services," *Social Work* 59, no. 1 (January 2014): 62–72; and Timothy Pippert and Rachel Zimmer Schneider, "'Have You Been to Walmart?': Gender and Perceptions of Safety in North Dakota Boomtowns," *Sociological Quarterly* 59, no. 2 (April 3, 2018): 234–49.

12. Paul Collier, "Doing Well Out of War" (paper prepared for Conference on Economic Agendas in Civil Wars, London, April 26–27, 1999), 147; Cynthia Arnson and I. William Zartman, eds., *Rethinking the Economics of War: The Intersection of Need, Creed, and Greed* (Baltimore: Johns Hopkins University Press, 2005), 4; and Bannon and Collier, *Natural Resources*, 147.

13. James Fearon, "Primary Commodity Exports and Civil War," *Journal of Conflict Resolution* 49, no. 4 (2005): 484; Karen Ballentine and Heiko Nitzschke, *The Political Economy of Civil War and Conflict Transformation* (Berlin: Berghof Center, 2005), 4; and Sara Balestri and Mario Maggioni, "Blood Diamonds, Dirty Gold and Spatial Spill-Overs," *Peace Economics, Peace Science and Public Policy* 20, no. 4 (2014): 563.

14. Markus Schultze-Kraft, *Getting Real about an Illicit "External Stressor": Transnational Cocaine Trafficking through West Africa*, Evidence Report no. 72, Addressing and Mitigating Violence, June 2014, p. 26; and Tom Parker, "Fighting an Antaean Enemy," *Terrorism and Political Violence* 19, no. 2 (April 6, 2007): 157.

15. Arnson and Zartman, *Rethinking the Economics of War*, 8; Philippe Le Billon, Jake Sherman, and Marica Hartwell, *Controlling Resource Flows to Civil Wars: A Review and Analysis of Current Policies and Legal Instruments* (paper for the International Peace Academy "Economic Agendas in Civil Wars" project conference, Bellagio, Italy, May 20–24, 2002), 37; and Paul V. Collier, V. L. Elliott, Håvard Hegre, Anke Hoeffler, Marta Reynol-Querol, and Nicholas Sambanis, *Breaking the Conflict Trap: Civil War and Development Policy* (Washington D.C.: World Bank, 2003), 4.

16. Ross, "Booty Futures," 3; Collier et al., *Breaking the Conflict Trap*, 90; and Augustine Ikelegbe, "The Economy of Conflict in the Oil Rich Niger Delta Region of Nigeria," *Nordic Journal of African Studies* 14, no. 2 (2005): 211.

17. William Reno, "The Business of War in Liberia," *Current History* 95, no. 601 (May 1996): 212; Naylor, *Wages of Crime*, 121; and Humphreys, "Natural Resource," 5.

18. Andrew Mumford, "Intelligence Wars," *Civil Wars* 7, no. 4 (Winter 2005): 390; and Loretta Napoleoni, *Modern Jihad: Tracing the Dollars behind the Terror Networks* (London: Pluto Press, 2003), 113.

19. Bannon and Collier, *Natural Resources*, 36; and Collier, "Doing Well Out of War," 13.

20. Naazneen H. Barma, "The Rentier State at Work: Comparative Experiences of the Resource Curse in East Asia and the Pacific," *Asia and The Pacific Policy Studies* 1 no. 2 (2014): 264; and Todd Moss, *Oil to Cash: Fighting the Resource Curse through Cash Transfers* (Washington, D.C.: Center for Global Development, 2011), 8.

21. Ballentine and Nitzschke, *The Political Economy*, 12; Heiko Nitzschke and Kaysie Studdard, "The Legacies of War Economies: Challenges and Options for Peacemaking and Peacebuilding," *International Peacekeeping* 12, no. 2 (2005): 235; and Laurence Juma, "'Shadow Networks' and Conflict Resolution in the Great Lakes Region of Africa," *African Security Review* 16, no. 1 (January 1, 2007): 10.

22. R. T. Naylor, *Patriots and Profiteers: Economic Warfare, Embargo Busting, and State-Sponsored Crime* (Montreal: McGill-Queen's University Press, 2008), 167; Philippe Le Billon, "Fatal Transactions: Conflict Diamonds and the (Anti)Terrorist Consumer," *Antipode* 38, no. 4 (September 2006): 783; and Nikos Passas and Kimberly Jones, "Commodities and Terrorist Financing: Focus on Diamonds," *European Journal on Criminal Policy and Research* 12, no. 1 (2006): 6.

23. Douglas Farah, "Digging Up Congo's Dirty Gems," *Washington Post*, December 30, 2001; Antonius Johannes and Gerhardus Tijhuis, *Transnational Crime and the Interface between Legal and Illegal Actors* (Nijmegen: Wolf Legal, 2006), 43; and Le Billon, "Fatal Transaction," 785.

24. Michael Renner, *The Anatomy of Resource Wars*, Worldwatch paper no. 162, ed. by Thomas Prugh (Washington, D.C.: Worldwatch Institute, October 2002), 33; Klejda Mulaj, ed., *Violent Non-State Actors in World Politics* (New York: Columbia University Press, 2010), 307; and Matt Potter, *Outlaws, Inc.* (New York: Bloomsbury, 2011), 107.

25. Douglas Farah, "Al Qaeda Cash Tied to Diamond Trade," *Washington Post*, November 2, 2001; and Douglas Farah and Stephen Braun, *Merchant of Death: Money, Guns, Planes, and the Man Who Makes War Possible* (Hoboken, N.J.: Wiley, 2007), 14.

26. Arnson and Zartman, *Rethinking the Economics of War*, 176; Collier et al., *Breaking the Conflict Trap*, 76; and Ross, "Booty Futures," 14.

27. Justine Rosenthal, "For-Profit Terrorism: The Rise of Armed Entrepreneurs," *Studies in Conflict and Terrorism* 31, no. 6 (2008): 484; Greg Campbell, *Blood Diamonds: Tracing the Deadly Path of the World's Most Precious Stones* (Boulder, Colo.: Westview, 2002), 72; and Judith Vorrath, *From War to Illicit Economies: Organized Crime and State-Building in Liberia and Sierra Leone* (Berlin: German Institute, November 2014), 10.

28. Naylor, *Patriots and Profiteers*, 167; Campbell, *Blood Diamonds*, 117; and Renner, *The Anatomy*, 33.

29. Naylor, *Patriots and Profiteers*, 96; Carl Anthony Wege, "Hizballah in Africa," *Perspectives on Terrorism* 6, no. 3 (August 2012): 47; and Mark Basile, "Going to the Source: Why Al Qaeda's Financial Network Is Likely to Withstand the Current War on Terrorist Financing," *Studies in Conflict and Terrorism* 27, no. 3 (June 2004): 172.

30. Farah, "The Role of Conflict Diamonds"; and Hubschle, *Unholy Alliance?*, 8.

31. Collier et al., *Breaking the Conflict Trap*, 142; and Campbell, *Blood Diamonds*, 199.

32. Philippe Le Billon and Eric Nicholls, "Ending 'Resource Wars': Revenue Sharing, Economic Sanction or Military Intervention?," *International Peacekeeping* 14 no. 5 (2007): 616; Khaled Fayyad, "The Kimberley Process and the Unfulfilled Promise of a Conflict-Free Diamond Industry," *Mellon Sawyer Seminar on Corporations and International Law*, May 7, 2018; and Joseph Kahn, "A Nation Challenged: The Money Trail; House Votes to Combat Sale of Diamonds for War," *New York Times*, November 29, 2001.

33. David Rhode, "The Kimberley Process Is a 'Perfect Cover Story' for Blood Diamonds," *Guardian*, March 24, 2014; Le Billon, "Fatal Transactions," 796; and France Desmarais, ed., *Countering Illicit Traffic in Cultural Goods: The Global Challenge of Protecting the World's Heritage* (Paris: ICOM, 2015), 21.

34. Passas and Jones, "Commodities and Terrorist Financing," 5; and Naylor, *Wages of Crime*, 311.

35. Daniel Kempton and Richard Levine, "Soviet and Russian Relations with Foreign Corporations," *Slavic Review* 54, no. 1 (1995): 88; Ballentine and Nitzschke, *The Political Economy*, 16; and Le Billon, "Fatal Transaction," 787.

36. Dan Henk, *The Botswana Defense Force in the Struggle for an African Environment* (New York: Palgrave MacMillan, 2007), 15; Robert I. Rotberg, *The Corruption Cure: How Citizens and Leaders Can Combat Graft* (Princeton, N.J.: Princeton University Press, 2017), 245; and Kempton and Levine, "Soviet and Russian Relations," 107.

37. Daniel Yergin, *The Prize: The Epic Quest for Oil, Money and Power* (New York: Simon and Schuster, 1990), 13; Naylor, *Patriots and Profiteers*, 227; and Sebastian Junger, "Blood Oil," in *Deviant Globalization: Black Market Economy in the 21st Century*, ed. Nils Gilman, Jesse Goldhammer, and Steven Weber (New York: Continuum, 2011), 109.

38. Gabriel Marcella, *American Grand Strategy for Latin America in the Age of Resentment* (Carlisle, Pa.: Strategic Studies Institute, 2011), 38; see also James J. Forest, *Confronting the Terrorism of Boko Haram in Nigeria* (MacDill Air Force Base, Fla.: Joint Special Operations University Press, 2012), 29; and Miroslav Nincic, *Renegade Regimes: Confronting Deviant Behavior in World Politics* (New York: Columbia University Press, 2005), 91.

39. Riley Post and Jeffrey Peterson, *Unconventional Economics: Operational Economics in Unconventional Warfare* (MacDill Air Force Base, Fla.: Joint Special Operations University Press, 2016), 41; and Mary Kaldor, *New and Old Wars: Organized Violence in a Global Era* (Stanford, Calif.: Stanford University Press, 2012), 109.

40. Giacomo Persi Paoli and Jacopo Bellasio, *Against the Rising Tide: An Overview of the Growing Criminalisation of the Mediterranean Region* (Santa Monica, Calif.: RAND, 2017), 23; Aderoju Oyefusi, "Oil and the Probability of Rebel Participation among Youths in the Niger Delta of Nigeria," *Journal of Peace Research* 45, no. 4 (2008): 539; and Francis Adyanga Akena, "Poornography and the Entrenchment of Western Hegemony: Deconstructing the Kony 2012 Video," *Socialist Studies* 10, no. 1 (2014): 56.

41. Beth Van Schaack, "Mapping War Crimes in Syria," *International Law Studies* 92 (2016): 325; Patrick B. Johnston, Mona Alami, Colin P. Clarke, and Howard J. Shatz, *Return and Expand? The Finances and Prospects of the Islamic State after the Caliphate* (Santa Monica, Calif.: RAND, 2019), 26; and Benjamin Bahney and Patrick Johnston, "To Defeat ISIS, Focus on Its Real Sources of Strength," *RAND Blog*, December 4, 2015.

42. Keith Johnson, "Islamic State Is the Newest Petrostate," *Foreign Policy*, August 4, 2014; see also Keith Crane, "The Role of Oil in ISIL Finances," testimony presented before the Senate Energy and Natural Resources Committee on December 10, 2015 (RAND Office of External Affairs, 2015), 8; and Janine Di Giovanni, Janine, Leah McGrath Goodman, and Damien Sharkov, "How Does ISIS Fund Its Reign of Terror?," *Newsweek*, November 6, 2014.

43. Post and Peterson, *Unconventional Economics*, 68; Jamie Hansen-Lewis and Jacob N. Shapiro, "Understanding the Daesh Economy," *Perspectives on Terrorism* 9, no. 4 (2015); and Aymenn Al-Tamimi, "Archive of Islamic State Administrative Documents," January 11, 2016, http://www.aymennjawad.org/2016/01/archive-of-islamic-state-administrative-documents-1.

44. Kenneth Watkin, "Targeting 'Islamic State' Oil Facilities," *International Law Studies* 90 (2014): 508; Crane, "The Role of Oil," 9; and Stefan Heißner, Peter R. Neumann, John Holland-McCowan, and Rajan Basra, *Caliphate in Decline: An Estimate of Islamic State's Financial Fortunes* (London: International Centre for the Study of Radicalisation and Political Violence, King's College London, 2017), 8.

45. Onur Burcak Belli, Andrea Böhm, Alexander Bühler, Kerstin Kohlenberg, Stefan Meining, Yassin Musharbash, Mark Schieritz, et al., "The Business of the Caliph," *Zeit Online*, December 3, 2014; and Crane, "The Role of Oil," 10.

46. UNODC, *Addressing Organized Crime and Drug Trafficking in Iraq: Report of the UNODC Fact Finding Mission* (Vienna: UN Office on Drugs and Crime, August 25, 2003), 11; and Lennox Samuels, "Al Qaeda in Iraq Ramps Up Its Racketeering," *Newsweek*, May 20, 2008.

47. Borzou Daragahi and Erika Solomon, "Fuelling ISIS, Inc.," *Financial Times*, September 21, 2014; and Anna-Lotta Aijala, "How Is ISIS Funded?" (Tallinn University of Technology, 2016), 17.

48. Channing May, *Transnational Crime and the Developing World* (Washington, D.C.: Global Financial Integrity, March 2017), 90; Forest, *Confronting the Terrorism*, 45; and Ikelegbe, "The Economy of Conflict," 222.

49. Michael Freeman, *Financing Terrorism: Case Studies* (Burlington, Vt.: Ashgate, 2011), 223.

50. Bannon and Collier, *Natural Resources*, 33; and Vanda Felbab-Brown, *Shooting Up: Counterinsurgency and the War on Drugs* (Washington, D.C.: Brookings Institution Press, 2010), 93.

51. Arnson and Zartman, *Rethinking the Economics of War*, 193; and Jon-Paul Maddaloni, *An Analysis of the FARC in Colombia: Breaking the Frame of FM 3-24* (Fort Leavenworth, Kan.: School of Advanced Military Studies, 2009), 13.

52. Pierre Englebert and James Ron, "Primary Commodities and War: Congo-Brazzaville's Ambivalent Resource Curse," *Comparative Politics* 37, no. 1 (2004): 69; Ross, "Natural Resources," 10; and James Ferguson, *Global Shadows: Africa in the Neoliberal World Order* (Durham, N.C.: Duke University Press, 2006), 203.

53. Humphreys, "Natural Resource," 2.

54. Xan Rice, "World Bank Cancels Pipeline Deal with Chad after Revenues Misspent," *Guardian*, September 11, 2008; Moss, *Oil to Cash*, 14; and Collier et al., *Breaking the Conflict Trap*, 131.

55. R. T. Naylor, "The Underworld of Ivory," *Crime, Law and Social Change* 42 (2004): 280; and Henk, *The Botswana Defense Force*, 4.

56. Ros Reeve and Stephen Ellis, "An Insider's Account of the South African Security Forces' Role in the Ivory Trade," *Journal of Contemporary African Studies* 13, no. 2 (1995): 230; see also Varun Vira, Thomas Ewing, and Jackson Miller, *Out*

of Africa: Mapping the Global Trade in Illicit Elephant Ivory (Horsham, U.K.: C4DS; Washington, D.C.: Born Free USA, August 2014); Naylor, *Wages of Crime*, 77; Naylor, "The Underworld of Ivory," 278.

57. Stephen Ellis, "Of Elephants and Men" *Journal of Southern African Studies* 20, no. 1 (1994): 58.

58. Naylor, "The Underworld of Ivory," 280; Ellis, "Of Elephants," 58; and Jeremy M. Weinstein, "Resources and the Information Problem in Rebel Recruitment," *Journal of Conflict Resolution* 49, no. 4 (2005): 614.

59. *Criminal Nature: The Global Security Implications of the Illegal Wildlife Trade 2008* (Yarmouth Port, Mass.: International Fund for Animal Welfare, 2008), 12.

60. Ranee Khooshie Lal Panjabi, "For Trinkets, Tonics and Terrorism: International Wildlife Poaching in the Twenty-First Century," *Georgia Journal of International and Comparative Law* 43, no. 1 (2014): 68; Rosaleen Duffy, "War, by Conservation," *Geoforum* 69 (February 2016): 242; and Jeffrey Gettleman, "Africa's Elephants Are Being Slaughtered in Poaching Frenzy," *New York Times*, September 3, 2012.

61. Johan Bergenas, *Killing Animals, Buying Arms: Setting the Stage for Collaborative Solutions to Poaching and Wildlife Crime* (Washington, D.C.: Stimson Center, 2013), 3; Tom Maguire and Cathy Haenlein, *An Illusion of Complicity: Terrorism and the Illegal Ivory Trade in East Africa* (London: RUSI, September 2015), 29; and Thomas Maguire, "Kenya's 'War on Poaching'," in *Militarised Responses to Transnational Organised Crime: The War on Crime*, ed. Tuesday Reitano, Lucia Bird Ruiz-Benitez de Lugo, and Sash Jesperson (Cham: Palgrave Macmillan, 2018), 65.

62. Natasha White, "The 'White Gold of Jihad'," *Journal of Political Ecology* 21 (2014): 466; Bergenas, *Killing Animals*; and Kasper Agger and Jonathan Hutson, *Kony's Ivory: How Elephant Poaching in Congo Helps Support the Lord's Resistance Army* (Washington, D.C.: Center for American Progress, June 2013), 3.

63. Rob Crilly, "African Nations Clash over Sales of Ivory," *Christian Science Monitor*, June 13, 2007; and Panjabi, "For Trinkets," 71.

64. Adrian Levy and Cathy Scott-Clark, "Islamic Militants Use the Trade in Rare Wildlife to Raise Funds," *Guardian*, May 5, 2007; see also May, *Transnational Crime*, 57; and Vanda Felbab-Brown, "Wildlife and Drug Trafficking, Terrorism, and Human Security," *PRISM* 7, no. 4 (2018): 127; and *Criminal Nature*, 10.

65. Gettleman, "Africa's Elephants"; and Bradley Anderson and Johan Jooste, "Wildlife Poaching: Africa's Surging Trafficking Threat," *Africa Center for Strategic Studies*, May 31, 2014.

66. Peter Gastrow, *Termites at Work: A Report on Transnational Organized Crime and State Erosion in Kenya; Comprehensive Research Findings* (New York: International Peace Institute, 2011), 56; Angus Nurse, "Policing Wildlife: Perspectives

on Criminality in Wildlife Crime," *Papers from the British Criminality Conference* 11 (2011), 41, https://eprints.mdx.ac.uk/11066/1/pbcc_2011_Nurse.pdf; and Vira et al., "Out of Africa," 17.

67. Rachel Nuwer, "How to Stop Poaching and Protect Endangered Species?," *New York Times*, September 24, 2018.

68. Panjabi, "For Trinkets," 27.

69. Andrew John Brennan and Jaslin Kaur Kalsi, "Elephant Poaching and Ivory Trafficking Problems in Sub-Saharan Africa," *Ecological Economics* 120 (2015): 323; Vira et al., "Out of Africa," 28; Felbab-Brown, "Wildlife and Drug Trafficking," 126.

70. Gettleman, "Africa's Elephants"; see also Felbab-Brown, "Wildlife and Drug Trafficking," 127; and Matthew Bolton, *Using the Arms Trade Treaty to Approach Wildlife Poaching in East Africa: A Human Security Approach* (New York: ControlArms, November 2015), 9.

71. Cathy Haenlein, Thomas Maguire, and Keith Somerville, "Poaching, Wildlife Trafficking and Terrorism," *Whitehall Papers* 86, no. 1 (2016): 59; Maguire, "Kenya's 'War on Poaching,'" 19; and Bolton, *Using the Arms Trade Treaty*, 6.

72. Christopher Jones, "What Central Africa's War on Poaching Can Teach Us about Fighting the Plunder of Antiquities," *Hyperallergic*, July 5, 2016, https://hyperallergic.com/303561/what-central-africas-war-on-poaching-can-teach-us-about-fighting-the-plunder-of-antiquities/; and Ferguson, *Global Shadows*, 47.

73. Henk, *The Botswana Defense Force*, 47.

74. Joel Konopo, Ntibinyane Ntibinyane, and Tileni Mongudhi, "Botswana's 'Shoot-to-Kill' Policy against Suspected Poachers," *Mail and Guardian*, March 18, 2016.

75. Alastair Leithead, "Dozens of Elephants Killed in Botswana," *BBC News*, September 3, 2018.

76. Goemeone E. J. Mogomotsi and Patricia Kefilwe Madigele, "Live by the Gun, Die by the Gun: Botswana's 'Shoot-to-Kill' Policy as an Anti-Poaching Strategy," *South African Crime Quarterly* 60 (June 2017): 53; Haenlein et al., "Poaching," 62.

77. Karl Jacoby, *Crimes against Nature: Squatters, Poachers, Thieves, and the Hidden History of American Conservation* (Berkeley: University of California Press, 2014); Ellis, "Of Elephants," 55; Jonny Steinberg, "The Illicit Abalone Trade in South Africa," in *Deviant Globalization: Black Market Economy in the 21st Century*, ed. Nils Gilman, Jesse Goldhammer, and Steven Weber (New York: Continuum, 2011), 163; and Justin S. Brashares, Briana Abrahms, Kathryn J. Fiorella, Christopher D. Golden, Cheryl E. Hojnowski, Ryan A. Marsh, Douglas J. McCauley, Tristan A. Nuñez, Katherine Seto, and Lauren Withey, "Wildlife Decline and Social Conflict," *Science* 345, no. 6195 (2014): 376.

78. Mimi Yagoub, "'First' Seizure of FARC's Illegal Mining Assets Could Worsen Dissidence," *InSight Crime*, October 26, 2016; Marina Jiminez, "In Latin America's Drug Hotbeds, Illegal Gold Is More Valuable Than Cocaine," *Toronto Star*, April 14, 2016; and May, *Transnational Crime*, 77.

79. Anthony Spaeth, "Kim's Rackets," *Time*, June 9, 2003.

80. Naylor, *Wages of Crime*, 200; and John Cassara, *Trade-Based Money Laundering: The Next Frontier in International Money Laundering Enforcement* (Hoboken, N.J.: Wiley, 2016), 105.

81. Audrey Cronin, "Behind the Curve," *International Security* 27, no. 3 (January 1, 2003): 49; Winer, *Illicit Finance*, 36; Naylor, *Wages of Crime*, 198; and Naylor, *Patriots and Profiteers*, 166.

82. Douglas Farah, *Blood from Stones: The Secret Financial Network of Terror* (New York: Broadway, 2004), 113; and Cassara, *Trade-Based Money Laundering*, 99.

83. Jeffrey Robinson, *The Laundrymen: Inside Money Laundering, the World's Third Largest Business* (New York: Arcade, 1996), 241; and Cassara, *Trade-Based Money Laundering*, 105.

84. May, *Transnational Crime*, 76; Bannon and Collier, *Natural Resources*, 31; and Arshi Saleem Hashmi and Muhammad Saqib, "Terror Financing and Growth of Terrorist Groups: A Case Study of Tehrik-e-Taliban Pakistan," *NDU Journal* (Pakistan), 2017, 75.

85. Naylor, *Wages of Crime*, 125; and Michael Jonsson, Elliot Brennan, and Christopher O'Hara, "Financing War or Facilitating Peace? The Impact of Rebel Drug Trafficking on Peace Negotiations in Colombia and Myanmar," *Studies in Conflict and Terrorism* 39, no. 6 (June 2, 2016), 553.

86. Bannon and Collier, *Natural Resources*, 201; John Daly, *The Deadly Convenience of Victor Bout* (Zurich: ETH, June 24, 2008), 3; and Nitzschke and Studdard, "The Legacies of War Economies," 225.

87. Muhyadin Roble, "Al-Shabaab Razes Somali Forests to Finance Jihad," Jamestown Foundation Terrorism Monitor, November 18, 2010.

88. Alfonso Daniels, "Battling Siberia's Devastating Illegal Logging Trade," *BBC*, November 27, 2009. See also Raffi Khatchadourian, "The Stolen Forests," in *Deviant Globalization: Black Market Economy in the 21st Century*, ed. Nils Gilman, Jesse Goldhammer and Steven Weber (New York: Continuum International Publishing, 2011), 181; and Louise Shelley, "A Tangled Web," *War on the Rocks* (blog), November 15, 2018.

89. William Reno, "War Markets and the Reconfiguration of West Africa's Weak States," *Comparative Politics* 29, no. 4 (1997): 500; Reno, "The Business of War in Liberia," 213; and Global Witness, *The Logs of War: The Timber Trade and Armed Conflict* (Oslo: Fafo Institute for Applied Social Science, 2002), 16.

90. Vorrath, *From War to Illicit Economies*, 10; and Le Billon and Nicholls, "Ending 'Resource Wars'," 616.

91. Spaeth, "Kim's Rackets"; Felbab-Brown, "Wildlife and Drug Trafficking," 127; and Peter Andreas, *Killer High: A History of War in Six Drugs* (Oxford: Oxford University Press, 2020), 137.

92. Eckart Woertz, "How Long Will ISIS Last Economically?," *Notes Internacionals CIDOB*, no. 98 (October 2014): 2; Naylor, *Wages of Crime*, 125; and Frédéric Lemieux and Fernanda Prates, "Entrepreneurial Terrorism: Financial Strategies, Business Opportunities, and Ethical Issues," *Police Practice and Research* 12, no. 5 (2011): 374.

93. Farah, *Blood from Stones*, 162; Napoleoni, *Modern Jihad*, 194; and Loretta Napoleoni, "The New Economy of Terror," *OpenDemocracy*, January 26, 2005.

Chapter 9. Drugs

1. David T. Courtwright, *Forces of Habit: Drugs and the Making of the Modern World* (Cambridge, Mass.: Harvard University Press, 2001), 78.

2. Peter Andreas, *Killer High: A History of War in Six Drugs* (Oxford: Oxford University Press, 2020), 184.

3. Richard Gunderman, "A Nazi Drug's US Resurgence: How Meth Is Making a Disturbing Reappearance," *The Conversation*, February 10, 2020.

4. Andreas, *Killer High*, 182.

5. Andreas, *Killer High*, 197.

6. Michael Knodt, "Why Do German Neo-Nazis Love Crystal Meth So Much?," *Vice*, January 16, 2015.

7. Pete George Simi, "Rage in the City of Angels: The Historical Development of the Skinhead Subculture in Los Angeles" (Ph.D. diss., University of Nevada, Las Vegas, 2003), 141.

8. Knodt, "Why Do German Neo-Nazis."

9. "Kleine Anfrage 2887: der Abgeordneten König (DIE LINKE)" (Thuringian Parliament, February 13, 2013); and Thomas Trappe, "Nazis auf Entzug," *Die Zeit*, December 12, 2012.

10. Simi, "Rage in the City of Angels," 114; and Michael Miller, "Meth, Torture and the Grip of the Aryan Brotherhood," *Washington Post*, June 10, 2015.

11. Travis Linnemann, *Meth Wars: Police, Media, Power* (New York: New York University Press, 2016), 93.

12. Seth G. Jones, Catrina Doxsee, and Nicholas Harrington, "The Escalating Terrorism Problem in the United States," *CSIS Briefs*, June 2020, p. 2; and Geneva Sands, "White Supremacy Is 'Most Lethal Threat' to the US, DHS Draft Assessment Says," *CNN*, September 8, 2020.

13. Vanda Felbab-Brown, *Shooting Up: Counterinsurgency and the War on Drugs* (Washington, D.C.: Brookings Institution Press, 2010), 164; John Horgan and Max Taylor, "Playing the 'Green Card,' Part 1," *Terrorism and Political Violence* 11, no. 2 (Summer 1999): 27; and Andrew Silke, "Drink, Drugs, and Rock 'n' Roll," *Studies in Conflict and Terrorism* 23 (2000): 117.

14. Mark Steinitz, "Insurgents, Terrorists and the Drug Trade," *Washington Quarterly* 8, no. 4 (Fall 1985): 146; Luis de la Calle and Ignacio Sanchez-Cuenca, "Killing and Voting in the Basque Country," *Terrorism and Political Violence* 25, no. 1 (2013): 107; and Grant Wardlaw, "Linkages between the Illegal Drugs Traffic and Terrorism," *Conflict Quarterly* 8, no. 3 (1988): 20.

15. Paul Clare, *Racketeering in Northern Ireland: A New Version of the Patriot Game* (Chicago: University of Illinois, 1989), 48; Horgan and Taylor, "Playing the 'Green Card,' Part 1," 26; and Michael Jonsson and Svante Cornell, "Countering Terrorist Financing," *Georgetown Journal of International Affairs* 8, no. 1 (2007): 73.

16. Howard Meehan, "Terrorism, Diasporas and Permissive Threat Environments" (master's thesis, Naval Postgraduate School, 2004), 47.

17. Chris Dishman, "The Leaderless Nexus: When Crime and Terror Converge," *Studies in Conflict and Terrorism* 28, no. 3 (2005): 247; Sam Cooper, "From Colombia to Lebanon to Toronto," *Global News*, March 25, 2019; and Victor Asal, H. Brinton Milward, and Eric W. Schoon, "When Terrorists Go Bad: Analyzing Terrorist Organizations' Involvement in Drug Smuggling," *International Studies Quarterly* 59, no. 1 (March 2015): 120.

18. R. T. Naylor, *Patriots and Profiteers: Economic Warfare, Embargo Busting, and State-Sponsored Crime* (Montreal: McGill-Queen's University Press, 2008), 116.

19. Alfred McCoy, *The Politics of Heroin: CIA Complicity in the Global Drug Trade* (Chicago: Lawrence Hill, 1991), 15.

20. Channing May, *Transnational Crime and the Developing World* (Washington, D.C.: Global Financial Integrity, March 2017), 11; and Linnemann, *Meth Wars*, 15.

21. Paul Rexton Kan, *Drug Trafficking and International Security* (Lanham, Md.: Rowman and Littlefield, 2016), 50; Christopher Thompson, "Fears for Stability in West Africa as Cartels Move In," *Guardian*, March 10, 2009; Antonio L. Mazzitelli, "Transnational Organized Crime in West Africa: The Additional Challenge," *International Affairs* 83, no. 6 (2007): 1075; and Markus Schultze-Kraft, *Getting Real about an Illicit "External Stressor": Transnational Cocaine Trafficking through West Africa*, Evidence Report no. 72, Addressing and Mitigating Violence, June 2014, p. 19.

22. Michael Miklaucic and Jacqueline Brewer, eds., *Convergence: Illicit Networks and National Security in the Age of Globalization* (Washington, D.C.: National

Defense University Press, 2013), 102; see also Stewart Patrick, *Weak Links: Fragile States, Global Threats, and International Security* (Oxford: Oxford University Press, 2011), 151.

23. Wolfram Lacher, *Organized Crime and Conflict in the Sahel-Sahara Region*, Carnegie Papers, Middle East (Washington, D.C.: Carnegie Endowment, September 2012), 8; Itziar Aguirre, "Financial Self-Sufficiency Fuels Terrorist Climate," *Global Risk Insights*, February 16, 2016; and Ajith Wickramasekara, "Transnational Organized Crime and New Terrorism in Sri Lanka" (master's thesis, Naval Postgraduate School, 2017), 60.

24. Benjamin Freedman and Michael Levitt, *Contending with the PKK's Narco-Terrorism* (Washington, D.C.: Washington Institute, December 8, 2009); Valpy FitzGerald, *Global Financial Information, Compliance Incentives and Conflict Funding* (Finance and Trade Policy Research Centre, University of Oxford, 2003), 14; and Mitchel Roth and Murat Sever, "The Kurdish Workers Party as Criminal Syndicate," *Studies in Conflict and Terrorism* 30, no. 10 (2007): 908.

25. Gretchen Peters, *Seeds of Terror: The Taliban, The ISI and the New Opium Wars* (New York: St. Martin's, 2009), 10; Vera Eccarius-Kelly, "Surreptitious Lifelines: A Structural Analysis of the FARC and the PKK," *Terrorism and Political Violence* 24, no. 2 (April 1, 2012): 248; and Asal et al., "When Terrorists Go Bad," 114.

26. Matthew Levitt, "Hizbullah Narco-Terrorism: A Growing Cross-Border Threat," *IHS Defense and Risk and Security Consulting*, September 2012, 41; Russell D. Howard and Colleen Traughber, *The Nexus of Extremism and Trafficking: Scourge of the World or So Much Hype?* (MacDill Air Force Base, Fla.: JSOU Press, 2013), 23; and Jo Becker, "Beirut Bank Seen as a Hub of Hezbollah's Financing," *New York Times*, December 13, 2011.

27. Stephen Ellis, "West Africa's International Drug Trade," in *Deviant Globalization: Black Market Economy in the 21st Century*, ed. Nils Gilman, Jesse Goldhammer, and Steven Weber (New York: Continuum, 2011), 118.

28. Howard Marks, *Mr. Nice: An Autobiography* (London: Secker and Warburg, 1996), 77.

29. John Picarelli, "Osama Bin Corleone? Vito the Jackal?," *Terrorism and Political Violence* 24, no. 2 (2012): 181; Javier Jordán, Fernando M. Mañas, and Nicola Horsburgh, "Strengths and Weaknesses of Grassroot Jihadist Networks," *Studies in Conflict and Terrorism* 31, no. 1 (January 2008): 30; and Joshua Alexander Geltzer, "Taking Hand-Outs or Going It Alone: Nationalization versus Privatization in the Funding of Islamic Terrorist Groups," *Studies in Conflict and Terrorism* 34, no. 2 (January 2011): 149.

30. Adam Dolnik, *Understanding Terrorist Innovation: Technology, Tactics and Global Trends* (London: Routledge, 2007), 74; and R. T. Naylor, *Economic Warfare:*

Sanctions, Embargo Busting, and Their Human Cost (Boston: Northeastern University Press, 1999), 63.

31. Anthony Spaeth, "Kim's Rackets," *Time*, June 9, 2003.

32. Bruce E. Bechtol Jr., "North Korean Illicit Activities and Sanctions: A National Security Dilemma," *Cornell International Law Journal* 51 (2018): 74; and Sheena Chestnut, "Illicit Activity and Proliferation: North Korean Smuggling Networks," *International Security* 32, no. 1 (Summer 2007): 87.

33. FitzGerald, *Global Financial Information*, 14.

34. Nick Reding, "The Inland Empire," in *Deviant Globalization: Black Market Economy in the 21st Century*, ed. Nils Gilman, Jesse Goldhammer, and Steven Weber (New York: Continuum, 2011), 144; "U.S. Drug Ring Tied to Aid for Hezbollah," *New York Times*, September 3, 2002; and Patrick Keefe, "How a Mexican Drug Cartel Makes Its Billions," *New York Times*, June 15, 2012.

35. Sulome Anderson, "These Are the People Making Captagon," *New York Magazine*, December 9, 2015; see also Andreas, *Killer High*, 203; and Jack Guy, Stephanie Halasz, Valentina DiDonato, and Gul Tuysuz, "Italian Police Seize over $1 Billion of 'ISIS-Made' 'Captagon' Amphetamines," *CNN*, July 1, 2020.

36. Dave Allen, Will Cafferky, Abdallah Hendawy, Jorache Horn, Karolina MacLachlan, Stefanie Nijssen, and Eleonore Vidal de la Blache, *The Big Spin: Corruption and the Growth of Violent Extremism* (London: Transparency International, February 2017), 23; Matt Herbert, "Partisans, Profiteers, and Criminals: Syria's Illicit Economy," *Fletcher Forum of World Affairs* 38, no. 1 (Winter 2014): 74; Anna-Lotta Aijala, "How Is ISIS Funded?" (Tallinn University of Technology, 2016), 23; and Boaz Ganor and Miri Wernli, "The Infiltration of Terrorist Organizations into the Pharmaceutical Industry," *Studies in Conflict and Terrorism* 36, no. 9 (September 1, 2013): 708.

37. Anderson, "These Are the People"; Courtwright, *Forces of Habit*, 15; Aijala, "How Is ISIS Funded?," 22.

38. Chavala Madlena and Radwan Mortada, "Syria's Speed Freaks, Jihad Junkies, and Captagon Cartels," *Foreign Policy*, November 19, 2015; Andrew Shepherd, "Getting High on Terrorism: Hezbollah's Drug Deal with ISIS," *The Intelligencer*, October 7, 2016; and Robert Bunker, ed., *Blood Sacrifices: Violent Non-State Actors and Dark Magico-Religious* (Bloomington, Ind.: iUniverse, 2016), 31.

39. Andrew Adams, "Money Laundering and TNOC" (lecture, Marshall Center, July 2019).

40. June Beittel, *Mexico: Organized Crime and Drug Trafficking Organizations* (Washington, D.C.: Congressional Research Service, 2019), 17; Sari Horwitz and Scott Higham, "The Flow of Fentanyl: In the Mail, Over the Border," *Washington*

Post, August 23, 2019; and Heidi Munro and Ron Granieri, "A Fatal Dose in 2 Milligrams," *War Room,* November 3, 2020.

41. Munro and Granieri, "A Fatal Dose."
42. Michael Odenwald, Harald Hinkel, Elisabeth Schauer, Frank Neuner, Maggie Schauer, Thomas R. Elbert, and Brigitte Rockstroh, "The Consumption of Khat and Other Drugs in Somali Combatants: A Cross-Sectional Study," *PLOS Medicine* 4, no. 12 (December 11, 2007): e341; Peter Gastrow, *Termites at Work: A Report on Transnational Organized Crime and State Erosion in Kenya; Comprehensive Research Findings* (New York: International Peace Institute, 2011), 35; and Courtwright, *Forces of Habit,* 55.
43. Timothy Wittig, *Understanding Terrorist Finance* (New York: Palgrave MacMillan, 2011), 120; Odenwald et al., "The Consumption of Khat"; Roland Marchal, *The Rise of a Jihadi Movement in a Country at War* (Paris: CNRS SciencesPo, March 2011), 68; and Bunker, *Blood Sacrifices,* 43.
44. Steinitz, "Insurgents," 143; Patrick Keefe, "The Trafficker," *New Yorker,* February 8, 2010; and Michael Pollan, *The Botany of Desire: A Plant's-Eye View of the World* (New York: Random House, 2001), 172.
45. Pollan, *The Botany of Desire,* 133.
46. Lacher, *Organized Crime,* 7; Zachary Abuza, "Funding Terrorism in Southeast Asia: The Financial Network of Al Qaeda and Jemaah Islamiya," *Contemporary Southeast Asia* 25, no. 2 (August 2003): 190; and Colin Clarke, "ISIS Is So Desperate It's Turning to the Drug Trade," *RAND Blog,* July 25, 2017.
47. Columbian Editorial Board, "Cannabis Industry Should Have Access to Banks," *Columbian,* May 28, 2019; Ephrat Livni, "Marijuana Money May Push California into Public Banking," *Quartz,* August 25, 2017; Yuki Noguchi, "Bags of Cash, Armed Guards and Wary Banks," *NPR,* April 10, 2019; and Kara Thorvaldsen, "RICO Suits against Cannabis Companies and Co-Conspirators," *National Law Review,* November 13, 2018.
48. "Cleaning Up Dirty Money," *Economist,* July 26, 1997, 13; Simon Mackenzie, "Illicit Deals in Cultural Objects as Crimes of the Powerful," *Crime, Law and Social Change* 56 (2011): 139; and Sylvia Longmire, "Legalizing Marijuana Won't Kill the Mexican Drug Cartels," *New York Times,* June 18, 2011.
49. This section's heading is a line from Bayard Taylor, "The Poet in the East," in *The Poems of Bayard Taylor* (New York: Thomas Crowell, 1907), 84.
50. Naylor, *Patriots and Profiteers,* 117; Peters, *Seeds of Terror,* 30; Christian Parenti, *Tropic of Chaos: Climate Change and the New Geography of Violence* (New York: Nation Books, 2011), 109.
51. Courtwright, *Forces of Habit,* 32.
52. Andreas, *Killer High,* 164; and McCoy, *The Politics of Heroin,* 123.

53. Felbab-Brown, *Shooting Up*, 114; and McCoy, *The Politics of Heroin*, 125.
54. Sam Dealey, "At War in the Fields of the Drug Lords," *GQ*, December 14, 2006; McCoy, *The Politics of Heroin*, 21; and Edward Zwick, dir., *Jack Reacher: Never Go Back* (Los Angeles: Paramount Pictures, 2016).
55. Fuat Salih Sahin, "Case Studies in Terrorism-Drug Connection: The Kurdistan Workers' Party, the Liberation Tigers of Tamil Eelam, and the Shining Path" (master's thesis, University of North Texas, 2001), 45; Jonathan Goodhand, "Frontiers and Wars: The Opium Economy in Afghanistan," *Journal of Agrarian Change* 5, no. 2 (April 2005): 201; McCoy, *The Politics of Heroin*, 21.
56. McCoy, *The Politics of Heroin*, 129; see also Andreas, *Killer High*, 165; Loretta Napoleoni, *Modern Jihad: Tracing the Dollars behind the Terror Networks* (London: Pluto Press, 2003), 12.
57. Ivelaw Griffith, "From Cold War Geopolitics to Post-Cold War Geonarcotics," *International Journal* 49, no. 1 (1993): 6; Svante E. Cornell, "The Interaction of Narcotics and Conflict," *Journal of Peace Research* 42, no. 6 (2005): 756; and Naylor, *Economic Warfare*, 386.
58. Wickramasekara, "Transnational Organized Crime," 55; and Mackenzie Institute, "Funding Terror: The Liberation Tigers of Tamil Eelam and Their Criminal Activities in Canada and the Western World," *Mackenzie Institute*, December 26, 1995.
59. Sahin, "Case Studies," 64; Rohan Gunaratna, "Bankrupting the Terror Business," *Jane's Intelligence Review* 12, no. 8 (August 2000): 55; and Colin Clarke, "Drugs and Thugs: Funding Terrorism through Narcotics Trafficking," *Journal of Strategic Security* 9, no. 3 (September 2016): 7.
60. Charles Wallace II, "Airpower against 'Irregular' Adversaries: How Terrorist Insurgent, and Guerrilla Forces Have Attempted to Negate Airstrikes" (thesis, Maxwell Air Force Base, Ala.: School of Advanced Air and Space Studies, 2006), 21; James Cockayne and Adam Lupel, eds., *Peace Operations and Organized Crime: Enemies or Allies?* (London: Routledge, 2011), 140; and Felbab-Brown, *Shooting Up*, 115.
61. McCoy, *The Politics of Heroin*, 436.
62. Ahmed Rashid, *Taliban: Islam, Oil and the New Great Game in Central Asia* (London: I. B. Taurus, 2009), 121; Felbab-Brown, *Shooting Up*, 119; and Peters, *Seeds of Terror*, 37.
63. Peters, *Seeds of Terror*, 45; Matt Potter, *Outlaws, Inc.* (New York: Bloomsbury, 2011), 45; and Naylor, *Patriots and Profiteers*, 73.
64. Kan, *Drug Trafficking*, 30; Naylor, *Patriots and Profiteers*, 89; and Potter, *Outlaws, Inc.*, 149.
65. Rashid Nugmanov, dir., *Igla* (Almaty, Kazakhstan: Kazakhfilm Studios, 1988).

66. Andreas, *Killer High*, 223.

67. Peters, *Seeds of Terror*, 89.

68. Felbab-Brown, *Shooting Up*, 126.

69. Felbab-Brown, *Shooting Up*, 131; and Andrew Mumford, "Intelligence Wars," *Civil Wars* 7, no. 4 (Winter 2005): 390.

70. Raphael F. Perl, "Taliban and the Drug Trade," *CRS Report for Congress*, October 5, 2001, p. 2; David Kilcullen, *The Accidental Guerrilla: Fighting Small Wars in the Midst of a Big One* (Oxford: Oxford University Press, 2009), 59; David L. DeAtley, "Illicit Drug Funding: The Surprising Systemic Similarities between the FARC and the Taliban" (Fort Leavenworth, Kan.: School of Advanced Military Studies, 2010), 44; and Dealey, "At War."

71. Felbab-Brown, *Shooting Up*, 131.

72. John Robb, "Brave New War: The Next Stage of Terrorism and the End of Globalization," in *Deviant Globalization: Black Market Economy in the 21st Century*, ed. Nils Gilman, Jesse Goldhammer, and Steven Weber (New York: Continuum, 2011), 263; and Cockayne and Lupel, *Peace Operations*, 140.

73. Wallace, "Airpower against 'Irregular' Adversaries," 83; and Peters, *Seeds of Terror*, 3.

74. Cockayne and Lupel, *Peace Operations*, 138; John Robb, *Brave New War: The Next Stage of Terrorism and the End of Globalization* (Hoboken, N.J.: Wiley, 2007), 144; Clarke, "Drugs and Thugs," 9; and Felbab-Brown, *Shooting Up*, 1.

75. Austin Long, "Whack-a-Mole or Coup de Grace? Institutionalization and Leadership Targeting in Iraq and Afghanistan," *Security Studies* 23, no. 3 (2014): 502; and Peters, *Seeds of Terror*, 125.

76. Geltzer, "Taking Hand-Outs," 160; DeAtley, "Illicit Drug Funding," 46; FATF, *Emerging Terrorist Financing Risks* (Paris: FATF, October 2015), 18; and Mary Beth Goodman and Trevor Sutton, "To Stem the Flow of Illicit Drugs from Afghanistan, Follow the Money," *Center for American Progress*, March 17, 2015.

77. Felbab-Brown, *Shooting Up*, 120; Mohammed Ehsan Zia, "Lessons Learned Interview," *Washington Post*, April 12, 2016, available on YouTube, https://www.youtube.com/watch?v=MLkwjn5Y870, 1; and Goodhand, "Frontiers and Wars," 201.

78. Zia, "Lessons Learned Interview," 2.

79. Chester G. Oehme III, "Terrorists, Insurgents, and Criminals—Growing Nexus?," *Studies in Conflict and Terrorism* 31, no. 1 (January 2008): 89; and Peters, *Seeds of Terror*, 189.

80. Felbab-Brown, *Shooting Up*, 142.

81. John Wood, "Lessons Learned Interview," *Washington Post*, June 17, 2015, 1; and Doug Wankel, "Lessons Learned Interview," *Washington Post*, April 19, 2016, 2.

82. James B. Love, *Hezbollah: Social Services as a Source of Power* (Hurlburt Field, Fla.: JSOU Press, 2010), 36; DoD, "Commanders' Emergency Response Program," in *Financial Management Regulation* (DoD7000.14-R), vol. 12, *Special Accounts, Funds and Programs* (Washington, D.C.: Department of Defense, December 2019); Tim Graczewski, "Lessons Learned Interview," *Washington Post*, January 11, 2015, 1; and Tooryalai Wesa, "Lessons Learned Interview," *Washington Post*, January 7, 2017, 3.

83. Courtwright, *Forces of Habit*, 32; Goodhand, "Frontiers and War," 207; and Sarah Chayes, *Thieves of State: Why Corruptions Threatens Global Security* (New York: Norton, 2015), 65.

84. Peters, *Seeds of Terror*, 2; see also Martin Strmecki, "Lessons Learned Interview," *Washington Post*, October 19, 2015, 18; Miklaucic and Brewer, *Convergence*, 194; and Cynthia Arnson and I. William Zartman, eds., *Rethinking the Economics of War: The Intersection of Need, Creed, and Greed* (Baltimore: Johns Hopkins University Press, 2005), 229.

85. Thomas Sanderson, "Transnational Terror and Organized Crime: Blurring the Lines," *SAIS Review of International Affairs* 24, no. 1 (Winter–Spring 2004): 58; see also Heiko Nitzschke and Kaysie Studdard, "The Legacies of War Economies: Challenges and Options for Peacemaking and Peacebuilding," *International Peacekeeping* 12, no. 2 (2005): 227; and Parenti, *Tropic of Chaos*, 109.

86. Goodman and Sutton, "To Stem the Flow"; Peters, *Seeds of Terror*, 186; and Chayes, *Thieves of State*, 64.

87. Michaela Martin and Hussein Solomon, "Islamic State: Understanding the Nature of the Beast and Its Funding," *Contemporary Review of the Middle East* 4, no. 1 (2017): 38; and Jeffrey Boutwell and Michael Klare, eds., *Light Weapons and Civil Conflict: Controlling the Tools of Violence* (Lanham, Md.: Rowman and Littlefield, 1999), 52.

88. Courtwright, *Forces of Habit*, 46; Richard Craig, "Illicit Drug Traffic and U.S.-Latin American Relations," *Washington Quarterly* 8, no. 4 (Fall 1985): 105; and *War and Drugs in Colombia*, Report 11 (Brussels: International Crisis Group, January 27, 2005), 3.

89. Courtwright, *Forces of Habit*, 51; and Kan, *Drug Trafficking*, 23.

90. *War and Drugs*, 3; Craig, "Illicit Drug Traffic," 106; and May, *Transnational Crime*, 87.

91. Courtwright, *Forces of Habit*, 61.

92. Wardlaw, "Linkages," 17; Hazel Smith and Paul B. Stares, eds., *Diasporas in Conflict: Peace-Makers or Peace-Wreckers?* (New York: United Nations University Press, 2007), 133; Felbab-Brown, *Shooting Up*, 73; and Jeffrey Robinson, *The Laundrymen: Inside Money Laundering, the World's Third Largest Business* (New York: Arcade, 1996), 224.

93. Stergios Skaperdas, "The Political Economy of Organized Crime: Providing Protections When the State Does Not," *Economics of Governance* 2 (2001): 178; and Horace A. Bartilow and Kihong Eom, "Busting Drugs While Paying with Crime: The Collateral Damage of U.S. Drug Enforcement in Foreign Countries," *Foreign Policy Analysis* 5 (2009): 97.

94. Naylor, *Patriots and Profiteers*, 205; R. T. Naylor, *Wages of Crime: Black Markets, Illegal Finance, and the Underworld Economy* (Ithaca, N.Y.: Cornell University Press, 2004), 75; Andreas, *Killer High*, 161; and Steinitz, "Insurgents," 143.

95. Michael Kenney, "Drug Traffickers, Terrorist Networks and Ill-Fated Government Strategies," in *New Threats and New Actors in International Security*, ed. Elke Krahmann (New York: Palgrave-McMillan, 2005), 71; Sanderson, "Transnational Terror," 56; Margaret Crahan and Alberto Vourvoulias-Bush, eds., *The City and the World: New York's Global Future* (New York: Council on Foreign Relations, 1997), 77; and Bartilow and Eom, "Busting Drugs," 97.

96. Shaylih Muehlmann, *When I Wear My Alligator Boots: Narco-Culture in the U.S.-Mexico Borderlands* (Berkeley: University of California Press, 2014), 11; Beittel, *Mexico*, 15; and Keefe, "How a Mexican Drug Cartel."

97. Keefe, "How a Mexican Drug Cartel"; see also Lisa Campbell, "Los Zetas: An Operational Assessment," *Small Wars and Insurgencies* 21, no. 1 (2010): 73; Peter McCabe and William Mendel, eds., *SOF Role in Combating Transnational Organized Crime* (MacDill Air Force Base, Fla.: JSOU Press, 2016), 30; and Michael Kenney, "From Pablo to Osama: Counter-Terrorism Lessons from the War on Drugs," *Survival* 45, no. 3 (Autumn 2003): 191.

98. Graham Turbiville, "Firefights, Raids, and Assassinations: Tactical Forms of Cartel Violence and Their Underpinnings," *Small Wars and Insurgencies* 21, no. 1 (2010): 124; see also Molly Molloy, "The Mexican Undead: Toward a New History of the 'Drug War' Killing Fields," *Small Wars Journal*, August 21, 2013; Kan, *Drug Trafficking*, 86; and Griffith, "From Cold War Geopolitics," 20.

99. Morten Boas, "Guns, Money and Prayers: AQIM's Blueprint for Securing Control of Northern Mali," *CTC Sentinel* 7, no. 4 (April 2014): 2; Nitsana Darshan-Leitner and Samuel Katz, *Harpoon: Inside the Covert War against Terrorism's Money Masters* (New York: Hachette, 2017), 202; and Lacher, *Organized Crime*, 6.

100. Celina B. Realuyo, "The Terror–Crime Nexus: Hezbollah's Global Facilitators," *Prism* 5, no. 1 (2014): 124.

101. Molly Dunigan, Dick Hoffmann, Peter Chalk, Brian Nichiporuk, and Paul deLuca, *Characterizing and Exploring the Implications of Maritime Irregular Warfare* (Santa Monica, Calif.: RAND, 2012), 72; Keefe, "How a Mexican Cartel"; Skaperdas, "The Political Economy," 181; and "How Russian Mafia Captured America," *ForumDaily*, July 2, 2018.

102. Miklaucic and Brewer, *Convergence*, 67; Peter Andreas and Thomas J. Biersteker, eds., *The Rebordering of North America: Integration and Exclusion in the New Security Context* (London: Routledge, 2003), 113; and H. Richard Friman and Peter Andreas, eds., *The Illicit Global Economy and State Power* (Lanham, Md.: Rowman and Littlefield, 1999), 134.

103. Keefe, "How a Mexican Cartel."

104. Pamela L. Bunker, Lisa J. Campbell, and Robert J. Bunker, "Torture, Beheadings and Narcocultos," *Small Wars and Insurgencies* 21, no. 1 (March 2010): 149; and Howard Campbell, "Narco-Propaganda in the Mexican 'Drug War': An Anthropological Perspective," *Latin American Perspectives* 41, no. 2 (2014): 66; and Keefe, "How a Mexican Cartel."

105. Steven T. Zech and Zane M. Kelly, "Off with Their Heads: The Islamic State and Civilian Beheadings," *Journal of Terrorism Research* 6, no. 2 (May 2015); and Luke Dittrich, "Four Days on the Border," *Esquire*, July 1, 2009.

106. Doug Bandow, "Will Mexico Declare Peace in the War on Drugs, and Will Obama Let Them?," *Forbes*, July 9, 2012; Bunker et al., "Torture," 150; and Bartilow and Eom, "Busting Drugs," 99.

107. Beittel, *Mexico*, 5; Kan, *Drug Trafficking*, 177; and Friman and Andreas, *The Illicit Global Economy*, 39.

108. Diego Cevallos, "Church Uproar over Drug Traffickers' 'Good Works,'" *Inter Press Service*, April 8, 2008; Mary Beth Sheridan, "Drug Lords Buy Way into Church's Heart," *Los Angeles Times*, October 21, 1997; and Associated Press, "Bishop Provokes Uproar in Mexico," *Denver Post*, October 5, 2005.

109. Ioan Grillo, "Drug-Dealing for Jesus," *Time*, July 19, 2009; and Bunker et al., "Torture," 170.

110. Muehlmann, *When I Wear My Alligator Boots*, 171; Philip Johnson, "How to Identify a Narcotrafficker," *Matador Network*, August 17, 2011; Campbell, "Narco-Propaganda," 61; and Campbell, "Los Zetas," 73.

111. Campbell, "Narco-Propaganda," 66; and Muehlmann, *When I Wear My Alligator Boots*, 102.

112. Nils Gilman, Jesse Goldhammer, and Steven Weber, Introduction to *Deviant Globalization: Black Market Economy in the 21st Century*, ed. Nils Gilman, Jesse Goldhammer, and Steven Weber (New York: Continuum, 2011), 4; see also Friman and Andreas, *The Illicit Global Economy*, 16; and Griffith, "From Cold War Geopolitics," 24.

113. *War and Drugs*, 6; Jon-Paul Maddaloni, *An Analysis of the FARC in Colombia: Breaking the Frame of FM 3-24* (Fort Leavenworth, Kan.: School of Advanced Military Studies, 2009), 9; Karen DeYoung, "For Rebels, It's Not a Drug War," *Washington Post*, April 10, 2000; and Francisco Gutiérrez Sanín, *Criminal Rebels?*

A Discussion of War and Criminality from the Colombian Experience (London: London School of Economics and Political Science, 2003), 19.

114. Maureen Orth, "Inside Colombia's Hostage War," *Vanity Fair*, November 2008; see also Mark Moyar, H. Pagan, and Wil R. Griego, *Persistent Engagement in Colombia* (MacDill Air Field, Fla.: JSOU Press, 2014), 25; Robert Bunker, ed., *Non-State Threats and Future Wars* (New York: Routledge, 2012), 71; and Louise Richardson, ed., *The Roots of Terrorism* (New York: Routledge, 2006), 94.

115. Bilal Saab and Alexandra Taylor, "Criminality and Armed Groups," *Studies in Conflict and Terrorism* 32, no. 6 (May 28, 2009): 465; Andreas, *Killer High*, 228; and Chris Dishman, "Terrorism, Crime, and Transformation," *Studies in Conflict and Terrorism* 24, no. 1 (January 2001): 50.

116. DeAtley, "Illicit Drug Funding," 31; and Justine A. Rosenthal, "For-Profit Terrorism: The Rise of Armed Entrepreneurs," *Studies in Conflict and Terrorism* 31, no. 6 (2008): 487.

117. Rosenthal, "For-Profit Terrorism," 484; "Unfunny Money," *Economist*, April 16, 2016, 28; Román Ortiz, "Insurgent Strategies in the Post-Cold War," *Studies in Conflict and Terrorism* 25, no. 2 (2002): 131; and Maddaloni, "An Analysis of the FARC in Colombia," 26.

118. Paul Saskiewicz, "The Revolutionary Armed Forces of Colombia—People's Army (FARC-EP): Marxist-Leninist Insurgency or Criminal Enterprise" (master's thesis, Naval Postgraduate School, 2005), 66; Mimi Yagoub, "What the FARC's Elusive Finances Mean for Peace," *InSight Crime*, April 20, 2016; and Mark Kennedy, "How Much Money Does the FARC Have?," *Colombia News*, August 14, 2015.

119. Felbab-Brown, *Shooting Up*, 84; Maddaloni, "An Analysis of the FARC in Colombia," 11; and Kyle Beardsley and Brian McQuinn, "Rebel Groups as Predatory Organizations," *Journal of Conflict Resolution* 53, no. 4 (2009): 632.

120. Sanín, *Criminal Rebels?*, 14; David Petraeus and James Mattis, *Counterinsurgency*, FM3-24/FMFM 3-24 (Washington, D.C.: Headquarters, Department of the Army, June 16, 2006), 18; and Saskiewicz, "The Revolutionary Armed Forces," 36.

121. Maddaloni, "An Analysis of the FARC in Colombia," 17; Rosenthal, "For-Profit Terrorism," 492; Eccarius-Kelly, "Surreptitious Lifelines," 248; and Douglas J. Davids, *Narco-Terrorism: A Unified Strategy to Fight a Growing Terrorist Menace* (Ardsley, N.Y.: Transnational, 2002), 9.

122. Adam Isacson, "Colombia's Human Security Crisis," *Disarmament Forum*, no. 2 (2002): 31; Moyar et al., *Persistent Engagement*, 27; and Ingrid Vaicius and Adam Isacson, *The "War on Drugs" Meets the "War on Terror": The United States' Military Involvement in Colombia Climbs to the Next Level* (Washington, D.C.: Center for International Policy, February 2003), 3.

123. Orth, "Inside Colombia's Hostage War"; see also Michael Jonsson, Elliot Brennan, and Christopher O'Hara, "Financing War or Facilitating Peace? The Impact of Rebel Drug Trafficking on Peace Negotiations in Colombia and Myanmnar," *Studies in Conflict and Terrorism* 39, no. 6 (June 2, 2016): 549; and Dunigan et al., *Characterizing and Exploring*, 71.

124. Moyar et al., *Persistent Engagement*, 50.

125. Douglas Farah and Stephen Braun, *Merchant of Death: Money, Guns, Planes, and the Man Who Makes War Possible* (Hoboken, N.J.: Wiley, 2007), 160; Saab and Taylor, "Criminality and Armed Groups," 461; and Bruce Zagaris, "The Merging of the Anti-Money Laundering and Counter-Terrorism Financial Enforcement Regimes after September 11, 2001," *Berkeley Journal of International Law* 22, no. 1 (2004): 155.

126. *War and Drugs*, 21.

127. Linnemann, *Meth Wars*, 191; Vaicius and Isacson, *The "War on Drugs" Meets the "War on Terror,"* 3; and Isacson, "Colombia's Human Security Crisis," 29.

128. DeYoung, "For Rebels"; Felbab-Brown, *Shooting Up*, 85; and Moyar et al., *Persistent Engagement*, 47.

129. Celina B. Realuyo, *"Following the Money Trail" to Combat Terrorism, Crime, and Corruption in the Americas* (Washington, D.C.: Wilson Center, August 2017), 17; "Unfunny Money"; and Richardson, *The Roots of Terrorism*, 95.

130. Andreas, *Killer High*, 248; Yagoub, "What the FARC's Elusive Finances"; and Mimi Yagoub, "'First' Seizure of FARC's Illegal Mining Assets Could Worsen Dissidence," *InSight Crime*, October 26, 2016.

131. Arnson and Zartman, *Rethinking the Economics*, 57; see also Napoleoni, *Modern Jihad*, 25; and Daniel Fitz-Simons, "Sendero Luminoso," *Parameters* 33, no. 2 (Summer 1993): 64.

132. Sahin, "Case Studies in Terrorism–Drug Connection," 76; and Felbab-Brown, *Shooting*, 41.

133. Davids, *Narco-Terrorism*, 21; Fitz-Simons, "Sendero Luminoso," 65; and Svante Cornell, "Narcotics and Armed Conflict," *Studies in Conflict and Terrorism* 30, no. 3 (April 2007): 221.

134. Felbab-Brown, *Shooting Up*, 46; see also Napoleoni, *Modern Jihad*, 25; and Arnson and Zartman, *Rethinking the Economics of War*, 71.

135. Mary Kaldor, *New and Old Wars: Organized Violence in a Global Era* (Stanford, Calif.: Stanford University Press, 2012), 112; David Palmer, "Peru, the Drug Business and Shining Path," *Journal of Interamerican Studies and World Affairs* 34, no. 3 (Autumn 1992): 71; and Arnson and Zartman, *Rethinking the Economics*, 72.

136. Ortiz, "Insurgent Strategies," 128; Shawn Flanagan, "Charity as Resistance: Connections between Charity, Contentious Politics, and Terror," *Studies in Conflict and Terrorism* 29, no. 7 (2006): 646; Palmer, "Peru, the Drug Business

and Shining Path," 77; and Arnson and Zartman, *Rethinking the Economics of War*, 77.

137. Griffith, "From Cold War Geopolitics," 28; Davids, *Narco-Terrorism*, 92; and Robinson, *The Laundrymen*, 218.

138. Felbab-Brown, *Shooting Up*, 39; and Mariano Castillo, "Chocolate Replaces Cocaine in Some Areas of Peru," *CNN*, February 10, 2010.

139. *War and Drugs*, 24; "Burn-Out and Battle Fatigue," *Economist*, March 17, 2012, 43; and Elizabeth Dickinson, "Legalizing Drugs Won't Stop Mexico's Brutal Cartels," *Foreign Policy*, June 22, 2011.

140. Kan, *Drug Trafficking*, 36; Felbab-Brown, *Shooting Up*, 17; and Peters, *Seeds of Terror*, 11.

141. Kan, *Drug Trafficking*, 26; Davids, *Narco-Terrorism*, 61; and Andreas, *Killer High*, 239.

142. Peter Andreas and Richard Price, "From War Fighting to Crime Fighting," *International Studies Review* 3, no. 3 (2001): 43; and Gregory Gatjanis, "Evolution of a National CTOC Strategy" (lecture, Marshall Center, July 16, 2019).

Chapter 10. Art and Antiquities

1. Roberta Mazzo, "Biblical History at What Cost?," *Biblical Archaeology Society*, July 24, 2017; and Alan Feuer, "Hobby Lobby Agrees to Forfeit 5,500 Artifacts," *New York Times*, July 5, 2017.

2. Noah Charney, "Museum of the Bible Is Busted," *Salon*, July 9, 2017.

3. Jason Felch, "Hobby Lobby's Legal Expert Speaks," *Chasing Aphrodite*, July 10, 2017.

4. Felch, "Hobby Lobby's Legal Expert Speaks."

5. Felch, "Hobby Lobby's Legal Expert Speaks"; see also Alex Capon, "U.S. Retailer Fined after Seizure of Illegally Imported Cultural Property," *Antiques Trade Gazette*, July 10, 2017; and U.S. Attorney's Office, "United States Files Civil Action to Forfeit Thousands of Ancient Iraqi Artifacts Imported by Hobby Lobby," July 5, 2017.

6. Isra Saghir, "Stealing, Smuggling, and Selling," *Society: Sociology and Criminology Review* 3 (2018): 35; U.S. Attorney's Office, "United States Files Civil Action"; and Charney, "Museum."

7. Tina Nguyen, "Did Hobby Lobby's C.E.O. Unknowingly Sponsor Terrorism?," *Vanity Fair*, October 29, 2015; see also Callaghan Todhunter, "Exhibiting Power: Proto-Museological Origins in the Empires of Antiquity" (honors thesis, University of Iowa, 2019), 9.

8. Michael Greshko, "'Dead Sea Scrolls' at the Museum of the Bible Are All Forgeries," *National Geographic*, March 13, 2020.

9. Katie Shepherd, "An Oxford Professor Allegedly Stole Ancient Bible Fragments and Sold Them to Hobby Lobby," *Washington Post*, October 15, 2019.

10. Caroline Goldstein, "The Museum of the Bible Must Once Again Return Artifacts," *Artnet News*, January 29, 2021.

11. Todhunter, "Exhibiting Power," 6; and Wayne Sandholtz, *Prohibiting Plunder: How Norms Change* (New York: Oxford University Press, 2007), 33.

12. Laurie Rush, ed., *Archaeology, Cultural Property and the Military* (Woodbridge, U.K.: Boydell, 2010), 4; and Mackenzie Warner, "The Last Poor Plunder from a Bleeding Land: The Failure of International Law to Protect Syrian Antiquities," *Brooklyn Journal of International Law* 42 (2016): 488.

13. Sandholtz, *Prohibiting Plunder*, 34.

14. Sandholtz, *Prohibiting Plunder*, 1; see also Noah Charney, ed., *Art and Crime: Exploring the Dark Side of the Art World* (Santa Barbara, Calif.: ABC-CLIO, 2009), 207.

15. Sandholtz, *Prohibiting Plunder*, 51.

16. Diana Panke and Ulrich Petersohn, "Norm Challenges and Norm Death: The Inexplicable?," *Cooperation and Conflict* 51, no. 1 (2016): 8; and Sandholtz, *Prohibiting Plunder*, 70.

17. Sandholtz, *Prohibiting Plunder*, 89; and Rush, ed., *Archaeology, Cultural Property*, 6.

18. Lauren Bearden, "Complex Destruction: Near Eastern Antiquities and the ISIS Spectacle" (master's thesis, Georgia State University, 2016), 13.

19. Hannah G. He, "Protecting Ancient Heritage in Armed Conflict: New Rules for Targeting Cultural Property during Conflict with ISIS," *Maryland Journal of International Law* 30 (2015): 170; Erik Nemeth, "Cultural Security: The Evolving Role of Art in International Security," *Terrorism and Political Violence* 19, no. 1 (2007): 24; and Tess Davis, "From Babylon to Baghdad: Cultural Heritage and Constitutional Law in the Republic of Iraq," *International Journal of Cultural Property* 21, no. 4 (November 2014): 454.

20. France Desmarais, ed., *Countering Illicit Traffic in Cultural Goods: The Global Challenge of Protecting the World's Heritage* (Paris: ICOM, 2015), 24; R. T. Naylor, *Patriots and Profiteers: Economic Warfare, Embargo Busting, and State-Sponsored Crime* (Montreal: McGill-Queen's University Press, 2008), 82; and Paul R. Williams and Christin Coster, "Blood Antiquities: Addressing a Culture of Impunity in the Antiquities Market," *Case Western Reserve Journal of International Law* 49, no. 1 (2017): 107.

21. Rush, *Archaeology, Cultural Property*, 29; Nemeth, "Conflict Security," 306; and Jennifer Anglim Kreder, "Guarding the Historical Record from the Nazi-Era Art Litigation Tumbling toward the Supreme Court," *University of Pennsylvania Law Review* 159 (2011): 257.

22. He, "Protecting Ancient Heritage," 178; Rush, *Archaeology, Cultural Property*, 28; and Sandholtz, *Prohibiting Plunder*, 185.

23. Michael Murali, "Black Beauty," *American University Criminal Law Brief* 7, no. 2 (2012): 55; Margaret M. Bruchac and Michael F. Brown, "NAGPRA from the Middle Distance: Legal Puzzles and Unintended Consequences," in *Imperialism, Art and Restitution*, ed. John Henry Merryman (Cambridge: Cambridge University Press, 2006), 193; Patty Gerstenblith, "The Destruction of Cultural Heritage: A Crime against Property or a Crime against People?," *John Marshall Review of Intellectual Property Law* 15 (2016): 369; and Samuel Andrew Hardy, "Is Looting-to-Order 'Just a Myth'? Open-Source Analysis of Theft-to-Order of Cultural Property," *Cogent Social Sciences* 1 (2015): 14.

24. Sandholtz, *Prohibiting Plunder*, 206; Charney, *Art and Crime*, 218; and Kaitlyn Armendariz, "Culturalcide: The Systematic Destruction and Rewriting of World History at the Hands of ISIS" (master's thesis, University of Arizona, 2017), 17.

25. Ömür Harmanşah, "ISIS, Heritage, and the Spectacles of Destruction in the Global Media," *Near Eastern Archaeology* 78, no. 3 (2015): 170; see also Katrina Bunyard, "ISIL and the Illegal Antiquities Trade" (honors thesis, University of Arizona, 2016), 9; and W. Andrew Terrill, *Antiquities Destruction and Illicit Sales as Sources of ISIS Funding and Propaganda* (Carlisle, Pa.: Strategic Studies Institute, 2017), 8.

26. Laurie Rush, "Cultural Property Protection as a Force Multiplier," *Military Review*, April 2012, 38; Noah Charney, "Saving Artifacts from Terrorists," *Journal of Art Crime* 15 (Spring 2016): 66; Matthew McGinnis, "Why Is ISIS Destroying Humanity's Heritage?," *Spectrum* 5, no. 1 (2015): 100; and Don Melvin, Ralph Ellis, and Salma Abdelaziz, "ISIS Executes Antiquities Prof Khaled Al-As'ad in Palmyra," *CNN*, August 20, 2015.

27. Heidi James Fisher, "Violence against Architecture: The Lost Cultural Heritage of Syria and Iraq" (master's thesis, CUNY, 2017), 7; Rim Lababidi and Hiba Qassar, "Did They Really Forget How to Do It? Iraq, Syria, and the International Response to Protect a Shared Heritage," *Journal of Eastern Mediterranean Archaeology and Heritage Studies* 4, no. 4 (2016): 341; and Rush, "Cultural Property," 36.

28. Lababidi and Qassar, "Did They Really Forget," 351; and Rush, *Archaeology, Cultural Property*, 36.

29. Nicole E. Dean, *Curse of the Mummy Snatchers: Protection of Cultural Property and the Prevention of Art and Artifact Looting in Conflict* (Ft. Leavenworth, Kan.: U.S. Army Command and General Staff College, 2017), 56; Benjamin Isakhan, "Heritage Under Fire: Lessons from Iraq for Cultural Property Protection," in *A Companion to Heritage Studies*, ed. William Stewart Logan, Máiréad Nic Craith, and Ullrich Kockel (Hoboken, N.J.: Wiley, 2015), 273; and Rush, *Archaeology, Cultural Property*, 37.

30. Bearden, "Complex Destruction," 25; David Grantham, "Antiquities and Conflict: Changing Military Strategy," *Norwich Review of International and Transnational Crime* 1, no. 2 (2016): 29; and Giorgio Buccellati and Marilyn Kelly-Buccallati, "Before the Flood: Systemic Prevention of Damage and Looting at Archaeological Sites; The Case of Tell Mozan" (lecture, Association for Research into Crimes against Art, Amelia, Italy, June 25, 2016).

31. Alessandro Chechi, "Rescuing Cultural Heritage from War and Terrorism: A View from Switzerland," *Santander Art and Culture Law Review* 2, no. 1 (2015): 93.

32. Maev Kennedy, "Kill Looters, Urges Archaeologist," *Guardian*, July 9, 2003.

33. Simon Mackenzie and Donna Yates, "What Is Grey about the 'Grey Market' in Antiquities," in *The Architecture of Illegal Markets: Towards an Economic Sociology of Illegality in the Economy*, ed. Jens Beckert and Matias Dewey (Oxford: Oxford University Press, 2017), 74; and Neil Brodie, "Protection Not Prevention: The Failure of Public Policy to Prevent the Plunder and Traffic of Cultural Property from the MENA Region (1990–2015)" (Oxford: School of Archaeology, 2017), 2.

34. Philipp Jedicke, "Germany Attracts Trade in Looted Artifacts," *Deutsche Welle*, October 24, 2014; and Lene Mariann Rødal, "Fear and Looting in Peru," *Nicolay Arkeologisk Tidsskrift*, January 1, 2017, 9.

35. McGinnis, "Why Is ISIS Destroying," 101; and Marc Balcells Magrans, "Contemporary Archaeological Looting: A Criminological Analysis of Italian Tomb Robbers" (Ph.D. diss., City University of New York, 2018), 25; and Charney, "Saving Artifacts from Terrorists," 64.

36. Rush, *Archaeology, Cultural Property*, 169; and Mackenzie and Yates, "What Is Grey," 75.

37. Laurie Rush and Luisa Millington, *The Carabinieri Command for the Protection of Cultural Property* (Woodbridge, U.K.: Boydell, 2015), 166; Mackenzie and Yates, "What Is Grey," 73; and Hamid Richard Beau Rahim, "Blood Antiquities: Cultural Property and the Political Economy of Armed Conflict" (master's thesis, Kings College London, 2015), 30.

38. Derek Fincham, "Social Norms and Illicit Cultural Heritage," in *Enforcing International Cultural Heritage Law*, ed. Francesco Francioni and James Gordley (Oxford: Oxford University Press, 2013), 223; and Russell D. Howard, Marc D. Elliott, and Jonathan R. Prohov, *IS and Cultural Genocide: Antiquities Trafficking in the Terrorist State* (MacDill Air Force Base, Fla.: JSOU Press, 2016), 18.

39. Cornelius Holtorf, "Can Less Be More? Heritage in the Age of Terrorism," *Public Archaeology* 5, no. 2 (2006): 106.

40. Blythe Alison Bowman Balestrieri, "Field Archaeologists as Eyewitnesses to Site Looting," *Arts* 7, no. 3 (2018): 52; and Kimberly Alderman, "Honor amongst

Thieves: Organized Crime and the Illicit Antiquities Trade," *Indiana Law Review* 45, no. 3 (2012): 607.

41. Paul M. Bator, "An Essay on the International Trade in Art," *Stanford Law Review* 34, no. 2 (1982): 318.

42. George Abungu, "Illicit Trafficking and Destruction of Cultural Property in Africa," *Journal of Art Crime* 15 (Spring 2016): 38.

43. Blythe A. Bowman, "Transnational Crimes against Culture: Looting at Archaeological Sites and the 'Grey' Market in Antiquities," *Journal of Contemporary Criminal Justice* 24, no. 3 (August 2008): 231; and Alderman, "Honor amongst Thieves," 614.

44. Jennifer Kreder, "The Revolution in U.S. Museums Concerning the Ethics of Acquiring Antiquities," *University of Miami Law Review* 64 (2010): 1007; Bowman, "Transnational Crimes," 230; and Noah Charney, "How the Sale of Stolen Antiquities Funds Organized Crime," *CNN Style*, July 13, 2018.

45. Samuel Hardy, "Using Open-Source Data to Identify Participation in the Illicit Antiquities Trade," *European Journal of Criminal Policy Research* 20 (2014): 472; see also Balestrieri, "Field Archaeologists," 52.

46. Tom Mashberg, "Khmer-Art Collector Linked to Statue," *New York Times*, December 12, 2012; see also Heather Pringle, "New Evidence Ties Illegal Antiquities Trade to Terrorism, Violent Crime," *National Geographic*, June 13, 2014; and Gerstenblith, "The Destruction of Cultural Heritage," 377.

47. Tess Davis, "Douglas Latchford: The Man Who Pillaged Cambodia," *Diplomat*, August 21, 2020; Tom Mashberg, "With a Gift of Art, a Daughter Honors, If Not Absolves, Her Father," *New York Times*, January 29, 2021; "Antiquities Dealer Charged with Trafficking in Looted Cambodian Artifacts" (press release, Department of Justice, November 27, 2019); and Antonius Tijhuis, *Transnational Crime and the Interface between Legal and Illegal Actors* (Nijmegen: Wolf Legal, 2006), 136.

48. Barbie Nadeau, "Italian Mob Trades Weapons for Looted Art from ISIS in Libya," *Daily Beast*, April 13, 2017; and Desmarais, *Countering Illicit Traffic*, 48.

49. Williams and Coster, "Blood Antiquities," 109; and Abungu, "Illicit Trafficking," 34.

50. Charles Hill, "A Euro Border Guard and Hybrid Warfare," *Connections* 15, no. 4 (2016): 111.

51. Terrill, *Antiquities Destruction*, 4; Rahim, "Blood Antiquities," 51; and Salon Staff, "Robbing the Cradle of Civilization, Five Years Later," *Salon*, March 20, 2008.

52. Raymond William Baker, Shereen T. Ismael, and Tareq Yousif Ismael, eds., *Cultural Cleansing in Iraq: Why Museums Were Looted, Libraries Burned and Academics Murdered* (London: Pluto, 2010), 26; Andrew McCalister, "Organized

Crime and the Theft of Iraqi Antiquities," *Trends in Organized Crime* 9, no. 1 (Fall 2005): 33; and Salon Staff, "Robbing the Cradle."

53. Helga Turku, *The Destruction of Cultural Property as a Weapon of War: ISIS in Iraq and Syria* (London: Palgrave MacMillan, 2018), 182; Pringle, "New Evidence"; and Charney, "Saving Artifacts from Terrorists," 65.

54. Loveday Morris, "Islamic State Isn't Just Destroying Ancient Artifacts," *Washington Post*, June 8, 2015; see also Micah Garen, "War Within the War," *Archaeology* 57, no. 4 (August 2004): 29; Salon Staff, "Robbing the Cradle."

55. Pringle, "New Evidence."

56. Matthew Bogdanos, "ISIS—The Destruction and Looting of Antiquities" (presentation at the 16th Conference of the City of David Studies of Ancient Jerusalem, Megalim Institute, Jerusalem, 2015), 21.

57. Jesse Casana, "Satellite Imagery-Based Analysis of Archaeological Looting in Syria," *Near Eastern Archaeology* 78, no. 3 (2015): 147; David Kohn, "ISIS' Looting Campaign," *New Yorker*, October 14, 2014; and Matt Herbert, "Partisans, Profiteers, and Criminals: Syria's Illicit Economy," *Fletcher Forum of World Affairs* 38, no. 1 (Winter 2014): 78.

58. Peter Campbell, "The Illicit Antiquities Trade as a Transnational Criminal Network," *International Journal of Cultural Property* 20, no. 2 (May 2013): 130; see also Casana, "Satellite Imagery-Based Analysis," 151; and Joe Parkinson, Ayla Albayrak, and Duncan Mavin, "Syrian 'Monuments Men' Race to Protect Antiquities as Looting Bankrolls Terror," *Wall Street Journal*, February 11, 2015.

59. Amr Al-Azm, "The Pillaging of Syria's Cultural Heritage," *Middle East* Institute (May 22, 2015), https://www.mei.edu/publications/pillaging-syrias-cultural-heritage, p. 14; Hannah D. Willett, "Ill-Gotten Gains: A Response to the Islamic State's Profits from the Illicit Antiquities Market," *Arizona Law Review* 58 (2016): 837; and Gerstenblith, "The Destruction of Cultural Heritage," 359.

60. Mike Giglio and Munzer al-Awad, "This Is How Syrian Antiquities Are Being Smuggled and Sold," *BuzzFeed News*, July 30, 2015; Mark Vlasic and Jeffrey Paul DeSousa, "The Illicit Antiquities Trade and Terrorism Financing: From the Khmer Rouge to Daesh," in *Palgrave Handbook of Criminal and Terrorism Financing Law*, ed. Colin King, Clive Walker, and Jimmy Gurulé (London: Palgrave MacMillan, 2018), 1379; and Jason Felch, "Inside the ISIS Looting Operation," *Chasing Aphrodite*, December 16, 2016.

61. Giglio and al-Awad, "This Is How"; and Armendariz, "Culturalcide," 37.

62. Felch, "Inside the ISIS Looting Operation"; Idahosa Osaherumwen and Adebayo Mutunrayo, "International Terrorism in the Middle East," *Science and World* 35, no. 7 (2016): 62; and Kohn, "ISIS' Looting Campagin."

63. Claire Stephens, "Blood Antiquities," *Chicago-Kent Law Review* 92, no. 1 (2017): 356; Turku, *The Destruction*, 42; and Al-Azm, "The Pillaging of Syria's Cultural Heritage."

64. Ben Taub, "The Real Value of the ISIS Antiquities Trade," *New Yorker*, December 4, 2015; and Stephens, "Blood Antiquities," 356.

65. Anshul Kumar Pandey and Nilotpal Bansal, "Mutilating the Past: The Islamic State and the Last Song of History" (paper presented at the 5th ILNU Conference on International Humanitarian Law, Ahmedabad, India, 2016), 3; Brodie, "Protection Not Prevention," 18; and Charney, "Saving Artifacts from Terrorists," 64.

66. David Gill, "The Auction Market and Due Diligence," *Journal of Art Crime* 15 (Spring 2016): 74; Turku, *The Destruction of Cultural Property*, 9; and Lorenzo D'Agostino and Judith Vonberg, "Two Spaniards Arrested over Smuggling of ISIS-Looted Artifacts," *CNN*, March 29, 2018.

67. Morris, "Islamic State"; Jenna Scatena, "Facebook's Looted-Artifact Problem," *Atlantic*, July 31, 2020; and Samuel Hardy, "Reassessing the Balance of Antiquities and Forgeries in Abu Sayyaf's Stash," *Conflict Antiquities*, July 17, 2015.

68. Chris Cooper, "Blockchain and the Battle for 'Blood Antiquities'," *DCEBrief*, September 26, 2016; Parkinson et al., "Syrian 'Monuments Men'"; and Matthew Bogdanos, "Thieves of Baghdad: Combatting Global Traffic in Stolen Iraqi Antiquities," *Fordham International Law Journal* 31, no. 3 (2007): 730.

69. Christopher Jones, "In Battle against ISIS, Saving Lives or Ancient Artifacts," *Hyperallergic*, April 17, 2015; Fisher, "Violence against Architecture," 15; Lelia Amineddoleh, "Cultural Heritage Vandalism and Looting," *Santander Art and Culture Law Review* 2, no. 1 (2015): 39; and Vlasic and DeSousa, "The Illicit Antiquities Trade," 1181.

70. Scatena, "Facebook's Looted-Artifact Problem."

71. William Lawrence, Laurie McGavin Bachmann, and Michael von Stumm, "Tracking Recent Trends in the International Market for Art Theft," *Journal of Cultural Economics* 12, no. 1 (June 1988): 63; and Matthew Hart, *The Irish Game: A True Story of Crime and Art* (New York: Walker, 2004), 25.

72. John Wilson, "Murdered Mob Boss Gave Stolen Boston Art to IRA," *Guardian*, November 4, 2018.

73. "The Cathedral of Oloron-Sainte-Marie Was Attacked in a Smash and Grab," *ARCA Blog*, November 4, 2019; and Rush and Millington, *The Carabinieri Command*, 22.

74. Celestine Bohlen, "Mafia and a Lost Caravaggio Stun Andreotti Trial," *New York Times*, November 8, 1996; and Jonathan Jones, "A Caravaggio for Christmas," *Guardian*, December 16, 2018.

75. Alex Marshall, "What Happened to the Stolen Gold Toilet?," *New York Times*, November 20, 2019; "Blenheim Palace Gold Toilet Theft," *BBC News*, November 14, 2019; and Charney, *Art and Crime*, 109.

76. Jennifer Kreder, "The Choice between Civil and Criminal Remedies in Stolen Art Litigation," *Vanderbilt Journal of Transnational Law* 38, no. 1199 (2011): 1206; Kate FitzGibbon, "National Stolen Property Act: Primary U.S. Cultural Property Law," *Cultural Property News*, November 26, 2018; and Alexis Shannon Baker, "Selling the Past: *United States v. Frederick Schultz*," *Archaeology*, April 22, 2002.

77. Kreder, "The Choice," 1211; and FitzGibbon, "National Stolen Property Act."

78. Daniel Kees, "ISIS the Art Dealer," *Regulatory Review*, April 13, 2020; Victoria Russell, "Don't Get SLAMmed into Nefer Nefer Land," *Pace Intellectual Property, Sports and Entertainment Law Forum* 4, no. 1 (Winter 2014): 220; and Lukas Padegimas, "How New York Investors Financed the Looting of Syria, Ukraine, and Iraq," *Global Business Law Review* 6 (2016): 137.

79. Davis, "From Babylon," 446; Chris Maupin, "Making Matters Worse? The Debate Over 'Repatriating' Antiquities to Failed States in the Middle East," *Clio Ancient Art and Antiquities*, May 15, 2015, https://clioantiquities.com/2015/05/15/making-matters-worse-the-debate-over-repatriating-antiquities-to-failed-states-in-the-middle-east/; and Sarah Cascone, "Reclaiming Seized Cuban Art Will Be Difficult," *Artnet News*, January 8, 2015.

80. FitzGibbon, "National Stolen Property Act"; Peter Lennon, "A Safe Little Earner," *Guardian*, March 15, 2003; and Bowman, "Transnational Crimes," 233.

81. Lennon, "A Safe Little Earner"; Kreder, "The Choice," 1207; and Stefano Manacorda and Duncan Chappell, eds., *Crime in the Art and Antiquities World* (New York: Springer, 2011), 59.

82. Jennifer Kreder, "State Law Holocaust-Era Art Claims and Federal Executive Power," *Northwestern Law Review* 105 (2011): 319; Jennifer Kreder, "The New Battleground of Museum Ethics and Holocaust-Era Claims," *Oregon Law Review* 88 (2009): 46; Kreder, "Guarding the Historical Record," 256; and Jennifer Kreder, "Executive Weapons to Combat Infection of the Art Market," *Washington University Law Review* 88, no. 5 (2011): 1362.

83. Patty Gerstenblith, "Controlling the International Market in Antiquities," *Chicago Journal of International Law* 8, no. 1 (2007): 193.

84. Bator, "An Essay on the International Trade in Art," 281; Campbell, "The Illicit Antiquities," 122; Bogdanos, "Thieves of Baghdad," 727; and Balestrieri, "Field Archaeologists," 57.

85. Gary Vikan, "Why US Museums and the Antiquities Trade Should Work Together," *Apollo Magazine*, January 30, 2017.

86. Kreder, "Guarding," 254; Bogdanos, "Thieves of Baghdad," 726; and Kreder, "Executive Weapons," 1355.

87. Bator, "An Essay on the International Trade in Art," 280; and Leila Amineddoleh, "Protecting Cultural Heritage by Strictly Scrutinizing Museum Acquisitions," *Fordham Intellectual Property, Media and Entertainment Law Journal* 24, no. 3 (2014): 746.

88. Bogdanos, "ISIS," 27; Bogdanos, "Thieves of Baghdad," 729; and Kate FitzGibbon, "New York District Attorney Goes after Art Collections," *Cultural Property News*, February 11, 2018.

89. Erin Thompson, "Married to a Smuggler: The Importance of the Social Networks of Antiquities Collectors," *Journal of Art Crime* 15 (Spring 2016): 10.

90. Geoff Edgers, "One of the World's Most Respected Curators Vanished from the Art World," *Washington Post*, August 22, 2015.

91. Alanna Martinez, "Disgraced Getty Curator Marion True Roars Back with Tell-All Memoir," *Observer*, August 25, 2015; see also Justin Walsh, "Marion True Does Not Deserve Our Sympathy," *Hyperallergic*, October 2, 2015; and Ulrike Knöfel, "Stolen Art," *Spiegel Online*, November 14, 2005.

92. Daniel Grant, "What Happens When Museums Return Antiquities?," *Hyperallergic*, March 18, 2014; Rush and Millington, *The Carabinieri Command*, 137; and Kanishk Tharoor, "Museums and Looted Art: The Ethical Dilemma of Preserving World Cultures," *Guardian*, June 29, 2015.

93. Chechi, "Rescuing Cultural Heritage," 94; Mwazulu Diyabanza, "I Steal from Museums," *Guardian*, November 20, 2020; and Bruchac and Brown, "NAGPRA," 199.

94. Lennon, "A Safe Little Earner"; see also Kumiko Mita, *Art Crimes and International Security* (Keio University: U.S.-Japan Research Institute, 2015), 8; Hart, *The Irish Game*, 136.

95. Andrew McCalister, "Organized Crime and the Theft of Iraqi Antiquities," *Trends in Organized Crime* 9, no. 1 (2005): 28.

96. Rob Portman and Tom Carper, "The Art Industry and U.S. Policies That Undermine Sanctions," Staff Report (U.S. Senate, Permanent Subcommittee on Investigations, Homeland Security and Governmental Affairs, July 29, 2020), 33; see also Will Fitzgibbon and Hamish Boland-Rudder, "Billionaire Putin Pals Evaded Sanctions through Art Deals," *International Consortium of Investigative Journalists*, July 30, 2020.

97. Campbell, "The Illicit Antiquities Trade," 123.

98. Alderman, "Honor amongst Thieves," 626; see also Mita, *Art Crimes*, 4; Baker, "Selling the Past."

99. Tijhuis, *Transnational Crime*, 155; Simon Mackenzie, "Conditions for Guilt-Free Consumption in a Transnational Criminal Market," *European Journal of Criminal Policy Research* 20 (2014): 506; and Manacorda and Chappell, *Crime in the Art and Antiquities World*, 82.

100. Manacorda and Chappell, *Crime in the Art and Antiquities World*, 74.

101. Mackenzie, "Conditions for Guilt-Free Consumption," 507; "Raider of the Lost Art," *Mail and Guardian*, June 27, 1997; and David Gill, "Antiquities and Jihadists," *Looting Matters* (blog), January 28, 2010.

102. Maxwell Lincoln Anderson, *Antiquities: What Everyone Needs to Know* (Oxford: Oxford University Press, 2016), 105; Mackenzie, "Conditions for Guilt-Free Consumption," 510; and Saghir, "Stealing," 35.

103. Saghir, "Stealing," 36; and Desmarais, *Countering Illicit Traffic*," 29.

104. Noah Charney, "Lessons from the Museum of the Bible's Fake Dead Sea Scrolls," *Salon*, October 29, 2018; Neil Brodie, "How to Control the Internet Market in Antiquities?," Policy Brief 3 (Antiquities Coalition, July 2017), 11; and Desmarais, *Countering Illicit Traffic*, 3. The Art Loss Register is found at https://www.artloss .com/, the red list is found at https://icom.museum/en/resources/red-lists/, and INTERPOL's ID-Art mobile app is found at https://www.interpol.int/en/Crimes /Cultural-heritage-crime/ID-Art-mobile-app.

105. Christopher Chippindale and David Gill, "On-Line Auctions," *Culture without Context*, no. 9 (Autumn 2001): 7.

106. Brodie, "How to Control the Internet Market," 7.

107. Lawrence et al., "Tracking Recent Trends," 65; and Ludo Block, "European Police Cooperation on Art Crime," *Journal of Art Crime* 13 (2011): 15.

108. Lennon, "A Safe Little Earner"; and Thomas Foley, "Art Loss and Databases: The Quest for a Free Single Unified System" (master's thesis, Sotheby's Institute of Art, London, 2015).

109. FitzGibbon, "New York District Attorney Goes after Art Collections"; Steve Schindler and Katie Wilson-Milne, "Art and Financial Crimes" *Art Law Podcast*, April 23, 2019, http://artlawpodcast.com/2019/04/23/art-and-financial-crimes/; and Amineddoleh, "Protecting Cultural Heritage," 749.

110. Rush and Millington, *The Carabinieri Command*, 171; Charney, "How the Sale"; Block, "European Police Cooperation," 17; and Amineddoleh, "Protecting Cultural Heritage," 751.

Chapter 11. Settling Accounts

1. Francis Akena, "Poornography and the Entrenchment of Western Hegemony: Deconstructing the Kony 2012 Video," *Socialist Studies* 10, no. 1 (2014): 51; and Lauren Hebing, "Persuasion in the Millennial Era: A Case Study of KONY 2012" (honors thesis, Western Oregon University, 2018), 7.

2. U.S. Department of the Treasury, "Treasury Sanctions Lord's Resistance Army Facilitators Involved in the Illicit Trade of Ivory, Weapons, and Money in Central Africa," press release, December 13, 2017; and Kara Moses, "Lord's Resistance Army Funded by Elephant Poaching," *Guardian*, June 4, 2013.

3. Jasmine Hogben and Fiona Cownie, "Exploring Slacktivism," *Journal of Promotional Communications* 5, no. 2 (2017): 204; Hebing, "Persuasion in the Millennial Era," 6; and Akena, "Poornography," 53.

4. Margaret Rundle, Emily Weinstein, Howard Gardner, and Carrie James, *Doing Civics in the Digital Age: Casual, Purposeful, and Strategic Approaches to Participatory Politics* (Chicago: MacArthur Research Network, September 2015), 7; Akena, "Poornography," 58; and Hebing, "Persuasion in the Millennial Era," 37.

5. Killian McCarthy, ed., *The Money Laundering Market: Regulating the Criminal Economy* (Newcastle upon Tyne, U.K.: Agenda, 2018), 25; and Khaled Alasmari, "Efforts of Controlling Money Laundering of Narcotics Money in Saudi Arabia," *European Journal of Interdisciplinary Studies* 6, no. 1 (2014): 33.

6. Anne L. Clunan, "The Fight against Terrorist Financing," *Political Science Quarterly* 121, no. 4 (2006): 575.

7. Donato Masciandaro, ed., *Global Financial Crime: Terrorism, Money Laundering and Offshore Centres* (Burlington, Vt.: Ashgate, 2004), 62; Wesley J. L. Anderson, *Disrupting Threat Finances: Utilization of Financial Information to Disrupt Terrorist Organizations* (Hurlburt Field, Fla.: JSOU Press, 2008), 40; and Bruce Zagaris, "The Merging of the Anti-Money Laundering and Counter-Terrorism Financial Enforcement Regimes after September 11, 2001," *Berkeley Journal of International Law* 22, no. 1 (2004): 138.

8. Anderson, *Disrupting Threat Finances*, 40; and André Standing, *Transnational Organized Crime and the Palermo Convention: A Reality Check* (New York: International Peace Institute, December 2010), 14.

9. Jake Bernstein, *The Laundromat: Inside the Panama Papers Investigation of Illicit Money Networks and the Global Elite* (New York: Picador, 2018), 76.

10. Eleni Tsingou, "Targeting Money Laundering: Global Approach or Diffusion of Authority?," in *New Threats and New Actors in International Security*, ed. Elke Krahmann (New York: Palgrave-McMillan, 2005), 95; and McCarthy, *The Money Laundering Market*, 27.

11. Nicole Healy, "The Impact of September 11th on Anti-Money Laundering Efforts," *International Lawyer* 36, no. 2 (Summer 2002): 742.

12. John Cassara, *Trade-Based Money Laundering: The Next Frontier in International Money Laundering Enforcement* (Hoboken, N.J.: Wiley, 2016), 2; Zagaris, "The Merging," 125; and Nicholas Ryder, *The Financial War on Terrorism: A Review of Counter-Terrorist Financing Strategies since 2001* (London: Routledge, 2015), 75.

13. Jeffrey Robinson, *The Laundrymen: Inside Money Laundering, the World's Third Largest Business* (New York: Arcade, 1996), 24; and Bernstein, *The Laundromat*, 63.

14. Clunan, "The Fight," 586.

15. Zagaris, "The Merging against Terrorist Financing," 126; Robinson, *The Laundrymen*, 91; and Tsingou, "Targeting Money Laundering," 91.

16. Darryle J. Grimes, "The Financial War on Terrorism: Grading U.S. Strategy for Combating the Financing of Terrorism" (master's thesis, Norfolk, Va.: Joint Advanced Warfighting School, 2006), 24; Lawrence Freedman, ed., *Superterrorism: Policy Responses* (Malden, Mass.: Blackwell, 2002), 59; and Douglas Farah and Stephen Braun, *Merchant of Death: Money, Guns, Planes, and the Man Who Makes War Possible* (Hoboken, N.J.: Wiley, 2007), 103.

17. Marieke de Goede, "Counter-Terrorism Financing Assemblages after 9/11," in *Palgrave Handbook of Criminal and Terrorism Financing Law*, ed. Colin King, Clive Walker, and Jimmy Gurulé (London: Palgrave MacMillan, 2018), 757; see also Clunan, "The Fight," 587; Sidney Weintraub, "Disrupting the Financing of Terrorism," *Washington Quarterly* 25, no. 1 (2002): 56; and Bernstein, *The Laundromat*, 73.

18. George W. Bush, Paul O'Neil, and Colin Powell, "Text: Executive Order Freezing Terrorists' Assets," *Washington Post*, September 24, 2001, https://www.washingtonpost.com/wp-srv/nation/specials/attacked/transcripts/bush092401.html.

19. Murray Weidenbaum, "Economic Warriors against Terrorism," *Washington Quarterly* 25, no. 1 (2001): 50.

20. Eric J. Gouvin, "Bringing out the Big Guns: The USA Patriot Act, Money Laundering, and the War on Terrorism," *Baylor Law Review* 55 (2003): 960; Nora Bensahel, "A Coalition of Coalitions: International Cooperation against Terrorism," *Studies in Conflict and Terrorism* 29, no. 1 (January 2006): 37; and Ryder, *The Financial War*, 79.

21. Nicholas Ryder, "Counter-Terrorist Financing, Cryptoassets, Social Media Platforms, and Suspicious Activity Reports: A Step into the Regulatory Unknown" (paper presented at the Centre for Financial and Corporate Integrity research seminar, March 20, 2019); Ryder, *The Financial War*, 98; and "UK National Risk Assessment of Money Laundering and Terrorist Financing" (London: HM Treasury, October 2015), 90.

22. Ken Booth and Timothy Dunne, eds., *Worlds in Collision: Terror and the Future of Global Order* (New York: Palgrave MacMillan, 2002), 82; Weidenbaum, "Economic Warriors," 48; Bensahel, "A Coalition of Coalitions," 38; Nicholas Ridley and Dean Alexander, "Combating Terrorist Financing in the First Decade of the Twenty-First Century," *Journal of Money Laundering Control* 15, no. 1 (2012): 49; M. Michelle Gallant, "Tax and Terrorism: A New Partnership?," *Journal of Financial Crime* 14, no. 4 (2007): 457; and Clunan, "The Fight," 581.

23. Sebastian Bae, "Shadow Networks: How Criminals, Terrorists, and Rogue States Collaborate," *Georgetown Security Studies Review*, February 24, 2015;

Christine Walsh, "Ethics: Inherent in Islamic Finance through Shari'a Law," *Fordham Journal of Corporate and Financial Law* 12, no. 4 (2007): 754; and Santha Vaithilingam and Mahendhiran Nair, "Factors Affecting Money Laundering: Lesson for Developing Countries," *Journal of Money Laundering Control* 10, no. 3 (2007): 363.

24. Phil Williams, "Crime, Illicit Markets, and Money Laundering," in *Managing Global Issues: Lessons Learned*, ed. P. J. Simmons and Chantal de Jonge Oudraat (Washington, D.C.: Carnegie Endowment for International Peace, 2001), 145; and Nicholas Lemann, "The Panama Papers and the Monster Stories of the Future," *New Yorker*, April 14, 2016.

25. Peter Andreas, *Killer High: A History of War in Six Drugs* (Oxford: Oxford University Press, 2020), 136; Jeff Smith, "Campaign to Boycott Salvadoran Coffee Was Part of the Grand Rapids Central American Solidarity Movement in the Early 1990s," *Grand Rapids People's History Project*, September 17, 2015; Deborah Tyroler, "Salvadoran Businesspersons Condemn Coffee Boycott Promoted by U.S. Organization" (Latin American Data Base, May 25, 1990); and Deborah Tyroler, "U.S. Humanitarian Organization Ends Two-Year Boycott of Salvadoran Coffee Exports" (Latin American Data Base, March 27, 1992).

26. Judith F. Posnikoff, "Disinvestment from South Africa: They Did Well by Doing Good," *Contemporary Economic Policy* 15, no. 1 (1997): 76–86; and Henry Foy, "The Invisible Man Who Changed the World," *Nouse/Muse*, January 26, 2010.

27. Ian Bannon and Paul Collier, eds., *Natural Resources and Violent Conflict: Options and Actions* (Washington, D.C.: World Bank, 2003), 112.

28. Majid Yar, "Teenage Kicks or Virtual Villainy?," in *Crime Online*, ed. Yvonne Jewekes (Abingdon, U.K.: Routledge, 2011), 97.

29. Gregory F. Treverton, Carl F. Matthies, Karla J. Cunningham, Jeremiah Goulka, Gregory Ridgeway, and Anny Wong, *Film Piracy, Organized Crime, and Terrorism* (Santa Monica, Calif.: RAND, 2009), 161; and Peggy Chaudhry and Alan Zimmerman, *The Economics of Counterfeit Trade: Governments, Consumers, Pirates, and Intellectual Property Rights* (Berlin: Springer, 2009), 85.

30. Xuemei Bian and Luiz Moutinho, "An Investigation of Determinants of Counterfeit Purchase Consideration," *Journal of Business Research* 62, no. 3 (2009): 368; Joshua D. Foss, "Plutonium and Picasso: A Typology of Nuclear and Fine Art Smuggling," *InterAgency Journal* 8, no. 2 (2017): 34; and Kameron Hurley, "Tech bros 'This is an emergency! No one can access books because the libraries are closed!,' tweet, March 29, 2020, https://twitter.com/kameronhurley/status/1244312494195322881.

31. Ian Phau and Min Teah, "Devil Wears (Counterfeit) Prada: A Study of Antecedents and Outcomes of Attitudes towards Counterfeits of Luxury Brands," *Journal of Consumer Marketing* 26, no. 1 (January 23, 2009): 24; Martine Stead, Laura

Jones, Graeme Docherty, Brendan Gough, Marilyn Antoniak, and Ann McNeill, "'No-One Actually Goes to a Shop and Buys Them Do They?': Attitudes and Behaviours Regarding Illicit Tobacco in a Multiply Disadvantaged Community in England," *Addiction* 108, no. 12 (2013): 2212–19; Elfriede Penz and Barbara Stottinger, "Forget the 'Real' Thing! Take the Copy! An Exploratory Model for the Volitional Purchase of Counterfeit Products," *Advances in Consumer Research* 32 (2005): 570; and Martin Eisend and Pakize Schuchert-Güler, "Explaining Counterfeit Purchases," *Academy of Marketing Science Review* 10, no. 12 (January 2006): 18.

32. Julia Sophie Woersdorfer, "When Do Social Norms Replace Status-Seeking Consumption? An Application to the Consumption of Cleanliness," *Metroeconomica* 61, no. 1 (2010): 38.

33. Varun Vira, Thomas Ewing, and Jackson Miller, *Out of Africa: Mapping the Global Trade in Illicit Elephant Ivory* (Horsham, U.K.: C4DS; Washington, D.C.: Born Free USA, August 2014), 48; and Franck Vigneron and Lester Johnson, "A Review and a Conceptual Framework of Prestige-Seeking Consumer Behavior," *Academy of Marketing Science Review* 1 (1999): 3.

34. Frank Langfitt, "Vietnam's Appetite for Rhino Horn Drives Poaching in Africa," *NPR*, May 13, 2013; Andrew John Brennan and Jaslin Kaur Kalsi, "Elephant Poaching and Ivory Trafficking Problems in Sub-Saharan Africa," *Ecological Economics* 120 (2015): 321; and Ranee Khooshie Lal Panjabi, "For Trinkets, Tonics and Terrorism: International Wildlife Poaching in the Twenty-First Century," *Georgia Journal of International and Comparative Law* 43, no. 1 (2014): 33.

35. J. C. Sharman, *The Despot's Guide to Wealth Management: On the International Campaign against Grand Corruption* (Ithaca, N.Y.: Cornell University Press, 2017), 10; Ethan A. Nadelmann, "Global Prohibition Regimes: The Evolution of Norms in International Society," *International Organization* 44, no. 4 (Autumn 1990): 484; and Kwame Anthony Appiah, *The Honor Code: How Moral Revolutions Happen* (New York: Norton, 2010), 38.

36. Zachary K. Goldman, Ellie Maruyama, Elizabeth Rosenberg, Edoardo Saravalle, and Julia Solomon-Strauss, *Terrorist Use of Virtual Currencies* (Washington, D.C.: Center for a New American Security, 2017), 5.

37. Michael Freeman, *Financing Terrorism: Case Studies* (Burlington, Vt.: Ashgate, 2011), 242.

38. Patrick Keefe, "The Trafficker," *New Yorker*, February 8, 2010.

39. Shina Keene, *Operationalizing Counter Threat Finance Strategies* (Carlisle, Pa.: Strategic Studies Institute, 2014), 35; David Sanger, "U.S. Cyberattacks Target ISIS in a New Line of Combat," *New York Times*, April 24, 2016; Jacob Shapiro and David Siegel, "Underfunding in Terrorist Organizations," *International Studies*

Quarterly 51, no. 2 (2007): 409; and Colin P. Clarke, Kimberly Jackson, Patrick Johnston, Eric Robinson, and Howard Shatz, *Financial Futures of the Islamic State of Iraq and the Levant: Findings from a RAND Corporation Workshop* (Santa Monica, Calif.: RAND, 2017), 11.

40. Graham Myres, "Investing in the Market of Violence: Toward a Micro-Theory of Terrorist Financing," *Studies in Conflict and Terrorism* 35 (2012): 698.

41. Katherine Bauer, "Survey of Terrorist Groups and Their Means of Financing," Hearing before the House Financial Service Subcommittee on Terrorism and Illicit Finance, September 7, 2018.

42. Richard DiGiacomo, "Prostitution as a Possible Funding Mechanism for Terrorism" (master's thesis, Naval Postgraduate School, 2010), 17.

43. Bauer, "Survey of Terror Groups."

44. Freeman, *Financing Terrorism*, 242.

45. Richard J. Aldrich, "Transatlantic Intelligence and Security Cooperation," *International Affairs* 80, no. 4 (2004): 742.

FURTHER READING

Allen, Dave, Will Cafferky, Abdallah Hendawy, Jordache Horn, Karolina MacLachlan, Stefanie Nijssen, and Eleonore Vidal de la Blache. *The Big Spin: Corruption and the Growth of Violent Extremism*. London: Transparency International, February 2017.

Amineddoleh, Leila. "The Role of Museums in the Trade of Black Market Cultural Heritage Property." *Art Antiquity and Law* 18, no. 3 (October 1, 2013): 227–54.

Anning, Stephen, and M. L. R. Smith. "The Accidental Pirate." *Parameters* 42, no. 2 (Summer 2012): 28–41.

Asal, Victor, Kathleen Deloughery, and Brian J. Phillips. "When Politicians Sell Drugs: Examining Why Middle East Ethnopolitical Organizations Are Involved in the Drug Trade." *Terrorism and Political Violence* 24, no. 2 (2012): 199–212.

Bakke, Kristin. "Help Wanted? The Mixed Record of Foreign Fighters in Domestic Insurgencies." *International Security* 38, no. 4 (Spring 2014): 150–87.

Barder, Owen. "A Policymakers' Guide to Dutch Disease." Working paper no. 91. Washington, D.C.: Center for Global Development, July 2006.

Basile, Mark. "Going to the Source: Why Al Qaeda's Financial Network Is Likely to Withstand the Current War on Terrorist Financing." *Studies in Conflict and Terrorism* 27, no. 3 (June 2004): 169–85.

Bechtol, Bruce E. "North Korean Illicit Activities and Sanctions: A National Security Dilemma." *Cornell International Law Journal* 51 (2018): 57–99.

Bensahel, Nora. "A Coalition of Coalitions: International Cooperation against Terrorism." *Studies in Conflict and Terrorism* 29, no. 1 (January 2006): 35–49.

Byman, Daniel, Peter Chalk, Bruce Hoffman, William Rosenau, and David Brannan. *Trends in Outside Support for Insurgent Movements*. Santa Barbara, Calif.: RAND, 2001.

Campbell, Howard. "Narco-Propaganda in the Mexican 'Drug War': An Anthropological Perspective." *Latin American Perspectives* 41, no. 2 (2014): 60–77.

Cochrane, Feargal, Bahar Baser, and Ashok Swain. "Home Thoughts from Abroad: Diasporas and Peace-Building in Northern Ireland and Sri Lanka." *Studies in Conflict and Terrorism* 32, no. 8 (2009): 681–704.

Cornell, Svante. "Narcotics and Armed Conflict." *Studies in Conflict and Terrorism* 30, no. 3 (April 2007): 207–27.

Cunliffe, Emma, Paul Fox, and Peter Stone. "The Protection of Cultural Property in the Event of Armed Conflict: Unnecessary Distraction or Mission-Relevant Priority." OPEN Publications. NATO Allied Command Transformation. Brussels: NATO, Summer 2018.

Felbab-Brown, Vanda. "Wildlife and Drug Trafficking, Terrorism, and Human Security." *PRISM* 7, no. 4 (2018): 124–37.

Ganor, Boaz, and Miri Wernli. "The Infiltration of Terrorist Organizations into the Pharmaceutical Industry." *Studies in Conflict and Terrorism* 36, no. 9 (September 1, 2013): 699–712.

Geltzer, Joshua. "Taking Hand-Outs or Going It Alone: Nationalization versus Privatization in the Funding of Islamic Terrorist Groups." *Studies in Conflict and Terrorism* 34, no. 2 (January 2011): 144–70.

Grynkewich, Alexus. "Welfare as Warfare: How Violent Non-State Groups Use Social Services to Attack the State." *Studies in Conflict and Terrorism* 31, no. 4 (2008): 350–70.

Herbert, Matt. "Partisans, Profiteers, and Criminals: Syria's Illicit Economy." *Fletcher Forum of World Affairs* 38, no. 1 (Winter 2014): 69–86.

Jacobson, Michael. "Terrorist Financing and the Internet." *Studies in Conflict and Terrorism* 33, no. 4 (April 2010): 353–63.

Jonsson, Michael, Elliot Brennan, and Christopher O'Hara. "Financing War or Facilitating Peace? The Impact of Rebel Drug Trafficking on Peace Negotiations in Colombia and Myanmnar." *Studies in Conflict and Terrorism* 39, no. 6 (June 2, 2016): 542–59.

Joosse, Paul, Sandra M. Bucerius, and Sara K. Thompson. "Narratives and Counternarratives: Somali-Canadians on Recruitment as Foreign Fighters to Al-Shabaab." *British Journal of Criminology* 55, no. 4 (2015): 811–32.

Kenney, Michael. "From Pablo to Osama: Counter-Terrorism Lessons from the War on Drugs." *Survival* 45, no. 3 (Autumn 2003): 187–206.

Lyall, Jason, and Isaiah Wilson. "Rage against the Machines: Explaining Outcomes in Counterinsurgency Wars." *International Organization* 63, no. 1 (2009): 67–106.

Makarenko, Tamara. "The Crime–Terror Continuum." *Global Crime* 6, no. 1 (February 2004): 129–45.

Miller, Gregory D. "Space Pirates, Geosynchronous Guerrillas, and Nonterrestrial Terrorists: Nonstate Threats in Space." *Air Power and Space Journal* 33, no. 3 (Fall 2019): 33–51.

Muro, Diego. "Nationalism and Nostalgia: The Case of Radical Basque Nationalism." *Nations and Nationalism* 11, no. 4 (2005): 571–89.

Myres, Graham. "Investing in the Market of Violence." *Studies in Conflict and Terrorism* 35 (2012): 693–711.

Nemeth, Erik. "Conflict Art: Scholars Develop the Tactical Value of Cultural Patrimony." *Cambridge Review of International Affairs* 23, no. 2 (June 2010): 299–323.

Orlova, Alexandra. "Russia's Anti–Money Laundering Regime." *Journal of Money Laundering Control* 11, no. 3 (2008): 210–33.

Panke, Diana, and Ulrich Petersohn. "Norm Challenges and Norm Death: The Inexplicable?" *Cooperation and Conflict* 51, no. 1 (2016): 3–19.

Picarelli, John. "Osama Bin Corleone? Vito the Jackal?" *Terrorism and Political Violence* 24, no. 2 (2012): 180–98.

Portman, Rob, and Tom Carper. "The Art Industry and U.S. Policies That Undermine Sanctions." Staff Report. U.S. Senate, Permanent Subcommittee on Investigations, Homeland Security and Governmental Affairs, July 29, 2020.

Renner, Michael. *The Anatomy of Resource Wars*. Worldwatch paper no. 162, ed. by Thomas Prugh. Washington, D.C.: Worldwatch Institute, October 2002.

Rosenthal, Justine A. "For-Profit Terrorism." *Studies in Conflict and Terrorism* 31, no. 6 (2008): 481–98.

Rosette, Daniela. "The Application of Real World Rules to Banks in Online Games and Virtual Worlds." *University of Miami Business Law Review* 16 (2008): 279–303.

Roth, Mitchel, and Murat Sever. "The Kurdish Workers Party as Criminal Syndicate." *Studies in Conflict and Terrorism* 30, no. 10 (2007): 901–20.

Selepak, Andrew. "Skinhead Super Mario Brothers: An Examination of Racist and Violent Games on White Supremacist Web Sites." *Journal of Criminal Justice and Popular Culture* 17, no. 1 (2010): 1–47.

Shapiro, Jacob, and David Siegel. "Underfunding in Terrorist Organizations." *International Studies Quarterly* 51, no. 2 (2007): 405–29.

Shaxson, Nicholas. "Oil, Corruption and the Resource Curse." *International Affairs* 83, no. 6 (2007): 1123–40.

Silke, Andrew. "In Defense of the Realm." *Studies in Conflict and Terrorism* 21 (1998): 331–61.

Standing, André. *Transnational Organized Crime and the Palermo Convention*. New York: International Peace Institute, December 2010.

Toloyan, Kachig. "Rethinking Diasporas: Stateless Power in the Transnational Moment." *Diaspora: A Journal of Transnational Studies* 5, no. 1 (Spring 1996): 3–36.

Tupman, W. A. "Ten Myths about Terrorist Financing." *Journal of Money Laundering Control* 12, no. 2 (2009): 189–205.

Vorrath, Judith. *From War to Illicit Economies: Organized Crime and State-Building in Liberia and Sierra Leone*. Berlin: German Institute for International and Security Affairs, November 2014.

Williams, Phil. *Violent Non-State Actors and National and International Security.* International Relations and Security Network. Zurich: Eidgenossische Technische Hochschule, 2008.

INDEX

413

ABOUT THE AUTHOR

Margaret Sankey earned a PhD in European military history at Auburn University and taught military history, security studies, and political science at Minnesota State Moorhead before joining the staff at the USAF Air War College as the director of research and electives. She is Air University's research coordinator in the Office of Sponsored Programs ("The Hub"), matching and supporting Air University assets with Department of the Air Force research problems. Her previous publications include *Jacobite Prisoners of the 1715 Rebellion: Preventing and Punishing Insurrection in Early Hanoverian Britain*, *Women and War in the 21st Century: A Country-by-Country Guide*, and the NACBS Love Prize–winning article, cowritten with Dr. Daniel Szechi, "Elite Culture and the Decline of Scottish Jacobitism, 1715–1745," in *Past and Present*.